CHRISTIAN MISSIONS.

CHRISTIAN MISSIONS:

THEIR AGENTS, AND THEIR RESULTS.

BY

T. W. M. MARSHALL

A FRUCTIBUS EORUM COGNOSCETIS EOS.—S. MATT. VII. 16.

VOL. II.

NEW YORK:
D. & J. SADLIER & CO., 31 BARCLAY STREET.
MONTREAL: COR. NOTRE-DAME AND ST. FRANCIS XAVIER STS.
MRS. HICKEY, 128 FEDERAL STREET, BOSTON.
1864.

RENNIE, SHEA & LINDSAY,
Stereotypers and Electrotypers,
81, 83 & 85 Centre-Street,
NEW YORK.

GEO. W. WOOD, Printer,
No. 2 Dutch-st., N. Y.

CHRISTIAN MISSIONS.

CHAPTER VIII.

MISSIONS IN THE LEVANT, SYRIA, AND ARMENIA.

MANY lands have now been passed in review, and each has proclaimed in turn the same unvarying tale. We have visited the Chinese and the Hindoo, the Cingalese and the Maori, the Philippine and the many tribes who people the island world of the Pacific. We have interrogated the Moor and the Copt, the Negro and the Abyssinian; and now at length the Kaffir and the Hottentot have added their voice, and have told us that they too, in spite of the mists which cloud both heart and brain, are learning to discriminate between the apostles of Jesus and the emissaries of man. All have bowed in turn before the meek but fearless pastors who went amongst them bearing the Cross, and have confessed, in love or in hate, that *they* indeed came from God; while all have agreed to spurn, as only men like themselves, the crowd of rival teachers having neither the gifts nor the calling of apostles, and to utter the testimony which the evil spirits have so often been forced to proclaim by the mouth of the heathen, "Jesus I know, and Paul I know, but who are you?"*

And now we approach the regions where the mightiest races of the human family have in turn reigned or served, and the lands, immortal both in sacred and profane story, where Christianity yielded its first martyrs, and won its earliest triumphs. They have changed since then, yet not as other lands have changed; for in this mysterious East, which still silently rebukes by its grave and solemn mien the fickle and clamorous races of the West, even error knows how to simulate the prerogatives of truth, and still wears the same outward form, after the lapse

* Acts xix. 32.

of centuries, in which it defied the sentence of God at Ephesus and Chalcedon. The lessons of a thousand years, and the abject misery of the last four hundred, have failed to admonish the disciples of Photius and Eutyches and Nestorius; until in these last days a new call to repentance and conversion has been heard amongst them, of which we are about to trace the noble results. We are going to speak of the Greek and the Syrian, of the Moslem who rules over both, and of the Russian who is planning in secret how he may set his heel on them all.

THE MEDITERRANEAN.

We have come from Africa, and must therefore enter the Mediterranean through that famous strait at whose mouth England keeps watch from her strongest fortress. Let us begin our new voyage from this spot; for even in Gibraltar, where but a few thousand men are crowded together, we shall find one more example, worthy of a moment's attention, of the eternal contrast between the children of the Church and the children of the world.

An Episcopalian clergyman, who had left his flock in America, but addressed to them from every place which he visited pastoral letters, of which the main object seems to have been to keep alive during his absence their aversion to the Catholic Church, found materials for an animated discourse even in Gibraltar. He visited both the Catholic and Protestant church in that place, and then dispatched to his remote congregation a description of what even he was constrained to call "the striking contrast." In the Protestant church, he tells them, he never saw "one of the attending soldiers on his knees;" and then he exclaims, "to what advantage do the Catholics appear in this striking contrast!" "The hundreds that stood *there*," he adds, when he had passed from the worship to the preaching, "were all eye and ear; but *here* (in the Protestant church) nothing could be seen but yawning, and drowsiness, and inattention."*

This unfavorable report of an American minister is more than confirmed by an Anglican writer, who observes: "The

* *Glimpses of the Old World*, by the Rev. John A. Clark, D.D., Rector of St. Andrew's Church, Philadelphia, vol. i., ch. ii., pp. 56, 68. An Anglican minister gives the same account of a church of the Waldenses, who are represented on English platforms as the most devout Christians of Italy. "There did not appear to be much external reverence among the congregation, who went in and out incessantly, nor was the attendance at all proportioned to the size of the church." *The Italian Valleys of the Pennine Alps*, by Rev. S. W. King, M.A., ch. x., p. 226.

state of religion when I was at Gibraltar was most disheartening. . . . There is literally no Church feeling in Gibraltar."*

It is perhaps worthy of remark, that a Russo-Greek traveller, the amiable Count Schouvaloff, seems to have owed the grace of conversion to his continual observation of the same "striking contrast" which produced only a transient impression on Dr. Clark. "What struck and edified me in the Catholic churches," he says, "was the profound recollection of the faithful in the act of prayer. I compared their modest and humble attitude with the often unbecoming movements, the deep *ennui*, and the distracted looks, of a great number of my co-religionists during the divine office; and I was obliged to confess, in spite of myself, that there was more piety among the Catholics than among the Greeks."†

Let us stay also for a moment at another fortress, also a symbol of Anglo-Saxon might, which we shall pass on our way to the isles of Greece. Malta has been for more than a quarter of a century the headquarters of Protestantism in the Levant. Nearly forty years ago Mr. Jowett recommended it to English missionary societies as a centre for their operations, because, as he said, "it is very far from unhealthy, British protection is here fully enjoyed, together with a degree of comfort seldom to be attained in foreign countries; rendering it a peculiarly eligible residence for a missionary family."‡ These characteristic considerations prevailed, and for thirty years an eruption of tracts and Bibles has flowed out of Malta, and covered both shores of the Mediterranean. In the single year 1831, they boast to have issued from this eligible residence "four millions seven hundred and sixty thousand pages, all in modern Greek."§ By the same year the Americans alone had dispersed "about three hundred and fifty thousand volumes, containing twenty-one million pages."‖ Both English and Americans have been dispersing them at an increased rate ever since. How many converts have been made by this abundant literature, and of what sort, we shall learn presently.

It is here also that the "Malta Protestant College" has been established, with the object of providing suitable instruction, as well as food and lodging, for any orientals who could be induced to enter it. Of the actual results obtained in this institution, which appears to have been hitherto a kind of

* *The Canary Isles*, &c., by the Rev. Thomas Debary, M.A., ch. xviii., pp. 213, 225.

† Schouvaloff, *Ma Conversion et ma Vocation*, ch. iii., p. 209.

‡ *Christian Researches in the Mediterranean*, p. 376, 3d edition.

§ *History of American Missions*, by the Rev. Joseph Tracy, p. 213.

‖ P. 235.

hospital for astute adventurers of every class, we shall have a sufficiently accurate notion when we have completed our review of missions in the Levant. It was here that Achilli found refuge; and it may be doubted whether any four walls in Christendom have contained within them, at a given moment, so singular an assemblage of adroit comedians as the Malta Protestant College. Even Achilli is not, as we shall see, an exaggerated specimen of its inmates. The gentleman who bears the title of "Bishop of Gibraltar," we are told, "said he was not pleased with Achilli, as he expected, after the friendly intercourse they had had, knowing the favorable opinion he had of the Church of England, that he would have joined himself to *our* Church, rather than have laid the foundation of another."*

No doubt Achilli, who is said to have become ultimately a Swedenborgian, had encouraged this expectation, and found his profit in affecting esteem for the Church of England. A person so fertile in resources would find little difficulty in outwitting the amiable gentleman of whom a well-known traveller gives this irreverent description: "Dr. Tomlinson acted like an Episcopalian tight-rope dancer, always balancing himself between Puseyism and Evangelicalism, and so distracted the few Protestants at Malta. He is eminently a man of no decision of character."† Achilli and his companions appear to have detected this infirmity. But the Malta College wanted recruits, and was willing to accept them on their own terms; and this fact becoming known throughout the Levant, the revenues of the College were constantly dilapidated by ingenious orientals, who adapted the new drama of "Achilli and the Bishop of Gibraltar," through every possible modification of comedy and burlesque, but always to their own advantage. A few examples, recorded by Protestant writers, deserve attention.

The first is the case of Dr. Naudi, reported at length by Dr. Clark. Professing to be a Protestant convert, Naudi was long supported by the Church Missionary Society, to whom he forwarded welcome periodical reports, setting forth the rapid increase of oriental Protestants, and the inconveniently crowded state of his own chapel in consequence. The "spread of Protestantism in the Levant" became the theme of many a glowing oration, till Dr. Joseph Wolff, always active and inquisitive, resolved to visit "Naudi's place of worship," in order to be an eye-witness of his evangelical triumphs; and then was revealed an unexpected fact. "He ascertained," says Dr. Clark, "that

* *Dr. Achilli, and the Malta Protestant College*, p. 9 (1851).

† Richardson, *Travels in the Great Desert of Sahara*, vol. i., ch. viii., p. 235.

Dr. Naudi *had never held service here*, although he had *for years* made his reports in relation to what he was doing, and received funds from England to enable him to carry on his operations!"*

The next case is related by Dr. Wolff himself. "Antonio Fabri, the Cancelliere of the British Consul, told us he was convinced of the truth of the Protestant religion." But Antonio was a very inferior performer to Dr. Naudi, and betrayed his secret too soon. "We found out," says Dr. Wolff, "that he said this in order to induce us to give our consent to his marrying our English maid-servant."†

Stephanos Carapiet was another of the same class of converts. "He arrived from Beyrout, and asked me to give him money to go to Malta, to join the American missionaries there, by whom he said he had been converted. He was a Greek priest." Apparently Dr. Wolff was generous enough to comply with the request, for he adds, "after he had stayed a few days he got extremely drunk, so we sent him away."‡

Dr. Carne also tells us, amongst other examples, of "two brothers," who came from Mount Lebanon,—the fame of the Protestant missionaries having evidently spread in all directions, —"clever and designing fellows both of them, who *agreed to be baptized* and become useful agents, on the promise of some hundred pounds, to be paid them by a zealous and wealthy supporter of the cause."§ We shall hear of many similar cases when we get into Syria, and these may suffice for the present. It is curious that these playful orientals never even attempt to practise their frauds upon Catholic missionaries, perhaps because they have detected that the latter do not pay for conversions; and that it is the English, who deem themselves the most discerning, and the Americans, who claim to be the keenest people in the universe, who are their only victims.

Let us leave Malta and its college, the value of which we shall learn to appreciate still more exactly hereafter, but not without noticing words which it seems to have chosen as its motto and device. "Here we are," says one of its officials, and the college printed and circulated the announcement, "safe from the withering influence of Puseyism, Romanism, and all the rest of Satan's isms."‖

* *Glimpses*, &c., ch. viii., p. 165.

† *Journal*, p. 161.

‡ P. 148.

§ *Letters from the East*, by John Carne, Esq., vol. ii., p. 115, 3d edition.

‖ *The Fifth Annual Report of the Malta Protestant College*, p. 13 (1853).

GREECE.

And now we come to Greece, famous for great actions which she has long ceased to imitate, more fruitful in words than in works, abounding rather in poets than in prophets, and as careless in the nineteenth century as she was in the fifteenth of the miseries which her errors have provoked, and the blessings which her crimes have forfeited. If there be a people in the world whose history may be compared to that of the Jews, and who seem, by the singularity of their fate, to have been struck by the heavy hand of God before the face of all nations, the Greeks are that people. From the hour in which the Photian schism was accomplished, and Michael Cerularius first uttered a curse, in 1053, against the Vicar of Christ, they have never ceased to endure such affliction and ignominy as no other Christian people ever knew.* Again and again reconciled to the Church, it was only to relapse into schism. Vainly they were warned by prelates of their own nation, perpetually affirming their allegiance to the Holy See, or admonished by chastisements which their pride refused to comprehend. But the Greeks were fast filling up the measure of their crimes, and judgment was at hand. Already, as Pachymeres, Gregoras, and other Greek historians relate, "there was scarcely a city in the empire which had not been twice or thrice in the presence of an enemy." Already they had this in common with that fated race to whom their prodigious calamities have caused them to be compared, that every fresh act of faithlessness was promptly followed by some signal judgment.† The West had sent forth the avenging hosts which scourged the one, and now the East was arraying the more terrible armies which were to crush the other. The fearful power which was destined to trample them under foot was gathering strength day by day. The Ottomans were knocking at their gates, and, like raging lions, "demanding their prey from God."

At this moment, fear and dismay, false and hypocritical even in their deep abjection, urged them once more to seek reconciliation with the chair of Peter; and at the Council of Florence, in 1439, *all* the prelates of the Greek and Oriental Churches again confessed, with one voice, that "the Roman Pontiff is the true Vicar of Christ and head of the whole Church,"—and

* A few lines are inserted here from a paper, written some years ago, on the "Russo-Greek and Oriental Churches," and printed by the author in the *Dublin Review*, Dec., 1847.

† Leo Allatius, *De Eccles. Occident. et Orient. Perpet. Consens.;* Maimbourg, *Histoire du Schisme des Grecs.*

Joseph, the Patriarch of Constantinople, bequeathed from his death-bed, as his last legacy to his nation and people, that famous exhortation to obedience and unity of which he had himself given an immortal example, and in uttering which he yielded up his soul to God.*

But Greek perfidy was still to provoke another and a final judgment. Gregory, the successor of Joseph, after struggling in vain against the new schism, retired to Rome in 1451, predicting the coming fall of Constantinople. Isidore, the metropolitan of Russia, and delegate of the Patriarch of Antioch; and Bessarion, once the ablest champion of the Greeks, followed his example. In vain the Sovereign Pontiff, Nicholas the Fifth, warned the twelfth and last Constantine, in the spirit of prophecy, that "if before three years they did not repent and return to holy unity, they would be dealt with as the fig-tree in the Gospel, which was cut down to the roots because of its sterility."† The prophecy was spoken in 1451, the Moslem gathered round the devoted city, and, in 1453, "struck by the hand of God," in the words of the Patriarch of Constantinople, the schismatical metropolis fell. Two hundred thousand barbarians, more merciless than the legions of Titus, ceased not to strike till their weary arms could no longer hold the sword. Here fell the last Byzantine emperor. Here the most gorgeous temple of the Christian faith, polluted by incurable schism, became a temple of the Arabian impostor. "Weep, oh, weep," said a Greek bishop, one of the captives of that sorrowful day, "weep for your miseries, and condemn yourselves rather than others; for like the Jews carried away captive to Babylon, you have despised the prophet Jeremy, foretelling the destruction and the captivity of Jerusalem."‡

The judgment so long provoked was now consummated. From that hour, misery, contempt, and oppression have been the bitter portion of the erring communities of the East. "Confounded with barbarians," says an eminent philosopher, "they bear the penalty of their schism, and remain—significant judgment!—the only Christian people subject to masters who are not so."§ The destruction of Constantinople by Mahomet II., and the subsequent fate of the Greek people, present, as Montesquieu observed, all the marks of a Divine judgment.‖ And to this hour, with the exception of those who have been reconciled to unity, and have recovered by a noble submission the freedom

* Maimbourg, liv. vi., ann. 1439.

† Gennadius, *Adv. Græcos: Theolog. Curs. Complet.*, tom. v., p. 480.

‡ Leonardi Echiensis, Episc. Mitylen, *Lib. de Captivitate Constantinopolis.*

§ M. De Bonald, *Législation Primitive*, tome iv., sec. v., p. 175.

‖ *Grandeur et Décadence des Romains*, ch. xxii.

and dignity which they had lost, the Photian sects are still the most degraded of all Christian races. "Since they fell away from the centre of unity," says one who has long dwelt among them, "they have been completely isolated from the movement of civilization and of science which is ever stimulating the onward march of the other people of Europe. All intellectual activity has died away among them. . . . . In losing the elevated sense of Christianity, they have transformed it into a religion of purely pharisaical ceremonies. The priests have no longer the virtue of the celibate; all the bishoprics, including the patriarchate of Constantinople, have become the object and the prize of base intrigue, upon which the temporal power eagerly speculates, while it openly exposes to auction these sacred dignities. Simony has spread itself like a leprosy over the whole hierarchy, and they make merchandise of holy things."*

"The sport which they make of the miserable dignities of the Greek Church," said Edmund Burke, "the little factions of the harem to which they make them subservient, the continual sale to which they expose and re-expose the same dignity, . . . is nearly equal to all the other oppressions together, exercised by Mussulmen over the unhappy members of the Oriental Church." "The secular clergy," he added, "by being married . . . . . are universally fallen into such contempt, that they are never permitted to aspire to the dignities of their own Church."†

But enough upon the well-known abasement of the Greek and other schismatical communities of the East. We shall visit them, one by one, in the course of this chapter. "Notre plume se refuse," says one who had traced their earlier history, "à tracer des tableaux qui ne sont que trop humiliants pour notre triste condition humaine."‡

The very Turks themselves, detecting the immense distinction between the Latin and Byzantine Christians, denote by certain habitual and emphatic designations their respect for the one and their contempt for the other; and as two centuries ago they styled Catholics *Beysadez*, or "the noble," and the Greeks *Taif*, or "the populace,"—so they still call the former *Francs*, the term of respect and honor, and the latter *Kaffirs*, the Mussulman synonym for "a man without any religion."

The Moslem, we are told by a modern traveller, "is astonished when he hears them classed among the great family of the Christians of the West." "They have preserved," he adds, "nothing of Christianity but the name. The clergy do not even compre-

* M. Eugène Boré, *Correspondance et Mémoires d'un Voyageur en Orient*, tome i., p. 152.

† *On the Penal Laws against Irish Catholics*, Works, vol. vi., pp. 285, 290.

‡ *Grèce*, par M. Pouqueville, Membre de l'Institut, p. 447.

hend the prayers of the liturgy. We have seen them selling prayers to Turkish women, who came secretly to drink the waters of some miraculous fountain. We have seen them selling brandy at the door of their church, and converting, so to speak, the sanctuary into a tavern, before the eyes of the Mussulmen, justly disgusted by the profanation." Even woman, who owes all her dignity and influence to the Christian religion, has relapsed, throughout the schismatical communities of the East, into a kind of barbarism; and while modern Protestants, who shall be quoted hereafter, notice the nobility and freedom of the *Catholic* women among the same races, sole exceptions to the general humiliation because they alone have kept, or recovered, the faith, "the schismatical Greeks and Armenians have caused their social system and their families to retrograde towards the Mussulman level. *Their* women fly from the sight of a Franc with a barbarism even more wild and senseless than that of the Turkish females."*

The facts here indicated are all confirmed, with ample details, by English and American Protestants of our own day, who have been eye-witnesses of them. "The utter desolation of the unhappy Greeks," says Dr. Carne, "forces itself on one's notice every day."† "The gross ignorance of the inferior clergy," observes Mr. Spencer, "not only in theology, but in the common rudiments of education, the dissolute habits of too many of the higher ecclesiastics, and the infamous practices carried on in the monasteries, have become household words throughout all Greece." And this applies to Greece Proper, of which, he adds, "the inhabitants are *more* demoralized than they were under the rule of the Turk."‡ "To the Greek," says Mr. Warrington Smyth, in 1854, "a large proportion of the crimes of the country is to be traced," even within the Ottoman dominions.§ "The Patriarchate," an American writer reports, in 1861, "is a seat of barefaced corruptions. Nine-tenths of the Greek clergy are ignorant, vulgar, drunken debauchees. . . . . They are, therefore, detested by a large majority of the members of that religion."‖ "Divorce is nearly, if not quite, as easy," says Sir Adolphus Slade, "in the Greek religion as in the Mussulman,"—and as it is now in the Anglican or Prussian. "The license is much abused, and the bishops, each of whom has the power, grant it on the slightest pretext." And then he adds, by way of contrast, of

* M. Boré. Cf. Ubicini, *Letters on Turkey*, vol. ii., Letter ii.

† *Letters from the East*, vol. i., p. 37.

‡ *Travels in European Turkey*, vol. ii., ch. xv., pp. 280, 289.

§ *A Year with the Turks*, ch. xiii., p. 295.

‖ Constantinople Correspondent of the *New York Herald*, April 16, 1861.

the *Catholic* population, "Divorce is not permitted among *them.*"* But we reserve the full exhibition of this contrast to a later period.

Yet there are not wanting men in our own country, who have agreed, for party purposes, to exalt the Greek as a convenient ally of Protestants against the Catholic Church. It is true that the Greeks, and all the oriental communities, have again and again anathematized the Anglican religion, and vehemently declined, in spite of their own miseries, even the semblance of intercourse with any of its professors. Not long ago, as an English writer lamented in 1854, the schismatical Greek Patriarch bluntly described its emissaries in the Levant, in an official document addressed to his co-religionists, as "satanical heresiarchs from the caverns of hell."† But this does not deter Anglican writers, always soliciting a recognition which they everywhere implore in vain, from an affectation of sympathy with communities which display such repugnance towards their own; and whose chiefs, after reciting on a solemn occasion—the deposition of Cyril Lucar—the tenets of Anglicanism as set forth in the "Thirty-nine Articles," declared all who hold them to be "heretics who vomit forth blasphemies against God," and then promulgated their decree, by the hands of Jeremy of Constantinople, as "A reply to the inhabitants of Great Britain," to whom its anathemas principally referred.‡

It is a notable feature in the oriental communities, that they spurn the modern errors which they have never accepted, as obstinately as they reject the ancient truth which they once held. When the advocates of Protestantism, vexed rather than convinced by the terrible array of evidence in Nicole's celebrated work, *La Perpétuité de la Foi*, appealed in despair to the oriental sectaries in support of their profane denial of the Sacrament of the Altar, they did not gain much by the appeal. Instructions were sent, as Prince Galitzin notices, to all the ambassadors and consuls throughout the Levant, and "professions of faith were received from the patriarchs, archbishops, and bishops of all the various Churches of the East, affirming in the most positive terms the doctrine of the Real Presence, and bitterly complaining of the calumny" which they thus effectually refuted.§ Let us see how they have replied in our own day to the same overtures which in earlier times they rejected with such vehement disdain.

* *Records of Travel*, &c., ch. xxiii., p. 444 (1854).
† *Journal of a Deputation to the East*, vol. ii., p. 816 (1854).
‡ Theiner, *Pièces Justificatives*, p. 363.
§ *Un Missionaire Russe*, par le Prince Augustin Galitzin, p. 83.

We are going to trace briefly the efforts which have recently been made by Protestants to introduce their opinions in the Levant. It is from Protestants exclusively that we shall, as usual, derive all our information. For more than a quarter of a century they have conducted their operations, distributing on every side, according to their wont, Bibles and gold, tracts and dollars. The Americans boast that by them alone "the annual sum spent for several years" is fifteen thousand pounds.* The English, as usual, have been still more profuse; and Dr. Wilson exults in the fact, that "the whole sum expended by Protestants in missionary efforts is annually double of that expended by Rome,"† though the former have neither churches nor flocks, while the latter numbers its converts alone by hundreds of thousands. Thirty years ago, the active emissaries of the United States were circulating, not only Bibles and tracts which nobody looked at, but "geographies and arithmetics, apparatus for lectures, and compendious histories," which received a much heartier welcome.‡ Indeed, for many years the education of the various sectaries of these regions was mainly in their hands. We should not perhaps exaggerate in supposing that the Protestant missionaries in the Levant have consumed already more than a million sterling. If we ask them what has been the actual result of efforts prolonged through so many years, they are willing to tell us.

Let us begin at Athens. The English, as usual, have employed only agents who could persuade no one to listen to them. An emissary of the British and Foreign School Society, as Dr. Wolff relates, "was sent for the purpose of establishing schools, but he soon gave up that project, and delivered lectures on political economy."§ The Americans have been more successful. "Our country," says an ardent American, "has reason to be proud of its missionaries here."‖ In the following year, another citizen of the United States, still writing from Athens, exclaims, "The cause of education and Christianity is making rapid progress."¶ It was not quite true, as we shall see, but it was hoped that it might be verified later. "In Greece," says a third transatlantic writer, with equal complacency, "the only schools of instruction are those established by American missionaries, and supported by the liberality of American citizens."** Nearly

* *Journal of a Deputation*, &c., p. 826.

† *Lands of the Bible*, by John Wilson, D.D., F.R.S., vol. ii., p. 599.

‡ *Excursions to Cairo*, &c., by the Rev. George Jones, ch. xxi., p. 321 (1836).

§ *Journal*, p. 97.

‖ *Wanderings in Europe and the Orient*, by Samuel S. Cox, ch. xiv., p. 197 (1852).

¶ *Yusef*, by J. Ross Browne, ch. xi., p. 100.

** *Incidents of Travel*, by J. L. Stephens, Esq., ch. xxviii., p. 212.

twenty years earlier, an English writer had noticed, that five hundred Greek children already attended the American schools in Athens; and that in those which were taught by Mrs. Hill, the wife of a missionary, "the daughters of many of the first Greek families of Constantinople, as well as of the most distinguished of Greece Proper," received their education.* Dr. King also rivalled Mr. and Mrs. Hill in influence and in the number of his pupils.

If, however, from these facts we infer that these gentlemen and their companions were making progress *as missionaries*,† the real aim to which all their efforts tended, later events will dispel the illusion. Like their brethren in all parts of the world, they were tolerated for such benefits as could be derived from them, but the moment they began to mistake their position, and to venture upon the subject of religion, grave incidents occurred to admonish them of their error. In spite of the influence which they had acquired by their relations with the higher classes,—in spite of the services which they had unquestionably rendered as secular teachers, and of the active sympathy of the Queen of Greece,—no sooner did they attempt to emerge from the humble function of schoolmaster to assume that of missionary, than a menacing murmur, which soon became a loud and universal outcry, revealed to them their real position. For twenty-four years Mr. and Mrs. Hill had conducted their schools in peace, and might well consider their permanence secured; but at the first hint they understood what was coming, "and thought it best to discontinue their school for boys."‡ Dr. King attempted to brave the storm, "in spite of episcopal and patriarchal anathemas," but the resistance was more energetic than effectual. The Greeks, though enfeebled by schism, were at least resolved to fall no lower; and so intense was their indignation at the attempt to introduce Protestantism among them, that, as Mr. Irenæus Prime relates, "there were serious and deeply concerted schemes for Dr. King's assassination,"§—whose life was only saved by transferring the consular flag to his residence, "a flag," as a sympathizing fellow-countryman observes, "containing quite a number of stripes, and more stars."‖

Finally, an English traveller informs us, in 1854, that "last year at Athens, an American missionary, the Rev. Dr. King, was tried by the civil courts, and condemned to fifteen days

* *Greece Revisited*, by Edgar Garston, vol. i., ch. v., p. 101.

† An English traveller speaks of one of them who "has named his four sons Leonidas, Miltiades, Themistocles, and Epaminondas!" *Narrative of a Yacht Voyage in the Mediterranean*, vol. ii., ch. vii., p. 160 (1842).

‡ *Notes of Travel in the East*, by Benjamim Dorr, D.D., ch. xv., p. 353 (1856).

§ *Travels in Europe and the East*, vol. ii., ch. xiv., p. 188 (1855).

‖ Cox, ch. xiv.

imprisonment, *and to be banished the country*, for preaching the Gospel to the natives in his own house, and publishing a pamphlet opposed to some of the doctrines of the Greek Church."* It seems that in his pamphlet he spoke against devotion to our Blessed Lady, a crime which even Greeks are not prepared to tolerate, nor able to witness with composure.

At the same time, a Mr. Buell, also a missionary, who refused to allow a crucifix to be suspended in his school at the Piræus, was summoned before the tribunals, his school closed by order of the government, and a fine of fifty drachmas imposed upon the profane schoolmaster.†

Such was the termination of the educational labors of a quarter of a century. The Greek conscience, though not fastidiously delicate, was outraged by the first accents of Protestantism, and while its agents were branded by the Patriarch as "heresiarchs from the caverns of hell," the people answered its invitations by a shout, which came from the heart of the nation, of "anathema" and "banishment."

It is not uninteresting to notice the effect of this popular outburst upon the Protestant missionaries and their supporters. Hitherto they had spoken, always with respect, often with a kind of reverence, of this "ancient" and "venerable" Church, in the hope that it might be induced to countenance their own more recent institutions. The language of praise was now to be heard no more. We have seen that in India, as soon as the Nestorians, upon whom so much courtesy had been lavished, declined the respectful overtures of the Anglican authorities, these disdainful heretics were consigned to ignominy by Protestant prelates, whose precarious "orders" they had refused to recognize, and even stigmatized as "worse than Romanists." The same thing happened in Greece. "The Greek Church," said Dr. Wilson, recording the discomfiture of his co-religionists, "agrees with the Church of Rome in most matters of the greatest moment. It has the essential characteristic of Antichrist."‡

It was thus that these gentlemen revenged themselves upon the Greeks, once objects of almost timid eulogy. "I would say," adds Dr. Wilson, confessing at length the futility of past missionary schemes, "that at present it seems a very difficult matter to impregnate the Greek Church with evangelical truth and influence; and that its circumstances are much less encouraging than those of the other oriental churches." So they

* *Journal of a Deputation*, &c., p. 590.
† *Journal d'un Voyage au Levant*, pp. 281, 311.
‡ *Lands of the Bible*, vol. ii., p. 466.

turned to these more promising fields, with what success, we shall see in the course of this chapter.

"In regard to the Greeks," says Dr. Hawes, an American Protestant minister, "the success of efforts made in their behalf has been less than was reasonably anticipated;" and then, as if he felt that this was hardly an adequate account of the matter, he adds, "The missionaries have felt themselves obliged, for the present, *to withdraw*, in a great measure, from this field."*

Messrs. Eli Smith and Dwight, more emphatic in their resentment, confound the Catholics with the Greeks, and even seem to attribute their misadventures to the influence of the former. "A missionary," they observe, "can hardly set his foot upon any spot in that field, the Mediterranean, without encountering some sentinel of the 'Mother of Harlots,' ready to challenge him and shout the alarm."† Yet the Greeks do not appear to have needed any suggestions from that quarter, and would certainly have received them with surprise if they had been offered.

Lastly, a representative of English Protestantism swells the gloomy chorus, and discovers, a quarter of a century too late, that "the Greek Church is opposed to the general circulation of the Bible;" and that "the priests have *always* strenuously opposed the distribution of the Bible in modern Greek."‡ Yet the Bible Society used to assure its subscribers, as we have seen, that they had no more promising sphere of action, and that even the Greek soldiery fortified themselves with the Protestant version during the intervals of combat, "while encamped, and in expectation of the enemy." It was, no doubt, to gratify this pious habit of the Greeks, that the English missionaries issued in a single year from their fortress at Malta "four million seven hundred and sixty thousand pages, all in modern Greek;" and that the Americans had already dispersed, thirty years ago, "about three hundred and fifty thousand volumes containing twenty-one million pages." And of this enormous but perfectly useless distribution, since increased fifty-fold, the Protestants of these two enlightened nations have cheerfully, but not wisely, defrayed the whole cost.

We must admit, however, before we pass from Greece to Turkey, that Protestant teaching has not been absolutely without effect in the former kingdom. Let us notice a single

* *Travels in the East,* by J. Hawes, D.D., p. 168.
† *Missionary Researches in Armenia,* Letter xi., p. 210.
‡ *Journal of a Deputation,* p. 594.

example of its influence. An accomplished Greek lady, of rare intelligence and attainments, the eloquent advocate of her race and nation, had the misfortune to lose her parents, and was brought up by a Protestant pastor. The result of his instructions, if we may judge by her own writings, has been to substitute for faith a cold and arrogant skepticism, to engender a fierce hatred of the Catholic religion, which this lady calls "Christian Mahometanism," and to give her courage to assert that divorce, which has become a kind of national institution in Greek and Protestant lands, is not an evil, but an engine of morality!* There is a good deal more of the same kind in the writings of this distinguished lady, which it would be both painful and unprofitable to notice, but which may at least confirm our conviction that Greece did well in crying "anathema" to Protestant missionaries.

What the Catholic apostles have done for the Greeks, by their own confession, we shall see a little later, but will first follow their rivals to Turkey, that we may complete the history of their operations in the Levant.

EUROPEAN TURKEY.

In European Turkey, the English do not appear to have organized any systematic missionary efforts; and throughout the Levant the Anglican Establishment has been represented, almost exclusively, as in India and elsewhere, by members of other communities. Mr. Perkins, an American missionary, to whom we shall have to refer presently, remarks that the employment of "so many men of a different religious communion reveals a painful deficiency in the missionary spirit of the Church of England, that men of devotion to the cause *cannot be found* in sufficient numbers within her pale to go in person and apply her missionary funds."† "At present," adds a Protestant historian of American missions, with quiet contempt, "she has more means than men."‡

Perhaps, however, the Church of England has no reason to regret this fact, considering the impression which her rare representatives usually produce upon the oriental mind. When Mr. Jowett, one of her clergy, was asked by a schismatical Greek bishop, what was the doctrine of his Church about the "Double Procession" of the Holy Spirit, his answer must have

* *Les Femmes en Orient*, par Mme. la Csse. Dora D'Istria, pp. 71, 84 (1860).

† *Residence in Persia among the Nestorian Christians*, by Rev. Justin Perkins, ch. iii., p. 52.

‡ Tracy, *History of American Missions*, p. 594.

astonished even such an inquirer. "It is a point, I replied, which, in the present day, has not been much controverted, being considered as somewhat indifferent!"*

But several years have elapsed since Mr. Jowett's visit, and the Greek prelates have had time to forget both him and his Church. So complete has been the oblivion, that when Mr. Curzon not long ago presented a letter of introduction from the Queen's Archbishop of Canterbury to the Sultan's Archbishop of Constantinople, the following curious conversation occurred.

"And who, quoth the Patriarch of Constantinople, the supreme head and primate of the Greek Church in Asia—who is 'the Archbishop of Canterbury?'

"What? said I, a little astonished at the question.

"Who, said he, is this Archbishop?

"Why, the Archbishop of Canterbury.

"Archbishop of *what?* said the Patriarch.

"*Canterbury*, said I.

"Oh! said the Patriarch. Ah! yes! and who is he?"†

The Church Missionary Society, in their sixty-third report, 1862,‡ give this quotation from their principal agent in Turkey. "Dr. Pfander takes this sober view of the mission at the close of the year 1861: 'Though there is no particular movement going on among the Mohammedans, yet there is the fact that they continue to visit the missionaries. . . . Our work is indeed but small as yet; still I am thankful that some progress has been made during the year, and, above all, that the translation and printing of the Miftah and the Mizan, through God's help, has been accomplished.'" Perhaps some may think that the only "help" in such proceedings came from the money of the Church Missionary Society.

The Americans have acquired more notoriety in these regions. Their operations in Turkey commenced in 1826, and by 1844 they had already thirty-one missionaries in that country.§ Not that they have "attempted any conversion except of *the Christians*," as Mr. Walpole remarks; the Turks, he adds, they are "afraid" of provoking.‖ But they are active enough amongst the Armenian sectaries, both here and in Armenia, as we shall see when we enter the latter country. Meanwhile, it seems to be a tranquil and jocund life which these thirty-one missionaries lead in Turkey. "Personal trials are very few," says the candid wife of one of them; "many are the comforts and

* *Christian Researches*, &c., p. 17.
† *Monasteries of the Levant*, ch. xxii., p. 336.
‡ P. 59.
§ Baird, *Religion in the U. S. of America*, book viii., ch. iii., p. 691.
‖ *The Ansayrii*, &c., ch. xvi., p. 366.

pleasant things about this life in the East."* And she was evidently not singular in her keen appreciation of them. The Rev. Justin Perkins tells us of a missionary wedding at Constantinople in these terms: "Mr. Schauffler was married to Miss Reynolds, February 25th. I could not help feeling that there was a moral sublimity in the scene presented."† Perhaps there was; but another witness, Sir Adolphus Slade, who knows these regions even better than Mr. Perkins, and is evidently much less impressed by the moral sublimity of missionary nuptials, gives the following candid account of the Protestant missionaries in Turkey and the Levant.

"To what purpose do the missionaries on the shores of the Turkish empire frequent them? to convert those *who are already Christians.* The utter unprofitableness of these gentlemen cannot be sufficiently pointed out. One comes to Malta, and settles there with his lady. Another comes to Tino, and while learning Greek, to be enabled to labor on the continent, falls in love, and marries an amiable Tiniote—his spiritual ardor takes another course. Another fixes himself at Smyrna, finding that demi-Frank city pleasanter than the interior of Turkey, whither he was destined. Another takes a disorder, and dies of it on the shores of the Persian Gulf. Another quietly pursues his own studies at Alexandria, regardless of others' souls, to qualify himself for a situation in one of the London colleges. All are living on the stipends granted by the missionary societies, and occupied in forwarding their particular views. Far be it from me to say that human weakness does not merit indulgence; but they who embark in a holy cause should quit it when they find that the flesh overpowers the spirit. Religion is the last asylum where hypocrisy should find shelter."‡

Admiral Slade adds, "It will scarcely be credited that missionaries arrive in the Levant, to preach, to convert, knowing absolutely no other than their mother tongue!" Yet we shall presently hear one of their number asserting, with perfect indifference to the more veracious testimony of a crowd of Protestant writers, that he and his friends had done more for education in Syria in twenty years than "all the Catholic missionaries" in two centuries; though the former have had neither scholars nor disciples, and were for the most part perfectly incapable of teaching them if they had.

A few words will suffice on the final results of Protestant missions in Turkey. The American Episcopalians sent Dr. Southgate, one of their bishops, to recommend their form of

* *Memoir of Mrs. Van Lennep*, ch. xi., p. 267 (1851).
† *Residence*, &c., ch. iii., p. 76.
‡ Ch. xxvii., p. 517.

religion to the inhabitants. He seems to have had some vague idea of ecclesiastical principles, and is even charged by his own countrymen, of other sects, with supporting the schismatical oriental bishops in their resistance to the proselyting schemes of the Protestant missionaries, whom he openly taxed with introducing amongst the Armenians "the revolutionary sentiments of European radicalism." He had, too, sufficient courage and honesty to confess, after ample experience, that the Protestant converts are "*infidels* and radicals, who deserve no sympathy from the Christian public."*

Dr. Southgate recommends also the employment of missionaries "unrestrained by family ties,"—though he does not suggest where they are to be found,—and after deploring the activity of "our brethren of other denominations," predicts this as the only fruit of their labors: "Horrid schism will lift itself up from beneath, and rend and scatter the quivering members of the body of Christ."† Yet this gentleman, who had so much distaste for horrid schism in others, actually intrigued to get a *firman* issued against the Catholics, whom he could only oppose by physical force, in favor of the Jacobite heretics, whose "numerous points of affinity" with his own sect he had detected with satisfaction.‡

We are not surprised to hear that Dr. Southgate failed. For a long time, he confesses, his mission at Constantinople received from a single congregation in Philadelphia one thousand dollars annually. But money could not save it. "The mission," we are told in 1852, "has been abandoned, at least for the present, after a heavy expenditure. Bishop Southgate has returned to the United States, and resigned the appointment of Missionary Bishop to Turkey."§ Two years later another Protestant authority says, "the bishop had to acknowledge the complete failure of his mission, and was *recalled* by his society."‖ It is exactly the tale which we have heard in so many other lands. Not one of the customary incidents is wanting, and they follow one another in their usual and invariable order: first, "horrid schism;" then, "heavy expenditure;" and finally, "complete failure."

Of the operations of the other American sects at Constantinople, there is no need to speak. We shall presently survey them on a larger scale in Syria and Armenia. Mr. Dwight, in a work which reveals the real designs of his co-religionists in

* *Christianity in Turkey*, by Rev. H. G. O. Dwight, ch. x., p. 244 (1854).

† *Narrative of a Tour in Turkey and Persia*, by Rev. Horatio Southgate, vol. i., ch. xxiii., p. 305.

‡ *Mr. Southgate and the Missionaries at Constantinople*, p. 27 (Boston, 1844).

§ *Colonial Church Chronicle*, p. 396 (1852).

‖ *Journal of a Deputation to the East*, vol. ii., p. 806.

the East, declares in 1850, that "at the capital the number of Armenians who declared themselves Protestants rapidly increased."* Their number is, in fact, perfectly insignificant; and many Protestant writers will tell us, before we conclude this chapter, as Dr. Southgate has already told us, what an Armenian really becomes when he professes to embrace Protestant tenets. They will also assist us to comprehend what even they consider the work of "corruption and demoralization" in which the American missionaries are engaged, though happily, up to the present date, within a narrow sphere. It is true, however, that they have succeeded, by lavish expenditure —we have been told that they consume thirty thousand pounds per annum in Turkey—in collecting together a few Jews and Armenians, who have more admiration for their dollars than their doctrines, and who abandon their old religion without adopting a new one; and that these form what they call the "Protestant Church," or, as Mr. Dwight styles them, "the people of God," in Constantinople. Such are the "wild grapes" of which they make sour wine, to set their own teeth on edge. "The Protestant Church of Turkey," says Mr. Cuthbert Young, "is now recognized by the government," owing to the energetic action peculiar to this branch of the Anglo-Saxon family, "with an officer of the Porte, *a Turk*, as its temporal head. This last circumstance cannot be regarded as auguring well for the interests of vital Christianity."†

A few years later, we learn from a competent witness, the prediction of Mr. Young was unpleasantly verified, and the Porte, though probably quite as capable of promoting "vital Christianity" as the Hebrew and Armenian Protestants to whom it lent a temporal head, proved to be only a Moslem Pharaoh, from whose ungentle sway Mr. Dwight's "people of God" are already desirous to escape. The Mahometan gentleman who consented to become the Caliph of Turkish Protestants has evidently formed a serious estimate of his own office. "All the Protestants in the country," we are told by a missionary in 1860, "must be enrolled in his books." And the enrolment is by no means a mere matter of form. From that moment, a marriage, an interment, or any other of the various ceremonies of joyful or sorrowing humanity, "*can only be done through him.*" And this is not all. "For the support of this officer," whose appointment the Protestant missionaries hailed with such lively satisfaction, "the Protestants all over the country have been called upon to contribute," apparently on a very liberal scale; and as this special tax does not exempt them from the burdens

* *Christianity Revived in the East*, p. 32 (1850).
† *The Levant and the Nile*, ch. iii., p. 76.

common to the rest of the population, "the Protestants are deeply in debt," says the same missionary, "and it has become a serious question with them, whether they should not dissolve their civil establishment entirely. This would doubtless open the way for a general persecution of the Protestants throughout the empire, the result of which none can foresee,"*—but which, considering the motives of Jews and Armenians in professing Protestantism, would certainly involve the final disappearance of all the unstable disciples who have been the costly stipendiaries of English or American missionary societies, but who, as Dr. Southgate ascertained, "are infidels and radicals, who deserve no sympathy from the Christian public."

CATHOLIC MISSIONS IN TURKEY.

And now let us speak briefly, before we enter Asia, of Catholic missions in the regions which we are about to quit. Not that we can hope to give, within the limits at our disposal, even a sketch of labors as distinguished by supernatural patience and charity as any which we have hitherto narrated. A few examples must suffice, but they will abundantly illustrate the familiar contrast which we have proposed to trace in all lands. We are going to speak, though unworthy even to record their names, of a band of apostles whom even a Protestant minister calls, with honest enthusiasm, "*the best instructed and most devoted missionaries that the world has seen since primitive times.*"† We have heard what sort of agents the Sects employ; let us contemplate for a moment another order of workmen, and see what the munificent bounty of God can do for men whom His own decree has called to the apostolic life. Too long we have listened to the mean sounds of earth—it is time to open our ears to voices from Heaven.

As early as 1610, the son of St. Ignatius had begun to convert both Jews and schismatics at Constantinople. So irresistible was the influence, here as elsewhere, of men in whom religion displayed its most fascinating form, and *self* was all but annihilated, that, as Von Hammer notices, the Grand Vizir told de Solignac, the French ambassador, that "he would rather see ten ordinary ecclesiastics at Pera than one Jesuit."‡ A century later, for these men do not change, a schismatical Armenian patriarch thus addressed a Catholic who had abandoned the schism, and

* *Three Years in Turkey, the Journal of a Medical Missionary to the Jews*, by John Mason, L.R.C.S.E., app., p. 373 (1860).

† Williams, *The Holy City*, vol. ii., ch. vi., p. 570.

‡ *Histoire de l'Empire Ottoman*, par J. Von Hammer, tome viii., liv. iii., p. 166, ed. Hellert.

was about to be martyred: "Your blood be upon the Jesuits who have converted you and so many members of our Church."*

In the single year 1712, for we must not attempt to trace the whole history, Père Jacques Cachod, to whom was given the noble title of "Father of the Slaves," reconciled three hundred schismatics to the Church.† Five years earlier, nearly one-third of the population of Constantinople died of the plague; and it was at that date that Père Cachod, compelled by holy obedience to give an account of actions which he would have preferred to hide, wrote as follows to his superior, Père Tarillon:

"I have just quitted the Bagnio, where I have given the last Sacraments to, and closed the eyes of, eighty-six persons. . . . The greatest danger which I have encountered, or to which I shall perhaps ever be exposed in my life, was at the bottom of the hold of a ship-of-war of eighty-two guns. The slaves, by the consent of their guards, had obtained my admission into this place in the evening, in order that I might spend the whole night in hearing their confessions, and say Mass for them very early in the morning. We were shut in with double locks, according to custom. Of fifty-two slaves whom I confessed and communicated, twelve were already plague-stricken, and three died before I quitted them. You may judge what sort of an atmosphere I breathed in this inclosed space, to which there was not the slightest opening. God, who by His goodness has preserved me in this danger, will save me also from many others." Twelve years later he perished, struck down by the pestilence which he thought he might henceforth defy. And the only reflection which such a narrative, and such a fate, suggested to the other Fathers was this: "If we were more numerous, how much more good we could do!"‡

But if these generous apostles displayed a zeal which knew not fear, it was regulated always by prudence and forethought. "During the seasons of the plague," says one of them, "as it is necessary to be close at hand in order to succor those who are seized by it, our custom is that only one Father should enter the Bagnio, and that he should remain there during the whole time that the pest rages. The one who obtains the permission of the Superior prepares himself for his duty by a retreat of some days, and bids farewell to his brethren, as one about to die. Sometimes his sacrifice is consummated, at others he survives the danger. The last Jesuit who died in this exercise of charity was Father Vandermans . . . . Since his death, the

* *Histoire de l'Empire Ottoman*, tome xiii., liv. lxii., p. 186.

† *Lettres Edifiantes*, tome i., p. 14.

‡ Ibid., p. 23.

only victim has been Father Peter Besnier, so well known for his genius and rare gifts."

It is impossible to trace here the details of the apostolic history of which this is only a characteristic episode. The public cemetery of Constantinople, filled with the bodies of Jesuits who died between 1585 and 1756, is their only monument. Smyrna, Aleppo, Trebizonde, and many other oriental cities, gave a tomb to missionaries of the same class. At Smyrna, where ten thousand perished by plague in the same year, a Jesuit bishop became a martyr of charity at eighty years of age. In Aleppo, Father Besson,—"who united to his immense labors perpetual mortification, allowed himself but scanty repose at night, and rose long before the dawn in order to spend many hours in prayer,"—"after having procured a holy death to a large number of persons, found the crown which he sought." He was followed, both in his life and death, by Father Deschamps; and almost at the same moment, Father de Clermont, of the illustrious family of that name, was added to the company of martyrs. It was at this time, and by the labors of such men, that the schismatical Patriarchs of Armenia (Erivan), of Aleppo, Alexandria, and Damascus, were all reconciled to the Church.

In 1709, Michael Paleologus becomes the disciple of Father Braconnier. Father Bernard Couder is the next in this band of Christian heroes. More than nine hundred families in the city of Aleppo were formed by him to a life of piety. Six times he solicited and obtained the coveted permission to devote himself to the plague-stricken; and so perfect was his obedience, that when ordered by his superior to quit a city in which he had attracted a veneration which might prove dangerous to his humility, "he began on the instant to make his preparations for departure."

In 1719, when the plague raged in Aleppo from March to September, "I was often obliged," says the celebrated Father Nacchi, "to bend down between two victims of the pestilence, to confess them by turns, keeping my ear glued as it were to their lips, in order to catch their dying sounds." And when death had done its work, these apostles, nurtured themselves in delicacy and refinement, often the most accomplished scholars of their age, and not unfrequently members of illustrious houses, would wash the bodies and clothes of the dead, "reeking with a horrible infection," and having borne them with their own hands to the common cemetery, hasten back to repeat the same office of charity for others.

Such deeds, which Catholics have learned to consider natural in their clergy, of whatever rank, would hardly deserve mention, but that we are tracing a contrast. There is probably not one of the thousand priests in our own England who would not imitate them to-morrow, and few of their number who have not already exposed their lives, many a time, with the same tranquil composure. It is not many years since an English bishop, and fifty priests, died within ten months, ministering to the victims of typhus. "The good shepherd giveth his life for the sheep." But let us complete the narrative which we have begun.

"Father Emanuel died in my arms," says the learned Nacchi, "after devoting himself incessantly for four months to the victims of the plague. After him I assisted Father Arnoudie, and Brother John Martha, both destroyed by the same disease." Father Clisson, after an apostolate of thirty years in Syria, met the same death; and was followed by Father Nau, of whom his companions used to say, "he has received from heaven all the gifts necessary for the apostolic life." Then came the noble brothers de la Thuillerie, Joseph and James, the elder dying on the bosom of the younger. The next was Father Réné Pillon, for they fell fast, whose only form of recreation was to visit and console the sick, and whose daily prayer it was "that he might die in the service of the dying." To him succeeded Father Blein, whose humility so touched the hearts of the Greeks that they flocked to see his dead body, and though he died of the plague, carried away fragments of his clothes as relics. Beyrout saw the last combat of Father John Amieu, "who predicted his own death to one who lay ill by his side, but assured the latter of his recovery."* And these are only a few names out of a multitude known to God, and written in the book of life. Of them it may be truly said that they resembled one another so exactly, that they were like brothers of one family. And even the most malignant spirit of heresy could not resist them. "*You* seek only our conversion," was a common saying of the sectaries, "the others ask for our money." And they often contrasted their manner of life with that of the Protestants who had already begun to dwell amongst them. "The English and Dutch in Aleppo," one of the missionaries remarks, "observe neither fast nor abstinence, to the scandal of everybody. The people of the country say that they cannot be Christians, and even the Turks regard them as void of religion." And the results of a contrast which even pagans have noticed, in every region of the world, were such as these. In Damascus, where there were only three Catholic families when the Jesuits arrived, there were in 1750 nearly nine thousand converts. In Smyrna and Aleppo, almost the whole schismatical population

* Ibid., p. 200. Cf. *Missions du Levant,* tome iv., p. 39.

has been converted; the work being continued in our own day, as Protestant travellers will presently assure us, by men in whom even *they* recognize the apostolic virtues of their predecessors. Throughout all Syria, as we shall learn from the same witnesses, the heirs of the martyrs are now laboring with such fruit, that from the banks of the Orontes to those of the Tigris and the Euphrates, the wanderers are flocking to the true fold, and even Chaldea, as we shall be told by men who vainly strove to mar the work, has become a Catholic nation.

When the Society of Jesus was suppressed, the enemy triumphed for a moment in Turkey and the Levant, as in so many other lands. But the Fathers of the Order of St. Lazarus were chosen by Providence to supply their place, at least for a time, and we must now say a word of *their* labors in the East.

In 1840, there were already in Greece Proper four bishops, one hundred priests, and twenty-three thousand Catholics. At the same date, in the three principalities of Moldavia, Wallachia, and Servia, there were three bishops, and seventy-one thousand Catholics. In the kingdom of Turkey there were eleven archbishops, four hundred and twenty-three priests, and two hundred and eighty-one thousand Catholics.* This total of three hundred and seventy-five thousand has probably trebled during the last twenty years, so that Ubicini reckons the whole number of Latin Christians in European Turkey alone, in 1856, at six hundred and forty thousand, of whom five hundred and five thousand were natives;† while the total number of Greeks under the sceptre of the Sultan had dwindled twenty years ago to one million.‡ It is even said that there is hope of the early reconciliation of the entire Bulgarian nation, though the influence of Russia will no doubt be employed to prevent it.

At the close of the year 1840, the celebrated Lazarist Father Etienne gave this report to the heads of his Order: "The chief obstacle opposed by error to the progress of the Gospel is profound ignorance, the common basis both of heresy and Islamism. The first means, therefore, of favoring the triumph of the Gospel is the education of youth. The Koran has still its disciples, but only because it proscribes all education. At present, however, this prohibition is no longer regarded by the great, whose contempt for the law of Mahomet is only imperfectly concealed under a few exterior practices." An English Protestant traveller confirms this account, when he says, that

* *Annals*, vol. i., p. 406.
† See Ubicini's *Letters on Turkey*.
‡ *La Turquie d'Europe*, par A. Boué, tome ii., ch. i., p. 21.

the present religion of the Turks "is a kind of gross epicurean skepticism."*

Father Etienne, however, gives interesting proofs of the respect which they begin to manifest for the Catholic religion, and the remarkable acquaintance which some of them display with its doctrines; and he adds, that "once permitted to frequent our schools, the Gospel and science will find them equally docile to their instructions. From the moment the Turks are allowed to enjoy liberty of conscience and the blessings oi education, the Church will be on the eve of counting them amongst the number of her children."†

Let it be permitted, at this point, to offer, under correction, a consideration suggested by the present aspect of Islamism. Perhaps there is nothing so marvellous in the annals of mankind as the history of the Mahometan religion,—its triumphant progress through the three continents of the Old World, checked only by the union of the Catholic nations under the inspiration of the Holy See,—and its puissant dominion of a thousand years. What providential scheme was this mystery, strange and unique in the annals of our race, designed to serve? The present condition of Islamism seems to suggest the explanation.

When the East was enslaved by heresy and schism, *then* the legions of the false prophet came out of Arabia. For centuries they have been permitted to scourge the oriental Christians, treading them under foot as vermin. In human history there are no such oppressors, no such victims. "Crushed and degraded below the level of humanity," in the words of Mr. Spencer, "generation after generation of the unhappy Christians have passed away like the leaves of the forest." Nor is this the darkest feature in their history. It was from *apostate Greeks* and monophysites that the legions of Antichrist were perpetually recruited by tens of thousands. "Mahommedanism," as Von Haxthausen forcibly observes, "represents the pure monotheistic direction which *the Eastern Church*, especially in its sects, had already indicated and followed, one-sided and dogmatical." Even in our own day it continues to enlist the same class of fallen Christians, helpless because severed from unity —Copts, Greeks, and Abyssinians. At Trebizonde, in 1838, we are told, "the Greeks professed Islamism abroad, but lived as Christians in the interior of their houses." "Apostasy is, in fact, so obvious a sin in these countries," says an English Protestant minister, "that even little children, as I was informed by the Bishop of Smyrna, will sometimes, when in a

* *Two Years' Residence in a Levantine Family*, by Bayle St. John; ch. xxiii., p. 267.

† *Annals*, vol. ii., p. 71.

violent passion, threaten their mothers that they will turn Turk."* Damascus, once wholly Christian, became almost entirely Mahometan; and the same fact occurred in most of the cities of the East. "Issuing from Arabia, *and absorbing in its passage the Christianity of the East*, the Mussulman torrent traversed the Bosphorus, and carried forward the crescent to the European provinces of the Greek Cæsars; for it was no longer with the degenerate Christianity of the East as with that which flowed, full of life and strength, from the apostolic Roman fount. The latter had quickly *absorbed into itself* all the conquerors of the empire; the former bowed down without resistance under the code of the Caliphs, and the Christian populations of Asia, deserting the faith of Christ, adopted, in vast numbers, that of the false prophet, and recruited the armies of his vicars."†

Such is the contrast between the Christianity of Rome and Byzantium; and such, for centuries, has been the influence of the Mahometan over the corrupt and schismatical communities of the East. But Islamism has done its work, and may now disappear. It came to chastise, by an unparalleled judgment, an unexampled offence. And now, when the oriental churches are visibly returning to unity, and the voice of the Supreme Pastor is once more heard amongst them, Islamism—as if conscious that it may no longer play the part of the Avenger—is hastening to decay. We seem to touch already that great epoch of Catholic unity,—of which the recent definition of the Immaculate Conception of the Mother of God is the surest pledge and precursor,—that consolidation of all believers into one household and family which Her love will obtain for the Church before the world is abandoned to its final judgment, and even the Church shall plead for it no more.

Let us return for a moment to Father Etienne, and to the account which he gives of religion in Turkey. "At Constantinople," he says, "the clergy of our congregation are at the head of a college, in which the children of the first families of the city are educated; they have also a school which is frequented by one hundred and fifty scholars." This refers to the state of things twenty years ago. "Three other schools are directed by the Sisters of Charity. The two hundred and thirty pupils whom they receive are not all Catholics; Russians, Arabs, Armenian and Greek schismatics come to the same source to obtain knowledge and wisdom." The Sisters had also under their care a hospital, towards the expenses of which the Sultan contributed

* Jowett, p. 23.
† *Persécution et Souffrances*, &c., p. 240.

one hundred pounds. Even the Mussulmen, he adds, filled with admiration for the charity of the Sisters, "who neither will nor can receive any recompense," are accustomed to ask, "*Whether they came down thus from heaven?*" "May we not presume," says M. Etienne, "that the Sisters of Charity are destined by Providence to effect the long wished-for union between Turks and Christians?"

An English Protestant writer, in spite of customary prejudice, thus confirms the account of Father Etienne: "Short as the time has been since these zealous Christians have entered upon this new field of labor, it must be owned in all justice that the progress they have made, and the beneficial effects of their judicious efforts, are most surprising. . . . The admiration, as well as confidence, with which both they and the Lazarists have inspired the Turks is unbounded."* And this is confirmed once more, in 1859, by another English Protestant, who considers "a visit to the convent of the Sisters of Charity interesting and instructive, as showing how human beings possessed of education and personal attractions can leave every thing which makes life dear for the sake of God. Here, as everywhere else, these ladies do a great deal of good, particularly in education of the Arab children." Of their hospital "for the special use of strangers," of all creeds, "who may chance to fall ill here"—Beyrout—he adds, that the sufferers, "when tended by the devoted Sisters, scarcely miss the absence of their friends."†

When we have shown that the missionaries have not degenerated from their fathers, but still resemble a Cachod, a Besnier, and a Vandermans, we may pass to other scenes. "M. Elluin," says Father Etienne, "catechizes the poor in Greek, and with the most consoling success; his instructions are frequented every Sunday by three hundred persons, children and adults. M. Bonnieux, another missionary, whose indefatigable zeal I could not but admire, spends his life in hearing the confessions of the Catholics, scattered throughout the city and the environs. Every morning he sets out, taking in his course both sides of the Bosphorus, penetrating into the interior of families, distributing consolation and advice, and often returning without having tasted food, except the morsel of bread he had taken with him. Often, too, surprised by the night far from his home, he passes it in some miserable hut, offers there the Holy Sacrifice in the morning before he leaves, and continuing his route of the previous day, returns at length to his brethren full

* *Wayfaring Sketches among the Greeks and Turks*, ch. ix., p. 184.
† *Two Years in Syria*, ch. xxvii., p. 235.

of joy. This laborious ministry is never interrupted, either by the rigor of the season or the ravages of the plague."

Such are "the comforts and pleasant things" which *these* men choose for their portion. And the results of their patient charity are such as the following: M. Bonnieux alone, in the course of a few months, reconciled to the Church one hundred and twenty-two heretics. The most conspicuous among his converts was Mgr. Artin, schismatical Archbishop of Van, in Armenia. An immense crowd of the former disciples of the converted prelate assisted at the ceremony of his abjuration; and after listening to the fervent exhortation which, from a heart newly kindled with Divine charity, he addressed to them, "more than twelve hundred persons were found to imitate this memorable conversion."*

The impulse given to education by the toils of the same workmen, is the only additional fact which we need notice. "It is very certain," says Ubicini in 1858, "that the number of the schools founded by the Lazarists, with the assistance of the Sisters of Charity and of the Christian Brothers, increases yearly in a remarkable degree." And then he observes, that already, in 1849, "the latter had six hundred children in their schools of Pera and Galata," while the former had, at the same date, eight hundred and sixty pupils.† Other writers will inform us that they are diffusing the same benefits in the principal cities of Asiatic Turkey.

We have no space for further details. For twenty years the work has progressed, everywhere by the same agents, and always with the same results. Even Protestants attest its power. "The Catholic religion in the East," says Admiral Slade, in 1854, appreciating these events from his own point of view, "has ever offered a secure asylum for wavering minds of the Greek and Armenian sects." He declares, also, from actual observation, "that it has made men *live in peace* among each other, and under their government, whatever that government be."‡

Dr. Wilson,—who has, perhaps, employed more intemperate language than any living writer, and has been more abundant in those vehement invectives which sound like imprecations, and remind one of the text, "Whoso hateth his brother is a murderer,"—is constrained by a Power which uses such men to proclaim the very truths which they abhor, to make the following confession. The Greeks, he says, when they become

* *Annals*, ii., 76.
† *Letters on Turkey*, vol. ii., Letter iii.
‡ *Records of Travels*, ch. xxvii., p. 511.

Catholics, "are amongst the most liberal and intelligent native Christians in the East."*

Dr. Robinson, an American writer of the same class,—who laments that the movement of conversion among the Greeks, after spreading through Syria, "has now extended itself into Egypt,"—admits with evident reluctance, that "the result is a certain elevation of their sect."† Dr. Durbin also, another American Protestant, declares without reserve of *all* the oriental communities, "It is not to be denied that their intercourse with the Roman Catholic Church tends to elevate them in the scale of civilization."‡ We shall hear many similar testimonies when we enter Syria.

ASIATIC TURKEY.

We may now cross the Bosphorus, and continue in Asiatic Turkey the investigations which we have hitherto confined to her European provinces. Let us begin at Smyrna. If we would find Protestant missionaries in pagan or moslem lands, much experience has taught us to look for them *on the coast.* They abound in Smyrna. "The number of missionaries who have been sent to *Turkey*," says an English Protestant, "and are established at *Smyrna*, is very considerable."§ "They find that demi-Frank city pleasanter," we have been told, "than the interior of Turkey;" and, as a matter of taste, they are probably right. M. de Tchihatcheff, a Russian traveller, found some of the American missionaries, in 1856, occupied in meteorological observations; a useful and honorable pursuit, for which he seems to think they had abundant leisure.‖ What else they have done, we may easily learn, either from themselves or their friends.

Two of the earliest missionaries from America were the Rev. Pliny Fisk and the Rev. Levi Parsons. Both have found admiring biographers. The Rev. Dr. Bond informs us that Mr. Fisk was dispatched to Syria by "the Prudential Committee of the American Board," and also that "his religious exercises were marked for pungency of conviction." He tarried at Malta on his way to Palestine, and "was for a season occupied in exploring the moral desolations which there prevailed," but to which it is not suggested that Mr. Fisk applied any remedy.

* *Lands of the Bible*, vol. ii., p. 581.
† *Biblical Researches*, vol. iii., sec. xvii., p. 456.
‡ *Observations in the East*, vol. ii., ch. xxxiv., p. 287.
§ *Wayfaring Sketches*, &c., ch. vi., p. 118.
‖ *Asie Mineure*, par P. de Tchihatcheff; ch. i., p. 5 (1856).

At length he reached Beyrût, and there "his spirit was much refreshed," apparently by the society of his countrymen. That he ever made a convert, from any class whatever, his biographer does not venture to insinuate; but his final retreat from these regions, after a residence which had been without a solitary incident for the pen of the historian, is thus described and accounted for: "Having sounded from the hill of Zion the trumpet-note of preparation," says Dr. Bond, "to awaken the Church to the glorious enterprise in which he had led the way, he retired, amid the commotion which his own efforts had excited, until the indignation was overpast."* The indignation, however, was so permanent, that Mr. Fisk was never again seen near the hill of Zion.†

The Rev. Levi Parsons, his companion, is thus sketched by the eloquent ardor of the Rev. Dr. Squier. "He was more like the good Samaritan than the Apostle Paul. If you classed him with the eleven disciples, it would be with John rather than Peter." The portrait is perhaps deficient in distinctness, but Mr. Parsons has added some touches with his own hand. "I was often," he says, "in Jerusalem, preaching with great success, and once I reasoned before the governor of Smyrna, as Paul did before Felix." Like Mr. Fisk, he never converted anybody, Greek, Jew, or Armenian, and least of all the governor of Smyrna; but his biographer adds, as if he owed this consolation to his readers, "he was among modern missionaries what Melancthon was among the Reformers."‡

The "eminent female missionary," Mrs. Sarah Smith, also visited Syria. Dr. Hooker, who celebrates her rare merits, appears to think that he has sufficiently indicated their character, when he adds, that "the Rev. Eli Smith, D.D., invited her to the relationship of a missionary wife." As this is the only fact in their joint career which he records, the rest of the biography, consisting of scripture texts interspersed with moral reflections, it is to be presumed that Dr. Hooker found nothing else to communicate.

The Rev. Daniel Temple was a more remarkable person. He took a printing-press, which did a great deal of work, and two wives, the latter at different dates, to the Holy Land. His life has been written by the Rev. William Goodell, himself a mis-

* *Biographical Sketches of Distinguished American Missionaries*, p. 188.

† The blunt and honest Dr. Wolff, who often stumbles on truth when his vanity does not lead him astray, relates, "without any invidious spirit," that while he travelled with Fisk and King, "they occupied themselves chiefly in examining ruins, and in collecting antiquities and mummies." *Travels and Adventures of Dr. Wolff*, ch. ix., p. 176.

‡ *Biographical Sketches*, &c., p. 198.

sionary. "Whoever saw him," observes Mr. Goodell, "would be likely to think at once of Abraham, Isaac, Jacob, Peter, or Paul." In spite of this advantageous personal appearance, Mr. Temple was as unsuccessful as his predecessors, and the close of his history, which exactly coincides with theirs, obliges us to conclude that his resemblance to the Patriarchs and Apostles was purely physical. Mr. Goodell, however, of whose own qualities we shall have a more accurate knowledge before we complete this chapter, assures his readers, that "Jews, Turks, and infidels," upon whom Mr. Temple produced only a faint impression while dwelling among them, "will some of them pronounce his name with something of the same reverence with which we should ever pronounce the name of 'Our Father in heaven!'" Mr. Goodell seems to have felt that he wronged his friend in only ranking him with "Abraham, Peter, and Paul." Yet in spite of the remarkable similitude by which he at length did justice to his merits, Mr. Goodell relates at last, and it is the only historical fact in the narrative, that "he left the mission in 1844:" and lest the world should misinterpret so unexpected a climax, evidently unworthy of a being who ranks above the Patriarchs and only a little below their Creator, Mr. Goodell adds disapprovingly, "*The Lord so remarkably hedged up his way among the Greeks.*"*

The English, who have had representatives at Smyrna for a long course of years, do not even claim any success, either with the Greeks, or with any other race. A gentleman who is apt to exaggerate their influence candidly admits, in 1854, that "although Smyrna has long had the advantage of resident missionaries, and of the faithful ministry of a devoted clergyman, in the Rev. W. B. Lewis, the British chaplain, there are few signs of religious life among the native population."† There are, in fact, ample signs of life, but not such as this writer could detect or appreciate, because they were all external to his own communion. Within its narrow limits his description is apparently accurate. "It is in the spirit of enterprise," says Mr. Jowett, "most especially that the Church of Christ," he means the Church of England, "appears defective."‡ "There is little of a practical and active missionary spirit to be found among the members of the Church of England," said the late Mr. Warburton. "When I was in Syria, there was not an English missionary who had taken a university degree; nor, with one exception, was there a Christian-born minister of

* Pp. 214–218.
† *Journal of a Deputation to the East*, vol. ii., p. 570.
‡ P. 392.

our Church."* Admiral Slade mentions a single Anglican clergyman, whom he considers an exception by character to his companions, and adds, "Where did his labors lie?—Among the Greeks, and without effect!"†

The Americans, as usual, have been, not more successful, but more ambitious and aggressive. Dr. Durbin, their fellow-citizen, informs us, in 1845, that they had printed in Smyrna up to that date thirty-two million two hundred and forty-seven thousand seven hundred and sixty pages. Dr. Wilson records, in his account, an increase of some twenty millions. What the inhabitants of Asia Minor have done with all this printed paper, amounting to about one hundred and fifty thousand octavo volumes, does not appear. Indeed, the only effect of the presence of the various Protestant sects, in Smyrna, who distribute pensions which are much esteemed, and books which nobody reads, has been to afford amusement to these languid Asiatics, though only for a brief space. The excitement lasted a few months, and then both Turks and Greeks decided, as Protestant travellers assure us, that the missionaries had ceased to be entertaining. "Even the Armenians themselves," says Dr. Valentine Mott, with unfeigned astonishment, "though professing Christianity, joined with the deluded Turks in suppressing the Protestant schools!"‡ And Dr. Durbin, also, an American preacher, relates that his co-religionists, of various denominations, were too much occupied in their accustomed pastime of fighting with one another, to allow a combination of their efforts against the oriental sects. "It is to be regretted," he observes, "that they have come into collision with each other in the midst of these ancient churches, and in the presence of the Turk. The chief ground of collision is the validity and authority of their respective ministries," a question which, he seems to think, they might have discussed more advantageously at home.§

Another sympathizing writer, who laments the trivial superstition which makes "keeping the Sabbath" the chief article of the missionary creed, says, "We draw down contempt on that which we seek to further, when we make it seem as though our religion consisted in the observance of the Sabbath."‖

* Ch. viii., pp. 117–18.

† P. 518.

‡ *Travels in Europe and the East*, by Valentine Mott, M.D., p. 404.

§ Vol. ii., ch. xxxv., p. 298. The incessant wranglings of these gentlemen have become so notorious, that when they wrote a complimentary letter to Earl Cowley, who foolishly encouraged them, according to the deplorable traditions of English diplomacy, that ambassador advised them "to prevent further quarrels," and "to respect the religious creed of others, as they desire to have their own respected." Mason, *Three Years in Turkey*, p. 241.

‖ *Wayfaring Sketches*, ch. viii., p. 170.

Yet the Protestant missionary always begins and ends with this precept.

Both the English and Americans have been especially unsuccessful with the Greeks, the very class to which they have mainly directed their attention Mr Arundell, a man of learning and intelligence, who was for some years British chaplain at Smyrna, expresses much dissatisfaction with their "ingratitude," as well as with the levities which they practised in their conduct towards himself. He sent a young Greek, after due instruction, and an expenditure from which he hoped better results, as schoolmaster to Kirkinge. Unfortunately he paid him in advance. "He went to Kirkinge, looked at it, said it was an *askemos-topos*, 'a horrible place,' and settled himself in Syria, without deigning to write me a word," a discourtesy which Mr. Arundell resented the more keenly, because he had "for some time assisted in keeping him and his mother from starving."*

But these Greeks are incorrigible—until they are brought within the influence of the Church. Anglicanism and Methodism are too weak to hold them, and only succeed in inspiring their ingenious malice. Nothing less mighty than the Church can baffle their intrigues, or rouse them from their petulant indifference. "Are you acquainted with Ephesus?" said the Count D'Estournel to a Greek, whom he wished to employ as a guide to the antiquities of the apostolic city. "Yes," replied the luxurious Demetrius; "I have eaten larks there with M. de Stackelberg, and drank Chian wine with Mr. Dodwell."† These were his recollections of Ephesus.

But there is a power in Smyrna which can stir the hearts even of such men as these. "The success which attended the Romish missionaries," says Mr. Jowett, "evidence of which exists in their numerous converts throughout every part of this region, should be an encouragement to Protestants."‡ He did not consider that if Protestants would emulate that success, they must first become Catholics. Thirty years later, another English writer, though he is unable to record any Protestant progress during that long interval, observes, that "the Romanists comprise probably *five-sixths* of the Frank population at Smyrna."§ In ten years—from 1830 to 1840—they more than doubled their numbers, though *they* have not been able to purchase a single convert, or bestow a single pension, and are

* *Discoveries in Asia Minor*, vol. ii., ch. xi., p. 271.
† *Journal d'un Voyage en Orient*, tome i., p. 213.
‡ P. 368.
§ Young, *The Levant and the Nile*, ch. iii., p. 74.

not only poor, but have sworn before the altar to remain poor to the end of their lives.

"My greatest hope," said the Archbishop of Smyrna some years ago, "is in our schools, in which the population of Smyrna, by the religious education imparted to them, are completely regenerated." Already the Lazarist Fathers had two hundred and fifty pupils in their male schools, and the priests of the *Missions Etrangères* one hundred and twenty students in their college. Twenty *native* priests, added to an equal number of European missionaries, attested the influence of the education which they had received. Noble institutions have since then been created, and Smyrna now rejoices in possessing those Sisters of St. Vincent who teach, by their presence and example, the charity which only the true faith can inspire. "In seasons of sickness," says Mr. Wortabet,—whose profession of Protestantism does not prevent his admiring the Sisters of Charity,—"whilst others flee to the mountains for a better atmosphere, *they* have been seen going from house to house, heedless of contagion from cholera, fever, or holes steaming with heat and stench, enough to make any one sick. One by one falls down by the bedside of the dying sufferer. They die, but their memory lives, and no wonder many rise up to call them blessed."*

If any further proof of the influence of the Catholic religion in Smyrna, and of the virtues displayed by its teachers, be required, it is impressively conveyed in the angry confession of a Protestant missionary, the Rev. I. Calhoun,—a confession appropriately recorded by the pen of Dr. Wilson,—that even "among the Protestants there are few who are decidedly anti-Roman Catholic."†

"The Rev. Messrs. Wolters, father and son," of Smyrna, thus report to the Church Missionary Society, in 1862:‡ "The number of native Christians connected with our mission has not increased." Their congregation, they say, "is mixed, consisting of native, English, and Dutch Protestants, and Greeks, the latter sometimes entering the chapel, but mostly standing at the open door." It was probably this disrespectful attitude which impelled the "father and son" to observe, with suitable emphasis, "the Greek Church is dead, dead in trespasses and sins. A missionary living long among them cannot but feel deeply for their spiritual welfare." "Mr. Wolters, junior," adds, "in conversing with Mussulmans it is impossible to avoid

* *Syria and the Syrians,* ch. xv., p. 104 (1856).
† *Lands of the Bible,* vol. ii., p. 577.
‡ *Report,* p. 61.

controversy. But I feel that this is not productive of much good." Yet these gentlemen, who are German-Anglican ministers, still remain, and will probably long remain, in the city of Smyrna, though the native disciples "have not increased," the Greeks amuse themselves at the open door, and the Mussulmans provoke a controversy in which the victory appears to be always on their side.

In Jaffa, Mr. Grühler, another German exponent of Anglicanism, informs the same missionary society that he has "six or seven boys" in his Protestant school. He does not say how these Syrian students were attracted, nor what progress they have made in abandoning their own religion, or in adopting his; but he adds, "I think we could have a nice school there, if the schoolmaster was as zealous as he is avaricious." This intelligent schoolmaster was apparently one of those who had not advanced beyond "the open door."

Beyrout is a more important place, but not more consoling to the supporters of Protestant missions. "There are ten thousand Christians in Beyrout," says the Rev. Dr. Durbin, "the great majority of whom are Roman Catholics." Yet a few years ago they were only a handful; and moreover, "Beyrout is the *centre* of the American missions in Syria," and "the missionaries have several presses here,"—which consume a good deal of paper, but do nothing else. Mr. Neale notices "the superb nunnery in course of erection here for the Sisters of Charity, whose advent has given great satisfaction to the Catholics of Beyrout;" as well as their "boarding-school for young ladies, day-school for poor girls and Arabs, and hospital for sailors."* Mr. Cuthbert Young observes, in 1848, that "the Jesuit establishment at Beyrout is said to be one of the most efficient, and many Maronite and Greek children are educated in their school." Lastly, the candid Mr. Warburton says: "I was much struck by the zeal, talent, and tact exhibited by the monks."

Sidon is no exception to the usual rule. It contains, we learn from a Protestant missionary in 1862, one thousand seven hundred and fifty Christians, of whom one thousand six hundred are Catholics, and one hundred and fifty separated Greeks.† Protestantism is wholly unfruitful.

Aleppo is still more worthy of our attention. Even Dr. Wilson tells us that the Jesuits here "applied themselves to the study of the Eastern languages with a devotion seldom surpassed." And then he adds: "They brought a considerable number of persons within the pale of the Romish Church, and

* *Syria, Palestine,* &c., vol. i., ch. xiii., p. 241.

† *The Land and the Book,* by W. M. Thomson, D.D., ch. ix., p. 108.

they paved the way for the ultimate establishment of the papal-Greek, papal-Armenian, and papal-Syrian sects." But if this gentleman finds nothing to say against the earlier missionaries, he seeks relief by informing his readers, without the least hesitation, that as to the present Jesuits in this region, "*their* morality is of the loosest kind."* Probably he never saw one of them, and knows nothing whatever about them; but it was a safe assertion, and was sure to be welcomed by his readers.

We need not reply seriously to such an assailant; but here is an example of these modern Jesuits, whose loose morality Dr. Wilson deplores. Father Riccadonna wrote a few years ago to his superior in these terms, in obedience to directions which required an exact account of his position: "I will tell you in confidence that we are living in destitution, without clothes, without shelter, without provisions. What others cast aside would be precious to us. A little thread, some buttons, and a packet of needles would be a most acceptable gift. For want of these we go for months together with our clothes in rags. Praise be to God! It is necessary to have tasted these precious sufferings to know their value and their sweetness. May it be my lot to suffer them always."†

Let us return to Aleppo. In 1818, the British Consul-General reported that "Aleppo is gradually drawing, and nearly drawn over to the Roman Catholics."‡ In 1854, a zealous Protestant relates, that of twenty thousand Christians, seventeen thousand five hundred are already Catholics.§

Monseigneur Brunoni, Archbishop of Taron, and Apostolic Legate in Syria, gave this account of them in October, 1855: "The Catholic community in Aleppo, governed by pious and zealous pastors, appear docile to their teaching, and animated with religious sentiments in a manner very consoling to witness. I speak of what I have seen, having been invited to celebrate the Holy Sacrifice in the churches of the different liturgies, on which occasions the evident devotion and fervor observable in all was very edifying. The day on which I officiated for the Armenians, the pious and learned Paul Balit delivered an excellent discourse in reference to the conversions of the previous year, and on the majesty and superiority of the Catholic religion. His words made the truth so evident that an inhabitant of the neighborhood, who was a schismatic, and happened to be present, was convinced of his errors, and renounced them on the spot."‖

* P. 573.
† *Annales*, tome vii., p. 241.
‡ *Asiatic Journal*, vol. vi., p. 503.
§ *Journal of a Deputation*, vol. ii., p. 822.
‖ *Annals*, vol. xvii., p. 137.

"In Aleppo," says a Protestant minister, the Rev. G. Badger, in 1852, "where they once numbered several hundred families, not more than *ten* Jacobite families now exist, the rest having joined the Church of Rome." This unwilling witness adds, that "the same secession has left them only a name at *Damascus*. The Jacobite community of *Bagdad* has followed the example set them by their brethren at Aleppo and Damascus." And then he performs the usual task for which Protestant travellers seem to be employed by Providence in all parts of the world. "If the truth is to be told, it must be confessed that, however much to be deplored this secession may be, the Syrian proselytes to Rome are decidedly superior in many respects to their Jacobite brethren."* Yet this gentleman "deplores" that they should cease to be heretics, sunk in corruption and ignorance, though they become "decidedly superior" as members of the Catholic Church. He does more; he rails at the Catholic missionaries for "forming a schism," and then proposes to the Anglican Establishment to re-convert these neophytes from their "Romish" errors! It seems that if we desire to find unequalled examples of this kind, we must now look for them in the Anglican clergy of the High Church school. But we shall hear of Mr. Badger again.

The Turks appear to discriminate more exactly than Mr. Badger between heretics and Christians. Bishop Bonamie reports, that at the Catholic funerals in Aleppo, "Janissaries, who are themselves Mahometans, precede the Cross, and oblige all whom they meet on the way, without excepting the Turks, to behave with respect and reverence before this sign of our salvation."†

Of the Protestants in Aleppo—for they have there also their usual printing press, which works night and day with the usual results—an eager advocate tells us, "On more than one occasion have the ecclesiastical authorities ordered all Protestant books, all Bibles from Protestant presses, &c., to be burned, destroyed, or delivered into their hands."‡ Of one school of missionaries in that city, Mr. Walpole says, "The Presbyterian mission here bides its time, and perhaps I may say *nothing* has yet been done by them." He remarks also that the missionaries do not even "kneel at prayers; which," he observes, "seems a cold form of adoration."§ Their Moslem neighbors are probably of the same opinion.

* *The Nestorians and their Rituals*, by the Rev. G. P. Badger, vol. i., pp. 63, 180.

† *Annales*, tome viii., p. 553.

‡ *Journal of a Deputation*, p. 822.

§ *The Ansayrii*, vol. i., ch. xiii., p. 205.

Returning towards the south, let us visit Damascus. Here also we meet the usual facts. "The Christians," says Mr. Warburton, "for the most part belong to the Latin Church." Times are changed since, in 1351, twenty-two Catholics were crucified in Damascus on the same day.* "I believe about twenty thousand are Christians," says Mr. Churton, in 1851, "principally *Greek* Catholics."† "The *Syrian* Catholics of Damascus," Dr. Robinson observes, "are *recent* converts."‡ It was in 1832 that the Syrian Bishop of Damascus was reconciled to the Church, together with his numerous household and relatives.§ At the present day, Dr. Wilson informs us, the Catholics have "the most splendid church which Damascus contains;"‖ and then he adds, as if to counterbalance these unwelcome proofs of their progress, "In its services it is difficult to recognize the simplicity of Christian worship."

The "simplicity" of his Presbyterian co-religionists, at Aleppo and elsewhere, who refuse to kneel in the presence of that God before whom the archangels hide their faces, and even their Immaculate Queen worships with awful fear, is more agreeable to Dr. Wilson. To insult the Most High, even while they imagine they are adoring Him, is commendable "simplicity," though Daniel "fainted away and retained no strength," even before the presence of an angel.¶ If Dr. Wilson had seen that other angel, "having a golden censer," to whom "was given much incense," that he might offer it "before the altar in heaven;"** he would perhaps have suggested to St. John, who did see it, that it was a very "unscriptural" ceremony, and extremely deficient in simplicity. If he had entered that temple, in which even the "nails of gold," and the "wings of the cherubim," and "the curtain rods" were all prescribed and fashioned by Divine inspiration, and where priests, arrayed in jewelled robes offered a mystical sacrifice by Divine command, he would perhaps have ventured on the same criticism. It would have been imprudent, for the Hebrews made short work of blasphemers. Yet Calvin, the author of the Presbyterian religion, pushed the claims of "simplicity" still further, and marvelled that the Son of God did not rebuke the "superstition" of the woman in the Gospel, who was healed by touching "the hem of His garment!" It was intolerable that God should

* Henrion, tome i., ch. xviii., p. 195.
† *The Land of the Morning*, ch. xv., p. 271.
‡ *Biblical Researches in Palestine*, p. 462.
§ *Annales*, tome vi., p. 291.
‖ *Lands of the Bible*, p. 581.
¶ *Dan.* x. 8.
** *Apoc.* viii. 3.

thus sanction the principle of relic worship, and the Genevan bade his disciples take note of the error.* Surely the Prussian philosopher had reason to exclaim, "The Calvinists treat the Saviour as their *inferior*, the Lutherans as their equal, and Catholics as their God."†

Let us return to Damascus. Another English writer, of the same school as Dr. Wilson, notices in 1854, that "there are in Damascus three Latin monasteries; the buildings are good, and have libraries attached to them, containing good collections of books in the oriental and other languages; there are also large day-schools under the direction of the priesthood:"‡ and then he scoffs at them as "concealed Jesuits." The Jesuits have not the habit of concealing themselves, and the objects of his dislike, were, in fact, Franciscans and Lazarists. That their schools are more accurately appreciated by the Damascenes than by this Protestant tourist, we learn from Dr. Frankl, who says, "It is worthy of notice that the Jews and Mohammedans sometimes send their children to the schools taught by the French missionaries of the order of St. Lazare." Ubicini also relates, that "their two schools were frequented, in 1856, by four hundred and fifty children,"—which perhaps accounts for the irritation of their English visitors,—and that at Beyrout, Salonica, Aleppo, and *wherever* the Lazarist missions extend, "*hundreds of children of all creeds* receive elementary instruction freely and gratuitously."

A well-known German Protestant, who visited the Franciscan schools at Damascus, expresses surprise and admiration at the patient charity of men who had abandoned all—they have since been massacred by Turks—to labor in this field, and exclaims, "The natural and primitive simplicity with which they follow their calling delighted me much."§ Yet an Anglican missionary, who, during a long residence in Syria, had only learned to defame the works which he knew not how to imitate; who spent his time in sneering at Franciscans and Lazarists, and even at those Sisters of Charity of whom the more discerning Moslem speaks with affection and reverence; affects to deplore the miserably defective education which attracted scholars of every class and creed, and of which other Protestants will presently describe to us the real character.‖ It is

* "Scimus quam proterve *ludat superstitio*. . . . Quod a veste hœsit potius, forte *zelo inconsiderato* paululum a via deflexit." *Comment. in Nov. Test.*, tome i., p. 220; ed. Tholuck.

† *Dictionnaire des Apologistes Involontaires*, introd., p. 31; Migne.

‡ *Journal of a Deputation to the East*, vol. ii., p. 488.

§ Countess Hahn-Hahn, *Letters*, &c., vol. ii., Letter xxi., p. 55.

‖ *Five Years in Damascus*, by the Rev. J. L. Porter, M.A.; vol. i., ch. iii., p. 145.

creditable to English and American travellers, that almost the only individuals of either nation who use such language are the missionaries themselves.

We should perhaps not err in attributing the exasperation which betrays itself in such expressions to the mortification of personal failure. After many years of lavish expenditure, they had so utterly wasted their time and money, that Mr. Wortabet unwillingly confesses, in 1856, that the *five* Protestant missionaries in Damascus had only secured *sixteen* precarious pensioners, who were probably all their servants and dependents;* and Dr. Frankl pleasantly adds, "The missionary society has as yet thrown out its golden net at Damascus *in vain*."†

On the other hand, English and American travellers attest in chorus the contrast to which they could not close their eyes, and the continual triumphs of the Catholic faith, throughout all Syria, in spite of the poverty of its apostles. "At *Diarbekir*, some years ago," says Mr. Badger, "the whole Greek community in the town became Romanists."‡ The Nestorians in the neighborhood quickly followed their example. "At *Aintab*, an American missionary," who had been distributing Bibles, "was driven out of the town by the Armenians," says Mr. Walpole; "not, I believe, without insults and some violence."§ And so uniform are these facts, as we shall see more fully hereafter, that a Protestant witness observes, that even in places "where a few years ago there were no Roman Catholics, we now find a fair share of the population belonging to that faith."‖ Mr. Jowett had reason to say, "All Syria is comparatively occupied by the Roman Catholics."

Before we quit Syria to enter Palestine, it seems impossible to omit one or two reflections upon what we have already heard. It is proved, by Protestant testimony, that throughout these regions the Church is constantly attracting to herself great numbers from the various dissident communities. "Men of virtue and piety," says a learned English writer, familiar with many of the forms of oriental society, "are often found to pass from the Eastern to the Roman Catholic communion, while no instance, perhaps, or scarcely an instance, can be adduced even of an individual of acknowledged piety and learning passing over to the Eastern Church."¶

* *Syria and the Syrians*, ch. vii., p. 203.
† *The Jews in the East*, vol. i., ch. viii., pp. 292, 7, 9.
‡ Badger, vol. i., p. 3.
§ Walpole, ch. xvi., p. 255.
‖ Wortabet, vol. ii., ch. xiv., p. 86.
¶ Palmer, *Dissertations on the Orthodox Communion*, p. 13.

Some Protestant writers are still more emphatic, and we must not conclude this portion of our subject without noticing their remarkable language. "Not one of the ancient Churches," says the Rev. George Williams, formerly a chaplain at Jerusalem, "but was visited by missionaries of the Propaganda, or the enterprising members of the Society of Jesus. . . . When we consider the zeal, ability, and persevering practice of the best instructed and most devoted missionaries that the world has seen since primitive times, it is no matter of surprise that their self-denying labors were crowned with abundant success."*

"It is difficult," says another English Protestant, familiar by long experience and observation with the East and its various races, "to meet and converse with the zealous and talented missionaries of the Propaganda in the East, and not feel warmly for their situation. They are exposed to no ordinary trial of patience. Educated at Rome, accustomed to Italian refinement and conversation, then sent to some remote spot—remote from causes of association rather than from distance—destined to pass their lives with a people as far beneath them in mental culture as separated by habits, they may be truly said to be banished men in the sharpest sense of the term. Still we might at times rather envy than pity them. Commiseration is lost sight of in our admiration at the disinterestedness and perseverance which they ever display in the performance of their duties—a good conscience their reward, heaven their guide. No shadow of preferment looms in the distance, no hope of distinction cheers them on, not one of the ordinary inducements to exertion prompts them. Courteous with the gentleman, confiding with the peasant, caressing with the distressed, they are, as St. Paul expressed himself to be, 'All things to all men.' Multiply the generations since the Osmanleys conquered the country, and it will appear that *millions of souls* have been saved by these advanced sentinels of Christianity, ever at their post to reclaim the wavering and confirm the steadfast."†

Dr. Durbin, an American Protestant minister, who visited the same lands, contents himself with admitting the facts. "It is not possible," he says, "to estimate the success of the Romish missions to the Oriental Churches, but the general fact is clear, that they have divided them *all;* so that there is in Asia a Papal-Greek Church, a Papal-Armenian Church, a Papal Church among the Nestorians, a Papal Church among the Syrians, and also many of the Copts in Egypt."‡

* *The Holy City,* vol. ii., ch. vi., p. 570.
† Slade, *Turkey, Greece, and Malta,* vol. ii., ch. xx., p. 425.
‡ Vol. ii., p. 287.

Other Protestant writers, deeply impressed, in spite of incurable and fatal prejudices, with the grave lessons which they have brought away from the East,—and especially with the demoralizing influence of Protestant missions,—do not hesitate to avow their condemnation of efforts which lead only to evil.

"I frankly avow my opinion," says the Rev. Mr. Spencer, who seems to be a Scotch Episcopalian minister, "that missions from the various religious bodies who contribute to the support of the gentlemen laboring in Syria *can never be productive of permanent results.* I was astonished to learn how little had, after all, been done." And again: "It deserves to be well weighed by Protestants at home, that no mission of theirs to the Oriental Christians has succeeded to any extent commensurate with the means, the men, the time devoted to their conversion: may it not properly be asked, *Are we ever likely to succeed any better?*"*

Dr. Wolff says, "I cannot help thinking that the Church Missionary Society, though they might send their Lutheran missionaries to the heathen, ought never to send them to the Eastern Churches. It is a gross insult to them,"†—and apparently a very unprofitable one. He adds, with characteristic frankness, that he "is sorry to make the declaration, that the worst people among the Eastern natives are those who know English, and have been converted to Protestantism!"‡

Mr. Williams also observes, though probably without much hope of obtaining a hearing, "There is surely an ample field in the East for the European and American missionaries, without encroaching on other Churches." Jews, Druses, Mahometans, Arabs, and others, are the avowed enemies of Christianity, as he remarks, yet the luxurious emissaries of Protestantism hardly even attempt to make any impression on *them*, and invariably fail when they do. "*They are merely playing at missions*," adds Mr. Williams—and with this frank confession we may conclude—"while they limit themselves to a task involving no risk, and requiring no sacrifices."§

It is impossible not to be struck by such unexpected language as has now been quoted, from Protestant writers of various and conflicting schools, in illustration of the eternal contrast which even they discern between Catholic and Protestant missionaries and the fruits of their labor. But there is yet another emotion, more painful than surprise, which such testimonies

* *Travels in the Holy Land,* by the Rev. J. A. Spencer, M.A., Letter xxii., pp. 483–4 (1850).

† P. 232.

‡ *Travels and Adventures,* ch. xv., p. 269 (1861).

§ *The Holy City,* vol. ii., ch. vi., p. 597.

awaken. The witnesses record their evidence, in spite of natural prejudice, and careless of the resentment of their less candid co-religionists; and this courage none will refuse to applaud. But we may be permitted to deplore that such men, so truthful and generous, should have been equally successful in banishing another kind of fear, more noble and legitimate —the fear of Him who has said, "*Out of thine own mouth will I judge thee.*"

JERUSALEM.

And now let us go to Jerusalem. The project of the King of Prussia, the chief of the Lutheran communities, was eagerly adopted by a Church always striving to make alliance with other heretical bodies, and always unsuccessfully. At last she has succeeded. The Church of England—in spite of the unmeaning protests of a class who seem to think, like Pilate, that it suffices to wash their hands in order to secure immunity for acts which they invariably make their own by acquiescence—consented to exercise, alternately with a Lutheran, the right of nominating a Protestant bishop at Jerusalem. The present holder of the office is Dr. Gobat, of whom we heard in Abyssinia. An English biographer, of similar religious opinions, tells us, that "Gobat, far from recognizing the Church of England as the sole, or even the most Scriptural Church upon earth, long declined receiving her ordination."* This writer plainly intimates that he would never have received it at all, but it was the turn of the Establishment to nominate, and he was obliged to submit. The accounts of the Protestant mission at Jerusalem, and of its results, are so absolutely uniform, with the exception of one or two writers who shall be noticed, that we may call our witnesses at random. The more serious class of Anglicans are ashamed of the whole proceeding, and would be glad to bury it in oblivion; we, however, have no motive for declining to discuss it.

Dr. Gobat's biographer, who is almost indiscreet in his frankness, reveals the secret aim of his party, when he says, "The Jerusalem episcopate ought to be a Protestant patriarchate." Let us inquire how far this project has been realized.

If we take the evidence in chronological order, it will run as follows. In 1841, an English visitor to Jerusalem says, "We went to church at the Consul's, and our congregation amounted to only *ten*, including an American missionary," and the

* *Evangelical Christendom*, vol. i., p. 79.

traveller's own party. "As to the advance of proselytism," adds the writer, "Mr. Nicholaison does not consider more than five converts have been made during the last period of his residence, nine years."*

In 1842, an Anglican clergyman still reports the congregation to consist of "the architect, the bishop's family, with a portion of his household, and two missionaries." But, on the other hand, this gentleman found about *eight hundred* Catholics at Nazareth, "particularly well conducted and habited for the country; indeed, the children who attend the school of the monastery were quite cleanly, and spoke Italian with fluency."† And one of the most distinguished of the Anglican clergy remarks of the same mission, where he heard Arab converts sing the chants of the Latin Church, "There is no church in Palestine where the religious services seem so worthy of the sacredness of the place;"‡ while another observes that the Catholic women of Bethlehem are "as noted for their independence and moral character as for their beauty."§

In the same year, an American traveller, who omits even to allude to the "Protestant patriarchate," as if he had failed to discover it, writes as follows: "Every traveller who has visited Jerusalem must have been struck with the contrast between the intelligence, wit, and learning of the friars of the *Latin* convent, and the besotted and gross ignorance of the *Greek* monks, whose superstitious fanaticism is but little removed above that of the Mussulmen."‖ And this is confirmed, with characteristic felicity of language, by the author of *Eothen*, when he says of the "Padre Superiore," and the "Padre Missionario" of the Jerusalem monastery, "By the natives of the country, as well as by the rest of the brethren, they are looked upon as superior beings; and rightly too, for nature seems to have crowned them in her own true way. The chief of the Jerusalem convent was a noble creature; his worldly and spiritual authority seemed to have surrounded him, as it were, with a kind of 'Court,' and the manly gracefulness of his bearing did honor to the throne which he filled. . . . . If he went out, the Catholics of the place that hovered about the convent would crowd around him with

* Mrs. Dawson Damer, vol. i., p. 309; vol. ii., p. 33.

† *Egypt and the Holy Land*, by W. Drew Stent, vol. ii., ch. ii., p. 44; ch. vi., p. 148.

‡ *Sinai and Palestine*, by Arthur Penrhyn Stanley, M.A., p. 437.

§ *The Pilgrim in the Holy Land*, by the Rev. Henry S. Osborn, M.A., ch. xvi., p. 200.

‖ *Tour through Turkey, Greece*, &c., by E. Joy Morris, vol. i., ch. vi., p. 116. Dr. Thomson also contrasts the "decorum and solemnity of deportment of the Latin monks" with the grossness of "the Greeks and Armenians." *The Land and the Book*, ch. xlii., p. 650.

devout affection, and almost scramble for the blessing which his touch could give."*

In 1843, Mr. Millard arrives at the gloomy conviction, "that Jerusalem is of almost all other places the least accessible by Protestant missionary labors."†

In 1844, a witness of a different class appears. The reader may possibly remember the Rev. I. Tomlin, an Anglican minister, who visited China and so many other places, always in submission to "calls" which he had not courage to disobey. Mr. Tomlin says, "The labors of the Protestant Bishop of Jerusalem have been remarkably blessed of the Lord." He says it quite seriously, and evidently without forecasting what later witnesses might possibly record on the same subject. Mr. Tomlin adds, "The Roman legions are gone forth, and are fast preoccupying the ground;" and then he exclaims, as if resenting a personal wrong, "They covertly creep in by the way which Protestant Britain has opened!"‡ The observation betrays some defect of historical accuracy. There was once a Christian "kingdom of Jerusalem," as Mr. Tomlin might have remembered, which lasted nearly two hundred years; and as Catholic missionaries have now been there for a good many centuries, we may perhaps say, without too much severity, that the notion of their recent and covert arrival under British protection is altogether worthy of Mr. Tomlin. Protestant Britain has not often been very generous to "the Roman legions," and has certainly not hitherto afforded them much assistance at Jerusalem.

In 1847, Dr. Rae Wilson, who had perhaps not read Mr. Tomlin, and was evidently unconscious of being "remarkably blessed" in his solitude, says, "At this time I was the *only* Protestant in Jerusalem."§

In the same year, Tischendorff gives this account of the operations of the "patriarchate" which Dr. Rae Wilson and Mr. Joy Morris failed to discern: "With respect to the baptism of converts in Jerusalem, it is, as far as I know, framed to an accommodation with the most modern Judaism. Six thousand piastres (about fifty pounds) are offered to the convert as a premium; other advantages are said likewise to be considerable."‖

In spite of these attractions, the results could hardly be deemed satisfactory; for in the same year Lord Castlereagh

* Ch. x.

† *Journal of Travels in Egypt*, by D. Millard, ch. xvi., p. 262.

‡ *Missionary Journals*, &c., introd., pp. 13, 15.

§ *Travels in the Holy Land*, &c., ch. xviii., p. 385.

‖ *Travels in the East*, by Constantine Tischendorff, p. 159.

expressed this opinion, founded on personal examination: "The progress of conversion, and the interests of Christianity, do not at present seem to require or warrant so large a church establishment as is here maintained. I inquired in vain for any number of converts that could be properly authenticated." And then he describes once more the scanty official audience with which we are already familiar, "The bishop has scarcely a congregation, besides his chaplains, his doctor, and their families."*

Dr. Gobat, however, did sometimes make a convert, as we saw in Abyssinia, in the case of the "noble Abyssinian" Girgis, who abandoned the Anglican tenets for Mahometanism. Here is one more specimen of Dr. Gobat's success. A certain "Joseph" was "acknowledged by the missionaries Gobat and Mueller as a sincere convert."† Indeed Admiral Slade says, and it is perfectly true, that he "figured more than once in the reports of the Bible Society, and has been cited as an instance of the success attending the missionaries' labor." He was even "strongly recommended as one admirably qualified to preach the Gospel among the Arabs." The qualifications of this favorite of the Bible Society were these. Dr. Wolff, to whom he gave lessons in Arabic, says that he was "the most infamous hypocrite and impostor I ever met with;" and he had good reason to say it, for this "admirably qualified" missionary broke open Dr. Wolff's trunk, stole all he possessed, and then ran away.‡ Dr. Gobat is evidently not happy in his converts, nor the Bible Society in its heroes.

In 1848, we have an official account by Dr. Gobat himself. "Our little congregation," he says, "goes its quiet way. I regret that we have not more spiritual life. . . . I believe there is growth in grace with some, and *there is less division*."‡ Yet Miss Bremer, an intimate friend of all the parties, laments several years later the "bitter schism between Christians who attend the same church," which was a jest among the English in Jerusalem, and particularly that Mrs. Gobat and Mrs. Finn, the Consul's wife, "do not speak to each other, because their husbands have become enemies!"‖

In 1852, an English clergyman, who describes the singular use made of "the Bibles and tracts so profusely spread among the Eastern nations," gives this grave account of the converts who had been obtained up to that date: "Their belief is a

* *A Journey to Damascus*, &c., vol. ii., ch. xix., p. 3.
† Wolff, p. 285.
‡ Slade, p. 521.
§ Margoliouth, vol. ii., p. 295.
‖ *Travels in the Holy Land*, vol. ii., ch. xi., p. 104.

blank, and their principles distinctly Antinomian. I maintain, from observation, that to one class or other of these all the proselytes made to Protestantism in the East belong. They are either worthless persons, or skeptics and infidels. The reports of the missionary societies themselves exhibit the truth of these allegations. . . . . The work of the Protestant missions is simply *destructive;* they first make a *tabula rasa* of minds, on which they never afterwards succeed in inscribing the laws of a sincere faith or consistent practice."*

Two years later, in 1854, the representative of an English missionary society still confesses of these ambiguous "converts," that "they have not unfrequently some hidden motive of worldly advantage."† We shall hear them presently discussing the real motive among themselves.

Admiral Slade, in the same year, prepares us for future revelations by this statement: "I will not say that any of them are gained by actual bribery, but they certainly are by promises of employment in the missionary line, promises often not fulfilled, in consequence of which the converts are reduced to distress."‡ The Rev. Moses Margoliouth, now an Anglican clergyman, incidentally confirms this unfavorable statement. This gentleman, an associate of Dr. Gobat, while he deplores the exceeding frailty of Hebrew Protestants, does not on that account permit himself to be discouraged. He even derives consolation from an unexpected source. "I do not affirm," he says, "that baptized Jews do not afford instances of consummate rascality. So do the clergy of our beloved Church."§

In 1855, Mr. Bayard Taylor, an intelligent American, relates that as they could not make converts at Jerusalem, Protestant Jews "were *brought hither* at the expense of English missionary societies, for the purpose of forming a Protestant community." The process was costly, for he adds, that "it is estimated that *each* member of the community has cost the mission about four thousand five hundred pounds; a sum which would have christianized tenfold the number of English heathen. The mission, however, is kept up by its patrons as a sort of religious luxury." On the other hand, this gentleman observes, "Many others besides ourselves have had reason to be thankful for the good offices of the Latin monks in Palestine. I have never met with a class more kind, cordial, and genial."‖

* Patterson, *Journal of a Tour in Egypt*, p. 455.
† *Journal of a Deputation*, vol. ii., p. 351.
‡ P. 519.
§ *A Pilgrimage to the Land of my Fathers*, vol. ii., p. 334
‖ *The Lands of the Saracen*, ch. v., p. 78; ch. vi., p. 100.

"The Latins," says a German Protestant—for all the independent witnesses use the same language—"receive all strangers with the greatest liberality—I mean liberality of sentiment." It is true this writer adds that Protestants would imitate the hospitality of the Catholic monks, if they could, for they see with displeasure their co-religionists dwelling as guests within the Latin monasteries; but "a Protestant establishment is quite out of the question," for the following reason: "The several parties would not easily agree to whom it should belong, whether to the Calvinists or to the Lutherans, to the Presbyterians or to the Anglican Church."* A little later, however, they escaped from their embarrassment; they could not unite in erecting a monastery or a church, but they combined their resources and built an hotel.

In 1857, Mr. Gibson repeats a tale which has now become somewhat monotonous. "As yet, few Hebrews have been induced here to profess Christianity. Some even of these have *gone back* to Judaism."†

The failure, after twenty years of prodigious expenditure, had now become so evident, and people at home were beginning to talk of it so loudly, that the missionaries seem to have resolved that they must make a diversion amongst the Christian sects rather than continue to do nothing. But there was this difficulty, that they were pledged not to attempt to proselyte the oriental sectaries. Relief came to Dr. Gobat in this perplexity from an unexpected quarter. The narrator of the incident is the Rev. Dr. Stewart, who tells us, that "Lord Palmerston has *authoritatively* stated that the bishop has a right to receive those from other communions who apply to him for instructions." This pontifical decision of the eminent statesman removed, as might be expected, all difficulty—except that of procuring the applicants for instructions. In this Lord Palmerston could not offer them any assistance. They were left, therefore, to their usual methods; and Dr. Stewart sufficiently indicates what they were, when he expresses his regret that "there is no way of making trial of a convert's sincerity before his admission into the institution;" and then frankly allows, that "the principle of giving support to *every* convert I deem faulty."‡

We have perhaps heard enough of the Jerusalem Protestant mission and its results, but we must not quit the subject without a brief notice of five important witnesses—Dr. Frankl, Dr. Wolff, Dr. Robinson, Mr. Williams, and Dr. Thomson,—a Jew, a

* Countess Hahn-Hahn, Letter xxix.
† *Recollections of other Lands*, by William Gibson, B.A., ch. xxxviii., p. 404.
‡ *A Journey to Syria and Palestine*, by Robert Walter Stewart, D.D. (Leghorn), ch. viii., pp. 294, 303.

proselyte, and three Protestants, who have all dwelt in Jerusalem, and who confirm each other's testimony in an unexpected way.

The first of these writers, whose work has been introduced to English readers by Mr. Beaton, gives this account: "The Protestants give earnest-money, and demoralize families. When a father sternly rebukes his children, it is not unusual for them to reply with the insolent threat, 'I will go to the mission.'" He mentions an example of a Jew who had got into difficulties by stealing two thousand five hundred piastres, and who, when his co-religionists "refused to intercede for him, out of revenge went to the mission;" but as the thief still had some religious prepossessions, he implored Dr. Frankl to lend him the sum abstracted, "to save him, his wife, and six children from being baptized!" Dr. Frankl adds, that this case "may serve as an example of the morals and principles of those who are converted;" and that so little importance is attached to the momentary profession of Protestantism by a Jew, that his family content themselves with observing, "He will soon come back after he has helped himself." Indeed, we are told by a friend and countryman of Dr. Gobat, that the Hebrew proselyte, when he has exhausted Protestant benevolence at Jerusalem, "has become *more than ever a Jew* by the time he has reached Jaffa, Hebron, or Tiberias."*

Dr. Frankl relates also the curious fact that "converts" from the Jews "receive baptism in different cities before they reach Jerusalem," where they are finally re-baptized, with a fresh payment for the operation; an account which is confirmed by the amusing authoress of *Travels in Barbary*, who is much defamed by Mr. Margoliouth for presuming to say of one of his Jewish converts, "This is at least the *twentieth* time he has been baptized." And even this was so far from a solitary case, that a Polish Jew remarked to some of his friends, "Baptism was the only good business we had, and who has spoiled it? The Jews themselves, *by underselling one another*."†

Dr. Wolff, who is a still better witness than Dr. Frankl, gives a sorrowful account of the London Society for the Conversion of the Jews. In fifty-two years, he says, not without reproaching himself for his own pleasantry, "they had spent eight hundred thousand pounds, and only converted two Jews

* Mislin, *Les Lieux Saints*, tome iii., ch. xxviii., p. 65.

† *The Jews in the East*, vol. ii., ch. ii., pp. 53, 54. Yet the Protestant missionaries, knowing what their employers expect from them, are never weary of supplying the materials for perpetuating the delusion of the home subscribers. Thus one of their number gravely assures his readers, on the authority of a Jew, that "in six years all the Jews would become Christians!" Mason, *Three Years in Turkey*, p. 137.

and a half!"* Nearly half a century ago, the Rev. Lewis Way, an Anglican minister, generously discharged all their liabilities, "took sixteen Jews into his own house, and baptized several of them; but, soon after their baptism, they stole his silver spoons, and one of them was transported to Australia, having forged Mr. Way's signature."

The history which began so inauspiciously never varied. A little later, "a young man of extraordinary talents, Nehemiah Solomon, was *ordained* by Bishop Burgess, ... and seemed to be going on well, when he suddenly ran away, after having drawn three hundred pounds from the society, and was never heard of afterwards." Other examples of the same kind so deeply affected Mr. Way, that "at last the dear man died at Leamington, broken-hearted."

Dr. Wolff himself was hardly less impressed by a similar series of disasters. "The Jews' Society for Promoting Christianity," he wrote to his friend, Mr. Henry Drummond, "has been disappointed by every Jew they took up. One became a Muhammedan, another a thief, a third a pickpocket," &c. At Cairo, "a Jew of high talent" visited Dr. Wolff, and confessed "that he had three times professed himself a Muhammedan, in order to make his fortune, and had divorced a dozen wives," &c. Upon which he adds, "Wolff preached to him the Gospel of Christ, and exhorted him to repentance." It does not appear that the exhortation was effectual.

At Damascus, Aleppo, Jerusalem, wherever he went, Hebrew "converts" were uniformly of the same type, so that his abundant experience constrained him to observe, "Jews who are converted by societies are like Eastern fruits cultivated in green-houses in Europe, and have not the flavor of those which are naturally grown." Yet he never seems to have suspected the true cause of so many failures, though he confesses that many Jews who had become Catholics have been Christians indeed. "Emanuel Veit, in Vienna," he says; "the two Veits, step-sons to Friederich Schlegel; Monsieur Ratisbon, of Strasbourg; are all true lights in the Church of Christ." He admits too, with his usual candor, that Ratisbon was converted like St. Paul, "suddenly, by miracle,"—an apparition of the Mother of God; and he adds, "Only those Jews who are converted in such an extraordinary way are worth any thing."†

Dr. Robinson, the author of a well-known work on the topography of Jerusalem, confirms all the other witnesses. "The efforts of the English mission" he seems to think unworthy of

* *Travels and Adventures of Dr. Wolff*, ch. xxiv., p. 417 (1861).

† Ch. v., pp. 80, 85; ch. vi., p. 131.

serious notice; while of his own countrymen, the Americans, he gives the following account: "The house of ——," one of the missionaries, "was large, with marble floors, and had on one side an extensive and pleasant garden, with orange and other fruit trees and many flowers. It furnished indeed one of the most desirable and beautiful residences in the city." We have been told by the wife of another American missionary, that "many are the comforts and pleasant things about this life in the East," and her countrymen evidently agree with her. Surrounded by so many enjoyments, to which they would probably have aspired in vain in Boston or Philadelphia, we are not surprised to learn from Dr. Robinson, that "the plague and other circumstances" soon scattered these opulent missionaries, and even "conspired to suspend wholly, for a time, the labors of the American mission in Jerusalem."

There is another class of missionaries whom the plague sometimes kills, but never puts to flight. The Protestant agents,—who would undertake at any moment to teach a St. Francis, a Bonnieux, or a Riccadonna, a more "scriptural" and enlightened piety,—prefer to run away when danger knocks at their doors; and so Dr. Robinson relates, as if the precaution of his missionary friends was too natural to require any comment, that though on this occasion the plague only acted "mildly," "the missionaries broke off their sittings, and those from abroad hastened to depart with their families!"*

It was almost at this moment that the author of a celebrated English book published the following narrative: "It was about three months after the time of my leaving Jerusalem that the plague set his spotted foot on the Holy City. The monks felt great alarm; they did not shrink from their duty. . . . A single monk was chosen, either by lot, or by some other fair appeal to destiny; being thus singled out, he was to go forth into the plague-stricken city, and to perform with exactness his priestly duties. . . . He was provided with a bell, and at a certain hour in the morning he was ordered to ring it, *if he could;* but if no sound was heard at the appointed time, then his brethren knew that he was either delirious or dead, and another martyr was sent forth to take his place. *In this way twenty-one of the monks were carried off.*"†

Dr. Robinson, who does not love Catholics, is fain to confess that they do not much resemble his own friends. Of their inflexible constancy, although surrounded by every evil example, he gives this instance: "The Christians of the Latin rite (native Arabs) are said to be descended from Catholic con-

* Pages 327, 368.
† *Eothen,* ch. x.

verts in the times of the Crusades." Centuries have left *them* unchanged. The Catholic college in Kesrawân, in which they teach Arabic, Syriac, Latin, and Italian, "takes a higher stand," he says, "than any other similar establishment in Syria." What he relates of the Maronites we shall learn hereafter. The Protestants, he superfluously observes, "do not exist in Syria as a native sect."

Lastly, Mr. Williams, a highly respectable Anglican clergyman, and once a chaplain in Jerusalem,—who, like most of his order, remains wholly unimpressed even by the lamentable facts which he discloses,—gives us the following information: "It was an unfortunate circumstance for our Church that it was first introduced to the Christians of Jerusalem, in later times, by a Danish Lutheran minister." The Church of Mr. Williams has usually been introduced by persons of the same class. This one, he says, was admitted "to orders in the English Church, on grounds of convenience rather than of conviction." But the Church of England, if she cannot produce missionaries of her own, is wealthy enough to pay for the services of others. "A church capable of accommodating four or five hundred persons was commenced," Mr. Williams remarks, "while as yet there were but eight or ten individuals for whom it would be available, and even they were there simply with a view to its construction!" They were, he adds, "the clergyman, the architect, and his clerk, the foreman of the works, the carpenter, an apothecary, and one other."* For this professional congregation a church was commenced, which, Dr. Durbin says, "will cost about one hundred and fifty thousand dollars."

Mr. Williams next describes the operations of the gentlemen who minister in this church: "The missionary operations of the society's agents have not been such as to exhibit to the natives an example of earnest zeal for the conversion of the Jews, nor the treatment of the converts such as to impress them with a favorable idea of their discretion." He laments the "serious errors and defects in the faith, scandalous irregularities and excesses in the practice, of the ill-instructed members of this small congregation." Finally, he observes, that "self-sacrifices and simple trust were not taught *either by precept or example* by the missionaries at Jerusalem."† Yet Mr. Williams has probably no doubt whatever that the system will continue, at

* *The Holy City*, pp. 579, 587.

† P. 593. "Mr. Salt complained that the London Society for promoting Christianity among the Jews had sent a most unfit missionary to Jerusalem... who was evidently a mere speculator. He sold medicine to the ladies, in order that they might be blessed with children, and pretended to know witchcraft." Dr. Wolff, *Travels and Adventures*, ch. vi., p. 107.

the same enormous cost, under the direction of the same class of men, and with precisely the same results.

This amiable writer, who records facts but seems never to draw conclusions, describes also "the very unsatisfactory native Protestants" made by the Americans,—during the intervals of "the plague and other circumstances,"—and gives examples of the class generally. One, an unfortunate Greek apostate, "the most favorable specimen by far," after being first an Independent, then an Anglican, "had fallen into a state of listless indifference and unconcern which it was most grievous to witness." A second, a Greek monk, "offered himself to Bishop Gobat as a Protestant convert." His sole motive was, "that the Patriarch had imposed upon him some discipline to which he did not choose to submit." Another, "a monk from Mount Lebanon, told me he wished to become a Protestant. 'Why?' 'I want to marry.' 'No other reason?' 'None.' "*

Lastly, in 1862, Dr. Thomson thus records his candid impressions, after an experience of twenty-five years as a missionary in Syria and Palestine: "Our missionary experience in this matter is most painful, and I hope *somewhat* peculiar. It would not be charitable—possibly not just—to say to every applicant, You seek us, not because you have examined our doctrines and believe them, but for the loaves and fishes of some worldly advantage which you hope to obtain; and yet it is difficult for me at this moment *to recall a single instance* in which this was not the first moving motive." Then relating an anecdote of a pretended disciple of Dr. Chalmers, who "almost kicked the mercenary wretch out of his house" when he found that he wanted to borrow money of him, he adds, that if Chalmers "had adopted the same summary mode in Palestine, he might just as well have remained at home in his mother's nursery for all the good he would have effected here."†

Such, by the testimony of her own clergy, as well as of strangers, is the history of the Church of England in Jerusalem. It resembles her history everywhere else, but in the Holy City such facts seem to acquire additional gravity. Nor is this all. Not only do Protestants fail, in Jerusalem as elsewhere, to propagate their own religious opinions, they appear even to lose in no small number of cases, whatever sentiment of religion they originally possessed. None but a Catholic can safely visit holy places, much less the scenes where the Son of God passed the years of His human life. "It is useless to deny," says Mr. Stanley, "that there is a shock to the religious

* Pages 578, 595.

† *The Land and the Book*, ch. xxvii., p. 408.

sentiment in finding ourselves on the actual ground of events which we have been accustomed to regard as transacted in *heaven rather than on earth.*"* In other words, only the believer, whose religion is *faith* and not sentiment, and who is able to penetrate with unerring glance all symbolical and sacramental veils, and quick to recognize the footsteps which the instinct of love alone can detect, may venture to put himself in contact with Hebron, Gethsemane, and Calvary. They are death to others. So like do they look to other places, so little do they reveal to the natural eye their stupendous secrets, that many who come to gaze cease even to believe. "The commander of an English man-of-war told me," says a writer of our own country, "that he once accompanied a party of twenty from his own ship to Jerusalem, and that, out of that number, seven returned unbelievers, not merely in the authenticity of localities, but in Christianity itself."† Such is the value of "religious sentiment."

And even when the results of their visit are less fatal than this, they are in a vast number of cases sufficiently serious. It is hardly possible to find a Protestant writer of any country who does not apply to the Holy Places precisely the same tone of criticism in which he would discuss the ruins of Pompeii or the fossils of Maine and New Jersey. Indeed he displays, not unfrequently, a far deeper interest in relics of the latter class than of the former, as well as a more intelligent submission to the testimonies of history and science. In Jerusalem he is "scandalized" at every step. "The American," says a missionary of that nation, "who has been pointed to (*sic*) Plymouth Rock, Bunker Hill, or Mount Vernon, and yielded to the hallowed impressions of certainty, must beware how he carries the same reverential feelings into the East."‡ What, he seems to say, are the true sites of the Scourging or the Anointing, compared with Bunker Hill and Plymouth Rock?

But Mr. Perkins is rivalled by English and German writers. "The one spot," says Mr. Dawson Borrer, "which arrested more especially my attention," in that city which was to him only "a horrid atmosphere of mockery," was not Calvary, nor the Cœnaculum, nor the Hall of Judgment; but a certain "spot," on which it was "*probable* that a bridge of Jewish construction once existed!"§

"I went without the slightest faith," says Miss Bremer, in a book which is nevertheless full of false sentiment and artificial

* Stanley, *Sinai and Palestine*, p. 426.
† Mrs. Dawson Damer, ch. iv., p. 92.
‡ *Residence in Persia*, &c., by Rev. Justin Perkins, p. 275.
§ *Journey from Naples to Jerusalem*, by Dawson Borrer, Esq., ch. xxiv., p. 404.

pathos, "to the sepulchre of Christ—the Church of the Holy Sepulchre." She confesses, indeed, that she was somewhat moved by "the evidently deep devotion of the pilgrims," though she considered the whole scene "a childish spectacle," and thinks that "our rational Protestant Church" may be excused for protesting against "custom and superstition, by standing rigid and stiff, where the Catholic and Greek Churches bend their knees and apply their ardent adoring lips."*

Another English traveller of great repute, the learned Dr. Clarke, tells his readers that St. Helena was "the old lady to whose charitable donations these repositories of superstition were principally indebted;" while of one tradition, referring to the dwelling-place of the Holy Family, a subject which only excited his merriment, he briefly remarks, "A disbelief of the whole mummery seems best suited to the feelings of Protestants."† Perhaps he was right.

It is certain, at least, that most of his co-religionists agree with him. "To Protestant Christians," says an Anglican bishop, as if resolved to show that men of his order could surpass all others in fanatical impiety, "it almost seems as if there were more need for a crusade to deliver the sacred scenes of Palestine from *Christian idolaters*, than there ever was to rescue it from the followers of the False Prophet."‡ A Mussulman, in this gentleman's opinion, is far less obnoxious than a Catholic. Another highly respectable Anglican minister considers the Turkish occupation quite a providential fact, expressly designed to check the growth of "idolatry," and quotes, apparently with approval, the saying of Mahomet in the Koran, "The Christians have forgotten what they received from God."§

And while some are content to revile the Christians, others avow their misgivings about Christianity itself. "As I toiled up the Mount of Olives," says a Protestant writer in 1855, "in the very footsteps of Christ, I found it utterly impossible to conceive that the Deity, in human form, had walked there

* *Travels in the Holy Land*, by Fredricka Bremer, vol. i., ch. iv., pp. 112–16. This writer, who is too much absorbed in self-worship to be able to worship any thing else, denies the site of Calvary altogether, doubts "the miracle of the re-awakening of Lazarus to life," and a good many other things "related in the Bible;" but on the other hand she admires Dr. and Mrs. Gobat, though she regrets that not many of their converts "have been considered as remarkably good Christians."

† *Travels in Various Countries*, by E. D. Clarke, LL.D., vol. iv., ch. iv., p. 174.

‡ *Palestine, or the Holy Land*, by the Right Rev. M. Russell, of St. John's College, Oxford, ch. ix., p. 380 (1860).

§ *Scripture Lands in connection with their History*, by G. S. Drew, M.A., Incumbent of St. Barnabas, South Kennington, ch. x., p. 357 (1862).

before me." And so, he adds, "I preferred doubting the tradition."*

Yet there is perhaps nothing in which all races of men, save only Protestants, are so absolutely of one mind, as in the traditions which relate to the holy sites. "Even the Mussulmans themselves," as a learned archæologist observes, "have always been of one mind with the Christians as to the authenticity of our sanctuaries."† "The voice of tradition at Jerusalem," says the author of *Eothen*, "is quite unanimous, and Romans, Greeks, Armenians, and Jews, all hating each other sincerely, *concur* in assigning the same localities to the events told in the Gospel." "The Biblical traditions," adds M. de Saulcy, "are imperishable. Here nothing alters connected with the Bible; nothing is changed, not even a name; the memory of human transactions alone has been lost."

But there is no admonition in these facts for men who would trace with a puerile enthusiasm the path of some favorite hero or national idol, and even strew it with costly monuments; but who, when it is a question of One who is to them little more than an historical phantom, or at best an object of "religious sentiment," prefer "doubting the tradition." "Many Protestants," says a well-known writer already quoted, "look upon *all* the traditions by which it is attempted to ascertain the Holy Places of Palestine as utterly fabulous."‡ The house of Shakespeare, the birthplace of Newton, or the coat of Nelson, are relics which they defend against all comers, for in these they avow a personal interest; but the house of Joseph, the birthplace of Mary, or the robe of Jesus,—these are only the theme of a jest, or scouted as "utterly fabulous." It is worthy of men and philosophers to guard in sumptuous shrines the mementoes of fellow-men, who no longer afford nourishment even to worms; but it is only a feeble superstition which is careful about the despised relics which the God-Man, or His Immaculate Mother, have left on earth. Protestants prefer "doubting the tradition" which relates only to such memorials.§ This method of obliterating importunate traditions which

* Bayard Taylor, ch. v., pp. 74, 84.

† *La Terre Sainte*, par M. l'Abbé Bourassé, ch. iv., p. 65.

‡ *Eothen*, ch. ix.

§ A learned English traveller observes, without so much as the thought of criticism in this case, that the "well authenticated relic" of Mahomet's beard "constitutes the sanctity which Moslems attach to the city of Cairwaan." Davis' *Ruined Cities*, &c., p. 272. Of the supposed Tomb of Hiram, near Tyre, for which there is not a single authority "except native tradition," a Protestant missionary says, "As there is nothing in the monument itself inconsistent with the idea, I am inclined to allow the claim to pass unquestioned." Thomson, *The Land and the Book*, ch. xiv., p. 196. It is only the Christian traditions which are denied,

they desire only to discredit, "meets with much approbation," we are told, "in speculative Germany;" where, however, they venerate Luther's inkstand, and other relics of the same value. "I have undertaken," says a German writer, "to convey to the American missionaries at Jerusalem the pamphlet of a Protestant clergyman, who disputes the locality of the Holy Sepulchre, without ever having been at the place!"* If he had been there, he would perhaps have disputed the Crucifixion.

Indeed, these gentlemen are prepared to dispute any thing. "Even the *Via Dolorosa*," Dr. Robinson gayly remarks, "seems to have been first *got up* during or after the times of the crusades;" although, as Tischendorff observes, "the real road along which Christ walked *must* have taken this direction." Dr. Robinson appears in this case to have been guilty at least of an anachronism. Half a century ago, people used to accept language of this kind in place of wit, and many reputations were cheaply gained by such means. The world has grown more exacting, and no longer regards a bad jest as a substitute for modesty, wisdom, and learning.†

"Alas! for the pilgrim," said the lamented Mr. Warburton,—to whose soul may God grant rest—"who can scoff within the walls of Jerusalem!" But there are men who can do worse than scoff, not only in Jerusalem, but within the precincts of the Holy Sepulchre. In that spot where Angels tread with fear and awe, but where schismatics jest and harangue, the writer was lately informed by a relative, an Anglican clergyman, that "the only visitors who were not prostrate on their faces were Turks and English Protestants, but that the former were much the more reverent of the two." And this very reverence at the tomb of Christ, before which the holy women once watched with heavy hearts, only moves the disdain of the disciples of Luther and Calvin and Cranmer. "I have never seen

and this very writer scoffs at the Holy Sepulchre, finds the tomb of Lazarus "every way unsatisfactory, and almost disgusting," and "came out of the Church of the Ascension with feelings of utter disgust." Ch. xliv., pp. 675, 697. Yet he is one of the most temperate of his class.

* Countess Hahn-Hahn, Letter xxvii.

† How different is the temper of Christian faith! "The faithful have a special light, over and above tradition," says one who appears to have been taught by the Holy Ghost, "to keep them right about the sites of the Holy Places." The same writer observes, "that devotion to the Holy Land is a hidden support to Catholic kingdoms,—that our Lady prayed that Catholics might always have the sanctuary of Bethlehem in their hands,—that heathen and misbelievers gain *temporal* blessings from living in the vicinity of the Holy Places,"—and finally, "that the sins of men have forfeited the peculiar custody of the Holy Places which our Lady established." Maria Agreda, quoted by F. Faber, *Bethlehem*, ch. vii., p. 382.

any thing *so abject*," says one of them, "as the conduct of the pilgrims before the altar in the Calvary chapel. You can scarcely recognize them as men."* To lie prostrate, and to weep, at the tomb of the Saviour, this gentleman deems abject degradation. "I plead guilty," says a distinguished British officer, "to having neither wept, pulled off my boots, nor performed *any other antics*" in the Holy Sepulchre; such is his rebuke to "pilgrims of another order, who advanced with bare feet and many tears."† And this exactly agrees with the equally cynical remarks of an Anglican missionary in Ceylon, who once witnessed certain ceremonies in a Catholic church which provoked a similar comment: "The great events of our Lord's conception, birth, and life; His last agony, trial, death, &c.; are all acted as upon a theatre. The *poor enthusiasts* are pleased and affected at these scenes."‡ He seems to marvel that they did not share his own indifference.

One effect of the temper displayed, with rare exceptions, by Anglican and American missionaries in the East, is to be traced in the intense scorn and indignation which they have excited amongst the oriental races. Thus the Maronites, we are told, "*now* confound under the common name of *biblicals* all who belong to the British nation, and the English tourist can hardly traverse the Libanus without peril."§

Mr. Farley, however, while he patriotically declares that, without compromising his personal opinions, he enjoyed, in every part of Syria, the most courteous and cordial reception both from priests and people, and that it is the fault of every English traveller if he does not experience the same hospitality, allows that the Americans, whom it was not his business to defend, are universally detested. "This, I think, is to be attributed to the manner in which they speak of every thing. Sterne says, 'I hate the man who can travel' from Dan to Beersheba, and say, ''Tis all barren;' but such is the usual mode of expression with American travellers. The traditions of ages are overturned, and the local prejudices of the people are shocked by the bold and free manner in which they express their thoughts. Kefr Kenna is not the Cana of Galilee; the Grotto of the Annunciation is not the veritable grotto; Mount Tabor is not the Mount of Transfiguration; the Workshop of Joseph is a myth; and so on. They would even deny that the Fountain of the Virgin is the true fountain; but, unfortunately, there is

* *The Wanderer in Syria*, by G. W. Curtis, ch. xi., p. 211.
† Colonel Napier, *Reminiscences*, &c., vol. ii., ch. ix., p. 137.
‡ Rev. Mr. Clough, quoted in *Asiatic Journal*, vol. i., p. 582.
§ *Correspondance d'Orient*, par M. Michaud de l'Académie Française, et M. Poujoulat, tome viii., p. 89.

not another fountain in the place. What a pity there is not a fountain at the other end of the town, so as to afford some reason for doubt!"*

It is creditable to the more enlightened class of Protestants, that the excesses of the missionaries are generally corrected by the spontaneous testimony, sometimes by the indignant rebukes, of lay travellers. The readers of Mr. Farley's work on Syria will remember the case of "the Rev. John Baillie, minister of the Free Church of Scotland," whose "vulgar and brutal bigotry" in the monastery of Mount Carmel was repudiated, with such eloquent disgust, by a multitude of English and Scotch tourists. But to return to Jerusalem.

It is true that the Holy City is the scene of almost daily scandals, which dishonor Christianity in the sight of the unbeliever; but this is only another of the bitter fruits of schism. "Il s'y passait des choses bien plus convenables à des salles de spectacles et à des bacchantes qu'à des temples et à des cœurs contrits."† Yet even these horrors are as nothing to those which were enacted on the same spot eighteen centuries ago, before the same two classes of spectators; of whom, then as now, the one "wagged their tongues and shook their heads," the other "smote their breasts," and went home to weep and pray.

It is no doubt with regret that France, Austria, and Spain, once the guardians of the Sepulchre of Jesus, look on in silence, and suffer the Russian to pollute that holy place. "The Greek Easter," says Mr. Stanley, and here we may agree with him, "is the greatest moral argument against the identity of the spot which it professes to honor; considering the place, the time, and the intention of the professed miracle, it is probably the most offensive imposture to be found in the world."‡ Yet it is patronized by Russia, and adopted by the whole Greek communion, although, as Dr. Wilson forcibly observes, "compared with the annual miracle of the Greek Church in the crypt of the Holy Sepulchre, the great festival of the Aztecs,"—the

* *Two Years in Syria*, ch. xxxiv. It is impossible to omit here the impressive admonition suggested in a recent work of the learned De Saulçy, whose cautious proceedings may serve as a lesson to jaunty tourists and supercilious "missionaries." When the "Arcade of the *Ecce Homo*" was first pointed out to this sagacious observer, its character and general appearance induced him to "reject the Christian tradition." Some time after, a tempest, which overthrew nearly forty houses in Jerusalem, disengaged the modern coating which had previously masked the House of Pilate, and revealed the circular arched gate behind it. "From that moment," adds M. de Saulçy, "I ceased to entertain the slightest doubt." *Narrative of a Journey round the Dead Sea*, ch. vii., p. 290, English edition.

† *Palestine*, &c., par S. Munk, p. 646.

‡ P. 464.

"rekindling of the holy fire,"—"was replete with significance and solemn grandeur, though stained with the blood of their hideous sacrifices."* But the nations are no longer one, and with division has come scandal, reproach, and dishonor. Hence the presence of the Muscovite, the Anglican, and the Calvinist in the Holy City—hence the scorn of the Moslem. "It is much to be deplored," says Mr. Curzon, "that the Emperor of Russia, by his want of principle, has brought the Christian religion into disrepute." But he is only fulfilling his mission as the head and pontiff of a "national" Church; nor does it concern him to purify this defiled temple. His spiritual subjects are only political agents, and both he and they know it. He knows, too, that the Protestants are his sure allies; that they, like him, would rather see the Turk ruling in Jerusalem than the Frank; and that even the "abomination of desolation" is less offensive in their sight than the Cross would be, if it were planted again on Mount Sion.

We have alluded to the influence of Russia in the East, and the selfishness of its aims. It will not be out of place to notice briefly her pretensions as a missionary church.

RUSSIAN MISSIONS AND SLAVONIC UNITY.

A certain school of English religionists, now more inveterately Protestant, in spite of their frequent use of Catholic words and names, than any other section of their community, profess a reverence for the Russian Church which the latter is far from reciprocating. The motive of this unrequited homage is transparent. The Divine unity of the Church, which is the glory of her children and the despair of her enemies, which no assault can weaken and no art counterfeit, but which the school in question have long ceased to contemplate either with admiration or desire, now only provokes them to anger. Unable to derive comfort from the dreary spectacle of their own confusion and disorder, and unwilling to receive the admonition which it suggests, their instincts impel them to seek in other communities the consolation which their own refuses to supply. Hence the affected admiration which the organs of this party now display for what they take pleasure in calling "Slavonic Unity."

Again: the fertility of the missions of the Catholic Church, the noble army of her martyrs, and the ever-increasing multitude of her neophytes, contrasted with the sterility of the Sects,

* *Prehistoric Man*, vol. i., ch. v., p. 126.

and the incurable earthliness of their salaried agents, inspires in the same men no higher feeling than fretful jealousy or impatient malice. Virtues which even the savage has confessed to be Divine leave *them* cold and indifferent; and sacrifices which have converted nations on earth, and have been greeted with hosannas in heaven, only kindle in their hearts new resentment and redoubled hate. They have fought so long against the Church, that even her most beneficent triumphs have become odious to them, and they have resisted with such fatal success the invitations of her Founder, that they have lost at last the power to recognize either His work or His presence. Hence the querulous zeal which they have lately manifested in exalting what they delight to call the efficacy of "Russian Missions."

Let us inquire, then, and chiefly from Protestant sources, what is the nature of Slavonic unity, and what are the pretensions of the Russian Church to be the mother of apostles.

In many countries, and notably in our own, political does not imply religious unity. In Russia, where so many races exist side by side, and over whose illimitable steppes Tartar, Slavonic, Mongol, and Hindoo tribes are scattered without being amalgamated, the one is only valued as an instrument to obtain the other. "We must gather around Russia," said Peter the Great, who was as incapable of a religious motive as of a political mistake, "all the Greeks scattered by discords, who are spread in Hungary, in Turkey, and in the south of Poland, make ourselves their centre, their support, and thus found by anticipation, *and by a sort of sacerdotal supremacy*, a universal hegemony."* Consistently with this first principle of Muscovite policy, thus crudely announced by the astute barbarian, the Church and the priesthood, as well as every secular influence, are employed with a tenacity of purpose which success does not relax and failure does not discourage, "simply to aid and cover the ever active ambition of the house of Romanoff."† Yet in spite of the efforts of a ruler as nearly omnipotent as a human agent can be, and of measures as nearly unscrupulous as human conscience will permit, both the political and religious unity of the Slavonic races have still no existence, save in the mortified hopes of the Russian Czar.

As respects the latter, in spite of ceaseless efforts to obtain even an apparent uniformity, there were already, thirty years ago, "*sixteen millions*, or about one-fourth of the entire popula-

* Leonard Choderko, quoted by Colonel Chesney, *The Russo-Turkish Campaigns*, app., p. 462.

† *The Baltic, the Black Sea, and the Crimea*, by Charles Henry Scott; ch. xv., p. 245, 2d edition.

tion, who did not profess the Greek faith;"* and as to those who do, while the educated orders, with hardly an exception, neither care nor affect to care for the state religion,—so that "with many of the mercantile classes, with most of the employés, and with the greater part of the landed aristocracy, all faith and confidence in their creed has long departed,"† the peasants are divided into about fifty sects, and "the hatred and contempt of these sects for one another, and the enmity between all of them and the orthodox church, are excessive."‡ And the evil assumes every year wider dimensions. Since 1840, as Golowine reports, the number of *Raskolniks*, or seceders, has swelled "*from nine to thirteen millions*," being an increase of four million dissenters from the national church in twenty years, or two hundred thousand per annum! § "It is by religious divisions," observes a well-known writer, "that the Russian empire will perish."‖

"There is not at this day," says Schouvaloff, "a single individual, priest or layman, who believes in the unity of his church." It is not possible that any Russian, conversant with its actual condition, should do so. "There are," as Mr. Kohl observes, "*five* independent heads of the Greek Church in Europe" alone;¶ viz., the Archbishop of Karlowitz in Hungary, now an independent Patriarch, with eleven suffragan bishops; the Greek Synod; the Bishop of Montenegro, an "*hereditary* metropolitan;"** the Patriarch of Constantinople; and the Emperor of Russia. And within the empire, where no two of the Russian bishops have any spiritual dependence upon or connection with each other, but are simply the paid officials of a common master, who appoints, degrades, or discards them at his pleasure, the fictitious harmony of the ecclesiastical fabric, in which such formidable breaches have already been made, is sustained by exactly the same machinery which controls its civil and military institutions. So utterly unknown in Russia is that religious unity which binds by a closer tie than that of blood or lineage Catholics of every tongue and race—"a oneness not to be brought about by human powers, oneness in believing, thought, and will."††

Many delusions have prevailed in England, and the supposed

* *The Russian Shores of the Black Sea*, by Laurence Oliphant, ch. xxvii., p. 373 (1853).

† *Revelations of Russia*, ch. xi., p. 334 (1844).

‡ *Russia*, by J. G. Kohl, p. 272 (1842).

§ Quoted by Döllinger, *The Church and the Churches*, p. 141, ed. MacCabe.

‖ *La Russie en* 1839, par le Marquis de Custine, *Lettre* xxii., p. 134.

¶ *Montenegro and the Slavonians of Turkey*, by Count Valerian Krasinski, p. 10 (1853).

** *Austria*, by J. G. Kohl, p. 259 (1843).

†† Moehler.

concord of the Russian, Greek, and Oriental Churches, is not the least notable among them. There is, in fact, no longer any such institution as the "Greek Church," or the "Oriental Church," in the sense in which those terms are employed by certain Anglican writers. When De Maistre remarked that "the words Oriental Church, or Greek Church, have no kind of meaning whatever,"* he stated a fact which no Greek or Russian would think of disputing. Indeed, a Russian writer of our own day, in proposing to the world what he considers the only defence which candor can offer or reason accept of his own ecclesiastical position, begins by affirming, with great energy, that the Russian Church has never had any part or lot with the so-called Greek Church, "in whose frightful aridity," he adds, "no one can fail to recognize the terrible effects of Divine justice."† We shall presently apply the same test to his own communion.

Long ago, Dr. Wolff expressed surprise and sorrow on discovering that the "Greek Church," like that of Russia, "is no longer under the Patriarch of Constantinople." It was Russia which suggested, from political motives, the final separation. "The new kingdom of Greece," we are told, "in imitation and by the counsels of Russia, has withdrawn itself from obedience to the Patriarch of Constantinople;" and this secession "was accomplished in Greece without a shock, and even without a rumor!"‡ So utterly extinct is the conception, or even the desire of ecclesiastical unity in all the Photian communities.

And Greece is not the only country which Russia has succeeded in detaching from the pretended chief of the Oriental Church, after abandoning him herself. "The clergy of *Georgia*," observes General Monteith, long ago negotiated with the Archimandrite of Moscow, expressly "to separate them from the Patriarch of Constantinople, under whom they had previously been."§ *Bulgaria*, now inclining towards Catholic unity, is nearly lost to the same chief; and the movement of repulsion is so general in the Danubian Principalities, that already there is a project of a national and perfectly independent "Moldavo-Wallachian Synod." Roumelia and the Herzegovina are said to be both ripe for a similar movement, which has actually been accomplished in the Churches of Cyprus and Montenegro.‖

The dethroned prelate of Byzantium, who would no more dare to make his voice heard in Greece or Russia than in France

* *Lettre à une Dame Russe sur le Schisme et sur l'Unité Catholique.*

† *La Russie, Est-Elle Schismatique?* par un Russe Orthodoxe, p. 21 (Paris, 1859).

‡ *Persécutions et Souffrances de l'Eglise Catholique en Russie*, p. 386.

§ *Kars and Erzeroum*, by General Monteith, ch. i., p. 17.

‖ Döllinger, p. 123.

or Spain, and who borrows from his dependants, or from Greek and Armenian merchants, the price of the See for which he is obliged to outbid his rivals, and which he is to repay by the spoliation of his own flock, has become at length a jest and a puppet. "His whole administration," as the learned Döllinger observes, "has now been for hundreds of years connected with an unexampled system of extortion, corruption, and simony. Every patriarch attains by these means to his dignity," and "is usually changed every two or three years, being deposed by the Synod for bad administration, or compelled to resign. The cases in which a patriarch dies in possession of his dignity are extremely rare, for those who make a profit by bargains for the patriarchate take care that they shall be transacted as often as possible."* "The patriarchate at Constantinople," says Leopold Ranke, "forms *a commercial institution or bank*, in which capitalists are well disposed to invest their money."† Such is the last end of the so-called Greek Church.

And not only have both Greece and Russia, after falling away from the Chair of Peter, abandoned at length the fallen usurper who has converted the sanctuary of St. Chrysostom into a den of thieves, and the throne of St. Gregory into a charnel-house of simony, but the solution at ecclesiastical affinity has become universal in Asia and Africa, as well as in Europe. There is now no other connection or bond of union between Athens and Constantinople, between Antioch and Jerusalem, or between Moscow and any of them, than the wages which they receive in common from the Czar, when it suits his purpose to employ their bishops and clergy as subaltern agents of his policy. "The most insignificant priest," we are told, not only in the great centres of Russian propagandism, but "in Albania, Corfu, Zante, and Cephalonia, receives a little yearly income from the ecclesiastical treasury at Nischnei-Novgorod."‡ And the nominal rulers of these clerical stipendaries accept without repugnance a similar lot. The three patriarchates which are supposed to share the jurisdiction of the Byzantine prelate, and of which the holders do not even reside in their shrunken dioceses, are now "scarcely more than titular dignitaries, for the patriarchate of Alexandria has but five thousand, that of Antioch fifty thousand, and that of Jerusalem twenty-five thousand souls,"§—the entire population of the once famous "Oriental

* Ibid.

† *History of Servia*, by Leopold Von Ranke, ch. ii., p. 30 (ed. Kerr). They are all alike. "The simoniacal manner in which every preferment is obtained in the Bulgarian Church" is described by Krasinski: *Montenegro*, &c., p. 143.

‡ Döllinger, p. 138.

§ Ibid., p. 126.

Church" being less than the number of Catholics in either of the modern dioceses of Westminster, Salford, Liverpool, or Glasgow!

And even this significant fact does not fairly represent the almost incredible humiliation of these Eastern patriarchs. In 1848, when Pius IX. reproached them with their "want of religious unity," and the shameful dissolution of ecclesiastical authority, these successors of St. James, St. Mark, and St. John replied that, "in disputed or difficult questions" they took counsel with each other, and "when they could not agree, referred the matter for decision to the head of the Turkish government!" And this singular pontiff of a Christian Church did not refuse the appeal. When some of the Armenian clergy had a quarrel not long ago with the Greek priests about the custom of mixing water with the sacramental wine, "the dispute was finally brought before the Turkish Reis-Effendi, who accordingly gave his decision. 'Wine is an impure drink,' he said, 'condemned by the Koran; pure water only, therefore, should be made use of.'"*

The ecclesiastical unity of the Russian, Greek, and Oriental Churches, which the Czar has so effectually destroyed, is hardly more fictitious than the pretended political unity of the Slavonic races, which he has vainly attempted to promote. Like other "scourges of God," he has found it easier to pull down than to build up. Indeed, the whole scheme of Panslavism is only a transparent artifice, subtly adopted for the consolidation of the heterogeneous elements of the Russian empire. At a very recent period, as Krasinski, an ardent Protestant advocate of Panslavism, clearly shows, it proposed "only a *literary* connection between all the Slavonic nations," and had no political element.† The Russians themselves, who wish to profit by it, have very little title to be considered a Slavonic nation. "Much has been written," says a competent authority, "about the Slavonism of the Russians. In blood, however, it is only a few that are purely Slavonic."‡ And if we examine the fortunes of the Panslavist movement, a multitude of facts will convince us how little progress it has made. Even nations long incorporated with the Russian empire are more than ever bitterly hostile to it. *Poland*, peopled by a Slavonic race, sinks on her knees, faint and exhausted by an unequal struggle, but still calls in her agony upon Europe for the recovery of her lost liberty, and upon the Holy See for the blessing of which

* Ibid.

† *Panslavism and Germanism*, ch. ii., p. 111.

‡ *The Nationalities of Europe*, by R. G. Latham, M.A., M.D., F.R.S., &c., vol. i., ch. xxxvi., p. 363.

she was never more worthy. *Finland* was united to Russia in 1808, yet an English writer tells us, in 1854, "We had some conversation with educated Fins, and never did we listen to more stirring words of burning hatred towards the oppressors of their country."* The Slavonic movement in *Turkey*, we are informed, "is *anti-Russian* in its tendency," though of the Turkish population more than seven millions are Slavonians.† "The struggle of the *Montenegrins*," again, though nominally of the same religion, "was beheld with indifference by their kindred race the *Servians*."‡ Far from converging to unity, religious or political, the populations whom Russia desires to amalgamate for her own purposes, and of whom she wishes to become the common centre, appear only to regard each other with increasing aversion. It is thus that Providence confounds a policy the success of which would be fatal to religion, and perhaps to civilization. "The Slavonic nations," we are told, "entertain as great a dislike to the Greeks as the Turks do."§ The celebrated Servian chief Kara George rejected a Russian agent at Belgrade, says Ranke, "because he was a Greek, and the Greeks had ever been suspected, nay even hated, by the Servians, who were at that very time on bad terms with the metropolitan, also a Greek."‖ The *Moravians*, again, though partly of Slavonic origin, have no more sympathy with Russia than with Brazil.¶ The *Armenians* also, who hate the Russians even while accepting their pensions, "are closely allied with, and much attached to, their Turkish masters."** In the *Danubian Principalities* generally, as well as in *Georgia*, while the Greeks are detested, connection with Russia has only generated a more profound aversion, except in the case of ecclesiastical and other agents, paid to extend Russian influence. "The Christians both of Wallachia and Georgia have been converted, by their contact with the Muscovites, from warm friends into sullen and suspicious foes."†† Lastly, of the *Greeks* themselves we are told, on the one hand, the singular fact that "the greater part of the Christians of European Turkey have no affinity with, and no sympathy for, the Greeks," though nominally of the same religion;‡‡ and, on the

* Scott, ch. i., p. 12.
† *The Frontier Lands of the Christian and the Turk*, by a British Resident of Twenty Years in the East, vol. i., ch. iii., p. 65 (2d edition, 1853).
‡ *Anadol*, by the same author, ch. xxviii., p. 356.
§ *Frontier Lands*, vol. i., ch. v., p. 106.
‖ *History of Servia*, ch. x., p. 127.
¶ See Spencer, *Travels in the Western Caucasus.*
** Chesney, *ubi supra.*
†† *Revelations of Russia*, vol. ii., ch. xii., p. 340.
‡‡ *A Year with the Turks*, by Warrington Smith, ch. xii., p. 275.

other, that "if the Greeks were once more in a tenable position as a free nation, they would undoubtedly become the most violent and active of Russia's enemies." So that this experienced observer might well resume the facts at which we have now glanced in this emphatic summary, "Russian Panslavism was outweighed in all the scales."*

It would be idle to offer any further evidence of an incontestable truth, disputed only by a few English writers of a particular school, who seem to think that they can dispense with unity in their own Church, by affecting to find it in another where it is quite as little known, and that the admitted disorder of one sect can be happily repaired by the supposititious harmony of another. It is no longer possible to deny in good faith that while, in the words of Dr. Döllinger, "the Greek patriarchate is in the most shameful and perishing condition to which an ancient and venerable Church has ever yet been reduced," the Greek, Russian, and Oriental communities have long since been dissolved into a number of perfectly independent Churches, often deeply hostile to one another, constantly engaged in conflicting aims and intrigues, and not even cemented together by the precarious tie of a common hostility to the Holy See. The next point to be noticed, and it is one which belongs more immediately to the general subject of these volumes, is the character of the Russian Church as a missionary power.

We have seen that a Russian advocate, while he denies that his own has any thing in common with the Greek and Oriental communities, appeals to the "frightful aridity" of the latter, as affording sufficient evidence of "the terrible effects of Divine justice." He admits, therefore, the efficacy of the test which we are about to apply to the Russian Church, after employing it to determine the character of the Protestant Sects.

"It is quite impossible," observes a spiritual writer of our own land, "for true love to coexist with an unmissionary spirit."† Yet Russia, as Schouvaloff remarks, "has never produced, since her schism, either a single missionary, or one Sister of Charity who deserves the name."‡ "In the Greek-Russian Church," says Mr. Kohl, "no such useful auxiliaries have ever been formed."§ And not only does she neither possess, nor affect to possess, any missionary organization, so supremely indifferent is she to all which does not concern her political interests; but even within her own territories, if the

* *Anadol,* ch. xxviii., p. 358.
† Dr. Faber, *The Creator and the Creature,* p. 242.
‡ Schouvaloff, *Ma Conversion et ma Vocation,* p. 361.
§ *Austria,* p. 476.

consolidation of national power can be more effectually promoted by the agency of pagan tribes, she condemns them to perpetual heathenism, and peremptorily *forbids* all attempts to convert them, even to the official religion. During a long series of years, this detestable policy has been adopted towards the captives from the Caucasus. "If these young mountaineers," we are told, "were converted to Christianity, they would be all the worse received by parents, who, once half Christian, have learned, thanks to Russian aggression, to view that faith with detestation."*

"Not only do the Russian government, and its slave the Synod," says a higher authority, "remain perfectly indifferent to the sad destiny of so many souls perishing in ignorance; the former even *opposes itself systematically* and by policy to their conversion to Christianity. The emperor has formed and taken into his pay several squadrons of cavalry, drawn from the populations of the Caucasus. All these men are Mahometans; they live in the midst of a Christian capital, where they have mosques constructed and ornamented at the expense of the treasury. Many children also from the countries of the Caucasus are brought to St. Petersburg, and there receive a gratuitous education. But it is most rigorously forbidden to admit them to Christian instruction with their companions, or to attendance at their church." In vain they sometimes "weep and lament" at this forced separation. The motive is imperious. "These children are destined to return one day to their native country, where their office will be to preach to their compatriots the advantages which they may derive from absolute and irrevocable submission to Russia." This they will do more effectually if they profess the religion of their parents, and *therefore* an infernal policy forbids their conversion. "And the 'most Holy and most Orthodox Synod' has no remonstrance to offer against measures so barbarous! *Dominus horum vindex est.*"†

It is difficult to conceive the profound degradation to which the national Russian Church must have fallen, when such crimes fail to elicit a solitary protest from one end of the empire to the other. But when we have read the testimonies of men of all sects and orders, to the actual condition of the Russian clergy, there is no longer room for surprise. "Nothing," says De Hell, an authority recognized even by the late emperor, "can be compared to the demoralization of the Russian clergy, whose ignorance is only equalled by their vice. The greater part of

* *Revelations of Russia*, pref., p. xxvi.
† *Persécutions et Souffrances*, &c., p. 519.

the monks and priests spent their lives in shameful inebriety, which renders them incapable of fulfilling decently their religious duties." They have lost all idea, he adds, of a "sacred mission,"—he is speaking, not of rare and exceptional instances, but of the whole body of the rural clergy,—and "the very aspect of the popes, or parish priests, excites equal disgust and astonishment. To see these men, whose uncombed beards, wine-bloated faces, and filthy dress, reveal a total absence of human respect, one cannot conceive that they are apostles of Divine truth."* "Not possessed of even the slightest shadow of influence or power in the empire," says an English writer, who is nevertheless a warm advocate of the Czar, "in ignorance, vulgarity, I may almost say degradation, they are perfectly without parallel in any religion throughout the world, not even excepting Greece, the natives of which country themselves admit the minor orders of their clergy to be the most abandoned miscreants in the world."† "In all street ballads and popular ribaldry," says a Russian author in 1850, "the priest, the deacon, and their wives, are always brought in as examples of the absurd and the despicable."‡ In four years, from 1836 to 1839,—as the so-called "Holy Synod" reported to its president, a cavalry officer, and aid-de-camp of the emperor,—thirteen thousand four hundred and forty-three ecclesiastics, or one-sixth of the whole Russian clergy, were under sentence of the public tribunals, and that, as the Supreme Procurator informed his master, "for infamous crimes."§ The "Synod" itself, which is supposed by a verbal fiction to rule over this clergy, is so avowedly a mere department of the state police, that, as Dr. Döllinger notices, "it cannot even appoint its own secretary and subordinate officials, who are all nominated and displaced by the Czar."

It is impossible to quote, without repugnance, such descriptions of a national clergy, who are, nevertheless, the spiritual teachers of some fifty millions of souls. But we are going to speak of the missionary operations of these very men, and we shall find them to be worthy, in every case, of ecclesiastics whom even Russians treat with scorn and outrage, and of whom they speak in exactly the same terms as the German, French, or English writers. Haxthausen, though a Russian advocate, confesses that they have no qualification "for the duties of a missionary," and even admits that the "sterility" of which we

* *Les Steppes de la Mer Caspienne*, &c., par Xavier Hommaire de Hell, Chevalier de l'Ordre de S. Wladimir de Russie, tome i., ch. viii., p. 120 (1843).

† *Personal Adventures in Georgia, Circassia, and Russia*, by Lieut.-colonel Poulett Cameron, C.B., vol. ii., ch. v., p. 205 (1845).

‡ Quoted by Döllinger, p. 137.

§ Theiner, *L'Eglise Schismatique Russe*, ch. vi., p. 138.

are about to furnish conclusive evidence, "is undoubtedly attributable to their separation from Rome."* Tourgeneff, who describes their fallen condition, and the "haughty disdain"† with which they are treated by all above the class of peasants, is confirmed by De Hell, who relates that the upper classes often strike them, and that they "bow their heads humbly to receive the correction." If a wealthy proprietor, we are told by M. Golovine, himself a Russian priest, "ask an archbishop to make a sacristan a priest, a priest he will be, even though he know not how to write."‡ And this is the case also in the churches subject to the Patriarch of Constantinople. "It might happen to any one," says a Greek writer, in letters addressed in 1856 to the Archbishop of Cephalonia, "to dismiss a servant one day for misconduct, and meet him on the morrow as a priest; people whom you have known as petty chandlers, day-laborers, or boatmen, you may see in a few days appear at the altar or in the pulpit."§ What marvel, if under such teachers "the Russians," as M. de Bonald observes, "have a religion entirely composed of words, ceremonies, legends, and abstinences, which is to genuine Christianity nearly what the Judaism of the Rabbis, followed by modern Jews, is to the Mosaic worship?"‖ What marvel if a Church of which such men are the ministers, should be described by Schnitzler as "stationary, withered by the spirit of formalism, and deprived of every principle of liberty?"¶

It would be endless to multiply such testimonies. They abound in the writings of men of every nation and every creed. And the higher classes of the laity, exercising an influence which the fallen prelates of Russia dare not dispute, are said to be themselves perfectly indifferent to the religion which has so little title to their respect, and in whose ministers they recognize only an inferior order of police. "Noblesse légère," says a French writer in 1860, "superficielle, égoïste, corruptrice, et corrompue."** "They show a strong tendency," says one who has lived among them, "to add infidelity to their immorality,"†† though they still affect the outward observance of religion, because, as Madame d'Istria observes, "*la religion est une partie de la consigne militaire*," and under the rule of the Czar even unbelief submits to discipline. Yet, as Golovine remarks,

* Haxthausen, *Etudes sur la Russie*, tome i., ch. xiv., p. 441.
† *La Russie et les Russes*, par M. A. Tourgeneff, tome iii., p. 103.
‡ *Mémoires d'un Prêtre Russe*, par M. Ivan Golovine, ch. x., p. 202.
§ Döllinger, p. 125.
‖ *Législation Primitive*, par M. de Bonald, tome iv., p. 176.
¶ *Histoire Intime de la Russie*, par M. J. H. Schnitzler; *Notes*, p. 472.
** *La Russie, son Peuple et son Armée*, par M. Léon Deluzy, p. 45 (1860).
†† *Dissertations on the Orthodox Church*, by W. Palmer, p. 293.

"every one knows that the number of unbelievers in Russia continually increases." M. de Gerebtzoff also admits "the general tendency—*entrainement*—to religious incredulity, and the unbridled gratification of brutal passions,"* which began to manifest itself in Russia during the last century, and of which every capital in Europe records proverbial examples in the present. The Russian Church has killed religion, by making it impossible to respect it. And yet, while corruption spreads like a gangrene through all ranks, and only a thin varnish of decency covers the universal license,—while even "in the public educational establishments," as the most competent witnesses report, "ignorance and immorality" prevail to such an extent, that, in the words of one of them, "respect for my readers prevents me from giving any detailed account of them,"† because a true account of Russian society would be a picture upon which no one could look; the worst crimes of all are still committed in the name of religion, and the titles of "Holy, Orthodox Russia," are invoked with solemn hypocrisy by men who have ceased even to believe in holiness, and who might boast more truly than the worst class of French sophists, "Nous sommes les enfants de Voltaire."

It is true that some believe, in spite of the facts which have now been noticed, that Russia, convinced at last that her schism has only defeated, instead of promoting, the political objects dearest to her ambition, will again be reconciled to the Holy See. There are even writers, still members of her national church, who avow, with such freedom of speech as a Russian may venture to use, that to this end all their hopes are directed. They know that Russia, once Catholic, was torn from unity mainly by the influence of princes who made themselves pontiffs in order to reign as kings, and whose ecclesiastical supremacy, sacred in the eyes of their subjects, is only an instrument of policy in their own. "I recognize," said Peter the Great, with a kind of savage candor, when solicited to restore the Russian Patriarchate, "no other legitimate patriarch but the Bishop of Rome. Since you will not obey him, you shall obey me alone. *Behold your Patriarch!*"‡

Perhaps also the hope to which we have referred is partly founded on the growth of a new sentiment in the highest class of Russian minds, created by increasing intercourse with the Latin world, and sometimes expressed in such language as the

* *Histoire de la Civilisation en Russie*, par Nicolas de Gerebtzoff, tome ii., ch. xii., p. 519.

† *Recollections of Russia during Thirty-three Years' Residence*, by a German Nobleman, ch. ix., p. 321; ed. Wraxall.

‡ Theiner, p. 46.

following. "The Russian Church," says one of her latest apologists, "is not, and never has been, schismatical of her own free will—*de son gré*—like the Oriental Church." "Catholic," he adds, "from her first entrance into the Christian family," she is still Catholic, "*without knowing it—à son insu.*" Her clergy, and all but a few of her bishops, are what they are, he says, solely through ignorance. And then this Russian advocate —after remarking that "the Greeks," with whom he disclaims the remotest sympathy, "were fourteen times reconciled to the Latins since the time of Photius," and always upon conditions prescribed by the latter—continues thus: "But what must sensibly afflict the friends of truth is to see that the Russian clergy are ignorant, or appear to be ignorant, that the liturgical books of the Russian Church contain the pure Catholic, *one may indeed say Ultramontane doctrine*, on the primacy of the Pope, and the authority of the See of St. Peter." This doctrine, he observes, which Russia received from her first apostles, is retained even in the liturgical books as reformed by Nikon, and as they still exist in every parish church in Russia, though the clergy are too ignorant or too careless to reflect upon the fact. Nay more, even the doctrine of the Immaculate Conception, regarded by Anglicans as peculiar to the Roman obedience, has always been held by the Russian Church, and is still proclaimed at this day in her public offices. On the feast of the Nativity of our Lady, the Church of Russia, living only to bear witness against herself, sings this canticle: "We proclaim and celebrate your Nativity, and we honor your Immaculate Conception." Finally, this writer—deploring as a mournful calamity what Anglicans affect to consider a privilege, repudiating as worthy only of the fallen "Greek Church" the pleas which *they* urge in behalf of their own, and seeing only grounds for self-accusation where they find motives of complacency—appeals earnestly *ad misericordiam*, and only ventures to suggest that Russia, since she confesses Catholic truth in her liturgical books, should be absolved from schism on the ground of "invincible ignorance."*

But it is time to approach, without further introduction, the subject of Russian missions, and to examine, as usual by the aid of Protestant witnesses, the actual condition of the various provinces of the Russian empire which have so long solicited missionary zeal, but which the national clergy have abandoned to heathenism, or only converted after the same fashion in which Anglican missionaries have converted the pagans of China, India, and Ceylon.

* *L'Eglise Russe, Est Elle Schismatique?* pp. 21–46.

"It is to the Russian Church," says Theiner, "that we must attribute the disgrace which attaches to Christian Europe, in seeing still in the nineteenth century so many pagans within her bosom. *Whole provinces*, united during many ages to the Russian empire, are still filled with gentiles." This is the fact which we are going to illustrate.

One observation is necessary by way of preface. It will be understood that neither the Church nor the government of Russia have any objection that pagan tribes should embrace the state religion, except when political interests may be better promoted by their continuance in heathenism. To the purely religious side of the question both are perfectly indifferent. In Russia a man may be a Mahometan, a worshipper of the Grand Lama, a Lutheran, a pagan, every thing but a Catholic, without giving umbrage to the civil or religious authorities. "The Greek Church has shown toleration," we are told, "because *indifferent* to the conversion of those of other creeds;" and reserves the lash and the dungeon chiefly for "those within the pale of its own fold who seem disposed to wander from the flock." "Two-thirds of the cabinet ministers," says the same writer, "a large proportion of the generals of the Russian army, and of the immediate courtiers of the emperor, profess the Lutheran religion."* But these are all devoted to Russian policy, and therefore their religious belief is a matter of indifference. "Religious toleration," as Krasinski observes, "had been a principle of Russian policy since Peter the Great," and was first renounced by the Emperor Nicholas, who strove to attain by violence the unity which his predecessors had failed to establish. Two exceptions were made in his reign to the universal toleration, and both from the same political motive. "Many hundreds of venerable men," says an English writer in 1844, "for years beloved and respected in their parishes, are now with irons on their legs, half-shaven heads, and in coarse party-colored garments, chained two and two, pursuing their weary journey to Siberia, some every day expiring on the road."† These were Catholic priests, as the Protestant Krasinski notices,‡ "whom an imperial ukase had united to the Russian Church," and who were torn from their flocks, lest the latter should imitate their example in refusing to deny their faith.

The other exception to Russian tolerance consists in the prohibition of conversion to any community but the National Church, and the punishment of all who attempt to do the work

* *Revelations of Russia,* ch. xi., p. 301.
† Ibid., p. 308.
‡ *Panslavism and Germanism,* p. 90.

which the Russian clergy leave undone. "Proselytism in Russia," says an Anglican writer in 1855, "whether from Mohammedanism or Lamaism, is not allowed, unless it be in favor of the Russo-Greek Church."* And now let us hear the witnesses who will tell us, from actual observation, what are the claims of that Church to the apostolic character, and what it has attempted towards the conversion of the heathen nations within the bounds of the empire.

From every province of the vast dominions of the Czar,—from Courland and Livonia, and all the eastern shores of the Baltic Sea; from Finland and Laponia; from both banks of the Volga, throughout its whole course, to where it flows into the Caspian Sea; from the sources of the Don to the plains which border the Sea of Azov; from Tobolsk to the Gulf of Obi; from Perm, Orenburg, and Astrakhan; from the White Sea to the banks of the Amur, and from the Ural to the Aleutian Isles; from Georgia and Circassia, and all the distant valleys of the Caucasus; from Archangel to Odessa, and from Kamshatka to the Tauric Chersonese, we have exactly the same reports. From the Kalmuks and Tchouwasses of the Volga, and the Lapes of the White Sea; from Ostiaks and Samoieds; from the Tschuktschi of the north, and the Ossets of the south; from the Tatars of Kazan, and those of Simferopol; from Georgians and Imeritians, and all the tribes of the Caucasus; the same cry is heard, proclaiming in a hundred dialects, that no sect of earth, though it wield the power of an empire and lavish the wealth of a continent, may hope to snatch a single soul from the powers of evil, nor do aught but reveal its own incurable impotence. To the emissaries of the all-powerful autocrat and his imperial Church, the barbarians of a hundred tribes, who bow their heads before the humblest messenger of the Vicar of God, reply with one voice, as they do to the baffled agents of English, German, and American sects, "Jesus I know, and Paul I know, but who are you?"

Let us begin with the provinces of the Baltic. The *Lettes*, who inhabit Courland and the southern half of Livonia, though long nominally Christian, and surrounded by Lutherans and Russo-Greeks, "sacrifice to household spirits," we learn from Mr. Kohl, "by setting out food for them in their gardens or houses, or under old oak-trees."†

Of the *Esthonians* the same Protestant writer says, after dwelling among them, "The old practices and ceremonies of

* *The Crimea, its Ancient and Modern History*, by the Rev. Thomas Milner, M.A., F.R.A.S., ch. viii., p. 281.

† *Russia*, p. 374.

heathenism have been preserved more completely among them than among any other Lutheran people. . . . There are many spots where the peasants yet offer up sacrifices."* Schnitzler adds of the Lithuanians generally, who are nominally Lutherans, "Ils sont ignorans, superstitieux, routiniers, et ivrognes;"† and Dr. Latham informs us that "so low is the present condition of the small peasantry which now represents the Lithuanic name and language," that no trace remains of their ancient character, and that "no small amount of heathendom underlies the imperfect Christianity of the Lithuanians," so that "with the single exception of the Esthonians, the Lithuanians are the *most pagan* of all the nations of civilized Europe."‡ Such has been the religious influence of the Russian national creed in the three Baltic provinces.

If now we cross the Gulf of Finland, continuing our journey through the northwestern provinces of the empire, we come to the home of the Fins, numbering about two millions, and already subject for more than half a century to the dominion of the Czar. "The Russians," says the great English ethnologist, "claim the credit of having converted them A. D. 1227. They may have done this, and yet have done it ineffectually; for the special charge that lay against the Fins was, that *there was nothing real* in their numerous conversions." It is a significant fact that at the present day, in spite of the threats or cajoleries of Russia, very few Fins profess the national religion, the great majority being nominally Lutherans, owing to their former connection with Sweden, "with a vast mass of the original paganism underlying their present Christianity."§

Passing out of Finland into Laponia, we have this account of the Russian Laps, who, unlike those of Sweden and Norway, profess the Greek religion. "They are indifferent to the Christianity which they have within a few years affected to embrace. . . . Instructed by a few drunken priests, and yielding from fear and complaisance, they mingle and confound the superstitions of the Russian Church with the old incantations of witchcraft."‖

The White Sea separates the province of Laponia from the government of Archangel, through which we enter those of Perm, Viatka, and Orenburg. In all we meet the same facts. The Permians, the Zirianians of Vologda, who "retain much of their original paganism," and in the south, where they have

* *Russia*, p. 388.
† *La Russie, la Pologne, et la Finlande*, lib. ii., ch. i., p. 546.
‡ *The Nationalities of Europe*, vol. i., ch. iii., p. 23.
§ Latham, vol. i., ch. xviii., p. 209.
‖ *Revelations of Russia*, vol. i., ch. xii., p. 350.

come in contact with the Bashkirs, have even in some instances become Mahometans;* the Votiaks of Viatka, who are hardly distinguishable from pagans, the Tsherimis, Tshuvash, and other tribes, who are Christians in name and pagans in belief, all bear witness to the indifference or incapacity of the Russian Church. The Tsherimis, who number nearly one hundred and seventy thousand, and abound chiefly in the governments of Kazan and Viatka, are thus described: "Some of them are pure pagans, the majority being but imperfect and approximate Christians, retaining, under the surface of their later creed, most of the essentials of their original heathendom."† The Tshuvash, numbering about four hundred and thirty thousand, are devil-worshippers, in spite of their outward profession of the Greek religion. "Their Christianity is nominal, and dashed not only with pagan but with Mahometan elements."‡ The *Bisermans* of Viatka are avowedly Mahometans, and Dr. Latham thinks they are "neither more nor less than Votiak converts of some standing."§ Yet the Votiaks themselves are supposed to be disciples of the Russian Church!

But there is nothing in this fact to surprise us. The Russians themselves, as many examples will convince us, often adopt the worst pagan superstitions, and practise them with a zeal proportioned to their religious earnestness. M. Pietrowski relates, and it is only one instance out of many, that during a voyage on the Dwina, which flows through the governments of Vologda and Archangel, his companions being all religious pilgrims of the National Church, visiting sacred places, "every soul on board, from the master to the poorest of the *bohomolets*, threw a piece of copper money into the stream, to render the Dwina propitious to their course along its breast."‖

Let us now accompany Mr. Laurence Oliphant on his journey to Kazan, and thence down the Volga to the Caspian Sea. Everywhere his experience is uniform. The *Kalmuks* whom he encountered were all still Buddhists. "The *Tartar* population," he says, "is precisely the same as it ever was." Near the mouth of the Volga he visits "a large and populous village in a state of utter heathenism, and apparently destined to remain so," because the Russian Church neither knows how to convert them herself, nor will suffer others to make the attempt. At Sarepta, near Astrakhan, where, out of a population of eleven hundred, eight hundred are Lutherans or Moravians, a new fact

* Latham, vol. i., ch. xix., p. 216.
† P. 218.
‡ P. 221.
§ P. 225.
‖ *Story of a Siberian Exile*, by M. Rufin Pietrowski, ch. viii., p. 160 (1863).

comes under his observation. The Moravians had begun to convert, after their mode, some of the neighboring heathen, for whom the National Church had no care. "The Greek clergy interposed, and insisted that the converts should be admitted into *their* Church." An appeal was made to the government, which supported the priests, and the Moravians gave up the contest. "No effort is made," observes Mr. Oliphant, "to atone for this wanton bigotry, by the establishment of missions by the Greek Church among these wandering tribes."*

Mr. Scott traversed in part the same ground, and thus confirms in 1854 what Mr. Oliphant had reported in 1853. Of one tribe he says, "Pagans in religion, they make a pretended adhesion to the Russian Greek Church;" of another, "They are followers of the Grand Lama;" of a third, "They are all Mahometans." The latter give no trouble to the State, and therefore nothing would be gained, according to Russian ideas of gain, by making them Christians. At Sarepta, Mr. Scott paid a visit to Mr. Louser, the Moravian minister. "The emperor stopped at once," he writes after the interview, "those noble efforts to rescue a people from the withering blast of paganism."†

It is, of course, impossible to defend either the emperor or his ecclesiastical agents, who were bound at least to attempt the work which they would not permit others to undertake; but it is some satisfaction to know that in prohibiting Protestant missions to the Tatars, they inflicted no injury on the latter. It appears that the Protestant missionaries in Russia, like so many of their brethren in other lands, are simply traders. Henderson, who confesses that "the Sarepta mission was the most unproductive of any they have established," discovered that at Karas also "little real progress has been made by the mission," and was shocked to find that its members were chiefly busy "in the temporal concerns of the colony."‡ Their later history is instructive. "It is to be feared," said Julius Von Klaproth, who also visited them, "that it will soon be nothing but a linen manufactory, for it is known that all the establishments of the Moravian Brothers in Russia have no other motive than the love of gain."§ Finally, the last phase of their career is described by Hommaire de Hell, who found that "at the present

* *Russian Shores of the Black Sea*, ch. iii., p. 52; ch. v., p. 70; ch. viii., p. 119; ch. xx., p. 272. Cf. *Oriental and Western Siberia*, by T. W. Atkinson, ch. xxii., p. 383.

† *The Baltic*, &c., ch. viii., p. 114; ch. x., p. 158; ch. xii., p. 194.

‡ *Biblical Researches in Russia*, by E. Henderson, ch. xvii., p. 412; ch. xx., p. 447.

§ *Voyage au Mont Caucase et en Georgie*, par M. Jules Klaproth, ch. x., p. 261.

day the original object of the establishment *is hardly remembered;*" and that "the colony, at Karas, essentially agricultural, no longer thinks of any thing but enriching itself at the expense of the strangers whom the mineral waters attract to the Caucasus!"* If the Russians have not even a conception of the character of an apostle missionary, their Protestant rivals can hardly reproach them with the fact.

It is true that in the neighborhood of Astrakhan Protestantism tried once more to do what Panslavism had failed to effect, but with no other result than to show that one form of human religion is as impotent as another. "The reception the Scotch missionaries met with from the Tatars," says Henderson, "was far from encouraging. . . . Sometimes they treated their message with mockery and scorn, hooted them with the utmost rudeness, and ordered them away."† It is also a curious example of the pretended religious unity of Russia, that in 1835 Astrakhan already contained, besides Russo-Greek churches, fifteen mosques, two Armenian churches, a Catholic church and convent, a Protestant temple, and a Hindoo pagoda.‡

We have now reached the mouth of the Volga, but must return for a moment to Kazan, once the capital of a powerful nation, before we continue our journey towards the East. Kazan, as Dr. Latham observes, is "the great seminary for missionaries and for agitators in behalf of religious and political designs of Russia in the direction of the East." Yet in this government, and throughout the whole course of the Volga, Russian missionary projects have been at least as fruitless as in every other region of the empire. Mr. Turnerelli confirms the statements of Latham, Scott, and Oliphant as to the paganism of the Tsherimis, Tshuvash, and other nominal converts,§ and adds that the great majority of these tribes do not even affect to profess the religion of their masters, in spite of the powerful inducements proposed to them. In the city of Kazan itself there are nearly twenty thousand Mahometans, and the immense Tartar population of the entire region, ranging as far as Astrakhan, remains either wholly uninfluenced by Russian teaching, or has adopted, as in the case of the *Tshulim* Tartars, to the number of fifteen thousand, and a few of the *Nogays*, a horrible compound of Christianity, Islamism, and Shamanism.‖ But the vast majority, as all the witnesses agree, are just what

* *Les Steppes de la Mer Caspienne,* tome ii., ch. vii., p. 206.

† *Biblical Researches,* ch. xviii., p. 431.

‡ Schnitzler, *La Russie,* &c., lib. ii., ch. iii., p. 699.

§ *Kazan, the Ancient Capital of the Tartar Khans,* by G. T. Turnerelli, vol. ii., ch. iv., p. 155.

‖ Latham, ch. xxiii., p. 258.

their forefathers were before the Khanat of Kazan was annexed to the Muscovite empire.

If we now advance eastwards, and cross the range which separates European from Asiatic Russia, we shall still encounter invariably the same facts. The *Voguls*, numbering about six thousand, in the two governments of Perm and Tobolsk, inhabit the district along the ridge of the Uralian chain. They invoke in all their expeditions the carved images of wild beasts.* The *Ostiaks*, who number nearly twenty thousand, and are found chiefly on the Obi and the gulf into which it flows, are thus described, in 1852, by Colonel Szyrma, whose work was published under the supervision of the Russian censorship: "Up to the present day, although a considerable number of the *Ostiaks* have been converted to Christianity, the neophytes have not discontinued the worship of ancient larch-trees, remnant of a sacred grove, which prevailed among their forefathers." On one occasion, the traveller whose notes he edited surprised a number of *Ostiaks* in a forest, who, "having accepted, or rather been compelled to accept Christianity, were performing the rites of their idolatrous worship in secret."†

The *Samoyeds*, the next great tribe of this part of eastern Siberia, are in much the same condition. No attempt was even made to convert them before 1830. "They are to this day," says Szyrma, and Latham gives the same account of them, "idolaters, following the tenets of their ancient Shamanic religion." "The Russians themselves," he adds, notwithstanding their profession of Christianity, "do not refuse belief in the prognostications of the Shamans;" and "Russians of all religious sects frequently consult them about what is to happen to them in the most important proceedings of life, and never doubt the truth of the revelations made to them." In this case, instead of pagans becoming Christians, we see Christians converted into pagans. Perhaps the Russian censor thought this too insignificant a fact to require suppression.

The same writer speaks of a couple of *Ostiaks* who came to the Greek church at Berezov on the river of Obi to be married, upon whom the ceremony of baptism had made so little impression, that "they had actually forgotten their Christian names." All these tribes, he observes, after their nominal conversion, display a brass cross on their breasts, to indicate their adhesion to Panslavism, "and carry the Shaitan in their pockets." And the Russian Church, which is only the instru-

* Id., p. 231.

† *Revelations of Siberia*, edited by Colonel Lach Szyrma, vol. i., ch. ix., p. 147; ch. xvii., p. 262; ch. xviii., p. 283; vol. ii., ch. ii., pp. 20–27.

ment of the policy of its lay pontiff, is satisfied with converts of this class, because they satisfy its master.

We have still to speak of the remoter governments of Yakutsk and Urkutsk, the newly-acquired region of the Amur, and the far eastern peninsula of Kamshatka. They have all the same tale to tell. The *Koriaks*, whether still nomads, or settled in villages, "are either Shamanists or imperfect Christians." The *Parenzi* and *Kamenzi*, of the Gulf of Pendzinsk, are Shamanists. The *Pallanzi* are partly heathen, partly Christians, if such a name can be applied to them, of the *Ostiak* and *Samoyed* type. The Olutorians are still more undisguisedly pagan. The Oronchons of the Upper Amur, as Ravenstein relates in 1861, "are nominally Christians, but they resort to the practices of Shamanism almost every night," and, though ostensibly members of the Russo-Greek Church, keep "idols made of wood and fur" in their dwellings.* The Russian *Tungús*, composed of various tribes, "as a rule are Shamanists, and imperfect converts to Christianity, rather than Buddhists," as the Chinese *Tungús* are.† The *Goldi* are Shamanists, as are the *Giliaks*, by whom the Abbé de la Brunière, who had gone to evangelize the region of the Amur, was lately martyred. The Russian Church has no martyrs, and its so-called missionaries undertake the work of which we have now seen the results from the same motive as the soldiers who accompany them, and in obedience to the same authority.

How willingly true missionaries would preach to these unhappy tribes, "without money and without price," the pure and holy doctrine which millions of men once equally degraded have accepted, in many a land, from teachers of the same order, we may infer from the heroic self-devotion of the four Polish priests, who, with the reluctant consent of the Russian Czar, carry to their exiled brethren in Siberia the consolations of religion. "No Christian mind," says one who profited by their charity, "can fail to appreciate the devotion of these poor priests. It cannot be too much admired, for it carries them along their ceaseless travels, and supports them as, in their sledges, they journey through the intense cold of Siberia, from Tobolsk to Kamshatka, and from Nertchinsk to the Polar Sea."‡

We have reached the extreme eastern frontier of the Russian empire, but only to find exactly the same proofs of spiritual impotence which we have seen in the provinces of the west, and in all the wide regions which lie between the Gulf of Finland

* *The Russians on the Amur*, ch. xx., p. 351.
† Latham, ch. xxii., p. 243; ch. xxv., p. 268.
‡ Pietrowski, ch. v., p. 102

and Bhering Straits, between the Polar Circle and the Caspian Sea. Everywhere the imperial church of Russia is equally sterile. Either she abandons to paganism whole nations, without an effort to kindle among them the light of the Gospel, or converts them into such "Christians" as the *Tshuvash* and *Voguls*, the *Ostiaks* and *Tsherimis*, the *Koriaks* and *Samoyeds*. Of the *Tschuktshi*, who had all received baptism, and were reckoned as converts by the Russian Church as the devil-worshippers of Ceylon are by the Anglican, Admiral Wrangell says, "It must be admitted that they are as complete heathens as ever, and have not the slightest idea of the doctrines or the spirit of Christianity."* Finally, the *Aleutians*, a race "much more powerful, bodily and mentally," than their congeners of Labrador or Greenland, and whose "blood is mixed largely with that of the Russians," "have been converted to an imperfect Christianity," faintly differing from paganism.†

If now we turn to the south, we receive from the banks of the Don and the Dneiper, from Georgia, Circassia, the Crimea, and all the Transcaucasian provinces, as well as from Russian Armenia, the same reports as from all the western, northern, and eastern governments of the empire. The *Cossacks of the Don*, among whom De Hell found evidence of strong religious feeling, call themselves "true believers," in opposition to the members of the State Church, "because a slight difference in the text of their Bible has occasioned a very great one in their religious sentiments." So difficult is it in Russia to conciliate religious zeal with attachment to the national creed.

The *Kalmuks*, on the banks of the Kouma, are thus described by the same witness. "Russian missionaries endeavored to convert them about the end of last century, but these attempts at proselytism, based upon force, had no result, and only created rebels." A few consented to be officially baptized, but "these pretended Christians are, with the Turcomans, the most formidable inhabitants of the steppes."‡

The *Douckoboren*, he adds, and the *Molokaner*—the latter already amounting to one million—"only abandoned the religion of their ancestors about sixty years ago," and were violently transported from their homes by the government, "alarmed at the propagation of their tenets," to New Russia. They now profess the fanatical tenets of the Mennonites, and belong to that dangerous class whose rapid increase suggested the pre-

* *Expedition to the Polar Sea*, by Admiral Wrangell, ch. vi., p. 121.

† Latham, ch. xxvi., p. 280.

‡ *Les Steppes*, &c., tome i., ch. xiii., p. 260 ; ch. xviii., p. 343 ; tome ii., ch. iv., p. 93.

diction of De Custine, "It is by religions divisions the Russian empire will perish."

The *Ossets* of the eastern slope of the Caucasus, numbering about fifty thousand, and subject to Russian authority, "have a strange mixture of Judaism, Christianity, Mahometanism, and Paganism for a creed."* The *Ossets* of Georgia "have been subject to Russia since the time Georgia was annexed to that empire. A portion of the tribe is said to have adopted a sort of nominal Christianity. It appears that, conversion being attended with certain advantages, the same proselytes had been repeatedly registered under different appellations."† The Rev. Mr. Percival gave us exactly the same account of the Anglican baptisms in Ceylon. "The majority of the *Ossets* are nominally Christians, and belong to the Greek Church," observes Haxthausen; "they are, in fact, semi-pagans; indeed some are wholly and avowedly heathens. They offer sacrifices of bread and flesh upon altars in sacred groves."‡ Yet the *Ossets*, whose connection with the Russian Church has only aggravated their misfortunes, were once, as Klaproth remarks, wholly Christian.

Of the *Georgians* generally, Bodenstedt speaks as follows, in a work commended by Humboldt. "It is incredible how ruinous and demoralizing Russian influence is. The manners and the customs peculiar to the country, which have occupied for centuries the place of laws, vanish before the foreign intruders, without being supplanted by any thing better. . . . . The Russians can only multiply the primordial ills and burdens of the people, without giving them a moral counterbalance. The only things they bring with them into the conquered lands are new coercive measures, new forms of deceit, of falsehood, and of abuse of the Church for objects of police." In *Circassia*, the same writer remarks, "Christianity has become hateful to them through the Russians."§

In the *Caucasus*, Mr. Spencer observes, "the Russians commenced their intercourse under the mask of proffered protection, friendly commerce, and a desire to instruct them in the civilizing truths of Christianity;" and the only result of their presence has been to "reduce their once fertile meadows to a desert," and to excite their "deadly hatred" against the religion which Russia has taught them to despise and abhor.‖ The fatal

* Latham, ch. xxix., p. 301.

† *Life and Manners in Persia*, by Lady Shiel, p. 51.

‡ *Trans-Caucasia*, p. 395.

§ *Life in the Caucasus and the East*, by Friedrich Bodenstedt, vol. i., p. 57; vol. ii., pp. 163, 175; ed. Waddington.

‖ *Travels in the Western Caucasus*, by Edmund Spencer, Esq., vol. i., ch. viii., p. 103; ch. xxix., p. 354.

effects of Russian influence upon all the Caucasian tribes subject to it are attested with impressive unanimity by various witnesses. The *Ingushes* acknowledge their power but detest their religion. "Every attempt," says Mr. Spencer, "of the Russian government to win them over to embrace the tenets of the Greek Church failed." "The *Kabardan* Circassians," we are told, "who had hitherto been Christians (of the Russian Church), abandoned their religion to escape her control, and became Mohammedans."* These men are believed by Klaproth to be descendants of the Greek colonies of the Lower Empire, and Latham remarks, that "ruins of Christian churches and monasteries in even the non-Christian parts of Caucasus are numerous; yet so utterly has every Christian tradition died away among them, that when Colonel Poulett Cameron inquired of them the meaning of the crosses still found in many of their highways, "their only answer was a careless and indifferent '*Allah billeer!*' 'God knows!' "†

When "some of the *Lesgians* are called Christians," says Latham, "little more is meant by the term than the suggestion that they are indifferent Mahometans." The *Abazes*, as Klaproth relates, professed also in earlier times the Greek religion, but became Mahometans in 1810.‡ The *Karatchai* had already deserted Photius for Mahomet in 1782.§ Finally, Henderson gives the following summary of the results of Russian missionary influence in all the Caucasian provinces; "The *Tcherkesses*, most of the *Lesgians*, the principal *Abkhasian* tribes, the *Tchetchenzi*, the *Nogais*, the *Kumaks*, and the *Karatchais*," numbering more than half a million, "*are Mohammedans*;" while the rest of the Caucasian tribes, with the exception of the Georgians, Armenians, and Jews, "*are in a state of heathenism*."‖

But even these facts, disgraceful as they are to the Russian Church, do not reveal the whole truth. Here, as elsewhere, not content with driving whole races into apostacy, by exhibiting to them only immorality, cruelty, and fraud, she has driven away the only missionaries who could have won them to religion and civilization. As early as 1612, Father Szgoda, of the Society of Jesus, allowed himself to be captured by the Tatars, and carried away as a prisoner to the Crimea, in the hope that he would find as a captive "the opportunity of preach-

* *The Progress and Present Position of Russia in the East*, ch. ii., p. 20; 3d edition (1854).

† *Personal Adventures*, &c., vol. i., ch. vi., p. 332.

‡ *Voyage au Mont Caucase*, ch. ix., pp. 202–225.

§ Ibid., ch. xi., p. 282.

‖ *Biblical Researches*, app., p. 538.

ing the Gospel to them."* Nearly two centuries later, Klaproth found a community of Jesuits at Mozdok, prepared to do what they had done in every other land, and already occupied in evangelizing the tribes of the Caucasus. One of them, the Père Henri, won the admiration of the great linguist by his zeal and talent, of which he gave a proof by preaching fluently in Armenian when he had been only nine months in the country. "The government," Klaproth observes, "ought to have afforded every possible facility to these religious, and would thus have spared itself a painful and costly task." But the authorities at St. Petersburg, who desired only to make Russians and not Christians, adhered to their usual policy, and have reaped the usual reward. The dishonor of religion, the waste of blood and treasure, and the ruin of whole provinces which might have become the fertile homes of a peaceful and Christian population, such have been the fruits of their unprofitable impiety. Had Russia continued Catholic, she would perhaps long since have attained both the religious and the political unity which she has hitherto vainly sought, and might have seen her flag float at this day on the castles of the Bosphorus, and been hailed by all Christian nations as the benefactor of Europe, instead of the baffled conspirator whose selfish intrigues have made her the common enemy of mankind.

Of the state of *Armenia*, now held in vassalage by Russia, we shall have occasion to supply ample evidence in a later section of this chapter. Tens of thousands of Armenians, we shall see presently, have been converted in our own day by Catholic missionaries, but it is in Russia that they have found their most implacable enemy. Pursuing everywhere a policy as profitless as it is criminal, and as fatal to the true interests of the empire as to those of religion, Russia, says M. Eugène Boré, "forbids the Catholic priests to give instructions to the Armenians who have passed into its territories, and interdicts the approach of every foreign ecclesiastic."† "The Catholic priests in Trans-Caucasia," adds Dr. Moritz Wagner, "are strictly forbidden to make any proselytes. One of the Capuchins informed me, that if they were allowed free scope, they could convert many hundreds of the Pagan and Mohammedan mountaineers." He added, that "multitudes of Suanetians and Abkhasians, most of whom were genuine heathens, had announced their wish to receive baptism in the convent of Kutais, *but they were ordered away;* for every priest who

* *Histoire du Royaume de la Chersonèse Taurique*, par Mgr. de Bohusz, Archevêque de Mohilew, liv. xvi., p. 377.

† *Correspondance et Mémoires d'un Voyageur en Orient*, tome i., p. 401.

endeavors to convert an idolater into a Roman Catholic is threatened with transportation to Siberia, a specimen of oppression and compulsion that, as far as I know, has never been devised by any potentate before."*

We have reached the shores of the Black Sea, having started from those of the Baltic, but only to receive in the southernmost province of the empire the same reports which we have gathered in every other. Even "the Tatars of the Crimea," says Mr. Milner, although educated, as M. De Demidoff asserts, by their masters,† "have suffered in manners and morals by contact with the knavish and notoriously sottish Russian peasantry."‡ Their contact wtth the Russian clergy can hardly have been more advantageous to them. Mr. Milner fully confirms the account which De Hell gives of their "ignorance and moral degradation," and mentions, as an illustration of their abject servility, that the chaplains of the Sebastopol fleet "are even directed respecting the points to be treated in their religious instructions to the seamen and marines, and an officer attends their services to ascertain if the orders of the commander are obeyed!" But, as De Hell observes, "religion has no influence upon them," and they accept their degradation without even being conscious of it. "Laziness, intoxication, and fanaticism, replace with them faith, kindliness, and charity."§ Meanwhile, as might be expected, the inhabitants of the Crimea cleave to the religion of their forefathers, and have only ceased, under Russian tuition, to practise their forgotten virtues.

One more fact will complete the tale of Russian missionary influence in the Crimea. Dr. Wolff, who preached in vain to the Caraite Jews at Jufut-Kaleh, observes in 1861, "It is most remarkable that though proselytism is prohibited in Russia, these Caraites have converted, not by their preaching, but by the integrity, uprightness, and honesty of their conduct, many of the Russians to the Jewish religion."‖

Such, by various and impartial testimony, has been the influence of the Russian Church even among tribes and races immediately subject to it, and such the gifts which she has imparted to populations which had so urgent a claim upon her charity, if she could have felt its Divine inspirations, and to regions which presented the most attractive field for the apostolic ministry, if she had possessed any apostles to bear her

* *Travels in Persia*, &c., vol. ii., ch. iii., p. 204.
† *Travels in S. Russia*, by M. Anatole de Demidoff, vol. ii., p. 41.
‡ *The Crimea*, &c., ch. ix., p. 309; ch. x., p. 367.
§ *Les Steppes*, &c., tome ii., ch. xii., p. 377.
‖ *Travels and Adventures of Dr. Wolff*, ch. xii., p. 228.

message to them. There is perhaps no darker page in the religious annals of mankind than that which records the indifference of the official Church towards the gentile populations of Russia, as there is nothing more shameful than the sterility, which would be monstrous and incredible if we did not know what befalls communities deserted by the Spirit of God, and which, as Haxthausen has candidly told us, "is undoubtedly attributable to its separation from Rome."

There are only two regions in the world, China and Syria, in which Russia maintains even the semblance of a *foreign* mission, and with a few words on each of them we may pass to other themes. In China, in spite of her long residence and advantageous position, we have seen that Russia has never even attempted, in a solitary case, to win a soul to Christ. "The members of the Russian mission in Pekin," we are told by Ravenstein in 1861, "have *never* engaged in missionary work," though established in that city since 1698!* Once, indeed, her agents converted a tribe, not in China, but on their way thither, and here is their own account of the event. Laurent Lange, who was sent in 1715 to Pekin, relates that the tribe in question were summarily baptized by the order of Prince Gargarin, and then frankly adds, "but they have not the slightest conception of the difference between Christianity and paganism."†

Lastly, in Syria, we have heard already from Protestant writers something of the character of Russo-Greek Monks, and of the contrast which even such travellers could detect, between their "besotted and gross ignorance," and the zeal, learning, and piety of the Latin clergy. It is on the sacred summit of Mount Sinai,—where "not one of the fraternity," we are told, "can carry on a conversation in any other than his native tongue,"‡—that the former have planted, during many centuries, the centre of Russian propagandism. Yet even here, where earthly projects seem out of place, the selfish schemes are rebuked by the sanctity of undying traditions; even here, where every motive conspires to stimulate them to religious fervor, or at least to the affectation of it, the representatives of the Russian Church still remain speechless and insensible, when it is only the glory of God and the salvation of souls which invite their sympathy. "The Convent of Mount Sinai," observes Dr. Stanley, "is a colony of Christian pastors planted amongst heathens, and hardly a spark of civilization, or of

* *The Russians on the Amur*, by E. G. Ravenstein, F.R.G.S., ch. ix., p. 72.

† *Journal du Voyage à la Chine*, par Laurent Lange, p. 93. Cf. *Nouveaux Mémoires de la Moscovie*, tome i., p. 193.

‡ *The Golden Horn*, &c., by Charles James Monk, M.A., vol. i., p. 103, (1851).

Christianity, so far as history records, has been imparted to a single tribe or family in that wide wilderness. It is a colony of Greeks, of Europeans, of ecclesiastics, in one of the most interesting and the most sacred regions of the earth, and hardly a fact, from the time of their first foundation to the present time, has been contributed by them to the geography, the geology, or the history of a country, which in all its aspects has been submitted to their investigation for thirteen centuries."* On the other hand, an ardent Protestant traveller, who had noted the same facts, remarks with admiration, that "for the care which is bestowed upon the remains of antiquity in Palestine, the whole of Christendom has to thank the Pope and the propaganda of Rome."†

Enough, then, of Russia and her National Church as a missionary power. Additional information with respect to both might have been obtained in abundance from Catholic sources, but we have decided in these volumes to limit our appeal to Protestant witnesses. We have seen, moreover, that we can dispense with any other testimony. If there be in the world a community which, while involuntarily testifying to Catholic truth, illustrates by its past history and actual condition the dismal penalties of separation from the Holy See, it is surely that fallen Church, which, even among its nominal members has bred only, with rare exceptions, superstition or incredulity, faith without virtue, or profession without belief; which loses every year tens of thousands, whose sincere but unenlightened zeal it cannot instruct, and whose distrust and aversion it cannot conciliate; and which, far from seeking to spread the light of the Gospel in foreign lands, regards with stupid indifference the perishing heathen nations in its own.

THE MARONITES.

If, now, after this long digression, we resume our journey in Palestine, and leaving the Holy City behind set our faces towards the north, we shall come to the forests and mountains of Lebanon. Here consolation awaits us and refreshment. Here we shall find a nation profoundly Catholic both in its social and religious life, contrasting in every feature with the less privileged tribes of the East, constant in the faith, steadfast in filial devotion to the Holy See, and recompensed by a generous Providence with gifts and qualities which have not only merited

* *Sinai and Palestine,* by Arthur Penrhyn Stanley, M.A., p. 56.
† F. Bremer, *Travels in the Holy Land,* vol. ii., p. 166.

the benedictions of the Church, but extorted the admiration of her enemies.

When we consider the position of the Maronites, surrounded on all sides by Mahometans, idolaters, or heretics; exposed to every evil influence which has gradually corrupted the other Christian natives of this land; weak, except by the nature of their country; owing all their security to their own valor, all their prosperity to their patient and cheerful industry; we are tempted to ask in surprise, by what mystery have they alone preserved through ages the dignity of character, the purity and simplicity of life, which even the most prejudiced travellers agree in ascribing to this favored race? The answer, which we need not anticipate, will be sufficiently revealed in the evidence which we are about to produce.

We have not hitherto had recourse to Catholic testimony in proving the contrast which it is the main object of these volumes to trace, both because the controversial value of such testimony would be insignificant, and because Providence, as we have several times observed, has forced Protestants to collect everywhere, and to publish to the world, all the facts which illustrate that contrast. We shall adhere to our rule in this case also, though it would be pleasant to quote some few at least of the magnificent eulogies which eminent writers have pronounced on the Maronite nation, the nobility of their character, and the unswerving constancy of their faith. Let us claim, for the first time, this indulgence.

"In spite of their great numbers," says M. Achille Laurent,—they are estimated by the French consular agents at five hundred and twelve thousand five hundred in the Libanus, and thirty thousand in the plain,*—"and though surrounded on every side by infidels, heretics, and schismatics, never, in relation to the faith, has the least difference been known amongst them; never has any schism disturbed their unity; never has one individual amongst them corrupted the purity of the Catholic doctrine."† "This Catholic colony," says M. Jules David, "seems to recall by its charity, by the simplicity of its manners, by its smiling industry and community of labor, the primitive Christian society; a society of united and active brothers, a society of equality before God, a veritable *communion* of which the Church is the sublime centre."‡ Lastly,—for we may not linger even over testimonies which are like music to the ear,—an apostolic missionary, one of that noble band of discalced Carmelites who

* De Baudicour, ch. vi., p. 246.

† *Relation Historique des Affaires de Syrie,* tome i., p. 403.

‡ *Syrie Moderne,* p. 21.

have dared to imitate their Lord in His utter poverty, gives this account of them in 1858. After describing their various neighbors,—the barbarous Moslem, the pastoral Turcomans, the reckless Ansayrii, the false and hypocritical Druses, the haughty Metualis,—disciples of the anti-caliph Ali, " of whom it would be difficult to say whether they hate a Christian or a Turk the most,"—and lastly, the schismatical Greeks, " the ignorance of whose priests is only equalled by the moral degradation of the people," he continues as follows: "We come now to the Maronites. The heart has been dried up and the soul saddened by the confused disorder of idolatry and schism. It is now our turn to rejoice. The ardent faith of primitive Christianity, its sweet piety, innocence, and simplicity of manners, is found reproduced amongst the Maronites. They appear like a people fresh from the hand of the Creator, or from the regenerating bath of the Baptism of Jesus. Oh, blessed people! how great are you in your oppression! how rich in your poverty!"*

It is not thus, of course, that Protestants speak of them, for they have attempted to creep into this paradise and have been somewhat rudely ejected; but their language, though tinged with resentment and mortification, abundantly confirms the reports of more impartial witnesses.

"The Maronites," says Colonel Churchill, who does not share the petty passions of the Protestant missionaries, " are still the 'fideles' who welcomed Godfrey de Bouillon and his associates."† While all has changed around them, centuries have left them unchanged. They are "the stanchest Romanists in the world," says the Rev. Mr. Williams; which only means that they resemble true Catholics everywhere. " So bigoted is this Romanist sect," says Mr. Drew Stent, " that very little can be effected;" that is, they spurned the heresies of Anglican and Calvinist teachers, and stoned the false prophets who tried to find an entrance amongst them. " The missionaries," says Mr. Wortabet, alluding to the Protestant emissaries, " had to retire before pelting stones and an angry mob." " They were driven out," says Mr. Walpole, " by the fanatic population, and I do not believe they ever procured the satisfaction they ought. The Maronites are very proud of the victory." He confesses, however, in spite of wounded sympathies, that " the attempt was worse than folly." And so purely spontaneous was the popular movement which expelled the foreign teachers, because they came, with money in their hands, blaspheming the Mother of God, the Sacrament of the Altar, and the Communion of

* *Annals*, vol. xix., p. 271.

† *Mount Lebanon*, by Colonel Churchill, vol. iii., ch. vi., p. 66.

Saints, so wholly independent of any political or ecclesiastical influence, that a Protestant Association confesses, in 1854, that "a strong proclamation came out from the Maronite and Greek Catholic Bishops at Beirût to all their people, requiring them to guard carefully and protect all the members of the American mission."*

Let us hear other witnesses. "They are most bigoted adherents of the Papacy," observes one writer, "allowing not merely the claims of his Holiness as Head of their Church, to dictate their creed, but submitting also to his paternal government in matters of discipline."† "The Maronites," says Dr. Robinson, and all Protestant writers use the same language, "are characterized by an almost unequalled devotion to the See of Rome." They have lately converted, he adds, two Emirs of the Druses, together with their families, "so that now almost all the highest nobility of the mountain are Maronites."‡

This may suffice. No one will deny, in the face of such testimony, that the Maronites are devoted Catholics. But perhaps they are servile, ignorant, and priest-ridden? The Rev. J. L. Porter, of whom we heard at Damascus, and who had to avenge both his personal misadventures and those of his colleagues, says with emphasis, "They are as ignorant a set of priest-ridden bigots as ever polluted a country, and no stranger," he means no Protestant missionary, "can pass through their streets without meeting insult and often abuse; they are as tyrannical, as unjust, and almost as bloodthirsty, as the haughty Moslems."§ We have said that it is only English and American missionaries, but chiefly the former, who soothe their mortification by outbursts of this kind; and as it is quite true that the Maronite nation owes its character, habits, and institutions solely to the influence of the Catholic religion, it may be well to compare Mr. Porter's account of them with that of other Protestants, not less prejudiced, but having more respect for truth, for themselves, and for their readers.

"They are," says Colonel Churchill in 1853, "a community of Christians who are virtually as free and independent as any state in Christendom."‖

"They are," exclaims Mr. Bayard Taylor, in 1855, "the most thrifty, industrious, honest, and happy people in Syria." "The women," he adds, "are beautiful, with sprightly, intelligent faces, quite different from the stupid Mahometan females;"

* *American Board for Foreign Missions*, Reports, p. 110 (1854).
† *North American Review*, vol. lxxxi., p. 78.
‡ *Biblical Researches*, &c., p. 460.
§ *Five Years in Damascus*, vol. i., ch. xvi., p. 279.
‖ *Mount Lebanon.*

and their home "is a mountain paradise, inhabited by a people so kind and simple-hearted, that assuredly no vengeful angel will ever drive *them* out with his flaming sword."*

"They are," writes the Countess Hahn-Hahn, "that industrious band of Christians who have adorned these mountains with cornfields and vineyards, with villages and convents."†

"Health and industry," says Colonel Napier, "appeared to be the chief characteristics of this hardy race. The men were a robust and fine-looking set of fellows, and their wives and daughters, availing themselves of the privileges of Christianity, were not ashamed to show countenances invariably beaming with smiles, and often possessing no inconsiderable share of beauty;" while the Greek schismatical women "lead nearly as secluded a life as the Osmanli ladies of Constantinople or Smyrna."‡

Mr. Farley has told us, in flat contradiction to Mr. Porter, that their kindness and hospitality, even to Protestant travellers were so universal, until they were irritated by the selfish intrigues and impertinent bigotry of missionaries whom they would have been content to despise if they had not been constrained to abhor them, that any Englishman was sure of a cordial welcome amongst them, and that he could never forget the "extreme courtesy" of the Maronite clergy towards himself.

Mr. Monro, an intelligent Anglican clergyman, who had the good sense not to insult his hosts, and had no personal motive for libelling them, not only contrasts their frank hospitality with the suspicious exclusiveness of other Syrian races, but adds, "The kind manners and energetic carriage of these people afforded a striking instance that, where industry prevails, the flowers of happiness will blossom, and abundance ever be the fruit."§

Colonel Napier, in 1847, and Mr. Monk, in 1851, rebuke with no less emphasis the peevish calumnies of the angry missionary; the latter reporting that he was "received in the most hospitable manner,"‖ and the former recording his experience in these words: "Nothing could exceed the kindness of our reception by the hospitable mountaineers, whose cottages were all thrown open to the strangers. . . . In every cottage on whose threshold we set foot, the welcome '*Faddal*' was pronounced."¶

* *The Lands of the Saracen*, ch. xii., p. 174.
† Countess Hahn-Hahn, Letter xxi.
‡ *Reminiscences of Syria and the Holy Land*, by Lieut.-Colonel E. Napier, vol. i., ch. v., p. 264.
§ *Travels in Syria*, by the Rev. Vere Monro, vol. ii., ch. xxiv., p. 107.
‖ *The Golden Horn*, &c., by Charles James Monk, M.A., ch. xx., p. 303.
¶ *Reminiscences*, ch. v., 261.

Mr. Walpole, in spite of strong religious antipathies, declares that their valor is as conspicuous as their industry and kindliness. "The Maronites rose against their oppressors, the Metuali, and drove them fairly out of the district. . . . The Metuali have a high character for warriors and courage. This shows what the Catholic population might become if united." The general prosperity, he says, was so remarkable, that "it exhibited a scene which made one feel proud that at last the Christian dared improve." He observes also, that the family of Sheebal, descended from Mahomet, had just been converted, and adopted into the Maronite nation.*

Mr. Keating Kelly cannot speak of them without enthusiasm. "The condition of this people is essentially happy. Its religion is free and respected; its churches and its convents crown the summits of its hills; its bells, that sound in its ears as a welcome token of liberty and independence, peal their summons to pray night and day; it is governed by its own hereditary chieftains, and by the clergy it loves; a strict but equitable system of police preserves order and security in the villages; property is respected and transmitted from father to son; commerce is active; the manners of the people *perfectly simple and pure.* Rarely is there seen a population whose appearance more bespeaks health, native nobility, and civilization, than that of these men of Lebanon."†

Lastly, even a Syrian Greek, who cordially hates both their religion and their nation, and who seems by converse with English Protestants to have become indifferent to his own religion without adopting theirs, makes the following confession. "They are a most industrious, contented, happy people . . . . and so manly and courageous that, until the year 1843, they had never been conquered by the Mahometans;" and then he adds the most magnificent eulogy which it was possible to pronounce upon a Christian people, that, "owing to the influence of the bishops, *crime is in a great measure unknown amongst the Maronites.*"‡

In reading these impressive testimonies, from writers of various creeds and nations, to the virtues of a Catholic people, we have almost forgotten Mr. Porter. Let us quote him once more, for the sake of adding a new example of the language in which passion finds vent while reason is mute, and of the class of agents whom Protestantism sends forth into every

* *The Ansayrii, with Travels in the Further East,* vol. iii., ch. i., p. 7; ch. xviii., p. 434.

† *Syria, and the Holy Land,* by Walter Keating Kelly, ch. viii., p. 97.

‡ *The Thistle and the Cedar of Lebanon,* by Risk Allah Effendi, ch. xvi., pp. 269, 273.

land, but only to augment everywhere the repugnance which is entertained, by all races of men, towards England and her representatives.

The Maronite clergy, Mr. Porter says, "are ignorant, bigoted, and overbearing," and their religion "senseless mummery." It is of the Syrian clergy, professors of the same faith, that a more enlightened English Protestant says, "It is a sublime spectacle to contemplate these men devoting themselves to deeds of charity and mercy, and welcoming a long martyrdom for conviction's sake."* "I can imagine St. Basil the Great," says another educated Englishman, "or the Gregories, just such persons in appearance."† "If Titian were about to paint a Doge of Venice," says an accomplished French traveller, speaking of the Maronite Patriarch of Cilicia, "he would ask for no other model."‡ Even Mr. Porter, in an access of involuntary admiration, confesses "their staid dignity and noble bearing;§ while the more candid Dr. Wolff declares that "the monks of the Maronite nation," though they "tried to convert him to the Church of Rome," "are usually men of great vigor and power."

But Mr. Porter speedily resumes his usual tone. "The education of the people," he observes, "they never think of;" and as if even this statement admitted of improvement, he adds, "the idea of imparting religious instruction is quite out of the question." Presently, as if the accounts of other Protestant travellers suddenly occurred to him, and suggested the necessity of caution, he says, "It is true a few schools have been established, but these are got up by the people," who, although "ignorant, bigoted, bloodthirsty, and polluters of the soil," he now represents as going beyond their pastors, to whom he declares they are slavishly subject, in promoting education!

Yet Mr. Ubicini has told us, that in every province of Asiatic Turkey, Catholic schools are multiplying in all directions, and are eagerly frequented by children of all sects. Dr. Robinson declares of the Maronite College of Kesrawân, in which the Jesuits teach Arabic, Syriac, Latin, and Italian, "that it takes a higher stand than any other similar establishment in Syria." Mr. Farley speaks in the same terms of the Lazarist College at Antoura, "where some hundreds of students who come from Beyrout, Aleppo, Damascus, and other towns in Syria, as also from Persia, Egypt, and even from Nubia and Abyssinia, are taught," in addition to "the usual branches of education,"

* Farley, *Two Years in Syria*, ch. xxxiv., p. 291.
† Patterson, p. 322.
‡ *La Syrie avant* 1860, par Georges de Salverte, ch. viii., p. 100.
§ Vol. ii., ch. xvi., p. 296.

"the Arabic, French, Italian, and Latin languages." M. de Salverte reports, in 1861, that the ecclesiastical seminary at Ghazir, in which he found ninety students, is so efficient, that its excellence dispenses them from seeking education in the colleges of Rome.* Mr. Wellsted relates, that even in Aleppo, "most of the children can read and write at an early age."† And even Risk Allah, though he affects, in order to please his English readers, to deplore what he has learned to call the "Romish tendencies" of the Maronites, honestly confesses that "their schools are really excellent;" and whereas the Protestant missionary affirms that the Maronite clergy "never think of education," this Syrian Greek avows, in spite of national and religious antipathies, that "one great advantage which the Maronites possess, and which must eventually prove very beneficial to them, is the fact, *that education is spreading universally amongst them.*"‡

Lastly, the accomplished M. de Saulçy furnishes the following example of the nature of the education imparted to all comers in the college at Antoura. A native pupil, who had only attained the modest position of assistant dragoman at Beyrout, is thus described by this competent judge: "He speaks and writes French very correctly, he is perfectly well read in all our first-rate authors, and altogether his education may vie with that of *the best French universities.* As to Arabic, his native tongue, he is complete master of it, and could, if required, fill the chair of the ablest professor."§

But in all this there is no lesson for Mr. Porter. He had a defeat to avenge, and after five years of unprofitable labor had convinced even himself that it was time to quit Syria. And so in his anger he forgot prudence as well as truth. Education is so literally *universal* among the Maronites, though their clergy "never think of it," that whereas, in the words of the late Mr. Warburton, "there is not an Egyptian woman who can read and write, except a daughter of Mehemet Ali and the few who have been educated in the school of Mr. Lieder, the Maronite women of the Lebanon, though of the same Arab race, *are generally instructed.*"‖ "Education," says Mr. Kelly, "though limited to reading, writing, arithmetic, and the catechism,"—we have seen that for the class above the peasants the course includes Arabic, Syriac, Latin, French,

* *La Syrie,* &c., ch. viii., p. 96.

† *Travels,* &c., by J. R. Wellsted, Esq., F.R.S., vol. ii., ch. v., p. 91.

‡ Ch. xvi. p., 270.

§ *Narrative of a Journey Round the Dead Sea,* by F. de Saulçy, vol. i., ch. i., p. 5.

‖ *The Crescent and the Cross,* vol. i., ch. xi., p. 100.

and Italian,—"is *universal* among them, and gives them a deserved superiority over the other tribes of Syria."* Whether such an amount of education can be said to be "universal" in England we need not stay to inquire.

But Mr. Porter had still something to add. It was possible to clothe his enmity in still more impressive language. The Maronites, like all the oriental tribes, severely exacting in their estimate of a Christian apostle, had rejected him and his companions, with an energy proportioned to the ardor of their faith, as ministers of the Evil one. Mr. Porter repays the indignity with the following announcement, in which he appears to have uttered his last farewell to Syria and the Syrian mission: "The Protestant missionaries have done more for the advancement of education within the short period of twenty years, than the combined priesthood of all Lebanon and all Syria has done during centuries." It is our turn to bid farewell to Mr. Porter, to whom we have perhaps given an undue share of attention, and we cannot do so more fitly than in the words of his co-religionists.

From Mr. Williams, himself a Protestant minister, we have learned, on the one hand, that the Protestant missionaries in Syria "are merely playing at missions," and that "self-sacrifice and simple trust" are not to be learned from their example; and on the other, that the Catholic Church has sent to this land "the best instructed and most devoted missionaries that the world has seen since primitive times." Dr. Southgate, a Protestant bishop, has assured us that the rare disciples of Mr. Porter and his colleagues "are infidels and radicals unworthy of the sympathy of the Christian public;" while Dr. Wolff has lately announced, after an experience of many years, that "the *worst* people among the Eastern natives are those who know English, and have been converted to Protestantism." To these emphatic statements Sir Adolphus Slade has added, that many of the missionaries themselves, who have "done more for education," though they have neither schools nor scholars, than all the Catholic clergy for centuries, "know absolutely no other than their mother tongue."

Finally, the same Protestant writer, long resident in Syria, conversant during many years with all which has occurred in that land, and full of admiration of the apostolic men by whom, as he observes, "*millions of souls have been saved*" in these regions, lends us the following appropriate words with which to take leave of Mr. Porter: "Protestant missionaryism is much extolled; it certainly costs a great deal; but the good it

* *Ubi supra.*

may effect *is as a drop of water, compared with the sea of benefits spread by the Roman Catholic Church*, silently and unostentatiously, all over Turkey."*

THE DRUSES.

It is time to quit the mountains and valleys of Lebanon, where we have found, in the heart of a land long abandoned to every error and impiety, a picture which a Christian may well love to contemplate: on the one hand, deep religious conviction, unshaken through ages, and that instinctive horror of heresy which is one of the surest signs of election; on the other, as even enemies allow, valor, dignity, purity, gentleness, industry, prosperity, and peace. Such, by Protestant testimony, is the influence of the Catholic religion upon generous natures, penetrated by its healing power, and such its results even among a people of Arab origin, though surrounded by races and tribes with whom faith is a dream, and virtue a jest.

It is characteristic of that singular form of religion which seems instinctively to prefer crime and ignorance in union with heresy to virtue and enlightenment in connection with the Church, that the only reflection suggested to another Episcopalian clergyman, of the same class as Mr. Porter, by the contrast which we have just delineated, found expression in these words: "How sad," exclaims the Rev. George Fisk, "that Popery should taint even the remains of the glory of Lebanon!" Greeks and Armenians, sunk in mental and moral decrepitude, Mr. Fisk would embrace with love, because, as he seriously observes, they hold "the great leading truths of the Gospel;" and though "in many respects superstitious, and manifestly corrupt," they have this merit, which amply supplies the want of every other, that "they have never merged in the apostasy of Rome."† Mr. Fisk has apparently not read, or perhaps forgotten, the testimonies of Protestant writers, who declare—as we have already heard and shall hear again presently—that the only Greeks and Armenians who deserve the name of intelligent or consistent Christians are precisely those who have derived new life from reconciliation with the Catholic Church.

Allusion has been made to the Druses, the implacable and hereditary foes of the Maronites. If we add a few words with respect to the former, it is only for the sake of noticing the

* *Turkey, Greece, and Malta*, vol. ii., ch. xx., p. 423.
† *A Pastor's Memorial*, ch. ix., pp. 398, 400, 410.

characteristic relations of the Protestant missionaries with them. Banished by the Maronites with every mark of contempt and disgust, they took refuge among their hostile neighbors, and endeavored to make alliance with them. The infamy of their character, and their indifference to any form of religion, was no impediment to the negotiations which now ensued. To protestantize the Druses, and to vex the Maronites, would be a double triumph; but it was one which they were not destined to enjoy. "The Druses," said Dr. Yates, with great confidence, "will unite with the Protestant Christians, and the power of the Osmanlis will cease."* Mr. Fremantle, an Anglican clergyman, was of opinion that they would become "independent Episcopalians;" and as if this were not enough to stimulate the hopes of his co-religionists at home, he gravely added—in a report which was actually published by the "Society for Promoting Christian Knowledge"—that "they desire to be united to the English Church."† Whether Mr. Fremantle really believed this, we need not question. The Druses, as Mr. Chasseaud observed in 1855, are unscrupulous hypocrites, and will affect to be of the religion of any society in which they happen to find themselves.‡ They pretend, says Mr. Paton, to be Mahometans when it suits them.§ All European writers agree in describing them as impious, false, and bloodthirsty. Dr. Clarke says, "Some among them certainly offer their highest adoration to a *calf*."‖ Risk Allah declares, apparently from his own observation, that "while they profess to be Mahommedans, they have no hesitation whatever in denouncing Mahommed as a false prophet;" and he adds, that the Druses, like the Kurds, have formed such an estimate of the creed of "English Protestants" as to assert, "that their religion is a species of free masonry, which very much resembles their own;" and one of their leaders assured him that "a tall English emir" had told him so.¶

How surely these atheists of Syria reckoned upon the sympathy of "English Protestants," and how much reason they had for doing so, is sufficiently revealed in the comments made by the latter upon the Turco-Druse insurrection of 1860. All their apologies are for the Druses, all their sarcasms for the Maronites. "The Maronites are mere savages," says one of the ablest organs of intellectual Protestantism; and as if this were

* *Modern History of Egypt*, vol. ii., ch. iv., p. 158.
† *The Eastern Churches*, pp. 44, 49.
‡ *The Druses of the Lebanon*, by George Washington Chasseaud.
§ *Modern Syrians*, p. 309.
‖ Clarke's *Travels*, vol. iv., p. 136.
¶ *Ubi Supra*, p. 292.

not venturesome enough, he gravely adds, that until "the hour of their triumph the conduct of the Druses had been unimpeachable!"* It is but a new version of the old cry, *Non hunc sed Barabbam.* The worshippers of a calf are preferred before the disciples of the Cross; and the latter, though travellers of all sects confess with enthusiasm their nobility and virtue, are peremptorily described, by that instinct of hate which can corrupt even genius into imbecility, as "mere savages."

An equally eminent authority observes, that "the great Druse chief Mohamed En-Nasar, the instigator of these butcheries, *counted on English support*, and therefore it need not be added on an English reward."† His calculation has been abundantly justified. "The Druses," observes a traveller who has lived amongst them, "seek refuge in the arms of England, because they know that *every other nation of Europe* has judged and condemned them;"‡ while another relates that he heard an Englishman say to a Maronite shiek, that England gave her support to the Druses solely in order to counterbalance the influence of France with the Christians. "You admit, then," replied the Maronite chief, "that as soon as France begins to labor for God, England takes up arms for the devil."§

Lord Carnarvon, who represents the official mind of England, and has composed, with much ability, an almost enthusiastic apology for the Druses, insists that the "strong connection of gratitude on the one hand, and of good offices on the other, which has existed between the Druses and England, ought neither on moral nor political grounds to be lightly severed."‖ In other words, it is worthy of England to become the patron of impiety, and an adversary of the Christian religion, if by accepting this mission she can counterbalance French influence in the East.

It appears, however, that in spite of the avowed sympathy and alliance between the Druses and the English, the former only amused themselves at Mr. Fremantle's expense when they encouraged his cheerful expectations; for Mr. Walpole tells us,—eleven years after that gentleman's sanguine prediction,—"With the Druses the Protestant missionaries have made, I believe, no progress." They are not yet affiliated to the "English Church," nor is there any immediate promise of that event. "Many professed themselves converts," says Mr. Walpole, "but directly the minister refused them some request, turned round and said

* *Saturday Review*, April 20, 1861.
† *The Times*, September 1, 1860.
‡ *La Vérité sur la Syrie*, par Baptistin Poujoulat, Lettre xliii., p. 489.
§ Mislin, *Les Lieux Saints*, tome i., ch. vi., p. 156.
‖ *Recollections of the Druses*, by the Earl of Carnarvon, ch. viii., p. 119.

We will listen to you as long as you pay us."* This was their view of the value of Protestantism.

In 1862, the agent of the Church Missionary Society reports thus of the Druses: "There does not as yet appear an opening for the reception of the Gospel among them; on the contrary, their hatred of Christians and Christianity seems, if possible, *to increase:* and direct missionary work is highly irritating to them, and excites their fanaticism."† Mr. Fremantle was apparently too sanguine.

These are not the only operations of Protestants in the Lebanon, though precisely the same result has attended all their efforts. We have heard of the two "designing brothers" who went to Malta, and "agreed to be baptized" on condition of receiving some hundred pounds. Others have imitated these neophytes of the Lebanon with still greater success. Dr. Carne relates the story of "the noted Eusebius, Bishop of Mount Lebanon," who far surpassed, as became his more elevated rank, the performances of his ingenuous flock. This Greek prelate "was chaperoned through many of the colleges at Oxford by one of the Masters." In such society his anti-Roman views made him a welcome guest; but the crafty oriental was only speculating on the inexhaustible credulity of his sympathizing hosts, by which he and his class have so often profited. Eusebius obtained, says Dr. Carne, "a capital printing press, and about eight hundred pounds in money. When we were at Sidon, we found that this eastern dignitary was living in a style of excessive comfort, and to his heart's content, at a few hours' distance. With this money, which was a fortune in the East, he has purchased a good house and garden; not one farthing has ever gone to renovate the condition of the Christians of the East, and the printing-press, or some fragments of it, were known to have found their way to Alexandria."‡ Oxford should have learned by this time to mistrust pseudo-converts, especially when they come from the East.

ARMENIA.

We may now take our departure from Syria, in order to pursue in Armenia the investigations which we have almost completed. It is in the latter province that the Protestant emissaries from America boast to have obtained the greatest

* *The Ansayrii,* ch. xvi., p. 356.
† *Sixty-third Report,* p. 66.
‡ *Letters from the East,* vol. ii., p. 115.

numerical results, and are at this moment engaged in operations which deserve particular attention. But we must first say a few words on Catholic missions to the Armenians.

Nearly twenty years ago, Dr. Joseph Wolff announced to Europe, that "about *sixty thousand* Armenians have joined the Church of Rome."* Since that date, the great movement of reconciliation among the Armenian nation has steadily progressed; and it may be said without exaggeration that, at the present time, hardly a week elapses without a fresh instance of conversions, often on a large scale, and all attesting the wonderful restoration of this people to unity.

And this remarkable fact is perpetually recurring, in spite of that "strong national bond" which, as Haxthausen notices, assimilates the Armenians to the Jews, "whose nationality no human power can destroy," and which knits them all into one tribe and family, from China to Morocco. So powerful is this ineradicable instinct of nationality,—a sentiment always more or less fatal to Christianity,—that Armenians, when converted to the Church, are obliged, like converts from certain European races, to repudiate that false and exaggerated patriotism which has rent Christendom into twenty jealous, selfish, and hostile bodies, "and proudly renounce the name of Armenians, to call themselves Catholics."†

During the last two centuries this consoling movement has received a constant impulse from the labors of European missionaries. In 1711, Père Ricard reconciled one bishop, twenty-two priests, and eight hundred and seventy-five lay persons.‡ Three years later, in 1714, Père Monier received the abjuration of more than seven hundred, and shortly afterwards, in company with Ricard, penetrated into Kurdistan. They were both chained and imprisoned by the Pacha of Kars, at the instigation of the Armenian schismatics, whose vengeance followed them to their new field of labor. By such men, and with similar results, the combat has ever since been maintained, the heretics always invoking Moslem aid, and seldom in vain. And these incidents have marked the conflict up to the present hour. "Recently," says M. Eugène Boré, "the schismatical patriarch purchased from the vizir for two thousand purses the right to prevent a member of his Church from becoming a Catholic."§ So uniform is their practice of seeking Mahometan auxiliaries in all their difficulties, that, as Mr. Walpole notices in 1851, the Bishop of Van "bribed the Pacha" to assist him in ejecting

* *Narrative of a Mission to Bokhara,* ch. iii., p. 114.
† Haxthausen, ch. vii , p. 224.
‡ *Nouveaux Memoires du Levant,* tome iii., p. 290.
§ *Arménie,* p. 138.

the American missionaries from the neighborhood of Etchmiadzin.

Even Protestant travellers are almost unanimous in affirming two facts,—the worthlessness of the schismatical and the superiority of the converted Armenian. "The Armenians," says the Rev. Mr. Dwight, "appear to hold a lower place in the scale than either the Greeks or the Latins,"*—after which he evidently felt that he had nothing more to say. He confesses, however, that even they are witnesses for the Church, since they hold all the Catholic doctrines controverted by Protestants, a fact confirmed by a Prussian writer, who lived in intimacy with the heads of the sect, and was led to make the following important reflections: "The Armenian Church bears a marked testimony to the antiquity of the Catholic Church. *All* the dogmas attacked at and since the Reformation are held by it,—the Saints, the Seven Sacraments, Transubstantiation, the Sacrifice of the Mass, and Purgatory. The dogmas which the Armenians hold in common with the Catholic Church must be of high antiquity, for as early as the Council of Chalcedon, in 451, the Armenian Church possessed an organization of its own, and jealously guarded itself from foreign influence."† This learned writer also observes, and proves by well-known examples, that the "Armenian Church not only acknowledges that its founder, St. Gregory the Illuminator, received the Armenian Patriarchate *from Rome*, but it has several times submitted to the Pope, as the centre of Unity and the Supreme Patriarch." He had reason to speak with confidence of the sentiments of the highest class of Armenian prelates, since Narses, the Patriarch of the separated Armenians, gave him the following explicit assurance with his own lips, when he met him at St. Petersburg in 1843: "On the whole we are in harmony with Rome; the Armenian Patriarch usually sends a notice to the Pope of his elevation to the Patriarchate. . . . There is no essential difference in doctrine between the Armenian and Latin Churches; indeed, perfect agreement has been repeatedly attained. Jealousies and disputes have been much more frequent with the Greek Church." It was impossible to omit testimony so interesting, though it probably reveals more accurately the convictions and wishes of Narses himself than of the corrupt and ignorant colleagues whom he nominally governs, and of whom Haxthausen declares with regret, "Avarice, envy, hypocrisy, and even gross sensuality are common amongst them."

Such are the penalties of separation from the Holy See, even

* *Christianity in Turkey*, p. 7.
† Haxthausen, ch. ix., p. 313.

where the apostolic doctrine is nominally retained. Captain Wilbraham observed at Etchmiadzin itself, the head-quarters of the schism, and in the cathedral, the "want of attention, and even of decorum," which was displayed by the congregation; and added, "There was none of that apparently sincere, though perhaps blind devotion, which I have so often remarked in Roman Catholic chapels." "The Catholicos," he says, or Patriarch, "nominally presides over the synod, but a *Moderator* has been appointed by the Russian government, without whose approval nothing can be done, which makes the emperor virtually the head of the Armenian Church throughout the world;"* a fact of which Narses bitterly complained to Baron Von Haxthausen, in these expressive words: "How undignified is the position of the Patriarch! Every letter must pass through the hands of the Governor-general of Caucasia, and is opened in his office, where every clerk may read it!" Narses, a man superior to most of his race and order, might have reflected, that this is the usual fate of those who consent to preside over "National" Churches.†

Mr. Walpole declares, from his own observation, that "the falsehood of the Armenian monks was dreadful, as they asserted that so and so was the belief of such and such a church."

Dr. Moritz Wagner, also a Protestant, confirms these dismal statements. "Gross ignorance, stupidity, covetousness, and immorality, are the predominant characteristics of these ecclesiastics. They readily assume an external show of virtue and self-denial, whilst, in secret, they indulge freely in vice. Envy and jealousy reign supreme among them. They do not appear to have a shadow of brotherly or neighborly love, or of kindliness and courtesy, in the Christian acceptation of those terms."‡ The whole community, including the Patriarch and "his bishops and monks," are described by Dr. Bodenstedt, who lived with them, as "a society blunted for all noble purposes, and wasted by unnatural lusts."§ And these are the men who perpetuate the schism.

Dr. Friedrich Parrot notices also the moral corruption in

* *Travels in the Trans-Caucasian Provinces of Russia*, ch. ix., pp. 95–98.

† Dr. Döllinger observes in his latest work, that all pagan religions were *national*, and that while it is the special glory of the Christian Church to have united all the tribes of the earth in one family, the Sects have always tended to restore the pagan element of nationality. It was thus with the Donatists, who speedily cast out the idea of a universal communion. "The whole course of the Reformation century," he adds, was in the same fatal direction, and "we find everywhere the victorious (*pagan*) principle of national distinct churches." *The Church and the Churches*, p. 31. In this, as in many other respects, Protestantism was a return towards Paganism.

‡ *Travels in Persia*, &c., vol. iii., p. 51 (1856).

§ *Life in the Caucasus and the East*, vol. i., p. 221.

which their priesthood is sunk," and gives this explanation of their profound and universal ignorance. "Every laic, provided only he be chosen by the congregation, and have passed fourteen days in the prescribed fastings and ritual observances in a church, may get ordination from the bishop, without either preparation or subsequent education." He agrees with Colonel Drouville, that "their priests and bishops are all as ignorant as it is possible to be;" and notices the usual phenomenon in all heretical bodies, that they have split into three sects. "There is an *independent* Catholicos at Sis, in Cicilia, and another, who has maintained himself in this dignity for seven hundred years, in the island of Akhthamar, in the lake of Van."*

Lastly, Dr. Wilson observes—though he would probably have said nothing about it if they would have welcomed his friends—"the Armenians partake in the monothelite as well as the monophysite heresy," a statement which is not true of the whole nation, especially in Western Asia.

Such, by Protestant testimony, are the unfortunate communities who are paying the penalty of heresy and schism, and whom the Church, with the patience and zeal of a mother, has resolved to restore to truth, charity, and obedience. How far she has succeeded in this aim we may now briefly state.

We have already heard from Dr. Wolff that sixty thousand had been reconciled when he visited them. Captain Wilbraham admits that "a considerable proportion have returned to the Catholic Church, from which this nation seceded, when, in the year 491, they rejected the authority of the Council of Chalcedon."† Dr. Parrot, though a Russian Imperial Councillor of State, allows that no small portion of the clergy and laity also have attached themselves to the Roman Catholic Church."‡ "Romanism," says the Rev. Justin Perkins, of whom we shall hear more presently, "is taking root and extending," which he considers "the conversion of the Armenians from bad to worse." "Very few of the Nestorians now remain," he adds, "on the western side of the Koordish mountains, who have not yielded to the intrigues and usurpations of Papal domination."§ This gentleman is apparently of opinion that the operations of the Americans, which shall be described immediately, involve neither intrigue nor usurpation.

But the conversions effected by Catholic missionaries have not been confined to Armenia Proper. "At Constantinople,"

* *Journey to Ararat*, ch. iv., p. 92; ch. v., pp. 105–110.
† Ch. xxxi., p. 352.
‡ P. 110.
§ *Residence en Persia*, p. 4.

says Mr. Curzon, "a great number of the higher and wealthier Armenians give their adherence to the Roman Catholic creed." Of the *Chaldean* Catholics, Dr. Wilson observes, "They form, I am sorry to say, a great portion of the Nestorians west of the mountains of Kurdistan." Bagdad and Mosûl have yielded to the same beneficent power. "Emissaries from Rome," says Mr. Perkins, "have been laboring, with a zeal and perseverance worthy of a better cause, to effect the conversion of the entire Nestorian Church. Mrs. Perkins received a letter from a pious English lady, who resides in Bagdad, in which the writer says, "the religious state of this city is very unsatisfactory; the Roman Catholics carry the day in every way. . . A large body of bishops and priests are going to Mosûl in a day or two, to form a convention to endeavor to bring over all the Chaldeans to the Papal faith." Fortunately, we can trace the results of this expedition; for a little later Mr. Walpole tells us, with an angry commentary hardly worthy of so intelligent a traveller, that of the fourteen Christian churches at Mosûl belonging to the different sects, several are now in the hands of Roman Catholics; . . . . whether by right or otherwise,"—how could a few poor missionaries gain them except by persuasion?—"the Catholics have gathered to themselves many congregations."

The expedition from Bagdad was evidently successful; indeed Dr. Southgate was able to report, with unfeigned regret, that "the whole body of the Nestorian Church is now a branch of the Church of Rome, and with a sad propriety may the Papal Nestorians assume the *national* name of Chaldeans."* "The Nestorians who once inhabited the Mosûl district," says Dr. Asahel Grant, "have *all* embraced the Romish faith."† "The whole Chaldean nation," adds an English traveller, "may now be esteemed Catholics."‡

Finally, the Patriarch of the Chaldeans, writing from Mosûl in 1853, could already report that thirty-five thousand wanderers from that nation alone had beon restored to the true fold, and that the "opposition of the Methodists"—he means the Anglican and other missionaries—was the chief impediment to the conversion of the few who were still in schism, but whose imperfect faith was in danger from contact with Protestant neology, as their morals were from the lavish distribution of Protestant gold.§ The mission of Protestantism seems to be everywhere the same. Its agents cannot make Christians

* Vol. ii., ch. xvi., p. 183.

† *The Nestorians,* ch. iii., p. 27.

‡ Patterson, app., p. 401.

§ *Revue Orientale et Algérienne,* tome iv., p. 357.

themselves, but they can prevent others doing so. By the banks of the Tigris, as by those of the Nile and the Jordan; in the cities of China, as in the villages of Hindostan; in the islands of the Pacific, as in those of the Mediterranean; their aim is to rend unity, to mar the work which they can neither understand nor imitate, to confirm the heathen in his unbelief and the heretic in his corruption; and the only triumph to which they aspire is to keep back a few, when all around are waking to a new life of truth and virtue, from sharing the blessings which, but for their presence, would perhaps regenerate the world.

Let us return for a moment, before we conclude this part of our subject, to Armenia Proper. The movement of Catholic regeneration of which Western Asia is now one of the most conspicuous theatres, has at last penetrated to the very heart and centre of the Armenian schism. Rumors had reached Europe towards the close of 1859 of extraordinary and almost unprecedented conversions in the regions which surround Etchmiadzin. An Armenian gentleman, who arrived in England in the month of September of that year, brought intelligence of the almost simultaneous conversion of ten thousand Armenians in the neighborhood of Erzeroum. Application was made to the proper authorities for authentic information with respect to so remarkable an event, and through the intervention of a venerable prelate a letter has been obtained from the Catholic Armenian Primate, dated Constantinople, October 26, 1859, which contains the following statement:

"I willingly communicate to you the details of the conversions which take place almost every week from the schismatical Armenian Church to the centre of unity in these latter times, and especially during the last two years, in which so great a religious movement has been manifested in various parts of Asia, that it might more fitly be called a religious revolution—*che potrei meglio intitolare una rivoluzione religiosa.* In Karput and Arabghir, cities in the neighborhood of Erzeroum, more than five hundred families with some of their priests have been converted to Catholicism. In Tadem, Sartorici, and Garmir, regions adjacent to Karput, about one hundred families. In Malatia and Adjaman, also contiguous districts, one hundred and fifty families with their priest. Last week I received letters from Palo, also in the territory of Karput, and containing more than two hundred villages, which inform me that fifty families have expressed their desire to be admitted to Catholic unity. In Marasci, near Diarbeker, more than six hundred families, with some of their clergy, have become Catholics, and other families in the neighboring districts. At Rodosto, near Adrianople, and again at Bandyrma, in the diocese of Byrsa in Bithynia, seventy families, besides others similarly disposed, have addressed petitions to me to be received into Catholic unity." The illustrious prelate does not state the exact numerical total of the converts, which was probably unknown to him; but as they amount already to about fifteen hundred *families*, besides others similarly disposed, we may easily form an approximate estimate. But even this is not all, for the Archbishop immediately adds: "I omit to speak of other districts in the like condition, and especially of one vast province, with respect to which I am also conducting negotiations, in favor of more than *ten thousand families*."

Such is the work of God, in these last times, among the schismatical communities of the East. Worn out by the exactions of simoniacal priests and bishops, scandalized by the ignorance and immorality of their fallen pastors, conversant in many cases with the superior virtue and dignity of their countrymen who have been reconciled to the Church, and above all touched by the compassionate grace of God, and the purity, wisdom, and goodness of the apostles whom He has sent amongst them,—they begin, in this eleventh hour of their history, to turn wistful eyes towards the source of unity and peace, and to marvel that they have so long despised the blessings which they knew not to be within their reach.

It only remains to show,—once more by Protestant testimony,—that as soon as they enter the Church, they begin to acquire the freedom, virtue, and enlightenment to which they had so long been strangers. This also, thanks to the copiousness and exuberance of Protestant literature, we shall be able to prove.

"The Roman Catholics," said an Anglican clergyman some years ago, "have compassed sea and land, have made and still retain proselytes to the Papal Supremacy from *every* Christian community and nation, Abyssinia excepted." If Mr. Jowett had written a little later, he would have been obliged to omit the exception. Other writers, who share Mr. Jowett's prejudices, will now tell us, in language more emphatic than could be expected from such witnesses, though far below the truth, what influence these conversions have produced upon the life and character of their fortunate subjects.

Let us begin with the *Greeks*. Of the converts from this nation we have been told, by men who can hardly speak with composure of the Catholic Church, such truths as the following: "They are," says Dr. Wilson, in words already quoted, "amongst the most liberal and intelligent native Christians in the East." They exhibit, since their conversion, says Dr. Robinson more cautiously, "a certain elevation." "Their intercourse with the Roman Catholic Church," adds Dr. Durbin, "tends to elevate them in the scale of civilization." And these are all vehement Protestants.

Of the Armenian converts, equally hostile witnesses give exactly the same account, though we may be sure they speak with reluctance and constraint. "Like the Christians in other parts of Turkey," says Messrs. Smith and Dwight, eager partisans of Protestant missions, "they who have embraced the faith of Rome are more respectable for wealth and intelligence than their countrymen." They add, that "most of the native Christians employed by Protestants in the Levant are of the Romish persuasion,"—a fact which they consider discreditable to the officials, merchants, and others, who employ them solely on account of their superior trustworthiness, because it encourages "the Pope's anti-Christian power."*

"The Catholic Armenians," says Captain Wilbraham, "are generally superior in education and intelligence to their countrymen,"—which this gentleman attributes, "in some measure, to the circulation of knowledge occasioned by the literary labors of the Catholic Armenian convent in Venice."† In other words, they are brought by their conversion into contact with Catholic intelligence and learning.

"The Roman Catholic branch of the Armenian Church," says Mr. Curzon, "has done much more for literature and civilization than the original body." Of the converts he says, "Their minds are more enlarged, they are less Oriental in their ideas," &c.;‡ an emphatic testimony, by a capable witness, to the civilizing influence of the Catholic religion. Mr. Curzon also observes, that "the Armenian monks at Venice printed the Armenian Bible in 1805; and entirely by their energy, the small spark which alone glimmered in the darkness of Armenian ignorance in the East has gradually increased its light." "The Mechitarists," says Haxthausen, "have printed Armenian translations from all the languages of Europe, and in every department of literature."

"It is a remarkable fact," says Dr. Joseph Wolff in his latest publication, "and it must not be concealed, that . . . . the native Christians of the Turkish empire in general, where Roman Catholic missionaries have not penetrated, are ignorant, rude, and uncouth, like buffaloes! Roman Catholic missionaries have carried everywhere the light of civilization."§

* *Missionary Researches in Armenia*, Letter i., p. 20.
† Ch. xxxi., 352.
‡ *Armenia and Erzeroum*, ch. xv., p. 230.
§ *Travels and Adventures of Dr. Wolff*, ch. xv., p. 274.

Of the *Syrians*, even Dr. Southgate notices the pregnant fact, that "the adherents of the Church of Rome have all been themselves converted *individually*," and that "they are zealously and intelligently attached to their new faith."*

Of the *Chaldeans*, we have heard that they have become a Catholic nation; and of the *Maronites*, who owe all the "deserved superiority" which even Protestants recognize in them to the influence of their religion, we need say nothing more than has been already related by English and American writers.

Of the converted *Jacobites*, Mr. Badger confesses, in spite of that uneasy dislike and jealousy of the Catholic Church which is now perhaps more intense in Anglicans than in any other class, "If the truth must be told, they are *decidedly superior*, in many respects, to their Jacobite brethren."†

Lastly, the eventual triumph of the Faith in all the long separated communities of the East appears so certain to a German philosopher who had watched, with cold but intelligent impartiality, its irresistible progress, that he does not hesitate to announce in these emphatic terms the inevitable issue: "*There is no doubt* that the theology of the West will in time penetrate the Eastern Church, with *all* its divisions, Greek, Armenian, Nestorian, and Coptic."‡

And now we have heard enough of Catholic missions in the Levant, Syria, and Armenia, of their uninterrupted success, and of the character both of the missionaries and their disciples. The history exactly agrees with what we have heard in every other land. On one side we have found God and his gifts, on the other only man and his frailties. The few Protestant converts, attracted only by offers of payment, and spurning the hand from which they receive it, are, as Dr. Southgate admits, "infidels and radicals;" or, as Mr. Williams, Mr. Patterson, and others report, notorious for "scandalous irregularities and excesses—either worthless persons, or skeptics and infidels;" while even a Protestant minister not only confesses the universal failure of his co-religionists in Syria, but candidly asks, "Are we ever likely to succeed any better?" Such is one more example of the momentous contrast which has not hitherto been revealed to the world, because neither genius nor learning could have anticipated, much less dispensed with, the facts which living writers have collected for our instruction.

And what explanation do Protestants offer, in *this* case, of the

* *Narrative*, &c., vol. ii., ch. xxiii., p. 284.
† Vol. i., p. 63.
‡ *Trans-Caucasia*, by Baron Von Haxthausen, ch. iii., p. 67.

success of Catholic missions and the failure of their own? In China, they assure us that, "in becoming Papists," and subsequently martyrs, "they *give up nothing*."* In India, "Popery is *better adapted*" to the illogical Hindoo. In Ceylon, and in other lands, it is "*ceremonial*" which accounts for the contrast. And what is it in Syria? In this province, the explanation is still more unexpected, and the very hypothesis which unites in itself the largest measure of extravagance and impossibility is precisely that which has been selected for the occasion. Who would have anticipated that, in the land of the Moslem, "where," as Mr. Walpole observes, "the Christian exists only on sufferance," it is by "cruelty and violence" that a few Lazarists, Franciscans, and Sisters of Charity win their way? "Romish tyranny," says the Rev. Mr. Fremantle, for the special instruction of the Anglican Church, "has been insulting and *persecuting*, and assisting the Mahommedans to oppress the fallen churches." And this account, which would be received with a shout of laughter by a Druse or a Mussulman audience, is repeated by other English writers, with various modifications, as the true history of Catholic victories in Syria.

Yet as late as 1845, we find a competent authority making this declaration, in the form of an appeal to Europe: "I know for a positive fact, that at this moment all classes, sects, and denominations, are crying aloud for European protection."† Fourteen years later, Mr. Wingfield still reports, that "the assassination of Christians, even of the richer class, is unhappily of no very rare occurrence."‡ Mr. Warrington Smyth relates, about the same time, that he himself saw a new church in Bulgaria wantonly destroyed, "crushing in an hour the hopes of years."§ "Never," adds a Protestant minister in 1862, "were the Christians throughout Turkey exposed to more atrocious cruelty than at the present day, when the Mahometan power is kept alive merely by the mutual distrust of the great powers of Europe."‖ "The various Christian sects who occupy the plains of Syria," says Colonel Churchill, "live in perpetual dread of some outbreak of Mohammedan fanaticism."¶ How reasonable that dread was, the dismal tragedy of 1860 once more proved. Even the Maronites, whose numbers and valor, as well as their geographical position, appeared to give them

* *The Land of Sinim*, ch. iv., p. 132.

‡ *Memoir on Syria*, by Charles Fiott Barker, formerly Secretary to Mr. Consul-general Barker, p. 50.

‡ *A Tour in Dalmatia*, &c., by W. F. Wingfield, M.A., ch. vi., p. 158.

§ *A Year with the Turks*, ch. ix., p. 239.

‖ *Servia and the Servians*, by the Rev. W. Denton, M.A., ch. i., p. 15.

¶ *Mount Lebanon*, vol. iii., ch. xxvii., p. 387.

an exceptional security, fell, betrayed and ensnared, in that cruel conspiracy of Druse, and Turk, and Metuali; and were at all times so exposed, in spite of the nominal protectorate of France, whose generous designs were thwarted by the policy of a jealous and non-Catholic nation, that as one of their bishops observed to Mr. David, "*Dieu seul est bon pour la Syrie.*" In Antioch itself, though it is, as Mr. Paton remarks, "nominally the metropolis of the orthodox Greeks," "the Moslems are so fanatical, that they do not allow the Christians to have a church in the town."* And it is in such a state of society as this, in which the Catholics exist, like the sectaries, "only on sufferance," and in daily peril of destruction, that helpless missionaries and religious women, who attract tens of thousands by the sweet odor of their virtues, from all ranks and sects, are said to do so by "insults and tyranny," and by "persecuting the fallen churches!" Such is the Protestant explanation of their success, and it is, as usual, an Anglican clergyman who suggests it.

PROTESTANT MISSIONS.

Before we close this chapter, let us add a few words, in further illustration of the contrast, on Protestant missions in Armenia. Hitherto we have encountered grave and earnest men, fit preachers of the evangelical truths of which their own apostolic lives were the most impressive illustration; having the counsels of Holy Writ in their hearts rather than on their tongues, and still more eloquent by example than in speech. Hence their peaceful triumphs, hence their acceptance among all the oriental races. We have now, in conclusion, to notice briefly a class of men towards whom we need not affect an esteem which even their co-religionists have refused: men to whom Holy Scripture appears to be every thing *except* a teacher; men whose mouths are full of imprecations against the pure and the just, while they do not even attempt to imitate their least merits; whose whole life is one unbroken course of littleness and self-indulgence, united with irrational contempt for the manly virtues which they hate without understanding; whose mission seems to consist in marring the Unity for which Jesus prayed, and in beguiling others to reject the blessings which they have forfeited themselves; and whose own friends confess, with one voice, that the few hearers whom they entice are only ten times more immoral and unbelieving than they were before.

The principal historian of Protestant missions in Armenia is

* *Modern Syrians,* ch. xix., p. 220.

the Rev. Justin Perkins. Let us hear his account of himself and his work.

Mr. Perkins quotes the following passage from the "Instructions" to the American missionaries by the society which employed them: "You are not sent among these Churches to proselyte. Let the Armenian remain an Armenian, if he will; the Greek a Greek, and the Nestorian a Nestorian." "The object of the American missions to Syria, and other parts of the Levant," says Dr. Robinson, "is not to draw off members of the Oriental Churches to Protestantism." Such was perhaps the original programme, and for a time caution restrained the American agents. They offered only secular education, the use of books, medical treatment, and other harmless boons. When they thought their position assured, they assumed their real character, and boasted, as we have seen, of the very operations which their nominal instructions forbade them to attempt.

They even claimed to have the field all to themselves, and warmly resented the intrusion of other Protestant sects, and especially of Anglicans. The report of the American Board for 1841 protests energetically against the English for entering into communication with the Nestorians, because such a proceeding may "tend to awaken the thought among the Nestorian ecclesiastics that there are rival Protestant sects and interests, upon which they may practice for the private gratification of avaricious desires." As a financial precaution, in order to keep down the price of converts by having only one bidder, there was much wisdom in this view; but the Anglicans answered, by the mouth of Mr. Badger, an Episcopalian minister, that the prudent suggestion was "as presumptuous as it is ludicrous." Mr. Badger even observed that his American rivals "seemed to lay claim to inspiration, and decided what was truth and what was error with the assurance of apostles." Meanwhile, the Nestorians looked on, and began to entertain "avaricious desires."

We have seen that Mr. Badger was no less indignant with the Catholic missionaries for their endeavor to draw the Nestorians out of the pit of heresy, ignorance, and corruption, which even Protestant writers of the most advanced school have described to us. This Anglican clergyman, attracted by their sounding titles, and rejoicing in their separation from unity, evidently thought them a far more privileged class than either Catholics or Protestants. It is true they deny the Incarnation, but they are outside the Church, and were therefore welcome allies for Mr. Badger. "The Nestorian Church," he says, "abounds in noble gifts and rightful titles!"*

* *The Nestorians*, &c., vol. ii., ch. xlvi., p. 351.

There was a time when even the most advanced Protestants, while Catholic traditions still lingered faintly amongst them, professed to reverence the Council of Ephesus, and to anathematize the Nestorian heresy. Now, it seems, they anathematize nothing; and in this new Pyrrhonism they see only a sign of their own progress and improvement. Geneva itself once taught its students to say, "I *abhor* all the heresies which were condemned by the first Council of Nice, *the first of Ephesus, and that of Chalcedon.*"* "We *detest* all sects and heresies," said the French Protestant communities, at what they called "the Synod of Paris," in 1559, condemned by the same Councils.† At the present day, even Anglican clergymen, especially those of the High Church school, celebrate the "noble gifts and rightful titles" of Nestorianism! The Rev. Webb Le Bas calls the title θεοτόκος a blasphemy,"‡ though even La Croze was ashamed to say less than that "the title has nothing contrary to sound theology;"§ and the celebrated Calvinist Baldæus flatly asserted, that the Nestorians "teach points *contrary to salvation.*"‖ But an Anglican clergyman, when he once begins to speak against the Catholic faith, is pretty sure to surpass both Calvinists and Lutherans. The Rev. Dr. Kerr, also an Anglican, called the monophysites of Malabar "a precious remnant of a *pure* and valuable people."¶ Dr. Southgate, a Protestant bishop, speaks of the Nestorian heresy, *if such it must be reputed,*"** implying that the Fathers of Ephesus were the real heretics. The Rev. Henry Townly considers the principal tenet of Nestorianism "a point of *orthodoxy* on which we are agreed."†† Mr. Layard says of the Chaldean Nestorians, "there are no sects in the East, and few in the West, who can boast of such purity in their faith,"‡‡ and Mr. Walpole adds of the same class, that they are "pure and untainted, professing nearly as we profess."§§ Lastly, Mr. Ainsworth, after enumerating the distinctive tenets anathematized by the Council of Ephesus, confidently asks, "In all this where is there any heresy?"‖‖ Evidently Mr. Badger is not alone in his admiration of the Nestorians, an admiration which, however, he would perhaps have concealed, if he had read the

* Ruchat, *Histoire de la Réformation de la Suisse*, tome vii., p. 291.
† Quick's *History of the Reformed Churches in France*, vol. i., p. 7 (1692).
‡ *Life of Bishop Middleton*, vol. i., ch. xi., p. 319.
§ *Histoire du Christianisme des Indes*, tome i., livre i., p. 16.
‖ Ap. Churchill, vol. iii., p. 576.
¶ *Report on the State of the Christians of Cochin and Travancore*, p. 8.
** *Narrative*, vol. ii., ch. xix., p. 224.
†† *Answer to the Abbé Dubois*, p. 230.
‡‡ *Nineveh and its Remains*, vol. i., p. 268.
§§ *The Ansayrii*, vol. ii., ch. i., p. 10.
‖‖ *Travels in Asia Minor*, vol. ii., ch. xli., p. 272.

historian Evagrius, who relates that the founder of their religion, the heresiarch Nestorius, was not only anathematized by an Œcumenical Council, but that he died, like Herod, by the judgment of God, his tongue being gnawed by worms.*

Let us leave Mr. Badger to accompany Mr. Perkins and his American colleagues. Here is a description, by Dr. Asahel Grant, of the country which they selected for their residence. "A plain of exuberant fertility is inclosed between the mountains and the lake, comprising an area of about five hundred square miles, and bearing upon its bosom no less than three hundred hamlets and villages. It is clothed with luxuriant verdure, fruitful fields, gardens and vineyards, and irrigated by considerable streams of pure water from the adjacent mountains. The landscape is one of the most lovely in the East." Some writers have suggested that it was the site of the terrestrial paradise.

Here the Americans established their dwelling, and here commenced the operations which Mr. Perkins has described. A few extracts from his narrative, supplemented by other witnesses, will explain their nature, and the character of the missionaries.

They hear that the Nestorian Patriarch at Julamerk is about to embrace the Catholic faith. In a few hours a messenger is bearing across the plain an urgent remonstrance, in which they address to him, amongst other inquiries, this question: "Is there Paul, or Peter, or the Pope at Rome, crucified for us?"† It does not appear how far he was affected by this interrogation.

Mr. Perkins professes much disdain for his Nestorian friends. "They are very degraded," he says, and their religion is "a revolting form of Christianity." On the other hand, they feasted with him, and jested with him, and by his advice took wives and begat children; and, above all, they accepted his Bibles and tracts, which, as he observes, "gives us a glorious field of common ground."

Here are some examples of his dealings with the Nestorian bishops who became his pensioners. Of one of them, he says, "Under the influence of *the mission*, he has got so much the better of his canonical scruples on the virtue of episcopal celibacy, that he has married a young wife, and is rearing a family." Mr. Perkins was much encouraged by this easy triumph, and his companions resolved to rival his success. "The American missionaries, Messrs. Goodell and Bird," says Dr. Wolff, "have succeeded in converting two Armenian bishops

* *Hist. Ecclesiast.*, lib. i., cap. vii.

† *Residence in Persia*, p. 163.

from the established Armenian symbols and ancient liturgy to the vague and uncertain creed of the Congregationalists of America; from their attachment to their Patriarch of Etchmiadzin to the half neological writings of Professor Moses Stuart, of Andover."* He adds that they did this "merely for the sake of a wife," that both of them married immediately, and that in order to quiet the troubled conscience of their wives, they frequently expounded to them "1 Tim. iii. 2,"—with the interpretation which their American friends had suggested.

And when they have pulled down these unfortunate men to their own level, they call it "bringing them under Zion's king;" and having collected together a few such as these, by exciting lust, or avarice, or both,—having sapped all faith and religion in them, and taught them to sing their shame in texts of Scripture,—they call them "God's infant Church!"† "Woe to you," said our Lord to such as these, "because you shut the kingdom of heaven against men, for you yourselves do not enter in, and those that are going in *you suffer not to enter*. . . . . For this you shall receive the greater judgment. Woe to you, because you go round about the sea and the land to make one proselyte, and when he is made, you make him the child of hell twofold more than yourselves."‡

Mr. Perkins took Mar Yohannan, an ex-Nestorian bishop, to the United States,—just as Tzatzoe and Africaner were conveyed to England,—and when he arrived there, the Episcopalian Protestants claimed him as an ally. "You belong to *us*," they said, in a formal address, and they protested against the indecency of his herding with Methodists, Presbyterians, Anabaptists, and other children of the "Reformation," from which they derived their own origin. Under the tuition of his American guides, this poor man, once a bishop, made the following official reply: "I do not wish to hear you say, You belong to us; I have not come here to make difference among Christians." And then he expounded his new ecclesiastical views: "I love Episcopalians, and Congregationalists, and Presbyterians, and Dutchmen, and Methodists, and Baptists. . . . . There is no difference in them with me."§

Such was the general result of the influence of Mr. Perkins. What the complexion of his theology was, we may infer from the following facts. Of Nestorius, and his denial of the θεοτόκος, he says, "Protestant Christians would certainly never have thought the worse of him;" and then, forgetting the description

* *Journal*, pp. 148–9.
† *Christianity in Turkey*, ch. v., p. 130.
‡ Matt. xxiii., 15.
§ *Residence in Persia*, p. 367.

which he had himself given elsewhere, of "the revolting form of Christianity" professed by Nestorians, he exclaims, "Their belief is orthodox and scriptural!" With respect to the sacrament of Baptism, he derides the oriental Christians because they "appeared to suppose that this rite possessed some mysterious charm that involved the agency of the Holy Spirit."* Such are the teachers whom America sends to promote the fortunes of Protestantism in the East.

Mr. Perkins would perhaps have remained in Armenia till the present hour, but the care of his wife and family, as usual, put an end to his labors. Armenia was a pleasant residence, but did not offer any career to his offspring. "The children of missionaries," he says, "should be to the Churches objects of deep interest, as well as of tender sympathy;" and for this reason, because the promise of our Lord to all who should *leave* "father or mother, or wife or children, for His sake," applies in a special manner "to the *children* of His missionary servants!"† It appears, therefore, that the Divine promise of special benediction to all who *abandon* these worldly ties means, in the opinion of Mr. Perkins, that "they shall have a double blessing who *retain* them." Finally, "Mrs. Perkins' health" suggested a return to America; and as he seems to have suspected that his retirement from Armenia might possibly suggest malevolent interpretations, he complains apologetically, and by way of precaution, that "there is a *sensitiveness* in the Christian community on the subject of the return of missionaries." It is probable, in spite of the protest of Mr. Perkins, that this sensitiveness will continue.

Perhaps we have now sufficient knowledge of the character of American missionaries; but here is one more, and it shall be the last illustration. In a series of volumes, bearing a grave title, and recommended to public attention by one of the scientific societies of America, the reader will encounter the following passage. "K. is on her prancing pony; Mrs. T. is on the lank, thin-chested, but deep-chested mountain horse; Mr. T. has mounted kicking Sâda; and I'm aloft on tibn-devouring Mahjûb." This is not, as might have been supposed, a sportive account of a pic-nic party, addressed by some Syrian Aspasia to a sympathizing friend, but the official narrative of "*a missionary tour*," extracted from "*Notes of a Tour in Mount Lebanon*, by a Missionary of the American Board in Syria," and solemnly read before the American Oriental Society!‡

* P. 247.
† P. 344.
‡ *Journal of the American Oriental Society*, vol. ii., p. 237.

Here we might have terminated our notice of Protestant missions in Armenia, but that Providence has provided a witness to their real character and results whose remarkable evidence it would be wasteful to neglect. In every country we have found Protestant writers to tell us, from personal observation, what the emissaries of England and America are really doing among the heathen, and what are their relations with other sects. Armenia is no exception to this rule. If there is a country in the world in which the agents of Protestantism have been more boastful and self-complacent than in any other, it is the province in which we are now going to resume their operations. Catholic travellers could have told us how fruitless, except in corruption and unbelief, those operations have been—but we have resolved not to hear Catholics on this point. It is from Protestants alone that we can receive such facts, since only by their unsuspicious evidence could they be adequately proved.

Dr. Moritz Wagner, who seems to profess some form or modification of Anglicanism, who was the intimate friend and constant guest of Mr. Perkins and his colleagues, who warmly professes "esteem and love" for his hosts, and considers "their devotion entitled to all praise," is exactly the witness whom we should desire to interrogate. Fortunately that intelligent naturalist has anticipated our wish, and here is his account of the Protestant missionaries and of their work in the fertile plains of Armenia.

Let us hear first what he relates of the manner of life of his opulent hosts. "The institution at Urmia," he says, "costs the North American missionary societies *about fifty thousand dollars annually;*" and he will tell us immediately how that substantial revenue is spent. A writer of his own nation, also a guest at Urmia, had already informed the world that the mansion of the missionaries "is furnished with so many conveniences and comforts, that it seemed to me as if I were not under the roof of simple followers of Christ and teachers of the Gospel, but in that of some wealthy private gentleman. Here were four ladies, a whole troop of children, &c."* Dr. Wagner modestly laments that he has not sufficient power "to depict the charms and features of this missionary residence," of which he declares with emotion that "the whole idyllic scenery" will never be effaced from his recollection. But this was only a portion of the missionary delights. They had also "a summer residence at Seir, scarcely four miles from Urmia, inclosed by a wall flanked with four towers, and covering the upper terrace of a hill, from which the eye commands a

* *Voyage Round the World,* by Ida Pfeiffer, p. 221.

wonderful prospect of the vast blooming plain of Urmia, with its three hundred and sixty villages." And these palatial mansions, with a suitable income of more than ten thousand pounds per annum, were the selected abodes of *five* missionaries, and of what Dr. Wagner calls, no doubt justly, "their amiable housewives." We are not surprised to learn from their privileged guest that "the missionaries not only live comfortably, but even luxuriously, as was testified by their stables, which were almost filled with horses of all oriental breeds." Dr. Wagner adds, however, without the least intention of jesting, that his friends had generously quitted America, where both their dwellings and their stables were probably on a smaller scale, "for the propagation of Christianity."

It was in these well-furnished halls that Mr. Justin Perkins held his court. "All the gentlemen," says Dr. Wagner, "were capitally mounted," but Mr. Perkins was distinguished even among his peers. "I have never seen throughout the East a finer horse than the snow-white mare of Mr. Perkins. Each movement of the beautiful animal, which had cost a considerable sum, was full of grace. It looked to the greatest advantage when kneeling down to drink."

But Mr. Perkins and his friends had one trial, in the midst of these fabulous enjoyments; they were obliged to share their wealth with the needy Armenians, who positively refused their proffered alliance on any other terms. The "Patriarch" led the band. "He had good reasons," our German informant observes, "for showing civility to Mr. Perkins, and allowing him to preach without interference the Gospel according to Presbyterian views, for he received a considerable subsidy from the mission, exceeding, by twice the amount, the income he received from his congregations. The same motive applied to the priests of lower degree, whose cringing politeness to the missionaries was sufficiently explained by their poverty, their love of lucre, and their monthly salaries."

And these were not the only classes who dilapidated the fifty thousand dollars which annually flowed into the missionary treasury from enthusiastic subscribers at home, who were perhaps not fully acquainted with the mode in which their contributions were consumed. "The missionaries showered their gold," says their favored guest, "with a liberal hand, and not only taught the youth gratis, *but gave them a weekly gratuity.* . . . . . . Each bishop receives from the Americans a monthly allowance of three hundred Turkish piastres, and ordinary ecclesiastics from a hundred and fifty to two hundred piastres. On the condition of this allowance being continued, the Nestorian clergy permit the missionaries to preach in their villages, to keep schools, &c. Without this payment, or bribery, of the priests for a good end, the missionaries could not maintain their footing in this country. Even the peasant is only carrying on a pecuniary speculation, in sending his child to school. Each scholar receives weekly, a sahefgeran; and though this gift is small, *the schools would become directly empty* if it were to cease."

Finally, if we ask Dr. Wagner to tell us frankly how many converts were really gained by this enormous expenditure—amounting, in thirty years, to one million and a half dollars, or more than three hundred thousand pounds sterling—he is willing to gratify our curiosity, and honestly confesses that it has converted nobody. Even Nestorians, though willing to accept any amount of American money, do not cease to despise American doctrine. Amongst the domestic servants in the palace of Mr. Perkins were two, the one a Jew, the other an Armenian, who professed to be disciples. Dr. Wagner, a very amiable man, was charitably disposed to think well of the Armenian, who constantly expressed an earnest desire to visit Europe and America; but the "other missionary servant, a converted Jew, who had been my guide to Seir, hinted slyly that it was not so much the devout impulse of a pilgrim which prompted his friend John to visit Europe and Christendom, as selfishness and ambitious aspirations. He implied that the shrewd Nestorian fancied that, if he knew the English tongue better, he could play the part of Messrs. Perkins and Starking among his countrymen." These intelligent "converts" evidently appreciated each other, and the acute Dr. Wagner seems at last to have appreciated them all. "As a missionary servant," he says, "John was a very unimportant personage in the land; but as missionary, and supported by the mission fund, even the higher clergy would have paid court to him, which was enough to excite the ambition of the Nestorian youth." And then follow these grave words, in which the true character of these costly missions,—always appealing to the meanest sentiments of the human heart, and openly conducted on the worst principles of human cunning,—is exposed by this friendly and capable witness. "If we except a few Jews, won over from motives of gain, *these expensive establishments have made no converts.*" This is all that has been accomplished, he says, by "America's evangelical apostles, who are so splendidly remunerated, and the wealthy members of the societies, who have never yet raised their voices against negro-slavery, and the hunting down of the poor red-skins by rifle-shots and bloodhounds, but who pay many hundred thousand dollars to support their *useless missions* in the East." "The American mission," he declares, and with this final testimony we may close our Armenian narrative, "cannot boast of splendid results in relation to the improvement of morality, stimulus by virtuous examples, or the advancement of culture. *Even Mr. Perkins admitted this.*" Yet in his official reports that gentleman only spoke of his continual triumphs, and even relates in his book such tales as the following: "The Rev. William Goodell dropped a copy of the tract entitled the *Dairyman's Daughter* in Nicomedia;" and this, he affirms, knowing what the home subscribers could bear, created, without the aid of any missionary, "a considerable number of enlightened, spiritual Christians!" And the man who could thus mock the well-meaning contributors to his own luxury, privately confessed to Dr. Wagner, who fortunately made a note of the words, that "he thought almost all hope must be given up in the case of the present generation."* Thus, by the aid of a little patience and industry, we have arrived at last, by exclusively Protestant testimony, at a full knowledge of the character and results of all the Protestant missions in Armenia, Syria, and Turkey.

GEORGIA AND PERSIA.

We need not pause to offer any reflections upon the history which we have now completed. Once more we have traced a contrast, and one which solicits no comment. Once more we have advanced a step in that controversy which, as we have said, God has already taken out of the hands of men, to decide it Himself. He knows how to distribute His own gifts, and we have seen upon whom He confers, to whom He refuses them. And the facts which we have now observed in so many regions, and which contain so momentous a lesson, are equally uniform in every part of Western Asia.

We might pursue our researches, at the risk of wearying the reader, in Georgia, and even in Persia, and everywhere we should find the same impressive phenomena, everywhere trace the same unvarying contrast. In Georgia,—where, as early as the thirteenth century, Catholics were detected by being ordered "to trample on the crucifix," and multitudes gained the crown of martyrdom,†—there are now German, American, and Scotch missionaries. Here is one example of each class. An English traveller, who visited the German colony near Tiflis, under the Lutheran missionary Dittrich, says, "I was sorry to learn from

* *Travels*, &c., vol. iii., ch. viii., pp. 234–258.

† *Histoire de la Georgie*, par M. Brosset, tome i., p. 504.

Mr. Dittrich that the German colonies had not flourished. . . . He told me that great disunion prevailed amongst the colonists, principally from differences of religious opinion."* Of those at Abbas Tuman, whom he also found in great misery, Dr. Bodenstedt says, "What silences compassion is the deplorable disharmony in which they live with each other."† Yet they thought themselves qualified to convert the Armenians to one or other of their own shifting creeds, or to all of them at once.

To the Americans at Shooshâ, in Georgia, the Russian Emperor sent the following admonition: "Learning by the real state of things that you, since the time of your settlement at Shooshâ, *have not yet converted anybody*, and, deviating from the proper limits," the conversion of the heathen, "have directed your views to the Armenian youth, which, on the part of the Armenian clergy, has produced complaints, the consequences of which may be very disagreeable; his Majesty's ministers have concluded to prohibit you all missionary labors, and for the future to leave it to your own choice to employ yourselves with agriculture, manufactures, or mechanical trades. It has pleased his Majesty the Emperor to confirm this decree."‡

It is true that the emperor tried to silence the Catholics also, not because they had failed, like the Americans, to convert the heathen, but because they would have converted the whole country if he had not prevented them. Yet Dr. Wagner found eight hundred Catholics "at or near Kutais," who all spoke the Imeritian dialect; while the pupils of the convent, to the number of thirty or forty, "could read and write Georgian, and read Italian with tolerable facility." He notices too "the respect and esteem which the Superior (of the Franciscans) had obtained in the town and country," and observes, "I frequently witnessed the child-like veneration in which he was held by the Armenian boys."§ Baron Von Haxthausen also mentions an Italian missionary, who "died thirty years ago, and the Georgians number him among their saints." Such men were opposed by the Czar, as the Americans were, but for very different reasons.

It is a curious illustration of the different policy of England, and of the deplorable influence which she everywhere exerts in support of seditious fanaticism or meddlesome unbelief, that when Mr. Perkins, whose operations we can now appreciate, solicited the sympathy of the Right Hon. Henry Ellis, British

* Wilbraham, *Travels in the Trans-Caucasian Provinces*, ch. xvii., p. 182.

† *The Caucasus*, &c., vol. ii., p. 27.

‡ Quoted by Perkins, p. 221.

§ *Travels*, vol. ii., ch. iii., p. 202.

Ambassador in Persia, in 1835, he received the following characteristic reply: "The proposed introduction of the pure doctrines of the Reformed Church among the Nestorian Christians in this country cannot fail to be a matter of deep and serious interest to his Majesty's government."* Russia, with more discretion, promptly dismissed the friends of Mr. Ellis as likely to prove "very disagreeable," and suggested to them the more congenial pursuit of manufactures or mechanical trades.

Lastly, for we need not stay to multiply testimonies of which we have learned by this time to appreciate the universality, Sir Robert Porter gives this account of the emissaries from Scotland. "A Scotch colony of missionaries have established themselves in the neighborhood of Konstantinogorsk; but it may be regarded as an agricultural society, rather than a theological college."†

In Persia,—where Jesuits once received honors, even in the tent of Nadir Schah, as their brethren did in that of Akbar;‡ and where in our own day Napoleon, comprehending with his infallible sagacity all that such men could effect, stipulated, by the treaty of 1808, for protection in favor of all Jesuits whom France might send to that land,—Catholic missionaries, having the apostolic graces of chastity and holy poverty, have won the respect even of the disciples of the false prophet, while a crowd of American missionaries dispense on every side the enormous funds intrusted to them. "The money they lavish," says the Prefect of the Armenian missions in Persia, "presents a strong temptation to certain Armenians, who follow them for a while, in order to profit by their profusion, but invariably adhere to the tenets of their own religion."§ The Armenian clergy, we are told by the wife of a British ambassador, "receive salaries" from them, like their fellows in the neighborhood of Urmia. Of the French Lazarists, the same lady says, "These gentlemen abounded in zeal and activity, but they were poor, and wholly unable to contend against the treasures of Boston."‖ Such is everywhere the influence, when they have any, of Protestant missionaries. To generate corruption and immorality, without producing even the semblance of religious conviction; to destroy faith, but never to inspire it; and to hinder those who, in spite of their poverty, know how to kindle the light of truth and charity in all hearts—such is

* *Residence in Persia*, &c., p. 219.
† *Travels in Georgia*, vol. i., p. 47.
‡ *Crétineau Joly*, tome vi., ch. i., p. 51.
§ *Annals*, vol. i., p. 95.
‖ *Life and Manners in Persia*, by Lady Shiel, p. 356.

their deplorable work. And their partisans at home are never weary of sending them money to be employed in such aims.

They do not even attempt, as might be anticipated, to convert the Persians, who suppose, like all orientals, that they are atheists. Indeed, Mr. Perkins incautiously relates an anecdote which shows that the Persians are quite as likely to convert the Protestants as to be converted by them. "A pious English family in Persia," he says, "were surprised and shocked on one day finding their little girl, then four years old, kneeling with her face towards Mecca, and lisping the devotions of the false prophet."*

But it is time to close this chapter, already extended to undue limits, and we may conclude it with an anecdote not less curious than that which we have just heard. Not long ago, a French traveller, journeying from Ispahan to Bagdad, came upon a small Catholic colony towards the close of a sultry day. They were assembled together in the house of one of them, and having recited vespers, were engaged, when the traveller joined them, not in asking gifts for themselves, but in praying for the conversion of England! They seem to have understood, even in their far home beyond the Tigris, that, in spite of the zeal of some, and the good intentions of many, England is still, by her relentless warfare against Unity, the great impediment to the conversion of the heathen; and that the surest way to obtain for *them* admission into the family of God, was to solicit for *her* the recovery of the gifts which she has lost, and of the faith which she has denied. And these Persian Christians were right. If England had remained Catholic, it is probable that at this hour there would not have been a pagan altar in the world.

* P. 343.

CHAPTER IX.

MISSIONS IN AMERICA.

PART I.

SOUTH AMERICA.

THE gifts and promises of God, it has been said, have travelled from East to West, from the rising to the setting sun. To each tribe of the human family in turn the Angel of the Covenant has delivered the message of peace, then passed on his way. In the appointed hour he crossed the great sea, with his face westwards. Then, for the first time, the name of Jesus was proclaimed in that mighty continent which stretches almost from pole to pole, and within whose boundless plains a new chapter of man's history has found its scenes and its actors. Here, among many tribes, and nations of various tongues, the ministers of light and darkness have long contended together for the mastery. When we have read the story of their conflict, we may close our book. Earth has nothing more to offer us. We shall have visited in turn all her provinces; and having started from the remote eastern sea which beats against the long coasts of China, we shall stand at length on the opposite frontier of man's narrow home, the western limits of his wanderings, and may once more look across the ocean to the land from which we commenced our journey.

No portion of the earth presents on a larger scale, none in more vivid colors, the contrast which it has been the business of these volumes to trace, than that whose religious history we are about to review. When Nature divided the great American continent into two parts, she seems to have prepared by anticipation a separate theatre for the events of which each was to be the scene, and for the actors who were destined to perform in either a part so widely dissimilar. The one was to be the exclusive domain of the Church, the other the battle-field of all the Sects.

A thousand writers have related, with sympathy or regret, but otherwise with unvarying uniformity, the historical results of a distribution which all seemed to have noticed, and in which may be traced, on the broadest scale, and with a clearness and precision which exclude even the risk of error, all the characteristic marks which have distinguished in every age the City of God from the City of Confusion. The races of the South, we shall see, have derived both their religion and their civilization from the missionaries of the Cross; the tribes of the North, doomed to swift destruction, have been abandoned to teachers of another school, and to prophets of another faith. And these have been the results of the unequal partition. In the *South*, the Church has united all, of whatever race, in spite of the ignorance or the ferocity of the barbarians, in spite of the follies or the crimes of some of her own children, into one household and family. In the *North*, the original heirs have been banished or exterminated, without pity, and without remorse, that the sects might build up in the desert which they had created a pandemonium of tumult and disorder, so full of division and discord, that the evil spirits might well congregate here from all the "dry places" of the earth, and deem that they had found at last their true home. Let us introduce at once a few of the witnesses whom we are hereafter to hear, that we may understand what is the history upon which we are about to enter, and what are the facts which it will disclose to us.

The contrast which we are going to trace is thus indicated, with frank, outspoken candor, by men who had analyzed all its features. "More than a million and a half of the pure aboriginal races," says the author of the *Natural History of Man*, "live in *South* America in the profession of Christianity."* "The history of the attempts to convert the Indians of *North* America," says the annalist of Protestant missions, "is a record of a series of failures."† This is the first great fact, in its broad outlines, which will be presented to our notice; and it is one, as an eminent English ethnologist observes, "which must be allowed to reflect honor on the Roman Catholic Church, and to cast a deep shade on the history of Protestantism."‡

A second and equally impressive fact, which has excited the attention of a multitude of writers of all nations, is thus expressed by a prejudiced traveller, who had lived among the tribes of the equinoctial regions. "Far from being diminished, *their* number has considerably increased. A similar increase has taken place *generally* among the Indian population in that part of America which is within the tropics . . . . the Indian population *in the missions* is constantly augmenting." On the

* Prichard, sec. xliv., p. 427.
† Quoted in *Monthly Review*, vol. lxxxiv., p. 143.
‡ Prichard, *ubi supra*.

other hand, "In the neighborhood of the United States, on the contrary, the Indians are fast diminishing in numbers. . . . . In the United States, as civilization advances, the Indians are constantly driven beyond its pale."* We shall trace this contrast hereafter in all its details.

Finally, a third feature of the prodigious contrast which we are about to examine is this—that while the innumerable native tribes who have been converted to Christianity between the thirtieth parallel of north and the thirty-fifth of south latitude, through a tract of more than four thousand miles in length and nearly three thousand in breadth, have never departed from the Catholic faith, and, as Protestant writers will assure us, cleave to it at this day as obstinately as ever: within the wide territories of the United States, where the Indian has only been corrupted or destroyed, nominal Christians of the Anglo-Saxon race have themselves become divided and subdivided into such a chaos of jarring sects, that, as their own leaders declare, with a sorrow which comes too late, there is nothing like it in the history of the world. "In the Western world," says a Protestant minister, "religion is made to appear too often as a source of contention rather than as a bond of union and peace."† Already, at the close of the seventeenth century, the English governor of New York reported of that province, that it swarmed with men of "all sorts of opinions, and the most part of none at all;" and a hundred years later, an English clergyman could still describe the inhabitants of his own district as "people of almost all religions and sects, but the greatest part of no religion."‡ In our own day, it has even become necessary to adopt a new nomenclature, in order to classify divisions and subdivisions which had elsewhere neither a form nor a name. "Two grand divisions of the Baptists," one of the innumerable offshoots from the Anglican Establishment, who already possess more than five thousand churches, are known, Mr. Olmsted says, "as the Hard Shells and the Soft Shells;" and even such titles are perhaps no greater outrage upon the religion of the Gospel than many which are daily uttered, with quiet complacency, in our own land. The relations of these cognate tribes to one another, Mr. Olmsted adds, are marked by "an intense rivalry and jealousy," as "persistent" as that which subsists between Druses and Maronites, between the followers of Ali and the disciples of

* *Journal of a Residence in Colombia,* by Captain Charles Stuart Cochrane, vol. i., ch. iii., pp. 218, 233.

† *The Western World Revisited,* by the Rev. Henry Caswall, ch. i., p. 9; ch. xii., p. 316.

‡ *Documentary History of New York,* vol. i., p. 186; vol. iii., p. 1113.

Omar.* "The dearest and warmest friends of the Republic," we are told, "look with fear and trembling on her sectional divisions, her party jealousies, the strange and anomalous divisions, subdivisions, and minor subdivisions of her interminable and contending religious denominations."† "Churches are divided," observes another Protestant writer, "Presbyteries are divided, Synods are divided, the General Assembly is divided;" and this is due, he considers, to "extreme looseness in doctrine and practice on the one hand, and a violent attempt to coerce it into orthodoxy on the other."‡ "The continual splitting of the numerous sections of Protestantism," Dr. Schedel remarks, in 1858, still recording the unwelcome phenomena to which the disciples of the Reformation feel that *they* can apply no remedy, and using them as an argument in favor of rationalism, "has had the effect of producing a deep impression of its danger for religion."§ "The clergy complain," says an English traveller of the same school, "of the enormous spread of bold books, from the infidel tract to the latest handling of the miracle question. There are schisms among all the more strict of the religious bodies, and large secessions and new formations among those which are bound together by slight forms."‖ Lastly,—for there is no need to multiply testimonies to a fact which no one disputes, or to the real nature of a religion of which these are so invariably the fruits, that its own professors now regard all unity as chimerical, except the diabolical unity of evil,—Dr. Stephen Olin, a respectable Wesleyan preacher, exclaims once more, "Twenty years of observation have produced in my mind a deliberate conviction that the sorest evil which presses upon the American Churches, the chiefest obstacle to their real progress in holiness and usefulness, is the spirit of sectarianism."¶

But even these three facts do not illustrate the whole contrast which we are about to trace in America, after proving it for every other land, between the work of the Church and the work of the Sects. The first has won a thousand tribes to the Cross; has seen them increase and multiply on every side under her gentle rule, and has preserved them for two hundred years, in spite of many calamities, in unbroken unity of faith. The second have not gained so much as a single tribe, have destroyed

* Olmsted, *Our Slave States.*

† *Statesmen of America,* by S. Maury, p. 483.

‡ Colton's *Thoughts on the Religious State of the Country,* p. 66

§ *The Emancipation of Faith,* by H. E. Schedel, M.D., vol. ii., p. 410 (New York, 1858).

‖ *Society in America,* by Harriet Martineau, vol. iii., p. 257.

¶ *Works,* vol. ii., p. 451.

without mercy the races which they could not convert, and have themselves become a proverb to the whole earth of religious division and discord. Yet this also does not exhaust all the facts of the contrast.

It would have been something if the sects could have pleaded that at least they had done their best, and only failed after earnest and courageous effort. Even this is a praise which they have not cared to earn, and which their own advocates refuse to allow them. We shall see presently what Protestant writers say of the dauntless courage and sublime virtue of the men who converted South America; of their own friends they speak as follows: "The pious men of America," says Möllhausen, with pardonable irony, "look with indifference on the heathen before their own doors, but send out missionaries to preach Christianity in the remotest parts of the world! When, through the covetousness of the white civilized races, the free inhabitants of the steppes shall have been ruined and exterminated, Christian love will find its way *to their empty wigwams*, and churches and meeting-houses rise over the graves of the poor victimized owners of the green prairies."* They leave *them* to perish with indifference, says another German Protestant, who, like Möllhausen, had lived among them, because "there are no territories to be won, there are no natives to be enticed into building comfortable houses for the Christian teachers, they would have to lead a wild life with *them*, no further profit in view as is the case with the South Sea Islands, but only the prospect of being driven with their pupils from one place to another, living on grubs, acorns, and other indigestible things; while, on the other hand, a comfortable life and a good income look far more inviting."† Such language need not surprise us, for we have seen many examples in the course of these pages both of the contempt which the more enlightened Protestants feel for their own missionaries, and the indifference with which they avow it.

Dr. Moritz Wagner, another German Protestant, who also had lived among American missionaries, has already told us, in the same tone of honest reprobation, that "America's evangelical apostles, who have never yet raised their voices against the hunting down the poor redskins, pay many hundred thousand dollars to support their useless missions in the East"—not because they love the orientals more, but simply, as Dr. Livingstone intimates with respect to South Africa, because they

* *Journey from the Mississippi to the Coasts of the Pacific*, vol. i., ch. xi., p. 220, ed. Sinnett.

† Gerstaecker, *Journey Round the World*, vol. i., ch. vi., p. 350.

cannot bear to be anticipated or excluded by the restless activity of rival sects. Mr. Buckingham, also, an English writer, who had dwelt among them, notices the characteristic fact, that while an American religious society voted by acclamation thousands of dollars at once to Persia, Siam, or the Sandwich Islands, which demanded nothing from them, and only asked to be left alone, they allotted, as if in derision, "for North American Indians," perishing at their own doors, the modest sum of two hundred!* And even when their cautious emissaries, moved by the attractions which alone prevail with such men, venture to follow the native to his forest home, it is only, as we shall see, to abandon after a brief space the unprofitable labor; so that Humboldt did not scruple to say, that the relics of the aboriginal races of North America, who have come into contact with the agents of English or American religions, are "sinking into a *lower* moral state than they occupied before."†

And this heavy reproach is repeated, in still more emphatic language, even by American Protestants. "While the Pequods and other northern tribes," says Judge Hall, of Cincinnati, "were being exterminated, or sold into slavery, the more fortunate savage of the Mississippi was listening to the pious counsels of the Catholic missionaries. *They* exercised, of choice, an expansive benevolence, at a period when Protestants, similarly situated, were bloodthirsty and rapacious."‡ "The Jesuit mission-farms," says Mr. Law Olmsted, in 1857, "are an example for us. Our neighborly responsibilities for the Lipans" —a tribe on the Texan frontier—"is certainly more close than for the Feejees, and if the glory of converting them to decency be less, the expense would certainly be in proportion."§ Lastly, Mr. Melville, also one of their own countrymen, noticing the vaunt that paganism is almost extinct in the United States, thus rebukes the hollow and impious boast: "The Anglo-Saxon hive have extirpated paganism from the greater part of the North American continent, *but with it they have likewise extirpated the greater portion of the Red race.*"‖

Such, by German, English, and American testimony, has been the work of Protestantism. On the other hand, a modern French naturalist, who visited in person thirty-nine existing nations of pure American race in the *Southern* continent, and

* *America,* by J. S. Buckingham, Esq., vol. i., ch. x.
† Preface to Möllhausen's *Journey,* p. xiii.
‡ *History of the Religious Denominations of the United States,* by J. D. Rupp, p. 163.
§ *Journey through Texas,* p. 298.
‖ *The Marquesas Islands,* ch. xxvi., p. 217.

collected statistics from which we shall borrow hereafter, declares, that he found indeed, scattered through the regions which he so painfully explored, ninety-four thousand one hundred and ninety-seven pagans; but that he counted also, within the same district, one million five hundred and ninety thousand nine hundred and thirty *native* Christians. And then he relates, speaking rather as a man of science than as a Christian, that these poor Indians, often robbed of their pastors and almost always wronged by their rulers, exhibit the same astonishing inflexibility of faith, even in cases where they have been enfeebled by ignorance or superstition, of which we have already seen so many examples; so that, as M. d'Orbigny observes, "they push their profession of the Catholic religion even to fanaticism."* Mendoza could say, at an earlier date, and in language more worthy of the subject, that "the natural people of South America, never since they were converted, have been found in any heresy, nor in any thing contrary to the Roman faith;"† and living Protestants will presently assure us, not only that all attempts to shake their faith are equally vain at the present day, but that in many parts of South America, and notably in Chili, where the emissaries of the English Bible Society have made their appearance, "the life of an Englishman is in danger among the peasantry," so vehement is their dislike of heresy, and of those who recommend it to them.‡ Finally, for we must not anticipate evidence which will claim our attention later, Sir James Mackintosh thus attests the memorable contrast which had not escaped his philosophical review, and of which the fact noticed by Mendoza is not the least instructive portion. "The natives of America, who generally felt the comparative superiority of the European race only in a more rapid or a more gradual destruction, and to whom even the excellent Quakers dealt out little more than penurious justice, were, under the paternal rule of the Jesuits,"—he might have added, under that of the Franciscans, the Dominicans, and many more,—"reclaimed from savage manners, and instructed in the arts and duties of civilized life."§ Such, in its leading features, is the history of which we are now going to trace the outlines.

In attempting to follow the course of events of which the details have filled hundreds of volumes, and which had for their theatre the whole extent of the vast American continent,—in

* *Voyage dans l'Amérique Méridionale*, par Alcide d'Orbigny, tome iv., p. 252.

† *Historie of the Kingdome of China*, vol. ii., p. 224, ed. Hakluyt Society.

‡ *Travels in Chili*, by John Miers, vol. ii., ch. xix., p. 223.

§ *Review of the Causes of the Revolution*, Works, vol. ii., p. 251 (1846).

the North, from California to the Gulf of Florida, and from the banks of the St. Lawrence to those of the Gila and the Colorado; in the South, from Carthagena to Buenos Ayres, and from the Andes to the mouths of the Amazon, the Orinoco, and the Plata; it is not a history which the reader will expect to find, hardly even a sketch, of a warfare which has filled the world with envy or admiration, which lasted more than two centuries, and in which the Church poured out like water the sweat and the blood of her children; while even her enemies have celebrated its final issue with an enthusiasm which the most inveterate prejudice could not silence, as one of the most astonishing of her many triumphs. The story of American missions includes names as venerable as any in the long catalogue of apostles, and tells of the deeds of a whole army of martyrs and confessors,—of Anchieta and Rodriguez, of Vieyra and d'Almeida, of D'Aguilar and Vénégas, of Herrera and Ugarte, of Betanzos and Las Casas, of Bracamante and Portillo, of Lopez and Barzana, of the Blessed Peter Claver and St. Francis Solano;—of the martyrs Suarez and Figuerroa, Baraza and Lizardi, Richler and Lucas Cavellero; of Aranda and Montalban, of Azevedo, whom the Huguenots cut in pieces, and Henri de la Borde, whom the English ensnared and then cruelly murdered; of Jogues and de Brébeuf, of Lamberville and Lallemand, and a thousand more—for, as M. Crétineau Joly observes, "the number of missionaries who fell is really incalculable;"—of that multitude of apostolic warriors of whom even American Protestants of our own day have said, that their monuments will yet be raised by the free people to whom they bequeathed examples of heroism which Americans know how to admire; who labored, as Mr. Washington Irving confessed, "*with a power which no other Christians have exhibited;*"* who excelled all others, as Mr. Schoolcraft admits, "in boldness, zeal, and indomitable efficacy;"† and who more than justified, as Professor Walters of Philadelphia remarks, whatever applause the admiration of mankind has lavished "upon their dauntless courage and their more than human charity and zeal."‡

It is of such men, and of their work, that we are now to speak—not fitly, but according to the measure of our capacity. It is a comparison of their life and death, of their labors, sufferings, and conquests, with the sterile career of men of another order, but ostensibly busy in the same calling, which will furnish the last but not the least instructive example of the

* *Knickerbocker*, June, 1838.

† *Notes on the Iroquois*, by Henry R. Schoolcraft, ch. xii., p. 403 (1847).

‡ Rupp, *Hist. of Religious Denominations*, &c., p. 119.

contrast of which we have already produced so many illustrations; and to which the Prophet pointed when he proposed this very contrast as the infallible test by which men should be able to distinguish, throughout the whole Christian era, between true and false apostles, *between the work of the Church and the work of the Sects.*

Let us begin with South America, and the world-famed missions of Brazil and Peru, of Chili and Paraguay. A little later we shall traverse Mexico in our way to the north, enter California and Oregon, visit the lakes of the northern continent and the plains of Canada, and trace the decay of the unhappy races whom the Saxon, unable to convert them to God, has pushed from their homes, or violently swept from the earth, that he might people after his own fashion the regions from which they have been banished forever.

We shall use, according to our custom, and as far as it is available, the testimony of Protestant writers. They have served us in all our former journeys, and will not refuse to aid us in this. Let us begin with their account of Catholic missions in Brazil. Mr. Southey—of whose sentiments towards the Catholic Church we shall presently see abundant tokens, and who did not hesitate to tell his countrymen, "I deprecate what is called Catholic emancipation"—has diligently compiled whatever relates to the history of Brazil. He will be our principal guide.

BRAZIL.

It was in 1549 that John III. of Portugal, solicitous, as Mr. Southey observes, "for the souls of his Brazilian subjects," resolved to dispatch to their aid missionaries of the Society of Jesus. Brazil was not the only land which owed eternal gratitude to the Christian zeal of that vigorous and enlightened monarch, who received from his contemporaries more honor than Mr. Southey is willing to allow him. "He was superstitious to the lowest depth of degradation," says this English historian, with that quiet composure which his countrymen usually display in judging such men. In spite of this defect, "he was truly and righteously anxious to spread his religion, such at it was, among the heathen."* So he sent Father Emanuel de Nobrega, and five others, chosen by St. Ignatius himself for this difficult mission; and it was under their auspices that the new city of St. Salvador, hitherto only a fortified camp, began to assume the dimensions which made it afterwards the

* *History of Brazil,* by Robert Southey, vol. i., ch. viii., p. 214 (1817).

capital of northern Brazil. "The Jesuits," says Mr. Southey, for Providence employs such men to proclaim the truths which they wish to hide, "immediately began that system of beneficence towards the natives from which they never deviated till their extinction as an order." From that hour the native of South America was to find, in every forest where he had made his home, and by the banks of every river on which his frail bark could float, a friend, a father, and a guide; who would save him from himself and from his oppressors, and teach him to love a religion which could move such as them to abandon home, country, and kinsfolk, in order to make such as him a partaker in its promises, its joys, and its rewards.

The attempt was bold, but not too bold. The missionaries, says Mr. Southey, had to encounter "obstacles great and numerous," and of these the almost universal practice of cannibalism was not the least formidable. But the children of St. Ignatius, like those of St. Francis and St. Dominic, who shared this field with them, knew how to combat the enemy, whatever form he might assume. They succeeded, therefore, in rooting out cannibalism. It was their first victory; but Mr. Southey, who will presently tell us how they did it, was so displeased with their proceedings, that he could only find relief by exclaiming, "Nothing is too impudent for the audacity of such a priesthood, nothing too gross for the credulity of their besotted believers."* Mr. Southey, however, will inform us hereafter, that when missionaries of another faith attempted to instruct the same savage disciples, it was contempt, and not credulity, which they excited among them.

Happily, like the rest of his class, this historian is not rigorously consistent. "These missionaries," he says, only a few pages later, "were every way qualified for their office. They were zealous for the salvation of souls; they had disengaged themselves from all the ties which attach us to life, and were therefore not merely fearless of martyrdom, but ambitious of it."† How such a temper, and such self-annihilation, were consistent with the grave demerits imputed to them by Mr. Southey, he does not explain. "They believed the idolatry which they taught," he says, as if he wished to excuse them as far as possible, "and were themselves persuaded that by sprinkling a dying savage, and repeating over him a form of words which he did not understand,"—it is Mr. Southey who says so—"they redeemed him from everlasting torments. . . Nor can it be doubted that they sometimes worked miracles upon

* *History of Brazil*, ch. viii., p. 230.
† P. 252.

the sick; for when they believed that the patient might be miraculously cured, and he himself expected that he should be so, faith would supply the virtue in which it trusted."*

This singular explanation of their supernatural power, which seems to have satisfied Mr. Southey, has one inconvenience; it leaves the missionaries under the reproach of idolatry, but it makes God their accomplice. Voltaire once said, with more than his usual wit and not more than his usual profaneness, "Si Dieu a fait l'homme à son image, l'homme le lui a bien rendu." The ductile divinity imagined by Mr. Southey, who was so easily persuaded to work miracles even at the risk of propagating "idolatry," had suffered not a little from that process, and was evidently fashioned after a human type. The infirmities of such a god disqualify him for ruling over Christians. But perhaps we may accept Mr. Southey's admission that the Catholic missionaries "worked miracles upon the sick," without adopting his explanation of the fact. Let us inquire of him, in the next place, how they extirpated cannibalism.

"All efforts at abolishing this accursed custom," he says, "were in vain. One day Nobrega and his companions heard the uproar and rejoicing of the savages at one of these sacrifices; they made their way into the area, just when the prisoner had been felled, and the old women were dragging his body to the fire; they forced the body from them, and in the presence of the whole clan, who stood astonished at their courage, carried it off. The women soon roused the warriors to revenge this insult. By the time the Fathers had secretly interred the corpse, the savages were in search of them." The barbarians were swift and eager in pursuit, but by the aid of the Portuguese authorities, the missionaries escaped their fury; and such was the impression which their intrepidity produced upon them, that "it was not long," says our historian, "before these very savages came to solicit their forgiveness, and promised not to repeat these feasts."

But Mr. Southey has more to tell us. "One of the Jesuits," he says, "succeeded in effectually abolishing cannibalism among some clans by going through them and flogging himself before their doors till he was covered with blood, telling them he thus tormented himself to avert the punishment which God would otherwise inflict upon them for this crying sin. *They could not bear this*, confessed what they had done was wrong, and enacted heavy punishments against any person who should again be guilty."† It was thus that the missionaries rooted out canni-

* *History of Brazil*, p. 253.
† P. 254.

balism. It is true that the process involved pain and suffering, and that they encountered every day the risk of death in its most intolerable forms; but, as Mr. Southey has remarked, "they were not merely fearless of martyrdom, but ambitious of it."

With more remote tribes, over whom they had not as yet acquired the personal influence which they were afterwards to exert throughout the whole country, the Fathers, we are told, "thought themselves fortunate in obtaining permission to visit the prisoners and instruct them in the saving faith, before they were put to death." It was a perilous ministry, which only such men would have accepted; and on these occasions, in order to escape the observation of the savages, while they complied with the Divine precept which makes Baptism a condition of salvation, "they carried with them wet handkerchiefs, or contrived to wet the skirt of their sleeve or habit, that out of it they might squeeze water enough upon the victim's head" to administer the Sacrament of Baptism. In recounting this proceeding, which excites his vehement disapprobation, Mr. Southey adds: "What will not man believe, if he can believe this of his Maker!" As it was his Maker who taught him the lesson, why should man be blamed for believing it?

When at length, by inexhaustible patience and intrepid valor, living the while on the roots of the earth and sharing the rude cabin of the savage, these men of gentle birth and cultivated tastes had laboriously won some ferocious tribe from its foul superstitions, taught them to pronounce with reverence the sweet names of Jesus and Mary, and planted in them the first rudiments both of faith and civilization, "they made the converts erect a church in the village, which, however rude, fixed them to the spot; and they established a school for the children, whom they catechised in their own language. . . . . They taught them also to read and write, using, says Nobrega, the same persuasion as that wherewith the enemy overcame man, 'Ye shall be as gods, knowing good and evil;' for this knowledge appeared wonderful to them, and they eagerly desired to attain it." And then Mr. Southey, unmoved even by the touching picture which he himself had drawn, haughtily exclaims, "Good proof how easily such a race might have been civilized!" More humane and candid writers will presently tell us, indeed he will tell us himself, in a later volume, when he had forgotten these hasty words, that they *were* civilized, and that this was the very process by which the arduous change was effected. Mr. Southey adds, that "reading, writing, and arithmetic were taught them; they were trained to assist at Mass," that is, to do an act which in itself is no mean education, "and to sing the Church service." Here was a beginning at least of "civilization;" and it was so complete in its later effects, so abiding in its influence, that three hundred years after we shall find even English writers not only celebrating the agricultural and economical results still visible in the Christian missions, but contrasting the courtesy and dignity, as well as the spiritual fervor of these children of the forest, with the boorish coarseness and animal instincts of their own countrymen.

Mr. Southey, however, was not satisfied, in this early portion of his work, with the efforts of the missionaries to civilize the natives of Brazil. Yet even he could understand, and he expresses the conviction in eloquent words, that "a ritual worship creates arts for its embellishment and support; habits of settled life take root as soon as a temple is founded, and the city grows round the altar." The Brazilians anticipated Mr. Southey in appreciating this important fact, and he will trace for us hereafter, in spite of himself, the prodigious work of civilization accomplished among races even more barbarous than these by the apostles of the Church; while others will tell us, that if to "assist at Mass," and to "sing the Church service," were the chief, they were not the only lessons which they taught, though they taught these so well, that, exactly three centuries after Emanuel de Nobrega landed in Brazil, M. d'Orbigny, who had listened with admiration to the ecclesiastical music sung by the Indians in the mission of San Xavier, confesses, "I could not but admire the labors of the Jesuits, when I reflected that previous to their arrival the Chiquitos, still in the savage state, were scattered through the recesses of the forest!" During twelve generations they have handed down, from father to son, the lessons which the Jesuits taught them; and d'Orbigny adds, that though they martyred the earlier missionaries, "once Christian, they have persevered, and at this day nothing would induce them to return to the life of the woods."* To what extent they were really civilized we shall learn hereafter, by the testimony of Protestant writers, including Mr. Southey himself.

The first missionaries in Brazil, to whom we must now return, had to contend not only with the ignorance and ferocity of its native tribes, but with the profound immorality of the reckless adventurers who had deserted Portugal to try their fortunes in the New World. In Brazil, as in Mexico, it was from men of this stamp, self-banished, and stained with many a crime, yet retaining even in their fall the faith which Catholics

* *Voyage*, &c., tome iv., p. 250.

so rarely lose, that the missionaries experienced the most obstinate and formidable opposition. Seeking only the goods of this world, they resented the admonitions of men who valued only those of the next. "As the Jesuits steadfastly opposed their cruelties," we are told by two Protestant ministers, "the Portuguese resorted to every means of annoyance against them. . . . . . As the Indians were driven back into the wilds of the interior, through fear of the slave-hunters, the Jesuits sought them out, and carried to them the opportunities of Christian worship and instruction."* Hence the implacable warfare which the Portuguese merchants waged against the missionaries. But this was only an additional motive with the latter for deeds of charity towards their enemies. With uncompromising firmness, but with gentle speech, they admonished them of their errors, refusing the Sacraments to all who maltreated their slaves or set them an unchristian example. "Many were reclaimed," says Mr. Southey, "by this resolute and Christian conduct." The immorality of professing Christians was vanquished, then, by the same fervent apostles before whose presence idolatry had already begun to flee away.

In 1553, a reinforcement of seven Fathers arrived in Brazil, the number already in the field being wholly unequal to a work which was destined to assume such vast proportions, and to require the co-operation of so great a multitude of laborers, that the day arrived when the Jesuits alone in South America numbered seventeen hundred, out of the *thirteen thousand* who, at the same moment, were preaching the Faith to the heathen in every part of the globe. Amongst the new-comers was one of that privileged order in whom the effects of the first transgression seemed to be almost effaced, and who are admitted, while still in the flesh, to that intimate union with God which the rest of the elect only attain in another life. Joseph Anchieta was in his twentieth year when he arrived in Brazil. Here, during forty-four years, he was to display before the eyes of Christians and Pagans a new example of those astonishing virtues which confirm the one in the obedience of the faith, and attract the other, by the force of their irresistible fascination, to put on its easy yoke. But as we have now to enter a region in which such guides will decline to follow us, we must separate for a while from Mr. Southey, and take for our companions men who do not start aside with instinctive repugnance from the presence of a saint, nor strive to reduce all the creatures of God to their own level, nor believe that the supernatural and the impossible are one and the same thing. We shall hear indeed

* *Brazil and the Brazilians*, by Kidder and Fletcher, ch. xx., p. 368.

what such men say of Anchieta, as we have already heard what they say of St. Francis, and de' Nobili, and their kinsmen in grace; but we must leave them for a moment, lest they disturb us in our contemplation of one to whom even nature, it is said, was sometimes obedient; whom the beasts of the forest attended as companions, forgetting their instincts of carnage; in whose presence the very heathen held their breath, amazed at the works which God wrought by his hand; and who renewed on the other side of the Atlantic the triumphs of that Divine ministry which had so often united heaven and earth in many a province of the old world.*

It was to a people among whom the graces of man's original state were so completely obliterated that they were hardly raised above the brute creation,—"utterly devoid of modesty, without any clothing, and so gross and inhuman as actually to devour one another,"—that Anchieta, confiding only in the omnipotence of the weapons with which the Church arms her apostles, announced the law of Christ. A Saint was needed for such a task, and a Saint was at hand.

Employed at first in teaching Latin in the school which de Nobrega had founded at Piratininga, Anchieta spent his earlier years in patience, humility, and obedience; yearning for the hour when he might proclaim the Holy Name to the tribes of Brazil, but waiting in silence for the permission which he was too meek to anticipate. Meanwhile he composed a Brazilian Grammar, which became afterwards a text-book in Portugal for all who were destined for the American mission. A little later, he produced a Dictionary of the same dialect; then an Exposition of the whole body of Christian doctrine; and soon after, a multitude of Canticles and devout Songs, in four different languages, in order to replace the profane or indecent songs which were in use among the people. His compositions "were continually sung, day and night," says his biographer, "in the streets and thoroughfares, so that the praises of the Christian doctrine everywhere resounded."

At length, having been admitted to the priesthood, he commenced the special work of a missionary. Alone, and with naked feet, fearing neither the pangs of hunger, nor the viper's sting, nor the jaw of the wild beast, he would penetrate the vast forests of this tropical land. On one occasion, having entered a wood, "without any conscious motive, and as if guided by another," he found an aged Indian supported against a tree, who greeted him with the assurance that he had for some time been expecting his arrival. He had journeyed from a remote

* The Life quoted is the Oratorian edition of 1849.

province on the borders of the distant Plata, and could only explain that he had been guided by an impulse which he could not resist to that spot, where, he was told, "he should be taught the right path." When Anchieta, who comprehended that a special grace had brought to him this unexpected neophyte, had unfolded the chief mysteries of the Catholic faith, he replied, "It is thus that I already received, but I knew not how to express them." A little rain-water, lodged in the leaves of some wild thistles, sufficed to baptize him; and when Anchieta returned to his companions, and related what had passed, he added, that he had just buried him, with his own hands, according to the rites of the Church.

But it was not always with such Indians as this that his apostolic journeys brought him in contact. The tribe of the Tamuyas, one of the fiercest and most warlike in Brazil, resenting the gradual advance of the Portuguese, and perhaps dreading the new power of which they might one day become the victims, fell suddenly on the colony of St. Vincent, massacred the white population, and ravaged the whole district with the blind and sanguinary fury of barbarians. Father de Nobrega, touched with compassion for the misery of these Christians, who were already preparing to abandon the country, conceived a project which only the heart of a true missionary could have entertained. Taking with him Anchieta, fitting companion for so perilous a mission, he boldly entered the territory of the Tamuyas. Received at first with unexpected reverence, the ambassadors hastened to propose terms of peace. Two months elapsed in fruitless negotiations, when de Nobrega was suffered to depart, in order to concert new measures at St. Vincent, leaving Anchieta as a hostage in the hands of the savages. As they parted at this critical moment, "Anchieta manifested to Father Nobrega three different circumstances which had been revealed to him in the same night, God then beginning to treat him as His familiar friend, and disclosing to him the hidden secrets of His Divine Providence." The first was, that the town of Biritioca, at the entrance of St. Vincent, from which they were distant at that moment about seventy miles, was already in possession of the savages; the second, that a person well known to Nobrega had been crushed to death; the third, that a Portuguese vessel, laden with supplies, was on the point of entering the port of St. Vincent. On the arrival of Nobrega, the two first statements were immediately confirmed; a little later, the third received its welcome fulfilment.

Meanwhile, Anchieta was alone with the savages, as calm and unmoved as if he had been in the company of little children. Outraged by their intolerable indecency, and his life perpetually menaced by their capricious fury, he had recourse to the usual weapons of apostles, prayer and mortification. "The continence of these Fathers," says Mr. Southey, to whom we may return for a moment, "had occasioned great admiration in their hosts, and they asked Nobrega how it was that he seemed to abhor what other men so ardently desired. He took a scourge out of his pocket, and said that by tormenting the flesh he kept it in subjection." Anchieta, he adds, "who was in the prime of manhood, made a vow to the Virgin that he would compose a poem upon her life, trusting to preserve his own purity by thus fixing his thoughts upon the Most Pure." Yet Mr. Southey, true to his instincts, could elsewhere call the prudent austerities of Catholic missionaries, "the frantic folly of Catholicism."

In spite of the difficulties of his position, Anchieta ceased not to preach the Gospel to his hosts, till "many of them were so well instructed, that he would have admitted them to the Sacrament of Baptism, if he had not feared their want of constancy, and deemed it prudent to leave the gathering of this harvest to his companions." But the more violent members of the tribe, irritated by the failure of the negotiations, and disappointed in their hope of plunder, resolved to put him to death without further delay. They announced to him, therefore, that he was to die at a certain hour, and that afterwards they should feast on his body. With perfect composure of soul and countenance he replied that they would certainly not kill him at the time appointed; and when they asked him in amazement how he could display such assurance, he answered,—that he had learned from the Mother of that God whom he had preached to them that he was not yet to die. His confidence was justified, and after a captivity of three months, a treaty of peace was established, and Anchieta was once more embraced by his fellow-missionaries at St. Vincent.

A few words will indicate his and their mode of life. They had not often a house to live in, and when they had, it was such as Anchieta describes in a letter to St. Ignatius, written from Piratininga, while he acted as professor under Manuel de Paiva. "Our house is composed of a number of long poles, of which the interstices are filled up with clay. The principal apartment, which is fourteen feet in length by ten in width, is at once our school, infirmary, dormitory, refectory, kitchen, and store-room." In fact, it was a cabin with one room, in which twenty-six inmates were lodged. "Yet all our brothers are delighted with it, nor would they exchange this hut for the most magnificent palace. They remember that the Son of God was born in a stable, where there was but little space, and died on a cross, where there was still less." Even Mr. Southey acknowledges that the only food they had was "what the Indians gave them," which was chiefly *mandioc* flour; and Anchieta himself, a man of noble birth, alluding to their rude manner of life, says jestingly, "We may be pardoned for not using napkins at a table on which there is nothing to eat."

It was in the midst of privations which they hardly deemed worthy of notice that these first apostles of Brazil prosecuted their work. Anchieta was one of them, and here is a description of his life. "Barefooted, with no other garment than his cassock, his crucifix and rosary round his neck, the pilgrim's staff and his breviary in his hand, and his shoulders laden with the furniture requisite for an altar, Anchieta advanced into the interior of the country. He penetrated virgin forests, swam across streams, climbed the roughest mountains, plunged into the solitude of the plains, confronted savage beasts, and abandoned himself entirely to the care of Providence. All these fatigues, and all these dangers, had God alone for witness; he braved them for no other motive than to conquer souls. As soon as he caught sight of a man, Anchieta quickened his pace; his bleeding feet stain the rocks and sands of the desert, but he still walks onwards. As he approached the savage, he stretched out his arms towards him, and with words of gentleness strove to retain him beneath the shadow of the cross, which to him was the standard of peace. Sometimes, when the savages rejected his first overtures, he threw himself at their knees, bathing them with his tears, pressing them to his heart, and striving to gain their confidence by every demonstration of love. At first the savages made small account of this abnegation, but the Jesuit was not discouraged. He made himself their servant, and studied their caprices like a slave; he accompanied them in their wanderings, entered into their familiarity, shared their sufferings, their labors, their pleasures." And the result of such a ministry, in which thousands were engaged at the same moment, from Lake Huron to Paraguay, and from Brazil to California, was this: "By degrees he taught them to know God, revealed to them the laws of universal morality, and prepared them for civilization after he had formed them to Christianity. The whole country of Brazil was the theatre of Father Anchieta's ardent zeal; but amidst those vast solitudes, that of Itannia, the land of stones, was his spot of predilection. It was so uncultivated, so rocky, that the very animals seemed to shun it; yet it was here that Anchieta, while toiling for the salvation of this ill-fortuned country, sought repose from the other dangers of his apostleship."* We might refuse to believe that a man like our-

* *Life of Anchieta,* p. 175.

selves could sustain such a life, and such labors during more than forty years, but that every other land presents to us, during the last three centuries, a thousand examples of the same virtues and the same victories.

In 1597 Anchieta died. The six Jesuits who landed with Nobrega had already increased to one hundred and twenty in Brazil alone, and a hundred more now hastened to fill the place of Anchieta, and to continue the work which he had begun. Before we pursue the history of their labors, let us notice briefly, as we have done in former cases, what Protestant writers relate of the men who had now departed.

Of Emanuel de Nobrega, even Mr. Southey says, that he died, "worn out with a life of incessant fatigue. The day before his death, he went abroad, and took leave of all his friends, as if about to undertake a journey. They asked him whither he was going, and his reply was, '*Home to my own country.*' No life could be more actively, more piously, or more usefully employed:"*—and then Mr. Southey, who, like all his class, would undertake to pronounce judgment at any moment on saints and angels, on principalities and powers, adds condescendingly, "the triumphant hope with which it terminated was not the less sure and certain, because of the errors of his belief." Singular belief, to which alone God imparts the virtues and the victories of the apostolic life, while he unaccountably forgets to purify it from its "errors;" singular contradiction, which makes God, in every age, the unintelligible ally of a "corrupt" religion,—so corrupt, in the judgments of its adversaries, that if, as an American Protestant ingenuously observes, their estimate of it were true, "decomposition and the last stages of decay had long ago been passed."†

Yet this Anglican historian adds, under an impulse which even he could not resist, "So well had Nobrega's system been followed by Anchieta and his disciples, that, in the course of half a century, *all the nations along the coast of Brazil*, as far as the Portuguese settlements extended,"—that is, through a range of more than two thousand miles,—"were collected in villages under their superintendence."‡ Never in the history of missions had so marvellous a triumph been obtained, except by the same class of men in the other provinces of America which we are still to visit. It is from Protestant writers alone that we can receive the evidence of that unparalleled triumph, since only by their testimony will it appear credible to their

* Ch. x., p. 310.
† *North American Review*, July, 1858, p. 283.
‡ Ch. xiii., p. 389.

co-religionists. Nobrega died at the close of the sixteenth century, and "in the beginning of the seventeenth," as Ranke observes, "we find the proud edifice of the Catholic Church completely reared in South America. There were five archbishoprics, twenty-seven bishoprics, four hundred monasteries, and innumerable parish churches." And even this does not represent the whole work accomplished in a land which had been tenanted, only a century earlier, by savages who had little more of the nature of man than his external form. "Magnificent cathedrals had sprung up, of which the most splendid of all was, perhaps, that of *Los Angeles*. The Jesuits taught grammar and the liberal arts; a complete system of theological discipline was taught in the universities of Mexico and Lima, ... Conquests gave place to missions, and missions gave birth to civilization. The monks, who taught the natives to read and to sing, taught them also how to sow and to reap, to plant trees and to build houses; and, of course, inspired the profoundest veneration and attachment." So that Ranke might well exclaim, "Catholicism produced a mighty effect in these countries."*

It was the contemplation of the same almost unexampled work, of which we shall better appreciate the character and extent when we have traced it in many provinces, which led Lord Macaulay to observe, in more emphatic phraseology, "The acquisitions of the Catholic Church in the New World have more than compensated her for what she has lost in the Old."†

Of Anchieta, the companion of Nobrega, and partner of his apostolic toils,—whose supernatural life has occasioned still greater perplexity to Protestant historians, they speak in such words as the following: "His self-denial as a missionary," we are told by two American preachers, who vainly endeavored to persuade even a solitary Brazilian to exchange a Divine religion for a human one, "his labor in acquiring and methodizing a barbarous language, and his services to the State, were sufficient to secure to him an honest fame and a precious memory." And then they exhaust all the resources of invective upon his biographers, by whom, they are not ashamed to say, "his real virtues were made to pass for little," that they might magnify "his pretended miracles."‡ If they had really read any history of the Saint, they would have found that his miracles are noticed simply as incidents in the life of one whose virtues were

* Book vii., vol. ii., p. 91.
† *Essay on Ranke's History of the Popes.*
‡ Kidder and Fletcher, ch. vii., p. 115.

more wonderful than his miracles, and perhaps more difficult to imitate.

Mr. Southey, as might be expected, uses similar language. "That Anchieta could work miracles," he says, "was undoubtedly believed both by the Portuguese and by the natives, each according to their own superstition. The former sent volumes of attestations to Rome after his death . . . . . the Tamuyas said there was a power in him which withheld the hands of men, *and this opinion saved his life.*" In other words, both Pagans and Christians were constrained to acknowledge a power of which they continually witnessed the exercise, and which multitudes, of all ranks and classes, solemnly attested on oath. It is Protestants alone, of all mankind, who deride the supernatural as the dream of superstition or the trick of the impostor; because they alone refuse to believe in the sanctity which they know to be unattainable by themselves, and believe to be impossible to others. When Dr. Horsley, a Protestant bishop of no mean repute, exhorted the English House of Lords to discourage all attempts to convert the Hindoos, because "the religion of a country is connected with its government," this Anglican prelate consistently added, that the apostolic power of working miracles having ceased, "he doubted whether the commission had not ceased also." And most of his co-religionists appear to agree with him. "One circumstance," say their representatives, "which must make all sensible and unprejudiced persons suspect very much the veracity of the Jesuits in general, is the account they give of miracles pretended to be wrought in the scenes of their several missions."* Yet these men profess to worship Him who said to the first missionaries, "*Ye shall do greater things than these!*" When did He who gave that promise recall it, or when did He first begin to send forth apostles without the gifts of apostles? And what new God is this, who has neither the will nor the power to interfere in human affairs, and who is as hopelessly fettered by the "laws of nature" as a plant or an insect? Is He, like the God of Baal, "asleep," or is he "on a journey," that he should forget to take note of man and his works? Or have Protestants agreed to accept the definition of the Creator which Kolben says was current among the Hottentots, who considered Him "an excellent man, who dwells far beyond the moon, and does no harm to any one?"

One thing is worthy of remark,—that a religion which professes to be founded on reason should despise all the laws of evidence; and that students of the Bible should scoff at miracles

* Lockman's *Travels of the Jesuits,* preface, p. xiv.

of which the sacred pages contain, according to human belief, some of the least credible examples. If Elias, "a man passible like unto us," forbid dew or rain to descend on the earth save at his word, in order to admonish a guilty king, the tale is venerable and true; if St. Francis Solano bring forth water in the deserts of Chili to save a perishing multitude, and to this hour the miraculous stream is called "the fountain of St. Solano," it is an execrable imposture. If the Eternal "stopped the mouths of lions" lest they should harm his prophet, let us marvel and adore; if the panther crouched by the side of His servant Anchieta as he prayed at midnight in the forest, or the viper dared not sting his naked foot when he trod upon it in the noonday, it is an impudent invention. If iron float at the bidding of Eliseus, though only to save a woodman's axe, let us fall down and magnify the Lord; if Anchieta is upheld on the waters of the San Francisco, that an apostle might not perish out of the earth, we should scorn the superstition which believes the fact, and the impostor who relates it. If a dead man spring to life again, as the Scripture affirms, because his corpse touched the bones of a Saint whom it was the will of God to honor,* who will refuse to praise and admire? If St. Augustine record the same fact of the bones of St. Stephen, in his own church, and before the very congregation who witnessed it, let us smile at the despicable fraud. If Agabus foretell a famine over the whole earth, "which came to pass in the days of Claudius,"† we should honor the prophet, though only a man like ourselves; if the Blessed Anchieta predict a coming storm when the sky had been cloudless for six months, and a vast multitude witness the miraculous rain-fall which ensued, let us be sure it was only the crafty jugglery of a priest, or the gross credulity of a besotted crowd. If Divine wisdom employ the voice of an ass to convey a warning to the rebellious prophet, let us accept without surprise both the messenger and his message; if Divine power command the jaguar to stop in full career at the feet of St. Francis Solano, and humbly kneel before the servant of the Most High, let us welcome the improbable tale with a shout of derision. If Elias raise the dead from corruption, though only to comfort a sorrowing widow, it shall be the text of our songs and our meditations; if St. Francis Xavier open a grave, in the presence of thousands, to show a whole nation what the God of Christians can do, it is a pitiable fiction. If Elias is fed by ravens or by angels, and then fast forty days and nights, let no

* 4 Kings xiii. 21.
† Acts xi. 28.

man doubt either his eating or his abstinence; if de' Nobili or de Britto instruct thousands unto righteousness by a whole life of austerity and mortification, it is only "the frantic folly of Catholicism." If the face of St. Stephen shone with glory, so that all who stood by "saw his face as it had been the face of an angel," let us acknowledge that grace can illuminate even this mortal body; if the blessed Peter Claver was transfigured before the eyes of a hundred witnesses, who saw the light play round his head, and covered their eyes with their hands, let us pity the degrading superstition which can accept the wretched tale. If a "handkerchief" or an "apron," which had only touched the body of St. Paul, could heal diseases and put demons to flight,* what more natural than that the Most High should thus sanction, before men and angels, the Catholic use of relics? If the same thing be told of St. Bernard or St. Philip Neri, of Anchieta, or St. Francis Regis, let us rend the heavens with our cry of anger, or stop our ears in indignant scorn.

Perhaps the true explanation of the inconsistency which accepts the one class of miracles without question, and rejects the other without inquiry, is found in the fact that very few Protestants have any more real faith in the one than in the other. They would deal in precisely the same manner with both, but that they have no pressing reason to reject the first, while they have an urgent personal motive for denying the last. Yet even the Hindoo and the Mahometan, witnesses against the credulous incredulity of modern sects, have manifested, with all their faults, a deeper insight than they into the mystery of holiness, and have confessed, in every age, that a god who ceased to display the power which he had once exerted, or to bestow the gifts which he had once conferred, would be only an impotent divinity, unworthy to reign over immortal men, and from whose palsied hand it would be lawful to pluck the feeble and useless sceptre. The instincts of the human heart, of the Pagan as well as of the Christian, reject such a god as Protestantism has invented; and the only race of men on earth who deny the wonder-working might of the True and Holy One in His saints and apostles, are they who acknowledge in their inmost soul, without shame and without regret, that it never has been and never can be manifested in themselves. Who dreams of an Anglican miracle, or a Wesleyan prophet, or a Presbyterian saint? Who can imagine Middleton bidding a stream spring forth in the plains of Bengal? or Buchanan respected by panthers? or Judson transfigured? or Heber raising the dead?

* Acts xix. 12.

This is no place to discuss at large the credibility of miracles. To the Christian, who is wisely familiar with Holy Scripture, and comprehends that the miracles of the New Testament are not isolated and abnormal, but typical and characteristic facts, proper to the whole dispensation which they adorn and illustrate, their cessation would be more inexplicable than their continuance. If they are rejected, it is by men who know neither God nor themselves; who, in spite of their profession of religion, have an instinctive fear and hatred of the supernatural, and who would rather believe that God is eternally silent than confess that it is in the Church alone that He deigns to speak. They would not, indeed, believe a miracle, even if they saw one; but what they *fear* in them is their exhibition of Divine power, what they *hate* is their testimony to the Catholic faith.*

Yet modern science, not always hostile to revealed truth, has lately protested, by the voice of one of its greatest adepts, against this irrational skepticism. A well-known English mathematician, refuting by a scientific process the infidel *formula* of Hume, has declared, and elaborately proved, that however that *formula* be applied, it will *always* be false. Hume had said that no amount of evidence can prove the truth of a miracle. Mr. Babbage, testing the proposition by a purely analytical method, arrives at exactly the opposite conclusion. "If independent witnesses can be found," he says, "who speak truth more frequently than falsehood,"—surely no intolerable postulate,—"it is *always* possible to assign a number of independent witnesses, the improbability of the falsehood of whose concurring testimony shall be *greater* than that of the miracle itself."† Yet the shallow incredulity of the Sects, though it annuls all the laws of evidence, and sets aside the most rigorous conclusions of science, affects to be a protest on behalf of the human intellect against the thraldom of superstition!‡

* "Image parfaite de Notre Seigneur Jésus-Christ, l'Eglise est en butte aux persécutions du monde, non pas parce que le monde oublie les prodiges qu'elle opère,.. mais tout au contraire parce que le monde *a en horreur* ces témoignages, . . . *ces miracles qui le condamnent.*" Donoso Cortes, *Œuvres*, tome iii., p. 128; ed. Veuillot. "The Church owes her very existence to miracles, and without them cannot at all conceive herself. . . . Our idealists and spiritualists have no need of miracles for the confirmation of their faith. No, truly, for their faith is one of their own making, and not the faith in Christ; and it would indeed be singular if God were to confirm a faith fabricated by man." Moehler, *Symbolism*, ii., 20.

† *Ninth Bridgewater Treatise*, app., p. 202, note E.

‡ "Miracles are evidently not only *not* impossibilities, but even not *improbabilities*. . . . Whatever is possible may occur, and whatever occurs ought, on the proper evidence, to be believed." Hugh Miller, *Footprints of the Creator*, p. 242.

If now we continue the history of missions in Brazil, and take Mr. Southey once more as our guide, we shall come to a new order of events. Hitherto we have seen men gradually converting the savages of half a continent by the display of supernatural virtues; and, except in a few instances which we have not stayed to notice, as in the case of the martyrs Soza and Correa, who fell in the very beginning of this apostolic warfare, accomplishing their work without even the customary tribute of blood. But that sacred debt was sure to be paid sooner or later, and we are about to witness the martyrdom of sixty-eight missionaries at once, massacred, not by pagan savages, but by more merciless heretics, whose fury no virtues could disarm, and who, in many a land, have made a compact with the heathen to slay the missionaries of the Cross.

In 1570, Father Ignatius Azevedo, by the nomination of St. Francis Borgia, conducted thirty-nine Fathers of the Society of Jesus from Madeira to Brazil. Thirty more started at the same moment from Lisbon, in two other vessels, as well as a number of postulants who had still to prove the strength of their vocation. The day after the ship which carried Azevedo sailed from Madeira, four French vessels, under the command of the Huguenot Jacques Sourie, bore down upon it. Sourie, says Mr. Southey, "was a man as little disposed to show mercy to any Catholic priests, as they would have been to show it towards him. . . . and he did by the Jesuits as they would have done by him and all of his sect—put them to death. One of the novices escaped, being in a lay habit, the rest were thrown overboard, some living, some dying, some dead." So smoothly does this English historian relate a tale which does not even provoke from him any other comment than this, that "when the tidings reached Madeira, the remaining missionaries celebrated the triumph of their comrades, a triumph which many of them were yet to partake." But this singular festival only inspired the mirth of Mr. Southey, who considers that the *Te Deum* chanted in honor of martyrs by men who in a few days were to be martyrs themselves, "was as much the language of policy as of fanaticism." St. Philip Neri would rather have said, as he was wont to say to the priests departing from Rome for the English mission, "*Salvete flores martyrum!*" St. Paul would have added, in his solemn accents, "*Quibus dignus non erat mundus!*"

A few days later, "one English and four French cruisers," according to the tranquil narrative of Mr. Southey, who does not mention that this time it was the Calvinist Capdeville who commanded, fell upon the remainder of the missionary fleet, and did their work so effectually, that "of sixty-nine missionaries whom Azevedo took out from Lisbon, only *one*, who was left behind at one of the ports where they touched, arrived at Brazil."

The blood of sixty-eight martyrs could hardly fail to win new graces for Brazil, and from that hour the work of conversion advanced with tenfold success. It was said, as Mr. Southey records with indignation, that supernatural incidents accompanied this holocaust of martyrs, whose fires the waves of the deep sea could not extinguish. "After Azevedo was killed, the heretics," Mr. Southey merrily observes, "could not force out of his hand a picture of the Virgin," which the martyr held in his dying grasp, and which, the English historian adds, with an appropriate and well-timed jest, "was a copy more miraculous than its miraculous original." This picture, found still in his embrace by the crew of another ship which sailed over the spot where the body had been flung into the ocean, "was shown," adds Mr. Southey, "by the Jesuits at St. Salvador, with heroic impudence, with the print of Azevedo's bloody fingers upon it;" but "ecclesiastical historians," he remarks, "enlarge as they go on, because every one adds his lie to the heap." If a martyrology were composed by demons, it is perhaps thus that they would write it.

Sixty years after the martyrdom of Azevedo and his companions, when their successors had reaped the full harvest of which the early seeds had been fertilized by their blood, a second drama of the same kind was enacted, and once more the knife and the axe were wielded by Protestants. This time it was the Dutch Calvinists who made war on defenceless missionaries, and here is Mr. Southey's narrative of their operations.

The unconverted natives of the district of Rio Grande had carried devastation into the territory of Pernambuco, and though chastised by the troops under the command of Manuel Mascarenhas, were still planning in their forests new expeditions. Soldiers could not reach these swift-footed marauders, but there were men in Brazil of the school of de Nobrega and Azevedo who could. Mr. Southey will tell us who they were. With no armor but prayer, and no weapon but the cross which they bore on their bosom, they advanced without fear into the retreats of the barbarians. "The Jesuits pacified them," says the Protestant annalist, "and brought *a hundred and fifty hordes* into alliance with the Portuguese." So true is that saying of Sir Woodbine Parish, who lived long in South America, that "the labors of the Jesuits were eventually more successful than all the military forces," and that, in every province of the land, on both sides of the Andes, and by the banks of all the rivers which flow from them, "these indefatigable missionaries reduced one tribe after another to a state of comparative civilization."

But the savage of the northeastern provinces was now to find an ally more fierce and cruel than himself, and by whose example he was to learn, that if there were Christians who were valiant only to suffer, to labor, and to bless, there were others who made religion itself the pretext of crimes from which even the savages would have shrunk. It was on Good Friday, in the year 1633, that the Dutch Protestants, passing at midnight through the smoking ruins of Olinda, attacked Garassu in the early morn, while the inhabitants were assembled at the celebration, proper to that sorrowful day, of the Mass of the Presanctified. The moment was skilfully chosen. No ignorant Tamuya or Chiquito, no blundering Mohawk or Oneida, could have matched the Calvinist in his craft; no bloodhound could have torn his prey with more pitiless cruelty, when once he had fastened his fangs upon it. "The men who came in their way," says Mr. Southey, "were slaughtered; the women were stripped, and the plunderers with brutal cruelty tore away ear-rings through the ear-flap, and cut off fingers for the sake of the rings which were upon them. Having plundered and burnt the town, they set out on their return, taking with them as prisoners some Franciscans, whom for their profession they especially hated, and driving in mockery before them the priest in his vestments, just as they had forced him from the altar."* It was thus they celebrated Good Friday.

The next year they attacked Paraiba, apparently because "it contained a Misericordia, a Benedictine Convent, a Carmelite, and a Capuchin." The inhabitants had capitulated, after a gallant defence, on the promise of "free exercise of the Catholic religion and the peaceable enjoyment of their property." "The most atrocious cruelties," says Mr. Southey, for once taking part with the victims, "were exercised upon these brave people by the conquerors, and they who possessed any property were *tortured* till they paid the full sum which was demanded as a life-ransom. By these means the Dutch raised twenty-eight thousand crowns, and it is by such means that they have rendered their history as infamous, and their names as detestable, in the East and in the West, as in their own country their deeds have been glorious."†

Yet these men professed to be exponents of the "reformed religion," and missionaries of the Gospel. It is true that even Mr. Southey admits, that it was only "for the sake of raising

* Vol. i., ch. xv., p. 486.
† P. 509.

sugar and tobacco" that they invaded Brazil; but they carried their religious ideas with them, and so, in the words of another historian, "from assassins they transformed themselves into missionaries." They were more successful in the first character than in the last. "They sent out preachers, and controversial books in the Spanish language were circulated;" but Mr. Southey shrewdly adds, "if the Brazilians hated their conquerors as heretics, they hated heresy still more because it was the religion of their oppressors. The Dutch have always been a cruel people, ... and there is no nation whose colonial history is so inexcusable and inexpiably disgraceful to human nature." He had perhaps read their history in Japan and Ceylon.

The Dutch were not destined to triumph in Brazil, either as soldiers or missionaries, but they were not finally ejected till a later period. Meanwhile, they continued to exhibit a new example of the nature and influence of Protestant missions, a new proof that they are everywhere, as we have said, the worst impediment to the conversion of the heathen, not only because they obstruct the ministry of the true apostles, but because their agents teach the barbarian to despise a religion of which *they* are the professors. In 1637, in all the districts under their rule, "the Catholics were ordered to confine their processions within the walls of the churches; no new church was to be built without permission from the senate; no marriages celebrated until the banns had been published after the Dutch manner," &c. There was even a certain refinement of ingenuity in some of their cruelties. Taking advantage of well-known customs which piety had consecrated in Brazil, they ordered, "that those persons who, when they created new sugar-works, chose to have them blessed, were to have the office performed"—by a Protestant minister! The Count of Nassau, who was their supreme ruler, "received orders to restrict toleration within the narrowest bounds, and the reformed clergy were calling upon him to enforce these imprudent orders."

In 1639, "Dutch missionaries labored," we are still quoting Mr. Southey, "to teach a Lutheran instead of a Popish creed." They failed indeed, but this was only, Mr. Southey considers, because "implements of conversion were wanting;" that is, "Lutheran theology had nothing wherewith to supply the deficiency of saints, images, beads, crosses, &c." The explanation seems to fall below the gravity of history. Lutheran theology, which the Brazilians rejected so decisively, does not appear to produce happy results even among those who profess to admire it. In Lutheran Prussia, where there is no deficiency of crosses and other symbols, it has all but extirpated Christianity; in Brazil, as we learn from two Protestant ministers in

1857, its results have been of the same unpleasant character. In "the Lutheran community at Nova Fribourgo," a colony of German settlers, they report that "there was but little Christian vitality; Lutherans of the old Church and State school are among the very last men to propagate the Gospel."* We need not wonder, then, that the Dutch failed to propagate such a gospel in Brazil.

But if they could not convert, they could destroy. In spite of every menace, and of unceasing cruelty and exactions, the people still clung to their old pastors. There was only one remedy for this obstinacy, and the Dutch adopted it. "The members of every monastic order were commanded within the space of a month to quit the Dutch possessions on the continent. The needful measure," it is Mr. Southey who speaks, "was carried into effect with brutal cruelty. The Dutch stripped them of their habits, and turned them ashore in their shirts and drawers, in such remote situations that most of them perished."†

When, in 1642, the Portuguese rose at last against the assassins, and recaptured Maranham, "those who were spared owed their lives," says our historian, "to the interference of a priest." He had asserted not long before that any priest "would have put all the sect to death," but now he relates that "he had borne the crucifix before his comrades as a standard beneath which they were to march to victory, and he stretched out that crucifix *to protect his enemies* now when the victory was won." But with all his efforts he could only save the other foreigners, because "a Catholic feeling incensed the conquerors against the Dutch, more hated for their heretical opinions than for their cruelty and perfidiousness." But we have heard enough of the Dutch, and it is time to return to the labors of a different order of missionaries.

In the middle of the seventeenth century, when the triumph of Christianity was already assured in Brazil, Portugal gave to this favored mission another of those apostolic workmen of whom in that age she produced so many. Father Antonio Vieyra, the friend of kings and the counsellor of statesmen, who had rejected all the honors of the world, and had told his admiring sovereign, when he entreated him to accept a bishopric in Europe, that he would not exchange the lowly habit of a missionary "for all the mitres in the Portuguese monarchy," had now entered Brazil. During many years this accomplished gentleman "ministered among the Indians and Negroes, for which purpose he made himself master, not only of the Tupi,

* Kidder and Fletcher, ch. xv., p. 29.
† Vol. ii., ch. xx., p. 65.

but also of the Angolan tongue." He was one, as Mr. Southey confesses, who "must ever hold a place, not only amongst the greatest writers, but amongst the greatest statesmen of his country." It is nothing new in the history of apostles that such a man should choose to devote his life to Indians and Negroes. The Catholic religion, in every age, has been able both to inspire and to reward such sacrifices. Once he wrote to the young prince of Portugal, who loved and honored him as a father, to send fresh laborers to Brazil; and he added, "I ask no provision for those who come, God will provide; what I ask is, that they may come, and that they may be many, and filled with zeal."

It is curious to see what the malice of heresy could force even a scholar and a poet to say of such a man as this—who was not only scholar and poet, but philosopher, orator, and statesman. "His devotion," says Mr. Southey, "had its root in superstition and madness." Festus estimated in the same manner the devotion of St. Paul, because he, like the English writer, could not understand an apostle. Yet he adds immediately, contradicting himself at every page, "Vieyra proceeded diligently with projects worthy of his order and of himself." Fifty Indian villages were organized by his labors to the north of Maranham, "along an extent of four hundred leagues of coast." So wonderful was the success of his labors, that on the 15th of August, 1658, he celebrated a solemn Mass of thanksgiving in commemoration of a treaty then concluded, "in the name of Jesus Christ," with the chiefs and representatives of more than *one hundred thousand natives.**

Such a victory might have contented even apostolic ambition, but for Vieyra it was only a motive for fresh exertions. He now resolved, therefore, says our historian, "to pursue the same system of civilization up the great rivers, and in the islands in the mouth of the Orellana." Two Jesuits were sent up the river of the Tocantins, a perilous journey of nine hundred miles, "to reduce a tribe of Topinambazes," famous for their courage and ferocity. "They were old enemies of the Para settlers," which increased tenfold the perils of the mission, but this did not daunt the companions of Vieyra, animated with his own spirit; and the Protestant historian is obliged to confess, that "these very enemies followed the missionaries, and agreed to send deputies back with them, who should treat concerning peace, and arrange measures for their conversion." More than a thousand of these hitherto irreclaimable barbarians, "of whom three hundred were warriors," returned with the Fathers to the

* Crétineau Joly, tome v., p. 114.

camp of their hated foes; and when the governor, Vidal—a man of such qualities that Vieyra wrote to the king, "if he had been in India, it would never have been lost to Portugal," —saw this multitude of neophytes approaching, "stern and inexorable as he was in war, he is said to have wept for joy at beholding this wild flock brought within the fold of Christ." Vieyra himself, though he might have been sitting in the courts of princes, started immediately to bring in the remainder of the tribe.

In every direction similar expeditions were undertaken, and always with the same results. No river was so broad or swift as to check their rapid march, no forest so dark or impenetrable as to bar their way. Whatever man, aided by the might of God, could do, they did. And the Indians, dazzled by their fortitude and valor, could resist neither the heroic courage which far surpassed their own, nor the patience which subdued and wore out their frowardness, nor the charity which they admired before they understood it. Everywhere and always, even by Protestant testimony, these apostles were the same. Take a few examples out of thousands. When the military expedition of Coelho against the people of the Sierra de Ibiapaba had completely failed, "and led to his own disgrace," the missionaries, says Mr. Southey, "prepared a peaceable expedition in the hope of reducing and civilizing its inhabitants. These mountains extended about eighty leagues in length, and twenty in breadth; they rise in waves, one towering above another. . . . To ascend them is the hard labor of four hours, in which hands and knees, as well as feet, must frequently be exerted." And when the missionaries, often men delicately nurtured, and of gentle lineage, had surmounted these first difficulties, they found themselves in presence of the Tapuyas, "the oldest race in Brazil," and so inconceivably barbarous, that "they ate their own dead as the last demonstration of love."* They had repulsed the soldiers of Portugal, but were vanquished by a few unarmed Jesuits.

In 1603, Father Rodriguez conducted another apostolic band to the territory of the cannibal Aymores. "The people ridiculed his project," says the Protestant historian, "thinking it impossible that the Aymores, fleshed as they were with human meat, could be reclaimed from their habits of cannibalism." Yet the savages themselves said of him and his companions, when they afterwards recounted their own submission, "The Fathers were good men who had neither bows nor arrows, nor ever did wrong to any one, and nothing which they requested

* Southey, ch. xiii., p. 377.

was to be denied." And so "two villages were soon formed, the one containing twelve hundred Aymores, the other four; and the captaincy, which had hitherto with difficulty been preserved from utter destruction by the help of frequent succors from Bahia, was effectually delivered from its enemies."*

In 1657, Fathers Emanuel Pires and Francis Gonsalvez were the first to ascend the Rio Negro, as Father Samuel Fritz was the first to trace the course of the Orellana, converting the Omaguas on the way—"a people," as Southey observes, "so famous in the age of adventure, and still, in his day, the most numerous of all the river tribes: thirty of their villages are marked upon his map." Before him, Fathers Christoval d'Acuna and Andres de Artieda, the one rector of a college, the other professor of theology at Quito, had accomplished an equally perilous mission at the request of the viceroy; for even the military adventurers of that age dared not accept, and refused to attempt, undertakings which the missionaries alone, in the interests of religion and science, could be persuaded to embrace, since they "were not merely fearless of martyrdom, but ambitious of it." We shall see hereafter how many found the crown which they sought. After a voyage of fifteen months, amid privations which we need not attempt to describe, Pires and Gonsalvez returned, bringing with them between six and seven hundred disciples; but Gonsalvez died of his fatigues. A little later, two others, who had taken another route, came back in their turn, "followed by more than two thousand Indians," who had consented to accept Christianity and civilization.†

In every province, and in each successive year, the same arduous apostolate continued. In 1662, Father Raymond de Santa Cruz perished by violence in the waters of the Pastaza. "His was truly a noble and well-spent life," says an English Protestant. "His usual dress consisted of an old battered hat, a coarse cotton shirt, and a pair of sandals;"—this was the "*gorgeous ceremonial*," by which Catholic missionaries, we are told, gain their converts!—"and his mode of life was more simple than that of the Indians who surrounded him . . . but it should be remembered that there were many other intrepid and devoted men on the banks of these rivers, at the same time, who were equally zealous in preaching to the Indians, and who generally, like Father Raymond, met with a violent death, as the welcome reward of their exertions."‡

As early as 1663, the fruits of these patient toils were so

* P. 388.

† Southey, p. 517.

‡ *Expeditions into the Valley of the Amazons*, by Clements R. Markham, F.R.G.S., introd., p. xxx.

abundant, that, as Mr. Markham notices, even on the banks of the upper Marânon "there were fifty-six thousand baptized Indians;" and from 1640 to 1682, no less than thirty-three different Christian settlements had been established in that region by this company of martyrs and apostles.*

In 1695, Henry Richler obtained the crown of martyrdom. "The most heroic devotion," says Mr. Markham, "could alone have enabled him to face the difficulties which surrounded him. During twelve years, he performed forty difficult journeys, through dense forests, or in canoes on rapid and dangerous rivers. He never took any provisions with him, but wandered bare-footed and half-naked through the tangled underwood, trusting wholly to Providence for support. His efforts were rewarded with success, and having learnt some of the Indian languages, he at last surrounded himself with followers."

Such were the men and such the toils which won all South America to the Cross. If sometimes they failed, or seemed to fail, it was only for a brief space. When Soto Mayor, one of the most valiant of this band of heroes, was rejected by a tribe which refused to be converted, he left with them his crucifix, assuring them with accents of patient love, that the God whom it represented would yet incline their hearts to truth. And when he was gone, their souls were stirred within them by the memory of his apostolic words; and one day they arrived in solemn procession, asking to be admitted to baptism, and bringing back with all reverence the crucifix, of which Mr. Southey, true to his instincts, observes, "*This idol* was deposited in the church of the Jesuits' college, where it was long venerated with especial devotion."

In 1661, the corrupt Portuguese traders, whose traffic in slaves had been well-nigh ruined by Vieyra and his companions, stirred up an insurrection, and cast the Fathers into prison. Vieyra himself, says the Protestant historian, "though treated more cruelly than any of his companions, betrayed not the slightest mark of irritation or impatience. . . . . An heroic mind, a clear conscience, and an enthusiastic sense of duty, produced in him that peace which passeth all understanding." They were dragged on board ship, and dispatched to Portugal, with a memorial to the king, setting forth their misdemeanors, and charging them with having ruined the prosperity of the colony. They were reinstated by a royal edict in the following year, with a sharp admonition to their accusers, but from that hour their enemies took counsel together to accomplish their destruction.

* *Expeditions*, &c., introd., p. xxx.

In 1676, Brazil being now divided into the three dioceses of Bahia, Pernambuco, and Rio de Janeiro, the first colony of Franciscan nuns arrived. "Such institutions," observes Mr. Southey, who records the arrival of these ladies and the establishment of their convent, "are better receptacles than Bedlam for the largest class of maniacs."* Presently, as if the expression pleased his taste, he calls even Anchieta, D'Almeida, and Vieyra—men adorned with every highest gift, both of nature and grace, which the Creator bestows on His creature—"harmless maniacs." If we quote such language, it is only to show how educated Protestants judge the men whom they cannot comprehend, and the works which they dare not imitate.

In reading words now almost habitual with Protestant critics, and of which we have seen too many examples in these pages, we are involuntarily reminded of the formidable sentence of Holy Writ, which announces the final lot both of the accused and their accusers. When the former, we are told, shall have received their crown, the latter, "seeing it, shall be troubled with terrible fear, and shall say within themselves, repenting, and groaning for anguish of spirit, These are they whom we had sometime in derision, and for a parable of reproach. *We fools esteemed their life madness*, and their end without honor. Behold, how they are numbered with the children of God, and their lot is among the saints."†

In 1696, Vieyra died, at the age of ninety. He had been seventy-five years a Jesuit, and Mr. Southey remarks, with real or affected surprise, that "his vows were never repented." He adds also, that "he had outlived the vexations as well as the joys of life; his enemies were gone before him to their account, and his virtues and talents were acknowledged and respected as they deserved."‡

We must hasten to an end. Twenty provinces still claim our attention, and we have barely glanced at the history of one. A hundred names might be added to those of Nobrega and Anchieta, of D'Almeida and Vieyra, but we have no space to recount them. They will pardon our silence. They are our fathers and kinsmen, but who can number all the links in such a genealogy? We have spoken only of the Fathers of the Society of Jesus, yet the children of St. Francis and St. Dominic, to whom America owes so much, might well have claimed the tribute of our respectful homage. "The Franciscans," says Mr.

* Vol. ii., ch. xxviii., p. 571.
† Wisdom v., 2–5.
‡ Vol. iii., ch. xxxi., p. 34.

Clements Markham, though he appreciates their courage rather than the religion which inspired it, "continued during a century and a half to send devoted men into the forests, who preached fearlessly, explored vast tracts of previously unknown land, and usually ended their days by being murdered by the very savages whom they had come to humanize."* In 1701, two Franciscan Fathers were martyred by the Aruans. Mr. Southey relates what befell their mutilated bodies. "They found them in a state of perfect preservation, although they had lain six months upon the ground, exposed to animals, insects, and all accidents of weather, and although their habits were rotten." It was no miracle, he adds, for he did not believe in miracles, "but fraud cannot be suspected." The evidence was so conclusive, that even he could not venture to reject it. "The whole city of Belem," he says, saw the bodies, which were ultimately interred in the Franciscan church in that town.

Finally, if we ask what signs there are at this hour in Brazil of the presence of the apostolic workmen of whose toils we may not offer here a more minute account; if we inquire how far, in this case, the promise has been fulfilled which declared of old, "*They* shall know their seed among the Gentiles, and their offspring in the midst of peoples;" it is an American Protestant who informs us, in 1856, that there are still, after all the calamities which have befallen that empire, "*eight hundred thousand domesticated Indians*," who call upon the name of Jesus, and invoke the protection of His Mother.†

Before we add a few words, in order to complete the narrative, upon the present state of Brazil, the fate of her earlier apostles claims a moment's attention. For two centuries they had toiled, with results which perhaps none but the Franciscans had ever rivalled, and having won the approval of God were now to receive their usual reward from man. St. Ignatius had dared to ask, it was his latest prayer, that his children "might be always persecuted." The petition, we know, has been heard. In 1753, the brother of the Marquis de Pombal was made Captain-general of Para and Maranham, and from that hour the fate of the Jesuits was sealed. By this man the requisite pleadings were prepared, and they were accepted with eagerness by the conspirators at Lisbon, as even Mr. Southey observes, "notwithstanding their falsehood and palpable inconsistency."‡ "A true statesman," says the same writer, singular witness in such a cause, "would assuredly have thought that

* *Valley of the Amazons*, introd., p. xxi.
† *Life in Brazil*, by Thomas Ewbank, ch. xxxviii., p. 432.
‡ Vol. iii., ch. xl., p. 510.

the Jesuits in America were worthy of his especial favor, protection, and encouragement." But Pombal, envious of a greatness which he could not share, had resolved to crush them. He knew that the Brazilian merchants would approve his design, for the Jesuits, as Mr. Southey remarks, "were the only unpopular order, because they were the only missionaries who uniformly opposed the tyranny of the Portuguese." Of the charges brought against them, the same unsuspicious witness says, "*All that are not absolutely false, are merely frivolous.*"* But Pombal was willing to suborn false witnesses, and if these had not been forthcoming, would have done without them. And so the decree went forth that the Jesuits should be banished.

Twice already they had been expelled from Brazil, and twice they had been restored amid the acclamations of the people. This time their exile was to last nearly a century. From Para *one hundred and fifteen* Fathers were deported, from Bahia *one hundred and sixty-eight*, from Rio Janeiro *one hundred and forty-five;* in all five hundred and twenty-eight, from this province alone. "The number expelled from all the Spanish Indies amounted to five thousand six hundred and seventy-seven."† We shall see hereafter what befell the Fathers in the other provinces. And this was the manner of their deportation: "They were stowed as closely as negro slaves," says Mr. Southey, whom we will quote to the last, "and confined below decks on the voyage to S. Luiz." Yet, as even he observes, "they were men whose innocence and virtue must most certainly have been known." And then he adds, his better nature triumphing for once over the instincts of heresy and unbelief, "They were treated with extreme cruelty upon the voyage; when they were suffering the most painful thirst, the captain would not allow, even to the dying, an additional drop of water, to moisten their lips, nor would he permit them the consolation of receiving the last sacrament in death. Five of them died (in one ship) under this unhuman usage."

And when at last this company of apostles reached Europe, followed by the sighs and tears of a whole continent, for eighteen weary years they languished in prison, till M. de Pombal passed to his account, with the horrible jest on his lips, "that the Jesuits were the longest lived body of men he ever knew." But they followed him to the judgment, for, as the historian relates, "in a few years thev were almost extinguished."

* P. 518.

† Southey, vol. iii., ch. xlii., p. 614.

Pombal had disappeared forever, but not so the Society of Jesus. In 1817, the revolted Spanish colonies of South America, justifying their separation, reproached their former mistress, in these earnest words: "You arbitrarily deprived us of the Jesuits, to whom we owe our social state, our civilization, all our instruction, and services with which we can never dispense." In 1834, the Argentine Republic recalled them with acclamation; in 1842, Columbia solicited their return; in 1843, they were re-established in Mexico; in Chili, they are once more the model and the admiration of their brethren. And where are their persecutors? When the Jesuits returned to the province of Coimbra, in 1832, more than one of them hastened to the town of Pombal, in order to offer in secret the suffrages of charity over the grave of the Marquis. To their amazement they found that the once imperious statesman had been so completely forgotten by all but them, that his body, covered with a ragged cloth, had remained without sepulture from 1782! But there is nothing in this fact to surprise us. The world, which pursues them with its heartless applause, abandons its heroes when the sword or the staff falls from their nerveless hands; and the Church alone, more tender than friends, more compassionate than kinsfolk, is found weeping over the tombs of her enemies, and praying for the pardon of their sins.*

And now let us see what were the results of their expulsion. Only twenty-five years after their departure, the noblest colony which Portugal had ever possessed was in ruins. "Decay and desolation," as Mr. Southey confesses, had succeeded "the prosperity which had prevailed in the time of the missionaries; houses falling to pieces; fields overgrown with wood; grass in the market-places; the lime-kilns, the potteries, the manufactories of calico"—for the Jesuits had introduced all these—"*in ruins.*"

Pombal, says the same writer whom we have so often quoted, while affecting to care for the welfare of the Indians, "removed the only persons who could have co-operated with him for this end; the only persons who would have exerted themselves disinterestedly to promote the improvement and happiness of the Indians; the only persons who for the love of God would have devoted themselves dutifully, cheerfully, and zealously to the service of their fellow-creatures. In their place such men as would undertake the office for the love of gain, were substi-

* A modern traveller relates of Joseph II., the Julian of Austria, "Nowhere is his name breathed; it is as if he had never existed, or as if a curse lay on his memory." *Austria*, by J. G. Kohl, p. 233 (1843).

tuted, and the immediate consequences were injurious in every way. The laws in favor of the Indians"—the missionaries had procured the abolition of slavery—"were infringed more daringly; the directors themselves had an interest in oppressing them, because their profits were in proportion to the work performed; they had the power of compelling them to work, and they had neither authority, influence, nor inclination to check those vices which certainly were not practised under the moral discipline of the *Aldeas*"—the Jesuit Reductions. "That process of civilization which had been going on so rapidly and with such excellent effect"—in an earlier volume Mr. Southey had scoffed at this civilization—"was stopped at once and forever; and a rapid depopulation began, because free scope was now given to drunkenness and to every other vice, and because many of the Indians fled into the wilderness, when they found that their state of filial subjection was exchanged for a servitude which had nothing either to sanctify or to soften it."* And it is Mr. Southey who writes this undesigned panegyric of Catholic missionaries!

But Mr. Southey is not the only writer of his class who makes these confessions. Dr. Kidder and Mr. Fletcher, two Protestant ministers, whose eager libels on the Catholic religion would perhaps excite our indignation if it were possible to treat them seriously, admit that the virtues of the Jesuits proved their ruin. "Their benevolence and their philanthropic devotedness to the Indians brought down upon them the hatred of their countrymen, the Portuguese."† "Centuries will not repair the evil done by their sudden expulsion," says a candid English traveller. . . . "They had been the protectors of a persecuted race, the advocates of mercy, the founders of civilization, and their patience under their unmerited sufferings forms not the least honorable trait in their character."‡ Prince Adalbert of Prussia, though apparently insensible to apostolic virtues, which he seems to have only contemplated with dull apathy or peevish dislike, confesses that "decay commenced with the expulsion of the Jesuits."§ Prince Maximilian of Wied-Neuwied, another modern traveller in Brazil, who observes that at Villa Nova, which he visited, "the Jesuits had collected six thousand Indians," adds "but most of them were driven away by the hard service exacted by the crown, and by the

* P. 534.

† Ch. xx., p. 368.

‡ *Journal of a Voyage to Brazil*, by Lady Calcott, pp. 13, 36 (1824).

§ *Travels in Brazil*, &c., by H. R. H. Prince Adalbert of Prussia, vol. ii., p. 149, ed. Schomburgh.

slavish manner in which they were treated."* Mr. Gardner also, who speaks, like these German princes, from actual observation, says: "It is handed down from father to son, particularly among the middle and lower classes of Brazil, that the destruction of the Jesuitical power was a severe loss to the well-being of the country. There are of course but few alive now (1846) who have personal recollection of the excellent men who formed the Company of Jesus, but the memory of them will long remain; I have always heard them spoken of with respect and with regret."† Lastly, for we need not multiply testimonies which we shall find to be identical for every province of America, another vehement Protestant goes a step further, and contrasts the Jesuits, as Lord Macaulay was wont to do, with the worldly and covetous missionaries of his own creed. "The early missionaries who ventured into the prairies and savannahs of America gave many indications of being animated by an apostolic spirit. . . . Destitute themselves, they had no lucrative employments to offer in the shape of subaltern offices in a richly endowed missionary establishment, to tempt the natives to enlist as retainers in the household of Christianity. They did not practise the simony of buying converts."‡ "They," says another English traveller, "have brought nearly the whole of the Indian population of South America into the bosom of their Church. Notwithstanding the numerous Church and Sectarian missionaries sent from England, I never met with one Indian converted by them."§ Thus, according to the words of our Lord, when He noticed the judgments of men upon Himself and His disciples, "is wisdom justified of all her children."

Before we finally quit Brazil, to pursue elsewhere the same inquiry, let us add, according to our custom, a brief account of the character and fortunes of Protestantism in that empire. The Huguenots of France, the Calvinists of Holland, and the Episcopalians of England, have all made attempts to acquire influence in Brazil. It would be impossible to say which class has failed most signally. It has often been observed, that heresy always presents itself under one of two aspects; when it does not act a tragedy, it performs a comedy; when it is not ferocious, it is ludicrous. The Dutch made the Brazilians groan; the English only made them smile.

Of the Dutch Protestants, "whose colonial history is so

* *Travels in Brazil*, by Prince Maximilian of Wied-Neuwied, ch. vi., p. 150 (1820).

† *Travels in the Interior of Brazil*, by George Gardner, F.L.S., ch. iii., p. 81 (1846).

‡ *Asiatic Journal*, vol. ix., p. 3.

§ *Nine Months' Residence in New Zealand*, by Augustus Earle, p. 171.

inexpiably disgraceful to human nature," we have heard more than enough. They were driven out, and went home to receive the condolence of their friends. The French Huguenots had scarcely a more brilliant destiny. Here is their sorrowful history, narrated by Protestant writers.

"Rio Janeiro," we are told by Messrs. Kidder and Fletcher, who always affect this florid style, "is fraught with interest to the Protestant Christian, as that portion of the New World where the banner of the reformed religion was first unfurled." As it was torn from its staff as soon as it was unfurled, these gentlemen were hardly prudent in calling public attention to this ill-starred banner. It was in 1556 that Villegagnon, himself an apostate, and who had once conducted Mary Stuart in safety through the English cruisers from Leith to France, landed at Rio with an *avant corps* of fourteen Calvinists, who seem to have been too much compromised in their own country to regret their forced emigration to another. It was their object, as Prince Adalbert sympathizingly observes, to form "the establishment of an asylum for Huguenots beyond the seas." This "interesting band," as the English historian of the London Missionary Society calls them, tried to introduce Calvinism among "the benighted savages;" but "it does not appear," Dr. Morrison adds, "that any of them were savingly wrought upon by the truth;"* indeed he presently confesses that they were bent chiefly on finding an "asylum," and that "the conversion of the heathen was a secondary object." Attacked by the Portuguese, who wisely objected to the presence of these seditious adventurers, their "banner" was speedily lowered. Villegagnon, recanting his errors, was reconciled to the Church, and left his companions to their fate. It was not likely that thirteen Protestant preachers would long "dwell together in unity;" and accordingly, as the Rev. Dr. Walsh relates, "weakened by their intestine dissensions,"† they became an easy prey. "Their squabbles," says Mr. Ewbank, "and the bitterness of spirit accompanying them, ruined all."‡ And so they came to a bad end; French Protestantism finally collapsed, and Brazil declined, once for all, to become "an asylum for Huguenots beyond the seas."

The English have hardly been more successful. Dr. Walsh, a minister of their Established Church, a gentleman whose integrity and kindly temper it is impossible not to admire, was honored by the friendship of the Bishop of Rio, "the excellent

* *The Fathers of the London Missionary Society*, vol. i., p. 60.
† *Notices of Brazil*, by Rev. R. Walsh, LL.D., vol. i., p. 153 (1830).
‡ *Life in Brazil*, ch. viii., p. 83.

José Caëtano da Silva-Coutinho, than whom a more learned or, I believe, a more amiable man does not exist." This prelate, Dr. Walsh says, "fasts all the year on one meal a day;" and he adds, perhaps with unintentional exaggeration, "he studies all night." In 1810, this excellent bishop was consulted by the civil authorities about a demand which the English residents in Rio had made for a public chapel in that city. He advised that it should be conceded, and for this reason: "The English have really no religion, but they are a proud and obstinate people; if you oppose them, they will persist, and make it an affair of infinite importance; but if you concede to their wishes, the chapel will be built and nobody will ever go near it." "The Brazilians say he was right," adds Dr. Walsh, 1830, "for the event has verified the prediction." The chapel, whose history the bishop had so sagaciously predicted, "had an air of dirt and neglect," says this clergyman, "quite painful to contemplate, and the congregation seemed to take no interest in it when it was built, notwithstanding their zeal to have it established."* Twenty-six years later, in 1856, to bring the history down to the present hour, Mr. Ewbank relates, that "the British chapel *never* received a native convert, while monks have drawn members from it."†

One more anecdote may close the history of Anglicanism in Brazil. Dr. Walsh had observed during his residence "the deep impression of rational piety" among the Brazilians, and that "the great body of the people are zealously attached to their religion;" and then he attests, with surprising candor, the supreme but good-humored contempt which they manifested for Protestantism. "An English merchant and his wife," he says, "had incurred the wrath of the Brazilians" by sneering at their processions in Passion Week, which these fervent islanders loudly condemned as "Popish idolatry." The people of Rio only replied, says Dr. Walsh, by adding to the images of Pilate, Judas Iscariot, and other malefactors, "two figures that exactly resembled the merchant and his wife—nothing could be more correct than the likeness."‡

Finally, in 1856, an American Protestant—evidently an amiable man, though he calls St. Francis of Assisi "an Italian devotee of the twelfth century," and looks upon the Catholic religion only as an incomprehensible mystery which defies analysis and baffles criticism—thus announces his view of the actual prospects of Protestantism in Brazil: "The more I see

* Vol. i., p. 328.
† Ch. xx., p. 238.
‡ Vol. ii., p. 398.

of this people,"—whom he lauds as "hospitable, affectionate, intelligent, and aspiring,"—"the more distant appears the success of any Protestant missions among them. . . . . The people avoid a missionary as one with whom association is disreputable, and they entertain a feeling towards him bordering on contempt, arising from a rooted belief in his ignorance and presumption."*

GUYANA.

If we now quit for a time the empire of Brazil at its northern frontier, we shall find, between the Amazon and the Oronoco, on the eastern coast, three narrow territories, which acknowledge respectively the dominion of England, France, and Holland. Of the Dutch proceedings we have already heard more than enough, but a few words may be allowed with respect to the English and French.

British Guyana has found a capable historian in Dr. Dalton. Two or three sentences from that candid writer will suffice to prove the contrast which we might have confidently anticipated, and which is not less conspicuous in this obscure region than in the wider fields which we have already visited. Of the negroes under the patronage of English missionary societies, he says, "Puritans in profession, they are liberals in practice,"—that is, as he explains, "they appeared to think that faith alone was necessary, and that good works were superfluous." And then he gives one more example of the real influence of Protestant Bibles. "The lazy, the dissolute, and the disaffected met every rebuke and remonstrance by *some scriptural phrase* or religious expression." Of the natives, he says, "After all," that is, after the usual enormous and perfectly useless expenditure, "the native Indian afforded but poor encouragement in the arduous task of Christianization."†

The negro appears to have profited as little by the presence of the English emissaries. His teachers have been aided during many years by the power and wealth of England, but with so little fruit, as an English writer notices in 1860, that though he considers the Guyana Protestant negro "somewhat superior to his brother in Jamaica," he thus describes the final influence of the teaching which he has received: "It seems to me that he

* Ewbank, ubi supra.

† *History of British Guiana*, by Henry G. Dalton, M.D., vol. ii., ch. iv., pp. 146–8.

never connects his religion with his life, never reflects that his religion should bear upon his conduct." Mr. Trollope adds, that his information was mainly derived "from clergymen of the Church of England," whose unusual candor is perhaps due to the fact that most of these singular "converts" had rejected their more tranquil ceremonies for the exciting harangues of the Baptist or Wesleyan preacher—whose sects have, as usual, accompanied the Church of England to Guyana. "They sing and halloa, and scream, and have revivals. They talk of their 'dear brothers' and 'dear sisters,' and in their ecstatic howlings get some fun for their money."* And this is all which the English have done in Guyana.

"The implements of conversion," as Mr. Southey speaks, appear to have been wanting; and Dr. Dalton does not conceal that all the English efforts were only cost.y failures. On the other hand, this Protestant writer generously observes of the Catholic missionaries in British Guyana, who do not receive much aid from patrons of any sort, and least of all from the government, "All are respected for their piety and zeal. The number of Roman Catholics in the colony is about ten thousand."

In speaking of the French mission in Guyana, we are obliged, for the first time, to use Catholic evidence, in default of any other. In 1560, the Spanish missionary, Sala, in company with another Dominican Father, entered this province, but both were immediately martyred. In 1643, the French Capuchins repeated the attempt, with the same result. Four years earlier, the Jesuits entered the country at another point, under Fathers Méland and Pelleprat, and evangelized the savage tribe of the Galibis, whose ferocity they appear to have disarmed by their contempt of suffering and danger, and whose obedience they won by patient wisdom and charity. In 1653, Father Pelleprat published a Grammar and Dictionary of their language. In 1654, Fathers Aubergeon and Gueimu, after converting many pagans, were martyred, the one after twenty, the other after fifteen years of religious life. At this time the Dutch seized Cayenne, and when they were cast out it was found that "Jews and Protestants had everywhere thrown down the crosses, the emblem of our salvation."† This was the only effect of their presence. At length, after the due proportions of martyrdoms, the work of conversion in French Guyana was so effectually accomplished, in spite of the peculiar difficulties of such a mission, and the impracticable character of the natives, that in

* *The West Indies and the Spanish Main*, by Anthony Trollope, ch. xii., p. 199.

† *Mission de Cayenne et de la Guyane Française*, par M. F. de Montézou, de la Compagnie de Jésus, introd., p. x. (1857).

1674, Fathers Grillet and Béchamel started from Cayenne for the interior, with the intention of renewing in its distant solitudes the same patient apostolate. Here, after fifteen years of prodigious toil, surmounting a thousand disgusts and disappointments occasioned by the inconstancy or the brutality of the savages, the celebrated Father Aimé Lombard was able to erect the first Christian Church at the mouth of the river Kourou. For twenty-three years he had labored among these barbarians, and at last could report to his friend de la Neuville, in 1733, in these words: "Acquainted as you are with the levity of our Indians, you will no doubt have been surprised that their natural inconstancy should at length have been overcome. It is religion which has effected this prodigy, and which every day fixes its roots deeper in their hearts. The horror with which they now regard their former superstitions, their regularity in frequently approaching the sacraments, their assiduity in assisting at the Divine office, the profound sentiments of piety which they manifest at the hour of death, these are indeed effectual proofs of a sincere and lasting conversion."*

Such were the fruits of the blood and the toil of men in whom even the most degraded races of the earth, hitherto unconscious of either truth or virtue, detected the presence of God. And this was only a part of their work. Along both banks of the Oyapoch, throughout its course, missions were established by apostles who seemed to have been almost exempt from human infirmity; and who, as a French historian relates, "formed the gigantic project, which had no terrors for the courage of these intrepid missionaries, of uniting by a chain of evangelical posts, both extremities of Guyana."

Already, in 1711, M. de la Motte-Aigron, lieutenant of the king, could report: "It has at length pleased God to reward by a success almost incredible the constancy of His servants." Fourteen years later, Father Arnaud d'Ayma, conspicuous for dauntless valor even among the one hundred and eleven Jesuits who labored in this difficult field, had fought his way to the remotest of all the known tribes; and in that distant spot, amongst the nation of the Pirioux,—"lodged in a miserable cabin, living like the savages, spending his day in prayer, in the study of their language, or the instruction of their children,"—he so won the hearts of the barbarians, that at length "they resolved to follow him whithersoever he wished to lead them." And then he founded the mission of St. Paul, on the Oyapoch, where he collected the Pirioux and the whole nation of the Caranes; as a little later Fathet d'Ausillac gathered

* P. 328.

by the banks of the Ouanari the tribes of the Tocoyenes, the Maourioux, and the Maraones; and Father Creulli performed those miracles of apostolic wisdom and charity which made Chateaubriand exclaim, "What he accomplished seems to surpass the powers of human nature."

In 1762, the evil day arrived for Guyana, as for every other land, and the madness of an hour put back the conversion of the heathen world to a future and unknown period. Once more the enemy triumphed; and there was a sound of mourning by the banks of the Oyapoch and the Ouanari, as by those of the Parana and the Paraguay.

In 1763, the Duc de Choiseul, imitating his compeer the Marquis de Pombal, formed the project of a grand scheme of colonization in Guyana, perhaps in order to show that he also could do without the missionaries of the Cross. Fourteen thousand persons were persuaded by magnificent promises to emigrate to this province, where Choiseul bade them surpass, by the aid of a sounder political economy, the triumphs of the Jesuits. They began by expelling the venerable Father O'Reilly, the last survivor and sole representative of the Company of Jesus, and the Christian Indians fled before them. Two years later, the Chevalier de Balzac could report to Europe, occupied in admiring its own wisdom and enlightenment, that only nine hundred and eighteen of the colonists remained alive. More than thirteen thousand dupes of M. de Choiseul, who proposed to eclipse the Jesuits in their own triumphs had perished in two years! In the following year, 1766, M. de Fiedmond, governor of Cayenne, wrote thus to the Duc de Praslin, who was probably as indifferent to this catastrophe as to the acts of which it was a natural sequel: "I have already informed the Duc de Choiseul how necessary it is to send priests to this colony." And then he describes the destruction of the once flourishing missions, the flight of the Indians, the growth of crime amongst the negroes deprived of their pastors, and the rapid ruin of the colony. Finally, this officer adds, "Religion is dying out among the whites, as well as amongst the colored races."*

For ten years he reiterated the complaint, but always in vain. How should "philosophers" condescend to entreat humble missionaries to repair the evils of which they had been themselves the authors? How should men in whom the light of faith had gone out, and whose intelligence was enfeebled by arrogant self-love, confess that the wide-spread ruin was the work of their own hands? At length the good King Louis XVI.,

* P. 335.

himself destined to be a sacrifice to the impiety which had already devoured so many victims, sent three Jesuits—Fathers Padilla, Mathos, and Ferreira—who had been banished with the others from Brazil; and then was seen a touching spectacle, which has been described in the Journal of Christophe de Murr. "The poor savages, beholding once again men clothed in the habit which they had learned to venerate, and hearing them speak their own language, fell at their feet, bathing them with tears, and promised to live once more as good Christians, since they had restored to them the Fathers who had begotten them to Jesus Christ."

In 1852, the Jesuits were once more in Cayenne. It was not the first time that a member of the family of Napoleon had understood that if the *impossible* was to be accomplished, it was the Fathers of the Society of Jesus who must be asked to attempt it. Between June, 1853, and September, 1856, eleven Jesuits died in the swamps of Cayenne of yellow fever. "Oh! how many souls has he delivered from hell!" was the exclamation of a poor French outcast over the body of one of them. But they have cheerfully accepted this "crucifying mission," as Father D'Abbadie called it; there were broken hearts to be comforted, and they asked no more. "Why do you weep?" said D'Abbadie to his brethren as they stood round his death-bed, in 1856; "I am going to heaven!" And it was always by the aid of the glorious and all-powerful mother of God that he and his companions recovered the unhappy souls committed to their care. "What led you," said one of the Fathers to an aged criminal who had obtained the grace of a happy death, "to seek at last the succors of religion?" "I have done nothing but evil during my whole life," he replied; "one thing only I have never failed to do, and that I owe to the councils of my mother: every day I have said the *Salve Regina*, in honor of the Holy Virgin." And that Blessed One, by her mighty protection, had saved him at last.

It is time to leave Guyana, where the same works are in progress at this hour, and where missionaries who have sacrificed all for the love of God, and do not repent the sacrifice, still display the apostolic virtues which forced not long ago from the French governor of Cayenne this cry of admiration, "You are happier than we; death itself has no terrors for such as you."*

* P. 460.

CARTHAGENA AND THE BLESSED PETER CLAVER.

If now we continue our hasty journey through the provinces of South America, and traverse Venezuela, without halting by the banks of the Cayuni or the Apuré, so often trodden by the messengers of peace, we shall enter New Grenada, and at Carthagena we shall find the traces of one whom the Church has already presented to the homage of the faithful, under the title of the Blessed Peter Claver.

Born towards the close of the sixteenth century, an age in which the most prodigious graces of heaven were poured out on every side, as if to counterpoise the irreparable calamities to which it also gave birth, this offspring of an illustrious Catalonian race displayed even in infancy the gifts with which he was to be more abundantly favored in his after career. In 1602, he was admitted as a postulant into the Society of Jesus, at Tarragona. In 1610, he left Seville, at the bidding of Claude Aquavivà, for the land in which he was to spend thirty-nine years of what has been truly called "a perpetual martyrdom." In 1615, he celebrated his first Mass at Carthagena, of which it was the will of God that he should become the apostle.

"Do every thing for the greater glory of God," was one of the rules found in a book containing his secret thoughts; and a second was this, "Seek nothing in this world but what Jesus Himself sought—to sanctify souls, to labor, to suffer, and if necessary to die for their salvation, and all for the sake of Jesus!" In these two rules, as Fleuriau observes, "his whole life was comprised."

At his solemn profession, he added to the customary engagements the special vow, "to be until death the slave of the negroes." How well he kept it, they know who have read the story of his life. As soon as a ship-load of negroes arrived from the coast of Africa,—from Congo, Guinea, or Angola,—"his pale emaciated face assumed a hue of health quite unusual to it." It was he who first hurried to the shore to greet the captives, astonished to receive such a welcome; who consoled them with loving words of peace, and poured into their seared hearts the balm of hope. It was he who followed them with a father's love to their wretched homes, that by sharing their sufferings he might teach them how to bear them, how to unite them with the sufferings of Christ. And then, in words of more than human wisdom, he spoke to them of Him whose name he could rarely mention without shedding tears. But who can describe that angelic ministry, unless filled with his own spirit? Who can bear to contemplate the terrible austerities with which it was accompanied, and of which, in an age like this, one can hardly venture even to speak?

Clothed in a hair shirt from his neck to his feet, and presenting such an aspect as St. John the Baptist when he came out of the desert to preach by his own example the doctrine of mortification, the man of God would sit during the long hours of the tropical day in the tribunal of penance, fainting with heat and with the fetid stench of the poor Africans who thronged round this physician of souls; and when evening came at last, and, nature having given way, they were obliged to carry him home in their arms, his only refreshment, we are told, was to spend hours in mental prayer. Even some of his companions, though members of that Society which has faced all trials and braved all dangers, sometimes lost their consciousness in the presence of sights upon which he calmly looked, both in the huts of the negroes, and in the hospitals of St. Sebastian and St. Lazarus. It was he who ministered to the most loathsome diseases, and even kissed the hideous wounds which they had traced in bodies half-devoured by scrofula or gangrene. . .* And in the midst of such scenes, at which angels are daily present in their invisible ministry, the spirit of God within him would sometimes break forth, so that the reflected glory of his Master shone around him. Once, at St. Sebastian's, the Archdeacon of Carthagena, who had gone to the hospital to distribute alms, "found him in the midst of the sick, with the look of a Seraph, his face shining like the sun, and a circle of light round his head." More than once, a company returning home in the darkness of the night thought the house of the Saint was on fire, but discovered on approaching, as they afterwards attested on oath, that it was filled, like the temple of old, "with the glory of the Lord," and saw him suspended in the air, and as it were transfigured before them. *Marabilis est Deus in sanctis ejus!* †

There is no need to describe at length the works of this apostle, nor their marvellous fruits. How should *such* a missionary not succeed? It was the Mahometan negroes from Guinea who gave him the greatest trouble. Yet he never ceased to pursue them with his cheerful pleasant speech, or sometimes with terrible menaces; as once when he held up his crucifix before a dying and obstinate unbeliever, and exclaimed in accents which reached even that obdurate soul, "Behold the God who

* "Malattia ordinaria è una certa specie di lebbra, che loro impiaga orribilmente la bocca e le gingive; indisi stende a comprendere tutte le membra e farne una sola piaga putrida e verminosa." *Compendio della Vita del B. Pietro Claver*, p. 25.

† Fleuriau, livre iii.

is about to judge you!" Multitudes of Turks and Moors owed their salvation to his ministry, for there was in him a power which few could resist. Once a ship containing more than six hundred English prisoners was captured in the bay of Carthagena. Among the captives was an Anglican dignitary, with his wife and family. Fleuriau calls him an "archdeacon," and Boero a "bishop." Touched, as the latter relates, by the "squisita affabilità e amorevolezza" of Claver, and rejecting the Catholic faith, like many of his sect, rather through ignorance and prejudice than from the malice of a disobedient heart, he strove in vain to resist the Saint; then he would promise to abandon his errors at some future period, declare "that he was in heart a Catholic," that there was no need for precipitation, "that if he were reconciled to the Roman Church he would be deprived of his revenues and his numerous family of their subsistence." But grace was too strong for him, and he died not long after in Father Claver's arms, rejoicing that he had escaped from delusions which still darken in our own day many a generous heart, and exulting in the light of that truth which had first dawned upon him in captivity. Almost all the other prisoners were converted in their turn, including one who had been accustomed to revile the Saint, and had called him to his face "a hypocrite and an impostor."

Such was the servant of God, and such his work. It was especially among the negroes that he labored, and with results which have disposed forever of the popular notion that this race is incapable of true conversion. "The authority he had gained over their minds," says one of his autobiographers, "and their affection for him, made them obey without reply or hesitation; the mere sight of him would check the most unruly, and even the vicious, when they met him, knelt down to ask his blessing." Finally, the number whom he gathered into the fold of Christ, either from Paganism or Mahometanism, was so great as to be incredible, if it were not certified by competent witnesses. "A religious questioned him on this subject shortly before he died, to whom he answered, that he thought he had baptized more than three hundred thousand; but as humility always led him to diminish the number of his good works, it has been asserted by persons likely to be well informed, that he had baptized at least four hundred thousand."

In his last mission, Father Claver penetrated for the first time to the dangerous country between the Magdalena and the Cordilleras, "where the ferocity of the Indians had hitherto prevented the entrance of Christianity." In 1654, he died. Three years later, his tomb was reopened; when Dr. Bartholomew Torrez, an experienced physician, affirmed on oath—

that although the very coffin, and every thing in it, was completely rotten and decayed, "the body, with all its skin, nerves, and other parts, was sound and healthy, notwithstanding the quantity of lime which had covered it."

PERU AND CHILI.

It is not a formal history of missions which we are writing, and for this reason we have not attempted to exhaust the facts which illustrate that history, even in a single province of the earth. Our purpose has been only to trace, in all lands, the contrast between the work of the Church and the work of the Sects; to show that God and His gifts have been ever with the first, never with the last; and to prove by testimony so various, impartial, and harmonious, that neither pride nor anger shall be able to gainsay it, that Catholic and Protestant missions have differed so enormously, both in their agents and their results, as to exclude all doubt in the mind of even the least thoughtful observer, of every man in whom the instincts of a Christian still survive, which were Divine and which human. We are not obliged, therefore, to trace with minute detail the missions of Peru and Chili, which exactly resemble, in every feature, those which have been already reviewed.

A few words will suffice with reference to the two famous provinces which lie between the Andes and the Ocean. In 1590,—fifty-seven years after the last Inca perished in the city of Cassamarca, by the order of Pizarro,—Fathers Antony Lopez and Michael Urrea were martyred in Peru. In 1593, eight Jesuits entered Chili. Aranda and Valdiva won to the faith the fierce and cruel Araucanians, but a little later, continuing their intrepid apostolate, Vecchi, Aranda, and Montalban were martyred; and when the Spaniards proposed to revenge their death, it was Valdiva who dissuaded them from this act of human justice, and afterwards established, by his own unaided ministry, four new missions in Chili. Vainly the trained soldiers of Spain tried to penetrate into the interior, where every forest concealed a hostile army, and every river must be forded in the midst of a storm of darts and arrows. And then these men of war had recourse to another order of warriors, bolder than themselves, because fighting in a nobler cause, and "missionaries were employed," as an English writer observes, "to penetrate into the retreats of the Indians, in order to civilize them by converting them to Christianity. In these attempts, rendered doubly hazardous by the exasperation of the Indians, many of the ministers of religion fell victims to their zeal." * But the work was never suspended. In 1598, de Medrano and de Figueroa had already penetrated the recesses of the Cordilleras. In 1604, a college had been founded at Santa Fé. Imperiali, D'Ossat, de Gregorio, and others carried the faith to one tribe after another, sometimes falling under the clubs or the arrows of the savages, but never crying in vain for new apostles to complete the work which they had left unfinished. In the single year 1614, fifty-six Fathers of the Society of Jesus arrived in Peru, to replace those who had fallen. At a still later date, Father Stanislas Arlet had traversed the most inaccessible forests and mountains of Western America, and gathered six nations into one family. Tucuman had become a Catholic province. The Dominicans were spread chiefly through the northern districts, the Franciscans were scattered at one time from Bogota to Buenos Ayres. The Jesuits were everywhere.

"From a corner of this department of Peru," says Dr. Archibald Smith,—candid and generous in spite of the prejudices of country and education,—" the voice of Christianity has penetrated into vast regions of heathen and savage tribes, and reached the unsettled wanderers among the thickest entanglements of the woods, which occupy a great portion of the widely extended missionary territory of Peru. From Ocopa issued forth those zealous, persevering, self-denying and enduring men, the great object of whose lives it has been, in the midst of danger, and in the name of the Saviour, to add to the faith of the Church, and to civilized society, beings whose spirits were as dark as the woods they occupied." † "All South America," observes Mr. Walpole, recording the same facts, " was explored under their direction. Overcoming every difficulty, surmounting toils, braving unheard-of and unknown dangers, smiling at and glorying in wounds, hardships, death itself, these zealous men spoke of Jesus and His love and mercy in the remotest nook of this vast continent." ‡ Yet neither of these Protestant travellers, nor any of their class,—differing in this respect from the more discerning savages, who were converted by such apostles, because even *they* could recognize the presence of God in them, —appear to have been in any degree impressed by the truths which they eloquently narrate, or to have derived the slightest admonition from them.

We may not stay to notice one by one the men who evangelized the Peruvian races, redeeming the violence and cupidity

* Stuart Cochrane, vol. i., ch. iii., p. 219.

† *Peru as it is*, by Archibald Smith, M. D., vol. ii., ch. iv., p. 114.

‡ *Four Years in the Pacific*, by the Hon. F. Walpole, vol. ii., ch. i., p. 25.

of the soldiers of Spain, and winning the love and reverence of the native tribes in spite of the injuries which they had received from Europeans; but there is one of their number whom it is impossible not to mention, because to him was given, in a special manner, the title of Apostle of Peru. It was in 1589 that Francis de Solano sailed for America, designing to labor in the province of Tucuman, which lies between the Cordilleras and Paraguay, "because there he might hope to find the greatest dangers, and to suffer most for the glory of God." Father Louis Bolanos, also a Franciscan, had preceded him, and having set out from Lima had travelled many a weary league on both banks of the Plata; but a greater than he was now to enter the same regions.

Perfectly conversant, like most of his order, with the dialects of the barbarous tribes whom he resolved to win, St. Francis Solano threw himself into the combat with all the ardor of an apostle. Already he had gathered thousands into the fold of Christ, when the remoter eastern tribes, who wandered through the country between the Dulce and the St. Tomé, came down in vast numbers, breathing fury and slaughter against their converted brethren, and threatening the most cruel torments to all who had become Christians. The neophytes began to fly in terror, and the new mission seemed to be menaced with swift and hopeless destruction. Then Solano went forth alone, confiding in the protection of the Mother of God, to meet the advancing multitude. He was a servant of Him who had said, "The good shepherd giveth his life for the sheep." The hour was come to die, and he would die as becomes an apostle. But he was only to be a martyr in desire; and "having by supernatural power arrested the advance of the barbarians, he addressed to them so moving a discourse on the Passion of our Divine Lord, and exhorted them with such burning words to embrace His holy religion, that in that single day more than nine thousand were converted."*

After this he went through the land, preaching everywhere "Jesus Christ crucified;" and everywhere he was accompanied, like the primitive missionaries, by "signs following." Even the wild beasts, as multitudes were able to testify, rendered him homage after their kind. And no marvel,—for as one of his biographers observes, "It is a principle of theology, that the revolt of irrational creatures against man is only a consequence of man's rebellion against his Maker." "The pre-eminence of the Blessed Lord over inanimate matter, and much more over the animal creation," says a living authority, is the true cause

* See his Life by Courtot, ch. viii.

that "as His Saints advance in holiness and in likeness to Himself, the animals obey their words, revere their sanctity, and minister to their wants."*

In 1610, St. Francis Solano died. Three hundred and four witnesses, of all ranks and classes, were examined on oath, and attested the prodigies which they had witnessed, and the heroicity of the virtues which had transformed a desert into a garden. Through a tract of two thousand miles he was numbered among the patrons and defenders of the faithful, and a hundred tribes burned lamps day and night in his honor, and called upon him to advocate their cause in heaven. Then Urban VIII., by his famous decree of 1631, peremptorily forbade all public devotion till the claims of the Saint had been further examined, and refused even to allow the process to continue until the apostolic edict was obeyed. For twenty years, the grateful Indians, who had loved their Father with all their hearts, refused to submit; till they comprehended at length that it was not by disobeying the Vicar of Christ that they could honor one of His apostles. And so, with heavy hearts, they brought in all the lamps which they had kindled in his honor; and in 1656, his body was removed from its shrine, and carefully hidden from their sight. Nineteen years later, the decree of Beatification was pronounced, and in 1726 he was canonized.

The faith which St. Francis Solano preached is still, in spite of many disasters, and of the crimes and follies of successive rulers, the light and the glory of Peru. Here, as in every other province evangelized by the sons of St. Ignatius, St. Francis, and St. Dominic, neither neglect nor oppression have been able to undo that mighty work, unparalleled since the first ages of Christianity, by which it was the will of God to replace the apostate millions of Sweden, Germany, and Britain by a multitude of new believers in China, India, and America. We have seen that in the two former countries persecution and suffering have only confirmed the faith planted in other days by the missionaries of the Cross; and it is time to show, once more by Protestant testimony, that in Brazil and Colombia, in Chili and Peru, in the valley of the Amazon and the plains of La Plata, the same astonishing stability attests at this hour by Whose power these nations were won to the service of Christ, by Whose protection they have been maintained in it.

* F. Faber, *The Blessed Sacrament,* book iv., sec. ii., p. 433.

PRESENT STATE OF THE SOUTH AMERICAN PROVINCES.

In Brazil, where de Nobrega and Anchieta once labored, eight hundred thousand domesticated Indians, as we have said, represent, even at this day, the fruits of their toil. Deprived during sixty years of their Fathers and guides, and too often scandalized by the example of men who were Christians only in name, the native races have not only preserved the faith through all their sorrows and trials, but have everywhere rejected the bribes and the caresses of heresy. Even Protestant writers, in spite of violent and incurable prejudices, do justice to the generous virtues of this people. Dr. Walsh, an Anglican minister, frankly confesses, as we have seen, the "deep impression of rational piety," and "zealous attachment to their religion," which he noticed during his long residence among them. Drunkenness and blasphemy, he says, were unknown; though once he heard, "on Sunday evening, at Rio, a desperate riot of drunken blasphemers, but they all swore *in English*."* Mr. Gardner also observes, in 1846, after pursuing during some years his scientific researches in these tropical climes, "It was on a Sunday morning that I arrived in Liverpool from Brazil, and during the course of that day I saw in the streets a greater number of cases of intoxication than, I believe, I observed altogether among Brazilians, whether black or white, during the whole period of my residence in the country."†

Before England had begun to educate her heathen masses, Brazil had inaugurated an elaborate system of public instruction. Dr. Walsh notices, not only the universality of primary education in Brazil, but the still more remarkable fact, that many of the colored races have been conspicuous for their success in various branches of knowledge. Speaking of the great public library at Rio, and the affluence of students of all ranks, he asks, "Is it not most unjust to accuse the Catholics as enemies to knowledge? Here is a noble and public literary institution, filled with books on all subjects,"—and with Bibles in almost every language,—"founded by a rigid Catholic monarch, and superintended and conducted by Catholic ecclesiastics, on a plan even more liberal, and less exclusive, than any similar establishment in our own Protestant country."‡

It would be too long to quote his interesting account of the *irmandades*, or religious brotherhoods; which "consist entirely

* *Notices of Brazil*, vol. i., p. 381.
† *Travels in the Interior of Brazil*, ch. i., p. 18.
‡ Vol. i., p. 438.

of the laity," and whose objects are to build and repair churches, found and maintain hospitals, bury the deceased poor, and to do, cheerfully and well, whatsoever else Christian charity can suggest. "It is quite inconceivable," he says, "to an Englishman, what immense sums of money these lay brothers annually expend in what they conceive to be pious and charitable uses." Even Messrs. Kidder and Fletcher, though less capable than most of their countrymen of appreciating such works, and despising the Brazilians because they refused to exchange the doctrine of St. Paul for the crude inventions of New England Protestantism, speak with reluctant admiration, in 1857, of "the philanthropy and practical Christianity embodied in the hospitals of Rio and Janeiro;" while they are obliged to confess that the devoted Italian Capuchins seem to be ever on errands of mercy, through tropic heats and rains."* And then they console themselves with coarse abuse of the "greasy friars." Yet Dr. Walsh, a man of purer instincts, commends the virtues even of the native clergy, some of whom, owing to the want of ecclesiastical training, and the mistaken policy of the government towards the seminaries, are the least edifying of their class. "I really cannot find," he says, "that the Brazilian clergy deserve the character imputed to them. From what I have seen myself and heard from others, they are, generally speaking, temperate in their diet, observant of the rules of their Church, assiduous in attending the sick, and charitable as far as their limited means permit."†

"The clergy," says another English Protestant, speaking of the order generally in South America, "are everywhere respected as friends worthy of double honor. Friendly, indeed, I have ever found them, in this and every other country where I have travelled; and Englishmen of every denomination must in gratitude acknowledge as much. They must own also, that our own prejudices, whether as a nation or a sect, soon appear to us as unworthy, inveterate, and unjust, as those of any other under the sun. They will admit that no set of men in their private character have been so injuriously aspersed by the cankered tongue of slander as the Roman Catholic priesthood."‡

Lastly, in spite of the gold of England and America, not a solitary Brazilian, white or black, has ever been induced to profess Protestantism; and Mr. Ewbank has informed us, no doubt with regret, that "the people avoid a missionary as one

* Ch. vii., p. 111.

† P. 374.

‡ *Travels in various parts of Peru*, &c. by Edmond Temple, vol. i., ch. xix., p. 418.

with whom association is disreputable," and regard him with sovereign contempt "from a rooted belief in his ignorance and presumption."

In that vast region which stretches from the mouth of the San Francisco to the Isthmus of Panama, watered by the mightiest rivers of our globe, and including the district of the Amazon with its "forty-five thousand miles of navigable water communication," the natives, who still find shelter in its forests or guide their barks over its myriad streams, "push their profession of the Catholic religion," we have been told, "even to fanaticism." Yet it is a kind of marvel, considering their past history, that they should have any religion at all. A less grievous trial sufficed utterly to destroy the apostolic churches of Asia; but it seems to have been the special privilege of those founded in the sixteenth century, that no power should prevail against them. Of the *modern* Indian population and the existing missions among them, many Protestant writers speak with admiration, though evidently perplexed by their obstinate adherence to the faith, in spite of their long calamities. Prince Maximilian notices the new mission at Belmonte, where he found "a race of civilized Indians converted to Christianity," who "have abandoned entirely their ancient mode of life, and are now quite reclaimed." * Prince Adalbert, though he writes in a more worldly and frivolous tone, speaks of meeting canoes on the river Xingu, all adorned with flags "bearing an image of the Virgin Mary,"—sufficient evidence of the Christian instincts of this people. Where She is honored, how should religion perish? What marvel if piety still linger in tribes who rejoice to be Mary's children, and confide in her protection whom highest angels honor with lowly reverence, as at once, by a prodigy of election and grace, the Mother, the Daughter, and the Spouse, of the Everlasting God?

From other Protestant travellers in these regions we learn that respect for the ministers of religion, as well as for the mysteries which they dispense, is also a characteristic of the same race.

Messrs. Smyth and Lowe, two British officers, who travelled by water from Lima to Para, from the Pacific to the Atlantic, repeatedly attest the powerful influence of the Franciscans of the present day. Thus, at Saposoa, on the river Huallaga, "the priest is treated by the people with great respect." On the banks of "the magnificent Ucayali," the only Europeans they met were "those excellent persons whose aim had been to rescue its inhabitants from the most miserable and horrid

* *Travels in Brazil*, ch. x., p. 277.

state of barbarism," in spite of the criminal indifference of "what is pleased to call itself a liberal government." At Sarayacu they are hospitably entertained by a Spanish missionary, and remark "the great influence his paternal care, during the long space of thirty-four years, gave him over the minds of all the civilized Indians, and his knowledge of their various languages." They add that, "during the long interval of nine years," through the *incuria* of the government, "he had not received any salary."*

Mr. Wallace, another English traveller, notices, in 1853, similar facts. Thus, at Javita, on the Rio Negro, "the girls and boys assemble morning and evening at the church to sing a hymn or psalm,"—a practice which is not usual in English villages. On the Amazon he meets negroes, who all join in the responses with much fervor," but, unfortunately, according to Mr. Wallace, "without understanding a word." He does not say how he ascertained the fact, but he relates immediately that some of them had just returned from a three days' journey to have a child baptized, which encourages us to believe that he was mistaken. Elsewhere he shows how religion enters into and colors the daily life of the Indians, so that at their frequent *festas*, "which are always on a Saint's day of the Roman Catholic Church," they will make a long tour to the various Indian villages, "carrying the image of the saint." Like the natives of China and Ceylon, they willingly spend their substance also in token of their piety. "The live animals are frequently promised beforehand for a particular saint; and often, when I have wanted to buy some provisions, I have been assured 'that this is St. John's pig,' or 'that is,' &c."† It is evident that, in spite of their misfortunes, their religion is still a reality. The English peasant does not refuse to sell his pig because it is promised to St. John, and would probably feel little respect for such self-denial, even if he knew who St. John was.

Mr. Campbell Scarlett relates the same characteristic anecdotes, and displays the same incapacity to appreciate them. "At least four nights out of seven," he says, speaking of the Indians of Panama,—for they are everywhere the same,—"I am indulged with a superstitious if not idolatrous ceremony." It was one which he might have witnessed in many a hamlet of Austria, Bavaria, or Spain, and even of France or Belgium, with the approval of men not much addicted to idolatry, and as remark-

* *Narrative of a Journey from Lima to Para,* ch. iv., p. 194.

† *Travels on the Amazon and Rio Negro,* by Alfred R. Wallace, ch. iv., p. 93; ch. ix., p. 270 (1853).

able for intellectual vigor as any in Europe; for it was simply a harmless procession which disturbed Mr. Scarlett's repose, wherein Christian Indians marched, "having on their heads a gorgeous image of the Virgin, under a canopy." But the same obnoxious spectacle, in which simple hearts displayed their filial affection towards the Mother of Jesus, met him everywhere. "Mummeries, disgraceful to Christianity," he angrily observes, "occur in these countries so frequently, that they appear to occupy the greater part of everybody's time and attention,"*—good proof of their being interested in Christianity, though it might perhaps be offensive to an English gentleman only anxious to sleep in peace.

In every region of the continent, the same spontaneous piety seems to manifest itself. Mr. Markham goes to Canete, in Peru, and in that tranquil valley meets this phenomenon: "Early in the morning one is roused by the voices of the young girls and women, when they all repair to the door of the chapel before going to work, and chant a hymn of praise upon their knees. This is repeated at sunset, when the day's work is concluded." Presently he is at Cuzco, where he finds the devout population "showering scarlet salvias" over a crucifix which was being borne in procession. Like Mr. Scarlett, he is offended, and gravely remarks, with the self-possession of a learned Englishman, that "such exhibitions supply the place of the worship of the Sun. It is a question which is the most idolatrous."† We shall not do justice to him without adding, that he is indignant with the Spaniards for having, as he says, "*polluted* the altars of the Sun!" In another work he repeats the sentiment with greater emphasis. "The Dominican friars," he observes, "succeeded in introducing far grosser and more degrading superstitions amongst the Indians than they had ever practised," and were particularly culpable in having set up "a picture of the Virgin," "which was to replace their former *simple* worship of the Sun and Moon!"‡

When Mr. Mansfield, also an English traveller, sees "the Peons and *Chinas* (the Guarani women) all fall on their knees in the street" at Corrientes, as Mr. Markham saw others do at Yanaoca, he exclaims with solemn complacency, "It is sad to see such a power of devotion thrown away!"§ It is true that he had detected, with the unerring sagacity of his countrymen,

* *South America and the Pacific*, by the Hon. P. Campbell Scarlett, vol. ii., ch. ix., p. 204.

† *Cuzco and Lima*, by Clements R. Markham, F.R.G.S., ch. ii., p. 27; ch. v., p. 155.

‡ *Travels in Peru and India*, ch. vii., p. 115.

§ *Paraguay, Brazil*, &c., by C. B. Mansfield, Esq., M.A., ch. ix., p. 265.

that these apparently devout people were in the habit of "worshipping a doll." When educated Englishmen undertake to criticize Christian devotion, they not unfrequently attain, as in these cases, the uttermost limits of unreason. Yet there are many of them who seriously marvel, when they are told that, in all which relates to religion, they are a proverb and a jest among all races of men; and this, as Mr. Ewbank has candidly informed us, "from a rooted belief in their ignorance and presumption."

Yet they seem all eager to prove that this estimate of them is perfectly just. Dr. Hartwig, a Protestant naturalist, goes to Peru, and having to speak of the *vicûna*, breaks out after this manner: "The Church manages to get the best part of the animal, for the priest generally appropriates the skin." In the next page, as if to enable his readers to appreciate his truthfulness and charity, he relates that, after a great chase in which one hundred and twenty-two *vicûnas* were caught, "the produce of their skins served for the building of *a new altar* in the village church."*

Another English traveller, this time a Protestant missionary, far surpasses even Mr. Scarlett, Mr. Markham, and Mr. Mansfield, in his repugnance to such manifestations of religious feeling. After observing that "the name of God is seldom long out of the mouth of any Central American," and sternly rebuking "a profane imitation of the Saviour riding upon an ass," he reveals unconsciously in these curious words the temper which makes Protestants shrink from such exhibitions. "Who can compute the amount of positive evil which must result from *familiarizing* the eye of a whole people with such objects as these?"† That persons whose religion is not Divine faith, but simply emotion, and who, like the Protestant visitors at Jerusalem, are only "scandalized" by familiarity with holy places and things, should dread any shock to their capricious and sentimental belief, is perhaps natural; but Catholics can bear to approach, and even to represent by sensible signs, the Divine mysteries which God has taught them both to know and to love.

Another Protestant Christian, also a witness to the devotion which he could not comprehend, after noticing the fervor displayed at a similar religious ceremony in Mexico, relates that he quitted the scene in disgust, and relieved his intelligent piety by an immediate visit to some Aztec ruins. "I contemplated the old Aztec god," he says, "and *could not but regret*

* *The Tropical World*, by Dr. G. Hartwig, ch. iii., p. 31.
† *The Gospel in Central America*, by Rev. F. Crowe, p. 278.

the change that had been imposed upon these imbecile Indians."* This gentleman is at least perfectly candid in the exhibition of his sympathies.

A learned Protestant professor, who would no doubt be shocked if any one doubted that he was a Christian, openly laments the conversion both of Mexico and Peru, but for other reasons. It was "not of such value," he says, "as to reconcile the student of that strange old *native* civilization of the votaries of Quetzalcoatl to its abrupt arrestment, at a stage which can only be paralleled by the earliest centuries of Egyptian progress." And he repeats the sentiment with great deliberation. "It is difficult to realize the conviction that either Mexico or Peru has gained any equivalent for the irreparable loss which thus debarred us from the solution of some of the most profoundly interesting problems connected with the progress of the human race."† It is impossible to conceive a display of impiety more bold or more unconscious. If a single act of supernatural faith or charity does more to promote the glory of God than the solution of many scientific problems, and tens of thousands of such acts are now daily made in Mexico and Peru, thanks to their conversion, Christians may venture to think that this is some "equivalent" for that "old native civilization," which was marked, as Dr. Wilson himself observes, by "cruel rites," and abominable demon-worship, involving the immolation of human victims, "in some cases even to the number of thousands."

On the river Magdalena, whose banks were once trodden by the Blessed Peter Claver, Captain Stuart Cochrane, who never mentions the Catholic religion without a jest or a curse, discovers the same offensive piety which his co-religionists deem an imperfect substitute for Aztec and Peruvian civilization. "Every time (the native crew) stopped to take their meals, one of them uttered a prayer, and invoked not only the Virgin and all the Saints in the calendar,"—which must have singularly protracted the repast,—but some, he is quite sure, "of their own invention." "This is a practice," Captain Cochrane naively adds, "which they would think it wrong to omit, and which, no doubt, originated in piety." When the meal was over, before they resumed their journey, they always "recited a prayer for the prosperity of our voyage," a habit which might have taught this English gentleman a useful lesson, but which he only found "highly diverting."‡ He confesses,

* *Mexico and its Religion,* by Robert A. Wilson, ch. xxi., p. 231.

† *Prehistoric Man,* by Daniel Wilson, LL.D., vol. i., ch. ix., pp. 302, 313; ch. xi., p. 362.

‡ *Journal of a Residence in Colombia,* vol. i., ch. iii., pp. 143, 150.

however, that education was spreading universally in Colombia, "not only in the capital, but in the most remote villages of the Republic."*

This, however, it must be confessed, in justice to the Spaniards, is only the perpetuation of fruitful traditions bequeathed by them. "The prudence of the clergy," said an earlier traveller, "and the education which the people have received from the Spaniards, have inspired all the Colombians with a profound respect for the exercises of religion, . . . the authority of the parish priests is absolute, ... the greatest decorum prevails in the churches, and the devotion of the faithful is no less striking."†

Everywhere the same facts, illustrating impressively the undying ministry of the first apostles of America, are recorded by Protestant travellers, though usually without any comprehension of their significance. On the Lake of Nicaragua and in the quicksilver mines of southern California, two of the most unpromising places in the world, Mr. Julius Froebel finds American Indians displaying the same generous and trustful piety. "I shall never forget," he says, "the impressions of one night and morning on the San Juan river. Our boat had anchored in the midst of the stream. . . . In the morning, a song of our boatmen addressed to the Virgin roused me from my sleep. It was a strain of plaintive notes in a few simple but most expressive modulations. The sun was just rising, and as the first rays, gilding the glossy leaves of the forest, fell upon the bronze-colored bodies of our men, letting the naked forms of their athletic frame appear in all the contrast of light and shade, while accents, plaintive and imploring, strained forth from their lips, I thought to hear the sacred spell, by which, unconscious of its power, these men were subduing their own half-savage nature. At once the same song was repeated from behind a projecting corner of the bank, and other voices joined those of our crew in the sacred notes. Two canoes, covered from our view, had anchored near us during the night. The song at last died away in the wilderness. A silent prayer, our anchor was raised, and with a wild shout of the crew, twelve oars simultaneously struck the water."‡ Can any one imagine such a scene on the Thames or the Clyde?

At another time, it is in the mines of New Almaden that he finds "fifteen or twenty men calling down the blessing of

* Vol. ii., ch. ix., p. 15.

† *Travels in the Republic of Colombia*, by G. Mollien, ch. xix., p. 354.

‡ *Seven Years' Travel in Central America*, by Julius Froebel, ch. ii., p. 20; ch. x., p. 585.

Heaven on their day's work in the interior of the mountain, before a little altar cut out of the natural rock;" and singing the same hymn to the Mother of Jesus, to the same air, at a distance of nearly two thousand miles. In both cases the only "spell" was that mysterious gift of faith which can illumine the darkness even of the Negro and the Indian, and both furnished an illustration of the truth imperfectly avouched by a travelled Protestant, when he exclaimed, "Catholicism has certainly a much stronger hold over the human mind than Protestantism. The fact is visible and undeniable."*

It is the *universality* of this fact which gives to it its deep significance. No race of men to whom the incomparable gift has once been imparted, however lowly their social or intellectual position, fail to bear witness to its marvellous power.† Millions of Englishmen, Swedes, and Germans, who have lost or never received it, have sunk almost to the level of animals, have less apprehension of Divine things than the very pagan, and neither know nor care "whether there be any Holy Ghost;"‡ yet the whole life of the untutored Indian is an unceasing manifestation of the *supernatural* principle within him. Peru is no exception to this rule. "The devotion of the population to Catholicism," says a well-meaning Protestant missionary after he had abandoned his hopeless undertaking, "is manifested in almost daily processions."§ So vehement is the repugnance of the Peruvians to heresy, a sentiment which could have no existence without deep religious conviction, that Dr. Archibald Smith mildly complains, "these good people believed we were but Jews." And then he relates that at Lima, on the death of a certain Englishman, "the good-natured bishop yielded his sanction to let the corpse have Christian burial; but subsequently to this permission, a mob was collected in the night, and the body was cast out from the church into the middle of the street."‖ Such facts, even if they be deemed

* Laing, *Notes of a Traveller*, ch. xxi., p. 430.

† A striking illustration is found in a well-known work. "If the London costermongers," who have not even the piety of heathens, "had to profess themselves of some religion to-morrow," says a competent witness, "they would all become Roman Catholics, every one of them." Even such men as these, have noted the familiar contrast between the two religions, and that while "the Irish in the courts will die for the priest," the English of the same class treat their ministers and their message with equal derision. "It is strange," adds this writer, "that the regular costermongers, who are nearly all Londoners, should have such a respect for the Roman Catholics, when they have such a hatred for the Irish, whom they look upon as intruders and underminers." *London Labor and the London Poor*, by Henry Mayhew, p. 21. Cf. p. 107.

‡ *Acts* xix. 2.

§ *A Visit to the South Seas in the U. S. Ship Vincennes*, by S. Stewart, A.M., vol. i., p. 197.

‖ *Peru as it is*, vol. i., ch. vii., p. 165.

to indicate excessive zeal, are at least incontrovertible evidence of the power which religion exerts over the hearts of these various races, and afford an instructive contrast to the dull apathy, or cheerless unbelief, of the same class in our own country. And though we have been told that "the life of an Englishman is in danger among the peasantry," because he has made himself odious by his shallow and presumptuous bigotry; yet even Protestant writers confess "the kindness and hospitality"* of these races to all who know how to conduct themselves with modesty and good sense. Even Captain Cochrane says, "John Bull may certainly improve his manners by imitating those of the peasants of South America;"† Mr. Kendall and Mr. Olmsted repeatedly attest the universal charity and kindliness of the Indians of Mexico; Mr. Markham celebrates the unbounded hospitality of the Peruvians, and not only acknowledges that the upper classes are "highly educated," but that "many Indians, too, have distinguished themselves as men of literary attainments;" while Mr. Froebel, contrasting "the unaffected kindness, good breeding, and politeness of the Mexican country people" with the manners of his own nation, declares, "In almost every respect they are superior to our German peasants."

An accomplished English writer, who would think it no reproach to be called a vehement Protestant, thus describes, in 1862, the effects of conversion upon this once heathen race: "I was thrown a great deal amongst the Indians, and had the most excellent opportunities of judging their character, and I was certainly most favorably impressed. . . . . *Crimes of any magnitude are hardly ever heard of amongst them.*" Their courtesy was equally remarkable, and that it was inspired by religious feeling was proved by the fact that they "always saluted with an '*Ave Maria,*' and a touch of the hat in passing." Travellers ignorant of their language may accuse them of want of intelligence, but "never was there a greater mistake; their skill in carving, and all carpenter's work, in painting and embroidery, the exquisite fabrics they weave from vicûna wool, the really touching poetry of their love-songs and *yaravis*, the traditional histories of their ayllus, which they preserve with religious care, surely disprove so false a charge."‡

Such, by Protestant testimony, have been the lasting fruits of conversion in the case of the Peruvians. And even this account, which contrasts so forcibly with that which a thousand

* Gerstaecker, vol. i., ch. x., p. 188.

† Vol. ii., ch. xii., p. 150.

‡ *Travels in Peru and India*, by C. R. Markham, F.S.A., F.R.G.S., ch. vi., p. 103; ch. ix., p. 178; ch. xiii., p. 221; ch. xviii., p. 311.

pens have given of the sottish peasantry of England, Holland, or Prussia, steeped in vice, and often as ignorant of religion, in spite of myriads of Protestant preachers, as the brutes of the field,—does not reveal all that St. Francis Solano and his successors have done for this nation. "Many Indians," says the same authority, "are wealthy enterprising men, while others have held the highest offices in the State." General Castilla, a native Peruvian, a man "of great military talent and extraordinary energy and intrepidity," became President of the Republic in 1858, and still held the office in 1862. General San Roman, also "a pure Indian," commanded at the same date the Army of the South. And wonderful as these facts must appear to men acquainted only with specimens of Protestant colonization, always attended by the degradation and destruction of the aboriginal races, they are found in every part of the continent. "Peru is far from being the best specimen of the South American republics, and the Chilians have displayed tenfold the ability, in governing, in commercial and agricultural pursuits, and in literature."

The only additional fact, in illustration of the enduring influence of religion over the Peruvian Indian, which we need notice here, has been recorded by Mr. Clements Markham. Beyond the lofty range of the Yquicha mountains lies the almost inaccessible home of the tribe of Yquichanos. "Distinguished by their upright gait, independent air, and handsome features,"—"true lovers of liberty,"—"an honor to the Indian races of South America," in the words of Mr. Markham, they have twice vanquished the military forces of the Peruvian Republic, and, persisting in their loyalty to the Spanish crown, have defied every effort to subdue their independence. "No tax-gatherer," he says, "dares to enter their country." But while this "most interesting people," in the words of the same Protestant writer, "refuse to submit to the capitation or any other tax, *they punctually pay their tithes to the priests* who come amongst them, and treat a single stranger with courteous hospitality."*

Perhaps the reader may be disposed to ask himself at this point, in the presence of facts at once so uniform and so incapable of a purely human explanation, what that Power can be, everywhere exerted by one class of teachers, and by one only, which even in the souls of negroes and savages has produced results so deep and so enduring? By what mysterious influence have they, in so many lands, subdued such natures to the law of Christ? By what spell have they engrafted on them

* *Cuzco*, &c., ch. iii., p. 71.

that supernatural faith which sixty years of utter abandonment could not weaken, nor evil example obliterate, nor bribes seduce, nor even ignorance corrupt, and which is as full of life and power in the rugged mountains of Peru and the far-spreading forests of Brazil, as in the mines of New Almaden and California, or by the banks of the Plata and the Maranon, of the San Juan, the Xingu, and the Ucayali?

In Chili,—as in Brazil, Colombia, and Peru,—a hostile witness reports, in 1840, that "education is certainly advancing;"* and he fully explains the progress when he adds, in 1847, "the influence of the Jesuits is gradually increasing."† Two years later, Mr. Walpole praises the "many excellent schools," and notices that those "attached to the various convents teach free of expense." There is even, he adds, at Santiago a normal school for the training of teachers, "who are afterwards sent into the provinces." "The priests," he says, "mostly taken from the higher classes, are educated at the university, and are a well-informed order of men."‡

Of the people we are told, by various Protestant writers, that, both by their industry and piety, they are worthy of their teachers. Dr. Smith declares that "the Christianized Indians of the Inca dynasty are truly hard laborers." Major Sutcliffe relates that *spiritual retreats* for this class "are held yearly on many of the large haciendas," at which they practise severe mortifications, using the discipline with such vigor that this gentleman, who judged the operation with the feelings of an Englishman and a Protestant, observes, "I frequently heard them, and wondered how they could stand such a self-flogging."§ They must at all events have been in earnest.

Of their invincible dislike of heresy Mr. Miers offers an explanation, when he relates the answer of the principal author of the modern constitution of Chili to the objection, apparently urged by an Englishman, that religious toleration was unknown in Chili. "Toleration cannot exist in Chili," he replied, in accounting for the absence of that word from the civil code, "because this presupposes a necessity for permitting it; but here we neither have any other, nor know any other religion than the Catholic."‖ Finally, a French traveller, busy only with economical and financial questions, but filled with admiration of the resources and the prosperity of this profoundly Catholic people, exclaims, "What an immense future is in store

* *A Visit to the Indians of Chili,* by Captain Allen F. Gardiner, ch. vi., p. 172.

† *A Voice from South America,* ch. i., p. 14.

‡ *Four Years in the Pacific,* vol. i., ch. viii., p. 165; ch. x., p. 349.

§ *Sixteen Years in Chili and Peru,* ch. ix., p. 320 (1841).

‖ *Travels in Chili and La Plata,* vol. ii., p. 219.

for this nation, which, to wise institutions and a prudent liberty, adds all the resources of an incomparable soil!"*

Yet Protestant missionaries, chiefly English or Scotch, careless of the fact, which their own experience has so often attested, that they only succeed in provoking the repugnance of these people towards themselves, their employers, and their opinions, continue to waste, year after year, the enormous sums imprudently intrusted to them, in efforts which always terminate in failure, and in operations which only excite ridicule. We have seen that, owing to such proceedings, the life of an Englishman is precarious in these regions, while his dead body is flung into the highway. It is certainly a grave question for the inhabitants of the British Isles, whether the annual expenditure of vast revenues in all parts of the world, with no other result than to kindle the contempt of every pagan, the disgust and indignation of every Christian nation, is a course of action likely to promote their own interests, or worthy of their proverbial sagacity. If England is abhorred, as is unhappily the case, by all races of men, from the White Sea to the Indian Ocean, and is even at this moment in considerable peril from the gradual accumulation of that universal hatred which may one day crush her, it is in no small degree to her foolish and offensive "missions," and especially to the complacent vanity and ignorance of which they are only one of the manifestations, that the evil is due.

The Argentine Republic, in spite of the crimes of its rulers, and the perpetual disorders of its social state, still remains so immutably Catholic, that all the overtures of opulent missionaries, whether English or American, have only been greeted with derision. Dr. Olin has told us, that the mission to Buenos Ayres was such a signal failure, that it suggested even to his ardent mind only motives of despair. The experiment, he says, "was formally given up in 1841–2, after an unsuccessful attempt to make some impression on the native Catholic population of that country." "No Protestant missions," he remarks, "have hitherto yielded so little fruit as those set on foot for the conversion of Roman Catholics;" and then this Wesleyan minister adds the suggestion already quoted, "We will trust that it will inspire the Board with great caution in entertaining new projects for missions among Catholics."

The same discouraging conclusion is adopted by a well-meaning English traveller, who endeavored to introduce Protestantism in the wide plains which stretch from the shores of the Plata and the Uruguay to the foot of the

* *Notice sur le Chili*, p. 42 (1844).

Cordilleras, but with such disastrous results, that he also was constrained to recognize the hopelessness of the attempt. "The Protestant missionary under the present arbitrary system,"—this is his way of describing the good-humored contempt of the people,—"appears to have little prospect of extending his ministerial labors beyond the members of his own Church, either American or English."* Yet Mr. Elwes reports in 1854, that "there is one English, one Scotch, and an American church, all in good situations in the main streets of Buenos Ayres, an instance of liberality towards the Protestant religion that I never before saw in a Catholic country."†

Such are the testimonies Protestants, of different nations and sects, still more astonished than mortified at the peremptory rejection of their various religions by all the South American races and tribes. Even the Carib and the Araucanian, the Peruvian and the Chilian, the vigorous Guacho who spurs his wild horse over the Pampas, and the milder Indian who urges his canoe over the swift waters of the Guaviare or the Ucayali, only laughs at the pretensions of a doctrine which outrages all his instincts of the holy and the true; which has banished every mystery, and, as far as the exuberance of Divine mercy will permit, suspended every grace; which displays itself only in words which awaken no echo, and in emotions which die away with the words; and whose salaried and effeminate preachers, all contradicting themselves and one another, so little resemble the saints and martyrs from whom his fathers received the faith which he still prizes more than life itself, that far from recognizing them as teachers of a Divine religion, he is accustomed to ask in surprise, like his fellows in other lands, "Whether they profess any religion whatever?"

MODERN MISSIONARIES IN SOUTH AMERICA.

Before we enter the last province which remains to be visited in South America, let us notice a few additional examples, not unworthy of a moment's attention, of the language in which Protestant travellers speak of *modern* missionaries in this land. It is well to learn from such witnesses that they have not degenerated from their fathers.

A British officer, who effected a few years ago the descent of the Amazon, had for a companion during a part of his voyage a

* Captain Gardiner, *Visit*, &c., p. 24.
† *Tour Round the World*, by Robert Elwes, Esq., ch. viii., p. 107.

Spanish Franciscan, who, by the toils of thirty-four years, had "founded many new missions," without aid from any human being, and whose career included the following incident:

A little to the northeast of Sarayacu, on the river Ucayali, dwelt the Sencis, a fierce and warlike tribe, still unconverted, whose solitary virtue was dauntless courage. With a courage greater than their own, Father Plaza, the Franciscan to whom our tale refers, resolved to enter their territory. He was seized at the frontier, as he had anticipated and desired, and then was enacted the following drama. "They asked him," says the English traveller, "whether he was brave, and subjected him to the following trial: Eight or ten men, armed with bows and arrows, placed themselves a few yards in front of him, with their bows drawn and their arrows directed to his breast; they then, with a shout, let go the strings, but retained the arrows in their left hands, which he at first did not perceive, but took it for granted that it was all over with him, and was astonished at finding himself unhurt." The savages had taken a captive who could give even them a lesson in fortitude; but they had another trial in store for him. "They resumed their former position, and approaching somewhat nearer, they aimed their arrows at his body, but discharged them close to his feet." The narrator adds, and perhaps no other comment could be reasonably expected from a Protestant, that "if he had shown any signs of fear, he would probably have been dispatched;" but that "having, in his capacity of missionary, been a long time subjected to the caprices of the Indians, he had made up his mind for the worst, and stood quite motionless during the proof." Finally, "they surrounded him, and received him as a welcome guest."* We can hardly be surprised that such a missionary—whom even Mr. Markham calls "a great and good man," whose "deeds of heroism and endurance throw the hard-earned glories of the soldier far into the shade"—should be able to "found many new missions," even in this nineteenth century.

But there are at this hour many such as Padré Plaza in the South American missions, as even the most prejudiced travellers attest. He himself, having recently finished his apostolic career as Bishop of Cuença, was succeeded at Sarayacu by Father Cimini and three other missionaries, who ruled "about one thousand three hundred and fifty souls, consisting chiefly of Panos Indians."† "The brave and indefatigable Father Girbal" was a hero of the same order; and through every Catholic

* Lieut. Smyth, ch. xii., p. 227.
† Markham, ch. viii., p. 257.

province of America, English and American travellers have discovered apostles who are ready to do in the nineteenth century what their predecessors did in the seventeenth and eighteenth. In Colombia, even Captain Cochrane applauds "the excellent Bishop of Merida." Mr. Gilliam, a consular agent of the United States, names "the celebrated and beloved Bishop of Durango."* Dr. Walsh has assured us that "a more learned or a more amiable man than the Bishop of Rio does not exist." Mr. Temple mentions "the Archbishop of La Plata, whose pious and benevolent character has caused him to be remembered throughout his vast diocese with every sentiment of veneration."† Mr. Markham celebrates, in 1859, "Don Pedro Ruiz, the excellent Bishop of Chachapoyas," in Peru. Sir George Simpson visits Monterey, and says, "Father Gonzalez is a truly worthy representative of the early missionaries."‡ Mr. Stewart is at Lima, and meets Padré Arrieta, "in extensive repute for piety and learning."§ Mr. Forbes is at San Luis Rey, where he sees Father Antonio Peyri, who, "after thirty-four years of incessant labor," had finished his career by "voluntary retirement in poverty to spend his remaining days in pious exercises."‖ M. de Mofras is on the Pacific shore, and finds Father Estenéga "teaching his neophytes how to make bricks;" and Father Abella, at sixty years of age, sleeping on a buffalo skin, and drinking out of a horn, refusing to retire, and declaring that "he will die at his post."¶ Mr. Walpole is in Chili, and meets one of whom he says, "If amenity of manners, great power of conversation, infinite knowledge of men and countries, could have won, his must have been a successful ministry. There was a soft persuasion, a seeming deep serenity in his words, very difficult to withstand."** Mr. Stephens is at Esquipulas, on the borders of Honduras, and says of the Cura, Jesus Maria Guttierez, already worn out at thirty years of age, "His face beamed with intelligence and refinement of thought and feeling," and "the whole tone of his thoughts and conversation was so good and pure that, when he retired to his room, I felt as if a good spirit had flitted away."†† Mr. Markham hears at Andahuaylas "the famous Chilian preacher, Don

* *Travels in Mexico*, by Albert M. Gilliam, ch. xvi., p. 288 (1846).

† *Travels in various parts of Peru*, &c., by Edmond Temple, vol. ii., ch. xii., p. 381.

‡ *Narrative of a Journey Round the World*, vol. i., ch. vii., p. 334.

§ Vol. i., p. 190. *Letter* v.

‖ *California*, ch. v., p. 229.

¶ *Exploration du territoire de l'Orégon*, par M. Duflot de Mofras, tome i., ch. vii., pp. 352, 380.

** Ch. x., p. 218.

†† *Incidents of Travel in Central America*, ch. viii., p. 184.

Francisco de Paula Taforo," and finds him escorted by "one continued triumphal procession;" while at Lima-tambo he makes the acquaintance of the Franciscan Father Esquibias, "whose good deeds it was refreshing to hear from his parishioners;" and at San Miguel that of "the excellent Father Revello, the true-hearted and devoted missionary of the Purus," the body of whose companion, a young monk from Cuzco, Revello found pierced with nine arrows, one of them passing right through his chest."* At El Paso, many a league to the north of Peru, Mr. Kendall, an American Protestant, encounters "the incomparable Ramon Ortiz," whose "charity and manly virtues adorn the faith which he professes and illustrates by his life."† At Ures, in Mexico, Mr. Bartlett commends "the learned and venerable Padré Encinas," the apostle of the Yaquis, and at Parras, "the courteous and intelligent Juan Bobadilla."‡ Lieut. Herndon is on the upper course of the Amazon, and finds in that remote solitude a Franciscan whom he thus describes: "Father Calvo, meek and humble in personal concerns, yet full of zeal and spirit for his office, was my beau ideal of a missionary monk."§ Mr. Wallace is on the Rio Negro, and meets Padré Torquato, "a very well educated and gentlemanly man, who well deserves all the encomiums Prince Adalbert has bestowed on him."‖ Lieut. Smyth is at Chasuta, where he finds Padré Mariana de Jesus, and notes in his journal not only "the devotion of the Indians," but that "their submissive obedience to the Padré, and the attention they show to the worship of the Church to which they have been converted, reflect great credit on their worthy pastor."¶ And this docility, he says, is the more remarkable, because "they seem to consider themselves on a perfect equality with everybody, showing no deference to any one but the Padré." Lastly, Mr. Cleveland is at Guadaloupe, in the Pacific, and observes, "The more intimately we become acquainted with Padré Mariano, the more we are convinced that his was a character to love and respect. He appeared to us of that rare class, who, for piety and love of their fellow-men, might justly rank with a Fenelon or a Cheverus."** We shall hear a little later exactly the same language applied, by the same class of

* Ch. iv., p. 92; ch. viii., p. 275.

† *Narrative of the Texan Santa Fé Expedition*, vol. ii., ch. ii., p. 41.

‡ *Personal Narrative of Explorations*, &c., by John Russell Bartlett, U. S. Commissioner, vol. i., ch. xix., p. 444; vol. ii., ch. xxxix., p. 488.

§ *Valley of the Amazon*, ch. x., p. 205.

‖ *Ubi supra*, ch. vi., p. 160.

¶ *Ubi supra*, ch. xi., p. 213.

** *A Narrative of Voyages*, by Richard J. Cleveland, ch. xiv., p. 57 (1842).

writers, to living missionaries in North America; let us close the list for the present with this reflection,—that everywhere Catholic missionaries are found having the graces and virtues of their calling, and everywhere Providence employs Protestant travellers to bear witness to both.

PARAGUAY.

One province only remains to be visited, before we complete our rapid survey, and turn our faces towards the North. Between the Parana and the Colorado, and stretching from Santa Cruz de la Sierra in Upper Peru to the Straits of Magellan, and from the frontier of Brazil to Chili, lies the vast region which gave a name to perhaps the noblest mission which the Christian religion ever formed since the days of the Apostles. Here was accomplished, amidst races so barbarous and cruel that even the fearless warriors of Spain considered them "irreclaimable," one of those rare triumphs of grace which constitute an epoch in the history of religion. Here one tribe after another, each more brutal than its neighbor, was gathered into the fold of Christ, and fashioned to the habits of civilized life. Here lived and died an army of apostles, who seem to have been raised up at that special moment, when whole nations were lapsing into apostasy, as if to show that the very hour which *they* chose for departing from the Church was marked in heaven as a season for pouring out upon her a flood of new graces. Here, as Muratori could say without exaggeration, amid a people so lately the sport of demons, "the sublimest virtues of Christians are become, if the expression may be used, common virtues."* Here, as even Voltaire confessed, was perfected a work which "seemed to be in some respects the triumph of humanity."† Here, as Sir Woodbine Parish declares in our own day, in spite of the prejudices of his class, "If we look at the good which (the Catholic missionaries) did, rather than for the evil which they did not, we shall find that, in the course of about a century and a half, *upwards of a million of Indians* were converted to Christianity by them, and taught to be happy and contented under the mild and peaceful rule of their enlightened and paternal pastors—a blessed lot when contrasted with the savage condition of the unreclaimed tribes around them."‡ Such was the mission of Paraguay, of which we are

* *Relat. delle Missioni*, p. 3.
† Ap. Crétineau Joly.
‡ *Buenos Ayres*, &c., ch. xvii., p. 260.

now to attempt to speak, though when we have said all which we know how to say, not the hundredth part will be told.

It was in 1586, as Charlevoix relates, that Don Francisco Victoria, the first Bishop of Tucuman, who had long labored like the humblest missionary, but hitherto almost alone in the formidable diocese committed to his oversight, implored the Society of Jesus to come to his aid.* He was himself a Dominican, "and this shows," observes Mr. Southey, whose evidence we shall once more use, "how highly the Jesuits were at that time esteemed." From the province of Peru, Barsena and Angulo were dispatched; from Brazil, of which Anchieta was at that moment the provincial, five Fathers were sent to Tucuman by way of Buenos Ayres, of whom the most celebrated, Manuel de Ortega, was to be associated with Barsena in that famous apostolate with which the names of these two heroes of the Cross are inseparably connected. The ship which carried Ortega and his companions was attacked in the Bay of Rio by the English,—at that time rivals of the Dutch in the war against Catholic missionaries,—and the Fathers, after being treated with the usual indignities, were carried out to sea, and finally flung into a boat, without either oars or provisions, and abandoned to the mercy of the waves. The boat drifted to Buenos Ayres, a distance of more than seven hundred miles, and when her passengers had returned thanks to Him who had saved them by so wonderful a providence, they crossed the Pampas to Tucuman, where they met the Fathers from Peru.†

It was Barsena and Ortega who commenced the celebrated Guarani mission, and afterwards that of the Chiquitos, a nation composed of about thirty tribes, speaking more than twenty different languages, all radically different from the primitive Guarani dialect. M. d'Orbigny observes that, at the present day, the Guarani has become the almost universal language of the natives inhabiting these regions; and an English historian of Brazil notices "the perfection with which the Jesuits spoke the Guaranitic idiom,"‡ of which they published Grammars and Dictionaries, and which perhaps owes its prevalence to their influence. Barsena spoke also the Tupi, a cognate dialect of the Guarani, and the Toconoté, of which he composed a Grammar. Among the innumerable works, of which M. Crétineau Joly says "it would be impossible to number even the titles," which the Jesuits produced in the department of philology, was a Dictionary of the language of the Chiquitos, in three volumes;

* Charlevoix, *Histoire du Paraguay*, tome i., liv. iv., p. 278.
† Ibid., p. 287.
‡ Henderson's *History of Brazil*, ch. vi., p. 135.

of which M. d'Orbigny, "the chief authority," as Dr. Latham allows, has lately declared, "nothing more complete exists in any American language." But such works were hardly more than relaxations amid their other toils.

We do not propose to follow Barsena, Ortega, and their companions through all the incidents of their apostolic career, which a few examples will sufficiently illustrate. They find a pestilence raging in the country around Asumpcion, and fling themselves at once, according to their custom, into the midst of the danger. Six thousand Indians are baptized, and even Mr. Southey pauses to acknowledge "the zeal and the intrepid charity with which they sought out the infected, and ministered to the dying." Barsena, worn out by labor as much as by age, died at Cuzco in 1596, his last missionary work being to convert the sole remaining prince of the family of the Incas of Peru, with whom he shortly after departed to his true home.

For Ortega, many a year of toil, many an hour of danger and suffering, were still in store. Some of the incidents of his laborious life may be compared with any thing which history records, or romance has invented, in the field of perilous adventure. On one occasion, travelling in a plain between the Parana and the Paraguay, with a company of neophytes, they were overtaken by one of those sudden floods with which the lowlands of South America are sometimes devastated. They climbed into trees, but the flood rose higher and higher. They were without food; wild beasts and monstrous serpents, surprised by the deluge, disputed with them their retreat. For two days they remained between life and death. In the middle of the second night, Ortega perceived an Indian swimming towards him. He had volunteered to carry tidings to the Father that three of his catechumens and three Christians, lodged in the branches of a neighboring tree, were at their last gasp; the first implored baptism, the others absolution. Binding his catechist, who shared his own refuge, more tightly to the branch which he had no longer strength to embrace, and having received his confession, Ortega leaped into the flood. A branch pierced through his thigh, inflicting a wound from which he never recovered, and which remained open for twenty-two years; but he swam on, baptized the three Indians, and saw them fall one after another into the gulf. Their struggle was over, but the three Christians still remained. Exhorting them, amidst the darkness of the night and the rushing of the waters, to fervent acts of contrition, which he recited with them, he saw two of them devoured in their turn by the flood. He had done all that charity could inspire or heroism perform, and returned to his own tree, in time to find his catechist with the water up to his neck. Hoisting him up by a final effort to a higher branch, he watched with him during the remaining hours of the night. On the morrow the flood abated, and the survivors pursued their way.

Ortega was now lamed for life, yet so little did he regard this additional obstacle, that on one occasion he performed a missionary journey of nine hundred miles at once. Every trial which could test his virtue befell him, and in all he was victorious. At Lima, the Holy Office of the Inquisition, to the amazement of the whole country, condemned him to prison. Ortega did not even ask what was his crime. He had been slanderously charged, though he knew it not, with revealing a confession. As he never opened his lips, his silence was accepted as an evidence of guilt. When he had been five months incarcerated, without a murmur or a question, his accuser died; and on his death-bed confessed, that it was Ortega's refusal to give him absolution which tempted him to invent the hateful calumny. Released from prison, with every mark of admiration and reverence, he resumed his apostolic career; and having brought multitudes into the Church, he died in 1622, surviving his companion Barsena by thirty years.

But he was only one in an army of soldiers as valiant as himself. We cannot even name the half of them; let it suffice to attempt a brief record of a few, and of their works. So like were they in their fortitude, their boundless zeal, and inexhaustible charity, that in describing one, we describe all.

Gaspard de Monroy, baffled in one of his journeys by the obstinate ferocity of an Omagua chief, who not only rejected the Gospel himself, but threatened the most horrible death to the missionaries and to all who should embrace their doctrine, formed one of those sublime resolutions of which the world applauds with enthusiasm the feeble imitation in its own selfish heroes, but refuses to praise the execution in warriors of a nobler class. He set out alone, and alone he entered the hut of the savage. "You may kill me," said the Father with a tranquil air, as soon as he stood in the presence of the barbarian, "but you will gain little honor by slaying an unarmed man. If, contrary to my expectation, you give me a hearing, all the advantage will be for yourself; if I die by your hand, an immortal crown awaits me in heaven."* Astonishment disarmed the savage, and admiration kept him silent. Then, with a kind of reluctant awe, he offered to his unmoved visitor a drink from his own cup. A little later, he and his whole tribe were converted.

* Charlevoix, liv. iv., p. 322.

In 1604, Marcel Lorençana, a friend of Monroy, and Joseph Cataldino, are wrecked in the Paraguay, and only saved by the daring of the Christian Indians. It was Lorençana,—"who was rightly considered," says Mr. Southey, "an accomplished missionary,"—who obtained permission to go to the Guaranis, when their caciques had publicly announced, "that they would never be satisfied till they had drunk the blood of the last Mahoma," a recently converted tribe, "out of the skull of the oldest missionary." The Guaranis became afterwards, as we shall see, a proverb for their Christian virtues.

But who shall estimate the toils by which these ferocious savages were converted into men and Christians? "The Guarani race," says a prejudiced English traveller in 1852,—two hundred and fifty years after Lorençana had dwelt amongst them, "are a noble set of fellows—Roman Catholic the creed."* It was no human power which wrought a change so marvellous and so enduring. "I was informed at Quito," says the celebrated navigator Ulloa, "that the number of towns of the Guarani Indians in the year 1734, amounted to thirty-two, supposed to contain between thirty and forty thousand families, and that from the increasing prosperity of the Christian religion, they were then deliberating on building three other towns."† From 1610 to 1768, seven hundred and two thousand and eighty-six Guaranis were baptized by the Jesuits alone, besides those who were admitted into the Church by the Franciscans.‡

It was Lorençana, for they were the same in all trials, who threatened the judgments of heaven against the Spaniards for their cruelty and avarice; and when commanded by an official of the church in which he was preaching to be silent and leave the pulpit, "immediately obeyed, without the slightest emotion of anger." "It is said," observes Southey, "that this moderation affected the Treasurer so much, that he went into the pulpit, and with a loud voice confessed his fault, for having insulted a good man in the discharge of his duty." A few days after, the Treasurer came to a miserable end.

In 1605, Diego de Torrez arrived in Peru as Provincial of Chili and Paraguay, bringing with him seven Fathers. In 1615, when his term of office expired, his successor de Onate found that the seven had become one hundred and nineteen. In 1617, thirty-seven more entered the field under the conduct of Viana. In 1628, forty-two arrived under Mastrilli. In 1639, thirty came with Diaz Tâno. And so to the last hour

* *Paraguay, Brazil, &c.*, by C. B. Mansfield, Esq., M.A., preface, p. 9.
† Ulloa, *Voyage to S. America;* Pinkerton, vol. xiv., p. 636.
‡ Dobrizhoffer, *Account of the Abipones*, vol. iii., p. 417 (1822).

they were recruited, more than five thousand Jesuits from Spain alone finding here their cross and their crown.

In 1623, Juan Romero, superior of the mission of Asumpcion, accepted a task which the viceroy had vainly proposed to his soldiers, that of tracing the Uruguay to its source. "None but a Jesuit," says Mr. Southey, "could make the attempt with any hope of safety," because they alone were not solicitous about safety. Escorted by a few Indians, he had already advanced a hundred leagues, when he was forced back to Buenos Ayres, unable to communicate his own intrepidity to his followers. It was Romero who replied to some Christians who wished to punish the murderers of Father Gonzalvez, "The blood of martyrs is not to be avenged by blood." In 1654, after a long life of apostolic toil, he was himself martyred.

Almost every year, from the beginning of this mission to its close, was consecrated by a martyrdom. Let us notice at least a few of these glorious dates. Gonzalvez, a man of illustrious birth, was one of the first. Often he had presented himself alone to the fiercest tribes, and when they lifted the bow or the club, he would say, "This cross which you see me carry is more powerful than the arms of the Spaniards, and it is my only defence;" and the club would fall harmless to the ground, the arrow would be withdrawn from the bow. In 1615, he was ascending the Parana without any companion. "No European," said an Indian cacique, who met him on his way, "has ever trodden this shore without dyeing it with his blood." "Think not," answered Gonzalvez, "to alarm me with your threats. I am a servant of the only true God, whose ministers count it the greatest happiness which can befall them to shed their blood for Him." A hundred times he encountered, and survived, the same perils, but his hour came at last. In 1628, on the 15th of November, just as he had finished the Holy Sacrifice, and had quitted the church, the savages rushed upon him: "One blow from a *macana* laid him lifeless upon the ground, and a second beat out his brains."* Father Rodriguez, running out of the church at the cry of the savages, found the same end; and two days later, Del Castillo, the companion of both, was also martyred.

Mr. Southey, who recounts these events after Charlevoix and other historians, admits that the barbarians were "impressed with astonishment," not only by the miracles which are said to have followed the triple sacrifice, but especially by "the public rejoicings in which all classes of men partook," in

* Southey, ii., 294.

celebration of the triumph of the martyrs. "Nor could they contemplate," says the English writer, "without astonishment the conduct of the Jesuits, their disinterested enthusiasm, their indefatigable perseverance, and the privations and dangers which they endured for no earthly reward." They became anxious, he adds, "to see these wonderful men," as of old the people of Lystra and Derbe thronged round Paul and Barnabas, "saying in the Lycaonian tongue, the gods are come down to us in the likeness of men;"* and when they "once came within the influence of such superior minds," even they discerned *Whose* messengers they were, and from murderers became disciples.

Montoya, whom Southey calls one of the most learned men of his age, and who was the author of a Grammar of the Guarani language, was a missionary of the same class as Gonzalvez and Rodriguez. A Guarani chief, Tayaoba, "who had long been the dread of the Spaniards," and whose tribe were some of the fiercest of their race, had resolved to kill him. The nation of which this man was the leader was so ferocious in its habits, that "their arrows were headed with the bones of those whom they had slain, and in weaning their children the first food which was substituted for the mother's milk, was the flesh of an enemy." To this tribe, with the more than human intrepidity which marked his order, Montoya presented himself; and when he told them that he had come to teach them how they might be saved from eternal torments, "they replied that he was a liar if he said they were to be eternally tormented, and then let fly a volley of arrows upon him and his attendants." Seven of the latter were killed, but Montoya, who seems to have been on this occasion miraculously preserved, retired with the rest; and when the savages had devoured the seven, "they expressed their sorrow that they had not tasted priest's flesh at the feast, and had the Jesuit's skull for a cup." Another chief, Pindobe, "laid in wait for Montoya, for the purpose of eating him." Yet even Tayaoba and his horrible crew were so impressed, as Mr. Southey relates, with the astonishing valor and dignity of the missionaries, that "this fierce warrior sent two of his sons secretly to the Reduction of St. Francis Xavier, to see whether what he had heard of these establishments was true." A little later, Tayaoba was instructed and baptized by Montoya, "with twenty-eight of his infant children."†

We have mentioned Cataldino, the companion of Lorençana, and the friend of Montoya. In 1623, he was one day super-

* Acts xiv. 10.
† Southey, p. 290.

intending the erection of a forest church, when Montoya suddenly appeared before him with the announcement, that a tribe of hostile savages were at his heels. "The will of God be done, my dear Father," said Cataldino, and then quietly resumed his work, without even turning his head towards the yelling crowd, who were rushing upon him. Amazed at his calm indifference, or restrained by an unseen power, they gazed upon him for a while, and then disappeared in the forest.

In 1632, Christoval de Mendoza, the grandson of one of the conquerors of Peru, was martyred by a tribe to whom he had been preaching. "It was his hope and faith," we are told by Mr. Southey, "that his life and death might atone for the offences of his ancestors against those Indians for whose salvation he devoted himself." "He is said," observes Dobrizhoffer, "to have baptized ninety-five thousand Indians." In 1634, Espinosa, who had been the companion of Montoya, Suarez, and Contreras, in all their toils, and whose own life had been a long series of dangers and sufferings, was martyred by the Guapalaches. He was on his road to Santa Fé, whither he was going to beg food and to buy cotton for his neophytes, suffering from the barbarity of the unconverted Indians. He knew his danger, but the famine was urgent, and he hurried on to fall into the snare which the savages had laid for him.

In 1636, Osorio and Ripario, who had founded a new Reduction in the country of the Ocloias, were tortured to death by the Chiriguanes. The former appears to have received a revelation of the death by which he was to glorify God, since he had himself announced it beforehand in a letter to the celebrated Cardinal de Lugo.*

In 1639, Alfaro gained in his turn the crown of martyrdom; and the death of so many victims had already been so prolific, according to the law of Christian missions, in graces to the heathen, that even at this early date there were already twenty-nine separate Reductions in the two provinces of Parana and Uruguay, in which more than three hundred thousand Indians had learned to practice all the virtues of the Christian life.

Let us pass at once to the close of the seventeenth century, and take up the narrative from the year 1683, in which Ruiz and Solinas, accompanied by a secular priest, Don Ortiz de Zaraté, who aspired to the crown of martyrdom, entered the mountain region of Chaco. Already they had formed a new Reduction, under the title of St. Raphael, in which four hundred families were assembled, and Ruiz had departed for Tucuman,

* Charlevoix, liv. ix., p. 377.

when Solinas and Zaratė were attacked by the Tobas and Macobis, and on the 17th of March, 1686, fell, under their arrows and clubs.

In 1690, Mascardi and Quilelmo, who had penetrated almost to the southern extremity of the continent, were martyred by the Patagonians, that so the blood of apostles might sanctify the land throughout its length and breadth; while Father Joseph Cardiel "was reduced to such straits as to be obliged to feed on grass, unless he preferred dying of emptiness."*

In 1694, some of the best and bravest of this company oi preachers,—de Arce, Centeno, Hervas, de Zéa, d'Avila, and others,—formed new Reductions on every side, amid perils which had no terrors for such men, though most of them were destined to lose their lives in the work. Twice de Arce attempted in vain to subdue the fierce Chiriguanes, "one of the most numerous and formidable of all the South American nations." They are supposed, Mr. Southey relates, to have killed in the course of two centuries "more than one hundred and fifty thousand Indians." When the missionary sought to arrest their attention by warning them of the fire of hell, they replied disdainfully, "that they should find means of putting it out." So his superiors removed him for a time, and sent him with Ignatius Chomé, "one of the most intelligent and most meritorious of the Jesuits," to the Chiquitos. Chomé had composed a Grammar and a Dictionary of both the Zamuco and Chiquito tongues; had translated Thomas à Kempis into the latter, and written a history of their nation. It is a circumstance worthy of remark, that of the seven companions who accompanied de Arce in this attempt, not two were of the same race. They were a Sardinian, a Neapolitan, a Belgian, an Austrian, a Bohemian, a Biscayan, and a Spaniard of La Mancha. "So curiously," says Mr. Southey, "was this extraordinary society composed of men of all nations. And what a pre-eminent knowledge of mankind must the Jesuits have possessed from this circumstance alone; this knowledge, of all others the most difficult of acquisition, was thus acquired by them as a mother tongue, and they were fitted for missionaries and statesmen almost without study." Yet this gentleman, intoxicated with self-love, thought himself qualified to pass sentence upon them all, and to rebuke their "superstition" and "idolatry!"

De Arce was now amongst the Chiquitos. Abandoned to the most extraordinary and eccentric superstitions, which it would be unprofitable to describe in detail, and brutalized by almost perpetual intoxication, they had killed the first mission-

* Dobrizhoffer, p. 150.

aries who went amongst them, and flattered themselves that they were now delivered forever from their importunate presence. But they were saved by the very blood which they had shed, as Saul owed his conversion to the martyrdom of St. Stephen. "From their first establishment," says the English historian, "the Chiquito missions were uniformly prosperous in all things. Here, as in other parts of America, the Jesuits were usefully, meritoriously, and piously employed; ready, at all times, to encounter sufferings, perils, and death itself, with heroic and Christian fortitude." And so they converted the whole nation; and with such lasting results, that as M. d'Orbigny observes, the Chiquitos, "happier than other tribes, all live to this day in the missions, under the old form of government established by the Jesuit Fathers."* It was amongst the Chiquitos that this traveller heard the ecclesiastical music which filled even his fastidious ear with admiration.

De Arce, to whom we must return for a moment, aspiring after new dangers and more arduous toils, now entered for the third time the territory of the Chiriguanes. It was almost certain death, but he was one of those missionaries who can say with St. Paul, who finished his career by martyrdom as they did, "The charity of Christ constraineth me." We have no space to relate his labors and tribulations, which were so fruitful, that when, at a later period, the enemies of these apostolic warriors came to count the final results of their warfare, they found forty thousand Chiriguanes, now fervent and docile Christians, collected together in a single mission. De Arce died as he had lived, and as it was fitting that such a man should die, martyred by the Payaguas, in 1717, together with his fellow-missionaries, Maco, Sylva, and de Blende.

Lucas Cavallero, also destined for martyrdom, was laboring at the same time amongst the Puraxis. Unable to resist his fearless charity, and captivated by his preaching and example, they also are won to Christianity and civilization. It would have been reasonable that he should have reposed, at least for a time, amongst these now peaceful neophytes; but he was willing to postpone thoughts of ease to another life, and once more plunged into the thick of the battle. In vain the Puraxis implore him not to expose himself to the fury of the barbarians. He leaves them his blessing, and confiding them to other pastors, hastens to the Manacicas. They also are subdued by his word, and he is next among the Sibacas. Everywhere he is victorious; and as the Quiriquicas had now become the most implacable enemies of his neophytes, and were thirsting for

* *Voyage dans l'Amérique Méridionale*, tome iv., p. 260.

his own blood, he presents himself among them. Such were the simple tactics of these soldiers of the Cross. They ask where danger is to be found, only to confront it. Four other tribes in succession are evangelized by the same indomitable missionary, and still he survives. But such a career could not last forever. His brethren, who knew how to judge apostolic gifts, were accustomed to say of him, "that St. Francis Xavier had no more perfect imitator than Lucas Cavallero." On one occasion he was saluted by a shower of arrows, but they inflicted no wound, though they rained on him from every side. At length his hour arrived, and he found amongst the Puyzocas, in 1711, the crown of martyrdom for which he had so long and so patiently labored.

Let us notice also Father Falconer, an English Jesuit, "of great skill in medicine," who succeeded in founding a mission in the Pampas, which he called Nuestra Señora del Pilar, and whose manner of life is thus described by the writer from whom Maria Theresa of Austria used to delight to hear such narratives, when he had been banished from America. "Wandering over the plains with his Indians to kill horseflesh, having no plate, either of pewter or wood, he always, in place thereof, made use of his hat, which grew at length so greasy, that it was devoured, while he slept, by the wild dogs with which the plains are overrun."*

Cyprian Baraza, says Mr. Southey, "was perhaps the most enlightened Jesuit that ever labored in South America."† He had set out from Lima with the martyr del Castillo, and ascended in a canoe the river Guapay. For twelve days they urged on their frail boat, till they reached the camp of the tribe whom they sought. It was among the Moxos, in the country to the south of the Portuguese territory of Mato Grosso, that Baraza was destined to toil for twenty-seven years. Recalled for a moment to Santa Cruz by his superiors, in consequence of a fever which had reduced him to what appeared incurable debility, he spent the long days of his convalescence in learning the art of weaving, that he might introduce it among his future disciples. At length he was able to resume the apostolate which had been interrupted, and found himself amongst a people so ignorant and barbarous that they had not even any chiefs, lived only for rapine and murder, and hunted men instead of beasts for food. Among these degraded savages this man of profound learning and elegant tastes consented to spend his life; sharing their filthy lodgings; studying all

* Dobrizhoffer, p. 145.
† Vol. iii., ch. xxxiv., p. 198.

their caprices; imitating their habits; and descending himself almost to the condition of a savage, in order to raise them to the dignity of Christians. And this life, for the love of God, he led for more than a quarter of a century; till on the 16th of September, 1702, being then in his sixty-first year, he was martyred by the Baures, whom he had visited in the hope of converting them, and who by his death were won to Christ.

Like all his fellows, he had not only planted but reaped, even in this rugged soil. At his death, fifteen colonies of Christian Moxos had been formed, from twenty to thirty miles apart from each other. "With his own hand," observes Mr. Markham, "he baptized one hundred and ten thousand heathens. He found the Moxos an ignorant people, more savage and cruel than the wild beasts, and he left them *a civilized community*, established in villages, and converted to Christianity."* The churches, of which he was often himself the architect, "were large, well built, and richly ornamented," says Mr. Southey. The Moxos, once so barbarous, had become, as the same writer relates, not only excellent workmen, but even skilful artists. "Cotton was raised in all the settlements," an active commerce created, and habits of intelligent industry formed. "More comforts," says Mr. Southey, "were found in the missions of the Moxos and Baures than in the Spanish capital of Santa Cruz de la Sierra."† And the apostle who had accomplished this amazing work, and who, during many years, had permitted himself no other couch than the bare ground or the steps of his church, was deemed happy and glorious by all his companions, because in his old age he attained to martyrdom, and after devoting all his faculties for forty years to the service of his Master, was beaten to death by the clubs of savages.

A century after his martyrdom, they were still, says Mr. Markham, "a thriving, industrious people, *famous* as carpenters, weavers, and agriculturists;" and an Anglo-Indian writer, alluding in 1857 to this prodigious and lasting work of civilization throughout the whole southern continent, asks how it can be explained that even "the slaves and mestijos of South America should be able to purchase of one single class of English manufactures, *twenty-four times as much* as the free, enlightened, and happily guided Hindus?"‡

Such as Baraza, and Cavallero, and Espinosa, they continued to the end. Dobrizhoffer, the apostle of the Abipones, "was contented," says Mr. Southey, though he hated and reviled the

* Introd., p. xli.
† Vol. iii., ch. xlii., p. 606.
‡ Mead, *The Sepoy Revolt*, ch. xxvii., p. 347.

very men whom he was forced to applaud, "to employ, in laboring among these savages, under every imaginable circumstance of discomfort and discouragement, talents which would have raised him to distinction in the most enlightened parts of Europe." Hénart, once a page of honor in the court of Henri IV., was a man of the same school, and chose the "riches of Christ" before the favor of the most popular of earthly kings; and Herréra, in whom the most learned men of Europe would have recognized a master, but whom the Abipones slew; and Hervas, who died of fatigue, after all his immense labors, by the banks of an obscure stream; and d'Aguilar, who governed the Reductions of the Parana, and at the head of seven thousand Christian Indians saved Peru to the crown of Spain; and Martin Xavier, a kinsman of St. Francis, who, with Father Balthazer Sena, was cruelly starved to death; and Sylva and Niebla, both martyred by the Payaguas; and Arias and de Arenas, who won the same crown; and Ugalde, whom the Mataguyos killed. Not inferior to these were Machoni and Montijo, the apostles of the Lulles; and Julian di Lizardi, who was martyred by the Chiriguanes, his body being found pierced with arrows, and his breviary lying open by his side at the office for the dead, as if he had chanted his own requiem; and Castanarez, who converted the Zamucos, when they had martyred Albert Romero, and was slaughtered himself, in 1744, by the Mataguyos, after forty years of toil; and Joseph de Quiroga, one of the most famous seamen of Spain before he put on the habit of St. Ignatius; and Juan Pastor, who at seventy-three years of age presented himself alone in the camp of the Mataguyos; and Juan Vaz, perhaps a kinsman of that other Vaz, of whom we heard in Ceylon, who died in old age of pestilence while ministering to the sick; and Alvarez, who dwelt alone among the fierce Caaïquas, whom the Spaniards could never reduce, and dared not provoke; and Philip Suarez, the martyr; and Altamirano, and Bartholomew Diaz, and a thousand more, whom we can neither name nor praise — whom God made what they were, who did all their works for His sake alone, and who found in Him their eternal reward.

We have still to show, in conclusion, and we shall be able to do so by the testimony of enemies, what were the actual and final results accomplished in Paraguay by the labors at which we have now glanced. But first let it be permitted to add a word upon the men themselves, of whom we have noticed only an inconsiderable number, because their lives sufficiently represent and illustrate those of their companions, and because thousands in that age left no other memorial on earth by which their passage may now be traced than the multitude of disciples from Canada to China, and from Paraguay to Abyssinia, who by their ministry were "renewed in the spirit of their minds," and gathered into the fold of Christ.

It would be a mere indiscretion to suggest reflections which the deeds of this great company of apostles, who will be imitated by Catholic missionaries to the end of time, will awaken in every Christian soul, and which they kindled even in the breast of the cannibal savage, half beast and half idiot, who wandered by the banks of the Parana and the Uruguay, guided only, till these men stood before him, by the instincts of an animal, and the passions of a demon. But it is well to observe, in contemplating the supernatural virtues of which we have witnessed the action, that they were the natural fruit of gifts and graces which were not only fair to look upon, and mighty to subdue the arts of the wicked one, and to unbind in every land the fetters of his victims, but which had a yet deeper and more awful significance, as even the barbarians of Asia and America understood, inasmuch as they revealed *the immediate and intimate presence of God*, as surely as the golden-fringed cloud tells of the great orb behind, whose rays it obscures but cannot hide. These men were mighty, but evidently not by their own strength; valiant, because they feared nothing but sin; patient, for they walked in the steps of the Crucified; and wise, beyond the wisdom of the children of Adam, because to them it had been said, by Him who once gave the same assurance to earlier missionaries, "*It is not you that speak, but the Spirit of your Father that speaketh in you.*"*

Yet it was at the very moment in which the loving providence of God was sending forth into all lands, from the crowded cities of the furthest East to the solitudes of the unknown West, such a multitude of apostles as the world had never before seen; and that His Spirit, with a mighty inspiration, was filling thousands at once with such graces, and leading them to such victories, as men had almost begun to reckon among the impossible glories of an earlier age; that a people of Saxon origin, newly separated from the Church to which they owed all their past happiness, all their noblest institutions, all their knowledge, and all their civilization, were filling the air with imprecations against the very religion upon which the Almighty was once more impressing, before the face of the gentiles now entering into *their* forfeited inheritance, the seal of His august sanction. It was at this time, when every pagan land was being newly fertilized with the blood of apostles, who died for the name of Jesus, and would have died,—as More and Fisher, Campion and Parsons, and many

* S. Matt. x. 20.

more, died in England,—as joyously and exultingly, for the Church which He illumined with His presence, or for the least of her doctrines; that the founders and promoters of the Anglican schism, less discerning than the pagans of India or China, more blind and perverse than the savages of Brazil and Paraguay, were blaspheming the faith which the Hindoo and the Omagua could no longer resist, when they had once heard the more than human wisdom which proclaimed it to them. It was in the very age in which St. Francis began that immortal apostolate, and those stupendous labors, which were to be continued during two centuries, and in which his brethren and kinsmen were to win to the Church more souls than all the powers of hell were about to snatch from her; that Cranmer, in language which none but an apostate could use, was stirring up the English against the Church which he called "the cursed synagogue of Antichrist;"* that Ridley was reviling her, with the accents of an energumen, as "the Beast of Babylon, that devilish drab, whore, and beast;"† that Bacon, the intimate of Cranmer, was shrieking like a maniac against "the pestiferous and damnable sect of the papists;" and declaring, in hideous words, that "the Sacrifice of the Mass came from hell;"‡ that Jewel, as if the powers of darkness used his mouth for a trumpet, was calling the Vicar of Christ, "the Man of Perdition;"§ that Grindal, who was called "Archbishop of Canterbury," was commanding all the altars in England, upon which the adorable Sacrifice of the New Law had once been offered, "to be utterly taken down, broken, defaced, *and bestowed to some common use;*"‖ that Sandys, who was styled "Archbishop of York," was raving like one possessed against "that synagogue of Satan, that man of sin, that triple-crowned beast, that double-sworded tyrant, that thief and murderer, that adversary unto Christ;"¶ and lastly, that the Anglican Church, the creation of these very men, was exhorting all her ministers diligently to teach the people of England, whether they would hear or no, that, till Cranmer and Beza arose, "*the whole world* had been sunk in the pit of damnable idolatry, by the space of nine hundred years and odd,"**—or, in other words, that Satan had dethroned the Author of Christianity, and brought to naught, in the early dawn of its strength and beauty, the

* *Against Transubstantiation*, book ii., p. 238; ed. Parker Society.
† *Piteous Lamentation*, p. 50; *Letters*, p. 409.
‡ *The Jewel of Joy*, p. 449; Cf. pp. 264, 380.
§ *Zurich Letters*, pp. 33, 47.
‖ *Remains*, p. 134; App., p. 480.
¶ *Sermon* xx., p. 389.
** *Homily on Peril of Idolatry.*

dearest, the most costly, and the most perfect work of His baffled love and unstable power!

We have heard the blasphemy, and have seen how God rebuked it. It was *at this moment*, long expected by the heathen world, but which England had chosen for the hour of her apostasy, that He resolved to create twice ten thousand apostles, who should gather from East and West, from lands hitherto unknown, a new company of guests to that Divine banquet which "they who were invited"* might never more taste, and preach in His name to nations lying in the shadow of death the mystery of salvation which England was now rejecting, and build up among them the very Church which England was vainly striving to uproot. And that all men might surely know whose messengers they were, He clothed them in armor brought out of the innermost sanctuary of heaven, and endowed them with gifts which the Seraphim might have consented to share. Once again the world saw an army of apostles, filled with the zeal of St. Paul, the tenderness of St. Peter, and the charity of St. John; austere as the Baptist, who fed on locusts and wild honey, yet merciful to the weak and infirm; ready to die, like St. Stephen, at the word of their Master, and rewarded in death with the same beatific vision which consoled his agony and theirs. England had begun, for the first time in her history, to invoke maledictions on the Church, and this was God's answer. The missions of the sixteenth century were *God's Protest* against Protestantism.

It is time to bring our account of the missions of Paraguay to a close. In estimating the actual fruits of those missions, it is not the evidence of Catholic writers which we shall interrogate. Protestant authorities, many of whom would read with sympathy, even if they hesitated to repeat, the horrible language of the authors of the Anglican religion, will tell us what the missionaries really effected in South America, and even, as far as such men could understand them, by what means they obtained their success. Mr. Southey, who uses such "intemperate language," as an English Protestant remarks, that "the general circulation of his book is rendered impossible;"† who declares that Vieyra, and Baraza, and Cavallero, and the rest, "never scrupled at falsehood when it was to serve a pious purpose;" who relates that Paraguay exhibited "the naked monstrosity of Romish superstition;" and who describes the sacred mysteries of the Christian Altar in terms which it would be profanation to repeat, and which the evil spirits would not dare to employ,

* S. Luke xiv. 24.

† *Voyage to Brazil*, by Lady Calcott, p 13.

because *they* "believe and tremble; will be our most appropriate witness. Here is his summary of the labors of the missionaries, as respects their geographical limits.

"A chain of missions has now been established in all parts of this great continent. Those of the Spaniards from Quito met those of the Portuguese from Para," thus connecting the Pacific with the Atlantic. "The missions on the Orinoco communicated with those of the Negro and the Orellana. The Moxo missions communicated with the Chiquito, the Chiquito with the Reductions in Paraguay, and from Paraguay the indefatigable Jesuits sent their laborers into the Chaco, and among the tribes who possessed the wide plains to the south and west of Buenos Ayres. Had they not been interrupted in their exemplary career, by measures equally impolitic and iniquitous, it is possible that ere this they might have completed the conversion and civilization of all the native tribes; and probably that they would have saved the Spanish colonies from the immediate horrors and barbarizing consequences of a civil war."*

Let us hear next what he says of their converts, who once wandered naked through the woods, fed on human flesh, and had almost lost the instincts of humanity. "At the close of the eighteenth century, the Indians of these Reductions were *a brave, an industrious, and comparatively a polished people.* They were good carvers, good workers in metal, good handicrafts in general, and the women manufactured calico of the finest quality, &c. &c."†

Again: "Considerable progress had been made both in the useful and ornamental arts. Besides carpenters, masons, and blacksmiths, they had turners, carvers, printers, and gilders; they cast bells and built organs. . . . . They were taught enough of mechanics to construct horse-mills, enough of hydraulics to raise water for irrigating the lands and supplying their public cisterns. A Guarani,"—we know what he had been in his unconverted state,—"however nice the mechanism, could imitate any thing which was set before him."‡

Once more. So universal was the industry of these populous communities, once disdainful of all toil but that of the chase, that the commerce of South America received a development under the prudent direction of their paternal guides, which

* Vol. iii., p. 372. "In fatto non v'ha in tutta l'America meridionale terra alcuna, dove non sieno penetrati i missionarii, e quasi nessuna tribù, a cui non sia stato bandito il Vangelo." *Storia Universale delle Cattoliche Missioni*, vol. i., chap. iv., p. 162.

† P. 842.

‡ Vol. ii., ch. xxiv., p. 350.

even the political economists of our own day might contemplate with admiration—if such philosophers could applaud a state of society in which none were poor and none rich; in which each worked for all; where there was labor without hardship and obedience without oppression; and in which was exhibited on a vast scale that wonderful spectacle which made even Mr. Southey exclaim, "Never has there existed any other society in which the welfare of the subjects, temporal and eternal, has been the sole object of the government!" and which forced from such a man the confession that "the inhabitants, for many generations, enjoyed a greater exemption from physical and moral evil *than any other inhabitants of the globe.*"*

We might stop here, dismissing all further details as superfluous, at least in such a sketch as this; but the educational and religious aspects of these communities claim also a moment's attention. "In every Reduction," says Mr. Southey, "not only was the knowledge of reading, writing, and arithmetic literally universal, but there were some Indians who were able to read Spanish and Latin as well as their own tongue." And, as at Carthagena at the other extremity of the continent, a university was founded under the immediate sanction of the Sovereign Pontiff, so at Cordoba, as Mr. Southey observes, "the university became famous in South America."

Lastly, the influence of religion among this vast population of converted savages was so powerful and all-prevailing, so utterly was vice in all its forms banished from among them, that, in 1721, the Bishop of Buenos Ayres, Don Pedro Faxardo, could report to Philip V. of Spain, "Their innocence is so universal, that I do not believe a mortal sin is committed in these Reductions in the course of a year."†

Mr. Southey offers an explanation, after his manner, of this almost fabulous innocence. "Few vices," says this gentleman with apparent seriousness, "could exist in such communities. Avarice and ambition were excluded; there was little room for envy, and little to excite hatred and malice." He forgets that there was human nature, with all its frailties; and that the enemy of man, who found an entrance even into Paradise, had probably free access to Paraguay. "Drunkenness," he continues, in order to prove that even the virtues of these Catholic Indians were not merits, "was effectually prevented by the prohibition of fermented liquors." Yet he relates in his next volume, forgetting, as such witnesses are apt to do, what

* Vol. ii., ch. xxiv., p. 360.
† Charlevoix, liv. v., p. 94.

he had previously said, that "the Indians of these Reductions cultivated the cane, both for sugar *and rum;* and *distilleries,* which in most places produce little but evil, may be regarded with complacency there, because the moderate use of ardent spirits appears to counteract the ill effects of marshy situations."*

Finally, as the absence of avarice, ambition, envy, and drunkenness, were perfectly natural in vast communities of many thousand persons, recently recruited from utter barbarism, and cannot reasonably be deemed Christian virtues; so the crowning grace of purity was also, according to this Protestant authority, a mere result of "precaution," and of "the spirit of monachism." Besides, as he gravely observes, "their idolatry came in aid of this precautionary system;" which means, it appears, that "no person who had in the slightest degree trespassed against the laws of modesty could be deemed worthy to be accounted among the servants of the Queen of Virgins." And so, in all these great communities, thanks to "monachism" and "idolatry," the law of chastity was kept inviolate.

And now we have heard enough. For two hundred years this work had been in progress, and these were its fruits. Once more the promise had been fulfilled which said of the apostles of the Church, "*They* shall build the places that have been waste from of old. And they shall know their seed among the gentiles, and their offspring in the midst of peoples." Once more the missionaries of the Cross had glorified their Master by one of those victories, of which the philosophers and the philanthropists of this world are always dreaming, always announcing the future promise to their credulous disciples, but always abandoning in impotent despair. Once more the Church had perfected one of those seemingly impossible triumphs which man may never compass or achieve by his own power; and of which all the stages—the first conception, the gradual progress, and the final execution—are traversed only by the succor and the inspiration of the Most High. But even the Church does not always triumph, or how would she imitate the life of her Lord? Like Him, to-day she is saluted with Hosannahs, to-morrow she puts on the Crown of Thorns. It was now the enemy's turn to triumph. Here, as in other lands, he understood, that if he would scatter the sheep, he must first smite the shepherds. While they watched the fold, no irreparable evil could befall the flock. Often, during those two hundred years, the Evil One had tried to force an entrance.

* Ch. xliv., p. 842.

At one time, his agents massacred the pastors who kept such careful watch, but a moment after their place was supplied by others as vigilant and undaunted. At another, he employed corrupt Europeans—filled with jealousy and malice, furious because the Indian had found a refuge from their oppression, or smarting with the shame of baffled cupidity—to plot their destruction. In the single year 1630, the infamous Paulistas—Portuguese and other slave-traders, of various nations—carried off by force fifteen hundred Indians from the Reductions. Fathers Mansilla and Manceta, as Mr. Southey relates, "had the courage to follow them as close as they could, trusting to what they might find in the woods for subsistence, and administering such consolation as they could to the dying, with whom the road was tracked." But these ravages, formidable as they were, could not mar the work of the missionaries, who during two centuries were affectionately supported in all their conflicts by the sovereigns of Spain and Portugal, and often led their Indian soldiers to victory against the enemies of religion and monarchy, when no other power in America could have saved either. The day was now at hand when the same troops would have fought with equal valor to save their Fathers from outrage, if the latter had not refused to use in their own defence the forces which they had constantly employed with success in that of others. "Upwards of a hundred thousand civilized Indians," says a Protestant author, "were ready to take arms in defence of their spiritual leaders, and it was only by their own earnest entreaties to their flocks that tranquillity was preserved."*

We have seen in the earlier chapters of this history how the Christian missions, just when they seemed about to embrace the whole heathen world, were suddenly overthrown in every land; not by the failure of apostolic laborers,—who were never so numerous as at that hour,—but by a conspiracy which had its agents in every court of Europe, and which enlisted the eager sympathies of statesmen, philosophers, and infidels, who attacked the Church through the Society of Jesus, and who despaired of executing the selfish or criminal projects which they had formed, so long as they were confronted on all sides by an army of indomitable warriors—more sagacious than the statesman, more subtle than the philosophers, more courageous than the infidels—whom they could neither divide by policy, nor bribe by favor, nor terrify by threats. And so these puritans of a pantheistic civilization, invoking with cynical hypocrisy the names of liberty, justice, and progress, and despairing of victory by any

* Mansfield, p. 443.

other means over their patient and accomplished adversaries, had recourse at last to vulgar and ignoble violence, the strategy of the bandit, and the craft of the highwayman. It was the only weapon in their armory, and they used it without remorse.

"The Jesuits were hurried into exile," says Mr. Southey, "with circumstances of great barbarity;" and then he shows, that even aged men, who had grown infirm in the work of the missions, actually died in the arms of the soldiers, as they were dragged along the road. And the same scenes occurred in every part of America. "Throughout Chili," says another English Protestant, "in deep midnight, the military governor of every town, attended by a military guard, took possession of every convent. The manner of performing the act was disgraceful to those who ordered its execution; it bore the appearance of performing an act of which they were ashamed."* Out of thirty, who were dispatched in one vessel from Buenos Ayres, "only five," says Dobrizhoffer, "reached Cadiz half alive."†

Let us add, in conclusion, a few additional testimonies from Protestant writers, who have honestly confessed not only the virtues of the missionaries, but the iniquity of the charges brought against them, the malignity of the treatment which they received, and the woeful results of their exile.

They were charged with amassing riches, and even Southey says, "that the Jesuits accumulated nothing from Paraguay is most certain." They were libelled for excluding the Spanish language from the missions, though, as Chateaubriand notices, "all the converts could read and write Spanish correctly," and Southey observes, "malice has seldom been more stupid in its calumnies." They were taunted with making converts "by violence," though they were every hour at the mercy of their own disciples, and the same unfriendly writer replies, "persuasion was their only weapon." They were accused of seeking to form a "principality," and of governing it independently of Spain, and of their own Order in Europe, and even Mr. Southey answers, "The charge will in itself appear incredible to those who reflect upon the character and constitution of the Company." They were all linked together, he observes, by "perfect unity of views and feelings;" whereas the very design imputed to them, "if successful, would in its inevitable consequences have separated the province from the

* Miers, vol. ii., ch. xviii., p. 208.
† Vol. iii., p. 415.

general system, and deprived the Jesuits there of those supplies without which their Order in that country would in one generation have been extinct. They had their root in Europe; and had the communication been cut off, it would have been barking the tree."*

Yet a respectable Anglican clergyman, reviving the very calumnies which even a Southey despised, and which the remorse of their original authors long since retracted and disavowed, was not ashamed to say a few years ago before the University of Oxford, as if sure of the sympathetic applause of such an audience, that "*it was not the Church* that was planted among the natives of Paraguay," though that mission was governed by Bishops and constituted by an Ecclesiastical Council, "but a *principality* of Jesuits!"† So true it is that, in our days, the clergy of this particular school, living only for their own theories and loving only their own inventions, abandoning even the pretence of reverence which they once affected for the Mother of Saints, and surpassing in intemperance the most thoughtless of their sect, have been willing, out of hatred to the Church which has only compassion for them, to catch up the abandoned weapons of the infidels of the eighteenth century, of the very men upon whose malignant fables the contempt of civilized Europe has long ago done justice.

Let us continue the chain of testimony which this digression has interrupted. "The King of Spain," says Mr. Prichard, "yielding to the advice of the enemies of religion and of monarchy, ordered their expulsion from Paraguay, and left one hundred and twenty thousand converts from one single aboriginal nation destitute of the advice and guidance of their spiritual and temporal instructors."‡

Sir Woodbine Parish, who ridicules, like Mr. Southey, the hollow pretexts of their enemies, and eloquently describes the true aim and character of the missions, says: "This was that *imperium in imperio* which once excited the astonishment of the world, and the jealousy of princes. How little cause they had to be alarmed by it was best proved by the whole fabric falling to pieces on the removal of a few poor old priests. A more inoffensive community never existed." And then he generously adds, "It was an experiment on a vast scale, originating in the purest spirit of Christianity, to civilize and render useful hordes of savages who otherwise would, like the rest of the

* Vol. iii., ch. xx., p. 501.
† Grant's *Bampton Lectures*, v., 152.
‡ Section xlvii., p. 466.

aborigines, have been miserably exterminated in war or slavery." He even confesses, that "its remarkable success excited envy and jealousy, and caused a thousand idle stories to be circulated as to the political views of the Jesuits in founding such establishments;" and that these very rumors, invented by malice and propagated by selfish cupidity, "contributed, there is no doubt, to hasten the downfall of their Order."*

"It is not easy," is the confession of a more prejudiced writer, "to find a parallel in history to the act of gigantic self-abnegation, so to speak, by which the Order renounced without a blow a dominion so vast, and seemingly so firmly founded, as that which they exercised in Paraguay."†

Even Robertson, though incapable of appreciating such men or their works, vindicates them from the calumnies of their implacable persecutors. "It is," he observes, "in the new world that the Jesuits have exhibited the most wonderful display of their abilities, and have contributed most effectually to the benefit of the human species. . . . The Jesuits alone made humanity the object of their settling there."‡

Sir James Mackintosh, a man who better deserved the title of philosopher, and who was able to admire "the heroic constancy with which they suffered martyrdom," declares, in his turn, that "the Jesuits alone, the great missionaries of that age, either repaired or atoned for the evils caused by the misguided zeal of their countrymen;" and, after quoting the well-known eulogy of Lord Bacon, he adds, "Such is the disinterested testimony of the wisest of men to the merits of the Jesuits."§

A multitude of American writers of our own day have delivered the same verdict; let the testimony of one suffice. "Their missionary zeal among the Indians in the remotest provinces," says a Secretary of Legation in Mexico, "was unequalled. The winning manners of the cultivated gentlemen who composed this powerful Order in the Catholic Church gave them a proper and natural influence with the children of the forest, whom they had withdrawn from idolatry and partially civilized." And then, denying "that there was just cause" for the affected "alarm" of the King of Spain, and hinting that "he and his council were willing to embrace any pretext to rid his colonial possessions of the Jesuits;" this

* *Buenos Ayres*, ch. xxii., p. 256.
† Mansfield, *ubi supra*.
‡ *Charles V.*, book vi., vol. vi., p. 203 (1817).
§ *Works*, vol. ii., pp. 250, 1.

gentleman notices, with just indignation, that "all expression of public sentiment, as well as amiable feeling, at this daring act against the worthiest and most benevolent clergymen of Mexico was effectually stifled."* Sir Woodbine Parish, an English diplomatic agent, repeats the same reproach, when he quotes the touching protest addressed by the Christian Indians of San Luis to the Governor of Buenos Ayres, in 1768. "Our children, who are in the country and in the towns, when they return and find not the sons of St. Ignatius, will flee away to the deserts and to the forests to do evil." The only reply of the sycophant Bucarelli was to send troops against them, but, adds Sir Woodbine, "he found them not in arms, but in tears."†

Lastly, another English writer of our own day, retracting with a noble candor earlier language, thus estimates the Society whose labors he had once misjudged. "I have formerly ranked its operations in Paraguay and Brazil amongst those of its worst ambition; but more extended inquiry has convinced me that, in this instance, I, in common with others, did them grievous wrong. . . Their conduct in these countries is one of the most illustrious examples of Christian devotion—Christian patience—Christian benevolence and disinterested virtue upon record." And then he adds, in words which he seems to have adopted from another, and which may fitly conclude these impressive confessions: "No men ever behaved with greater equanimity, under undeserved disgrace, than the last of the Jesuits; and the extinction of the Order was a heavy loss to literature, a great evil to the Catholic world, and an irreparable injury to the tribes of South America."‡

The evil was consummated, and, as Sir Woodbine Parish observes, "upwards of a million of Indians" were now deprived of the pastors and guides by whom they had been, as it were, created anew; and whose gentle rule they obeyed with such docile and loving confidence, that, as Ulloa relates, "even if they had been punished unjustly, they would have believed that they deserved it." We have seen, by the unsuspicious testimony of Protestant writers, to what degree of civilization they had attained. No longer dwelling in huts composed of branches, or lying naked on the untilled earth, from which they gathered only the fruits which it spontaneously offered, the Fathers had taught them to build stone houses, and to roof them with tiles; agriculture, directed by science and aided by an effective system of irrigation, gave birth to new products of which they had not

* *Mexico, Aztec, Spanish, and Republican,* by Brantz Mayer, vol. i., ch. xiii., p. 243 (1852).

† *Ubi supra.*

‡ Howitt, *Colonization and Christianity,* ch. x., pp. 121, 141.

suspected the existence; their wide pastures nourished vast herds of cattle; public magazines afforded a safeguard against famine, and carefully organized hospitals a refuge against disease or accident; noble churches, decorated with no mean skill by their own art, displayed treasures of silk and jewels and gold which only their own intelligent industry, and the profits of a well-regulated commerce, had enabled them to procure; they had troops and arsenals, ever at the service of the king, never employed against him; they had become, by the prudent cultivation of their own resources, almost independent of foreign productions; they grew their own sugar, and their own tea, and distilled enough alcohol for the wise uses to which they applied it; they were artists and manufacturers, as well as soldiers and herdsmen; they made all kinds of musical instruments, even the organs, whose tones filled their vast churches, and sung with a sweetness and precision which modern travellers still attest with admiration; and lastly, though the ecclesiastical Council of Lima—mindful, perhaps, that they had but lately been hunters of men, and eaters of human flesh—prescribed the most rigorous precautions in admitting the Indians to the Sacraments, even refusing Holy Communion till after seven years of blameless life, so great was their purity and devotion that these injunctions had become well-nigh superfluous, and the Bishop of Buenos Ayres, who had minutely examined them by virtue of his office as "apostolic visitor," could report to astonished Europe, "They form, perhaps, the most precious portion of the flock of Jesus Christ."

And now the apostles, who out of such rude materials had built up so fair an edifice, were taken from them. "Here ended," says Mr. Southey, whom we quote for the last time, "the prosperity of these celebrated communities. The 'administrators'"—who now supplanted the missionaries—"*hungry ruffians from the Plata*, or fresh from Spain, neither knew the native language, nor had patience to acquire it."

Before these "rapacious and brutal" agents, emissaries of rapine, fraud, and obscenity, the Indian sunk down in despair, or fled away in dismay. The administrators were appointed, as the new authorities—apt representatives of Pombal, Choiseul, and Aranda*—gravely announced, "to purify the Reductions

* Even English Protestants have sometimes appreciated these men and their fellows. "Well read in Voltaire, D'Alembert, and Helvetius," says the late Lord Holland, speaking of Aranda, "jealous of the Church, inveterate against the Jesuits, who had been suppressed during his first ministry, and not insensible to the somewhat exaggerated praises lavished upon him for that measure by those who had rendered infidelity fashionable in Paris." And the school has continued the same to the present day. The "ignorant, rash, and presumptu-

from tyranny;" and the immediate result of their presence was, that "the arts which the Jesuits had introduced were neglected and forgotten; their gardens lay waste, their looms fell to pieces; and in these communities, where the inhabitants, for many generations, had enjoyed a greater exemption from physical and moral evil than any other inhabitants of the globe, the people were now made vicious and miserable. Their only alternative was, to remain to be treated like slaves, or fly to the woods, and take their chance as savages."

Such is the last chapter of a history more full of sadness than any in the modern annals of our race. Out of "a population of one hundred thousand persons, inhabiting thirty towns under the control of the Jesuits," by the borders of the Parana and the Uruguay, which were more exposed than remoter districts to the arts of the "hungry ruffians" who now devastated them, "not a thousand souls," observes Sir Woodbine Parish, "remained in 1825!" "Upwards of *four hundred towns*," says Dobrizhoffer, "which formerly stood around Guadalcazar, a city of Tucuman now destroyed, utterly perished." Other tribes, it is true, suffered less, because the agents of European infidelity could not reach them; but these also were deprived of their Fathers and teachers, and left to find their way in darkness. And yet they have kept the faith, by that special privilege which distinguishes every church founded in the sixteenth century, and have survived a trial hardly paralleled in ecclesiastical story; nay more, their number is again steadily increasing, and "many of the missions at this day," as M. d'Orbigny has told us, "push the Catholic religion even to fanaticism,"—which probably means no more, in the mouth of such a witness, than that they are fervent Christians. The same writer,—who seems to belong to that class, of which France unhappily produces so many, who classify the phenomena of religious life with the same frigid composure with which they arrange the statistics of the animal or vegetable world,—furnishes in his elaborate work many deeply interesting proofs of that marvellous inflexibility of faith of which the history of Catholic missions supplies examples in every land, and which, to a Christian reader, are the most valuable portion of his remarkable volumes. All the Chiquitos, he has already told us, "have persevered, and at this day nothing would induce them to return to the life of the woods."

ous" Urquijo is thus described by the same critic. "So fanatically hostile was he to the Church of Rome, that when, being *Chargé d'Affaires* in London, he first heard that General Bonaparte, by the peace of Tolentino, had spared the Papal Government, he ran like a maniac from his house for more than a mile, on the Uxbridge road, and threw himself in despair into a pond." *Foreign Reminiscences,* by Henry Richard Lord Holland, pp. 75, 100 (1851).

Amongst other nations, he observes, the customs introduced by the missionaries "are still maintained;" and he relates that whenever an old sermon of one of the Jesuit Fathers is read to them, they eagerly assemble, and listen with profound attention. "The old men still remember with sorrow the expulsion of the Fathers in 1767, and all repeat, 'By them we were made Christians; by them we were brought to the knowledge of God, and the possession of happiness.'"*

Wherever he goes, and he went everywhere, M. d'Orbigny says: "I am never weary of admiring the unparalleled results which the Jesuits obtained in so short a time amongst men who had so lately quitted the savage state." And then he contrasts their social and religious condition before and after the suppression of the Society. "Under the Jesuits a severe morality was observed; their present rulers are themselves examples to the Indians of misconduct." "The epidemics which now afflict them were unknown," he says, "in the time of the Jesuits," being kept at a distance by rigorous sanitary arrangements. Besides, the Jesuits nursed them in all their sickness, and now they are left to die like the beasts of the field. Finally, contrasting the economical and agricultural statistics under the Religious and under the Civil administration, he declares, in eloquent words, that "Nature herself seems to have resumed her original aspect."†

Sir Woodbine Parish also, who speaks, like M. d'Orbigny, after personal experience, gives examples, which would be surprising if the fruits of such apostolic toils could excite astonishment, of the abiding power and influence of the missionaries. Thus at Cordoba, which was a sort of metropolis of the missions, "the effects of the preponderating influence of the monastic establishments *are still visible in the habits of the generality of the people.*"‡

Lastly, for it is time to bring this sketch to a close, an official French writer, who was attached to the diplomatic mission to the Plata, confirms, in 1850, all the other witnesses. M. de Brossard is not wholly exempt from the vulgar prejudices of his day, and has not shaken off the superstition, which makes the Jesuits a bugbear and a scarecrow in the eyes of so many shallow and half-educated Frenchmen; but he was capable of expressing with energy the generous impressions which actual observation produced in his mind. "One thing is certain, and ought to be declared to the praise of the Fathers, that since their

* Tome ii., p. 606.
† Tome i., p. 281.
‡ Part iii., ch. xviii., p. 281.

expulsion the material prosperity of Paraguay has diminished; that many lands formerly cultivated have ceased to be so; that many localities formerly inhabited present at this day only ruins. What ought to be confessed is this,—that they knew how to engrave with such power on their hearts reverence for authority, that *even to this very hour*, the tribes of Paraguay, beyond all those who inhabit this portion of America, are the most gentle, and the most submissive to the empire of duty."*

* *Les Républiques de la Plata,* par M. Alfred de Brossard, ch. iv., p. 31.

PART II.

NORTH AMERICA.

It is time to quit South America, that we may search in the northern continent for the last and most notable example which the world offers of the contrast between the work of the Church and the work of the Sects. In tracing this final chapter of a history which we have now almost completed, we shall once more use, as we have done throughout these volumes, the testimony of Protestant authorities; and if we have had reason to feel surprise at the vigor with which they have denounced the operations of their co-religionists in all other lands, the astonishing candor and truthfulness which, with rare exceptions, are the honorable characteristic of American writers, including the eminent names of Washington and Franklin, of Irving and Channing, will be found to supply evidence at least as valuable as any hitherto produced, and perhaps still more remarkable than any for copiousness, precision, and emphasis. It is impossible not to be struck by the fact, that while, on the one hand, the inhabitants of the United States have pushed the right of religious division, and the sovereign independence of the individual, to results which have appalled even the boldest thinkers among them, and have generated at last that chaos of spiritual confusion which their own writers have partly described to us; on the other, a large portion of their literature, since they became a distinct nation, is a protest against the unappeasable jealousies, the eager malice, and fierce resentments, which breathe in every line of the polemical writings of British Protestants. In refusing to transplant to her free shores the effete feudalism of England, America has declined also to become the heir of her arrogant and superstitious bigotry.* Almost the only, certainly the most conspicuous, exceptions to this rule are found, as we might have anticipated, among the members of the American Episcopalian sect; as enamored at this hour of their dull and frigid forms, as incapable of generous and expansive life, as when they first provoked the disgust of the Virginians by their petty tyranny, ignoble greed, and querulous self-love. Imitating the model which they had left behind, they have attempted to restore it in their new home, but without success; and while the majority of American sects, wisely allowing the echoes of sectarian fury to die away, and refusing the heritage of cruel traditions and implacable hatred which have given a special tone both to the literature and the legislation of England, have frankly acknowledged that the Church wears as noble a front in a Republic as in an Empire, and have even been willing to draw their own ranks closer together, not to oppose, but to make room for her; the Episcopalians, affecting to be neither wholly Catholic nor frankly Protestant, but doomed in all lands to restless jealousy and the pangs of that unfruitful labor in which "there is not strength to bring forth," still repeat the fretful maledictions which seem, with them as with others, to be the sole positive element of their religion.

In the United States, whose religious phenomena, as far as they relate to the history of missions, we shall presently review, there is hardly room, except in one sect, for that peculiar form of the passion of hate which is begotten by the memory of wrongs inflicted but not repented. The Americans never decapitated, in the interests of a new religion, a More or a Fisher, nor tortured a Campion, nor tore out the bowels of a Lacy; and being guiltless of the blood of the righteous, have no motive for cherishing hatred against them. Hence the marked contrast between their controversial writings and those of British Protestants. What the English can say of the Church of God, and of her works, we have seen; the Americans will tell us, in their turn, how they have learned to estimate both.

* A single example will serve to illustrate effectively the absence of mean and fretful passions which distinguishes the American people from their English co-religionists. In 1862, the authorities of Harvard University, who are Protestants of an advanced school, spontaneously offered their highest academical degree to the Catholic Bishop of Boston, and being trustees of a plot of land in that city which the Prelate desired to purchase, afforded him every facility in completing his design, which included the conversion of a Protestant into a Catholic church.—*Boston Pilot,* October 25, 1862.

GUATEMALA.

The first province which we must traverse in our way towards the North after passing the Isthmus of Panama, is Guatemala. If we stay here for a moment, we have at least a sufficient apology to offer for what might otherwise be deemed a needless delay. The history of the early missions in this comparatively obscure province has been recently sketched, by an English Protestant writer, with such rare fidelity of research and humanity of temper, that it would be unpardonable to neglect altogether his interesting record. "It will be a pleasure," he says, and his readers will confirm the declaration, "to recount the proceedings of the Dominican monks of Guatemala, instinct with the wisdom of the serpent, as well as the harmlessness of the dove."

It was by Pedro de Alvarado, one of the most famous of the *conquistadores* of the New World, that this province had been annexed to the crown of Spain, in 1523. Animated, like all the warriors of his age and class, by a burning religious zeal which even their many faults never quenched, he had announced to the natives of Guatemala that he "came to show the Indians the way to immortality." The promise was to be abundantly fulfilled, though not by himself. In 1529, the celebrated Dominican, Domingo de Betanzos,—of whose life and character Mr. Helps gives an account almost as remarkable for elevation of sentiment as for purity of style,—set out from Mexico for the scene of Alvarado's conquest. It was a weary journey of four hundred leagues, but he went on foot, "eating little, and that only of wild fruits, and sleeping in the open air." He had scarcely reached the new city of Santiago, when he was summoned back to Mexico to attend a Council of his Order. In the spirit of patient obedience he retraced his steps, though not till he had commenced the building of a humble monastery, which was to be governed a little later by a disciple of his own, who became, as often happens, more illustrious than his master.

It was in 1532 that Las Casas, also a Dominican, arrived in Nicaragua, on his return from Peru. Four years later he entered Guatemala, and "took up his abode in the convent which Domingo de Betanzos had built." With him went Luis Cancér, Pedro de Angulo, and Rodrigo de Ladrada, "all of whom," observes the English historian, "afterwards became celebrated men." "These grave and reverend monks," he continues, "might any time in the year 1537 have been found sitting in a little class round the Bishop of Guatemala (Francisco de Marroquin), an elegant scholar, but whose scholarship was now solely employed to express Christian doctrines in the Utlatecan language, commonly called Quiché. As the chronicler says, 'It was a delight to see the bishop, as a master of declensions and conjugations in the Indian tongue, teaching the good Fathers of St. Dominic.' This prelate afterwards published a work in Utlatecan, in the prologue of which he justly says, 'It may, perchance, appear to some people a contemptible thing that prelates should be thus engaged in trifling things solely fitted for the teaching of children; but, if the matter be well looked into, it is a baser thing not to abase one's self to these apparent trifles, for such teaching is the marrow of our Holy Faith.' The bishop was quite right. It will soon be seen what an important end this study of the language led to; and, I doubt not—indeed it might almost be proved—that there are territories, neighboring to Guatemala, which would have been desert and barren as the sands of the sea but for the knowledge of the Utlatecan language acquired by these good Fathers—an acquisition, too, it must be recollected, not easy or welcome to men of their age and their habits."*

In the neighborhood of Guatemala, on its northeastern frontier, was the province of Tuzulútlan, called by the Spaniards, "The Land of War," because they had thrice invaded and been thrice repulsed from it. Las Casas, whose whole life was a struggle in favor of the Indian against his oppressors, engaged on behalf of the Dominican Fathers to attempt the conversion of this formidable people, "whom no Spaniard dared to go near," but only on a condition that the battle should be waged with spiritual weapons alone, and that no Spaniard should be suffered to enter the province for the space of five years. The Governor of Guatemala accepted the "compact," and then they made their missionary preparations, "using," says Mr. Helps, "all the skill that the most accomplished statesmen, or men of the world, could have brought to bear upon it." It is probable that the Fathers themselves relied still more, as St. Paul was wont to do, upon "the most fervent prayers, severe fasts, and other mortifications," which, as he relates, preceded their perilous attempt.

It would be pleasant to transcribe the whole narrative of Mr. Helps, in which he traces, with rare refinement of language and feeling, the gradual progress of the Fathers and the means by which it was effected. One of the points, he says, to which "the cautious Cacique" of the province directed the most careful attention, in order to test the real character of the new teachers, was "to observe whether they had gold and silver

* Helps, book xv., vol. iii., ch. v., p. 331.

like the other Christians, and whether there were women in their houses." The Dominicans, as we might have anticipated, endured with success an investigation which would have been fatal to certain "missionaries" of whom we have read in these pages; and so, when this point was sufficiently cleared, the prudent Cacique "was the first to pull down and burn his idols; and many of his chiefs, in imitation of their master, likewise became iconoclasts."*

"The mission was extremely successful," says Mr. Helps, as such missions are apt to be; and Las Casas, who was always looking ahead, and providing with all his might against possible dangers, was gladdened by the arrival of a brief from Paul III., pronouncing "a sentence of excommunication of the most absolute kind against all who should reduce the Indians to slavery, or deprive them of their goods." And then "the great Protector of the Indians," as Mr. Helps justly styles Las Casas, passed through Tuzulutlan, and penetrated to Coban. Being well received, he hastened to inform the other Fathers, "and they all commenced with great vigor studying the language of Coban. Each success was with these brave monks a step gained for continued exertion."

After a while the converted Cacique of Tuzulutlan came on a visit to the monastery at Santiago, and was presented by the learned bishop to the governor Alvarado. "Now Alvarado," says our eloquent historian, "though a fierce and cruel personage, knew (which seems to have been a gift of former days) when he saw a man. When the bold Adelantado met the Cacique, the Indian chieftain's air and manner, his repose, the gravity and modesty of his countenance, his severe look and weighty speech, won so instantaneously upon the Spaniard, that, having nothing else at hand, he took off his own plumed hat, and put it on the head of the Cacique." The soldiers who stood round murmured when they saw the great captain pay honor to an Indian; but Alvarado was a better judge than they of the qualities of the new Christian, and continued to treat him with the same distinction during his stay in Guatemala. By this specimen also he understood what sort of converts the Fathers had won in that "Land of War," which his own troops once dared not enter, "but which now," as Mr. Helps observes, "deserved that name less than any part of the Indies."†

Indeed, the once dreaded province had already received from Charles V. the significant name which it bears to this day of

* Ch. vii., p. 350.
† P. 369.

Vera Paz; and Mr. Helps remarks that it is a notable instance "of an aboriginal tribe being civilized and enlightened by their conquerors, and not being diminished in numbers nor restricted in territory." Its prosperity has lasted during nearly three hundred years; and the English historian, alluding to the final success of the great undertaking of Las Casas, observes, in words worthy of himself and of the subject, "It seems something wondrous when any project by one man really does succeed in the way and at the time that he meant it to succeed. We feel as if the hostile Powers, always lurking in the rear of great and good designs, must have been asleep, or, in the multiplicity of their evil work, have, by some oversight, let pass a great occasion for the hindrance of the world."*

Of the four great and good men who accomplished this noble work, and by their wisdom and fortitude added provinces to the kingdom of Christ, two will meet us again in Mexico; let us add a word upon the other two, Luis Cancér and Pedro de Angulo. The latter was appointed Bishop of Vera Paz, in 1556, but "did not live to enter his diocese." His memory long survived, says Mr. Helps, who has carefully studied all the original records, and never begins to write till he has examined every thing relating to his subject, and "the Indians forty years afterwards were wont to quote things which they had heard him say in the pulpit. He gained their love, it is said, so much, that 'they did not know where they were without him.'" One of them, "giving an account of the effect which his preaching produced, used an expressive metaphor—especially expressive in that country—comparing the excitement in the hearts of his Indian audience to that of ants in an ant-heap when some one comes to disturb it with a stick."

Luis Cancér, the first of the four to enter the province of Vera Paz, was the only one honored with the crown of martyrdom. He was put to death by the Indians of Florida, who knew not how to distinguish him from the violent and unjust Spaniards whom they feared and hated. "How seldom," says Mr. Helps, in allusion to this martyrdom, "do men recognize their true friends!"

It is time to pursue our journey. Three provinces more had been won to religion and civilization, and this time the work was done by Dominicans. But if they succeeded, and the fruits of their apostolic toils remain to this day,—for paganism is almost unknown in these regions,—it was not because they were Dominicans, not because they were learned, patient, and wise,

* Ch. ix., p. 398.

but because they had received from God a special vocation to this work, and had been sent forth by the Church to accomplish a task which none but her chosen apostles have ever undertaken, and in which none but they may ever hope to triumph. This is the only reflection which we miss, and which we could hardly expect to find, in the graceful and learned pages of Mr. Helps.

CENTRAL AMERICA.

It would detain us too long to speak in detail of the various provinces of Central America. If we refer to them for a moment, it is with the object of recording the experience of an English Protestant missionary, who was not indeed of the school of Angulo or Las Casas, but should not on that account be passed over in silence. It is our business to trace a contrast. This gentleman announces, then, in 1850, after a somewhat disastrous career in these regions, and in language which his English friends would perhaps applaud, that "Romanism is the putrescent heart of Central America." The rest of his book is in the same style. He observes with displeasure that even "the Carif women," who are not, socially speaking, a high class, "have been seen joining in the prostrate adoration of an image of the Virgin," and that he and his companions tried in vain "to preserve them from these calamities."

From his own account, the state of the Protestant mission was not consoling. All its members were fighting together, within hearing of "the Carif women," and with the usual lavish expenditure of Scripture texts. One of them retired "for want of a congregation," a trial which the rest endured with greater fortitude. The narrator himself got into jail, and seems to have stayed there a good while. Finally, the "mission house" was sold, and converted into a lunatic asylum. Such was the issue of Protestant efforts in this region.

But this is not the most important information which we derive from this gentleman, whose "violent extramission" from Guatemala was related in an earlier chapter, and may perhaps account for his lively resentment. The people of Brazil, Mr. Ewbank has told us, despise a Protestant missionary, "from a rooted belief in his ignorance and presumption;" in Guatemala, as Mr. Crowe relates with indignation, "a Jew is something akin to a demon, and a Protestant is something lower and more dangerous than a Jew." He adds, however, as if to excuse this misconception on the part of the Guatemalians, that "the general deportment of the Anglo-Saxon visitors, or residents, has not been such as to raise the respect of the inhabitants for the Protestantism which they profess," and that his own attempts to apply a remedy "have signally failed." And so he returned to England, and the people of Central America still rank him and his co-religionists below the Jew.*

It was apparently, as we have said, the memory of his own discomfiture which inspired Mr. Crowe's volume. Other Protestant travellers, who had a much more extensive knowledge of Central America, thus correct his unfavorable report. Mr. Stephens, unconsciously reproving, like so many of his candid and intelligent countrymen, the ignoble malice of mortified missionaries, gives a very different account, in his well-known work, both of the inhabitants of these tropical regions and of their pastors. Of a large tribe of Carib Indians, dwelling within the British territory, on the Gulf of Honduras, he says, "Though living apart, as a tribe of Caribs, *they were completely civilized.* . . . . . In every house was a figure of the Virgin, or of some tutelary saint; and we were exceedingly struck with the great progress made in civilization by these descendants of cannibals, the fiercest of all the Indian tribes whom the Spaniards encountered."

A little later, he assists at a religious service in the same tribe, conducted by a strange priest, an Irishman, whose total ignorance of their language "led to confusion; but all were so devout and respectful, that, in spite of these tribulations, the ceremony was solemn."

"From the moment of my arrival," says the same writer, "I was struck with the devout character of the city of Guatemala," of which Mr. Crowe retained such unpleasant recollections. "Every house had its figure of the Virgin, the Saviour, or some tutelary saint, and on the doors were billets of paper with prayers." One of these, which Mr. Crowe perhaps failed to notice, was as follows: "May the true blood of Christ our Redeemer deliver us from pestilence, war, and sudden death. Amen."

Mr. Stephens visited every part of Central America, and was constantly the guest of the clergy in every province. Speaking of "the whole Spanish-American priesthood," he says, in spite of Protestant sympathies, exactly what Mr. Temple and others have already told us of the same class. "They were all intelligent and good men, who would rather do benefits than an injury; in matters connected with religion they were most reverential, labored diligently in their vocations, and were without reproach

* *The Gospel in Central America*, by Rev. F. Crowe, ch. xii., p. 242; ch. xiv., pp. 294, 306, 457.

among their people." He remarks that he "had an opportunity of seeing throughout all Central America the life of labor and responsibility passed by the cura in an Indian village . . . . . looked up to by every Indian as a counsellor, friend, and father," and declares, after coming out on one occasion from a church in which all the Indians had assisted at Vespers, "I could but think, what subsequently impressed itself upon me more and more in every step of my journey in that country, Blessed is the village that has a padré."*

Perhaps we may now cease to wonder that Mr. Crowe and his companions only succeeded in getting into jail, and that their mission-house was converted into a lunatic asylum.

MEXICO.

And now let us enter Mexico. The conquest of Mexico by Spain has been compared by Lord Macaulay with that of Hindostan by the English. Only one point of contrast between the two events was left unnoticed, perhaps because unheeded, by the great Essayist. He nowhere reminds either himself or his readers that Mexico became a Christian nation, while India has only been confirmed in her worship of demons. Such is the familiar contrast which history records, for the admonition of mankind, between the fruits of a Catholic and a Protestant conquest.

Mexico is Christian. Count up all the misdeeds of the violent men who subdued the Aztec race,—exaggerate, if it be possible, all their faults, and add a darker shade to their crimes,—still, when all is told, the fact remains, which you will never be able to obliterate, that paganism is extinct in Mexico, and triumphant in India.

And how was this conversion of a whole people, hitherto abandoned to a dark and bloody superstition, brought to a prosperous issue? How was this mighty work of renovation accomplished, the contemplation of which forced an eminent American writer of our own day to exclaim, "How easily has the Indian element in Mexican nationality been developed into civilized and productive co-operation!"† By what mysterious and persuasive arts was this new triumph of Christianity effected, of which a French writer epitomizes the whole history in a few emphatic words, when he says, "The progress of religion in

* *Incidents of Travel in Central America*, by John Lloyd Stephens, ch. ii., pp. 13, 15; ch. viii., pp. 104, 108; ch. xxxv., p. 442 (1854).

† *Texas*, by F. Law Olmsted, p. 297.

America, by the preaching of a few poor religious, notably of the order of St. Francis, was so universal, that in the space of forty years, six thousand monasteries and six hundred bishoprics were founded in that land?"*

It is only a brief answer which we can give to this question. No doubt it was to the labors of apostolic men,—such as Betanzos and Motolinia; Martin de Valencia and Peter of Ghent; Francisco de Soto, Las Casas, and Zumarraga; such, in a word, as that great company of valiant and gifted men who at the same hour were toiling for God's glory in every land, from Lake Huron to the Gulf of Siam—that this magnificent conquest was chiefly due. But justice claims even for the mailed warriors of Spain, who fought, like Cortez, with the sword in one hand and the cross in the other, some share in the noble work to which it is their glory, and almost their justification, to have contributed. It has been the fashion, with all but a few cautious and patient students of history, to load with undiscriminating obloquy the men who overthrew, by a prodigy of valor and policy, the throne of Montezuma. Yet something may be said in their behalf. It is not, indeed, to such red-handed warriors, impetuous as Jehu and resolute as Joab, that we can point as types of the Christian character. Yet even these imperious soldiers, who shouted from morning till night their war-cry of "Santiago,"—Cortez and Alvarado, Sandoval and Pizarro,—will be monuments to the end of time of the power and majesty of that Faith from which, in spite of their errors, they derived all their strength, and without whose inspirations they would neither have attempted nor accomplished the immortal enterprise with which their names are forever associated.

A tardy justice has begun to recognize in our own day the truth of this allegation. Even Protestant writers will tell us, that it was not a thirst for gold which was, or could be, the sole spring of action with a man so truly great as Cortez. "There is much to blame," says one of the most elegant and discerning historians of this memorable epoch, "in the conduct of the first discoverers in Africa and America; it is, however, but just to acknowledge that the love of gold was not by any means the only motive which urged them, or which *could* have urged them, to such endeavors as theirs."† They were penetrated, he adds, with the most profound conviction of "the fatal consequences of not being within the communion of the Church." He does not, of course, share their belief, but he is keen enough to see that it affords the only rational explanation of their conduct.

* Migne, *Dictionnaire des Conversions*, introd., p. 18 (1852).
† Helps, vol. i., ch. i., p. 28.

A French writer, equally devoid of partial sympathies, detects also the same motive in all their actions. "They redeemed," says M. de Brossard, in words which we cannot accept without modification, "the disorders of their private life by deeds of charity and an ardent faith." And this was especially true of Cortez. "An object which Cortez never lost sight of," says Mr. Helps, "was the conversion of the natives." It was Cortez who first requested that religious might be sent from Spain. "I supplicate your Imperial Majesty," he says in one of his letters, alluding to the possibility of converting the natives, "that you would have the goodness to provide religious persons, of good life and example, for that end." And when the Franciscans arrived, it was in the following words that he presented them to the people of Mexico. "These are men sent from God, and ardently desiring the salvation of your souls. They ask neither your gold nor your lands, for despising all the goods of this world, they aspire only after those of the next."*

It is an error to suppose that Cortez, a man filled with tender and generous thoughts, was cruel by nature, or that he was as careless of the blood of others as he was of his own. He never slew for the sake of slaying, and was as calm in victory as he was terrible in battle. He deplored, with perfect sincerity, the very actions in which he took part, and only inflicted death upon those who refused mercy. It must be remembered too, that he had entered with Montezuma that infernal shrine in which the hearts of men smoked in golden platters before the idols of the nation, and that he quitted it trembling with religious horror and indignation, and became thenceforward as truly the minister of the Most High in chastising the demon-worship of this guilty race, as Joshua was when he led the armies of Israel across the Jordan. Nor let it be forgotten that to him is due, at least in part, the significant and atoning fact that the noblest temple which has ever been reared in the New World stands on the very site of that foul and impious den, from which Cortez hurled with his own hand both the blood-stained priests who were lodged within it, and the idols which, but for him, might perchance have been worshipped at this hour.†

Lastly, it is evident that Cortez was otherwise appreciated, both by the Mexicans themselves and by the prelates and mis-

* Henrion, tome i., ch. xxxvi., p. 390.

† "On the same lofty platform, where Cortez converted the half-burned temple of the great 'teocalli' to the purposes of a Christian church, now stands a more modern ecclesiastical structure, dedicated to Our Lady *de los Remedios*, whose shrine is tended *by an Indian priest* of the blood of the ancient Cholulans." *Prehistoric Man*, vol. i., ch. xiv., p. 433.

sionaries who were their most courageous and devoted protectors, than by the crowd of careless or half-informed critics who have neither done justice to the merits nor rightly discriminated the faults of this illustrious man. When he returned from his first visit to Spain, "he was received," we are told, "with vivid demonstrations of delight by great numbers of the people in New Spain, both Spaniards *and Indians*."* Zumarraga, the first bishop of Mexico, and Domingo de Betanzos, men as valiant as himself though in another cause, and always strenuous protectors of the Indians, were not only his personal friends, but the chosen executors of his will; while another prelate of the same class, Sebastian de Fuenleal, who would have refused homage to any mortal potentate, unless he could offer it with a good conscience, chose him for his counsellor. "Far from looking upon Cortez as an enemy," says Mr. Helps, "the wise bishop acted entirely in concert with the Captain-General. It was Don Sebastian's practice to take counsel with many persons as to what ought to be done, but with the Marquis alone, or, at least, with very few persons, as to the mode of executing what had been resolved upon."†

Cortez was a warrior who had something of the temper of St. Louis, and more of Richard Cœur de Lion. Like the last, he turned aside neither to right nor left, but clove a straight path through all that barred his way; like the first, every blow he dealt was a defiance to the pagan, a victory for the Cross. He was inconsistent, as men of war are wont to be; but he was no vulgar swordsman, battling only for wealth and honors. His great heart was filled to the brim with that faith which meaner men call "fanaticism," but which alone made him what he was, which gave lustre to all his actions, and which he assisted to plant so deeply in the soil of Mexico, that, in after days, it overshadowed all the land.

Even Alvarado and Pizarro, men far inferior to Cortez, were no such graceless ruffians as modern critics, possessing neither their heroic valor nor their religious instincts, would have us believe. It is no small praise to the first, that, with all his faults, he was honored with the friendship of the learned and saintly Bishop of Guatemala. His last will remains to prove that he knew at least how to deplore his injustice and violence, and desired to atone for them; and when he lay on his death-bed, mangled by that avenging rock which had crushed his stalwart limbs, and was asked where his pain was sorest, the spirit within him broke forth in the sorrowing cry, "My soul! my soul!"

* Helps, vol. iii., ch. vi., p. 198.

† Ch. viii., p. 218.

Pizarro, too, an adventurer and an outcast from his youth, whether he was starving in the island of Gorgona, with his fourteen dauntless followers, or leading on his handful of comrades to battles in which they were one against a thousand, or plucking the Inca with his own hand from his litter in the great square of Cassamarca, was ever, after his kind, a soldier of the Cross. "In the midst of all their misery," says a Protestant historian, "they did not forget their piety." In Gorgona, where they spent three heavy months of doubt and suffering, while "subsisting upon shell-fish, and whatever things, in any way eatable, they could collect upon the shore;" "every morning they gave thanks to God: at evening-time they said the *Salve* and other prayers appointed for different hours. They took heed of the feasts of the Church, and kept account of their Fridays and Sundays."* And when the decisive hour arrived, and Pizarro stood face to face with Atahuallpa, it was Father Vicente de Valverde who, at the conqueror's request, "advanced towards the Inca, bearing a cross in one hand, and holding a breviary in the other," and explained to the Peruvian prince, still at the desire of Pizarro, the mysteries of "the true Catholic Faith," and "the history of Jesus Christ." Finally, when this intrepid warrior came to his end, and the violent man fell under the swords of assassins, he drew the sign of the cross on the floor with his own blood, kissed with his dying lips the emblem of salvation, and with that supreme act of love and contrition Pizarro passed to his account.

Compare these men, who in every case won kingdoms for their Divine Master, and who banished paganism from every land which they entered, with the English captains who scattered the hosts of the Mogul or the Mahratta. Little recked *they* of the glory of God, or of the progress of the Faith. Fanaticism, as they would have called the sublime enthusiasm of a St. Paul or a Las Casas, was not their line. No word did *their* tongues ever utter in honor of the Cross, no hymn did they chant in praise of the Crucified. "Not a temple has been thrown down *by the English*," says a Protestant writer, "not a single deity removed by proclamation from the calendar."† To live as the heathen blushed to live, and sometimes to die as even the heathen would have been ashamed to die; to smile complacently on the foul superstitions which they neither rebuked themselves, nor would suffer others to rebuke; to "*discountenance Christianity as a most dangerous innovation*," while they attended banquets in honor of Ganesa, fired royal salutes to do

* Helps, vol. iii., p. 447.
† Mead, *The Sepoy Revolt*, ch. xix., p. 245.

homage to Sivah, or gathered wealth from the worship of Juggernaut; such, as their own historians have told us, were the tactics of the English conquerors of Hindostan. And they were the same from first to last. The hero of Plassy, almost as great a soldier as Cortez, found an exit from life through the shameful gate of suicide; the victor of Assaye and Seringapatam died as his own war-horse died, and with scarcely more thought of the Unseen. No province did they, or such as they, ever win to Christ. They found India pagan, and they left it pagan. One lesson only they imparted to Hindoo or Mahometan, which he learned but too well. They taught him, by their own example, to hate and despise the religion of which *they* were professors, and to deride a doctrine the very preachers of which, when at last they arrived in India, were so manifestly types of worldliness and self-indulgence, that, far from producing any impression upon the mocking pagans who doubted "whether they believed their own Scriptures," a conspicuous member of their order ingenuously confessed, "Your profession of religion is a proverbial jest throughout the world."

There is no need, even if we had space, to recount the toils by which men of another faith, and other gifts, won Mexico to the cross of Christ. Here, as in every other land in which they encountered only such impediments as were common to St. Paul or St. James, they did the work for which God raised them up, and for which He endowed them with adequate gifts. They failed only, where St. Paul or St. James would perhaps have equally failed, in countries where the heathen have been fatally prejudiced against Christianity, by the divisions and contradictions, the irrational precepts or the effeminate habits, of Protestant teachers. Against *such* obstacles even apostles contend in vain, or only at a fearful disadvantage.

In Mexico they had a fair field, and had to fight only against the corruptions of the human heart, and the devices of the Evil One. They overcame both. All South America, from the Isthmus of Panama to the frontiers of Patagonia, and from the valleys of Peru to where the floods of the Amazon and the Orinoco mingle with those of the Atlantic, was converted by them; and then they spread their conquests in the North, through Guatemala, Nicaragua, Mexico, Texas, and California. They had done all that apostles could do. Canada and the United States, which would have shared the same privilege, were snatched from them; because *there*, as we shall see, a hundred spurious forms of Christianity, stripped of every Divine element, and each battling against every other, had inspired only the disdain of the barbarian, who formed such an estimate of the doctrine and its teachers, that he not unfrequently went down to his untimely grave, imprecating with his latest breath a malediction upon both.

One special trial beset the apostles of Mexico, and it should be noticed, because there is perhaps nothing in their career more admirable than the struggle by which they overcame it. It was not from such men as Cortez or Pizarro that they ever encountered opposition in their holy work, but from a later generation of ignoble adventurers, vulgar soldiers or greedy lawyers, who soon swarmed in the fair regions which the great Marquis had added to the crown of Spain. Against these men, whose crimes were often unredeemed by a single virtue, Las Casas and Zumarraga, and all their brethren, fought with a patient but unyielding courage which even the most prejudiced writers have celebrated with applause. "The Roman Catholic clergy in America," says the unbelieving Robertson, "uniformly exerted their influence to protect the Indians, and to moderate the ferocity of their countrymen."* "We must express our admiration," says an English naturalist, "for the exalted piety of the Roman Catholic missionaries, who, in these countries, inhabited by human beings in the lowest state of degradation, endured poverty and misery in all forms, to win the Indians to better habits and a purer faith."† "The learned and thoughtful men," says Mr. Helps—"for such the monks and ecclesiastics must be held to be, looking before and after, knowing many of the issues of history, and often appealing to great and general principles, are steadily arrayed against the mere conquering soldier,—the good Bishop Zumarraga and his confraternity, against Nuno de Guzman and his followers."‡

Sometimes the civil authorities, who wished to employ the Indian only as a beast of burden, cunningly affected in their appeals to Spain to defend "the prerogatives of the State" against "the encroachments of the Church;" but Charles V. was too sagacious a monarch to be much moved by arguments of which he appreciated the real character, but which the same class of statesmen use in our own day to frighten feebler potentates.

On the other hand, notable examples are found of active and generous co-operation with the clergy on the part of the lay Auditors of Mexico. In 1531, when there were only a hundred Dominicans and Franciscans in the whole country, the Auditors "sent to the Emperor, beseeching him to send out more monks, being, doubtless, of the same mind with a subsequent Viceroy

* *Charles V.*, notes, vol. x., p. 400.

† *Narrative of the Voyage of H.M.S. Herald*, by Berthold Seemann, F.L.S., vol. ii., ch. ix., p. 153 (1853).

‡ Book xiv., ch. v., p. 186.

of Mexico, who, when there was much question about building forts throughout the country (a suggestion urged upon him by the authorities at home), replied, that towers with soldiers were dens of thieves, but that convents with monks were as good as walls and castles for keeping the Indians in subjection."*

Again: when a new generation of Auditors "made the noble endeavor to provide homes and instruction for the numerous orphans who had lost their parents by reason of the cruel work imposed upon them in the mines," Quiroga, one of their number,—"who, it must be remembered, was a lawyer, and therefore less likely to be led away by a love for monastic institutions,"—urgently recommended the Council of the Indies "to make a settlement of the young Indians in each district, at a distance from other *pueblos*, and in each settlement to place a monastery with three or four *religiosos*, who may incessantly cultivate these young plants to the service of God." And so perfectly did these shrewd men of the world of that age comprehend, what the same class affect to doubt in our own, that monasteries are both cheaper and more potential institutions than prisons or workhouses, that Quiroga, filled with admiration at what the monks had already done, exclaims, "I offer myself, with the assistance of God, to undertake to plant a kind of Christians such as those were of the primitive Church; for God is as powerful now as then. I beseech that this thought may be favored."†

Nor was this the language of mere enthusiasm. What the Religious could do had been already sufficiently proved in many a province of America, and Mexico was not destined to be an exception. Already the Indian, refusing to see in them the emissaries of a foreign power, had learned to regard the Fathers first with astonishment, and then with veneration. "Their poverty, their temperance, their simplicity of life," says a Protestant writer, "recommended them at once to the Indian."‡ And as time went on, and fresh colonies of Dominicans and Franciscans arrived, all filled with the same charity, and displaying the Christian religion in its noblest and most attractive form, the Mexican understood that these men came to him with hands filled only with gifts and blessings. It was they who obtained from the Holy See the menace of excommunication against his selfish oppressors, and from the royal authority such decrees as the following: "That no Indian should carry any burdens against his will, whether he was paid for it or not;" that "when they were sent to the mines they

* Helps, book xiv., ch. vi., p. 200.
† Id., p. 208.
‡ Id., ch. xv., p. 313.

were to be provided with clergy there;" that the "Protectors," of whom the noble and generous Las Casas was one, should "cause that the Indians be well treated, and taught in secular things, and instructed in the Articles of the Holy Catholic Faith."*

What marvel if the Indian abandoned himself with love and confidence to such teachers as a bountiful Providence had now provided for him? How should men who are thus described even by Protestant writers fail to win his heart? Of the Bishop-President of Mexico, Don Sebastian Ramirez de Fuenleal, who arrived in 1531, Mr. Helps gives the following portrait: "No single subject of government occupied his attention to the exclusion of others. He founded churches; he divided Mexico into parishes; he established a college, and was the first man to propose *that a learned education should be given to the Indians.* His efforts in this matter were successful; and it is curious that one of the best chroniclers of the bishop's proceedings (Torquemada) was instructed in the Mexican language by a most accomplished Indian, who had been educated at this college."†

"The clergy," says the same careful and conscientious historian, "not only taught spiritual things, but temporal also. They converted, they civilized, they governed; they were priests, missionaries, schoolmasters, kings. A considerable share in the credit of this good work must be given to the unwearied labors of the Franciscan and Dominican monks. That the missionary spirit in that age was so potent and so successful as it was must in some measure be attributed to the intense belief which the missionaries entertained of the advantage to be derived from outward communion of the most ordinary kind."

St. Paul seems to have shared the same "intense belief," if we may judge from his summary exhortation to Titus how to deal with "*a man that is a heretic*,"‡ or his equally emphatic warning to the Philippians, "*Beware of dogs.*"§ "Earth has no privilege," is in every age the confession of loving faith, "equal to that of being a member of His Church; and they dishonor both it and Him who extenuate the dismal horrors of that outer darkness in which souls lie that are aliens from the Church." Only they who have received this "royal grace" can understand their unutterable calamity who possess it not, or the "appalling difficulties of salvation outside the Church. This

* Helps, book xiv., ch. xiv., pp. 175–177.
† Id., p. 219.
‡ Tit. iii. 10.
§ Philip. iii. 2.

is the reason why the saints have ever been so strong in the instincts of their sanctity, as to the wide, weltering, almost hopeless deluge which covers the ruined earth outside the ark. Harsh, to unintelligent uncharitable kindness intolerably harsh, as are the judgments of stern theology, the saints have even felt and spoken more strongly and more peremptorily than the theologians. The more dear to the soul the full light and sacramental life of Jesus, the more utter the darkness, the more dismal the death, of those who are without that light and life, in their fulness and their sacramentality. The eternal possession of Mary's Immaculate Heart, together with all the intelligences of the countless angels, would not suffice to make one act of thanksgiving for the single comprehensive mercy of being Catholics, and of acknowledging St. Peter's paternal supremacy."*

But this ardent conviction, of the "advantage to be derived from communion" with the Catholic Church, which alone has inspired all apostolic works, and which St. Peter and St. Paul, St. James and St. Jude, expressed in such startling words, "would not alone have caused the rapid progress of these missionaries," Mr. Helps truly observes, "had there not been to back it the utmost self-devotion, supreme self-negation, and also considerable skill in their modes of procedure." Was not the "supreme self-negation" a result of the "intense belief," and were not both the fruit of Divine grace, which during some twenty centuries has always lavished these noblest gifts upon one class of men, and always refused them to every other?

Sometimes the same English historian whom we have so often quoted, and always with pleasure, gives individual examples of that great company of preachers by whom Mexico was evangelized. Of the Franciscan Martin de Valencia, head of the Order in Mexico, he speaks thus: "When he arrived in Mexico, he maintained the most rigid mode of life. He went barefoot, with a poor and torn robe, bearing his wallet and his cloak on his own shoulders, without permitting even an Indian to assist in carrying them. In this fashion he used to visit the convents under his jurisdiction. Being already an old man when he arrived in Mexico, he could not learn the language with the same facility as his companions; so that what he most devoted himself to was teaching the little Indian boys to read Spanish. . . . . He sang hymns with the little children, and, as we are told, did great good in the Indian villages where he resided." Like Moses, he would sometimes go apart from the

* Father Faber, *The Blessed Sacrament*, book iv., sec. 5, p. 502.

world to draw nearer to God, for whose sake he lived this life, and was accustomed to "retire to an oratory on a mountain, where he might enjoy the most profound contemplation."

Francisco de Soto, "a man of singular piety, who afterwards refused the bishopric of Mexico," was a missionary of the same class; and Toribio Motolinia, who wore out his life in "teaching, catechizing, and baptizing the Indians;" and of whom it is said, that "he baptized no less than four hundred thousand of them."

But it was Peter of Ghent, Mr Helps assures us, "who perhaps did most service." He was a Flemish lay brother, "who, in his humility, never would be any thing but a lay brother." From him the Mexicans learned "to read, to write, to sing, and to play upon musical instruments. He contrived to get a large school built," in which, besides more elementary matters, he taught them painting, carving, and other arts. "Many idols and temples owed their destruction to him, and many churches their building. He spent a long life—no less than fifty years—in such labors, and was greatly beloved by the Indians, amongst whom he must have had thousands of pupils. The successor of Zumarraga one day generously exclaimed, 'I am not the Archbishop of Mexico, but brother Peter of Ghent is!'"

Of Domingo de Betanzos, who became "the principal Dominican in New Spain," we have already heard in Guatemala. It was a sharp life which he and his brethren led, following the strictest rule of their ascetic Order, and "so versed in self-denial," as our historian observes, that "the sternest duties of a missionary were easy to them." They were men thoroughly penetrated with the maxim of St. Paul, "No man being a soldier of God entangleth himself with secular business."* They could be merciful to the poor, for none were so poor as they. They could rebuke the rich, for they had often resigned wealth and honors in order to have the right to do so. The very sight of them suggested thoughts of penance, hope, and manly effort. Of Betanzos, to whom "his brethren were attached beyond measure,"—for monks have more loving hearts than the egotistical votaries of pleasure, who are too feeble even to love in earnest,—we read as follows: "The principal men in New Spain held him in high estimation; the Indians were delighted with his disinterestedness; and the whole country reverenced him, and looked up to him as a father."† When he had done his work in Mexico, the brave old man, "moved by a desire for martyrdom," wanted to go to China, and so kindled

* 2 Tim. ii. 4.
† Helps, ix. 407.

the heart of the noble Bishop Zumarraga, says Mr. Helps—though he only considers it a proof of "high-souled fanaticism,"—that he was ready to resign his bishopric to go with him. The Pope, however, refused permission, and they both died in the land for which they had done so much.

Ortiz, afterwards Bishop of Santa Martha, was of the same school, and Julian Garces, "a very learned man and an elegant Latin writer," who was the first Bishop of Los Angelos in Tlascala; and Antonio de Montesino, subsequently martyred in India, and Lorenzo de Bienvenida, who boldly admonished Philip II. not to peril his own soul by tolerating the injustice of the Spaniards;* and a hundred more, who displayed in Mexico the same virtues, waged the same battles, and gained the same victories, as their fellow-laborers in other lands.

And now if we inquire, without attempting to enter into impossible details, what was the final result of all this apostolic toil, the kindly and accomplished historian whom we have followed will tell us. "Two important letters," he observes,—the one addressed by Bishop Zumarraga, in 1551, to a General Chapter of the Franciscan Order, held at Toulouse; the other by Bishop Garces a year or two later to Pope Paul III.,—afford information from which "we are able to form something like a complete picture of the state of this early Church in relation to the Indians."

The Bishop of Mexico relates, that already more than a million Indians had been baptized by the Franciscans alone; "five hundred temples have been thrown down, *and twenty thousand idols broken in pieces, or burnt.* In place of these temples have arisen churches, oratories, and hermitages. But, as the good bishop says, that which causes more admiration is, that whereas they were accustomed each year in this city of Mexico to sacrifice to idols more than twenty thousand hearts of young men and young women, now all those hearts are offered up, with innumerable sacrifices of praise, not to the Devil, but to the Most High God."†

Both the venerable writers speak with enthusiasm of the piety and docility of the Indian children, and the Bishop of Tlascala says of those in his own diocese, "they not only imbibe but exhaust the Christian doctrines'—'non hauriunt modo, sed exhauriunt, ac veluti ebibunt.'" Of their exactness in frequenting the Divine office, and in the practice of confession, as well as of "the dove-like simplicity" with which they accused themselves

* *Voyages, &c., pour servir à l'histoire de la Découverte de l'Amérique,* par H. Ternaux Compans, tome ii., p. 307. See also the letter of Juan de Zumarraga in tome v.

† Helps, iii., 300.

of their faults, they speak with equal admiration; while "the Bishop of Mexico mentions that the children steal away the idols from their fathers, for which, he says, some of them have been inhumanly put to death by their fathers; but they live crowned in glory with Christ."

Lastly, the English writer whom we have so often quoted, referring to that final victory of the Faith which was accomplished in Mexico by "the untiring efforts of such men as Las Casas, Betanzos, Zumarraga . . . and the various prelates and monks who labored with or after these good men," not only declares with a noble frankness that "it is a result which Christians of all denominations may be proud of and rejoice in,"—an excessive statement, since only one "denomination" has ever had the smallest share in producing such results,—but is led to make the following weighty reflection upon the whole history: "We are told that in the sixteenth century there was a revival throughout Europe in favor of the Papacy, which set the limits to Protestantism—those limits which exist even in the present day; but we cannot say that any such revival appears to have been greatly needed, or to have taken place in Spain. The fervent and holy men, whose deeds have been enumerated, were in the flower of their youth or their manhood before the Reformation had been much noised abroad; and it is evident, from the whole current of the story, that the spirit of these men *was not a thing developed by any revival*, but was in continuance of the spirit with which they had been imbued in their respective monasteries. All honor to their names!"

Let us conclude, according to our custom, with a few Protestant testimonies to the fact, which we have noticed in every other land, that neither suffering, nor neglect, nor lapse of years, have been able to shake the faith of the converted Mexican. Las Casas and Zumarraga, Betanzos and Peter of Ghent, are no longer among them; the disorders of Europe have reached, and sometimes convulsed, even their remote dwellings; profligate rulers, whom their want of political education obliges them to accept, have involved their nation in shameful disorder; but the Mexican people, innocent of the crimes which scandalize without corrupting them, are still Catholic in their inmost heart, still preserved by the Mother of God, who always guards her own, from the taint of heresy.

A few witnesses will suffice; and that we may take extreme cases, they shall include an agent of the Bible Society, an English lawyer, two American Protestants, and a Scotch Presbyterian. "Every man," says the Rev. Mr. Norris, whose Bibles and discourses the Mexicans seem to have rejected with amused contempt, "professes himself a Catholic, and is very devout and religious in his way; in some respects they are worthy of imitation by enlightened Christians."* It is true that elsewhere Mr. Norris calls their religion "idolatry;" but men whose own "worship" hardly equals the decent courtesy which one civilized man offers to another, and who have still to learn in what the union of the creature with his Creator consists, may well deem that homage idolatrous which is so far deeper and more tender than their own, even when the objects of it are only the Saints in heaven. Of worship in its true sense, that which is due to God alone, such men would speak with more profit if they had any personal experience of it.

Of one Mexican province, Mr. Brantz Mayer speaks as follows, in 1852. "The aborigines of Jalisco, formerly warlike and devoted to a bloody religion, are most generally tillers of the ground, *adhering to the doctrine of the Catholic Church*."†

Even the most frivolous writers suspend the jibe or the jest to notice the deep religious feeling of the Mexicans, in spite of neglect or scanty instruction. An American traveller of this class, who confesses that he drew his knife on a priest, and scoffs at the "ridiculous mummeries" of processions and prayers, notices with a sneer that "the Mexicans are jealous of their churches, and do not, willingly, allow a heretic to enter alone;" and then he sums up his impressions in these words: "The religious feeling which pervades all classes, young and old, is remarkable. Never do you see any of them pass a church without uncovering their heads, and turning their faces thitherwards; while, at the sound of the bell, every hat is removed and all stand uncovered where they are, until the sound is over."‡

Dr. Lempriere relates that "*funciones solemnes*, or other religious performances, may be witnessed in the principal towns and cities *almost daily*," in which fact his legal education might have taught him to see at least a proof of the influence of religion; but it suggests to him quite another comment. Superbly ignorant of religion in general, and of the Christian religion in particular, this ornament of the Inner Temple goes on thus: "You enter a church and invariably encounter *a motley crowd*, exhaling unseemly odors, and dispensing small vermin on every side." A few "well dressed, well-appearing individuals" he encountered, but not enough to leaven the mass, and so he adds, "It is impossible for an individual of respectable education and ordinary delicacy of feeling to join a

* Strickland, *Hist. of American Bible Society*, ch. xx., p. 175.
† *Mexico*, &c., vol. ii., ch. viii., p. 295.
‡ *A Campaign in New Mexico*, by Frank S. Edwards, ch. vi., p. 92.

crowd *in one of these pagodas or jos temples, called churches,* without feeling ineffable disgust."* Witnesses of this class should always be allowed to speak for themselves. Alas! for Lazarus, if he should venture to display his sores at Dr. Lempriere's gate.

A more humane writer, Madame Calderon de la Barca, speaks thus of modern Mexico: "There exists no country in the world where charities, both public and private, are practised on so noble a scale; generally speaking, charity is a distinguishing attribute of a Catholic country." And this is confirmed by an American Protestant, who visited Mexico as a prisoner, and had some reason to speak of its rulers with resentment. "It is not in Mexico alone," says Mr. Kendall, after describing "the institutions for relieving the distresses of the unfortunate, and the different orders of Sisters of Charity, those meek handmaidens of benevolence, whose eyes are ever seeking the couch of sickness," "that this holy feeling of charity exists; but wherever the religion of Rome is known, there do we find the same active benevolence exerted, the same attention to the wants of the suffering."†

Of the existing race of monks, usually the butt at which every witless traveller aims his shafts, Madame de la Barca, in spite of the prejudices of her Scotch training, candidly observes: "I firmly believe that by far the greater number lead a life of privation and virtue." "Throughout the whole country," this lady adds, "at every step you see a white cross gleaming among the trees . . . *here every thing reminds us of the triumph of Catholicism.*" Of the Indians themselves, their "superstitions," and perpetual "religious processions," she gives much the same account, though with less bitterness of language, as we received from Mr. Scarlett, Mr. Mansfield, and others, with respect to their brethren in the south; she adds, however, while vehemently disapproving such external manifestations, which are usually dramatic representations of facts in the life of our Lord or of the Saints: "It is singular, that, after all, there is nothing ridiculous in these exhibitions; on the contrary, something rather terrible."‡

If it be true that "out of the abundance of the heart the mouth speaketh," and that national customs represent national feelings, we may perhaps conclude, that a people who spend a large part of their lives in devout processions and religious

* *Mexico in* 1861 *and* 1862, by Charles Lempriere, D.C.L., of the Inner Temple, and Law Fellow of St. John's College, Oxford, ch. iii., p. 103; ch. v., p. 175.

† *Narrative of the Texan Santa Fé Expedition,* by George Wilkins Kendall, vol. ii., ch. xvii., p. 340.

‡ *Life in Mexico,* by Madame C. de la Barca, Letter xxiii., pp. 177, 288.

exhibitions, can hardly be indifferent to religion. Such spectacles are not indeed witnessed in England or Holland, and no man expects to see them. The Mexicans, who have received the gift of Faith, may fitly represent the scenes of the Nativity, the Passion, or the Resurrection, for these events are to them realities. Such sights are familiar to the eye and heart, and kindle the sad or joyous sympathies of every inhabitant of the land. If any one should attempt to introduce them in any village of England, the incongruous spectacle would be speedily suppressed, and perhaps with reason; for every one would feel that it awakened only uneasiness and repugnance, by forcing them out of their habitual train of thought, and rudely disturbing the ordinary current of their life.*

TEXAS.

If now we once more pursue our journey northwards, we shall find two provinces, one on the eastern, the other on the western frontier of Mexico, which deserve a moment's attention. Texas and California, both lately absorbed by that energetic and all-devouring race which is perhaps destined one day to overrun the whole continent, will introduce us, not only to that order of missionaries with whose labors and successes we are now sufficiently familiar, but also, for the first time in America, to the agents of another religion, who have already nearly completed the work of ruin, violence, and demoralization which has marked their presence in every other land. A few words must suffice for each province.

A well-known American writer, who published in 1857 an account of the present state of Texas, will give us, in two or three pregnant sentences, all the information we need in illustration of the contrast which we have so often traced. Speaking of the work of the Catholic missionaries, he says, "The missions bear solid testimony to the strangely patient courage and zeal of the old Spanish Fathers."† Yet one hun-

* Dr. Lempriere scoffs, as becomes "an individual of respectable education," because "the people take off their hats," not only to every ecclesiastic, but "whenever they pass an image, and also, whenever the bells indicate that some performance is going on inside any one of the churches they happen to be passing." *Mexico*, ch. ii., p. 64. English Protestants, he rejoices to think, do nothing of the kind. Why should they? To *them*, a clergyman is only a gentleman with a fair income, while the "performance" in their churches is more apt to create drowsiness than reverence.

† Olmsted, *Texas*, p. 154.

dred and thirty years have passed away since the *latest* mission of San Antonio was founded by the Franciscans, in which, after so long an interval, such evident traces of their wisdom and goodness are still apparent even to Protestant eyes.

It is certainly a notable fact, which even the political economist may contemplate with interest, that the very ruins of Catholic missions present tokens of the mighty civilizing power which created them, such as no Protestant effort of the same kind has ever exhibited, though sustained by the co-operation of civil and military officials, and aided by temporal resources which Catholic missionaries neither desire nor enjoy. "A noble monument of the skill of the Fathers," says an American writer, "and of the improvement of their neophytes, remains in the many churches, aqueducts, and other public works, *built by Indian hands*, which still remain on Texan soil."*

Of the Indians themselves, Mr. Olmsted says, "We were invariably received with the most gracious and beaming politeness and dignity. Their manner towards one another is engaging, and that of children and parents most affectionate." And then follows the usual account of the woful results of their unwilling contact with a Protestant people. "Since 1853 the diminution has been rapid. . . . *At all points of contact with the white race they melt gradually away.*"† There is, then, no exception to the universal law. Wherever the Anglo-Saxon sets his foot, bringing in his train selfishness, arrogance, and insatiable cupidity, the aboriginal races disappear; and if he is accompanied, as sometimes happens, by the ministers of his religion, they disappear so much the quicker. A little later we shall find the Indians themselves noticing this invariable fact.

Nor can this doom surprise us, as respects Texas, when we learn from Protestant evidence how the natives are treated by their new masters. "It is," says Mr. Olmsted, in expressive language, "the mingled puritanism and brigandism" of his fervid countrymen which make it impossible for them "to associate harmoniously" with the mild and courteous Mexican. "Inevitably they are dealt with insolently and unjustly. They fear and hate the ascendant race." Mr. Froebel also notices "the injustice and overbearing with which the Anglo-Americans everywhere treat the Hispano-American and Indian population;" and Mr. Russell Bartlett, one of their countrymen, not only describes "their shameful and brutal conduct," but deplores their participation in "outrages which make one who has any national pride blush to hear recited."‡

* Shea, *Missions among the Indian Tribes*, &c., ch. v., p. 87.
† P. 296.
‡ *Personal Narrative*, &c., vol. i., ch. xviii., p. 423.

Yet the Mexicans, of all ranks, could teach their rude guests a lesson of charity and courtesy, if the latter were capable of profiting by it. When the Americans who invaded Mexico from Texas, most of whom were brigands of the vilest class, were happily captured, and marched as prisoners through the whole country to the capital, Mr. Kendall, who shared their fate without deserving it, gives this account of "the Mexican population generally," through whom the lawless adventurers were conducted. "They seldom manifested any feelings of exultation in our presence. On the contrary, the mild and subdued eyes of the poor Indians were turned upon us invariably in pity, while the crowds through which we passed, in all the large cities, appeared rather to be actuated by commiseration than triumph or hatred, Jews and heretics though they thought and termed us."*

The lesson appears to have been unfruitful. At Bexar, Mr. Olmsted relates how the Mexican householders, using a right which American institutions are supposed to guarantee, voted at a certain election against "the American ticket," and apparently against the introduction of slavery, which Catholic Mexico has suppressed. For this act of citizenship they were publicly assailed, in terms which may suffice to warn us that we are once more coming into the presence of Protestantism, as "political lepers, voting at the bidding of a rotten priesthood."† We may easily anticipate the fate of the Mexican in Texas.

But he will not perish without an effort to save him. There are missionaries at this hour in Texas whom the best and bravest of other days would have welcomed as brothers. Even Zumarraga and Las Casas might have rejoiced to claim for a colleague Bishop Odin, the Vicar Apostolic of Texas; even Betanzos and Peter of Ghent would have recognized as fellow-laborers such men as Timon and Domenech, Dubuis and Chazelle, Calvo and Estany, Clark and Chanrion, Fitzgerald and Hennessy; who now toil, or have recently finished their course, in that arduous field. The Abbé Domenech has lately described their labors, their sufferings, and their patience. If we refer for a moment to his well-known pages, it is for the sake of adding one more proof that the Church still produces the same class of missionaries—Spanish, French, English, or Irish—as have borne her message to all lands from the time of St. Paul to our own.

When Bishop Odin visited Europe in 1845, and appealed in

* *Narrative*, &c., ch. vi., p. 131.
† P. 499.

the city of Lyons to the Levites of France to follow him, for the love of Christ, to the banks of the Brazos, the Nuèces, and the Rio Grande, these were the attractions which he offered to their zeal. "You will not always find any thing to eat or drink; you will be without ceasing in travels through unknown regions, where the distances are immense, the plains boundless, and the forests of vast extent. You will pass your nights on the moist earth, your days under a burning sun. You will encounter perils of every kind, and will have need of all your courage and all your energy."*

The invitation was accepted as frankly as it was given. Amongst those who embraced the proposed career was the Abbé Emanuel Domenech, who arrived in Texas in 1846. From the window of his humble dwelling in Castroville he looked out upon the tomb of his predecessor the Abbé Chazelle. Excessive labor, and the want of all nourishing food, had reduced the latter, as well as his companion the Abbé Dubuis, to that mortal languor and exhaustion for which in their utter poverty they could find no remedy. The one lay on the ground, the other on a table, both stricken with typhus fever. They had none to succor them, and water, of which a neighbor placed every morning a pailful at their door, was their only medicine. On the tenth day of their illness,—it was the great Feast of the Assumption,—the Abbé Dubuis resolved to make an attempt to offer once more the Holy Sacrifice. "Let us confess for the last time," he said to his dying companion; "the strongest of the two shall then say Mass, and give Holy Communion to the other." With difficulty Dubuis accomplished the pious design, and then Chazelle fell to rise no more. He was in his last agony, when his companion staggered to his side, and in a feeble whisper pronounced over him the final blessing of the Church. A little later, he bore him with tottering steps to a grave in the garden, and there "the dying interred the dead."†

The Abbé Dubuis recovered. You think, perhaps, that he now abandoned a scene so full of sorrowful memories in the past, of formidable anticipations in the future? But men who have received the apostolic vocation accept all that it imposes. At the close of the year 1847, we find the Abbé Dubuis writing from Castroville to his friend the Curé of Fontaines, near Lyons, a letter which concludes with these words: "To this hour I have never known one moment of disgust or regret;

* *Journal d'un Missionaire au Texas et au Mexique,* par l'Abbé E. Domenech, ch. i., p. 2.

† Ch. ii., p. 50.

and if I were still in France, I would quit it immediately for the mission of Texas, which I shall only abandon when strength and life are taken from me."*

Yet it was a hard life which these brave missionaries led in Texas. Salary they had none, not even the traditional twenty pounds a year which their brethren receive in India and China. They lived on alms, when alms were offered, and dispensed with them when they were not. Sometimes they dined on a rattle-snake, sometimes on a cat, and oftener still they did not dine at all. Once the Abbé Dubuis failed to say Mass, though the congregation were assembled; he could not speak, not having tasted food for forty-eight hours. He and the Abbé Domenech were joint proprietors of a single cassock,—for as they sometimes galloped eighty miles to administer a sick person, their vestments were subject to dilapidation,—so that while one said Mass, the other stayed at home in his shirt-sleeves.

Nor does their bishop, whom the Holy See subsequently raised to the dignity of Archbishop of New Orleans, seem to have fared much better than his clergy. The Abbé Hennessy relates to a friend in Paris the manner of living in the Episcopal Palace. "To give you an idea of the comfort and luxury of our life, let it suffice to say, that here, in Galveston, the whole amount of our weekly expenditure, for the Vicar Apostolic and the three priests who live with him, is four dollars, or about sixteen shillings. Monseigneur Odin, choosing poverty and straitness for himself, is only rich and lavish towards the poor."† In a letter which this apostolic bishop, who lived upon four shillings a week, addressed to his parents, he says, "Sometimes discouragement almost seizes me, when I know not what means to adopt to procure even the most indispensable provisions; but God is so good a Father that He always comes to our help."‡

We are not surprised to learn from the Abbé Domenech that the Protestant clergy in Texas had no sympathy with such a mode of existence. Each of them, he says, had five hundred pounds a year, besides what he could earn by the ingenious operations in which such men are skilled. One of them, who had three marriageable daughters, announced to his flock,—he had chosen for his text the appropriate words, "Increase and multiply,"—that he would give three thousand piastres with each of the young ladies to any eligible suitor; and his

* App., p. 471.
† P. 465.
‡ *Annales de la Propagation de la Foi,* tome iii., p. 533.

congregation probably saw nothing unusual or incongruous in this form of paternal solicitude.*

But if the Protestant ministers lived in Texas as they are wont to live everywhere else, carefully limiting their prudent operations to the principal cities, and diligently avoiding even the remote possibility of unwelcome perils; the Catholic missionaries would have taught them, if they could have comprehended the lesson, what men can do who have forsaken all for Christ's sake. The Abbé Domenech, amongst others, was familiar with startling scenes. He is on one of his ordinary errands of mercy, journeying from Dhanis to La Leona, and comes suddenly upon the bodies of seven Mexicans, pierced with arrows, scalped and mutilated. The still smouldering embers of their camp-fire showed how recent the massacre had been. A few miles beyond La Leona,—for he had boldly continued his way where charity called him,—he finds a woman suspended to a tree, still living, though her scalp had been torn off; and at her feet three Mexicans, just slaughtered by a party of marauding Indians. The missionary pursued his course unhurt.

At another time the house of the Abbé Estany is attacked by the *Comanches*. He makes his way through a storm of arrows, and receives no wound; but all he possesses, clothes, books, and church vessels, are carried off or destroyed.

The Abbé Dubuis, who had braved a hundred deaths, is surprised in his turn by a party of savages. There is no escape, and he quietly advances to meet them. "Do me no harm," he says, with a calm voice; "I am a captain of the Great Spirit, and a chief of prayer." They leave him in peace.

But death had no terrors for such men as these; it was but the passage to eternal life. Once the Abbé Domenech received an express, bidding him hasten to the assistance of Father Fitzgerald, dying at Victoria. He sets out at a gallop, almost leaps over a panther lying in his path, and at length stands by the bedside of his friend. "I spoke to him," he says, "but he did not answer. I wished to embrace him; his lips were rigid. He was just dead. At twenty-six years of age, far from his family, his country, and his friends, without even the succors of religion at his departure out of the world, he had breathed his last. In beholding this youthful victim of Christian charity, my heart was oppressed; I fell on my knees, and being unable to pray, I wept. . . . But in spite of the sad end of my poor friend, I envied his lot; for him no doubt any

* Domenech, ch. iii., p. 281; 2d voyage.

longer existed about the future; he had died in the midst of his work."*

But it is time to leave Texas, where missionaries of the same class continue at this hour the same valiant and patient apostolate, calmly expecting, amid all their toils, sufferings, and dangers, the hour when they shall be joined to their brethren who have gone before, and receive the recompense to which St. Paul looked forward during all the vicissitudes of his ministry,—the bonds and scourging, the hunger and thirst, the perils and contradictions,—and which such as they have earned a right to share with him.

CALIFORNIA.

The history of California, a land which effectively illustrates the peculiar civilization of the nineteenth century, has been written by Venegas and others. Here the same facts meet us, which we have noticed in every other region of the earth. Not one of the usual phenomena is wanting. The zeal and devotion of the Catholic missionaries; their unbounded success; the love and veneration which the converted natives displayed towards them; the commercial and agricultural prosperity which existed, as Humboldt observes, under "the strict though peaceful rule of the monks;" and finally, the swift havoc and ruin introduced by men of the Saxon race; all recur in their accustomed order, and all are eagerly attested, as usual, by Protestant writers.

"The name of California," says Mr. Berthold Seemann, in 1853, "is forever united with the unselfish devotion of the Franciscan friars."† Yet the children of St. Francis had been preceded by men of whom another Protestant traveller thus speaks: "The Jesuits, before they were supplanted by the Franciscans," observes Sir George Simpson, "had covered the sterile rocks of Lower California with the monuments, agricultural, architectural, and economical, of their patience and aptitude; not only leaving to their successors apposite models and tolerable workmen, but also bequeathing to them the invaluable lesson, that nothing was impossible to energy and perseverance."‡ We shall presently hear what the same impartial writer says of the Protestant missionaries in the same regions, and the results of their apparition.

* Ch. vi., p. 176.
† *Voyage of H.M.S. Herald*, vol. ii., ch. ix., p. 153.
‡ *Journey Round the World*, vol. i., ch. vii., p. 334.

Mr. Forbes,—who celebrates with frank admiration "the pure and disinterested motives of the Jesuits," whom he generously lauds as "true soldiers of the Cross," and contrasts in energetic terms with the "illiterate fanatics" whom the Sects have sent to take their place,—records also, like Sir George Simpson, "the minute but not uninteresting warfare which they maintained for so many years against the rude natives of California and its still ruder soil, until at length they triumphed over the former, and as much over the latter as was possible."*

He describes, too, the work of their successors, after careful observation of it. "The best and most unequivocal proof of the good conduct of the Franciscan Fathers is to be found in the unbounded affection and devotion invariably shown towards them by their Indian subjects. They venerate them not merely as friends and fathers, but with a degree of devotedness approaching to adoration." And then he exclaims, as if he found it impossible to restrain the unwelcome confession, "Experience has shown how infinitely more successful the Catholic missionaries have been than the Protestant." He even becomes enthusiastic in tracing the contrast, and adds, "Nor can there be agents more fitting than the persevering and well-disciplined friar, whose whole life and studies have been directed to this end; whose angry passions no injury can rouse, whose humility and patience no insult or obstacle can overcome. *With him our missionaries can bear no comparison.*"†

Sir George Simpson is more cautious, for he was a British official, yet he also relates how the Protestant missionaries abandoned in despair their attempts on the natives of Colombia, because "they soon ascertained that they could gain converts only by *buying* them;" and he adds, almost resentfully, "The Church of Rome is peculiarly successful with ignorant savages." Yet so intelligent a person can hardly suppose that *these* were the easiest class of disciples to win—much less, that they were the easiest to retain.

Let us hear other eye-witnesses, but all Protestants. "We visited the missions," says Dr. Coulter, in 1847, "making a few days' stay at each, enjoying the lively, humane, and agreeable conversation of the padrés, who were, without an exception, a pleasant set of men. . . . . The padrés now have perfect control over the Indians of the missions."‡

Captain Beechey had made exactly the same observation a few years earlier. "The converts are so much attached to the

* *California*, ch. i., p. 17.

† Ch. v., pp. 230, 242.

‡ *Western Coast of South America*, vol. i., ch. xv., p. 154; ch. xvi., p. 170.

padrés, that I have heard them declare they would go with them if they were obliged to leave the country."*

Mr. Walpole, writing two years after Dr. Coulter, and with scant sympathy for Catholics, says, "To me the Catholic missionaries of America always appeared far superior to all other Catholics; under their fostering rule the rude savage ceased his wars, settled down and tilled the land in peace,—witness Paraguay and California!"†

These witnesses are all English Protestants; let us hear what Americans say on the same subject. Captain Benjamin Morrell visits the mission of St. Antony of Padua, near Monterey, and this is his report: "The Indians are very industrious in their labors, and obedient to their teachers and directors, to whom they look up as to a father and protector, and who in return discharge their duty towards these poor Indians with a great deal of feeling and humanity. They are generally well clothed and fed, have houses of their own, and are made as comfortable as they wish to be. The greatest care is taken of all who are affected with any disease, and every attention is paid to their wants."‡ Such testimonies are instructive, yet every one must feel that they deal only with the surface of things, and do not lay bare the hidden sources from which all these blessings spring.

Captain Morrell finds one thousand two hundred Christian Indians in the mission of St. Clara. "No person of unprejudiced mind," he exclaims, "could witness the labors of these Catholic missionaries, and contemplate the happy results of their philanthropic exertions, without confessing that they are unwearied in well-doing." And then he adds, that although "the Mexicans and Spaniards are very indolent, and consequently very filthy," "the converted Indians are generally a very industrious, ingenious, and cleanly people."§

Mr. Russell Bartlett, who notices in 1854 that at the mission of Cocopera, in Sonora, "the increase of cattle in a single year amounted to ten thousand head," adds that in that of San Ignacio, founded in 1687, "though abandoned for many years, the results of Jesuit industry are *still* apparent." "The mission of San Gabriel," he says, "at one time branded fifty thousand calves, manufactured three thousand barrels of wine, and harvested one hundred thousand fanegas (two hundred and sixty-two thousand bushels) of grain a year. The timber for a brigantine was cut, sawed, and fitted *at the mission*, and then

* *Voyage to the Pacific*, vol. ii., ch. i., p. 21.

† *Four Years in the Pacific*, vol. ii., ch. i., p. 25.

‡ *A Narrative of Four Voyages*, ch. vi., p. 208 (1832).

§ P. 212.

transported to and launched at San Pedro. Five thousand Indians were at one time collected and attached to the mission. They are represented to have been sober and industrious, well-clothed and fed. . . . . They constituted a large family, of which the padrés were the social, religious, and, we might almost say, political heads." Then noticing the ruin which other men and other principles have wrought among thom, this candid Protestant adds: "Humanity cannot refrain from wishing that the dilapidated mission of San Gabriel should be renovated, and its broken walls be rebuilt, its roofless houses be covered, and its deserted halls be again filled with its ancient industrious, happy, and contented population."

But Mr. Bartlett appears to have understood, from his own observations, and from converse with the unhappy survivors of these tribes, that the Power which made them what they were is withdrawn, and that his co-religionists, incapable of emulating such triumphs, will infallibly complete the work of destruction which they have commenced. At the great mission of Los Angeles, once a proverb throughout the whole region, "the Indians have now no means of obtaining a living, as their lands are all taken from them. . . . No care seems to be taken of them by the Americans; on the contrary, the effort seems to be, to exterminate them as soon as possible!" Such is the contrast between Catholic and Protestant colonization. At the modern mission of San Luis Rey he converses with an aged chief. "On inquiring as to the state of things when the padrés were here, the old man heaved a deep sigh. He said his tribe was large, and his people all happy, when the good Fathers were here to protect them. That they cultivated the soil, assisted in rearing large herds of cattle, were taught to be blacksmiths and carpenters, as well as other trades, and were happy. . . . He spoke with much affection of Father Peyri, its original founder, who had resided here for thirty-four years." Now his tribe were scattered, "without a home or protectors, and were in a miserable starving condition."

In a few places, not yet overwhelmed by the Anglo-Saxon flood, the Fathers still linger, and here is the result of their presence, attested by the same official witness: The Yaqui Indians of Sonora, he says, are "invariably honest, faithful, and industrious. They are also the fishermen and the famous pearl-divers of the Gulf of California." They were "among the first to be converted by the Jesuits." Originally "extremely warlike, on being converted to Christianity, their savage nature was completely subdued, and they became the most docile and tractable of people. They are now very populous in the southern part of Sonora."

Finally, the Opate Indians, whom he also visited, though "noted for their bravery, being the only ones who have successfully contended with the savage Apaches," "have ever remained faithful to their religion. Of their attachment to law, order, and peace, they have given the most unequivocal proofs."*

One exception there is to these candid testimonies, and it is found, as might be anticipated, in the writings of a Protestant minister. The Rev. Joseph Tracy gravely informs his readers, in the face of all the evidence which Protestant travellers of various classes have offered on this subject, that the Jesuits and Franciscans in California taught only the "forms of religion," "without improving their intellects, their morals, *or their habits of life!*"† Perhaps there are no two works, in the whole range of Protestant literature, at once so trivial and so profane,—so full of false and idle words, childish vaunts, and παντολμορ 'αμαθια,—as Mr. Tracy's history of American missions, and the "Reports of the American Board for Foreign Missions."

Once more we have noticed one of those peaceful triumphs, rich in blessings to suffering humanity, and which have extorted the admiration even of men whose unhappy prejudices they fail to correct, and whose conscience they leave unawakened. The poor Indians were wiser. *They* could discern Whose ministers such workmen were, and that it was only by the communication of His Spirit that they found strength to lead such lives, or accomplish such victories.

But the history of California does not end here. The Catholic missionaries had done, in this land as in every other, all that men having the gifts and the calling of apostles could do. They had forced the rugged soil to yield ample harvests, they had fertilized the yet more barren heart of the savage with the dew of heavenly graces. Two other classes were now to enter these regions,—Mexicans who had forfeited their birthright as Catholics, and Protestants who had never possessed it. Both have inflicted irreparable injury upon the tribes of the Northwest.

Let us speak of the Mexicans first. Affecting to follow the precedents of modern European policy, of which the chief maxim seems to be the exclusion of all ecclesiastical influence in the government of human society, the civil authorities resolved to secularize all the missions. The result has been, as in every land where the same experiment has been tried, a swift relapse into the barbarism from which the Church alone has saved the

* *Personal Narrative of Explorations in Texas, New Mexico, California,* &c., vol. i., ch. xix., pp. 442–4; vol. ii., ch. xxv., pp. 82, 92.

† *History of American Missions,* p. 197.

world, the immediate decay of material prosperity, and a vast augmentation of human suffering. History might have taught the Mexicans to anticipate these inevitable fruits.* When England laid her hand on the possessions of the Church, which had been for centuries the patrimony of the poor, she took her first step towards her present social condition. Prisons and work-houses became the dismal substitutes for monasteries, and jailers supplanted monks. England has not profited much by the change. The new institutions are at least ten times more costly than the old, and the benefits derived from them have been in inverse proportion. They now receive only prisoners, and disgorge only criminals, while a whole nation of heathen poor, a burden on the present resources of the country and a menace for her future destiny, have sunk down, as even English writers will tell us, to the level of the most degraded tribes of Africa or America, and are as utterly void of religion or of the knowledge of God, as the Sioux, the Carib, or the Dahoman.

Here is the history of the same proceedings in California. "In 1833," says Möllhausen, "the government of Mexico, jealous of the great influence of the clergy, secularized the missions, and confiscated their property to the State." It was Gomez Farias who devised the felony, and, as Mr. Brantz Mayer relates, ruined in a single province twenty-four missions, inhabited by twenty-three thousand and twenty-five Christian Indians. We will quote immediately the exact statistics of the operation and of its results.

It was not long before the spoilers were ejected in their turn by the Americans, a more energetic race, who, not content with destroying the missions, have proceeded to destroy the Indians also. They would have been ashamed not to surpass so pusillanimous a criminal as Gomez Farias, who contented himself, like a mean robber, with appropriating the property of others. "When California became attached to the United States," says Möllhausen, "the former property of the missions of course passed into the hands of the American government, and their dwellings are now lonely and desolate, and falling rapidly to decay; the roofs have fallen in, the stables are empty, the once blooming gardens and orchards are choked by a wild growth of weeds, and it will probably not be long before the waves of commercial activity will sweep over them and obliterate the last traces of their existence."†

* "I asked what they thought of the abolition of tithes, and confiscation of Church property? (in Spain.) The answer was, 'The poor man pays more, and the rich less.'" *The Pillars of Hercules*, by David Urquhart, Esq., M.P., vol. i., ch. v., p. 77.

† *Journey from the Mississippi to the Coasts of the Pacific*, ch. xv., p. 334.

A few merchants may perhaps improve their fortunes by the change, but it will be at the expense of the whole Indian population, whom they are now busy in exterminating, and who, at no remote day, will have ceased to exist. Already, except in a few of the missions, where the Franciscans still linger, starving amid ruins, but protecting the Indian to the last, they begin to be "brandy-drinking, wretched creatures," says Möllhausen; and then he adds, "It is impossible not to wish that the missions were flourishing once more, or to see without regret the fallen roofs and crumbling walls of their abode, a mere corner of which now serves as a shelter for a few Catholic priests. . . . . . The energetic and heroic sacrifices of such missionaries as the Padrés Kino, Salvatierra, and Ugarte, obtained their reward; and, up to 1833, when three new missions had been founded, they enjoyed the fruits of their labors."

"The spoliation of the missions," says Sir George Simpson, "excepting that it opened the province to general enterprise, *has directly tended to nip civilization in the bud.*" And even the new "enterprise" to which it has furnished a field is so unfruitful, as he admits, except in unprincipled speculations, which enrich a few and ruin many, that whereas in the time of the missions the province exported wool, leather, soap, wheat, beef, and wine, the policy of its actual possessors has annihilated almost all these branches of commerce.

Before we notice, in conclusion, the effect of the American conquest upon the Indians, and the characteristic operations of American missionaries, let us show what have been the admitted results, up to the present date, of the suppression of the missions. In 1844, M. Duflot de Mofras published his work on Oregon and the Northwestern provinces of Mexico. Here is the evidence of this intelligent and impartial writer.

It was not till 1842 that Santa Anna robbed the Bishop of California of all the religious funds which still remained from former spoliations, and committed their administration to a coarse and greedy soldier of his own class. "You see," said an Indian Alcalde to M. de Mofras, "to what misery we are brought; the Fathers can no longer protect us, and the authorities themselves despoil us."* The Indians have learned once more to regard the white man as their natural enemy, and, as M. de Mofras observes, "*since* the destruction of the missions" it has become dangerous to travel from Sonora to California. A few Fathers still linger in the scene of their once happy labors; the rest have been driven from the country, carrying

* *Exploration du Territoire de l'Oregon*; tome i., ch. vii., p. 345.

with them for all their wealth the humble robe of their order. In 1838, Father Sarria died of exhaustion at the foot of the altar, at the mission of St. Soledad, when about to say Mass, after an apostolate of thirty years. Father Guttierrez received a daily but insufficient ration, dispensed by a man who had formerly been a domestic servant, but who was now civil administrator of the mission! The Father President Sanchez died of grief, when he beheld the havoc and ruin to which he could apply no remedy.

The mission of San Francisco Solano was only founded in 1823 by Father Amorós. It increased so rapidly, that at the time of the suppression it contained one thousand three hundred Christian Indians, and possessed eight thousand oxen, seven hundred horses, and other property in proportion. Don Mariano Vallejo, the new civil administrator, seized every thing which it was possible to carry away or sell, and pulled down the mission house to build himself a dwelling out of the materials.*

Yet some of the missions still remain, perhaps because neither Mexicans nor Americans have yet found time to destroy them, and still present something of their former aspect. "We cannot express the surprise," says M. de Mofras, "with which the traveller is struck, on seeing, in the neighborhood of Indian villages, where the land is cultivated with extreme care, and there exists a perfect system of irrigation, the *pueblos* of the whites in a state of profound misery, under the *free* government of most of the so-called Republics!" The common salutation, he says, of a Dominican or a Franciscan to an Indian is still "Amar a Dios, hijo!" and the answer, "Amar a Dios, padré!" The Americans will probably introduce another language.

Perhaps it would be impossible to indicate more briefly or more impressively the historical results of the secularization of the missions, after their long career of peace and prosperity, than M. de Mofras has done in his interesting pages. Even men who are careful only about financial success can appreciate such statistics as are exhibited in the following table. It has sometimes been said in jest that there is nothing so eloquent as figures; let the reader consider, in sober earnest, what lesson he may derive from these.

UPPER CALIFORNIA.

UNDER THE ADMINISTRATION OF THE RELIGIOUS, IN 1834.

Christian Indians,	30,650
Horned Cattle	424,000
Horses and Mules	62,000
Sheep	321,500
Cereal Crops	70,000 hectares.

* P. 445.

UNDER THE CIVIL ADMINISTRATION, IN 1842.

Christian Indians	4,450
Horned Cattle	28,220
Horses and Mules	3,800
Sheep	31,600
Cereal Crops*	4,000 hectares.

It appears, then, that in the brief space of eight years, the secular administration, which affected to be a protest against the inefficiency of the ecclesiastical, had not only destroyed innumerable lives, replunged a whole province into barbarism, and almost annihilated religion and civilization, but had so utterly failed even in that special aim which it professed to have most at heart,—the development of material prosperity,—that it had already reduced the wealth of a single district in the following notable proportions: Of horned cattle there remained about *one-fifteenth* of the number possessed under the religious administration; of horses and mules less than *one-sixteenth;* of sheep about *one-tenth;* and of cultivated land producing cereal crops less than *one-seventeenth.* It is not to the Christian, who will mourn rather over the moral ruin which accompanied the change, that such facts chiefly appeal; but the merchant and the civil magistrate, however indifferent to the interests of religion and morality, will keenly appreciate the cruel and blundering policy of which these are the admitted results, and will perhaps be inclined to exclaim with Mr. Möllhausen, "It is impossible not to wish that the missions were flourishing once more!"

And these facts, which even worldly craft may teach men to deplore, are everywhere the same. Far away to the South, in the plain where the Lake of Encinillas lies, on the borders of Chihuahua, is "one of the richest and most valuable localities in the world for cattle-grazing, in times past supporting innumerable herds. *Now it is almost a desert!*"† It is the history of Paraguay on a smaller scale.

Yet there are American writers, whom no official rebuke has ever disavowed, who appear almost to exult in this universal ruin. Lieutenant Whipple, a highly respectable officer of the United States, from whom Mr. Schoolcraft derived some of the materials for his great work on the Indian nations, after noticing, in 1849, that the Lligunos, converted by the Franciscans, still number eight thousand, continues as follows: "They profess the greatest reverence for the Church of Rome,

* P. 321.

† Froebel, ch. ix., p. 340.

and, glorying in a Christian name, look with disdain upon their Indian neighbors of the desert and the Rio Colorado, calling them miserable gentiles." He confesses, too, speaking of the single mission of San Diego, that "for many miles around, the valleys and plains were covered with cattle and horses belonging to this mission; yet the only reflection which the Christian zeal of the Indians and the skilful administration of their pastors suggested to him is expressed in the silly taunt, that they were "slaves of the priests," and the worse than silly boast, that "now they are freed from bondage to the Franciscans," his countrymen will teach them "their duties as Christians and men!"* We shall see immediately what they have really taught them.

The Americans, whom Mr. Whipple dishonors by such indiscreet advocacy, are in fact completing the work of destruction with characteristic energy; and here is an account of their proceedings. After emptying every other province of the United States, they are now rapidly effecting the same process in California. On the 15th of March, 1860, the *Times* newspaper contained the following extract from the *San Francisco Overland and Ocean Mail Letter:* "Never, as journalists, have we been called upon to comment on so flagrant and inexcusable an act of brutality as is involved in General Kibbe's last Indian war—a scheme of murder conceived in speculation and executed in most inhuman and cowardly atrocity. If the account of Mr. George Lount, a resident of Pitt river, be true, General Kibbe and all the cowardly band of cut-throats who accompanied him should be hung by the law for murder; for murder it is, most foul and inexcusable. Sixty defenceless Indian women and children killed in their own *rancheria* at night, by an armed band of white ruffians! The massacre of Glencoe does not afford its parallel for atrocity. *This band of Indians were friendly*, had committed no outrage, were on their own lands, in their own homes." But this was only a beginning; later operations are thus narrated by the same witness.

"The Indians have been driven from their hunting-ground by the white man's stock. Their fishing racks have been destroyed by the caprice or for the convenience of the white man. Their acorns are exhausted by the white man's hog, and, *driven to desperation* by actual want and starvation, they have stolen the white man's ox." This was the pretext for another onslaught. "When Governor Weller authorized W. J. Jarboe to organize a

* *Historical and Statistical Information respecting the Indian Tribes of the U. S.*, by H. R. Schoolcraft, LL.D., part ii., p. 100 (1851).

company to make war on the Indians . . . in seventy days they had fifteen battles (?) with the Indians; killed more than four hundred of them; took six hundred of them prisoners, and had only three of their own number wounded, and one killed. . . . Under the licence of the law; under the cover of night; in the security of your arms; in the safety of your ambush; you have murdered in cold blood more than four hundred sleeping, unarmed, unoffending Indians—men, women, and children. Mothers and infants shared the common fate. Little children in baskets, and even babes, had their heads smashed to pieces or cut open. It will scarcely be credited that this horrible scene occurred in Christian California, within a few days' travel from the State capital." And not only were the actors, or promoters, of this enormous crime a General of the United States army and a Governor of a province, but "a bill of nearly seventy thousand dollars is now *before the Legislature* awaiting payment, to be distributed, in part, among these crimsoned murderers!"

More than forty years ago, an American Protestant clergyman, alluding to the early atrocities of his Protestant countrymen against the Indian race, exclaimed, "Alas! what has not our nation to answer for at the bar of retributive justice!"* If this writer had lived to hear of the scenes just described, he would perhaps have felt that his nation has done little as yet to propitiate the justice of God, and that it would have been well for California to have been left, as of old, to the Jesuits, the Franciscans, and the Dominicans.

We have been told that, at least in one case, the victims were "friendly and unoffending." In the early history of North America, as we shall see when we come to speak of the Atlantic States, this was almost invariably the case. The Catholic colonists on both banks of the St. Lawrence, as well as those in Maryland under Lord Baltimore, were always on the best terms with the natives. Even Penn, who was admonished by the religious maxims of his society to eschew rapine and war, had no difficulty in making amicable treaties with the Indians in his neighborhood, though he appears to have always made them to his own advantage. It was not till Protestants had robbed and murdered them, and had repaid their good offices, as the Indians afterwards reminded them, with horrible outrage and ingratitude, that the latter swore eternal enmity against them. They became cruel and vindictive, because the white man had set them the example. If North America had been colonized by Catholics alone, there would have been at this day, as in the Southern continent, whole nations of native Christians.

* *A Star in the West*, by Elias Boudinot, LL.D., ch. viii., p. 255 (1816).

But it was the doom of the red man to perish before the face of the Anglo-Saxon. He might be friendly and unoffending, but this could not save him. "I never found," says Mr. Gerstaecker, speaking of the Wynoot Indians of California, "a more quiet and peaceable people in any country than they were." While of the tribes of this region generally he adds, "They are really the most harmless nations on the American continent, let white people, who have driven them to desperation, say what they please against them." And then he quotes Mr. Wozencraft, United States Indian agent, who made this official report. "A population perfectly strange to them has taken possession of their former homes, destroyed their hunting-grounds and fisheries, and cut them off from all those means of subsistence a kind Providence had created for their maintenance, and taken away from them the *possibility* of existing. But not satisfied with that, these men deny them even the right we have granted to paupers and convicts—the right of working and existing."* "Goaded by hunger," says a Wesleyan writer, "and stimulated by revenge, they have begun to trespass on the lands of the colonists,"† because they can no longer find subsistence on their own. Yet Mr. Kirkpatrick reported, in 1848, of the Oregon Indians, "Long before a missionary went into that country, these people were as honest, kind, and inoffensive as any I have ever met with, either civilized or savage." Mr. Townshend declared the same thing of the Chinook and Walla-Walla tribes, whose "honesty and uprightness," as well as friendly and cordial hospitality, he satirically compares with "the habits and conduct of our Christian communities;"‡ and Dr. Rattray reports, in 1862, of those in British Columbia, "the natives are quiet and inoffensive to a degree, unless provoked or made victims of intemperance."§

And now a word, in conclusion, on the Protestant missionaries. There are not many of them here, because, as Mr. Gerstaecker has told us, "there is no profit in view;" but there are a few, and of the usual class. The same writer tells us that he encountered two of them, of rival sects, "but as we find in the present age only very few men who really teach the gospel for Christ's sake"—he means among his co-religionists—"the two pious brethren had long given up preaching to the heathen. *With the natives they would have nothing at all to do.* Should they live upon acorns and young wasps, and sleep in the wet

* *Journey Round the World,* vol. i., ch. vi., pp. 343–7.
† *Colonization,* by Rev. John Beecham, p. 7.
‡ *Rocky Mountains,* ch. xi., p. 272.
§ *Vancouver Island and British Columbia,* by Alexander Rattray, M.D. R. N., ch. x., p. 172.

woods all for nothing? They did not find sufficient encouragement."* Yet some of them appear to have remained there, for Mr. Chandless observes, in 1857, "Religious freedom, I suppose, exists; there seemed to be a sort of Protestant Church there (in South California), with a bishop, self-ordained, and pretending to some direct revelation from heaven."†

Few men, we may believe, are so undiscerning as to need any assistance in reflecting upon the contrast between the Catholic and Protestant history of California."‡ Yet it is impossible to omit the following observations of a distinguished American official, who presided over the commission for the settlement of the Mexican boundary, and who sums up the facts of that history in terms scarcely less honorable to himself than to the subjects of his candid and generous eulogy.

"Christian sects may cavil about their success among the Indian tribes, but it is an undeniable fact, that the Jesuits during their sway,"—he probably counts the Franciscans with them—"accomplished more than all other religious denominations. They brought the tribes of Mexico and California under the most complete subjection, and kept them so until their order was suppressed. And how was this done? Not by the sword, nor by treaty, nor by presents, nor by Indian agents, who would sacrifice the poor creatures without scruple or remorse for their own vile gains. The Indian was taught Christianity, with many of the arts of civilized life, and how to sustain himself by his labor. By these simple means the Society of Jesus accomplished more towards ameliorating the condition of the Indians than the United States have done since the settlement of the country. The Jesuits did all this from a heartfelt desire to improve the moral and social as well as the spiritual condition of this people, and at an expense infinitely less than we now pay *to agents alone*, setting aside the millions annually appropriated for indemnities, presents, &c."§

OREGON.

Let us pass from California to Oregon. We will speak of the Protestant missionaries first, and all our information will be

* Vol. ii., p. 10.

† *A Visit to Salt Lake*, by William Chandless, ch. x., p. 316.

‡ It is an instructive fact, that when the Fathers of the Society of Jesus were banished from Piedmont, the exiles immediately resumed their apostolic labors in California! In 1857, they had already one hundred and fifty-one students in their college at San Francisco, under the direction of thirteen Fathers and five lay professors. *Prospectus of Santa Clara College*, San Francisco, 1858.

§ Bartlett, *Personal Narrative*, vol. ii., ch. xxxix., p. 432.

derived, as in other cases, from themselves or their friends. When Oregon was annexed to the United States, the various sects endeavored, according to their wonted policy, to get the start of each other in appropriating the promising field. The very first missionaries, however, who arrived, and whose instructions were to labor amongst the Flatheads, positively declined, after a brief trial, to execute their mission. Mr. Townshend, who travelled with them, discovered that they had "arrayed themselves under the missionary banner, chiefly for the gratification of seeing a new country, and participating in strange adventures."* The motive of their retreat was characteristic. "The means of subsistence," we are told by two of their number,—for as they see no dishonor in the confession, they are not ashamed to make it,—"in a region so remote and so difficult of access, were, to say the least, very doubtful."† The doubt was enough to put them to flight. Yet these gentlemen were probably familiar with certain words of St. Paul, in which he thus describes the life of a true missionary: "Even unto this hour we both hunger and thirst, and are naked, and are buffeted, and have no fixed abode."‡ We shall presently meet with missionaries of the school of St. Paul who *did* stay with the Flatheads, in spite of "the doubtful means of subsistence," and who will tell us what was the result of their residence among them.

One of the most influential of the American sects is the Methodist Episcopal body. Here is an account, by an eminent Methodist preacher, of their proceedings in Oregon. It exactly resembles their proceedings everywhere else.

"No missionary undertaking has been prosecuted by the Methodist Episcopal Church with higher hopes and a more ardent zeal. That the results have fallen greatly below the usual average of missionary successes, and inflicted painful disappointment upon the society and its supporters, none, we presume, any longer hesitate to confess." This particular mission, he adds, "involved an expenditure of *forty-two thousand dollars in a single year;*" nor can we be surprised even at such enormous prodigality, when we learn how it was composed. "At the end of six years, there were *sixty-eight* persons connected with this mission, men, women, and children, all supported by this society! How such a number of missionaries found employment in such a field, it is not easy to conjecture, especially as the great body of the Indians never came under

* Townshend's *Rocky Mountains*, vol. i., ch. i., p. 29 (1848).
† *Ten Years in Oregon*, by D. Lee and J. H. Frost, missionaries, ch. xii., p. 127.
‡ 1 *Cor.* iv. 11.

the influence of their labor." And then follows this curious narrative: "They were, in fact, mostly engaged in secular affairs—concerned in claims to large tracts of land, claims to city lots, farming, merchandizing, blacksmithing, grazing, horse-keeping, lumbering, and flouring. We do not believe that the history of Christian missions exhibits another such spectacle." We have seen that it exhibits a good many such, and in every land. "The mission," he continues, "*became odious to the growing population* . . . irreconcilable differences arose among the missionaries, which led to the return of several individuals to the United States, and to a disclosure of the real state of the mission." Finally, he adds, that of all the Indians who had ever held relations of any kind with these men, "*none now remain.*"*

Another American writer gives the same account of the Wesleyan operations, especially at the *Great Dalles* of Columbia. After describing a murder of a very atrocious kind, committed in the very presence of the preacher, while surrounded by his nominal flock, and by one of his own congregation, he adds, "The occurrence is but a type of a thousand atrocities *daily* occurring among these supposed converts to the merciful precepts of Christianity. . . . . Yet these men had been, and still are, represented as evangelized in an eminent degree!"†

Another Wesleyan mission was established in the Wallamette. Here an English Protestant traveller found one hundred families, "by far the greater part Catholics, *a very regular congregation*, ministered to by M. Blanchette, a most estimable and indefatigable priest of the Roman Catholic faith." The Wesleyans, he adds, consisted of four families, "a clergyman, a surgeon, a school-master, and an agricultural overseer!"‡ But if they had no disciples, they had their salaries, an arrangement which they probably considered quite satisfactory.

The Rev. C. J. Nicolay, apparently an English Episcopalian minister, gives exactly the same account of the other sects in Oregon. "It has ever," he says, "been thought a just ground of complaint against men whose lives are devoted to the service of God," if they try to make "a gain of godliness." But this reproach, he remarks, "will appear, by their own shówing, to lie at the door of the American missionaries who have established themselves in Oregon. In their settlements at Okanagan, &c., &c., this charge is so far true, that their principal attention is devoted to agriculture, but in the Wallamette they sink into

* *The Works of Stephen Olin*, LL.D., vol. ii., pp. 427–8.
† *Traits of American Indian Life*, ch. x., p. 174 (1853).
‡ *The Oregon Territory*, by Alex. Simpson, Esq., p. 38.

political agents and would-be legislators." Presently he adds, after quoting the statement of the American navigator Wilkes, that "their missionary intentions have merged in a great measure in others more closely connected with ease and comfort;"—that "the missionaries had made individual selections of lands to the amount of a thousand acres each." Finally, this gentleman cautiously observes, "It appears that the Roman Catholic missionaries were placed in advantageous contrast to their Protestant brethren."*

The same familiar contrast is thus indicated by another Protestant traveller, at the same date, with more emphasis than could be fairly expected from an Anglican clergyman: "There are at this time between thirty and forty semi-religious semi-political pioneers. The religious mission of too many has been adopted merely as the means of securing snug locations for themselves and families in this western paradise . . Several French priests are also laboring in this wilderness, and putting to shame *their* efforts after self-aggrandizement by a singleness of purpose, which purpose is propagandism, and entire devotion thereto."† The heathen make the same observation, but comprehend, unlike Protestants, the lessons which such facts inculcate. God, they argue, must be with those upon whom alone He confers His gifts. And they hasten to seek communion with Him and them.

But if the candid narratives of Messrs. Lee and Frost, Olin and Nicolay, Wilkes and Simpson, reveal the true character and results of all the Protestant missions in this region, we must not suppose that the missionaries themselves admitted, as long as they had any hope of concealing them. Their commercial and agricultural pursuits; their dealings in "city lots;" their "horsekeeping, lumbering, and flouring;" were too importantly aided by their ample salaries to permit them to indulge in such imprudent candor. They sent home, therefore, exactly the same periodical reports which missionaries of the same class were constantly forwarding from every other land, and which the societies at home expected and *required*, as the only means of obtaining a fresh stream of subscriptions. Their employers were willing to forgive them any thing, even the cupidity which had made them "odious to the growing population," so long as they abstained from the additional and unpardonable crime of confessing their failure. And so, in 1844, these well-instructed agents wrote home thus: "A gradual advance in Christian knowledge is perceptible!"‡ They knew

* *The Oregon Territory*, by Rev. C. J. Nicolay, ch. vii., pp. 155, 177, 183, 184 (1846).

† *The Oregon Territory*, by Alexander Simpson, Esq., p. 31 (1846).

‡ *U. S. American Board for Foreign Missions*, Reports, p. 212 (1844).

it was untrue, and when they had nothing more to gain, they crudely confessed it. "It is acknowledged on all hands," we are told *in this very year*, by two of their number, who were candid because they were abandoning the hopeless work, "that the present prospects in respect to civilizing and christianizing these natives are exceedingly gloomy."* But this did not prevent the missionary societies from publishing reports which they *knew* to be false, in order to raise fresh means for perpetuating the same lamentable schemes, in which the agents, as they had already ascertained, were only sordid speculators, merchants, and horse-dealers, who had adopted for a season the title of missionaries. Let us notice a few examples of their inexhaustible ingenuity.

In 1843, only a few months before their own agents confessed the whole truth,—it is by a careful collation of dates that we learn to appreciate the fidelity of Protestant missionary reports,—the bait held out to languid subscribers at home was contained in the published statement, that "Mr. Spalding," one of the Oregon missionaries, "believes a considerable number have experienced the renewing grace of God."† Mr. Spalding believed nothing of the kind, as they very well knew, and had such excellent reasons, as we learn from American writers, for repudiating the opinion imputed to him, that he was himself only saved by the influence of a Catholic missionary, at the risk of his own life, from being slaughtered by the homicidal fury of these "renewed" savages." "For this," we are told, "he was indebted to the timely aid and advice of the Rev. Mr. Brouillet, of the Roman Catholic mission. . . his Catholic friend assisting him from his own small stock of provisions."‡ For two days the Indians appear to have pursued him, but without success, Father Brouillet having nobly exposed his own life by putting them on a wrong scent, a trick which only their respect for him induced them to pardon. But he was too late to prevent the massacre of Dr. Whitman and his wife, by the Cayoux Indians, and "the entire destruction of Wai-let-pu mission," consisting of fourteen members, over which that unfortunate gentleman presided. All he could effect was to rescue their bodies from further dishonor; and Mr. Paul Kane, who had been the guest of Dr. Whitman just before this lamentable event, relates that "the Catholic priest requested permission to bury the mangled corpses, which he did,"—here Mr. Kane is certainly mistaken,—"with the rites of his own

* Lee and Frost, ch. xxiii., pp. 215, 311.
† *Reports*, p. 171 (1843).
‡ *Traits of American Indian Life*, ch. vi., p. 121.

Church. The permission was granted the more readily, as these Indians are friendly towards the *Catholic* missionaries."* "This terminated the mission," says the Rev. Dr. Brown, "among the Indians west of the Rocky Mountains."† Such is the instructive history from which we may appreciate, not only the relative influence of Catholic and Protestant missionaries, but the immoral fictions by which the revenues of Protestant "societies" are annually recruited.

Eighty miles from the *Dalles*, by the banks of the Atinam, another mission is thus described by a Protestant traveller from Boston, who had learned to despise what he calls "the crude and cruel Hebraism" of his Puritan forefathers. "The sun was just setting as we came over against it on the hill side. We dashed down into the valley, that moment abandoned by sunlight. My Indians launched forward to pay their friendly greeting to the priests. But I observed them quickly pause, walk their horses, and noiselessly dismount.

"As I drew near, a sound of reverent voices met me,—vespers at this station in the wilderness! Three souls were worshipping in the rude chapel attached to the house. It was rude, indeed,—a cell of clay,—but a sense of the Divine presence was there, not less than in many dim old cathedrals, far away, where earlier sunset had called worshippers of other race and tongue to breathe the same thanksgiving and the same heartfelt prayer. . . . . . . Never in any temple of that ancient faith, where prayer has made its home for centuries, has prayer seemed so mighty, worship so near the ear of God, as vespers here, at this rough shrine in the lonely valley of Atinam."

A friendly welcome greeted the Protestant traveller, who thus sums up his reflections on this church in the wilderness: "A strange and unlovely spot for religion to have chosen for its home of influence. It needed all the transfiguring power of sunset to make this desolate scene endurable. The mission was a hut-like structure of adobe clay, plastered upon a frame of sticks. It stood near the stony bed of the Atinam." Here dwelt two Fathers of the Society of Jesus, "cultivated and intellectual missionaries," who had forsaken all to labor among the Yakimah Indians. "The good Fathers were lodged with more than conventual simplicity. Discomfort, and often privation, were the laws of missionary life in this lonely spot. Drearily monotonous were the days of these pioneers. There

* *Wanderings of an Artist among the Indians of North America*, ch. xxi., p. 320.

† *Hist. Prop. Christianity*, vol. iii., p. 155.

was little intellectual exercise to be had, except to construct a vocabulary of the Yakimah dialect." . . . And the traveller, familiar with missionaries of another order, marvelled greatly that such men could accept such an existence.*

But there were many other missions in these distant regions, conducted like that on the Atinam, by men who were not anxious about "means of subsistence," knew nothing of "lumbering" or "city lots," and who have succeeded, after long and patient toil, in converting multitudes of the very tribes with whom the Protestant agents, as their own friends have told us, would have nothing at all to do." We have seen, by their own confession, how speedily the latter abandoned the *Flatheads;* let us inquire how the Catholic missionaries fared amongst them.

ROCKY MOUNTAINS.

The Fathers of the Society of Jesus entered twenty years ago the territories which lie to the west of the Rocky Mountains Here such men as de Smet and Hoecken, Dufour and Verhaegen, have emulated the courage and fortitude which for more than three centuries have been a tradition in their Society. When Father de Smet, a name honored throughout Christendom, presented himself to the *Flatheads*, they had already acquired some knowledge of Christian truth from a band of Catholic *Cherokees*, who had been driven from their own hunting-grounds, and found a refuge with the *Flatheads*. The hospitality of the latter was to be nobly recompensed. "During twenty years," says Father de Smet, "according to the counsel of the poor *Cherokees*, who had established themselves amongst them, they had approached, as much as possible, towards our articles of belief, our morals, and even our religious practices. In the course of ten years, three deputations had the courage to travel as far as St. Louis, that is to say, to cross more than three thousand miles of valleys and mountains, infested with *Black-Feet* and other enemies. At length their prayers were heard, and beyond their hopes."†

The Christian *Cherokees*, solicitous to impart their own blessings to others, had done what they could, and their work was now to be completed. In October, 1841, Father de Smet

* *Adventures among the North-Western Rivers and Forests,* by Theodore Winthrop; ch. xi., pp. 225, 232 (Boston, 1863).

† *Annals,* vol. iv., p. 231.

could already give the following report: "All that is passing before our eyes in the Rocky Mountains strengthens us in the hope, which we have long since conceived, of seeing once more a new Paraguay, flourishing under the shadow of the Cross, with all its marvels and affecting recollections. . . . . What proves to me that this pleasing imagination is not merely a dream, is, that at the moment while I write these lines, the noisy voices of our carpenters, and the smith whose hammer is ringing on the anvil, announces to me that we are no longer projecting the foundations, but fixing the roof, of the house of prayer. This very day, the representatives of *twenty-four different tribes* assisted at our instructions; while three savages, of the tribe of the *Cœurs-d'Alène*, who had heard of the happiness of the *Flatheads*, came to entreat us to have compassion upon them also." In spite of these successes, and of still greater ones to be noticed presently, there will be no new Paraguay in Oregon, for a reason which the course of this narrative will sufficiently indicate.

Of the converted *Flatheads*, the same missionary gives an account, full of interest and importance, but which we are compelled to abbreviate, and which shall be confirmed immediately by Protestant evidence. "They never attack any one," he says, "but woe to him who unjustly provokes them." In other words, in becoming good Catholics they have not ceased to be valiant warriors. On one occasion they were assaulted by a band of a thousand *Black-Feet.* "Already the enemy poured down upon them, while they were on their knees, offering to the Great Spirit all the prayers they knew, for the chief had said, 'Let us not rise until we have well prayed.'" The fight lasted five successive days, when the *Black-Feet* retired, leaving the ground strewed with their dead and wounded.

And these brave *Flatheads*, whose chief, says Father de Smet, "considered as a warrior and a Christian, might be compared with the noblest characters of ancient chivalry," are as remarkable, in his judgment, for their virtues as for their valor. "I have spoken of the simplicity and courage of the *Flatheads;* what more shall I say? that their disinterestedness, generosity, and rare devotedness towards their brethren and friends, their probity and morality, are irreproachable and exemplary; that quarrels, injuries, divisions, enmities, are unknown amongst them. I will add, that all these qualities are already naturalized in them through motives of faith. What exactness do they show in frequenting the offices of religion! What recollection in the house of prayer! What attention to the catechism! What fervor in prayer! What humility, especially when they relate actions which may do them honor!"* The Protestant governor of the State will presently give us his testimony on the same subject.

Elsewhere he says: "Often we remark old men, even chiefs, seated beside a child ten or twelve years old, paying for hours the attention of a docile scholar to these precocious instructors, who teach them the prayers, and explain to them the principal events of the Old and New Testament." And once more. On Christmas Eve, 1843, "Fathers Mengarini and Zertinati had the happiness of seeing, at the midnight Mass, almost *the whole nation* of the *Flatheads* approach the Holy Table. Twelve little musicians, trained by Father Mengarini, performed with admirable precision several pieces of the best German and Italian composers. The history of this tribe is known to you; its conversion is certainly well calculated to show forth the inexhaustible riches of the Divine mercy."† Such was the work of Catholic missionaries among a tribe whom the Protestants had abandoned, because "the means of subsistence were, to say the least, very doubtful."

It is not uninteresting to learn how the apostles who had once more accomplished such a triumph as this were content to live, in the earlier years of the mission, among their wild flock. The "means of subsistence," about which our Lord enjoined His disciples, and principally such as were to teach others, to "take no thought," were meagre and precarious. The Protestant ministers, who loved not this distasteful precept, had promptly made the discovery, and fled away to more genial regions. Father de Smet, who might have been taking his ease in his own fair land, gayly describes what he calls "a supper," which he ate with his disciples, and which "consisted of a little flour, a few roots of *camash*,"—a species of wild onion,—"and a bit of buffalo grease. The whole was flung together into the cauldron, to form a single *ragout*. A long pole, for the heat kept us at a respectful distance, was transformed into a ladle, which it was necessary to turn continually, until the contents of the kettle had acquired the proper thickness. We considered the dish delicious! We had but one porringer for six guests. But necessity makes man industrious. In the twinkling of an eye my Indians were ready for the attack on the cauldron. Two of them provided with bits of bark, two others with bits of leather, the fifth armed with a tortoise-shell, plunged again and again into the cauldron with

* IV., 353.
† VII., 360.

the skill and regularity of a smith beating on his anvil. It was soon drained."

At another time, by way of varying their delicacies, it was "wild roots and moss-cakes, as hard as dried glue," which furnished their table, and of which a broth was composed "which has the appearance and taste of soap." But enough of these trivial hardships, to which the missionaries rarely refer, and then only by way of jest.

The *Flatheads* were not the only tribe won to Christianity by the Jesuits in this remote western world. When *they* had been gathered into the fold, Father de Smet started for Columbia; where, as Sir George Simpson has told us, the Protestant missionaries "soon ascertained that they could gain converts only by *buying* them." The Jesuits, like St. Peter, had "neither silver nor gold;" but they worked, as he did, "in the name of Jesus of Nazareth," and with similar fruits. "During the journey," says Father de Smet, "which lasted forty-two days, I baptized one hundred and ninety persons, twenty-six of whom had arrived at extreme old age. I announced the word of God to more than two thousand Indians, who will not delay, I hope, to place themselves under the standard of Jesus Christ." And then he relates an anecdote of a certain Protestant, a Mr. Parkers, one of that class who have inflicted so much injury upon the heathen in every land. This gentleman had wilfully broken a cross, erected over the grave of an Indian child, and had announced that he did it "because he did not wish to leave in this country a monument of *idolatry*, set up in passing *by some Catholic Cherokees.*" "Poor man!" says Father de Smet, "if he now returned to these mountains, he would hear the praises of the Holy Name of Jesus resounding on the banks of the rivers and lakes; in the prairies as well as in the bosom of the forests; he would see the Cross planted from shore to shore, over a space of three hundred leagues, commanding the loftiest summits of the *Cœurs-d'Alène*, and the principal chain which separates the waters of the Missouri from those of the Columbia; and saluted with respect in the valleys of Wallamette, of Cowlitz, and of the Bitter-Root. At the moment that I write, Father Demers has gone to carry it to the different nations of Caledonia; everywhere the word of Him who has said that this glorious sign would attract men to Him begins to be verified in favor of the poor sheep so long wandering over the vast American continent. Would that this cross-breaker might pass again through these same places. He would see the image of Jesus suspended from the necks of more than four thousand Indians; and the youngest child, who is but learning the catechism, would tell him, 'Mr.

Parkers, it is God alone whom we adore, and not the cross; do not break it, for it reminds us that a God has died to save us.' "*

Father de Smet, whom we must now quit, has been joined since that date by many fellow-laborers of his own school. In 1852, he could already report, speaking only of his personal toils amongst the Indians *west* of the Rocky Mountains, "The total number of baptisms administered by me in the different tribes amounts to one thousand five hundred and eighty-six." And he was then contemplating a still more perilous ministry. "The account which I receive of the dispositions of the *Black-Feet*," he says in one of his letters, "is frightful. . . . I place all my confidence in the Lord, who can change, at His good pleasure, and soften these implacable hearts. My business is to carry the Gospel to the very places where the excursions of these marauders are most frequent. No consideration can turn me aside from this project."† It appears to have been at least partially executed, as we learn incidentally from the following statement in an English journal: "An interesting marriage ceremony has been recently performed at Illinois. The parties were Major Culbertson, the well-known Indian trader and agent of the American Fur Company, and Natowista, *daughter of the chief of the Blackfoot Indians*. . . . They were married a few days since by Father Scanden, of St. Joseph's, Missouri, according to the ritual of the Catholic Church. Mrs. Culbertson is said to be a person of fine native talent, and has been at times a very successful mediator between the American government and the nation to which she belongs."‡

The Potawattomies are another tribe who have accepted in great numbers the teaching of the Catholic missionaries. At the request of their chiefs, Father Verhaegen did not hesitate to present in person to the government at Washington the petition which they had intrusted to him. Fortified by the generous co-operation of General Clark, agent for Indian affairs in the district west of the Mississippi, this missionary commenced his labors among them, accompanied by Father Hoecken. They had peremptorily rejected, like the Omahas, and many other tribes, the Protestant teachers offered to them by the government. They had detected, as Father de Smet observes, that "the chief solicitude of the ministers is reserved for their commercial speculations, and when they have amassed large profits, they return to their native country, under pretence that there is nothing to be done among the savages."

* IV., 367.
† *An.* vii., 382; xiii., 319.
‡ *Weekly Register*, October 15, 1859.

Twelve months after Father Hoecken had entered the territory of the *Potawattomies* he could give this description of them: "They are sincerely attached to the practices of religion, respectful towards the missionaries, assiduous in approaching, at least every three weeks, the sacred tribunal (of penance) and the Holy Table. Scarcely a day passes that some one of them is not seen approaching one of those sacraments. On festivals, the number of those who receive Holy Communion varies from twenty to thirty." Already more than a thousand Potawattomies professed the Catholic faith; and the same missionary adds, that they manifest "an entire obedience, not only to the commands of the priest, but to the slightest intimation of his wishes."*

Yet these missionaries were, if possible, poorer than the savages themselves, willingly accepted their humble food and lodging, and abased themselves to share their daily life. "For myself," says Father Hoecken, in one of his letters to a member of the same society, "I have no other wish than to live among the Indians, and to find on the other side of the Rocky Mountains the spot from which I am to rise at the last day."

The same apostolic missionary, though he would have displayed only charity and courtesy towards the men who had abandoned in disgust the work to which he had devoted his life, gives this account of the reception which they experience from the Indians: "The Protestant ministers have endeavored to obtain followers among these savages, but their efforts have not been attended with success. Instead of listening to them, they are questioned, and put to a severe examination. 'Where is your wife?' said an Indian to one of them; a gesture was the only answer of the minister, who pointed with a finger to his residence where his wife was. 'Your dress, no doubt,' continued the savage, 'is a black robe?'—'No,' replied the minister, 'I do not wear one.' 'Do you say Mass?'—'Oh, never,' answered the minister eagerly. 'Do you wear the tonsure?'—'No.' 'Then,' they all exclaimed together, 'you may go back from whence you came.'"†

The *Winnebagoes* display the same dispositions. Father Cretin relates that they have repeatedly petitioned the government authorities to send them Catholic priests, but that their prayer was always answered by an embassy of Protestant ministers. When a treaty was negotiated in 1845 between

* An English gentleman who lately visited a large Potawattomie village, several days' journey beyond the Missouri, found that "they were all of them educated in the Roman Catholic faith." *The English Sportsman in the Western Prairies,* by the Hon. Grantley F. Berkeley, ch. xix., p. 320 (1861).

† II., 40.

this tribe and the United States, a solemn assembly was convened, and the Governor of Wisconsin unfolded the terms which he was commissioned to offer them. Their territory consisted of two million three hundred thousand acres of excellent land, watered by six considerable rivers. This magnificent tract they were asked to abandon, the invitation being equivalent to a command, for a recompense which they neither wished to accept nor dared to refuse. After a day's deliberation, the Indians again met the governor, prepared to give a reply to his proposals. *Wakoo*, an aged chief, the most celebrated orator of the tribe, rose to speak in the name of his nation, "a large crucifix glistening on his breast." From his noble address we extract the following words:

"If I alone speak to-day, far be it from you to suppose that I am the only one able to express the feelings of my tribe. All the chiefs here present know how to make known their thoughts, but being accustomed from my youth to speak in the councils of my nation, I have been chosen as the eldest to defend, in the name of all, our common interests. Thou comest on the part of our great father (the President) to demand the cession of our territory. But can he have forgotten the magnificent promises which, on two different occasions, he gave me at Washington? I remember them, for my part, as if they had been spoken only to-day. . . . 'Depend upon me,' said our great father, 'I will always defend you. You shall be my children. If any wrong be done to you, address yourselves always to me. Your causes of complaint shall cease so soon as they shall be known to me, and I will defend you.' And I, a child of nature, who have but one tongue, believed in the sincerity of these promises. Yet, in spite of our remonstrance, all our affairs have been arranged without our being even consulted. They have sent away agents whom we loved, to give us others, without asking our opinion. We have forwarded petitions, to which no attention has been paid. They promised us that they would leave us always the lands which we occupy, and already they wish to send us I know not where. My brother, thou art our friend. Tell our great father, that his children require a longer halt here, before they enter on the path of a new exile. *The tree which is continually transplanted must quickly perish.*"

Here the orator interrupted himself, to notice the charges brought against his tribe as a pretext for "dispensing with justice towards them," and for palliating the tyranny of which they were to be victims. "Why," said he, "reproach us with vices which you have yourselves encouraged? Why come to the very door of our tents to tempt us with your fire-water?"

And then he went on thus: "Our great father has said to us, 'I will send to you men who will teach you how to live well.' These men have come, but though they are tolerably good, *our young men do not listen to them any better than to ourselves; we wish for Catholic priests.* They will make themselves heard, be assured of it. I take God to witness that what I say expresses the wishes of my nation." And then he sat down amid the applause of the assembled chiefs.*

We have seen, in every chapter of this work, the triumphs of Catholic missionaries attested by the unsuspicious evidence of Protestant witnesses. Here is their testimony to the same order of facts in the valleys of the Rocky Mountains. In 1855, Governor Stephens forwarded to the President of the United States an official report on the territory committed to his charge, to which the President himself referred in his annual "Message to Congress." Of the *Flatheads* he speaks as follows: "They are *the best Indians in the territory*, honest, brave, and docile. They profess the Christian religion, and I am assured that they live according to the precepts of the Gospel." After describing their manner of life, the same authority adds, that they are "sincere and faithful," and "*strongly attached to their religious convictions.*"†

Of the tribe called *Pend-d'Oreilles*, Governor Stephens observes, that the mission established among them has been in existence nine years, and that for a long time the missionaries lived in huts, and fed on roots. "They have now a church," he says, "of which all the ornaments are so well executed, that one is tempted to suppose they must have been imported;" yet they are entirely the work of the missionaries and their neophytes. "When the missionaries arrived," he adds, "these Indians were impoverished, wretched, and almost destitute of clothes. They were in the habit of burying alive both the aged and infant children. *At this day almost the entire tribe belongs to the Saviour's fold.* I have seen them assembled at prayer, and it appears to me that these savages are, in every respect, in the way of true progress. These Indians have a great veneration for their Fathers, the Black Robes. They say if the missionaries were to leave them, it would certainly cause their death." He then praises their habits of industry, and adds, that while the Fathers have brought one hundred and sixty acres under cultivation, "the produce of the harvest belongs to the Indians, because very

* VI., 364.

† Quoted in the work entitled, *Cinquante Nouvelles Lettres du R. P. de Smet*, pp. 292 et seq. (Paris, 1858).

little suffices for the wants of the missionaries." Finally, after noticing their "pious fervor," the Governor remarks, that "religion has destroyed the state of slavery in which woman groans in all the unbelieving tribes."

Of the *Cœurs-d'Alène*, of whom there are five hundred Christians, the same official reports thus: "Thanks to the labors of these good Fathers, they have made great progress in agriculture. Instructed in the Christian religion, they have abandoned polygamy; their morals have become pure, and their conduct edifying. *The work effected by the missionaries is really prodigious.* There is a magnificent church, almost finished, entirely built by the Fathers, the Brothers, and the Indians."

Lastly, he declares of the *Potawattomies*, among whom Father Hoecken desired to live and die, and who are one of the latest conquests of the children of St. Ignatius, "*they are hardly Indians now!*" Such, by Protestant testimony, are the works of men by whom the Most High delights to display His power, and whom He fills with the abundant graces by which alone apostolic victories are gained. And as this favored tribe has found in the Fathers of the Society of Jesus masters and doctors, from whom they have received "the promise of the life that now is, as well as of that which is to come;" so their daughters, once half-naked savages, doomed to bondage and degradation, have become the pupils of those *Sisters of the Sacred Heart of Jesus*, who have not feared to traverse an ocean and a continent, that they might carry religion and civilization to the most hidden recesses of the Rocky Mountains, and dispense in their obscure valleys the same instruction which the noblest of other races receive at their hands in all the capitals of Europe.

BRITISH COLUMBIA.

In the year 1862, two British officers, whose frank but inoffensive Protestantism colors every chapter of their works, assist us to trace, in Vancouver's Island and British Columbia, the contrast which witnesses of the same class have detected in the other provinces of Western America. It is right to add that nothing was further from their intention than to do what they have unwittingly done.

"The close contiguity of the Soughies Indians to Victoria," says Commander Mayne, "is seriously inconvenient;" and the sentiment was so universal among the English authorities, that the colonial legislature, he adds, has already devised "various plans for removing them to a distance." To get the natives out of their way was, therefore, the first thought of these British colonists.

"In consequence of their intercourse with the whites," continues the same authority, "this tribe has become the most degraded in the whole island," or, as he observes in another place, "the most debased and demoralized of all the Indians." In these two reports he unconsciously records the prompt and invariable results of Protestant colonization.*

"The Cowichens," we learn from this gentleman, "are rather a fine and somewhat powerful tribe, numbering between three thousand and four thousand souls;" but "the Nanaimo Indians, who at one time were just as favorably spoken of, have fallen off much since the white settlement at that place has increased." Now the Nanaimos have sunk morally by contact with Protestants, while the superiority of the Cowichens, we are told by Captain Barrett Lennard, is owing to their conversion to the Catholic faith. "The missionaries of the Romish Church," says that officer, "have long labored assiduously among these different Indian tribes, and with considerable apparent success, in some instances, especially among the Cowichens, a good many of whom attend Mass in the little chapel of the mission." He adds, indeed, that "there is *now* a very effective staff of Protestant missionaries in Vancouver," but his sympathy with their projects does not impel him to say a word about their disciples, nor even to inform us if they have any.†

At the mouth of the Harrison River, Captain Lennard found the tribe of the Skaholets. "These Indians," he observes, in reluctant and somewhat ungenerous phrase, "make a great profession of their adherence to the Roman Catholic faith,"—a sufficient proof that at least they are not indifferent to it. They were very exact, he confesses, in the due observance of Sunday, earnest in rejecting "any kind of intoxicating drink," and both brave and industrious, as his own account of their habits sufficiently indicates.‡

Near Fort Hope he visits the Tum-Sioux Indians, and, though no missionary was then with them, he finds "a party of Indians, to the number of thirty or forty, engaged in bowing and crossing themselves in the intervals of chanting." Most Protestants would probably give much the same account of a

* *Four Years in British Columbia and Vancouver Island,* by Commander R. C. Mayne, R.N., F.R.G.S., ch. ii., p. 30 (1862).

† *Travels in British Columbia,* by Capt. C. E. Barrett Lennard, ch. iv., p. 57 (1862).

‡ Ch. x., p. 143.

Catholic congregation in Paris or London. "I doubt," he adds, "whether these poor savages attached any particular meaning or significance to any of the rites and ceremonies in the performance of which they were engaged."* It was perhaps only to pass away the time that they were secretly occupied in chanting hymns, and in what Captain Lennard calls "bowing and crossing themselves," though it was certainly an unusual mode of recreation for savages. Protestant witnesses of this school are invaluable. Their utter inability to comprehend the most impressive phenomena, and their diligent perversion of the simplest facts, only lend additional force to their testimony.

Commander Mayne, who is more copious in details, gives us the following information. "While in Henry Bay we witnessed the arrival of some Roman Catholic priests, which caused the greatest excitement among the natives. They were scattered in all directions, fishing, &c., many on board and around the ship"—that is, the ship of Commander Mayne—"when a canoe with two large banners flying appeared in sight." Both profit and curiosity, the strongest passions of the uncivilized man, were overpowered in a moment by a deeper sentiment. "Immediately a shout was raised of 'Le Prêtre! Le Prêtre!' and they all paddled on shore as fast as they could to meet them. There were two priests in the canoe, and in this way they travelled, visiting in turn every village on the coast. A fortnight afterwards, when I was in Johnstone Strait with a boat-party, I met them again. It was a pouring wet day, cold, and blowing hard, and they were apparently very lightly clothed, huddling in the bottom of their canoe, the Indians paddling laboriously against wind and tide to reach a village by night, and the sea washing over them, drenching them to the skin. I never saw men look in a more pitiable plight. . . . Certainly if misery on this earth will be compensated hereafter, those two priests were laying in a plentiful stock of happiness."† We cannot be surprised when this officer goes on to observe that these missionaries, who, he says, are "thorough masters" of the native language, "undoubtedly possess considerable influence over the Indians."

"I remember one Sunday in Port Harvey," says the same gentleman, "when we were all standing on deck, looking at six or eight large canoes which hung about the ship, they suddenly struck up a chant, which they continued for about ten minutes, singing in beautiful time, their voices sounding over the perfectly still water and dying away among the trees

* P. 149.
† Ch. xiii., p. 175.

with a sweet cadence that I shall never forget." And the singers were Vancouver Indians! "I have no idea," he adds, "what the words were, but they told us they had been taught them by the priests. The Roman Catholic priest has indeed little cause to complain of his reception by the Indians."*

Once more. "At Esquimalt *all* the Indians attend the Romish mission on Sunday morning, and at eight o'clock the whole village may be seen paddling across the harbor to the mission-house, singing at the top of their voices." For a moment the contemplation of these scenes puts to flight national and religious prejudices, and he goes on thus. "Certainly the self-denying zeal and energy with which the priests labor among them merit all the success they meet with. To come upon them, as I have done, going from village to village, alone among the natives, in a dirty little canoe, drenched to the skin, forces comparisons between them and the generality of the laborers of other creeds that are by no means flattering to the latter."†

We have seen so many examples in these volumes of inveterate prepossessions conquered by the same irresistible influence, and have read so many similar confessions of unwilling sympathy and admiration, that this particular instance claims no special comment. But we must not conclude without a few details in further illustration of the contrast which this officer attests.

"Before 1857," he observes, "no Protestant missionary had ever traversed the wilds of British Columbia, nor had any attempts been made to instruct the Indians." The statement is not quite exact, as he seems to have felt, for he adds immediately, "I must except the exertions of the Roman Catholic priests." *They* had not waited till forts were built, commerce established, and a military police organized. Before even the trapper or the hunter, they had tracked the streams and penetrated the forests of Columbia, without protection, and without salary, except from Him who "rewardeth in secret." They were now to be jostled on every side by men of another order. By 1859, "eleven missionaries of different denominations," of whom four were Wesleyans, each receiving the annual stipend

* Ch. xi., p. 274.

† P. 275. Commander Mayne makes an exception in favor of "Mr. William Duncan," a Protestant missionary, of whose energy and perseverance he speaks in terms which the conduct of that gentleman appears to merit. Mr. Duncan has judiciously labored for their "temporal welfare," and endeavored to establish schools for their instruction; but we can see little more in Commander Mayne's account of his work than the skilful adaptation of natural means to a natural end. We are so far, however, from questioning Mr. Duncan's merits, that we should be glad to be forced to recognize them in all his co-religionists. When Protestants can be found, who, from supernatural motives, are willing to devote themselves without reserve, and without salary, to the service of God, they will soon cease to be Protestants.

which was deemed an appropriate recompense of his labors, had entered this region; but "their mission," says Commander Mayne, "like that of our own Church, *has been more to the whites than the Indians.*"* The Anglican bishop "reached Esquimalt in 1860," bringing "an iron church which had been sent from England," but which had cost so much money that "the edifice was not free from debt when I left the island." What this Protestant functionary will do for the natives in general we may judge from the operations of his colleagues in other lands; what he will accomplish at Esquimalt in particular, may be inferred from the fact already recorded, that "at Esquimalt *all* the Indians attend the Romish mission."

But we are not without information as to the proceedings of this gentleman. Mr. Macdonald, who speaks of him with warm friendship, relates in 1862 such facts as the following. "Although the magnificent gift of twenty-five thousand pounds by that most estimable Christian lady, Miss Burdett Coutts, is a fit foundation, nevertheless *more* money is urgently required." Yet the immense sums already expended seem to have been utterly fruitless as far as the heathen are concerned. "It is well known," says Mr. Macdonald, "that the Rev. Mr. Cridge has labored zealously amongst these Indians for years, without even the shadow of a hope of success. The Rev. W. Clark and family also failed, and have left the country; and another highly esteemed clergyman has likewise left." These facts, he adds, are so notorious, that "it does seem rather marvellous that Dr. Hill," the Anglican bishop, "should, in *a few days* after his arrival in the colony, produce the following effect upon some Indian children." The words quoted are from an official report by Dr. Hill himself. "We sang heartily, . . . and when we finished, we found a remarkable impression to be produced. *All were reverently hushed in a fixed and thoughtful manner!*" It is probably the fatal necessity of producing a sensation at home, and the fact that "more money is urgently required," which alone compel a man of education thus to expose himself to the satire of his own friends and adherents.†

Mr. Macdonald, differing in this particular from Captain Lennard and Commander Mayne, insinuates that the Catholic missionaries have had only feeble success. But in this case his testimony is no longer founded on personal observation. Père Cheroux, he observes, "*is said* to have exclaimed, 'He who would sow the seed of instruction in the heart of these savages has selected a soil truly sterile;'" while Père Lamfrett is

* Ch. xii., p. 341.

† *British Columbia and Vancouver's Island*, by Duncan G. F. Macdonald, C.E., ch. v., pp. 162–9 (1862).

reported to have remarked, that "they were spoiled by their intercourse with the white man." If it be so, it is only a fresh example of the fact which we have encountered in every land, that Protestants not only fail to convert the heathen themselves, but make it almost impossible, by their presence, for Catholics to remedy the evil.

Yet we have reason to hope that the remarkable instances cited by Captain Lennard and Commander Mayne, in spite of their religious prepossessions, are found throughout a wider region than they were able to explore. Father Demers, we have been told by Father de Smet, quitted him a few years ago, to preach the Gospel in these very provinces. He does not seem to have preached in vain. "On the 15th of October (1861)," says a Californian Protestant journal, "the Right Rev. Bishop Demers left here (San Francisco) for British Columbia, to attend a muster meeting of Indians *in that colony*. The bishop is known by all the Indians, and has great influence over the tribes. When the news reached the camp that the bishop had arrived, one hundred Indians in forty canoes were sent to escort him. . . . The Indians know a great deal about religion. It must have been grand and solemn to hear in the wilderness of the far North one thousand five hundred Indians praying and singing together."*

It is not expedient to pursue with further detail the history of missionary labors in these remote western regions, nor to multiply the illustrations which it affords both of the character of the missionaries and the results of their toil. We have sufficiently traced, here as elsewhere, the contrast which it is the main object of these volumes to exhibit. One remark, however, may be added, before we enter those more famous provinces of the East which lie between the frozen wastes of Hudson's Bay and the sun-lit waters of the Gulf of Mexico.

We have read the words in which Father de Smet avows the noble ambition, worthy of himself and his order, of reviving on the other side of the Rocky Mountains the glories of Paraguay. Would that it were possible for us to share his generous hopes. If such a triumph could indeed be accomplished in Oregon or Columbia, Father de Smet and his colleagues sufficiently resemble their illustrious predecessors of the Society of Jesus both to attempt and to effect it. Even Protestant writers have recognized this fact. "There is an unseen element at work," says one of those candid witnesses of whom we have quoted so many, "in the remote wilderness of the Oregon, whose success is guaranteed by all the precedents of history; *it is the agency*

* *San Francisco Monitor*, quoted in *Weekly Register*, January 4, 1862.

of the Catholic Church."* But the conditions of her warfare are no longer the same. In Paraguay, the enemy whom the missionaries of the Cross fought and vanquished, rescuing more than a million victims from his grasp, had no such army of auxiliaries as are now doing his fatal work on the shores of the Pacific. The apostles who converted, one after another, the ferocious hordes of South America, and built up whole nations of peaceful, civilized, and Christian men, where before their coming only bloodthirsty savages dwelt, owed their astonishing success, not only to their own patient valor and invincible charity, but to the oneness of the faith and the unalterable harmony of the doctrine which they carried with them. Never during two centuries was the half-awakened pagan of the *Southern* continent embarrassed by the divisions, the contradictions, or the worldly lives of another order of teachers, who have made Christianity hateful to his brethren in so many other lands, both in the east and west. And thus it came to pass, as we have seen, that even the brutal Omagua or the cannibal Chiriguana confessed, at first with reluctant admiration, a little later with loving reverence, that men who were always pure, meek, and just, came forth from God, and that the message which they brought, since it never varied, must have come from Him also. This is an advantage which the less fortunate tribes on the other side of the Rocky Mountains are now losing forever. Twenty sects will soon be fighting together before their eyes. The Anglicans have recently entered Columbia, carrying with them the two weapons which they have used in other lands,—unlimited pecuniary resources, and undying hatred of the Church. They cannot convert the heathen themselves, but they can prevent others doing so. This is their mission. And therefore there will be no new Paraguay to the west of the Rocky Mountains. "I am fully impressed with the belief," is the official report of Mr. Nathaniel Wyeth, "that these Indians *must* become extinct under the operation of existing causes."† There are indeed laborers in that distant field who, if they had fair play, could convert, as their fathers did, the inhabitants of a whole continent; but even hope hides her face in the presence of the deadly evils which Protestantism generates in every pagan land. The inevitable fate of the Indian, when once he comes in contact with its emissaries, is to perish from the face of the earth. We are about to consider the last and most afflicting proof of this fact in the sorrowful history of Canada and the United States.

* *The Statesmen of America in* 1846, by S. Mytton Maury, p. 309.
† Schoolcraft, part i., p. 226.

CANADA.

The first European settlements in Canada, as in India, were made by a company of merchants; in the former country by French Catholics, in the latter by English Protestants. The usual significant contrast marked the proceedings of the two classes. "The stockholders and directors of the East India Company," says an English writer, "never gave education or religion a thought in their earliest enterprises; and when they had attained to sovereign power in the East, the use they made of it was to *prohibit* both the one and the other for a long period. . . . The French Company for trading to Canada were, on the contrary, so impressed with the duty of providing instruction and religion for the Indians among whom they were going to place settlers, that they undertook"—and then he describes at length the noble efforts which they made, and of which we are going to examine the results.*

The Canadian Company established under the auspices of Cardinal Richelieu, who wisely prohibited the admission of Protestant colonists as sure to be fatal to the welfare of the heathen, bound themselves by a solemn compact, "to maintain missionaries for the conversion of the savages."† The pledge was faithfully observed, in the same religious spirit which made Champlain exclaim, "The salvation of one soul is of more value than the conquest of an empire." "The principal design of French settlements in Canada," says Mr. Alfred Hawkins,—we shall quote, as usual, only Protestant authorities,—"was evidently to propagate the Christian religion." With this object, they sent the agents whom the Catholic Church always provides for such labors, and it is in the following words that Mr. Hawkins attempts to describe them.

"The early history of Canada teems with instances of the purest religious fortitude, zeal, and heroism; of young and delicate females relinquishing the comforts of civilization to perform the most menial offices towards the sick, to dispense at once the blessings of medical aid to the body, and of religious instruction to the soul, of the benighted and wondering savage." He alludes, no doubt, though he does not name them, to such ministers of consolation as Marguerite Bourgeoys, Marie Barbier, Marguerite Le Moine, Marie Louise Dorval, and a hundred more, "renowned for their piety," as the Swedish traveller

* J. S. Buckingham, *Canada*, ch. xv., p. 203

† *Histoire du Canada et de ses Missions*, par M. l'Abbé Brasseur de Bourbourg, tome i., ch. ii., p. 33 (1852).

Kalm observed in the last century,* and of whose labors Mr Hawkins thus speaks: "They must have been upheld by a strong sense of duty. But for such impressions, it would have been beyond human nature to make such sacrifices as the *Hospitalières* made, in taking up their residence in New France. Without detracting from the calm philosophic demeanor of religion at the present day,"—it is a Protestant who speaks,—"it is doubtful whether any pious persons could be found willing to undergo the fatigues, uncertainty, and personal danger, experienced by the first missionaries of both sexes in New France. Regardless of a climate to whose horrors they were entirely unaccustomed, of penury and famine, of danger, of death, of martyrdom itself; sustained by something more than human fortitude, by Divine patience, they succeeded at length in establishing, on a firm foundation, the altars and the faith of their country and their God."†

We shall see them presently at their work, but a preliminary consideration claims a moment's attention. Before we examine their labors, it is necessary to show, by a few examples, what kind of reception the new teachers met with from the Indians, before the latter were finally estranged by actions which would have embittered a more forgiving temper than theirs. In the *South*, we know what greeting awaited the missionaries of the Cross; let us see how they were welcomed in the *North.*

"The untutored Indians," says Mr. Hawkins, "treated the first Europeans with true Christian charity. The efforts of the Jesuits for the conversion and instruction of the savages, the universal kindness and benevolence of the missionaries wherever they succeeded in establishing themselves, perpetuated this friendly spirit *towards the French.*"‡

When the Ursulines arrived at Quebec in 1639, "as the youthful heroines stepped on shore," observes Mr. Bancroft, "they stooped to kiss the earth which they adopted as their country, and were ready, in case of need, to tinge with their blood. The governor, with the little garrison, received them at the water's edge. Hurons and Algonquins, joining in the shouts, filled the air with yells of joy. Is it wonderful that the natives were touched by a benevolence which their poverty and squalid misery could not appal?"§

A little later Mr. Bancroft will tell us, that the sympathy of the Indians *towards the French* never waned, and that as the

* *Travels in North America,* Pinkerton, vol. xiii., p. 658.

† *Picture of Quebec, with Historical Recollections,* ch. x., p. 177.

‡ Ibid., ch. i., p. 5.

§ *History of the United States,* by George Bancroft, vol. ii., p. 787; ed. Routledge.

latter "made their last journey" down the valley of the Mississippi, after the English conquest, "they received on every side *the expressions of passionate attachment* from the many tribes of red men." In the last years of the eighteenth century, when Chateaubriand visited them, they still remembered the flag of France, and "a *white* handkerchief," says the illustrious traveller, "is sufficient to insure you a safe passage through hostile tribes, and to procure you everywhere lodging and hospitality."* Familiarity, therefore, had only confirmed the love which they had inspired on their first arrival, and which had been deepened by an intercourse of more than a century. It is not easy to exaggerate the importance of this fact, from which impartial writers have justly concluded, that if the French alone had colonized America, conversion, and not extermination, would have been the lot of its native tribes.

But a welcome as sincere, though less enthusiastic, had greeted the Protestant emissaries from England and Holland. They confessed it themselves. "To us," said the Rev. Mr. Cushman, one of the early Protestant missionaries, "the Indians have been like lambs; so kind, so submissive and trusty, as a man may truly say, many Christians are not so kind or sincere."†

From every part of the Eastern States came the same reports. "The Virginia tribes," destined to be repaid with merciless cruelty and ingratitude, "literally sustained the colony planted at Jamestown with supplies of Indian corn from their own fields."‡ Of those in New England an Anglican minister gave this account: "The Indians doe generally professe to like well of our comming and planting here."§ When the English first arrived at Pokanoket, where they afterwards massacred men, women, and helpless children, leaving not a soul alive, "the native inhabitants received them with joy, and entertained them in their best manner."‖ Even the so-called "Pilgrim Fathers," though they made not so much as an attempt to convert them, reported soon after their arrival, "We have found the Indians very faithful in their covenant of peace with us, very loving, and ready to pleasure us."¶

In the Carolinas, the same facts occurred, though we learn from a public petition presented to "the Lords Proprietors of

* *Genius of Christianity*, p. 561 ; ed. White.

† Schoolcraft, part i., p. 25.

‡ Id., part ii., p. 29.

§ *New England's Plantations*, by a Reverend Divine now there resident, p 13 (1630).

‖ *History of the Town of Plymouth*, by James Thacher, M.D., p. 39 (1835).

¶ *The Pilgrim Fathers*, by George B. Cheever, D.D., p. 73.

Carolina," that "the Indian nations in the neighborhood of the said province had been so inhumanly treated, that they were in great danger of revolting to the French."* Lastly, in that region which was more than any other exclusively English in its character, laws, and traditions, but of which the injured natives learned to cherish a more deadly hostility towards their guests than in any other part of America, Mr. Howison relates, that on their first arrival, "a friendly interchange of courtesies took place." In the Isle of Roanoke, where the English landed, "the wife of the chief ran, brought them into her dwelling, caused their clothes to be dried, and their feet to be bathed in warm water; and provided all that her humble store could afford of venison, fish, fruits, and hominy for their comfort." And when "the English, in unworthy distrust, seized their arms, this noble Indian woman obliged her followers to break their arrows, in proof of their harmless designs"—so that the colonists themselves described them, in letters to England, as "gentle and confiding beings."†

We shall see hereafter more ample and affecting illustrations of the same truth, and these may suffice for the present. Enough has been said to indicate the contrast which we shall presently exhibit in all its details, and to prepare us for the future consideration of these two impressive facts,—that while in the *South*, where the preachers of the Gospel were everywhere received with clubs and arrows, and everywhere dyed the soil with their blood, *they converted the whole continent;* in the *North*, where a simple and confiding hospitality greeted the emissaries of Protestantism, *they have only created a desert.* This is the lesson which we shall learn from the history upon which we are about to enter.

It was not at the same date, nor in the same spot, that the English and Dutch began to arrive in America, but they brought with them the same religious ideas, as well as the same motives and aims; and as their sole object was to acquire territory and amass wealth, they began by deliberately bribing the *unconverted* tribes, after stimulating them with strong liquors, to make war on the *Christian* Indians in alliance with France. Even Gookin, a fierce adversary of the Catholic religion, who vehemently deplored the rapid success of the early missionaries among the natives, confessed, that "this besetting sin of drunkenness could not be charged upon the Indians before the English and other Christian nations came

* *An Historical Account of the Protestant Episcopal Church in South Carolina,* by Frederick Dalcho, M.D., p. 83.

† *History of Virginia,* by Robert R. Howison, ch. i., p. 53.

to dwell in America."* He had reason to say it. When Hendrick Hudson was received by the Indian tribe with whom he came in contact on landing, his first act was to intoxicate them all with whiskey, which they drank with repugnance, and only to show, by an admirable courtesy, their confidence in their new visitors.† Monseigneur de Laval, Bishop of Quebec, who anticipated the terrible effects which intemperance would produce among the inhabitants of North America, denounced the penalties of mortal sin upon all who should give spirits to the Indians;‡ and Mr. Bancroft will tell us hereafter that the admonition was entirely successful; but the English and Dutch were not subject to his authority, and would have laughed at his censures. And the natives quickly distinguished the different policy of their Catholic and Protestant guests. "You yourselves," they said to the Dutch, "are the cause of this evil; you ought not to craze the young Indians with brandy. Your own people, when drunk, fight with knives, and do foolish things; you cannot prevent mischief, till you cease to sell strong drink to the Indian."§ To the English they addressed, again and again, still more earnest reproaches. "It is the English," they were accustomed to say, "who corrupt us."‖ When their chiefs implored that the traders might not be permitted to bring rum into their villages, the English officials, incapable of any higher ambition than commercial success, haughtily replied, "that the traders could not be prevented from going where they might best dispose of their goods."¶ And the natives appreciated the brutality which did not even affect any disguise. When the English governor of Boston, striving to alienate the natives from the French, made them enticing offers, on condition that they should consent to admit "an English minister," the answer which he received from their representatives is perhaps as worthy of record as any which the Indian annalists have preserved.

"Your speech astonishes me," said the orator whom they deputed to speak on their behalf. "I am amazed at your proposal; you saw me long before the French did; yet neither you nor your ministers *ever spoke to me of prayer, or of the Great Spirit.* They saw my furs, and my beaver-skins, and they thought of them only. These were what they sought.

* Gookin's *Historical Collections*, sec. 3, p. 7 (1772).

† Schoolcraft, part ii., p. 24.

‡ Brasseur de Bourbourg, tome i., ch. vii., p. 140. Cf. *Relations des Jesuites dans la Nouvelle France*, Année 1671.

§ Bancroft, vol. ii., p. 563.

‖ Henrion, tome ii., 2de partie, p. 609.

¶ *An Inquiry into the Causes of the Alienation of the Delaware and Shawanese Indians from the British Interest*, p. 32.

When I brought them many, I was their great friend. That was all.*

"On the contrary, one day I lost my way in my canoe, and arrived at last at an Algonquin village near Quebec, where the Black Robes taught. I had hardly arrived when a Black Robe came to see me. I was loaded with peltries. The French Black Robe disdained even to look at them. He spoke to me at once of the Great Spirit, of Paradise, of Hell, and of the Prayer which is the only path to heaven. I heard him with pleasure. I stayed long in the village to listen to him. At length prayer was pleasing to me. I begged him to instruct me. I asked for baptism, and I received it. Then I returned to my own country and told what had happened to me. They envied my happiness, and wished to share it. They set out to find the Black Robe, and asked him to baptize them. This is how the French behaved to us. If when you first saw me, you had spoken to me of prayer, I should have had the misfortune to learn to pray like you, for I was not then able to find out if your prayer was good. But I have learned the prayer of the French. I love it, and will follow it till the earth is consumed and comes to an end. Keep, then, your money and your minister. I speak to you no more."†

The Swedish traveller Kalm appears to allude to this, or to some similar oration, when he says, to the great displeasure of his editor, Pinkerton, "The English do not pay so much attention to a work of so much consequence as the French do, and do not send such able men to instruct the Indians as they ought to do."‡ Mr. Talvi, also, an American author, but contrasting unpleasantly with the candid and generous writers of that country,—his solitary allusion to the Catholic missionaries being a vulgar and heartless jest,—confesses, that "the Indians themselves, now that the Christianity was to be enforced upon them which the whites," he means the English, "had not taught them to love, asked, why the latter had been silent about it twenty-six years, when the matter was so weighty that their salvation depended upon it?"§ And lastly, Mr. Halkett forcibly observes, "It cannot be doubted that the Indians, for successive generations, have looked upon the whites as a fraudulent, unjust, and immoral race, preaching what they did not practice.

* In one of the earliest excursions of the so-called "Pilgrim Fathers" into the interior of Massachusetts, the same sordid temper was displayed. "*Some few skins* we got there," is the characteristic entry in the Puritan journal, "but not many." Of any attempt to convert the natives, they make no mention. *The Pilgrim Fathers*, by George B. Cheever, D.D., p. 60.

† *Lettres Edifiantes et Curieuses*, tome vi., p. 211.

‡ Pinkerton, vol. xiii., p. 588.

§ Talvi's *History of America*, vol. ii., ch. xix., p. 78.

We need not, therefore, be surprised to find that the Indians do not scruple, even at the present day, to express, through their chiefs, their decided reluctance to receive the instructions of the missionaries."*

We shall see presently further examples, both of the contrast and of the native comments upon it; meanwhile, let us endeavor, by the aid of Protestant writers, to sketch the outlines of the history of missions in Canada, and of the fortunes of its aboriginal tribes.

The first mission to the Hurons was commenced in 1615, by one whom Mr. Bancroft calls "the unambitious Franciscan, Le Caron," who, "years before the Pilgrims anchored within Cape Cod, had penetrated the land of the Mohawks, had passed to the north into the hunting-grounds of the Wyandots, and, bound by his vows to the life of a beggar, had, on foot, or paddling a bark canoe, gone onward and still onward, taking alms of the savages, till he reached the rivers of Lake Huron." "It was neither commercial enterprise," says the same distinguished writer, "nor royal ambition which carried the power of France into the heart of our continent; the motive was Religion;" and he adds, the only "policy" which inspired the French conquests in America "was congenial to a Church which cherishes every member of the human race without regard to lineage or skin."†

By the year 1636, fifteen Fathers of the Society of Jesus had entered Canada, and commenced that astonishing warfare, celebrated with honest enthusiasm by American writers, of which the fruits were long ago described by Father Bressany, who had himself no mean share in producing them. "Whereas at the date of our arrival," he says,—writing with the hand which the savages had cruelly mutilated, after tormenting him for a whole month,—"we found not a single soul possessing a knowledge of the true God; at the present day, in spite of persecution, want, famine, war, and pestilence, there is not a single family which does not count some Christians, even where all the members have not yet professed the faith. Such has been the work of twenty years."‡ A little later, as is well known, the whole Huron nation was Christian.

It was in June, 1611, that Fathers Biart and Masse arrived in Canada; and it is a notable fact that the first Jesuit slain in America, in 1613, fell by the hands, not of the savages, but of

* *Notes on North American Indians*, by John Halkett, Esq., ch. xiii., p. 305.

† Vol. ii., p. 783.

‡ *Missicns dans la Nouvelle France*, par le R. P. F. G. Bressany, S.J., p. 109; ed. Martin (1852).

the English.* American Protestants have described the labors of these first missionaries and of their successors. A few examples of the language which they employ will fitly introduce the history which we are briefly to trace.

"Long before the consecration of Plymouth Rock," observes Mr. Bartlett, an official of the United States government, "the religion of Christ had been made known to the Indians of New Mexico; the Rocky Mountains were scaled; and the Gila and Colorado rivers, which in our day are attracting so much interest as *novelties*, were passed again and again. The broad continent, too, to cross which, with all the advantages we possess, requires a whole season, was traversed from ocean to ocean, before Raleigh, or Smith, or the Pilgrim Fathers, had touched our shores."*

"Within thirteen years," says professor Walters, "the wilderness of the Hurons was visited by sixty missionaries, chiefly Jesuits." One of them, Claude Allouez, discovered Lake Superior. Marquette, of whom Mr. Bancroft says, "the people of the West will yet build his monument," "embarks with his beloved companion and fellow-missionary, Joliet, upon the Mississippi, and discovers the mouth of that king of rivers, the Missouri. A third member of this devoted band," continues Mr. Walters, "the fearless Ménan, settles in the very heart of the dreaded Mohawk country, on the banks of the river which still bears that name. The Onondagas welcome the missionaries of the same illustrious society. The Oneidas and Senecas likewise lend an attentive ear to the sweet tidings of the Gospel of peace. When we consider that these missionaries were established in the midst of continual dangers and life-wasting hardships, that many of the Jesuits sealed with their blood the truth of the doctrines they preached, and the sincerity of their love for these indomitable sons of the American forest, we are not surprised at the eloquent encomiums which have been passed upon their dauntless courage and their more than human charity and zeal." And then he adds, with that singular freedom from peevish bigotry and irrational prejudice which is the characteristic of so many American Protestants, "We have sufficient data to prove, that there is not a State of our Union wherein Catholicity has obtained a footing, whose history does not exhibit many interesting traits of heroic self-denial, of dangers overcome, of opposition meekly borne, of adversaries won to our faith by the Catholic missionaries."‡

* Charlevoix, *Histoire de la Nouvelle France*, tome i., liv. iii., p. 211 (1744).

† *Personal Narrative of Explorations in Texas, New Mexico*, &c., by John Russell Bartlett, U. S. Commissioner, vol. i., ch. viii., p. 183 (1854).

‡ Rupp, *Hist. of Rel. Denominations of U. S.*, pp. 119–20.

Mr. Washington Irving is not less emphatic in his generous admiration of the same great company of apostles. "All persons," he observes, "who are in the least familiar with the early history of the West, know with what pure and untiring zeal the Catholic missionaries pursued the work of conversion among the savages. Before a Virginian had crossed the Blue Ridge, and while the Connecticut was still the extreme frontier of New England, more than one man whose youth had been passed among the warm valleys of Languedoc, had explored the wilds of Wisconsin, and caused the hymn of Catholic praise to rise from the prairies of Illinois. The Catholic priest went even before the soldier and the trader; from lake to lake, from river to river, the Jesuits pressed on unresting, and, with a power which no other Christians have exhibited, won to their faith the warlike Miamis and the luxurious Illinois."*

Even Protestant ministers, forgetting, in presence of so much heroism and virtue, their conventional phraseology, which they seem to have agreed to suspend over the graves of martyrs, have caught up the strain. "How few of their number," exclaims the Rev. Mr. Kip, "died the common death of all men!" And then, after enumerating the various kinds of death by which they finished their course, he continues thus: "But did these things stop the progress of the Jesuits? The sons of Loyola never retreated. The mission they founded in a tribe ended only with the extinction of the tribe itself. Their lives were made up of fearless devotedness and heroic self-sacrifice. Though sorrowing for the dead, they pressed forward at once to occupy their places, and, if needs be, share their fate. 'Nothing,' wrote Father Le Petit, after describing the martyrdom of two of his brethren, 'nothing has happened to those two excellent missionaries for which they were not prepared when they devoted themselves to the Indian missions.' If the flesh trembled, the spirit seemed never to falter. Each one indeed felt that he was 'baptized for the dead,' and that his own blood, poured out in the mighty forests of the West, would bring down perhaps greater blessings on those for whom he died, than he would win for them by the labors of a life. He realized that he was 'appointed unto death.' '*Ibo, et non redibo*,' were the prophetic words of Father Jogues, when for the last time he departed for the Mohawks. When Lallemand was bound to the stake, and for seventeen hours his excruciating agonies were prolonged, his words of encouragement to his brother were, 'Brother! we are made a spectacle unto the world, and to angels, and to men.' When Marquette was

* Ibid., *Knickerbocker*, June, 1838.

setting out for the sources of the Mississippi, and the friendly Indians who had known him wished to turn him from his purpose, by declaring 'Those distant nations never spare the stranger,' the calm reply of the missionary was, 'I shall gladly lay down my life for the salvation of souls.'" *

Yet these candid men, who could thus applaud in all sincerity the gifts and graces which they recognize in the missionaries of the Cross, and sometimes confess in glowing words the supernatural "constancy and patience which," as Mr. Hawkins observes, "must always command the wonder of the historian and the admiration of posterity," were content to utter barren applause! Less impressed by actions which they often attribute only to enthusiasm, or peculiarity of temperament, than the more discerning Huron or Oneida, who knew how to trace them to their true source, and who quickly comprehended that only the "Master of Life" could form such men or inspire such actions, these Protestant historians derive no lessons from deeds which they record without comprehending, and of which their own annals contain not even a solitary example, and deem their task fully accomplished when they have elaborated the unprofitable panegyric which they would apply, with hardly the variation of a phrase, to the prowess of a Hannibal or the constancy of a Regulus.

One advantage, however, we derive from their unsuspicious testimony, that it renders all Catholic evidence superfluous; one inference we draw from the facts which they proclaim, that the missionaries would have done in the Northern what they did in the Southern continent, if they had not been hindered in the former by a fatal impediment, from which they were delivered in the latter. If Canada and the United States had belonged to France or Spain, instead of to England or Holland, no one can doubt, with the history of Brazil and Paraguay in his hands, that the inhabitants of both would have remained to this day; and that the triumphs of Anchieta and Vieyra, of Solano and Baraza, would have been renewed by the banks of the St. Lawrence and the Ohio, in the forests of Michigan, the prairies of Illinois, and the savannahs of Florida and Alabama.

In both fields of apostolic warfare, the agents were exactly the same. "Every tradition," says the most laborious historian of the United States, "bears testimony to their worth. They had the faults of ascetic superstition,"—they shared them with St. Paul and St. Francis Xavier,—"but the horrors of a

* *The Early Jesuit Missions in North America*, by the Rev. Wm. Ingraham Kip, M.A.; preface, p. 8.

Canadian life in the wilderness were resisted by an invincible passive courage, and a deep internal tranquillity. Away from the amenities of life, away from the opportunities of vain-glory, they became dead to the world, and possessed their souls in unalterable peace. The history of their labors is connected with the origin of every celebrated town in the annals of French America; not a cape was turned, not a river entered, but a Jesuit led the way."* Let us see through what perils and sufferings it conducted them.

In 1641, a bark canoe left the Bay of Penetangushene, for the Sault Ste. Marie, at the invitation of the Chippewas, who had heard of the messengers of the Great Spirit. "There, at the falls, after a navigation of seventeen days, they found an assembly of two thousand souls. . . . . Thus did the religious zeal of the French bear the Cross to the banks of the St. Mary and the confines of Lake Superior, and look wistfully towards the homes of the Sioux in the valley of the Mississippi, five years before the New England Eliot had addressed the tribe of Indians that dwelt within six miles of Boston harbor!" Raymbault and Jogues travelled in that canoe. The former perished by the rigor of the climate, the latter was destined to a more tragical fate. Returning by the Ottawa and the St. Lawrence to Quebec, with "the great warrior Ahasistari" and a party of Christian Hurons, he was attacked by a band of Mohawks. The Hurons leaped ashore, to hide in the thick forest. "Jogues might have escaped also; but there were with him converts who had not yet been baptized; and when did a Jesuit missionary seek to save his own life, at what he believed the risk of a soul? Ahasistari had gained a hiding-place; observing Jogues to be a captive, he returned to him, saying, 'My brother, I made oath to thee that I would share thy fortune, whether death or life: I am here to keep my vow.'"†

Ahasistari was burned alive. He had been baptized, after due trial of his sincerity, Mr. Bancroft relates, "and enlisting a troop of converts, savages like himself, 'Let us strive,' he exclaimed, 'to make the whole world embrace the faith in Jesus!'" The noble barbarian accepted martyrdom with exultation, and sang at the stake, not his own warlike deeds, but the praises of Jesus and Mary. Réné Goupil, a novice, in the act of reciting the rosary with Father Jogues, was killed by the blow of a tomahawk, "lest he should destroy the village by his charms." Jogues was not yet to die. They allowed him, because of his infirmities, to wander about, and often "he wrote

* Bancroft, ii., 783.

† Ibid., 791.

the name of Jesus on the bark of trees, as if taking possession of these countries in the name of God." His torments were long and horrible, but his martyrdom was to be postponed for four years. They tore out his hair and nails by the roots, cut off his fingers by one joint at a time, and only suspended his tortures when they seemed likely to deprive him of life. Yet he never wavered. Ransomed at length by the Dutch, he was released, and having visited Rome to obtain a dispensation to say Mass in spite of his mutilated hands, the Sovereign Pontiff replied, "*Indignum esset Christi martyrem Christi non bibere sanguinem.*" Having obtained the permission which he solicited, instead of seeking the repose which his sufferings seemed to have earned, he returned immediately to America, and being recaptured by the Iroquois in 1646, was again cruelly tortured, and finally obtained, on the 18th of October, the crown of martyrdom.* His actual murderer was burned to death in the following year by the Algonquins, "but the holy martyr seems not to have abandoned him in his last hour," says Charlevoix, "for he died a Christian."

On the 4th of July, 1648, Father Antoine Daniel, while laboring in a Huron village, was surprised in his turn by the Mohawks. His flock was cut down on every side, while he moved amongst them, calm and fearless, baptizing the catechumens and absolving the Christians, and when his task was done, quietly advanced to meet his murderers. "Astonishment seized the barbarians," says Mr. Bancroft, who thus describes the closing scene: "At length, drawing near, they discharge at him a flight of arrows. All gashed and rent by wounds, he still continued to speak with surprising energy, now inspiring fear of the Divine anger, and again, in gentle tones, yet of more piercing power than the whoops of the savages, breathing the affectionate messages of mercy and grace." At last they slew him, "the name of Jesus on his lips." The whole Huron nation mourned him, and some of them related, as Mr. Bancroft notices, "that he appeared twice after his death, youthfully radiant in the sweetest form of celestial glory."†

On the 16th and 17th of March, 1649, Fathers Jean de Brebeuf and Gabriel Lallemand, both apostles of the Hurons, passed to their eternal reward through one of the most appalling trials which man ever inflicted or endured. The first had been twenty years in the mission, and had converted more than seven thousand Indians; the last was weak and delicate, and had only just commenced the apostolic career. Among his

* Charlevoix, tome i., liv. vi., p. 390. "Verissimum patientiæ et in proximum charitatis portentum." Tanner, *Vita et Mon. Martyr. Soc. Jesu*, p. 510.

† Bancroft, ii., 796.

private papers was found, after his death, a writing in which he devoted himself to martyrdom. "Oh, my Jesus, sole object of my love," he had written, "it is necessary that Thy blood, shed for the savages as well as for us, should be efficaciously applied to their salvation. It is on this account that I desire to co-operate with Thy grace, and to immolate myself for Thee."*

They were both captured by the Iroquois, allies of the English, and implacable enemies of the Hurons, after a battle in which every combatant of the latter tribe was either killed or taken. Occupied during the conflict in baptizing the dying, and in exhorting all "to have God alone in view," they only ceased to teach and console when there was no longer a Huron left to need their ministry. De Brebeuf was first led to the stake, and as he continued to proclaim with a loud voice the faith for which he was about to die, "the savages, unable to silence him, cut off his lower lip and his nose, applied burning torches to all parts of his body, burned his gums, and at length," for he still continued to admonish them, "plunged a red-hot iron into his throat." And then they brought forth his young companion, stripped him naked, and covered him with sheets of bark that he might be slowly roasted. It was at this moment, when he saw the horrible condition of his venerable friend, that he cried out, "We are made a spectacle to the world, to angels, and to men!" De Brebeuf replied to him by a gentle inclination of the head, when Lallemand, whose fetters had been consumed by the fire, ran to him, cast himself at his feet, and respectfully kissed his wounds. Shortly after De Brebeuf was scalped, while still living, and then Lallemand's agony began. They poured boiling water on his head, in mockery of baptism; they plucked out one of his eyes, and placed a burning coal in the empty socket; the smoke from the burning sheets of bark filled his mouth so that he could no longer speak, but as the flame had again burst his bonds, he lifted up his hands to heaven. Finally, after an agony which was skilfully protracted during *seventeen hours*, the victim was immolated, and the sacrifice complete. "The lives of both," says Mr. Bancroft, "had been a continual heroism; their deaths were the astonishment of their executioners." The Protestant historian omits to add the impressive fact, that many of their murderers were afterwards converted, and that it was from *their* voluntary account that the details of their martyrdom were collected.†

* Bressany, p. 258.
† Charlevoix, tome ii., liv. vii., p. 18; Bressany, ch. v., p. 251.

"It may be asked," adds Mr. Bancroft, "if these massacres quenched enthusiasm? I answer, that the Jesuits never receded one foot." Father Bressany, who wrote his own history with his mutilated hand, has described, as if speaking of another, the tortures which made him say, "I did not think it possible for man to survive such an ordeal." Yet he lived to return to Europe, where he had professed literature, philosophy, and mathematics, before he devoted himself to the conversion of the heathen; and it was a common remark of those who heard him preach in the churches of Italy, "*He* has no need to say, 'I bear in my body the marks of the Lord Jesus.'" Even the Indians used to say to him, "Show us your wounds, they speak to us of Him for whom you received them."

In the same year which saw the death of De Brebeuf and Lallemand, Father Garnier was also martyred. He had already been pierced through the breast and stomach, and was dragging himself along the ground in order to give absolution to a dying Huron, when he was cut in two by a hatchet. On the 18th of December, still in the same year, Father Noël Chabanel met a similar fate. Léonard Garreau, Nicolas Viel, and "the fearless René Mesnard;" Buteux and Poncet; Le Maistre and Vignal; Souel and Constantine; Du Poisson and Doutreleau; all gave their lives for the faith, after toils which only Divine charity could inspire or support. Besides these, the historian of the United States, as if a moment of transient enthusiasm made him almost a partaker in their faith, celebrates Pinet, "who became the founder of Cahokia, preaching with such success that his chapel could not contain the multitude that thronged to him;" and Binnetau, "who left his mission among the Abenakis to die on the upland plains of the Mississippi;" and Gabriel Marest, "who, after chanting an ave to the cross among the icebergs of Hudson's Bay," was captured by the English, but found his way back to America; and Mermet, "whose gentle virtues and fervid eloquence made him the soul of the mission at Kaskaskia," far away in the valley of the Mississippi; and Marquette, "still honored in the West;" and Guignes, who had travelled six hundred leagues from Quebec to the territory of the Sioux, and when on the point of being burned alive by the Kickapoos, was saved by an aged chief who adopted him as his son;* and Pierron, of whom the Mohawks said, "this Frenchman has changed our hearts and souls, his desires and thoughts are ours;" and Du Jannay, whose memory is still preserved at Detroit, and his name dear to the Ottawas; and Milet, whom

* *Lettres Edifiantes,* tome vii., p. 67.

the Onondagas called "the one who looks up to heaven;" and Etienne de Carheil, "revered for his genius as well as for his zeal," and "who spoke the dialects of the Huron-Iroquois tribes with as much facility and elegance as though they had been his mother tongue;" and Druillettes, whom even the English, after plotting his death, extolled for his incomparable charity;* and Picquet, who for more than thirty years labored amongst the savages, and in three years gathered round him three hundred and ninety-six heads of families,—of whom the Marquis du Quesne used to say, "The Abbé Picquet is worth more than ten regiments,"—whom de Bougainville eulogized as "theologian, orator, and poet,"—and whom Amherst tried to conciliate, after the conquest of Quebec, though the English had often set a price on his head.†

To these let us add one whom Mr. Bancroft calls "the faithful Senat," who, "when D'Artaguette lay weltering in his blood, might have fled," but "remained to receive the last sigh of the wounded, regardless of danger, mindful only of duty;" and Lamberville, who, as an English writer observes, captivated even the hereditary enemies of the Christian Hurons, and "so won the confidence of the Iroquois by his unaffected piety, his constant kindness, and his skill in healing their differences and their bodily ailments," that even these irreclaimable savages, hired by the English to fight against their Christian brothers, "looked upon him as a father and a friend;"‡ and Marest, who, after travelling many weeks to the distant home of the Potawattomies, "carrying with him only a crucifix and a breviary," found himself clasped in the arms of a brother whom he had not seen for fifteen years, but who, in the interval, had become a Jesuit like himself, and whom he was destined to meet for the first time in an Indian cabin more than two thousand miles from the sea.

Lastly, let us allude to, though we cannot name them, that multitude of generous apostles who, like Anne de Noué, tasted the *martyrium sine sanguine*, drowned, starved, or frozen to death, and "whose fate," as Mr. Halkett observes, "was not ascertained, and who were never afterwards heard of."§

Yet their labor was not in vain, and its fruits survive even to this hour, in spite of the multiplied disasters of every kind which have concurred to blight them. "If any Indians still remain in Canada," says M. Brasseur de Bourbourg, "it is to

* *Relations des Jesuites dans la Nouvelle France,* Année 1652; ch. viii., tome ii., p. 29.

† Bancroft, ii., 838, 916, 964; *Lettres Edifiantes,* tome xxvi., pp. 18–63.

‡ Howitt, *Colonization and Christianity,* ch. xx., p. 321.

§ *Notes on N. American Indians,* ch. ii., p. 43.

the Catholic Church alone that their preservation is due." We shall see presently how much reason he had to say it. The whole Huron nation was converted, and Protestant writers will tell us that its survivors still do honor to their apostolic teachers. Abenakis and Algonquins, Ottawas and Onondagas, received the message of peace, "and in the heart of the State of New York the solemn services of the Roman Church were chanted as securely as in any part of Christendom."* The Cayugas and Oneidas, the Senecas and Miamis, welcomed the preachers of the Gospel; and a single missionary, Claude Allouez, "lighted the torch of faith for more than twenty different nations."† "To what inclemencies, from nature and from man," says the Protestant historian, "was each missionary among the barbarians exposed! He defies the severity of climate, wading through water, or through snows, without the comfort of fire; having no bread but pounded maize, and often no food but the unwholesome moss from the rocks; laboring incessantly; exposed to live, as it were, without nourishment, to sleep without a resting-place,—to carry his life in his hand, or rather daily, and oftener than every day, to hold it up as a target, expecting captivity, death from the tomahawk, tortures, fire." And yet, as he judiciously adds, these heroes had abundant consolation. "How often was the pillow of stones like that where Jacob felt the presence of God! How often did the ancient oak seem like the tree of Mamre, beneath which Abraham broke bread with angels!"‡ One reflection only he fails to make,—that the doctrine which such men delivered in every land was the same which St. Paul or St. Philip preached, by the same method, and which *they* also illustrated by the same actions, and sealed by the same death.

The men who preached the faith in Canada continued to the end such as its first apostles had been. One after another they displayed the same supernatural character, and even their enemies acknowledged in them the marks of the same apostolic vocation. But they were now to encounter that peculiar obstacle, unknown, as we have several times observed, in the age of St. Peter and St. Paul, and which has proved fatal in so many lands to the salvation of the heathen. They were rapidly converting one tribe after another, as their brethren had done in the South, and would not have rested from their labor till they had converted them all; but a price was now to be set on their heads, by men calling themselves Christians, and

* Bancroft, ii., 799.
† Id., 804.
‡ Id., 806.

representing the government and the religion of England! "*In* 1700, *the legislature of New York made a law for hanging every Popish priest that should come voluntarily into the province;*"* and Lord Bellamont, the English governor, declared his intention to execute the law immediately upon every Jesuit whom he could seize.† They had tried every other plan; they had surpassed even the Mohawk, whom they made their ally in hunting down the missionaries of the Cross; and now they announced to the world, by a solemn legislative enactment, that they were prepared to murder every Catholic priest, upon whom they could lay hands. Their success, it must be admitted, was complete; but in accomplishing it, they not only destroyed Christianity and those who alone could propagate it, but extirpated by the same fatal policy the nations whom they could neither convert themselves, nor would suffer others to convert.

The conduct of Lord Bellamont, who only executed faithfully the instructions of his masters, was thus noticed by Mr. Talbot, an Anglican missionary in America, in 1702. After expressing generally his reluctant admiration of the "zealous and diligent papists," the Protestant preacher continued as follows. "'Tis wonderfully acted, ventured, and suffered upon that design; they have indeed become all things, and even turned Indians, as it were, to gain them. One of their priests lived half a year in their wigwams without a shirt; and when he petitioned my Lord Bellamont for a couple, *he was not only denied but banished;* whereas one of ours, in discourse with my Lord of London, said, Who did his Lordship think would come hither that had a dozen shirts?"‡

The Dutch, though they twice humanely ransomed a Catholic missionary, were not in other respects superior to their co-religionists of England. As early as 1657, they were established at Orange, now the city of Albany, where they lived after a fashion which provoked such comments as the following. Of one preacher, who was sent out by the "Lutheran Consistory at Amsterdam," his Dutch Calvinist colleagues gave the following graphic account. "This Lutheran parson is a man of a godless and scandalous life, a rolling, rollicking, unseemly carl, who is more inclined to look into the wine-can, than to pore over the Bible, and would rather drink a can of brandy for two hours than preach one." He and his flock were accustomed, "when full of brandy, to beat each other's heads black and

* Bancroft, ii., 835.

† Brasseur de Bourbourg, tome i., ch. xii., p. 216.

‡ *Missions of the Church of England in the N. American Colonies*, by Earnest Hawkins, B.D., ch. ii., p. 33 (1845).

blue," their pastor being "excessively inclined to fight whomsoever he meets."* The disciples of the Dutch clergy generally are thus described, in 1710, by the Rev. Thomas Barclay, an Episcopalian minister, in an official report on the "State of the Church in Albany." "There are about thirty communicants of the Dutch Church, but so ignorant and scandalous, that they can scarce be reputed Christians."† It is fair, however, to add, that we shall hear exactly the same account, by their own friends, of the Episcopalian clergy and *their* flocks. It was probably their experience of such teachers and such congregations which made the neighboring Indian tribes reason as follows. "What a difference between the Christians and the Dutch! They say that they all acknowledge the same God, but how unlike are they in their conduct! When we go to visit the French, we always come back with a desire to pray. At Albany they never say any thing to us about prayer. We do not even know whether they pray there at all."‡

Yet at this very date, the Indians collected in the island of Montreal had been so effectually converted to God,—and in many of the fixed missions, notably at the Sault Ste. Marie, the same thing was true,—that European visitors could report, "The whole island of Montreal resembles a religious community;"§ or, as the Bishop of Quebec observed in 1688, "You would take this village for a monastery, so extraordinary is their daily life."‖ At Kaskaskia, far away in the valley of the Mississippi, Mr. Bancroft says, "the success of the mission was such, that marriages of the French emigrants were sometimes solemnized with the daughters of the Illinois according to the rites of the Catholic Church;" while the Indians, he allows, were so thoroughly converted, that not only did they all assemble "at early dawn" to assist at Mass, and again "at evening for instruction, for prayer, and to chant the hymns of the Church," but, as the Protestant historian adds, "every convert confessed once in a fortnight," and "at the close of the day, parties would meet in the cabins to recite the rosary, in alternate choirs, and sing psalms into the night."¶ By the end of the seventeenth century, as Mr. Owen observes, "the total of the Confederacy (Six Nations) who professed the Roman Catholic religion was computed to exceed eight thousand."** And this was only one

* *Documentary History of New York,* vol iii., p. 105.
† Ibid., p. 898.
‡ Charlevoix, tome ii., liv. viii., p. 80.
§ Ibid., liv. ix., p. 163.
‖ *Lettres Edifiantes,* tome vi., p, 126.
¶ Bancroft, ii., 839.
** *History of the Bible Society,* vol. i., p. 128.

example of their success. "The whole Abenakis nation," the martyr Rasles could say in 1722, "is Christian, and full of zeal for their religion." "Among the Five Nations," as a bitter Puritan lamented, "there is a great number of French Jesuits, and the chief of the poor silly Indians do entirely confide in them."* As early as 1670, Roger Williams, a famous Protestant preacher, confessed to Mason, in the frightful language of his class, that "the French and Romish Jesuits, the firebrands of the world for their god-belly sake, are kindling at our back in this country their hellish fires, *with all the natives of this country*."† So that Judge Hall could truly observe, "The French Catholics, at a very early period, were remarkably successful in gaining converts, and conciliating the confidence and affection of the tribes;" while, as he adds, with singular candor, "Protestants, similarly situated, were bloodthirsty and rapacious."‡

In truth, as respects the fruits of their labors, it was the history of Brazil and Peru in another clime. In many a mission, from the Mohawk to the Genesee, and from the Hudson to the Mississippi, were gathered Christian Indians, who, as one whom Mr. Bancroft styles "the honest Charlevoix" has recorded, "would have done honor to the first ages of Christianity." "I give my life willingly," said Tegananokoa, a native martyr, "for a God who shed all His blood for me." When his fingers had been cut off by the heathen, because he lifted them up in prayer, and he was scoffingly bidden to continue his supplications, "Yes," he replied, "I will pray," and then made the sign of the cross with his mutilated hand. But men who could defy all the arts of the pagan, and who were once more converting a continent, were vanquished by the more subtle wickedness of so-called Christians. The Iroquois, a nation remarkable for their natural gifts, so that even Dr. Timothy Dwight compares them with "the Greeks and Romans," appear to have become perfectly demoniacal after intercourse with their white allies, by whom they were paid to fight against the French. They were, says a Protestant ethnologist, "a people advancing in many ways towards the full initiation of a self-originated civilization, when the intrusion of Europeans abruptly arrested its progress, and brought them in contact with the elements of a foreign civilization pregnant only with the sources of their degradation and final destruction."§ "I have often," says Charlevoix, "asked some of our

* *Discoveries of the English in America*, Pinkerton, vol. xii., p. 410.
† *Massachusetts Historical Collections*, 1st series, vol. i., p. 283.
‡ Rupp, *Hist. Rel. Denom.*, p. 163.
§ Dr. Wilson, *Prehistoric Man*, vol. i., ch. vii., p. 225.

Fathers, with many of whom who labored longest in this part of the Lord's vineyard I had the happiness of living, what had hindered the seed of the Word from taking root amongst a people whose intelligence, good sense, and noble feelings they so much praised. All gave me the same reply,—that the chief cause of this evil *was the neighborhood of the English and Dutch*, whose want of piety, though professing to be Christians, had induced these savages to regard Christianity as a mere religion of caprice—*comme une religion arbitraire.*"

But we have not been accustomed in these volumes to rely upon Catholic evidence, however weighty, and the testimony of Charlevoix, as we shall see immediately, is amply confirmed from other sources. On the 10th of August, 1654, at a general council of all the Iroquois nations, as we read in the *Documentary History of New York* they solemnly invited the Catholic missionaries, in a moment of freedom from English influence, to take up their abode amongst them. "It is *you*," they said, "who ought to possess our hearts." And it was from *Christian Huron captives*, the very race whom they had most hated and injured, that they had learned "the great value of the Faith, and to prize without being acquainted with it." They had seen the Catholic Indian suffer, and they had seen him die, and the lesson had not been lost upon them. Nor can it be reasonably doubted that, but for the counsels and example of the English, these noble tribes would all have been won to Christianity and civilization. It was not till they had learned to despise the religion of their Saxon allies, and to imitate their vices, that they closed their hearts forever against the message of peace. It has been the mission of the English, in all lands, to make the conversion of the heathen impossible. Here are fresh examples, recorded by themselves, of their mode of proceeding in the Atlantic provinces of America.

In 1687, Governor Dongan of New York, after reporting officially to the Lords of the Committee of Trade, that the Iroquois were "a bulwark between us and the French," added these characteristic words, "*I suffer no Christians to converse with them* anywhere but at Albany, and that not without my licence." It was more advantageous to English interests that they should continue pagans, because if they embraced Christianity they were sure to be Catholics. He even avowed, with crude brutality, the odious treachery which he knew the English government would approve and reward. "The French Fathers have converted many of them,—Mohawks, Senecas, Cayugas, Oneidas, and Onondagas,—to the Christian Faith, and doe their utmost to draw them to Canada, to which place there are already six or seven hundred retired, and more like to doe, *to* *the great prejudice of this government*, if not prevented;" and then he tells his masters how he had induced some to return by fraud, promising "to furnish them with priests,"—a promise kept, thirteen years later, by enacting a law "to hang every Popish priest that should come into the province."* It was against such deadly influences that the apostles of North America contended, till both they and their flocks were annihilated.

Yet not a few even of the Iroquois had proved how powerfully grace could work in them, when they were suffered to come within its reach. All the early Canadian records speak, amongst others, of the Iroquois Saint, Catherine Teguhkouita. Born in 1656, and converted in early youth by the missionaries from Montreal, she led until her death, in 1680, a hidden life of prayer, seeking by her austerities to make atonement for the errors of her tribe. "She had placed a cross in the trunk of a tree, by the side of a stream, and this solitary spot served her for an oratory. There in spirit she placed herself at the foot of the altar, united her intention to that of the priest, and implored her angel guardian to assist at the sacrifice of the Mass in her place, and to apply to her the fruit of it." Accustomed to practise in secret the most painful mortifications, and making her bed of rough thorns, a Christian companion suggested to her that this was an error in the sight of God, who does not approve austerities performed without the sanction of authority, and not consecrated by obedience. "Catherine, who dreaded even the appearance of sin," says Father Cholenec, "came immediately to search for me, to acknowledge her fault, and ask pardon of God. I blamed her indiscretion, and directed her to throw the thorns into the fire. This she instantly did." When she died, at the age of twenty-four, the same missionary relates that the very sight of her corpse filled the spectators with surprise and edification: "It might be said that a ray of glory illuminated even her body."†

Margaret, another of these Indian virgins, was martyred by the pagan members of her own tribe, and, amidst the greatest tortures which savage cruelty could inflict, "continued to invoke the holy names of Jesus, Mary, and Joseph." The agony of thirst made her crave for water, yet when they offered it to her, she refused, saying, "My Saviour thirsted for me on the cross; it is just that I should suffer the same torment." She survived so long under her tortures, that her murderers exclaimed with surprise, "Is this dog of a Christian unable to die?"

* *Documentary History of New York*, vol. i., pp. 41, 154.
† *Lettres Edifiantes*, tome vi., pp. 67, 97.

The apostles who had raised up to God, in many an Indian tribe, such worshippers as these, would not have failed in due time to renew the triumphs which their brethren had effected in Brazil, Peru, and Paraguay. They had begun, and would have completed, the same work. The Indian of the North, until brutalized by drink and maddened by cruelty, was at least as capable of appreciating Christian heroism and sanctity as his fellow-barbarian of the South; and when he saw both displayed before his eyes, did homage after his kind. "The North American Indian," says an eminent English writer, "is of a disposition peculiarly religious,"* though the emissaries of Protestantism could not turn the disposition to account. When the tribes of Kentucky had declared implacable war against the seed of the oppressor, they still respected, even in the paroxysm of their rage, one class, and one alone. The French Trappists, far from all human succor, dwelt without fear in the midst of them; and "the monks themselves," though blood was flowing all around them, were never molested in their own establishment. The savages seemed even to be awed into reverence for their sanctity; and often did they pause in the vicinity of the rude Trappist chapel, to listen to the praises of God chanted amidst the bones of their own fathers."†

Such is the spell, as we have seen in many lands, which Catholic holiness exerts even over the rudest natures. "So wide," says Mr. Bancroft, with his usual candor, "was the influence of the missionaries in the West," that when Du Buisson, defending Fort Detroit with only twenty Frenchmen against the forces of the English, "summoned his Indian allies from the chase; Ottawas, and Hurons, and Potawattomies, with one branch of the Sacs, Illinois, Menomonies, and even Osages and Missouris, each nation with its own ensign came to his relief. 'Father,' said they, 'behold! thy children compass thee round. We will, if need be, gladly die for our father.'"‡ Multitudes, no doubt, would have shared the fate of Jogues and Lallemand and De Brebeuf, before the victory was finally accomplished; but others would immediately have taken their place, until Mohawk and Sioux, Shawnee and Delaware, subdued by their invincible courage, and won by their surpassing charity, would have imitated the Moxos and Chiquitos of the southern continent, and, like them, would have survived

* *Lectures on Colonization*, by Herman Merivale, A.M., Professor of Political Economy; lect. xix., p. 526.

† *Sketches of the Early Catholic Missions of Kentucky*, by M. J. Spalding, D.D., ch. x., p. 173.

‡ II., 858.

to this day, dwelling in the land of their fathers, and praising the God of Christians. But an enemy had now entered the field, before whom both the missionary and his flock disappeared, and whose operations it is time to notice. Two or three examples, out of many, will sufficiently indicate their scope and character.

"On the banks of the Kennebec," says the historian whom we have so often quoted, "the venerable Sebastian Rasles, for more than a quarter of a century the companion and instructor of savages, had gathered a flourishing village round a church which, rising in the desert, made some pretensions to magnificence. Severely ascetic,—using no wine, and little food except pounded maize,—he built his own cabin, tilled his own garden, drew for himself wood and water, prepared his own hominy and, distributing all that he received, gave an example of religious poverty. . . . Following his pupils to their wigwam, he tempered the spirit of devotion with familiar conversation and innocent gayety, winning the mastery of their souls by his powers of persuasion. He had trained a little band of forty young savages, arrayed in cassock and surplice, to assist in the service and chant the hymns of the Church, and their public processions attracted a great concourse of red men."*

The apostolic labors of Father Rasles, and their success, made him odious to the English. They tried two plans for his destruction, of which Mr. Bancroft mentions only one. "The government of Massachusetts," he says, "attempted, in turn, to establish a mission; and its minister made a mocking of purgatory and the invocation of saints, of the cross and the rosary. . . . Thus Calvin and Loyola met in the woods of Maine. But the Protestant minister, unable to compete with the Jesuit for the affections of the Indians, returned to Boston."†

Their first project having failed, they adopted a second; and the English authorities now offered by proclamation one thousand pounds sterling for the head of the too successful missionary! "The English regard me," said the venerable man who was soon to be their victim, "as an invincible obstacle to the design which they have formed of acquiring all the lands of the Abenakis."‡ His crime was unpardonable, but it will be well to learn by Protestant testimony how it was avenged. "After vainly soliciting the savages," says Mr. Bancroft, "to surrender Rasles, in midwinter, Westbrooke led a strong force to Norridgewock, to take him by surprise." They had often hunted him before,

* Bancroft, ii., 938.
† Ibid., p. 939.
‡ *Lettres Edifiantes,* tome vi., p. 148.

but this time they were to be successful. In vain his flock had implored him to fly betimes. "The aged man, foreseeing the impending ruin of Norridgewock, replied, 'I count not my life dear unto myself, so I may finish with joy the ministry which I have received.'" When the English arrived, "Rasles went forward to save his flock, by drawing down upon himself the attention of the assailants; and his hope was not vain." Many of them escaped, "while the English pillaged the cabins and the church, and then, heedless of sacrilege, set them on fire."* Mr. Bancroft omits to add, what we learn from another source, that they "horribly profaned the sacred vessels, and the adorable Body of Jesus Christ."†

And what was the fate of one who for thirty-seven years had devoted himself, in poverty and suffering, to the welfare of the natives? Mr. Bancroft has recorded it. "After the retreat of the invaders, the Abenakis," to whom the generosity of the missionary had given time to save their women and children, "returned to nurse their wounded and bury their dead. They found Rasles mangled by many blows, *scalped*, his skull broken in several places, *his mouth and eyes filled with dirt;* and they buried him beneath the spot where he used to stand before the altar." Such was the work of a British military force conducted by three British officers.

The vengeance of England was complete, and from that hour the fate of the red man in all the Eastern States was sealed. It is Mr. Bancroft who draws the conclusion. "Thus died Sebastian Rasles," he says, "the last of the Catholic missionaries in New England; *thus perished the Jesuit missions and their fruits*,—the villages of the semi-civilized Abenakis and their priests."‡ Is it wonderful that there has been no new Paraguay in Canada or the United States?§

One hundred and eight years after the martyrdom of Sebastian Rasles, Dr. Fenwick, Bishop of Boston, purchased the land which had been dyed with his blood, to build a church on the spot consecrated by his death.‖ In the following year, 1833,

* II., 859.

† Charlevoix, tome iv., p. 12.

‡ II., 941.

§ Let it be observed, too, that the English never faltered in their crusade against religion and its ministers. Thirty-five years later, Amherst led a force against the Indian village of St. Francis. The inhabitants were all Catholics. "These Indians," we are told, "had a handsome Catholic chapel, with plate and ornaments." Taken by surprise, they were almost all slain. "The village, *as had happened so often in New England*, was first plundered, and then burned." Hildreth, vol. ii., ch. xxvii., p. 487. If the natives of North America have remained unconverted, it is to English Protestants alone that this result is due.

‖ *Annales de la Propagation de la Foi*, tome vi., p. 274.

the same bishop met the grandson of one of the English who had slain him, by whom the prelate was informed, that to the hour of his death his grandfather ceased not to shed tears at the thought of that sorrowful day; and often called to mind that, having been wounded, he had been charitably nursed by one of Father Rasles' disciples, though her own husband had been killed by his English companions. It is worthy of notice, too, that a century after his death, a deputation of the Abenakis brought to Dr. Carroll, Archbishop of Baltimore, the crucifix of the martyr, a relic which they only agreed to transfer to his custody, "on condition that he would send them a priest."* So well had they kept the faith, during that long interval, that when Sir Guy Carleton sent to them Protestant ministers in 1785, "they drove them out of their village;" and the governor, generously appreciating their constancy, not only dispatched to them a Catholic priest, but offered him a stipend of fifty pounds a year.†

The action of the Indian woman noticed above, whose charity would perhaps be rarely imitated by European Christians, affords an interesting example of the influence of religion among the disciples of the martyred missionary; a still more striking case, in which the hand of the Indian warrior was restrained in the very heat of battle by the power of Catholic sympathy deserves notice. Nearly a century after the death of Father Rasles, in the war of 1812–13, an Irish Catholic, fighting with a body of American troops against a native tribe, was about to be overtaken by a chief. Falling on his knees, "he made the sign of the cross, and endeavored as well as he could to prepare himself for death. The warrior suddenly stopped, dropped his tomahawk, and falling likewise on his knees, embraced the white man, exclaiming, "You are my brother!" It is Bishop Fenwick who records this touching anecdote, which he received from the very man who owed his life to the forbearance suggested to a savage by a religious sentiment, which taught him to recognize a brother even in an enemy, whose hand had just been raised against him.‡

The fate of the venerable Sebastian Rasles overtook many an apostle in the midst of his toils, and would have been shared by all if the English could have laid hands on them. The celebrated Abbé Picquet, who united rare energy and ability to the higher virtues of his calling, was also tracked by the English

* Brasseur de Bourbourg, *Histoire du Canada*, &c., tome i., ch. xxi., p. 85.

† Id., ch. xxii., p. 88.

‡ Spalding, ch. ii., p. 30.

as a wild beast, and a price set on his head.* Yet he was one who could have converted half the tribes of the North. In 1749, he commenced his mission at Ogdensburgh with six heads of families; in 1750, he had eighty-seven round him; in 1751, three hundred and ninety-six. "People saw with astonishment several villages start up almost at once; a convenient, habitable, and pleasantly situated fort; vast clearances covered almost at the same time with the finest maize." This was the system by which the Jesuits and Franciscans had conquered South America, but it was only a small part of his work. At the mission of *la Présentation*, "the most distinguished of the Iroquois families were distributed in three villages." The Bishop of Quebec, "wishing to witness and assure himself personally of the wonders related to him," visited *la Présentation*, "and spent ten days examining and causing the catechumens to be examined. He himself baptized one hundred and thirty-two, and did not cease during his sojourn blessing Heaven for the progress of religion among these infidels." Yet Picquet was hunted by the English, after gaining the illustrious title of "Apostle of the Iroquois," and finally, in 1760, was obliged to quit Canada forever, in consequence of the death of Montcalm and the capture of Quebec.†

But he has not been, as we shall see more fully hereafter, without successors of his own school. Thirty-two years after Picquet was driven from Canada, an illustrious traveller described the following incident. "I myself met one of these apostles of religion amid the solitudes of America. One morning, as we were slowly pursuing our course through the forests, we perceived a tall, venerable old man, with a white beard, approaching us. He proved to be a missionary of Louisiana, on his way from New Orleans, returning *to the country of the Illinois.* He accompanied us for several days, and however early we were up in the morning, we always found the aged traveller risen before us and reading his breviary while walking in the forest. This holy man had suffered much. . . . . He seemed to possess great attainments of many kinds, which he scarcely suffered to appear under his evangelical simplicity. Like his predecessors, the Apostles, though knowing every thing, he seemed to know nothing."‡

* We are not surprised to learn that he revenged himself in a manner worthy of an Apostle. When an English officer, who was actually in search of him, was captured by the Indians, and their clubs were already raised to beat him to death, Picquet forbade them to harm the baffled assassin. *Memoire sur la Vie de M. Picquet,* par M. de Lalande, de l'Académie des Sciences; *Panthéon Littéraire,* tome i., p. 742 (1838).

† *Documentary History of New York,* vol. i., p. 432.

‡ Chateaubriand, *Genius of Christianity,* p. 592; ed. White.

We have now perhaps sufficient knowledge of the men who announced the Gospel in Canada, and of the policy by which their work was frustrated. The English became masters of all the lands which lie between Cape Gaspé and the western shores of Lake Superior, and the same fate awaited the doomed native which has crushed, under the same masters, the aborigines of South Africa, of Australia, of Tahiti, and New Zealand. It only remains to show, by a few characteristic examples, how complete the ruin has been.

It may be allowed, however, in noticing the condition to which Protestantism has reduced the natives of British America, to indicate, as usual by the aid of Protestant witnesses alone, the traces which still exist of the Catholic missions, and the character of those who conduct them. In spite of murder, fraud, and oppression, English writers will assure us, both that the Catholic Indians of Canada are the *only* Christians who deserve the name, and that their teachers at this hour exactly resemble those who died to save their fathers.

The evidence is copious, but shall be confined within narrow limits. Exactly a century ago, the Rev. John Ogilvie, an Anglican missionary agent in America, thus addressed his employers: "Of *every* nation, I find some who have been instructed by the priests of Canada, and appear zealous Roman Catholics, extremely tenacious of the ceremonies and peculiarities of that Church. . . . . How ought we to blush at *our* coldness and shameful indifference in the propagation of our most excellent religion. The Indians themselves are not wanting in making very pertinent reflections upon our inattention to these points."*

Other witnesses notice the same invariable facts at the present day. The *Chippeways*, Sir George Simpson relates, met him at Fort William, and represented to him that, "*being all Catholics*, they should like to have a priest among them."† Like the Christian natives of Hindostan, of China, and of Paraguay, they had preserved their faith, though separated for more than *half a century* from those who had declared it to them.

It is related of Cardinal Cheverus, whose character excited so much admiration in America, to whom the State of Massachusetts voted a subsidy, and the first subscriber to whose church at Boston was John Adams, President of the United States, that when he visited the Penobscot, he found an Indian tribe, who had not even seen a priest for half a century, but

* Ernest Hawkins, *Missions*, &c., ch. xii., p. 289.
† *Journey Round the World*, vol. i., ch. i., p. 35.

were still zealous Catholics, carefully observed the Sunday, and "had not forgotten the catechism!"*

In 1831, Bishop Fenwick found a whole tribe of *Passamaquoddies*, constant in the faith, and, as he observed, "a living monument of the apostolic labors of the Jesuits."†

Of the *Hurons*, the beloved disciples of the early missionaries, Mr. Buckingham, an English traveller, speaks as follows: "They are faithful Catholics, and are said to fulfil their religious duties in the most exemplary manner, being much more improved by their commerce with the whites than the Indian tribes who have first come into contact with Protestants usually are." Of the Indians in the neighborhood of Montreal, the same Protestant writer says, "They are *always* sober, a rare occurrence with Indians of either sex." "This difference," he candidly observes, "is occasioned by the influence of Christianity, as the *Caghnawaga* Indians *are Catholics*."‡

Of the *Abenakis*, whose fathers listened one hundred and fifty years ago to the voice of Sebastian Rasles, Protestant missionaries angrily relate, in 1841, after vainly attempting to subvert them, that they could do nothing against the "controlling influence of the Romish priesthood."§

Of the Indians at *l'Arbre Croche*, on the east shore of Lake Michigan, "for sixty years or more the seat of a Jesuit mission," Dr. Morse, a Protestant minister, reported thus to the United States government: "These Indians are much in advance, in point of improvement, in appearance, and in manners, of all the Indians whom I visited."‖ Do we not say with reason that in Catholic missions, we see everywhere the power of God rather than of man?

Of the *Wyandots*, the same official witness reported, "nearly all the aged people still wear crucifixes."

Of the *Onondagas*, Mr. Schoolcraft observes, "They were ever strongly opposed to all missionaries *after* the expulsion of the Jesuits."¶

"The *Ottawa-Chippewa* mission," in Upper Michigan, we are told, "is greater than it ever was in the most flourishing time of the old Jesuit Fathers."**

Of the *Micmacs*, in Prince Edward's Island, Colonel Bouchette says, "They are *all* still Catholics;" of the tribes in

* *Vie du Cardinal de Cheverus*, liv. ii., p. 68 (4me édition).

† *Annales*, tome v., p. 449.

‡ *Canada*, &c., ch. xi., p. 151; ch. xvii., p. 251.

§ *History of American Missions*, by Rev. Joseph Tracy, ch. xxxiii., p. 331.

‖ *A Report to the Secretary of War of the United States on Indian Affairs*, by the Rev. Jedidiah Morse, D.D., app., pp. 24, 91, 327.

¶ *Notes on the Iroquois*, ch. xii., p. 443.

** Shea, ch. xxi., p. 392.

New Brunswick, "the greater part of the Indians profess the Romish religion;" of those at Cape Breton, "*All* the Acadians are Roman Catholics;" and of the Indians *generally*, who are in communion with the Church, "they are *a quiet, temperate race.*"*

"The *Micmacs* of Restigouche," says a Protestant professor at Toronto, "are a highly civilized band of the Micmac nation . . . . . industriously engaged in the manufacture of staves, barrel-hoops, axe-handles," &c.†

Of the great mission in the Manitouline islands, the gentleman who is Protestant bishop at Toronto cautiously says, in 1842, "A considerable portion consists of half-breeds, of French and Indian extraction, and these being *all* Romanists, possess a good deal of influence among the natives."‡

More ingenuous witnesses give a less meagre account of them. "There are upwards of *two thousand* natives in the island," says Mr. Kingston in 1856, "the greater proportion of whom profess the Romish faith. At a settlement on the other side, a considerable number reside under four Jesuit Fathers"—the Jesuits re-entered Canada in 1842,—"and they are said to be a very obedient, industrious, and intelligent set, and superior to the Protestants; but of the truth of the assertion I have no means of judging."§ Yet in a later portion of his work, when he had perhaps acquired ampler experience, Mr. Kingston frankly describes the so-called *Protestant* Indians as "a very inferior race," and observes that the only effect of their pretended conversion is, "that now they wear blanket coats, weave mats, receive alms from the white man, and get drunk whenever they can."‖

Let these details be pardoned, for the sake of the lesson which they teach, and which is certainly of sufficient importance to merit ample illustration. We have seen in every other land the same contrast between the work of God and the work of man, and it is our business to trace it here also. For this reason, at the risk of repetition, we will continue the subject.

"The whole body of these Indians," said a respectable American Puritan, some years ago, speaking of the Pequods, "are a poor, degraded, miserable race of beings. The former

* *British Dominions in North America*, vol. ii., ch. vii., p. 85; ch. x., p. 148; ch. xi., p. 178.

† Wilson, *Prehistoric Man*, vol. ii., ch. xxii., p. 373.

‡ *The Church in Canada;* Journal of a Visitation by the Lord Bishop of Toronto in 1842, p. 10.

§ *Western Wanderings*, by W. H. G. Kingston, vol. i., ch. viii., p. 180.

‖ *Western Wanderings*, vol. i., ch. xvii., p. 314.

proud heroic spirit of the Pequod is shrunk into the torpor of reasoning brutism. All the vice of the original is left: all its energy has vanished. . . . . Their children, when young, they place in English families as servants. In the earlier parts of life these children frequently behave well, but, when grown up, throw off all that is respectable in their character, and sink to the level of their relatives,"*—a proof of the impotence of Protestantism which we have seen in every other land.

Sometimes we are told, not of tribes or nations, but of selected individuals, who had enjoyed every advantage, including a liberal education, which Protestantism could offer them; but the result was always the same. Dr. Timothy Dwight admits that even Indians who had taken academical degrees in the Protestant colleges of New England "returned to the grossness of savage life!"† Mr. Kingston tells us of one Indian, brought up "in the house of a clergyman," married to an American woman, and finally employed as an assistant missionary. "He saved a good deal of money, built himself a house, and furnished it nicely . . . . . but he was not content. He was ambitious of becoming a chief, and of forming a settlement of his own." The spiritual influence of Protestantism never seems to go beyond this point.

Mr. Buckingham also notices the case of "Peter Jones," another Indian Protestant, who has been exhibited in England as a preacher, and married an English woman. In spite of much acuteness, and a superior education, he not only "met with no success," but even flatly denied "that any who had passed the middle period of life would ever be prevailed upon to change their religion."‡

Jones was a Methodist, and one of the leaders of that denomination thought it expedient to write his life. "He ever sought to promote the glory of God," says Dr. Osborn, who seems to have made the same use of him as others made of Tzatzoe and Macomo, and pretended converts of the same class. Thus he quotes from him a statement that the "River Credit Indians" were devout Protestants, and bright ornaments of the Wesleyan body. Fortunately, a well-known English writer, who actually visited his flock, has published her impressions of them. "The Indians whom I saw wandering and lounging about," says Mrs. Jameson, "*filled me with compassion.*" Three or four half-caste women, she observes, and some of the young children, showed signs of intelligence, "but these are exceptions, and dirt, indolence, and drunkenness were but too prevalent."

* Dr. Dwight, *Travels in New England*, vol. iii., p. 20.
† Vol. ii., p. 99.
‡ *Canada*, ch. iv., p. 46.

Then contrasting them with the sober and prosperous *Catholic* Indians, of whom she candidly says, "I heard them sing Mass with every demonstration of decency and piety," this accomplished writer adds, that the very different behavior "of the *Methodist* Indians, as they lie grovelling on the ground in their religious services, struck me painfully."* Yet Dr. Osborn, nine years later, deliberately asserts, and quotes Jones in proof of the assertion, that "the Wesleyan missionaries have never yet failed to introduce Christianity among a body of Indians!"†

And these cases, bad as they are, represent, not the average results of Protestant teaching, but its choicest examples. The *mass* of the fallen and degraded Indians who have come, rather as pensioners than as "converts," under its fatal influence, are described by travellers of all classes in the same terms. The Catholic Indians invariably refuse to associate with them, and consider them the most abject of mankind. And Protestant witnesses freely confess that their estimate is perfectly just. Thus Mr. Kane, one of the latest writers on the western continent, while he lauds "the agricultural skill and industry" of the *Catholic* Indians near Manitouline, candidly describes the *Protestant* mission at Norway House in these words: "It is supported by the Hudson's Bay Company with the hope of improving the Indians, but, to judge from appearances, with but small success, as they are decidedly the dirtiest Indians I have met with, and the less that is said about their morality the better."‡

Miss Harriet Martineau, who is both a capable and an impartial witness, and who speaks, like all the rest, from actual observation, indicates the same contrast with her usual candor and emphasis. The most vaunted of the Protestant establishments is at Mackinaw, and here is Miss Martineau's account of it: "There is reason to think that *the mission* is the least satisfactory part of the establishment. A great latitude of imagination or representation is usually admitted on the subject of missions to the heathen. The reporters of *this* one appear to be peculiarly imaginative." And then follows the usual contrast: "The Indians have been *proved*, by the success of the French among them, to be capable of civilization. Near Little Traverse, in the northwest part of Michigan, within easy reach of Mackinaw," as if to make the invariable contrast more impressive, "there is an Indian village, *full of orderly and industrious inhabitants*, employed chiefly in agriculture. The

* *Sketches in Canada*, by Mrs. Jameson, part i., p. 40; part ii., p. 287 (1852).

† *History of the Objibway Indians*, by the Rev. E. Osborn, D.D., pp. 228 et seq. (1861).

‡ *Wanderings of an Artist*, ch. viii., p. 105.

English and Americans have never succeeded with the aborigines so well as the French; and it may be doubted whether the clergy have been a much greater blessing to them than the traders."* Mrs. Jameson also, in spite of religious prejudices, uses the same frank expressions. The Ottawas, she says, under the care of Father Crue, "have large plantations of corn and potatoes, and have built a chapel for their religious services, and a house for their priest." And then, although the relative and associate of Protestant ministers, she thus announces the final result of all her observations: "*One thing is most visible, certain, and undeniable, that the Roman Catholic converts are in appearance, dress, intelligence, industry, and general civilization, superior to all the others.*"†

Other Protestant writers go still further, and do not hesitate to avow that, like all other barbarians under Protestant masters, the natives are doomed to inevitable destruction. Where Divine charity is absent, and the sacraments of the Precious Blood, mere human benevolence, however active, only reveals its own impotence. "Our system of trade and intercourse with the Indian tribes," says Governor Chambers in an official report, "*is in this region of country rapidly destroying them.*"‡ "They hardly dare cultivate the soil," observes Mr. Beecham, even on the nominally "reserved" lands, "lest some reason should be found for dispossessing them!"§ Dr. Shaw declares, in 1856, that "*the authorities* frequently swindled the poor Indians."‖ "I am satisfied," adds Mr. Bradford, "that at least one quarter of the annuity paid to the Menominis is collected by traders, at the annuity payment, for whiskey."¶ "Many an Indian," says Mr. Kane, from actual observation, "returns to his wigwam poorer than he left it;" and he relates that, at a distribution of the government bounty which he personally witnessed, "there was scarcely a man, woman, or child old enough to lift the vessel to its mouth, that was not wallowing in beastly drunkenness."** Yet the Protestant clergy, incapable of dealing with evils which can only be alleviated by another ministry than theirs, do nothing whatever, either here or in the United States, to mitigate these disasters; so that Mr. Bradford, with a candor not unusual in Americans, contrasts them with "the pious, peaceful, and

* *Society in America*, by Harriet Martineau, vol. ii., ch. i., p. 18.

† *Sketches in Canada*, part ii., p. 287.

‡ *Notes on the North West*, by Wm. J. A. Bradford, part ii., p. 195 (1846).

§ *Colonization*, p. 9.

‖ *A Ramble through the United States*, &c., by John Shaw, M.D., F.G.S., F.L.S., ch. iii., p. 67 (1856).

¶ *Ubi supra.*

** Ch. ii., p. 41.

zealous disciples of the Cross," as he styles the Catholic missionaries, surmounting "with comparative ease" the complicated evils to which their rivals, with all the aid of opulence and of government support, despair of applying a remedy. "The Frenchman," says this American writer, "forgets not that the uncivilized, as well as civilized man, is his brother, and he deports himself as man to man. The sturdy Saxon treats the Indian like a dog. The American thinks every thing is to be accommodated to him."*

It would be idle to attempt to exhaust the Protestant witnesses, who record, from actual observation, the contrast which these passages illustrate between the influence of Catholic and Protestant agency upon the life and fortunes of the Indian. Let us close the series with these statements by two venerable prelates, whose testimony we may well accept, after what we have already heard, as conclusive: "These Indians," says Monseigneur Gaulein, Bishop of Kingston, in 1838, "are all excellent Catholics, and seem to me industrious and fond of labor; a large number of savages have been recently baptized." "I had often been told," observes Monseigneur Loras, Bishop of Dubuque, in 1839, "that the savages when converted make excellent Catholics, and having become acquainted with them, have had occasion to admire their fervor."†

Such are the disciples, by the testimony both of friends and enemies, and such the inflexible constancy of their faith, even where every influence has combined to destroy it. And now a word on the missionaries. "*They* are not inferior," says Mr. Buckingham, "in zeal and devotion to the first founders and propagators of the Faith on this continent;" while of their efforts to convert the pagan savages, in spite of the cruel disadvantages which attend them in a country under Protestant domination, he observes, "Of late years they are *more than usually* successful." And then he contrasts the dignity of these apostolic teachers with the "inferiority" of the Episcopalian ministers, and laments to notice in that opulent body "more than the usual portion of formality in the ministers, and coldness in the congregations."‡ A more distinguished Anglican writer, after quoting the observation of "one of our most intelligent Indian agents," that "the English Church either cannot or will not, certainly *does not*, sow, and therefore cannot expect to reap," asks, "what she is about?" and gives this reply: "Here, as in the old country,

* *Notes on the North West,* part ii., p. 89.
† *Annals,* vol. i., pp. 470–79; English edition.
‡ Ch. xv., p. 220.

quarrelling about the tenets to be inculcated, the means to be used!"*

Mr. Sullivan, another British traveller, of no mean capacity, frankly declares of the Catholic missionaries, "They exercise extraordinary influence amongst their proselytes, and also amongst several tribes of Indians."†

Mr. Halkett, also an eye-witness, observes as follows. "There is one point which cannot be disputed, that the Indians of British North America are treated by their present Roman Catholic instructors with great kindness and consideration. So far as benevolence, charity, and paternal care can afford comfort to the Indian, he receives it at their hands."‡ In other words, they still display the same patient, unwearied charity by which, two centuries ago, their predecessors first subdued the frowardness and captivated the affections of their wild flock; when, as Nicolini allows, "they visited daily every house in which lay a sick person, whom they served as the kindest nurse, and to whom they seemed to be ministering genii. By such conduct they brought this primitive population to idolize them."§

The Honorable Charles Murray, after noticing, in the generous language which might be expected from him, "the zeal and enterprise with which the Roman Catholic religion inspires its priests to toil, travel, and endure every kind of hardship," continues thus: "In this labor, especially among the Negroes and Indians, they put to shame the zeal and exertions of all other Christian sects; nor do they labor without effect. During my stay in Missouri, I observed that the Romish faith was gaining ground with a rapidity that outstripped all competition."‖

It would be easy to multiply these confessions of Protestant travellers, but surely we have heard enough. One witness only shall be cited in addition, because a peculiar interest attaches to his evidence, with which we may fitly terminate this series.

In 1860, Mr. Kohl published his journal of travels on the shores of Lake Superior. "I may take it on myself," says this gentleman, in eulogizing "those excellent men, the learned pastors of the Canadian mission," "to speak on this subject, for I have read all the old journeys of the early messengers of

* Jameson, *Sketches in Canada*, part i., p. 116; part ii., p. 287.

† *Rambles in North and South America*, ch. iii., p. 60.

‡ *Notes on North American Indians*, ch. x., p. 232.

§ *History of the Jesuits*, by G. B. Nicolini, ch. xiii., p. 302 (Bohn).

‖ *Travels in North America*, by the Hon. C. A. Murray, vol. ii., ch. xiii., p. 309. In 1851, the "Vicariate of the Indian territory" was established, and the bishop, aided by such men as Father Van Quickenborne, counted in a few years more than five thousand Catholic Indians in his Vicariate.

the Church, and followed them with sympathizing zeal. In our day, when religious martyrdom no longer flourishes, it is especially refreshing to travel in a country where this epoch has not entirely died out, and to associate with men who endure the greatest privations for lofty purposes, and who would be well inclined even to lay down their lives for their Church. In fact, every thing I heard here daily of the pious courage, patience, and self-devoting zeal of these missionaries on Lake Superior, caused me to feel intense admiration. They are well educated and learned men,—many better educated, indeed, than the majority,—and yet they resign not only all enjoyments and comforts, but also all the mental inspiration and excitement of polished society. They live isolated and scattered in little log huts round the lake, often no better off than the natives. They must draw their inspirations entirely from their own breast, and prayer. Only the thought of the great universal Church to which they belong keeps them connected with society and the world. It is true, however, that they find in this an incitement to exertion which our Protestant missionaries lack. The latter, broken up into sects, labor only for this or that congregation, while the former are animated by a feeling that, as soldiers of the Church, they are taking part in a mighty work, which includes all humanity, and encircles the entire globe."*

Mr. Kohl lived much, during his wanderings, with the men whom he thus describes, and whose labors appear to have excited his astonishment. Even a baptism, a wedding, or a funeral, he observes, involves in such a climate almost the privations and sufferings "of an Arctic expedition." He is lodging on one occasion in the hut of a Jesuit Father, who had retired after the toils of the day. It was "the blessed cold Christmas season," and the missionary was sitting over the evening fire with his guest. "All at once there was a knock at the door, and a breathless stranger, covered with snow and icicles, walked in." His message was soon told. Forty miles away, through swamps and forests, his mother lay ill, and implored the succors of religion. On the instant the Father rose and left the hut, "the missionary and the Indian walking side by side in their snow-shoes." They cross a frozen river, the ice parts asunder, and they fall through "up to their waists." "At the end of the *third* day," adds Mr. Kohl, "the missionary was enabled to give the poor dying Indian woman extreme unction, and to see her eyes gently close in death. Would an Oxford gentleman rejoice at being presented to such a living?"

* *Wanderings Round Lake Superior*, by J. G. Kohl, ch. xix., p. 306.

And these missionaries, he says, are all of the same class.* Of one, whom he calls his "honored friend," and who was the author of an Ojibbeway Lexicon, Mr. Kohl remarks, "There is hardly a locality on Lake Superior which is not connected with the history of his life, either because he built a chapel there, or wrote a pious book, or founded an Indian parish, or else underwent dangers and adventures there, in which he felt that Heaven was protecting him." And then he relates a tale, which he received from a Canadian *voyageur*, and which he did well to communicate to his readers. A message had been brought from the other side of Lake Superior to one of these martyrs of charity with whom Mr. Kohl dwelt. It was night, a tempest was raging, and seventy miles of water must be crossed, for to go round the lake would occupy many days; but the case was urgent, and the missionary did not hesitate. In an open canoe, paddled by a Canadian, who only consented to brave the perilous voyage on the Father's reiterated assurance that God would protect them, the darkness of night resting on the waters which the storm had lashed into fury, the missionary encouraged his faithful companion to strain every nerve. The weary hours of the night were passed in prayer and toil, and when the Canadian approached the long line of foaming breakers which beat against the opposite shore, with a cry of anguish he exclaimed, "Your Reverence, we are lost!" "Paddle on, dear Dubois," said the calm voice of the missionary, "straight on. We *must* get through, and a way will offer itself." "My cousin shrugged his shoulders," said the narrator to Mr. Kohl, "made his last prayers, and paddled straight on he hardly knew how. . . . All at once a dark spot opened out in the white edge of the surf, which soon widened," and they were saved. "Did I not say, Dubois," was the only remark of the missionary, "that I was called, that I must go, and that thou wouldst be saved with me? Let us pray." And then they knelt down by the shore of the lake, and gave thanks to God.

On the very spot where they landed, Mr. Kohl adds, a large cross has since been erected by a rich merchant, "which can be seen a long distance on the lake," and is known throughout

* They never change, of whatever nation they may be. In 1840, the American mission lost one of whom we have this account. "In 1799, a young priest took up his abode among the most rugged summits of the Alleghanies." For forty years he labored alone, and "after expending one hundred and fifty thousand dollars of his fortune in this admirable work, he died, leaving ten thousand Catholics in the mountains, where he had found only twelve families." He was known in life as the "Rev. Mr. Smith," but when his humility could no longer be wounded, the world learned that this solitary apostle was the Prince Demetrius Gallitzin, a convert from the Russo-Greek Church. De Courcy, ch. xviii., p. 128.

the region as "the Cross of ——'s Traverse." When Mr. Kohl had heard the tale, he says, "I laid myself down on the knotted flooring, by the side of this excellent, gently slumbering man."*

Such are the missionaries who still labor, as Lallemand and De Brebeuf once labored, among the North American Indians. Two centuries have passed away since the first martyrs of this land entered into their reward, and not a single grace has been withdrawn, not a single gift diminished, which Divine bounty once lavished upon *them*, and still confers upon their successors. It is no grateful task to compare them with their Protestant rivals, but we are tracing a contrast, and must needs go on with it. An amiable Anglican minister, very superior to many of his colleagues, has published to the world in what manner *he* set out upon his mission in Canada, and with what appliances. "Our own carriage," he says, "a sort of double dennet, drawn by my own horses, brought up the rear," the van being formed by wagons of furniture and provisions. "This contained myself, my wife, and our eldest son, every corner being filled up with trunks, bandboxes, and endless et ceteras." After this description of his going forth, the writer, who had evidently good feelings and intentions, gravely observes, "I may not presume to class myself with those heroic and warlike churchmen of old," but the disclaimer appears to betray a lurking hope that, in spite of his equipage and his bandboxes, his readers might be of a different opinion.†

The same clergyman informs us that his missionary colleagues in Canada "absolutely ridiculed the idea" of baptism conferring grace; while from higher authorities of the same sect we learn, that all the other religious phenomena which characterize the present state of England are being successfully reproduced in Canada. "We remark, far and wide," says the gentleman who is Protestant bishop at Toronto, "the prevalence of religious division, and its attendant is too frequently in this diocese a feeling of hostility to the Church of England,"‡—a statement confirmed, with ample details, by his colleague at Quebec, and by the Rev. J. P. Hincks, who also laments "a general coldness towards the Church." Another Protestant bishop, in Huron, reports in 1862, that "many of the emigrants are almost as destitute of religious knowledge as if they came from a heathen country." In the so-called diocese of Ontario, only one-fifth of the population even profess to belong to the Establishment, the

* Pages 182, 183, 307, 309.

† *Memoirs of a Church of England Missionary in the North American Colonies,* ch. xii., p. 73; ch. xxii., p. 141.

‡ *The Church in Canada,* p. 37.

rest being divided into a multitude of jarring sects, or "having relapsed into a state which may well be called infidelity."* It is to be observed also, as an example of the influence of Protestantism which we have found in all the British colonies, that in the census of 1861, eighteen thousand five hundred of its nominal disciples were returned as of "no religion."†

On the other hand, the episcopal officer of the Anglican community at Montreal sorrowfully recognizes, amongst the *Catholics* of Canada, amounting to nine hundred and forty-two thousand seven hundred and twenty-four in the lower province alone, "the order, unity, discipline, habitual and unquestioning conformity to rule, common and fraternal feeling of identity with the religious institutions of the whole race," which, as he had detected, "attaches to the system of the Roman Catholic Church," and which, he considers, "carries with it a great lesson to the Protestant world."‡ And this statement is more than confirmed by Lord Durham, when he says, "In the general absence of any permanent institutions of civil government, the Catholic Church has presented almost the *only* semblance of stability and organization, and furnished the only effectual support for civilization and order."§

On the whole, when we combine the facts which have now been hastily reviewed,—when we compare the admissions of Mr. Buckingham and others, that the *Catholic* Indians "fulfil their religious duties in the most exemplary manner" and "are always sober," with the confessions of Mr. Kingston and Mr. Kane, that the *Protestant* natives are "a very inferior race," and "get drunk whenever they can;" when we find English writers admitting that the Catholic missionaries are, even at this day, "more than usually successful" in converting the heathen, while the most competent Protestant agents freely confess that adult Indians "can never be prevailed upon to change their religion;" when we note, on the one hand, the peaceful and industrious progress of the natives under their Catholic guides, in spite of the coldness of the civil authorities, and on the other, the squalid misery of the pensioners under an official patronage which, as Mr. Bradford laments, "is rapidly destroying them;" when we consider the frank declaration of such witnesses as Miss Martineau and Mrs. Jameson, that the "superiority" of the Catholic Indians is "most visible, certain, and undeniable;" and lastly, when we compare "the order, unity, and fraternal feeling" which cements the one, with "the prevalence of

* *Report of S.P.G.F.P.*, pp. 77, 83, 88 (1862).
† *The Times*, February 12, 1862.
‡ *Church in the Colonies*, No. ix., p. 12.
§ *Report and Despatches of the Earl of Durham in Canada*, p. 97 (1839).

religious division" which dissolves and scatters the other, and contrast, by the aid of Protestant witnesses, the character and mode of life of the two orders of missionaries, of whom the one are destitute strangers, scowled upon by the rulers of the land, the others opulent representatives of British power and influence; we may surely accept without surprise the conclusion announced by an English traveller, whose scrutiny of all these facts compelled the reluctant avowal, "It appears to me that Roman Catholicism is best adapted for civilizing the Indians."*

We might now quit Canada, to examine in the wide territories of the American Union the final example of the contrast which we have traced in every other region, but a special motive compels us to linger for a moment among the people who have found a home by the banks of the St. Lawrence. The religious history of the French Canadians is perhaps only indirectly connected with the immediate subject of this work, yet there are sufficient reasons for a brief allusion to it. Like some other races of whom we have read in these volumes,—like the Maronites in Syria, the Chinese in Corea and Annam, and the Indians in Paraguay,—the Canadians are what they are solely by the power of the Catholic religion. By it they have been created and sustained. To its penetrating influence their whole social and individual life bears witness. Take away the faith which has been the light of their homes and hearts, and the Canadians would have no place on earth. They would be absorbed in the dull, inert mass of semi-pagan life by which they are surrounded.

The resistance which the Catholics of British America, and especially the Canadians, have opposed to the deadly influences which threatened for more than a century to destroy their peaceful communities, and to dry up the fountains of their life, forms one of those chapters of modern history at which the statesman glances with indifference or disgust, but in which the Christian loves to trace the providence of God. Subject to masters of an alien race and creed, who could neither appreciate their virtues nor respect their independence, every thing has been tried which eager malice could invent, or unscrupulous fraud devise, or shameless violence execute, to exhaust their constancy. In a single year, as Haliburton relates, nearly fifteen thousand Catholics were forcibly deported from the province of Nova Scotia, and their goods confiscated, by the authority of the British government.† And the policy

* *Letters from the United States, Cuba, and Canada*, by the Hon. Amelia M. Murray, letter ix., p. 127.

† *History of Nova Scotia*, quoted by Brasseur de Bourbourg, tome i., ch. xvi., p. 290.

which suggested this crime prevailed in Canada, as Burke indignantly reminded his nation, until the fear of rebellion provoked a tardy and calculating justice. "All the laws, customs, and forms of judicature," says Mr. Bancroft, "of a populous and long-established colony were in one hour overturned, by the ordinance of the 17th of September, 1764; and English laws, even the penal statutes against Catholics, all unknown to the Canadians, and unpublished, were introduced in their stead. . . . . In the one hundred and ten rural parishes there were but nineteen Protestant families! The meek and unresisting province was given over to hopeless oppression. The history of the world furnishes no instance of so rash injustice."* Mr. Bancroft appears to have forgotten Ireland.

The same acts occurred throughout all the regions then acquired by England on the American continent. "The council at Halifax voted all the poor Red Men that dwelt in the peninsula to be 'so many banditti, ruffians, or rebels;' and by its authority, Cornwallis, 'to bring the rascals to reason,' offered for every one of them 'taken or killed,' ten guineas, to be paid on producing the savage *or his scalp*." The Catholic inhabitants of Acadia were treated even worse than those of Canada. Under the French, says the Protestant historian, "they formed, as it were, one great family. Their morals were of unaffected purity." But this did not save them. The possession of virtue and innocence was a slender title to the esteem of the English; and so, continues our authority, "the Acadians were despised because they were helpless. Their papers and records, the titles to their estates and inheritances, were taken away from them. . . . . When they delayed in fetching fire-wood for their oppressors, it was told them from the governor, 'if they do not do it in proper time, the soldiers shall take their houses for fuel.'"

Finally, as these too lenient measures failed to destroy their faith, or to exhaust their patience, all their remaining property was seized by the crown officers, and they were banished *en masse*. "Some were charitably sheltered from the English," says Mr. Bancroft, "in the wigwams of the savages!" But even this did not satisfy their new masters. "To prevent their return, their villages, from Annapolis to the isthmus, were laid waste. The live-stock was seized as spoils, and disposed of *by the English officials*. . . . . The Lords of Trade, more merciless than the savages, wished that every one of the Acadians should be driven out; and when it seemed that the

* IV., 151.

work was done, congratulated the king that 'the zealous endeavors of Governor Lawrence had been crowned with an entire success.' I know not if the annals of the human race keep the record of sorrows so wantonly inflicted, so bitter and so perennial, as fell upon the French inhabitants of Acadia."*

Long years after, the successors of Cornwallis, and Lawrence, and the Earl of Loudoun, still resembled their predecessors, still imitated their example as closely as they dared; and Lord Durham, whose fretful but honest temper was soothed by the simple virtues of a people whom he learned to love, and strove to defend, could tell his government, with a warmth which he did not care to subdue, that "*they* had done nothing to promote education, though they had applied the revenues of the Jesuits, destined for educational purposes," and whose college the English converted into a barrack, to the miserable schemes of official patronage; and reminded them, that with cynical contempt of truth and honor, they gave a large annual stipend, out of these very revenues, to an Anglican preacher, as "chaplain of the Jesuits!"

The fate of the once famous college of the Jesuits at Quebec, now tenanted by the military police of the province, will be regretted by all who appreciate the objects which it was destined to promote. "From this seat of piety and learning," says a Protestant writer, "issued those dauntless missionaries who made the Gospel known *over a space of six hundred leagues*, and preached the Christian faith from the St. Lawrence to the Mississippi."†

Yet the Canadians, who received from England, until the time of Lord Durham, only coarse insult or heartless oppression, have steadfastly maintained, by the counsels of their spiritual guides, a sincere and manly loyalty to their foreign rulers. In 1755, Canada would have been lost to England, but for the vigilant action of the Catholic clergy. Half a century later, as Colonel Sleigh remarks, "the Canadian population" once more displayed a "chivalrous devotion and faith which find not in the records of the past a more noble example. In 1812, the defence of the country mainly depended upon the French Canadians. A second time they proved their loyalty; the Americans were repulsed on all sides, and Canada was saved."‡ "England holds the Canadas," observes another Protestant writer, "by the influence of the Roman Catholic hierarchy

* III., 138, 146.

† Hawkins, *Quebec*, &c., ch. x., p. 193.

‡ *Pine Forests and Hacmatack Clearinge*, by Lieut.-Col. Sleigh, ch. xi., p. 275; 2d edition (1853).

alone. The Sulpicians of Montreal are her vicegerents."* "A large part of the Catholic clergy," said Lord Durham, "support the government against revolutionary violence."† But if the Catholic people of Canada have hitherto refused, though often urged by agents from the United States, to rebel against their hard and unsympathizing rulers, they have rejected with inexpressible repugnance both their religion and their habits, while they have jealously preserved their own distinctive life, their language, their faith, and their traditions. Let us see what Protestants say, in spite of religious and national prejudices, of a people whom they have so deeply wronged, but whom they are constrained to praise, even when they wish to revile.

"The French Canadians," says Sir Francis Head, "retain all the social virtues of the French, without their propensity to war."‡ "They are mild and kindly," observes Lord Durham, "frugal, industrious, and honest, very sociable, cheerful, and hospitable, and distinguished for a courtesy and real politeness which pervades every class of society."§ "They vastly surpass," observes Dr. Shaw, in 1856, "the people of England in the same rank of life;" and then, alluding to the religion which has made them what they are, he adds, "I have seen them flocking in great numbers, as early as five o'clock in the morning, and have been informed that they frequently assemble as early as four A.M., proving one thing at least, that they are not indolently religious."‖ "I confess," says Mr. Godley, an Anglican Protestant, "I have a strong sympathy for the French Canadians; they are *si bons enfants*—contentment, *gaitié de cœur*, politeness springing from benevolence of heart, respect to their superiors, confidence in their friends, attachment to their religion,"—these are among the qualities which he detected in them.¶ "Every thing we saw of the French Canadians," writes Mr. Buckingham, "induced us to believe that they are amongst the happiest peasantry in the world. . . . I think the Canadian more sober, more virtuous, and more happy than the American."**

Such are the Canadians, in the judgment of upright Protestants, willing to acknowledge, even when slow to imitate, the virtues of the simple and winning race whom they describe. But these frank and cordial eulogies of amiable and discerning

* *The Statesmen of America*, p. 305.
† *Despatches*, p. 11.
‡ Sir Francis Head's *Narrative*, p. 194.
§ *Despatches*, p. 17.
‖ *Ramble through the United States*, &c., ch. iii., p. 90.
¶ Godley's *Letters from America*, vol. i., letter v., p. 89.
** *Canada*, &c., pp. 211–18–20, 264, 270. Cf. Lieut.-Col. Cunynghame's *Glimpse at the Great Western Republic*, ch. xx., p. 252.

witnesses have not been allowed to pass, and the fact is worthy of notice, without the protests of that uneasy rancor which heresy inspires, and which could awaken even in a woman's heart the thoughts expressed in the following words: "The enslaving, enervating, and retarding effects of Roman Catholicism are nowhere better seen than in Lower Canada, where the priests exercise despotic authority." And as if this were too weak to do justice to her feelings, this English lady presently adds, that all the evils of that country, whatever they may be, are due to the "*ignorance* and terrorism caused by the successful efforts of the priests."* Her book was intended for English readers, and she appears to have anticipated that they would welcome such statements. Yet in the next page she confesses, that "there are in Lower Canada *upwards of eleven hundred schools*," of which, it may be added, nearly one hundred are at this moment under the direction of Christian Brothers;† and Mr. Buckingham informs us, speaking of the religious schools in Quebec, "So highly is the tuition given here prized by *all* classes, that Protestant families send their daughters quite as freely to the Ursuline convent for education as Catholics."

Elsewhere, the lady whom we quote, forgetting her own gloomy picture of the "enslaved" Canadians, gives the following account of these victims of a "despotic priesthood." "The peasants of Lower Canada are among the most harmless people under the sun; they are moral, sober, and contented, and zealous in the observance of their erroneous creed. They strive after happiness rather than advancement, and who shall say that they are unsuccessful in their aim? On Sundays and Saints' days they assemble in crowds in their churches. Their wants and wishes are few, their manners are courteous and unsuspicious, they hold their faith with a blind and implicit credulity,"—she neither knows what their faith is, nor how they hold it,—"and on summer evenings sing the songs of France as their fathers sang them in bygone days on the smiling banks of the rushing Rhone."‡ Yet after this description of a charming people,—whom she calls, in various places, "moral, sober, contented, amiable, courteous, not ambitious, sincere, and devout,"—she scoffs complacently at the Divine religion which has generated these very virtues as "the great antidote to social progress." All her own ideas of an unexceptionable religion appear to be connected with railroads, steamboats, much commerce, and a diligent police. Unfortunate Canadians, who refuse to say to such objects of worship, "These

* *The Englishwoman in America*, ch. xiv., p. 312.
† *The Metropolitan Catholic Almanac*, Baltimore, 1860, p. 278.
‡ Ch. xiii., p. 284.

are thy gods!" "With *them*," says an English Protestant of a higher class, "churches come first, railroads afterwards, which appears to *us* a very paradoxical arrangement. They make the church the *first* object, and we the *last*."* And for this reason it is,—because their souls are penetrated with the Divine admonition, "*Unum necessarium*," and Christian faith counsels them not to be "*troubled about many things*,"† that the Canadians have found grace to remain what they are; for this reason their life contrasts so visibly, in purity and dignity, in true wisdom and enlightenment, in familiar knowledge of God and of holy religion, with the feverish "progress" and restless greed of the American, or the dismal sottishness of the English boor.

Yet it is simply untrue that the material progress of this Catholic province is unworthy to be compared with that of its non-Catholic neighbors. On the 26th of September, 1862, the Hon. A. T. Galt, late Finance Minister of Canada, announced the following facts in the Town Hall of Manchester: In 1852, the population of Lower Canada was eight hundred and ninety thousand; in 1861, it was one million one hundred and eleven thousand, being an increment of 25 per cent. in nine years.

In 1852, the quantity of land held by lease or freehold was eight million one hundred and thirteen thousand acres; in 1861, ten million two hundred and twenty-three thousand, or 27⅜ per cent. more.

In 1852, the number of bushels of grain other than wheat, for the cultivation of which the climate and soil of the Lower are less favorable than those of the Upper province, was twelve million one hundred and forty-seven thousand; and in 1861, twenty-three million five hundred and thirty-four thousand—an increase of 93¾ per cent., "or very nearly as much as was shown by the whole British population of Upper Canada." And these facts have a tenfold significance, as Mr. Galt remarked, inasmuch as "the French Canadians had not had the advantages of a fresh influx by emigration, and all *their* advances had proceeded *from themselves*."

Mr. Galt did not add, though this fact was also revealed by the census of 1861, that, in spite of the constant influx of Protestant emigrants, the proportion of the Catholic inhabitants of Canada to the Protestants was *higher* than in 1852. He did, however, observe that, "as there was a school *in every parish*, where every child received a free education, they were, or ought to be, beyond the reach of any stigma."‡

* Godley, letter iv., p. 71.
† S. Luke x. 42.
‡ *The Times*, September 27, 1862.

Colonel Bouchette, who knows more of the Canadians than the English tourist whom we have quoted, and who observes that neither the crimes nor the social misery of England exist among them, declares with energy, that "the Catholic religion is in Canada no more the instrument of the people's degradation than is the Quaker religion in Pennsylvania;" and he not only confesses that English destitution is as little known in Canada as English unbelief, but that "*a bold spirit of independence* reigns throughout the conduct of the whole population," and that "its priesthood use only the influence of the understanding, are merely the advisers, and not the rulers of their flocks."*

As Canada is often referred to by English writers as an example of the social stagnation of a Catholic people, it may be permitted to add a few words on this familiar theme. Catholic States, we are told, rarely emulate the material progress of their Protestant rivals. Yet nothing is more incontestable than this, that in Canada, as in every other Catholic land, neither social misery nor social crime have ever attained the proportions which distinguish England, Prussia, and other non-Catholic nations. As respects Great Britain, a Protestant authority affirms the notorious fact, that "in no country is so large a proportion of the inhabitants sunk in pauperism and wretchedness."† In Prussia, the same experienced writer, honestly comparing the Catholic and Protestant districts together, affirms as follows with respect to the Rhine provinces: "The people are Roman Catholic; and in manufactures, trade, capital, and industry, *are very far in advance* of any other portion or people of the Prussian dominions."‡ Belgium, the most Catholic province of Northern Europe, is also the most prosperous. In France, where the products of the so-called Reformation are held in lower esteem than in almost any country of the world, successive revolutions, which would have utterly destroyed the financial equilibrium of England or Holland, have scarcely inflicted a shock either on the national credit or the public welfare, so solid is the basis of her prosperity. And, lastly, whereas it is usual to point to Spain and Portugal as notable instances of the decay of Catholic States, they are, in fact, pregnant examples of exactly the

* *British Dominions*, &c., ch. xvii., p. 414.

† Laing, *Residence in Norway*, ch. iv., p. 156.

‡ Laing, *Observations on Europe*, ch. xiii., p. 316 (1850). A vehement German Protestant, consenting to refute one of the popular libels of his co-religionists, says of the Neapolitans between the gulfs of Naples and Salerno, "the diligence of our vine-growing peasants on the Rhine, whose laborious cultivation has become proverbial, is nothing compared to that of the Neapolitans on these mountains; and yet they have become proverbial for indolence!" *Wanderings through the Cities of Italy*, by A. L. Von Rochau, ch. xvii., p. 222; ed. Sinnett.

opposite truth. It is history which teaches us, that both those kingdoms attained the summit of their opulence and might precisely at the moment when Catholic principles and traditions most powerfully influenced their rulers and people, and that *they began to decay* only when their degenerate statesmen first adopted the political maxims which Protestantism introduced into the world, and broke that intimate alliance with the Catholic Church to which they owed all their glory and renown. If Portugal, once so illustrious in arms and in commerce, has become contemptible in Europe, it is because she has suffered her religious life to ebb away, and though of old she filled the world with her apostles, has now hardly vigor enough to produce even a domestic clergy; while the great Spanish nation, after a temporary eclipse, is resuming at the same moment, amid the applause of Christendom, both the Catholic instincts which made her in other days the mightiest empire in the universe, and the material prosperity which she knew how to create under Ferdinand and Isabella, to develop under Charles the Fifth, to preserve under Philip the Second, and to restore once again under the daughter of Ferdinand the Seventh.*

Let us return for a moment to Canada, and to the English lady, who, as a specimen of the singular pertinacity of British prejudice, deserves additional notice. The Canadian clergy, whose despotic influence, she informs us, creates "ignorance and terrorism," but who "only use the influence of the understanding," as Colonel Bouchette observes, and number among them, as Mr. Kohl has told us, the most learned men on the western continent, and "are a most gentlemanly and enlightened class," as Colonel Sleigh observes, are thus described by Lord Durham: "The Catholic priesthood of this province have to a very remarkable degree conciliated the good-will of persons of all creeds; and I know of no parochial clergy in the world

* It is not, of course, denied that the influence of religion, in proportion to its energy, will generate indifference to the material progress which the world esteems so highly. It was the doctrine of St. Paul, and the world has always resented it, that Christians should use this world "*as if they used it not.*" "The world," says an eminent writer, "is a counterfeit of the Church of God, and in the most implacable antagonism to it. . . The view which the Church takes of the world is distinct and clear, and far from flattering to its pride. It considers the friendship of the world as enmity with God. It puts all the world's affairs under its feet, either as of no consequence, or at least of very secondary importance. . . It provokes the world by looking on progress doubtingly, and with what appears a very inadequate interest, and there is a quiet faith in its contempt for the world extremely irritating to this latter power." Dr. Faber, *The Creator and the Creature*, ch. iii., p. 378. It is perhaps only an incidental and subordinate, but still a startling illustration of the mortal apathy of our countrymen, that this wonderful book should exist in their own language, and remain utterly unknown to them.

whose practice of all the Christian virtues is more universally admitted, and has been productive of more beneficial consequences."* And if this be not a sufficient rebuke to the lady whom we are quoting, perhaps her own words will supply whatever is wanting. She is noticing the ravages of the cholera at Toronto, and these are the reflections which she makes: "The priests of Rome then gained a double influence. Armed with what appeared in the eyes of the people supernatural powers, they knew no rest either by day or night; they held the Cross before many a darkening eye, and spoke to the bereaved of a world where sorrow and separation are alike unknown."† But no virtues could soothe her enmity, instruct her prejudice, nor inspire the thought of imitating, however feebly, the charity which these priests could have taught her; and so, after exhausting the vocabulary of disdain and reproof, she finishes, as she began, by a general defiance to all Catholic people and nations, and by the peremptory declaration, addressed to humanity at large, that "America and Scotland are the two most religious countries in the world!"

If we accept the imprudent challenge conveyed in these words, we shall hardly be led into a digression, for we shall still be illustrating one of the facts proper to our subject. "Scotland," says Dr. Shaw, contrasting her expressly with Canada, "claims the honor of standing pretty near *first* in the catalogue of crime."‡ "Nearly every tenth Scotsman," says another local witness, "is a bastard;"§ and, speaking of the country districts, it is the *exception* and not the rule if a master has not been chargeable, some time or other, with corrupting those under him."‖ The latest Report of the Scottish Registrar-General (1860) reveals once more, with almost unofficial candor, "the excessive incontinence" of this Presbyterian nation, and deplores that "the immorality is not confined to the humbler classes."¶ A well-known Presbyterian writer attests with equal frankness the enormous inebriety of the same people, and records the characteristic fact,—indicating, as he observes, "the moral and religious condition of Edinburgh,"—that the sum of two thousand one hundred and seventy pounds is spent *every Sunday* in that metropolis of Calvinism "in drinking whiskey or other spirits."** Dr. Barclay registers the popular proverb, "As besotted and as

* *Despatches*, p. 97.
† Ch. xii., p. 263.
‡ *The United States*, &c., ch. iv., p. 106.
§ Quoted in *The Times*, July 17, 1858.
‖ *Banffshire Journal*, quoted in the *Times*, February 24, 1859.
¶ *The Times*, November 26, 1860.
** Laing, *Observations on Europe*, ch. ii., p. 37.

pharisaical as Glasgow;" and another authority adds, "If Scotland is the most Sabbatarian and Calvinistic country upon earth, its town populations at least are the most drunken of drunkards."* "Drunken," says one of her own children, "in a greater measure than other countries, fiercer in crime, surely Scotland can scarcely point to the success of her theories in the evidence of her training."†

Lastly, the decaying influence of religion, in spite of the fierce and peremptory tone of its self-confident teachers, is thus attested by two eminent Scotchmen, who were perhaps better qualified than most of their countrymen to speak with authority. "If we are to believe one-half of what some religious persons themselves assure us," says Lord Cockburn, "religion is now almost extinct," and this in spite of the fact, which he notices in the same sentence, that "it is certainly more the *fashion* than it used to be."‡ "A people sunk into an abyss of degradation and misery," says Mr. Hugh Miller, "and in which it is the whole tendency of external circumstances to sink them yet deeper, constitute the weakness and shame of a country;" and this fact, he adds, is being more and more plainly revealed by "the ominous increase which is taking place among us in the worse class."§ "It is not fashionable," says the same writer in another work, "in the present age openly to avow infidelity, save in some modified rationalistic or pantheistic form, but in no age did the thing itself exist more extensively."‖

America, where the disintegrating power of Protestantism has never been resisted, as in England, by lingering Catholic traditions, is thus described by a competent witness, Dr. Onderdonck, a Protestant bishop. "A spirit of misrule, of impiety, of infidelity, of licentiousness, is stalking through the length and breadth of our land, threatening ruin to every interest connected with individual, domestic, social, and civil welfare. It must be resisted, it must be kept at bay, it must be crushed, *or we are a ruined people*."¶ "I greatly fear," says another American preacher, at a still later date, "that we are advancing by certain, and by no means slow steps, in the direction of complete absence of religion, and moral ruin."** This is not a cheerful description of "the most religious country in the world;" in which, we are further informed, "nearly four-fifths

* *Saturday Review*, April 20, 1861.
† *The Times*, November 5, 1862.
‡ *Memorials of his Time*, by Henry Cockburn, ch. i., p. 44 (1856).
§ *Rambles of a Geologist*, by Hugh Miller, ch. viii., p. 135 (1858).
‖ *The Testimony of the Rocks*, lecture ix., p. 345 (1862).
¶ *Sermon preached at the Consecration of Christchurch.*
** Quoted by Döllinger, p. 248.

of the children, and two-thirds of the male population, are unbaptized!"* "There is not a country," adds Mr. Francis Wyse, "where infidelity is more generally diffused amidst the bulk of the population;"† and this infidelity, an American writer will presently assure us, "is *the usual recoil*" of his countrymen "from the Puritanism of their childhood:" another proof that atheism is the logical result of a religion which, in its best form, can only appeal to emotion and sentiment, and when these are exhausted, dies away in apathy and gloom. "A great portion of our country," observes an Episcopalian minister, in 1858, "is witness to the most alarming theological progress towards the Rationalism of Germany."‡ In other words, the mass have no religion at all, and the few have a religion which is either a profitless rehearsal of dead forms, or an explicit denial of the principal truths of revelation.§ Again: the total absence of any moral result from Protestant *education* in America, the universality of which has been so much vaunted, is so notorious, as to force from candid and experienced observers the following avowals: "It trains up men," says an American theological periodical, "to make them cold, calculating scoundrels."‖ "Many well-judging persons, of different religious persuasions, have assured me," says another, "that the only really *useful* and *corrective* education is that of the Catholic schools and colleges. So far as I have known, these seminaries are crowded, not only with pupils of their own creed, but with those of other sects. And I have high official authority for saying, that the ministers and missionaries of the Roman Catholic Church are at this moment doing more good for the cause of virtue and morality throughout the whole continent of America, than those of any other religious denomination whatever."¶

And if we ask, in conclusion, what have been the fruits of that peculiar system which America has borrowed from Scotland, for reawakening religious emotion where it has ebbed away or become extinct, every witness, of whatever creed, except those who trade in that form of hysterical mania, will

* Godley, *Letters from America*, vol. ii., p. 102.

† *America, Its Realities and Resources*, vol. i., ch. ix., p. 270.

‡ Rev. A. C. Coxe, *Statements and Documents concerning the Board of Managers of the American Bible Society*, p. 28 (New York, 1858).

§ A recent traveller observes that "to such an extent does oblivion of the Sabbath day go, that for want of one day of rest to distinguish from the other six days, not one man in ten of the Far West settlers can tell you, if you ask him, the day of the week. All days are alike, and not one of them is set apart for rest and worship." *The English Sportsman in the Western Prairies*, by the Hon. Grantley Berkeley, ch. xxii., p. 373.

‖ Quoted by Döllinger, *The Church and the Churches*, p. 223.

¶ *The Statesmen of America in* 1846, p. 491.

give us the same reply. "If a victorious army," says a conspicuous American preacher, "should overflow and lay us waste, or if a fire should pass over and lay every dwelling in our land in ashes, it would be a blessing to be coveted with thanksgiving, in comparison to the moral desolation of *one* ungoverned 'revival' of religion."* "Had the inhabitants of Bedlam been let loose," observes Mr. Fearon, in describing one of these orgies, "they could not have exceeded it."† Yet this is the mode by which Protestant ministers, of many sects, endeavor to acquire a transient influence over souls from which Divine faith is absent, and which can therefore only be reached through the medium of disorderly sentiment and fluctuating emotion. This is their remedy for evils which their unblessed ministry can only aggravate. The physical excitement of an hour is followed by furious impiety or cold despair; and "neither revivals, nor cholera, nor any thing,"‡ can again stimulate even the spasmodic life which the rude experiments of an unhallowed art have quenched forever.

It does not appear, then, that Canada, to which we will now return, has much reason to envy the condition of Scotland or America. Even the writer, whose idle words have suggested these remarks, and who does not seem to affect consistency, deplores "the obliquity of moral vision which is allowed to exist among a large class of Americans," declares that "Mammon is the idol which the people worship;" and confesses that "the most nefarious trickery and bold dishonesty are invested with a spurious dignity if they act as aids to the attainment of that object. Children from their earliest years imbibe the idea, that sin is sin—only when found out."§ And this is "the most religious country in the world!" Perhaps we may conclude, either that this writer attaches no meaning whatever to her own words, and neither believes them herself nor wishes others to believe them; or that the energy of her religious tastes induces her to prefer the immoral and impure Scotchman, or the "nefarious and Mammon worshipping American," to the "sober, moral, courteous, and devout Canadian," so long as the former consents to revile what the latter reverently esteems—the Faith which was preached in America by Vieyra and Monroy, by Lallemand and De Brebeuf, and of whose influence the Canadian nation is one of the noblest monuments.

* Quoted in *Visit to the American Churches,* by Andrew Reed, D.D., vol. ii., pp. 41, 49.

† *Sketches of America,* by Henry Bradshaw Fearon, p. 164.

‡ Dr. Reed, vol. ii., p. 187.

§ Ch. xv., pp. 326, 423.

NEWFOUNDLAND, GREENLAND, AND LAPLAND.

The events of which we have thus far attempted to trace the outlines, but which it would have been beside our purpose to review with the minute precision of historical detail, have conducted us over a wide field, and have demanded, even in so rapid a survey, a large and conspicuous place in this too meagre and crowded narrative. Yet we have suppressed at every page illustrations which our limits warned us to exclude, and have altogether omitted several provinces, of which the religious history would have furnished exactly the same facts which we have gathered elsewhere.

Thus in Newfoundland, where the Faith was once proscribed, and the Catholic population harassed by every torment and vexation which the agents of Anglicanism could inflict upon them, the result has been the same as in every other land. Far from persuading the Catholics to apostatize, it is their own disciples, as the Anglican clergy sorrowfully report, who have deserted them by hundreds. "It is a lamentable fact," says the Rev. G. M. Johnson, in 1862, "that the whole shore between Petty Harbor and Cape Race, originally settled by numerous *English* colonists, has fallen to the Church of Rome, and that of all the large population, *most of whom once were members of our Church*, scattered along that fifty miles of coast, the small remnant kept together by the presence of your missionary at Ferryland are all who remain steadfast to the Church and religion of their country."*

Everywhere there is the same conflict between the apostles of Divine truth and the agents of human systems, and everywhere the issue is the same. From Rupert's Land and the Red River district the reports of Anglican misadventures, faintly qualified by vague predictions of possible future success, are identical with those from every other region. "In reviewing the past year," say the Rev. W. Stagg and the Rev. J. Settee, "there has been very little done." And then they explain their failure. "We could have done more for the instruction of the Indians than what has been done, had they come forward to obtain Christian knowledge: but they stand away from the truth." This means, it appears, that they prefer to become Catholics. "A Chipewyan chief," the Rev. R. Hunt reports, informed him that his tribe "had been given over to ministers (the Romanists)

* *Report of the Society for the Propagation of the Gospel in Foreign Parts*, p. 45 (1862).

who, *we told them*, were not ministers of the Lord Jesus Christ."* Apparently they told them in vain.

But it is not only the ministers of the Church of England who record these incidents. The Rev. S. Maudsley, a Wesleyan missionary, reports thus from his sphere of labor: "In some localities the Romanist majorities tell with an unhappy influence on isolated Protestants, inasmuch as several families have been drawn within the coils of the Man of Sin."† And this was not his greatest trial, for he adds, "the past ecclesiastical year has been one of unexampled scarcity of cash."

Of another place the Methodists say, "This mission might well be compared to an island in the sea, with this difference, instead of cooling water, it is surrounded with Romanism." Of a third the missionary despondingly observes, "The battle is a hard one; Romanism on one side, and Dippers on the other." The Dippers, or Baptists, are in all lands particularly odious to Wesleyans.

From St. Armand another missionary writes, "The past year has not been a year of so much prosperity as I had desired, owing to the great exertions of the Roman priests." But he assures his society that there is not the smallest doubt of his ultimate victory. From Pierreville, a name of evil augury for Protestantism, another reports that "some persons have ceased to have confidence in Popish ceremonies," which would probably have been much more consoling to his employers if he had not added, "but the ceaseless efforts of the Romish priests to destroy Protestantism retard the work of evangelization."

From the Mackenzie River district, the Rev. W. Kirby, a Church of England missionary, writes as follows: "You will gather from my journal that the Romanists are endeavoring to concentrate their efforts for the conversion of the Indians of this district. When I came they were just establishing their *first* mission in it; now they have Fort Resolution, Fort Rae, Good Hope, and, I fear, will have Liard also!"‡ He had seen them

* *Church Missionary Society's Report*, p. 222. Such is everywhere the action of Anglican Missionaries. Incapable of imitating the apostolic works of the Catholic evangelists, they are content to revile them. Thus a person who calls himself "Bishop of Mauritius," and who represents the Church of England in that island, claims additional "contributions" from his co-religionists, because he is "bearing the witness of the Church of England against Roman assumption and error." *Report of S.P.G.F.P.*, p. 135. One should have thought the Church of England might be sufficiently occupied just now in bearing witness against her own members.

† *Report of Wesleyan Missionary Society*, 1862, pp. 174 et seq.

‡ Captain Palliser, who commanded the British-America exploring expedition in 1859, speaks also of Fort Edmonton, on the Saskatchewan, where "two French priests" had acquired their usual influence, so that the natives, to whom they have taught agriculture, "sometimes realize very fair crops of barley and potatoes." *Journal of Royal Geographical Society*, vol xxx., p. 309

at their work, had ascertained "their perfect knowledge of the language," sometimes travelled with them, and received from them only compassionate courtesy. For a moment he is constrained to confess the truth. "*They possess in a great degree the sympathy of the Indians* . . . . They are really heart and soul in their work, and would verily compass sea and land to make one proselyte." And then, untouched by virtues which even savages learn to admire and strive to imitate, the poor sectary, knowing nothing of Christianity but a few names and words, throws his cap into the air, and shouts, "Great is Diana of the Ephesians!" "The worst is," he cries, "their zeal so completely overleaps all sense of truth and justice, that the most unscrupulous means are used to accomplish their purposes. The most extravagant falsehoods and frauds are freely laid under tribute, but of this the poor Indians are at present too ignorant. . . . Little else is to be heard but the praises of Mary. Oh, my country, what a rebuke is this to thee! . . . Britain, why is this?" &c., &c.*

It is a curious commentary upon this gentleman's observation, that in the next page of the same report, his colleague, the Rev. J. Horden, thus describes *his* disciples at Rupert's House, where he was located with "his wife and four children." "Two professedly *Christian* Indians, forgetting all the instructions they had received on the matter, strangled their poor infirm mother during last winter." By this summary process these Indian Protestants, fruits of Anglican missionary skill, economized the cost of her food. "This," adds Mr. Horden, "hurt me deeply."

In the frozen regions which lie between the St. Lawrence and the Arctic Circle, we find, by the testimony of Protestant writers, missionaries of the same class as we have encountered in the valley of the Amazon and the mountains of Peru, in the forests of Michigan and by the shores of the Canadian lakes. We learn also, by the same evidence, what manner of men the Sects have dispatched to these gloomy wastes, and what has been the fruit of their unwilling sojourn in the tents of Greenland and the huts of Labrador.

Every Protestant traveller seems unconsciously to attest the same truth, and to lend his aid in tracing the same contrast. Mr. Loring Brace visits Norway in 1857, and meets Father Etienne, a missionary in *Iceland*. "I heard him speak five languages," he says, and then he gives his history. In the world he had been the Baron Djunkowsky, a Russian nobleman, deprived of his estates for becoming a Catholic. And now, possessing nothing but the robe of his order, and being, accord-

* *Church M. S. Report*, pp. 226–8.

ing to this American Protestant, "such a man as the holy Xavier was," he had devoted his life to the conversion of the Icelanders. Nor does he appear to have labored in vain. A young Icelander accompanied the missionary, of whom Mr. Brace says, "He spoke German and French as well as he did English;" and that he had learned better things also was proved by the fact that he had forsaken all to follow Christ in the same religious order as his master.*

The facts are everywhere and always the same. A learned Protestant ethnologist observes, in 1862, that the ecclesiastical ruins in the *Arctic* regions, "are memorials alike of the pious zeal and the architectural skill of the first Norse colonists." But these zealous and devout sea-rovers were Catholics. The mortuary tablet, bearing a Runic inscription, which was found at Igalikko in 1829, "indicates the recognition of the Christian faith, and the presence of Christian worshippers in *Greenland*, certainly not later than the twelfth century."† And the missionaries, even at that early date, appear to have shared the zeal for science as well as for religion which their successors have so often displayed. "In 1266," says Professor Rafn, "some priests at Gardar, in Greenland, set on foot a voyage of discovery to the Arctic regions of America. An astronomical observation proves that this took place through Lancaster Sound and Barrow's Strait to the latitude of Wellington's Channel."‡ Six centuries have made no change in the character of Catholic missionaries, either in Greenland or elsewhere. Let us inquire what the Protestant emissaries, to whom these northern regions have been abandoned for eighty years, have done for their inhabitants.

In a recent work by Dr. Rink, Danish Superintendent of South Greenland, which is said to have excited much attention in Stockholm, and throughout the Scandinavian peninsula, the results of Protestant teaching amongst Finns, Greenlanders, and other northern races, appear to be revealed with unusual candor. Dr. Morrison had admitted, at an earlier date, the futility of all the Lutheran projects in these regions, and had confessed, in guarded phrase, that "the moral and spiritual results of this mission were not such as to warrant any glowing picture of its successful issue." The Danish Superintendent seems to have spoken with less reserve. In a letter from Stockholm, dated the 5th of September, 1858, and published in English Protestant journals, Dr. Rink's unwelcome revelations are thus noticed.

* *Home Life in Norway and Sweden*, by Charles Loring Brace, ch. vii., p. 57.

† Quoted by Wilson, *Prehistoric Man*.

‡ Id.

"During the last few years, religious movements have taken place amongst the half-civilized Lappanian and Finnish tribes, which excited their minds to so great a degree, and animated them to such tumultuous excesses, that the Swedish-Norwegian government found it necessary to send troops to that distant region in order to restore peace. . . . . The excitement of the public mind is still so great, that measures have been taken to suppress any possible new outbreak at its very birth."

The source of these "tumultuous excesses," it appears, was a monstrous kind of religious fanaticism, generated by the rival schemes of Lutheran missionaries. "There can be no doubt," says the Swedish narrative, "that these commotions have arisen from a gross misunderstanding *between the Christian teachers*. . . So far has been proved from the most minute investigations, that Christianity, as yet, is by no means deeply rooted amongst these tribes,"—although the missionaries, we are told, have been at work "more than a century!" "Remains of heathenism, gross superstition, credulity, as well as inclination to religious fanaticism and enthusiasm, have, on the contrary, shown themselves as fully developed. Here is ground, the working of which would yield a rich harvest to different religious sects. The Roman Catholic missionaries who are settled at Quananberfjore, and amongst whom are several Jesuits, were doubtless aware of this state of affairs before their arrival, and will assuredly not fail to draw from it every possible advantage."

The account then proceeds to furnish examples of the effects of Protestant religious instruction upon the Greenlanders, constantly exhibiting the same phenomena during the last seventy years. "Disturbances have in former times repeatedly broken out amongst the Greenlanders, the origin of which is alone to be found in their misconceived religious views. In 1790, and in 1803, several women gave themselves out as holy; and one who was called Mary Magdalene declared herself to be a prophetess, spoke of the visions and revelations she had had, and gained a considerable number of followers. She took advantage of the activity of her disciples to bring about a blind obedience to her commands, and had two of her enemies killed. Some bad deeds of her husband, to whom she had given the name of Jesus, brought her after a few months so glaringly into notice, that the missionaries endeavored to bring the lost sheep back into the bosom of the Church." Whether they succeeded, does not appear; but these events induced them "to carry out the plan of training the most able and intelligent among the natives as catechists," a project which led to unpleasant results. "It is from one of these Greenland pupils that the last excitement has proceeded. . . . . In the summer of 1854, a young man of Frederikstal, who had been selected as catechist, became unusually still, and sought retirement. Shortly afterwards, unusual meetings were held by the Greenlanders of this place and its neighborhood, and soon the usual religious services were obliged to be discontinued *for want of worshippers*." The next event was that "the catechist declared himself to be a prophet, and that it was his intention to form a new company entirely distinct from the Europeans. He pretended to have had revelations and interviews with the Saviour; assumed, in consequence, the name of Gabriel, and gathered together many followers, all of whom promised him implicit obedience. The falling away was so universal, that but few Greenlanders remained true to the missionaries."

But this was not the end. "The new Gabriel performed religious ceremonies, married several couples amongst the new believers, and sent people to the next mission station in order to gather followers thence. Then other Greenlanders pretended to have had visions, and a feverish madness possessed the whole population. Some pricked their hands, and allowed others to suck out the flowing blood in order to taste the sweetness of the Saviour's blood! Some were commanded to open their mouths, when Gabriel breathed into them the Holy Ghost." The madness lasted a year, and then seems to have died out. "But who," says the Scandinavian writer, "can answer for it that no mishap will arise in future from the same religious delusions? It is by no means impossible that the safety of the Europeans may be by such cases endangered,"—this is what they seem to have felt most acutely in Sweden,—"and the usefulness of the missionaries brought into question."

The same facts are related both of Norway and Lapland. Professor Kooslef informed Mr. Bayard Taylor, in 1858, that "through the preaching of Lestadius and other fanatical missionaries, a spiritual epidemic, manifesting itself in the form of visions, trances, and angelic possessions, broke out among the Lapps." They committed murder and other crimes to force their countrymen "to acknowledge their Divine mission." "Those missionaries have much to answer for," adds Mr. Taylor, "who have planted the seeds of spiritual disease among this ignorant and impressible race."*

The peculiarity in the Protestant missions of Greenland and Lapland appears, then, to consist in this; that while in every other land they have encountered only apathy, indifference, or aversion, here they have engendered fierce religious

* *Northern Travel; Sweden, Lapland, and Norway*, by Bayard Taylor, ch xi., pp. 115–122 (1858).

mania. In the torrid climes of Asia, or of Central and Southern America, they hardly attract attention, or at most provoke a smile; in the icy wastes of the North they breed "religious delusions," "feverish madness," and "tumultuous excesses." The Chinese may rob or the Hindoo revile them; the wily Armenian may become their pensioner and the Red Indian sink under their patronage to a lower depth of shame; but the Greenlander, refusing to imitate such examples, takes a line of his own, and learns from them just enough of Christianity to burlesque its doctrines and profane its mysteries, to usurp the titles of the Saviour, and to parody the functions of His archangels. It is satisfactory to know that a better day has dawned for him, and that the Jesuits have arrived in Greenland.

UNITED STATES.

And now we approach the final scene of that long series which we have contemplated in so many lands, from where the sun rises in the furthest East to where it sinks in the distant West, and in which we have recognized everywhere the same unvarying forms, and have read the same eternal truth—how great man becomes when upheld by the might of God, how little when abandoned to his own.

In that famous Republic, now as conspicuous for social as for religious schism, and whose almost unrivalled prosperity only a political and moral corruption still more unexampled could have so grievously menaced, we find the last and saddest example of the contrast which we have reviewed in other lands. Yet here dwells a people from whom we might have hoped better things. Capable, in the natural order, of the most arduous efforts which man can conceive or sustain, it is only in that which touches the life of the soul that they are feeble, uncertain, and perplexed. Vigorous beyond all other races in the pursuit of material goods, they are blind and impotent only in spiritual things. The gift of Divine faith, without which man is only an intellectual animal, they have lost, or never possessed. Hence the weakness of the supernatural element in all classes of Americans; whose religion oscillates between a pretentious but shallow infidelity and a coarse and sensual fanaticism,—between the impiety of the mass, to whom religion is only a name, and the degrading *man-worship* of the few, who have put away Christian liberty to become the serfs of smooth-tongued preachers, or the captives of mercenary zealots. "In the United States," said a Protestant bishop, in September, 1862, before a

"General Convention" of his community in New York, "there is less religion, with more pretence, than in any other country in the world professedly Christian."*

The story of Protestant missions in the United States is told in a single sentence by an American writer, from whom we have already learned that paganism is nearly extinct, because the pagans are nearly annihilated. *That* is the history of religion in North America, as far as the natives are concerned. But the reproach of this unexampled catastrophe does not rest with Americans. The causes which produced it were already in operation a century before the Union existed. The destruction of the red man, like the institution of slavery, was a legacy bequeathed by England. It was by British colonists, and British officials, that the Indian was first provoked to deeds of blood, and then hunted to death like a wild beast when he had yielded to the temptation. It would have been easy to make him a friend, as was proved by Lord Baltimore in Maryland, by Penn in Virginia, and by the French everywhere. But the friendship of the credulous savage would only have been importunate to men who coveted his lands and not his alliance. The Indian soon discovered that he was doomed, and resolved, since he was tracked as a beast of prey, to die like one. And therefore he fell, rending and tearing, with teeth and claws, the hunter who had brought him to bay. This was the explanation which he often gave, with an energy of language peculiar to himself, of the atrocities which the white man had taught him to commit. "When you first arrived on our shores," said an Indian sachem of Long Island to the masters of New York, "you were destitute of food; we gave you our beans and our corn; we fed you with oysters and fish; and now, for our recompense, you murder our people. The traders whom your first ships left on our shore to traffic till their return, were cherished by us as the apple of our eye; we gave them our daughters for their wives; among those whom you have murdered *were children of your own blood*."† And the greatest historian of the United States justifies the argument of the Indian, when he shows that from all classes,—from Puritans, from Dutch Calvinists, and from English Episcopalians,—they received the same treatment. "New England," he says, and we shall see presently how true it was, "waged a disastrous war of extermination; the Dutch were scarcely ever at peace with the Algonquins; the laws of Maryland refer to Indian hostilities and massacres which extended as far as Richmond.

* Dr. M'Croskey, quoted in the *Times*, October 16, 1862.
† Bancroft, ii., 564.

Penn came without arms; he declared his purpose to abstain from violence; he had no message but peace; *and not a drop of Quaker blood was ever shed by an Indian.*" Elsewhere the same writer notices, in words already quoted, the impressive fact, that the *French* authorities, who had treated the native as a brother, "as they made their last journey through Canada, and down the valley of the Mississippi, on every side received the expressions of passionate attachment from the many tribes of red men."

Such was the influence of Catholic colonists, here as in other lands. "*To this day*," says General Cass, "the period of French domination is the era of all that is happy in Indian reminiscences." "When the Frenchmen arrived at these Falls," said a Chippewa chief, in 1826, to the American agent at the Sault Ste. Marie, "they came and kissed us. They called us children, and we found them fathers. We lived like brethren in the same lodge. *They* never mocked at our ceremonies, and they never molested the places of our dead. Seven generations of men have passed away, but we have not forgotten it. Just, very just, were they towards us."* "The French," Mr. Bancroft observes, "had won the affection of the savages, . . . and retained it *by religious influence.* They seemed to be no more masters, but rather companions and friends. More formidable enemies now appeared, arrogant in their pretensions, scoffing insolently at those whom they superseded, *driving away their Catholic priests*, and introducing the traffic in rum, which till then had been effectually prohibited."† Surely we had reason to say, that if the French had retained possession of America, her aboriginal tribes would have survived to this day to worship the God of Christians; and we may add, that if they had not lost India, Buddhism, as Ranke and others more than insinuate, would have been vanquished by the religion of the Cross.

The present condition of the Indians of North America is, then, the direct and inevitable result of the proceedings inaugurated nearly two centuries ago, and constantly renewed, by the Protestants of England and Holland. They have perished because the English could make more profit by their death than by their life; and they have perished without leaving a trace behind. "All the Indian tribes," says M. de Tocqueville, "which formerly inhabited the territory of New England, the Narragansets, the Mohicans, the Pequods, no longer exist but in memory; the Lenape, who received Penn one hundred and fifty

* Jameson, part ii., p. 148.
† Bancroft, iv., 79.

years ago on the banks of the Delaware, have at this day disappeared. I myself saw the last of the Iroquois; they were begging alms! . . . . These savages have not simply *retreated*; they have been *destroyed*."* It was in allusion to such facts that a Protestant minister already quoted, and who had dwelt amongst the Delawares, was led to exclaim, "Alas! what has not our nation to answer for at the bar of retributive justice!"

The three classes, as we have said, who made war on the Indian, were the Dutch, the Puritans of New England, and the English Royalists. The operations of the first we need not stay to notice, but a few words may be allowed with respect to the other two.

THE PILGRIM FATHERS.

The "Pilgrim Fathers" of New England have been the heroes of many a romance which has been accepted by the world as history. Even Mr. Bancroft, though he reveals something of their real character, avows the customary sympathy with their supposed "love of freedom," maintenance of "individual rights," and defence of "intellectual liberty." Yet the annals of mankind contain, perhaps, no such example of unrelenting tryanny on the one hand, of abject bondage to human traditions on the other, as that which is displayed in the acts, the laws, and the literature of the Puritans of New England. Professing to frame their daily life by the maxims of the New Testament, it may be affirmed without exaggeration, that no race of men, since the Gospel was first preached on earth, have ever violated its spirit with such remorseless consistency. They were not, perhaps, conscious hypocrites, for most of them had deceived themselves before they deceived others; but this, if we judge them by the narratives of their own historians, is nearly the only crime of which these Arabs of the Reformation were guiltless. It would be difficult to find in them so much as one lineament of the true Christian character. Humility, modesty, meekness, patience, forbearance, obedience, charity—against these, and all the kindred graces of the disciples of the Cross, every word and deed of their life was an unvarying protest. Never were they so utterly unchristian, in every thought, feeling, and desire, as when they were preaching what they called "the Gospel;" never were they so full of cruel arrogance, haughty defiance, bitter menace, and incurable self-righteousness, as when they vehemently

* *De la Démocratie en Amérique*, tome iii., ch. v., p. 115.

called God to witness that they were His peculiar people. They had fled from England to enjoy "liberty of conscience," and they proved their love of liberty by refusing it to all who dared to interpret a text otherwise than themselves. "I came from England," said Blackstone, an ex-Anglican minister, "because I did not like the Lord Bishops; and I cannot join with you, because I would not be under the Lord Brethren."* But they quickly punished his temerity. "To say that men ought to have liberty of conscience," exclaimed one of their oracles, "*is impious ignorance*."† And they proceeded forthwith to chastise what they called, in their singular jargon, "the profaneness of *polypiety*." It would almost seem as if they had bound their souls by a vow to abhor and revile all creatures of God, save only themselves. At one moment they rejoiced to have placed an ocean between themselves and "the iron yoke of wolvish bishops;" at another to have broken asunder "the chains of Presbyterian tyrants." Baptists were mulcted in heavy fines, and when they failed to pay, "were unmercifully whipped." Quakers they branded with a hot iron, or lopped off their ears, or hung up by the neck. Every male Quaker "was to lose one ear on the first conviction, and on a second the other; and both males and females, on the third conviction, were to have their tongues bored through with a red-hot iron."‡ "Witches," a title which included all their opponents for whom they could find no other, and especially rival ministers of religion, were executed in troops. "'There hang eight firebrands of hell,' said Noyes, the minister of Salem, pointing to the bodies swinging on the gallows."§ When Burroughs, an obnoxious preacher, was hanging from the gibbet, and the spectators showed symptoms of tardy regret, "Cotton Mather, on horseback among the crowd, addressed the people, cavilling at the *ordination* of Burroughs, as though he had been no true minister! . . . . . and the hanging proceeded." "By what law," said Wenlock Christison, a Quaker, "will ye put me to death?" "We have a law," it was answered, "and by it you are to die." "So said the Jews to Christ." "But who empowered you to make that law?—We have a patent, and may make our own laws." "I appeal then," said their victim, "to the laws of England." It was a luckless appeal, and only provoked the prompt reply, "The English banish Jesuits on pain of death, and with equal justice we may banish Quakers. The jury returned a verdict of guilty; the vote was put a

* Cheever, *The Pilgrim Fathers*, ch. xvii., p. 243.
† Bancroft, i., 336.
‡ Hildreth, vol. i., ch. xii., p. 405.
§ Bancroft, ii., 762.

second time, and there appeared a majority for the doom of death."*

It is worthy of remark, that *seventy-seven* of the New England Puritans "were in orders in the Church of England,"† and that, as Burke notices, "several who had received episcopal ordination" joined them; yet, as he adds, "The truth is, they had no idea at all of freedom. The very doctrine of any sort of toleration was so odious to the greater part, that one of the first persecutions set up was against a small party which arose amongst themselves. . . . The persecution which drove the Puritans out of England might be considered as great lenity and indulgence in the comparison." Then describing some of their unrelenting atrocities, he adds, "Things of this nature form the greater part of the history of New England for a long time. In short, this people, who in England could not bear being chastised with rods, had no sooner got free from their fetters than they scourged their fellow refugees with scorpions, though the absurdity, as well as the injustice, of such a proceeding in them might stare them in the face." Lastly, referring to the charges of "witchcraft" which these ex-Anglican ministers brought against their rivals, Burke says, "A universal terror and consternation seized upon all. The prisons were crowded; people were executed daily; yet the rage of the accusers was as fresh as ever." A magistrate, he adds, who has just committed forty persons for sorcery, and then refused to go on with his disgusting task, "was himself immediately accused of sorcery, and thought himself happy in leaving his family and fortune, and escaping with his life out of the province." "Several of the most popular ministers, after twenty executions had been made, addressed Sir William Phips," the Anglican governor, "with thanks for what he had done, and with exhortations to proceed in so laudable a work."‡ The exhortation was hardly needed. "To such a degree did the frenzy prevail," says one who deliberately defends all their acts, "that in a single month the grand jury indicted almost fifty persons for witchcraft."§ A child under five years was imprisoned on such a charge. An Indian woman, "after lying some time in prison, escaped without any further punishment," says Dr. Dwight, "*except* being sold to defray the expense of her prosecution!" "At Andover, a *dog* was accused of bewitching several human beings, and put to death." Giles

* Bancroft, i., 342.

† Rupp, *Hist. Rel. Denominations*, p. 271.

‡ *An Account of the European Settlements in America*, pp. 151, 159, 160, (1758).

§ Dwight, *Travels in New England*, vol. i., p. 417.

Corey "was pressed to death for refusing to plead." "Neither age nor sex . . . furnished the least security. Multitudes appear to have accused others merely to save themselves." Yet this writer, two hundred years after these events, could formally defend the Puritans, on the ground that "the existence and power of witches has been the universal belief of man," and was not afraid of avowing that their spirit still lingers among their New England descendants by declaring, with reference to their most arbitrary enactments against "Quakers, Ranters, and such like notorious heretics," "*I can find no justification* either for the Anabaptists or for the Quakers."*

Even Mr. Bancroft, beguiled by that bastard philosophy which puts words in the place of things, could commend in swelling phrase the attachment to freedom, to intellectual vigor, and to the great principles of human progress and enlightenment, displayed by the New England Puritans!

This is not the place to examine the whole history of the "Pilgrim Fathers," with which indeed we are not immediately concerned; yet something we may learn from it incidentally, in considering the fortunes of the unhappy Indian tribes who dwelt within their reach. It was not likely that zealots who spared neither man nor woman in their cruel vanity, and who, as Mr. Bancroft observes, "would not bow at the name of Jesus, nor bend the knee to the King of kings," would learn mercy in dealing with Indians, much less that they would sacrifice themselves in order to labor for their salvation. "No one," says Dr. Wilberforce, "had so much as a thought of attempting to convey to the unhappy tribes around them the blessed message of salvation."† So easily does fanaticism coexist with utter godlessness; so wide is the gulf between Sectarian zeal and Christian charity. "It is requisite to recollect," says a recent Protestant writer, "that the Puritans, although burning with religious zeal, did little for the conversion of the American Indians."‡ Little in truth! But, on the other hand, they did more than any of their contemporaries, perhaps more than all of them put together, to kindle the fires of that inextinguishable hate which made the Eastern States a field of blood, and which only the utter annihilation of their primitive inhabitants could appease. "The Puritans," says Mr. Howitt, "gave at length as much as one thousand pounds

* Vol. iv., p. 242.

† *A History of the Protestant Episcopal Church in America*, by Samuel Wilberforce, ch. iii., p. 82.

‡ Dr. Thomson, *New Zealand*, vol. i., part ii., ch. iii., p. 303.

for every Indian scalp that could be brought to them!"* The very first "Pilgrims" who landed rifled the Indian graves, stole their corn,—which might have been excused on the plea of necessity,—and when they resented the indignity, massacred them; and then, with their hands still red with blood, they gravely recorded in their journal, "Thus it pleased God to vanquish our enemies."† "O how happy a thing had it been," said Robinson, with reference to this slaughter, "that you had converted some before you killed any!" Yet he himself had preached to them at the moment of their departure, as Dr. Cheever approvingly observes, "from the appropriate text, '*I will deliver the Philistines into thine hand.*'"‡

"They seized without scruple," says the Protestant bishop of Oxford, "the lands possessed of old times by the Indians, and it is calculated that *upwards of one hundred and eighty thousand of the aboriginal inhabitants were slaughtered by them* in Massachusetts Bay and Connecticut alone."§ This was their mode of effecting conversions; and these men were not Spanish soldiers, nor Portuguese slave-dealers, but "Ministers of the Gospel," and champions of the "Reformation!" These were the Vieyras, the Clavers, and the Las Casas of Protestantism. "As long as slavery was profitable," says a living American writer, the Puritans not only enslaved *both the Indians and the Negroes*, making them 'taxable property,' but carried on a brisk traffic in their flesh, selling them in the best markets to the highest bidder."‖ As late as 1810, there were more than fifteen thousand *slaves* in the State of New York.¶

Cotton Mather, who ruled among them as prophet and pontiff, and who was ready at any moment to prove or disprove any thing which any other man could affirm or deny by a torrent of Scripture texts, not only hounded on his fierce sectaries to thirst for their blood, but publicly offered thanks to the God of heaven when it covered the land as with an inundation. In a book which he entitled *Prevalency of Prayer*, exulting, like some Mexican hierophant, as he counted with gleaming eyes and dripping hands the reeking hearts which he had piled around him, the Puritan leader exclaims, without pity and without remorse, "God do so to all the implacable enemies of Christ, and of his people in New

* *Colonization and Christianity*, ch. xx., p. 317.
† *The Pilgrim Fathers*, by George B. Cheever, D.D., pp. 23–31.
‡ Ibid., ch. vii., p. 140.
§ *Ubi supra.*
‖ *New York Herald*, January 20, 1861.
¶ Dwight, *Travels in New England*, pref., p. xvii.

England!"* "The efficacy of prayer for the destruction of the Indians," we learn from Dr. Thacher, was a favorite topic also with Dr. Increase Mather, who told his hearers not to "cease crying to the Lord against Philip," the chief of the New England Indians, "until they had prayed the bullet into his heart." Yet, as Thacher admits, "Philip possessed virtues which ought to have inspired his enemies with respect."† But this could not save him. Apostles have shed their own blood, during eighteen centuries, that by dying they might purchase life for their enemies; but it was reserved for Protestant ministers to shed the blood of the heathen, and then claim the approval of heaven for doing it.

It would be only too easy to multiply illustrations of the demoniacal spirit of the New England ministers. Their only thought towards the heathen was to slay them. "Many heathens have been slain," cries one of them; and then he adds with exultation, "Another expedition is about to set out!" The letter, addressed to sympathizing colleagues, which announces this view of the relations of Puritans to the Indian nations, concludes with these words: "May we see each other hereafter in our bridegroom's chamber, securely sheltered behind the blue curtains of the heavens, in the third heaven of Abraham's bosom."‡

One of the many tribes annihilated by men, who, in spite of their profession of Christianity, were far more cruel and implacable than the ill-fated barbarians whom they massacred, was the Pequods. In a single battle against these naked and half-armed Indians, who might easily have been won to religion and civilization, as the fiercer Chiquitos and Omaguas of the South had been won, between eight and nine hundred were killed or taken, while the colonists lost only two men. Such of the Indians as were spared were immediately *sold as slaves.* When Underhill, one of the leaders of this expedition, was taxed with cruelty, he answered, "We had sufficient light from the Word of God for our proceedings."§ Others compared themselves to David, and claimed the approval of the Most High in language which would make one blush for Christianity, if it were possible to admit that such men were Christians.‖

* *History of the Indians of North America,* by Samuel G. Drake, book ii., ch. vii.

† Thacher, *Hist. of Plymouth,* p. 391.

‡ *Documentary History of New York,* vol. iii., p. 964.

§ Hildreth, voi. i., ch. ix., p. 252.

‖ It deserves to be noticed, as an illustration of the mental as well as moral obliquity of these men, that when some fossil bones, probably of the mastodon, were found in New England in 1712, Dr. Increase Mather reported to the Royal

There is no need to examine more minutely the dealings of the Puritans with the natives, nor to trace the history of the furious dissensions which raged amongst themselves. In spite of banishment, tortures, and death,—in spite of enactments only matched in the penal code of Great Britain,—new sects continually sprang into being, equally confident and imperious, by whom the peculiar and exclusive religious polity of the New England pulpit oligarchy was finally stifled and quenched. It was a marvel that it lasted so long. Every innocent joy, the fruit and blossom of true religion, was suppressed by the founders of Salem, "because their followers regarded gayety as sinful."* "All those that weare long locks," was one of their judicious rules for their Indian victims, "shall pay five shillings."† And this hideous burlesque of Christianity, which substituted for grace and virtue fierce animal excitement or hysterical delusions, and that blasphemous arrogance to which the Prussian monarch alluded when he said, "The Calvinists treat the Saviour as their inferior," perished at last, devoured, like a putrid corpse, by the worms which it had bred. "If the account given by Dr. Mather of the colony of Rhode Island be correct," says Mr. Halkett, "its red aborigines must have been somewhat bewildered with the variety of Protestant sectaries who had planted themselves among them." It was truly a singular exhibition of Christianity, by Mather's own account. "It has been," he confessed, when his reign was over, "a *colluvies* of Antinomians, Familists, Anabaptists, Antisabbatarians, Arminians, Socinians, Quakers, Ranters,—every thing in the world except Roman Catholics and real Christians," by which latter phrase he designated himself and his diminished flock, "so that if a man had lost his religion, he might find it at that general muster of Opinionists."‡ Well might Ninigret, a celebrated Indian sachem, reject Mayhew's offer to preach to his tribe, with the scornful reply, "If my people should have a mind to turn Christians, *they could not tell what religion to be of.*"§ And even Mather himself, after his long career of pride and cruelty,—"an example," as Mr. Bancroft admits, "how far selfishness, under the form of vanity and ambition, can stupify the judgment, and dupe consciousness

Society of London, that they were remains of extinct giants, "particularly a *tooth*, weighing five pounds and three quarters, with a *thigh-bone* seventeen feet long! To have doubted the New England philosopher's conclusions might have been even more dangerous then, than to believe them now." Dr. Wilson, *Prehistoric Man*, vol. i., ch. iv., p. 113.

* Chalmers, *History of the Revolt of the American Colonies*, vol. i., p. 40.

† *The Day-Breaking of the Gospel with the Indians in New England*, *Mass. Hist. Coll.*, 3d series, vol. iv., p. 20. Cf. *Hutchison Papers*, vol. i.

‡ Halkett, ch. xii., p. 281.

§ Drake, book ii., ch. iv., p. 82.

itself,"—betrayed at last the hollowness of the earth-born creed which he had once imposed with such terrible penalties, fell headlong into the abyss prepared for those who mistake blind self-confidence for Christian faith, and "had temptations to atheism, and to the abandonment of all religion as a mere delusion."*

Such was the beginning and end of one of the most hateful sects to which the Church of England, the cradle of almost every modern heresy, ever gave birth. And its fruits were confessed, even by the cruel sectaries who had watched their growth. A general decay of all religious sentiment followed the fierce animal excitement which they had mistaken for the meek spirit of holiness, until Cotton Mather, repeating language which was then universal in New England, could say, in 1706, "It is confessed by all who know any thing of the matter, that there *is a general and horrible decay of Christianity* among the professors of it."† The monstrous delusion revealed itself at last. The first Anglican church in Boston became the first Socinian temple,‡ and this was only a presage of what was to come. "Latitudinarianism continued to spread," says an historian of the United States; "some approached even towards Socinianism, carefully concealing, however, from themselves their advance to that abyss."§ Concealment has long ceased to be necessary. "The university of Boston," we are told in 1853, "is attended by about five hundred students yearly. It is *wholly* a Unitarian establishment, and belongs to the Unitarian Church."‖ "Infidelity," says an American Protestant, "has made rapid strides in New England; and at present, not one-half of the adult population are in the habit of attending *any* religious worship, or even belong to any Christian sect."¶ And even they who profess some corruption of Christianity, some human doctrine which has its roots deep in the earth, and shoots upwards with rank luxuriance only to shut out the pure light of heaven, are for the most part avowed or concealed Unitarians, blaspheming the Incarnate God, and enemies of the Cross of Christ. "They are introducing themselves," we are told, "into every village;"** so that, "of all the Congregational ministers in New England, there are not probably, at this day, twenty-five who believe the

* Bancroft, ii., 766.

† Gillies, *Hist. Collections*, vol. ii., ch. ii., p. 19.

‡ Wilberforce, ch. xii., p. 446.

§ Hildreth, vol. ii., ch. xxiii., p. 309.

‖ F. Bremer, *Homes of the New World*, vol. i., letter vii., p. 144.

¶ *New York Churchman*, vol. ix., No. 25.

** *First Annual Report of the Executive Committee of the American Unitarian Association*, 1827. Cf. *Church Advocate*, vol. i., p. 90; Colton's *Church and State in America*, p. 39; *Remarks on the Moral and Religious Character of the United States*, p. 51.

doctrines of the Nicene Creed! "Boston," says a capable witness, "is the headquarters of *cant*. . . . . There is an extraordinary and most pernicious union, in more than a few scattered instances, of profligacy and the worst kind of infidelity with a strict religious profession, and an *outward* demeanor of remarkable propriety."* "Infidelity," says another witness, in 1858, "has been cultivated. Young America's *usual* poor recoil from the Puritanism of its childhood."† Yet there are men who believe that New England theology was one of the most auspicious products of Anglicanism, and that the "Pilgrim Fathers" were benefactors of mankind.‡

That the Puritans should have exterminated, instead of converting, the Indian tribes of the northeastern States, can hardly surprise us. The savage had sufficient intelligence to comprehend, and sufficient wit to express his conviction, that the professors of a religion which formed such characters and produced such fruits, must be as hateful in the eyes of the "Great Spirit" as they were mean and odious in his own. "It is very remarkable," says Hubbard, speaking of Massasoit, the famous sachem of the Narragansetts, who for forty-five years was the constant associate and firm ally of the English, "that how much soever he affected the English, he was never in the least degree well affected to their religion."§ The unhappy barbarian, whose whole nation was afterwards to be destroyed by them, knew it too well by its fruits. He knew also, by a sorrowful experience, that in spite of their grim affectation of integrity and contempt for earthly goods, none were so greedy and insatiable as they. Winthrop was one of the most famous among them, and Gorton hardly of lower repute; yet both these preachers, to say nothing of others, had learned the profitable art which Anglican missionaries were to practise elsewhere, at a later date and on a larger scale. "In the records of the United Colonies for the year 1647," observes an American writer, "it is mentioned that 'Mr. John Winthrop *making claim to a great quantity of land* at Niantic by purchase from the Indians,"—have we not reason to say that these men are always and everywhere the same?—"although he was a famous 'saint' among his party,

* H. Martineau, *Society in America*, vol. iii., ch. i., p. 31.

† *The Life and Times of Aaron Burr*, by J. Parton, ch. iv., p. 63.

‡ It is worthy of observation, that America owes to Great Britain Mormonism as well as Puritanism. "It is to Protestantism that we must look for the origin of the New Faith," says Mr. Burton, "which we find to be in its origin English, Protestant, anti-Catholic." Great Britain supplies to this newest form of Protestantism "five times more than all the rest of the world, except Denmark." *The City of the Saints*, by Richard F. Burton, ch. vi., p. 359; ch. ix., p. 440 (1861).

§ *Indian Biography*, by B. B. Thatcher, Esq., vol. i., ch. vi., p. 139.

'the commissioners set aside his claim with considerable appearance of independence.'"* Four years earlier, the Rev. Samuel Gorton obtained lands in the same manner from Miantunnomoh, "which was grievous to the Puritan Fathers of Massachusetts," not because they condemned a proceeding which they would gladly have imitated, but because Gorton had collected disciples of his own, and presumed to set *them* at nought.† And this acquisitiveness, which clung like a garment to their limbs, marked their proceedings to the end. As late as 1768, we still find Sir William Johnson indignantly complaining to General Gage of certain "New England ministers" in these expressive words: "I was not ignorant that their old pretensions to the Susquehanna lands was their *real*, though religion was their assumed, object."‡ And once more, in 1746, the Council of New York informed Governor Clinton that Whitfield, the celebrated preacher, "had purchased several thousand acres of land at the forks of the river Delaware," and requested his attention to the transaction. "This scheme," the council added, "was carried on by Whitfield till he had gulled a sufficient sum out of the deluded people, under color of charity for the orphan house at Georgia and this Negro Academy, but as most rational to suppose, with real design under both pretexts to fill his own pockets; and when he had carried on the farce so far as he could well expect to profit by, *he sells this estate* at Delaware to Count Zinzendorf."§ But we have heard enough of the "Pilgrim Fathers" and of their kindred, and it is time to speak of the operations of the Church of England in the same land, and of the agents by whom they were conducted.

ANGLICAN MISSIONS.

The history of Anglican missions in the American colonies has been written by the Rev. Ernest Hawkins, a highly respectable minister of the Establishment. It does not take a wide range, is somewhat barren of incident, and will not detain us long. "The Church of England is not rich in missionary annals," says this gentleman, just three centuries after she had come into existence; and his own account does not permit us to believe that change of climate has removed her sterility, or

* Drake, book ii., ch. vi., p. 108.
† Id., book iii., ch. v., p. 73.
‡ *Doc. Hist. N. York*, vol. iv., p. 398.
§ Ibid., vol. iii., p. 1024.

that she has enjoyed a more fruitful career in the New world than in the Old. There is indeed some reason for surprise that Mr. Hawkins should have thought it necessary to write a history which has neither a plot nor a hero, and which contains absolutely nothing, from the first page to the last, except the continual repetition of the same statement, that the Anglican missionaries had no success in America, and sincerely regretted the fact. Here is a list of some of them, whom we reasonably infer to have been the most conspicuous of their number, since they occupy the most prominent place in the pages of Mr. Hawkins.

The reader will observe how exactly they resemble one another in this particular, that they all visited America and all ran away again. Mr. Urmston, he says, after "vainly demanding the payment of his dues," returned to England. Mr. Rainsford "abandoned his mission," "being unable," says Mr. Hawkins,—whose *dramatis personæ* are constantly escaping from him,—"to undergo the fatigues of an itinerant mission." Mr. Gordon only stayed a year, being driven away "by the *distractions* of the people, and *the other* inconveniences in that colony." Mr. Adams was just going to "set out for Europe," but died before he could start. Mr. Wesley stayed one year and nine months, and then "shook off the dust of his feet, and left Georgia." Mr. Neil complained, as late as 1766, "Few Englishmen that can live at home will undertake the mission." Mr. Moor, however, stayed three years before he ran away. Mr. Barton announced his opinion about the same time, that "in the conversion of Indians many difficulties and impediments will occur which European missionaries"—he meant to say English—"will never be able to remove;" and then he recounts the "hardships" which such a work entailed, and which always put his Anglican friends to flight. Mr. Talbot wrote a little earlier to the "Society for the Propagation of the Gospel in Foreign Parts" this characteristic tale: "*All* your missionaries hereabouts are going to Maryland, for the sake of themselves, their wives, and their children." We shall see presently what they did in Maryland. Lastly, Mr. Hawkins adds, "Nor must it be concealed that cases occurred of clergymen dishonoring their holy calling by immorality, or neglect of their cures."* And this is about the sum of the information which we derive from his book.

In reading such a narrative, two conclusions appear to suggest themselves; the first, that the Anglican clergy would hardly

* *Missions of the Ch. of Eng. in the N. A. Colonies*, ch. iv., pp. 72, 86; ch. v., p. 97; ch. vi., pp. 125, 131; ch. vii., p. 146; ch. xi., p. 265.

condemn their colleague who candidly observed to "my Lord of London," "Who did his lordship think would come hither that had a dozen shirts?"—and the second, that if Mr. Hawkins has not succeeded in producing a "history," it was only for want of materials.

Yet he might have indefinitely swelled the catalogue of fugitive ministers, if he had not deemed his own sufficiently ample. He might even have assisted his readers to form a more exact estimate of their real character, if that had been his object. Colonel Heathcote, an ardent Protestant, informed the Society for the Propagation of the Gospel, in 1705, that Mr. Talbot, whom Mr. Hawkins would fain represent as a true missionary, ran away, "having not thought it worth the while to stay at Albany." The Rev. Thomas Barclay deserved also a conspicuous place in the same series of missionary portraits. This gentleman informed the English society in 1710, that his Dutch colleague at Albany was "a hot man, and an enemy to our Church, but a friend to his purse, for he has large contributions from this place." And then he added, with that admirable self-possession with which most English people are familiar, "As for myself, *I take no money*, and have no kind of perquisite." Yet two years later, this ascetical Anglican minister, to whom money was an offence, was publicly tried before the commissioners at Albany, for employing a person "to get fifty pounds for him upon interest to pay his debts, which his wife was to know nothing of," and then sorely libelling his agent because he failed to get the loan.* Mr. Hawkins might have filled his volume with equally dramatic incidents. He might also, if that had been his design, have informed his readers that the congregations of these Anglican ministers were worthy of such pastors. As late as the eighteenth century, Colonel Morris, another sympathizing correspondent of what is called the Society for the Propagation of the Gospel, gave this description of the English in America: "Whereas nine parts in ten of ours will add no credit to whatsoever Church they are of, nor can it be well expected otherwise; for as New England, excepting some families, was the scum of the Old,"—though the teaching class was mainly composed of ex-Anglican ministers,—"so the greatest part of the English in this province was the scum of the New, who brought as many opinions almost as persons, but neither religion nor virtue, and have acquired very little since."†

Another Anglican writer, deservedly esteemed, like Mr. Hawkins, for character and ability, has applied himself to the

* *Doc. Hist. N. York*, vol. iii., pp. 125, 898, 904.
† Ibid., p. 247.

production of a much larger work on the same subject. He also tells us of Mr. Morrell, who, after spending a year in New England, "was compelled to retire baffled and discomfited."* Mr. Bancroft has described to us another class of missionaries, "who never receded one foot;" and Mr. Washington Irving has added, that "*they* pressed on unresisting, with a power which no other Christians have exhibited." Mr. Hawkins, having other matters to discuss, dismisses this class briefly as—"*French Romanists!*" This is what an educated Anglican clergyman deems a suitable description of men whom St. Paul would have greeted with the kiss of charity, and whom the God of St. Paul endowed with gifts and graces which American Protestants have celebrated with respectful enthusiasm, and of which even the American savage recognized the supernatural beauty. Mr. Hawkins, however, reserving his sympathy for the hirelings whose career he has described, appears to approve the verdict of Dr. Selwyn—who, as we have seen, is so little impressed by the ministry of apostles such as Lallemand and De Brebeuf, St. Francis and De Britto, Schaal and Verbiest, that he cannot endure even the sound of their names, forgets even self-respect in his eagerness to defame them, and deems their very existence "a blot on the mission system!"†

Mr. Anderson concludes from *his* researches, that in the seventeenth century, "the vital energies of the whole body of the Church throughout the colony were rapidly sinking beneath the baneful influences which oppressed her." He relates also, from original records, that the worst influence of all was that of the clergy, of whom he quotes this animated description. "Many came, such as wore black coats, and could babble in a pulpit, roar in a tavern, exact from their parishioners, and rather by their dissoluteness destroy than feed their flocks."‡ If Mr. Anderson and Mr. Hawkins could have found more cheerful topics, we may assume that they would have selected them.

When so distinguished a person as Mr. Anderson undertakes to write a "History of the Colonial Church," we may be sure

* *History of the Colonial Church*, by the Rev. J. S. M. Anderson, vol. i., ch. xii., p. 457.

† "There are many," says a spiritual writer, whose words are not without application in this case, "to whom the perfections of God are not so much terrible as they are odious. When they come in sight of some manifestation of His sovereignty, or even some beautiful disclosure of His tenderness," as in the supernatural lives of Catholic missionaries, "they are like possessed persons. They are so exasperated as to forget themselves, until their passion hurries them on to transgress, not only the proprieties of language, but even the decorum of outward behavior." F. Faber, *The Creator and the Creature*, ch. iv., p. 231.

‡ Vol. ii., ch. xiv., p. 132.

that nothing will be omitted which industry could detect, or art embellish, to adorn and illustrate the theme. It is probable, however, that in spite of the attraction of his name, few persons would attempt, without a special motive, the continuous perusal of volumes of such dimensions, and that fewer still would succeed in the attempt. The impossibility of accomplishing such a task is due, not to the incapacity of the writer, but to the weariness and aridity of the subject. Never, perhaps, was so vast a collection of pages illumined by so slender an array of facts. In reading Mr. Anderson's immense volumes, which profess to trace the fortunes of Anglicanism in the colonies, we seem to be invited to examine a history in which there are neither scenes nor actors, neither agents nor events; wherein much is said, but nothing is done; and in which the solitary truth which struggles to the surface, but which might have found adequate expression in fewer words, consists in the patient iteration of one fact—that the Church of England was always *going* to do something worthy of record, and never did it. So absolutely void are these endless pages, not only of any semblance of incident or vestige of action, but even of any definite character by which one chapter may be distinguished from another; so full of words which reveal nothing and suggest nothing, of sentences which incessantly resolve themselves into mist; that the reader can only ascertain by diligent reference to notes and index where he is, whither he is going, and to what point of the narrative he is supposed to be giving his attention.

There are certain regions, described by American writers, the interminable prairies which stretch many a league along the northern frontier of Mexico, in which, as they relate, the eye discovers neither tree, nor shrub, nor hillock, to serve as guide or landmark, but only one dead level, which has everywhere the sky for its boundary, and in which any living form, though it were the meanest of God's creatures, would be welcomed with enthusiasm. Here the hapless traveller wanders, without aim and almost without hope, tracing again to-day the path which he vainly followed yesterday, and ever returning to the spot from which he set out; moving in a fatal circle, which grows less and less, as strength fails and courage ebbs away; till he falls in despair on the earth which refuses to aid his baffled sense, or to give him so much as a hint which way lies the road that leads to the haunts of men. In reading Mr. Anderson's illimitable volumes we seem about to share the fate of this doomed traveller; but a movement breaks the spell, and closing his book, we find that we have already quitted the desert into which he had beguiled us, and which, by the prescriptive rights of prior discovery, he has chosen to call, "The History of the Colonial Church."

What the Anglican Church really did in America, and what sort of agents she employed, there as elsewhere, we learn only imperfectly from Mr. Anderson and Mr. Hawkins; but other writers, of similar religious persuasions, will supply the information which they thought it prudent to withhold.

Berkeley, a Protestant bishop, filled with generous but unfruitful designs for the welfare of the American colonies, detected, by actual observation, that the clergy who possessed "a dozen shirts," and the position which such an estate implies, rarely crossed the Atlantic. "The clergy sent over to America," says this celebrated person, "have proved, too many of them, very meanly qualified, both in learning and morals, for the discharge of their office. And, indeed, little can be expected from the example or instruction of those who quit their country on no other motive than that they are not able to procure a livelihood in it, which is known to be often the case."* The Church of England, however, sent such representatives, in default of others, and continued to send them, during the seventeenth and eighteenth centuries. Berkeley, who seems to have understood that the character of the missionaries "hath hitherto given the Church of Rome great advantage over the Reformed Churches," not only deplored the fact, but indicated its probable results. "In Europe, the Protestant religion hath of late years considerably lost ground," he says; and then, looking across the sea, he anticipates still more unwelcome events. "The Spanish missionaries in the South, and the French in the North, are making such a progress as may one day spread the religion of Rome throughout all the savage nations in America."† We have seen that in the South the work which he dreaded is done; and if in the North they failed to convert all the savage tribes, it was only because England massacred both them and their flocks, till she left them none to convert.

The principal scene, as is well known, of the operations of Anglicanism in America lay between Cape Cod and the Chesapeake Bay; though the great majority of its agents confined their wanderings to the still narrower tract between the mouth of the Hudson and the mouth of the Potomac. English soldiers and traders carried their arms and their strong liquors to the foot of the Alleghanies and the shores of Lake Erie and

* *A Proposal for the better supplying of Churches in our Foreign Plantations*, Works, vol. ii., p. 422 (1784).

† P. 432.

Lake Michigan; but English missionaries preferred to spend their stipends in the cities of the coast, and left the wilderness to the savage and the apostles of France. Massachusetts, Maryland, and Virginia were the chief fields of English enterprise; and with a few words upon each of them,—upon Boston, Baltimore, and Richmond,—we may sufficiently indicate both the method of their operations and their effect upon the aboriginal tribes.

There is not a State of the Union which has not found, and merited, at least one historian, and there is not a difference of opinion among them all as to the character of the English proceedings. But it would be a mere ostentation of research to affect to quote the original records, when all have been collected in one work, and all cited by the same author. Mr. Bancroft's voluminous history, supplemented by English witnesses, will furnish all the facts which in such a sketch as this demand our attention, or which our limits will permit us to notice.

Beginning at the extreme northern point of the country which we are now to visit, and selecting the least dishonorable epoch of the English sway,—when Eliot, an exile from England and a fugitive from her National Church, by whose officers he had been "deprived," had gathered together a certain number of "praying Indians," soon to be dispersed and annihilated,—we find this account of the actual and final result of all which had been accomplished at that date among the Indians. "Christianity hardly spread beyond the Indians of Cape Cod, Martha's Vineyard, and Nantucket, and the seven feeble villages round Boston. The Narragansetts, a powerful tribe, counting at least a thousand warriors, retained their old belief; and Philip of Pokanoket, at the head of seven hundred warriors, professed with pride the faith of his fathers."* While the few scattered villages, scanty in number and exhausted in strength and vigor, which nominally accepted the religion of their masters, are thus described by the same historian. "The clans within the limits of the denser settlements of the English, especially the Indian villages round Boston, were broken-spirited, from the overwhelming force of the English. In their rude blending of new instructions with their ancient superstitions—in their feeble imitations of the manners of civilization—in their appeals to the charities of Europeans, they had quenched the fierce spirit of savage independence. They loved the crumbs from the white man's table."

So well was the character of these unwilling "converts," sorrowful pensioners of a niggard bounty, understood even on

* Bancroft, i., 421.

this side of the Atlantic, that a distinguished English writer did not scruple thus to describe them and their pastors. "The missionaries always quarrelled with their flocks, and made but few converts; nor among them produced any real improvement." And again: "The instruction of the Indians in schools, among the Europeans settled in great towns, was another method which was adopted, and with no better success. . . . . These pupils returned to their naked and hunting brethren *the most profligate and the most idle members of the Indian community.*"*

But their end was at hand. A little later, Pokanoket, who asked only permission to live, and "who is reported to have wept when he heard that a white man's blood had been shed," consented at length to a war which might relieve, but could hardly augment, the sufferings of the Indians, and the last remains of the New England tribes hurried to their doom. "The Indian cabins were soon set on fire. Thus were swept away the humble glories of the Narragansetts; the winter's stores of the tribe, their curiously wrought baskets, full of corn, their famous strings of wampum, their wigwams nicely lined with mats,—all the little comforts of savage life were consumed. And more—*their old men, their women, their babes, perished by hundreds in the fire.* Then, indeed was the cup of misery full for these red men."† "Sad to them," adds the historian, "had been their acquaintance with civilization. The first ship that came on their coast kidnapped men of their kindred, and now the harmless boy," the only son of Philip, that had been cherished as the future sachem of their tribes, the last of the family of Massasoit, was sold into bondage to toil as a slave under the sun of Bermuda!"‡ Such were the deeds of Englishmen in America. When the inevitable hour of England's reckoning arrives, the cry of the American native will surely mount up to heaven, and add a heavier burden to the maledictions already registered against her.

But we have as yet no adequate conception of the patient cruelty with which England uprooted Christianity in every part of America where her power was felt. In Florida, as a French writer observes, "the ardent zeal of several generations of martyrs," Jesuits, Dominicans, and Franciscans, "received

* *Edinburgh Review,* vol. viii., p. 444.

† Bancroft, i., 427.

‡ P. 430. Dr. Wilson notices the characteristic fact, that "after a discussion as to his fate, in which Increase Mather *pleaded against mercy,* the boy's life was spared. The New England divine urged the case of Hadad, of the king's seed in Edom," and insisted upon the death of the unoffending child. *Prehistoric Man,* vol. ii., ch. xix., p. 152.

its recompense, and the natives embraced Christianity. Villages and neophytes gathered round the Spanish posts." At length the English arrived from Carolina. "In 1703, the valley of the Appalachicola was ravaged by an armed body of covetous fanatics; the Indian towns were destroyed, the missionaries slaughtered, and their forest children hurried away, and *sold as slaves* in the English West Indies."* But the work of destruction was not yet complete. Sixty years later, by the treaty of Paris, 1763, Florida was ceded by Spain to England. "This was the death-blow of the missions. The Indians were expelled from the grounds cultivated by their toil for years, and deprived of their church, which they had themselves erected. All was given by the governor to the newly established English church. In ten years not one was left near the city." From that hour the natives of Florida took the name of Seminoles, or Wanderers, and being deprived of all guidance and instruction, gradually lost the faith, but retained an implacable hatred against the race which had robbed them both of their lands and their religion. When General Jackson tried to deport them beyond the Mississippi, "the Seminoles, so gentle under the paternal care of the Franciscans, had become ungovernable." The "Florida war" cost the United States twenty thousand men, and forty million dollars, lasted for seven years, and "produced no result." "The Seminoles are a striking monument of the different results obtained by the Catholic government of Spain, and the Protestant government of England. The one converted the savages into Christians, a quiet, orderly, industrious race, living side by side with the Spaniards themselves, in peace and comfort; the other replunged the same tribes into barbarism and paganism, and converted them into a fearful scourge of her own colonies."†

Let us turn again to the North, and come to Maryland. Here dwelt a Catholic colony, under a Catholic lawgiver, and Protestants will tell us how the one governed and the other throve. "Within six months," says Mr. Bancroft, "the colony of Maryland had advanced more than Virginia had done in as many years. . . . But far more memorable was the character of the Maryland institutions. Every other country in the world had persecuting laws: 'I will not,'—such was the oath of the governor of Maryland,—'I will not, by myself or any other, directly or indirectly, molest any person professing to

* *The Catholic Church in the United States,* by H. de Courcy de Laroche Héron, ch. i., p. 15.

† *Catholic Missions among the Indian Tribes of the United States,* by John Gilmary Shea, ch. iii., p. 75. A multitude of similar examples will be found in this valuable work.

believe in Jesus Christ, for or in respect of religion.' Under the mild institutions and munificence of Baltimore, the dreary wilderness soon bloomed with the swarming life and activity of prosperous settlements; the Roman Catholics, who were oppressed by the laws of England, were sure to find a peaceful asylum in the quiet harbors of the Chesapeake; and there, too, Protestants were sheltered against Protestant intolerance. Such were the beautiful auspices under which the province of Maryland started into being. . . . . . Its history is the history of benevolence, gratitude, and toleration."*

Fenimore Cooper, and a multitude of eminent American writers, have noticed the relations which were quickly formed between the Catholics of Maryland and the Indian tribes. *They*, as an English Protestant observes, "fairly paid" the natives for their land, and "their generosity won the hearts of their new Indian friends."† But let us continue Mr. Bancroft's account.

"The happiness of the colony was enviable. The persecuted and the unhappy thronged to the domains of the benevolent prince. If Baltimore was, in one sense, a monarch, his monarchy was tolerable to the exile who sought for freedom and repose. Numerous ships found employment in his harbors. . . . . Emigrants arrived from every clime; and the colonial legislature extended its sympathies to many nations, as well as to many sects. From France came Huguenots; from Germany, from Holland, from Sweden, from Finland, the children of misfortune sought protection under the tolerant sceptre of the Roman Catholic. Bohemia itself, the country of Jerome and of Huss, sent forth its sons, who at once were made citizens of Maryland with equal franchises."‡

Such was Catholic Maryland, the solitary oasis of the northern desert, and the refuge for all who found elsewhere only cruelty and oppression. Lord Baltimore died, and "immediately on the death of the first feudal sovereign of Maryland, the powerful influence of the Archbishop of Canterbury had been solicited to secure an establishment of the Anglican Church, which clamored for favor in the province where it already enjoyed equality. The prelates demanded, not freedom, but privilege; an establishment to be maintained at the common expense of the province. . . . . The English ministry soon issued an order, that offices of government in Maryland should be intrusted exclusively to Protestants. Roman

* Bancroft, i., 188.
† Buckingham, *America*, vol. i., ch. xx., p. 388.
‡ Bancroft, i., 523.

Catholics were disfranchised in the province which they had planted!"*

"It is a striking and instructive spectacle to behold, at this period," says Professor Walters of Philadelphia, "the Puritans persecuting their Protestant brethren in New England, the Episcopalians retorting the same severity on the Puritans in Virginia, and the Catholics, against whom all others were combined, forming in Maryland a sanctuary where all might worship, and none might oppress, and where even Protestants might find refuge from Protestant intolerance." Yet these very men, he adds, "with ingratitude still more odious than their injustice, projected the abrogation not only of the Catholic worship, but of every part of that system of toleration under whose shelter they were enabled to conspire its downfall!"†

If any thing be wanting to complete the picture, it is supplied in the fact, noticed by Mr. Baird, an American minister, that the character of many of the Anglican clergy who were now dispatched to Maryland to supersede the Catholic missionaries, was notorious for "shocking delinquency and open sin."‡ "*A great part of them*," was the confession of the Protestant Bishop of London to the celebrated Dr. Doddridge, "can get no employment at home, and enter into the service more out of necessity than choice. Some others are willing to go abroad to retrieve either lost fortunes or lost character."§ "Ruffians, fugitives from justice," adds Mr. Bancroft, "men stained by intemperance and lust (I write with caution, the distinct allegations being before me), nestled themselves in the parishes of Maryland."‖ And it was to procure an "Establishment," on the Anglican model, for men who are thus described by those who knew them best, but who sent them in spite of this knowledge, that religious liberty was suppressed, and Catholics disfranchised, in the English colony of Maryland. "In the land which Catholics had opened to Protestants," says Mr. Bancroft, "the Catholic inhabitant was the sole victim to Anglican intolerance."¶

Not that this was an exceptional incident in the history of Anglicanism, for, as the historian observes, it displayed exactly the same character in Ireland. Here also, in the words of Edmund Spenser, the Anglican ministers who supplanted the pastors of the ancient faith, "were generally bad, licentious,

* Bancroft, p. 528.
† Rupp, p. 115.
‡ Baird, *Religion in the U. S. of America*, book ii., ch. xx., p. 210..
§ Ibid., ch. xx., p. 211.
‖ III., 98.
¶ II., 717

and most disordered;" "men of no parts or condition," as Mr. Bancroft adds, "and as immoral as they were illiterate."*

Let us hear a single witness from our own country, and then pass on to Virginia. "While the Catholics of Maryland," says Mr. Buckingham, who visited America twenty years ago, "acted with so much liberality to their Protestant brethren, these last, who had many of them come to seek refuge from Protestant persecution in the north, returned this liberality with the basest ingratitude, and sought by every means to crush those by whom they had been so hospitably received." And finally, when "the Church of England was declared, by law, to be the constitution of the State of Maryland, Catholics were prohibited under the severest penalties from all acts of public worship, and even from exercising the profession of teachers in education."†

It is satisfactory to learn from the same witness the ultimate result of this conflict between cruel bigotry, working by profligate agents and distrustful of its own power, and the unquenchable life of faith, surviving injustice and barbarism, and accomplishing in weakness what all its combined enemies could not effect in their pride of strength. We shall see that, in the words of Mr. Bancroft, "persecution never crushed the faith of the colonists." Of all the religious bodies who inhabit Baltimore at this day, "first come the Roman Catholics," says Mr. Buckingham, "who far outstrip any other separate sect, in numbers and in zeal. . . . . The Catholic Archbishop, and all the subordinate priesthood," who now serve nineteen churches within the city itself, "are learned, pious, and clever men; the Sisters of Charity have amongst their number many intelligent and devoted women; and these, with the seminary for the education of Catholic youth,"—there are now seven seminaries and six colleges,—"secure not merely the permanence of the present supremacy of Catholic numbers and Catholic influence, but its still further steady and progressive increase."‡

It only remains to speak of Virginia, the special domain of Anglicanism as long as Virginia was English, and whose history is, perhaps on that account, more full of reproach to its former masters than that of any other State in the Union.

The accounts of the Anglican clergy in Virginia, even as late as the second half of the eighteenth century, appear to surpass every thing in the annals of Church of England missions, and throw even New Zealand into the shade. Sir William Berkeley, Governor of Virginia, used to ask, with a not unreasonable curiosity, "Why the worst are sent to us?"

* Bancroft, iv., 45.
† *America*, ch. xx., p. 387.
‡ Ibid.

"In Virginia," says Mr. Bancroft, who had examined all the original records, "some of the missionaries, of feeble minds and uncertain morals, prodigious zealots, from covetousness, sought, by appeals to England, to clutch at a monopoly of ecclesiastical gains. . . . The crown incorporated and favored the Society for Propagating the Gospel in Foreign Parts."* Under the patronage of that society, as the Protestant historian relates, "the benefices were filled by priests ordained in England, and for the most part of English birth, too often ill-educated and licentious men, whose crimes quickened Virginia to assume the advowson of its churches."† Yet the people of Virginia could have endured a good deal in this way, if the crimes of their clergy had not exceeded what prescription permitted; but it was one effect of their enormity that the Episcopalian Sect finally sunk into contempt in Virginia. "The Episcopal Church in Virginia," says Dr. Reed, "became slothful and impure under its exclusive privileges, so as to have made itself despised by the people."‡ "For want of able and conscionable ministers," was the joint confession of a multitude of Anglican witnesses, "they of the Reformed religion themselves are becoming exceeding rude, more like to turne heathen, than to turne others to the Christian faith."§ And it is admitted that this state of things, characteristic of Anglican missionary operations, continued for two centuries. Between 1722 and the beginning of the nineteenth century, observes Dr. Samuel Wilberforce, "instead of any growth throughout an extent of country one hundred miles long and fifteen broad, *every church and chapel had been forsaken*. . . . Such was the deadly trance which had fallen on the Church." And then this English prelate, unwilling, perhaps, to avow the real causes of the decay, and the mingled avarice and sensuality which had made episcopalian ministers hateful throughout the colony, refers it all to "the absence of endowment," of which he had learned to appreciate the importance in his own community, but the want of which in America, he adds, with a *naïveté* remarkable in so acute a person, "impairs its character and moral weight."‖ Yet it was

* II., 769.

† III., 95.

‡ *Visit to the American Churches*, by Reed and Matheson, vol. ii., p. 100.

§ *A Petition exhibited to the High Court of Parliament*, by William Castell, Parson of Courtenhall, which Petition is approved by seventy able English Divines (1641; ed. Force).

‖ Ch. viii., p. 276; ch. xii., p. 436. Dr. Wilberforce no doubt agrees with the following announcement of a great authority. "The Church of England deprived of its estates would become merely an episcopal sect in this country, and it is not impossible in time might become an insignificant one." *The Times*, October 31, 1862.

at this very time that men of another faith, already apostles, and soon to be martyrs, were traversing in hunger and poverty, utterly unmindful of "the absence of endowment," the shores of Lake Superior, the banks of the Mohawk, and the valley of the Mississippi, and showing the wondering savage what was the religion of St. Paul, and how men trained in *his* school could live and die.

The Anglican missionaries in America appear to have taught them a different lesson, and sometimes by a method which does not seem to have been ever adopted by any other class of religious teachers but themselves. On the 18th of May, 1725, as an American annalist relates, a British officer shot a poor unoffending Indian, who was actually scalped on the spot by the Rev. Jonathan Frye, a military chaplain, whose prowess is appropriately celebrated by another missionary, the Rev. Mr. Symmes. We learn, without excessive regret, that Frye was killed the same day by the tribe of the murdered man, after a battle which was one of the great events of the epoch, and which was recorded in a popular song described by Mr. Drake as "for several years afterwards the most beloved song in all New England." The following verse, as an illustration of the character of English missionaries in America, deserves particular notice. We may hope, for the honor of humanity, that no such action was ever celebrated in similar language. Here is the triumphal dirge:

"Our worthy Captain Lovewell among them there did die;
They killed Lieutenant Robins, and wounded good young Frye,
Who was our English Chaplain; he many Indians slew,
And some of them he scalped, when bullets round him flew."*

American Protestants have observed, and the fact is worthy of note, how strangely the history of the Anglican colony of Virginia contrasts, from its earliest origin and in every particular, with that which was formed by Lord Baltimore. Even at the first moment of their arrival, "the emigrants themselves were weakened by divisions and degraded by jealousy." A large proportion of them perished by sickness or famine, and "disunion completed the scene of misery."† Unlike the Catholics of Maryland, they soon made the Indians their enemies, and reaped, during many years, till they had created a desert around them, the fruits of their own want of charity.

Towards the close of the seventeenth century, an English colonist, explaining how the "Virginians, Susquehanians, and

* Drake, book iii., ch. ix., p. 130.
† Bancroft, i., 95.

Marylanders, of friends became engaged enimyes," relates, that "the English had (contrarie to the law of arms) beate out the braines of six grate men *sent out to treate a peace;* an action of ill consequence, as it proved after."* "It has been to many a source of wonder," says another writer, more than half a century later, who gives innumerable examples of the savage cruelty of his countrymen, "how it comes to pass that the English have so few Indians in their interest, while the French have so many at command;" and that "those neighboring tribes in particular, who, at the first arrival of the English, showed every mark of affection and kindness, should become our most bitter enemies." And then he explains the mystery from his own point of view, omitting altogether the question of religious influence. "The English, in order to get their lands, drive them as far from them as possible, *nor seem to care what becomes of them,* provided they can get them removed out of the way of their present settlements; whereas the French use all the means in their power to draw as many into their alliance as possible, and, to secure their affections, invite as many as can to come and live near them, and to make their towns as near the French settlements as they can."†

Mr. Howison, the historian of Virginia, who records touching examples of the generous confidence and hospitality with which the Indians welcomed the English settlers, notices, that a poor native having stolen a silver cup, of which he probably did not know the value, "for this enormous offence the English burned the town, and barbarously destroyed the growing corn. Had the unhappy savage stolen the only child of the boldest settler, a more furious vengeance could not have followed! To such conduct does America owe the undying hatred of the aboriginal tenants of her land, and the burden of infamy that she must bear when weighed in the scales of immaculate justice."‡ The whole history, he says, "is a dark record of injuries sustained, and of insult unavenged."§

But no misfortunes could instruct either the insatiable avarice or the cruel bigotry of the Anglican colonists. The fee of their clergy for a funeral sermon, we are told by Mr. Hildreth, was "four hundred pounds of tobacco;" and for a marriage by

* *An Account of our late Troubles in Virginia,* by Mrs. Ann Colton (1676).

† *An Inquiry into the Causes of the Alienation of the Delaware and Shawanese Indians,* written in Pennsylvania, p. 48 (1759).

‡ *History of Virginia,* ch. i., p. 57.

§ Ch. v., p. 260. As late as 1763, "a company of Presbyterians" murdered a band of Conestoga Indians, though they were descendants of the very men who had welcomed Penn with so much hospitality, and this without the slightest provocation. *Events in Indian History,* ch. xxi., p. 492 (1842). Cf. Heckewelder's *Narrative.*

licence, half that amount of the same weed. It was natural that such men should fight for what Mr. Ernest Hawkins calls "the payment of their dues." And so in 1643, "it was specially ordered, that no minister should preach or teach, publicly or privately, except in conformity to the constitutions of the Church of England, and non-conformists were banished from the colony." "The government of Virginia," says Mr. Bancroft, "feared Dissenters more than Spaniards;"* and yet so incapable was the Anglican Church of performing the functions which she had violently usurped, and which she sent "ill-educated and licentious men" to perform, that "there were so few ministers that a bounty was offered for their importation!" St. Paul had said, "The charity of Christ constraineth me;" but the Anglican clergy could only be attracted by a "bounty." And they never varied, either in their character or in their operations, till the day of their downfall. "The English Episcopal Church became the religion of the State; and though there were not ministers in above a fifth part of the parishes, yet the laws demanded strict conformity, and required of every one to contribute to the support of the Established Church . . . no non-conformist might teach, even in private, under pain of banishment; no reader might expound the catechism or the Scriptures. The obsolete severity of the laws of Queen Elizabeth was revived against the Quakers. Absence from church was for them an offence punishable by a fine of twenty pounds sterling."† "So late as the year 1748, the Rev. Dr. Rogers, of New York, was sent out of Virginia by the General Court of that province, for preaching to some Presbyterians who had invited him into the country for that purpose."‡ "Virginia," says Mr. Howison, "is the proper field for those who wish to study one of the closing pages of American intolerance."§

Yet England pursues exactly the same policy at the present day, wherever she can do so with safety. Thus in Prince Edward's Island, the *Established* religion is that of the Church of England, though it has perhaps fewer professors than any denomination known there!"‖ We are not surprised to learn that the religious condition of this colony is worthy of the "Church of England." The population, says a British official in 1853, "are generally a very ignorant race," immorality is almost universal, and "the sight of a book or a newspaper in the house of a yeoman is a rare and exceptional occurrence; the only

* I., 1028.
† I., 497.
‡ Dwight, *Travels in New England*, vol. ix., p. 241.
§ Ch. vii., p. 431.
‖ Bouchette, *British Dominions, &c.*, vol. ii., ch. xi., p. 178.

literature to be seen consists of a few musty theological works of *dissenting* divines, or some temperance tracts."* In 1862, the "Society for the Propagation of the Gospel" inform their subscribers, that, in spite of emigration, and general increase of the population, "the whole Church population is only seventy-one more than in 1855.†

The same contrast which distinguished the clergy marked the conduct of the civil rulers in the Catholic and Protestant colony. Under Lord Baltimore, "the virtues of benevolence and gratitude ripened together," and "the people held it a duty themselves to bear the charges of government, and they readily acknowledged the unwearied care of the proprietary for the welfare of his dominions. . . . The colony which he had planted in youth, crowned his old age with its gratitude."‡ Very different were the rulers of Virginia. "The illegal grants favored by Sir John Harvey had provoked the natives into active hostility."§ His successors surpassed him. Berkeley was greedy, selfish, and cruel. When they had captured an Indian sachem, more than a hundred years old, and exposed him in Jamestown, mortally wounded, to die amidst the jeers of the English, "Had I taken Sir William Berkeley prisoner," was the rebuke of the savage, "I would not have exposed him as a show to my people." Culpepper, the confederate of Arlington, was still worse. "He valued his office and his patents only as property. Clothed by the regal clemency with power to bury past contests, he perverted the duty of humanity into a means of enriching himself, and increasing his authority. Nothing but Lord Culpepper's avarice gives him a place in American history. . . . . All accounts agree in describing the condition of Virginia, at this time, as one of extreme distress. Culpepper had no compassion for poverty—no sympathy for a province impoverished by perverse legislation—and the residence in Virginia was so irksome, that in a few months he returned to England." He was succeeded, in his turn, by Lord Howard of Effingham, a man as shameless as himself. "It is said he did not scruple to share perquisites with his clerks. In Virginia, the avarice of Effingham was the public scorn; in England, it met with no severe reprobation."‖ The governors of Virginia, then, were worthy of its clergy; and both continued to represent with equal dignity the Crown and the Church of England, till the colonists, weary of the cruelty of the one and the immorality of the other,

* *Pine Forests*, &c., by Lieut.-Col. Sleigh, ch. xvi., p. 383.
† *Report for* 1862, p. 40.
‡ Bancroft, i., 525.
§ Howison, ch. v., p. 285.
‖ Bancroft, p. 533.

gave the signal of that righteous revolution out of which sprang the great American Union. It was surely a fitting retribution, that Virginia, once a proverb for its royalism, should be the first to shake off the yoke which English bigotry, injustice, and cupidity had made intolerable; and the national historian might well relate, with honest exultation, that "*Virginia* rang the alarum bell—Virginia gave the signal for the continent!"*

It is a characteristic fact, which should not be omitted even in this hasty sketch, that the only remonstrants against the American Revolution were a few of the Episcopalian clergy, dreading the loss of their incomes and privileges, and warring to the last against the liberties of their fellow-creatures. "The present rebellion," says Dr. Inglis of New York, in 1776,—and the sentiment appears to have gained for him the Protestant bishopric of Nova Scotia,—"is certainly one of the most causeless, unprovoked, and unnatural that ever disgraced any country;" and then he ventured upon a prediction equally creditable to his discernment, and exclaimed, "I have not a doubt that, with the blessing of Providence, his Majesty's arms will be successful, and finally crush this unnatural rebellion."†

One or two names there are, in the dark religious annals of British America, which contrast favorably with those of the adventurers whose career we have traced, and whose misdeeds hindered the conversion of a hundred tribes, and lost half a continent to the crown of England. Eliot and Brainerd, both witnesses against British oppression, appear to have been animated by a real desire for the improvement of the heathen, and to have done their best to promote it. So far as they were sincere in their good intentions they deserve our sympathy and respect. Eliot had collected at one time, apparently by the kindness of his deportment, and frequent relief of their necessities, a considerable number of "praying Indians." "I never go unto them empty," he says himself, "but carry somewhat to distribute among them;"‡ which he was enabled to do by a subsidy of three thousand dollars annually from England. Naturally attracted by conduct which contrasted so strongly with the usual habits of his countrymen, they came to consider him as their friend, and had good reason to do so. Yet it may be doubted whether he ever produced even a superficial impression upon their conscience. Often they perplexed him with questions to which his barren theology could suggest no reply. An Indian sachem, as we are told, having embarrassed

* Bancroft, iv., 196.

† *Doc. Hist. of N. York*, vol. iii., pp. 1052, 1064.

‡ Dr. Morrison, *Fathers of the London Missionary Society*, vol. i., p. 82.

him with such inquiries, "the good man seemed at a loss for an answer, and waived the subject by several Scripture quotations!"* He has been called, with the usual unreality of Protestants, "the apostle of the Indians;" yet, as Mr. Hildreth candidly remarks, there was an army of Catholic missionaries "not less zealous than Eliot and far more enterprising." and, as the same historian observes, "Eliot's scheme for civilizing and Christianizing the Indians proved in the end an almost total failure."† "The natives of our forests," says his American biographer, "derived no permanent benefit from the exertions of Mr. Eliot and others."‡ He confessed himself, just before his death, "There is a dark cloud upon the work of the Gospel among the poor Indians."§ Even of his nominal disciples, Mr. Drake admits, "there is not the least probability that even one-fourth of them were ever sincere believers in Christianity;"‖ and Mr. Conyers Francis relates, that among the English themselves, "there was little or no confidence in their sincerity."¶ When "Philip's war" broke out, his whole work came to an end; and whereas the Catholic Indians, until they were slain by the English, would always prepare for battle by the reception of the sacraments, and fight in the name and the defence of their religion, "many that had been at the head of the 'praying' towns, the Indian *ministers* themselves, were found in arms against their white Christian neighbors," and flung off altogether the disguise of Christianity. Lastly, it is an unpleasant fact, which one would have gladly missed in the history of such a man as Eliot, who was at least superior to his contemporaries, that one of his grandchildren claimed "a tract of one thousand acres of land at a place called the Allom Ponds, given by the Indian proprietors *to the late Rev. John Eliot.*"**

Brainerd, who seems, like Henry Martyn, to have been devoured by melancholy, and who was never of the same mind many hours together, confesses his own failure, and others account for it. "The prevailing defect of his character," says Dr. Morrison, was a tendency to deep brooding and melancholy depression." But he seems to have had other infirmities quite as little suited to the office of a missionary,

* Drake, book iii., ch. vi., p. 85.

† *The History of the United States of America,* by Richard Hildreth, vol. i., ch. xii., p. 412; vol. ii., ch. xviii., p. 85.

‡ *Life of John Eliot,* in *Library of American Biography,* by Jared Sparks, vol. v., ch. xv., p. 301.

§ Ibid., ch. xvii., p. 335.

‖ Ch. viii., p. 115.

¶ *Life of John Eliot,* by Conyers Francis, ch. xiv., p 272.

** Jared Sparks, Appendix, p. 354.

"Mr. Brainerd acknowledges," said Dr. Boudinot half a century ago, "that he *dared not* go among them."* And when he did, but always, like Eliot, in the immediate neighborhood of the English, it was not with much profit. "His account of the Delawares," observes Mr. Bancroft, "is gloomy and desponding: 'they are unspeakably indolent and slothful,' he says; 'they discover little gratitude; they seem to have no sentiments of generosity, benevolence, or goodness.'"† Yet we have heard Catholic missionaries commending tribes less happily endowed than the Delawares as "industrious and fond of labor," and Protestants confirming their report. Even the few whom Brainerd employed as assistants appear to have exactly resembled the same class in China, and one for whom he procured "ordination," and who became his own successor "in the charge of his congregation," is thus described by Dr. Smith: "Whatever professions this man might have made, or whatever opinion might have been formed of him, it is too evident that he was a stranger to the vital influence of religion."‡

So uniform were these results of Protestant missionary labor, here as elsewhere, even in cases where the agents employed were men of pure intentions, that an American writer confessed, as late as 1792, "*There never was an instance* of an Indian forsaking his habits and savage manners," under the influence of Protestantism; and then he cited the case of the Rev. Samuel Kirkland, a well-known missionary, "who has taken all the pains that man can take, but his whole flock are Indians still!"§ Mr. Kirkland himself declared to Sir William Johnson, "In general they treat me with no more respect than they would show to a dog."‖ Yet these same Indians clung to missionaries of another creed with so much love and reverence, that they willingly exposed their own lives to save them, and even displayed such delicacy and refinement in their respect, as they continue to do at this hour, that, as one of the latter relates, when a Father knelt down in their tents to recite his office, they not only suspended every occupation, but "hardly moved or breathed lest they should interrupt him."¶

Lastly, the Quakers, in spite of their temperance and humanity, were as unsuccessful as the rest. "The Quakers," Mr. Bancroft observes, "came among the Delawares in the

* *Star in the West*, ch. vi., p. 227.
† Bancroft, ii., 916.
‡ *History of the Missionary Societies*, by Rev. Thomas Smith, introd., p. 16.
§ *Documentary History of New York*, vol. ii., p. 1110.
‖ Ibid., vol. iv., p. 358.
¶ *Annales*, tome iii., p. 558.

spirit of peace and brotherly love, and with sincerest wishes to benefit the Indian; but the Quakers succeeded no better than the Puritans—not nearly as well as the Jesuits." In 1822, Dr. Morse could still report of this tribe, who seemed worthy of a better lot, "They are *more* opposed to the Gospel and the whites than any other Indians with whom I am acquainted." It is exactly the same history as in China, Ceylon, Africa, and everywhere else; the more familiar they become with Protestant missionaries, the deeper is their hatred of Christianity. "It cannot be denied," said Dr. Timothy Dwight, in 1823, "that the attempts which have been made in modern times to spread the influence of the Gospel among the Indians have in a great measure been unsuccessful;"* and long after, for every chapter of this sad history resembles that which preceded it, when Mr. Elisha Bates was examined by a parliamentary committee, and was asked what had been effected among the heathen by the well-intentioned efforts of the Society of Friends, he candidly confessed, "I do not know that we could say that we have brought them to a habit of prayer; I know of *no instance* that would warrant me in saying so."†

In 1861, an English traveller once more says, "The Europeanization of the Indian generally is as hopeless as the Christianization of the Hindoo. The missionaries usually live under the shadow of the different agencies. . . I do not believe that an Indian of the plains ever became a Christian."‡ Finally, an English society, which has done perhaps more than any other to make Christianity an object of derision, by depriving it of all truth and robbing it of all dignity, confesses unwillingly, and in terms which suggest rather than announce a falsehood, that the failure applies equally to all the tribes, "Cherokees, Choctaws, Pawnees, Oregons, Sioux, and others." And then they explain, for the instruction of their subscribers, the cause of the failure. It was, they inform them, with imperturbable assurance, "the opposition of Papists"§ which alone prevented the success of Protestant missions,—and probably their subscribers believe them.

AMERICAN PROCEEDINGS.

We have now perhaps reviewed with sufficient detail the history of Protestant missions in North America, fitly described

* *Travels in New England*, vol. iii., p. 71.

† *Parliamentary Papers*, vol. vii., p. 545 (British Museum).

‡ Burton, *The City of the Saints*, ch. ii., p. 140.

§ *The Indians of North America*, by the Religious Tract Society, p. 295.

by a partial annalist as "*the record of a series of failures.*" We have seen also, by sufficient testimony, why Jogues and Lallemand and de Brebeuf labored in vain, and why the apostolic triumphs of their brethren in the South—in Brazil, Peru, and Paraguay, in Guatemala, Mexico, and California—were not renewed in Canada and the United States. It was not that the English massacred the apostles who were already rapidly effecting, among various tribes and nations, the same supernatural work which their brethren had accomplished in the South, for this was a trial which they had encountered and overcome in every other land, and which would only have contributed to their final success. They would have offered their heads to the English, as they did to the Baures or the Chiquitos, and the victims would, sooner or later, have worn out their executioners. But in British America it was not the pastors only who were slain. This was a loss which could have been repaired. But what power could gather together or summon back to new life the flocks whom the persecutor had maddened by oppression, or driven far away from the graves of their fathers, or exterminated by fire and sword? A new race of apostles might indeed have entered the land, but it would have been only to find a desert.

We have said that for this calamity, without parallel in the history of pagan lands, and which overwhelmed the inhabitants of a continent in hopeless ruin, Americans are not responsible. It must be confessed, however, that if the crime was not theirs, they have done little to repair it. It was an evil legacy which the English bequeathed to them, but they have made an evil use of it. Nearly forty years ago, Dr. Morse implored the government to "provide an asylum for the *remnant* of this depressed and wretched people, who have long been insulated, corrupting and wasting away in the midst of us;" but the Americans have shown more zeal to complete their ruin, and to deprive them of their remaining lands, than to grant them the "unmolested home" which Morse foresaw they would never enjoy.* A few testimonies will suffice to prove, that their present masters have dealt almost as hardly with the scattered fragments of the Indian nations as the English did with their yet unbroken masses, while they wandered in thousands, ignorant of their coming doom, by the rivers and lakes where God had given them a home. If the English left a curse behind them, the Americans have not substituted a blessing.

When that Union of many States was formed by the patient valor of a generation which nobly refused to accept the fate of

* Morse, *Report on Indian Affairs*, pp. 24, 30.

Canada or Ireland, but whose unwilling fault it was that it left no heirs of its virtue, its genius, or its patriotism,* two races of suffering men asked from the children of the new Republic the humblest lot which misery ever consented to implore or charity to concede—the right to labor and live. And they asked it in vain. "The African race, bond and free, and the aborigines, savage and civilized, being *incapable* of assimilation and absorption," says a well-known American statesman of our own day, with almost brutal frankness, "remain distinct, and may be regarded as *accidental*, if not disturbing, political forces."† Negroes and Indians, both victims of English cupidity and violence, were refused from the beginning, and are still refused wherever Protestant principles prevail, even the smallest measure of the rights which their vigorous masters had known how to win for themselves. Let us inquire what has been their fate in this paradise of freedom and independence, and what American Christianity has attempted or achieved to improve their lot. We will speak of the Negro first.

AMERICAN NEGROES.

Let it be permitted, however, in alluding briefly to this grave subject, which will afford a new test of the relative power of the Church and the Sects, to disclaim all sympathy with the professional advocates of Negro emancipation. Wherever the Church exercises her civilizing influence, the Negro tends towards complete liberty, and, while still in bondage, is being wisely prepared for it; but though she utterly condemns the traffic in human flesh, in the words of Gregory XVI., "as injurious to salvation, and disgraceful to the Christian name," she tolerates, like St. Paul, while she everywhere strives to abolish, the state of slavery. She knows that the negro has no worse enemy than the partisan of unconditional emancipation. She knows also, that however little may have been done for his soul, the American negro has both more happiness and more liberty in his bondage than he would have possessed in his native land; that, with rare exceptions, he is better fed, better clothed, more lightly tasked in his strength, and more

* "Few things have more surprised the world than the deterioration of the political men of America. . . Few of their public men would pass in Europe for tolerable second-rates." *Slavery in the United States*, by Nassau W. Senior, Esq., p. 15.

† *Speech of Mr. Seward*, 1850, quoted by D. W. Mitchell, *Ten Years in the United States*, ch. viii., p. 115 (1862).

mercifully tended in his old age, than any class of white laborers, in any country whatever; and finally, that the colored man is the object of far more charity in the *slave* than he is in the *free* States. In the former, he *generally* receives only benevolence and consideration; in the latter, in spite of the hollow professions of men who trade even in philanthropy and religion, he *always* encounters contumely and neglect. "As a slave," says an American authority, with full knowledge of all the facts, "he is happy and contented; as a free man, despised and contemned."* "The thoughtfulness of masters, mistresses, and their children about, not only the comforts, but the indulgences of their slaves, was a frequent subject of admiration with me,"† observes an English writer; while in the free States, and especially in those which are the abode of the Abolitionist party, even "the schools for the colored children are, unless they escape by their insignificance, shut up, or pulled down, or the school-house wheeled away upon rollers over the frontier of a pious State, which will not endure that its colored citizens should be educated!"‡ "I have sometimes thought," says one who has recently marked the contrast between the tenderness of the Southern slave-owner and the merciless brutality of the Northern abolitionist, "that there is no being so venomous, so bloodthirsty, as a professed philanthropist; and that when the philanthropists' ardor lies negro-wards, it then assumes the deepest venom and bloodthirstiness."§

Half a century ago, a Protestant missionary, who had assured the Delawares that the religion which he taught would secure their happiness, received from them a reply which he records in these words: "They had determined," they told him, with solemn irony, "to wait, in order to see whether all the *black* people among us were made thus happy and joyful, before they would put confidence in our promises; . . . . . that therefore they had sent back the two missionaries, with many thanks, promising that when they saw the black people among us restored to freedom and happiness, they would receive our missionaries." Dr. Boudinot adds, that this was "close reasoning," and considers the incident "too mortifying a fact to make further observations upon."‖

It was England, as is well-known, who introduced slavery into the United States. "English ships," says Mr. Bancroft, "fitted out in English cities, under the special favor of the

* *New York Herald*, January 25, 1861.

† Martineau, *Society in America*, vol. ii., ch. v., p. 314.

‡ Id., vol. i., ch. iii., p. 194.

§ *North America*, by Anthony Trollope, vol. i., ch. xvi., p. 354 (1862).

‖ *Star in the West*, ch. viii., p. 234.

royal family, of the ministry and of parliament, stole from Africa, in the years from 1700 to 1750, probably *a million and a half souls*, of whom one-eighth were buried in the Atlantic, victims of the passage; and yet in England no general indignation rebuked the enormity, for the public opinion of the age was obedient to materialism. . . . . Protestantism itself had, in the political point of view, been the *triumph of materialism* over the spiritual authority of the Church."*

But Protestantism, having substituted the material for the spiritual, was, at least in this case, consistent with itself, as the negro found to his cost. "From New England to Carolina," we are told by Mr. Bancroft, "the notion prevailed, that '*being baptized is inconsistent with a state of slavery;*' and this early apprehension proved a main obstacle to the culture and conversion of these poor people."† Apparently the obstacle has never been removed, or only to give place to others equally fatal. Governor Dongan, of New York, reported officially, at the close of the seventeenth century, that while the English colonists generally wished "to bring up their children and servants in that opinion which themselves profess, I observe that they take no care of the conversion of their slaves."‡ Their American descendants have not rebuked them by a display of greater charity. The immense majority of the American negroes, amounting to four millions, confessedly remain, as respects their spiritual development, in much the same position as their kinsfolk in Dahomey or Ashantee. "They exist among us," says Mr. Howison, the historian of Virginia, "a huge mass of mind, *almost entirely unenlightened.*" And even in exceptional cases, in which, by the connivance of benevolent owners, and in spite of legal prohibitions, they receive some sort of religious instruction, there is too much reason to believe that it has only generated that terrible malediction to which Holy Scripture points, when it tells us of men whose "last state is worse than the first." Two modes of dealing with negroes are recorded by Mr. Law Olmsted, and other American writers, both of which deserve our attention.

One of them is described by Mr. Olmsted, in quoting "Bishop Meade, of the Church of England in Virginia," whose compositions the author of *Our Slave States* judiciously selects, as affording the fairest specimen of "the most careful kind of preaching ordinarily addressed by the white clergy" to negro audiences. When we have seen how Dr. Meade appreciates the

* Bancroft, ii., 997.
† P. 994.
‡ *Doc. Hist. N. York*, vol. i., p. 187.

relations of that class to Christianity, we shall have no reason for surprise at the estimate furnished by Mr. Howison of their actual condition in the State of Virginia. The extracts cited from this Protestant bishop by Mr. Olmsted are taken, he tells us, "from a published volume of his sermons, recommended by him to masters and mistresses in his diocese, *for use in their households*;" and of which the contents, as Mr. Olmsted appears to intimate, resemble rather the menaces of a turnkey than the exhortations of a Christian minister. "Your bodies, you know,"—it is thus that Dr. Meade counsels masters and mistresses to address their slaves,—"are not your own; they are at the disposal of those you belong to." And the rest is in harmony with this beginning. "Poor creatures! you little consider when you are idle, when you are saucy and impudent . . . . that what faults you are guilty of towards your masters and mistresses are faults done against God Himself." And so he goes droning on, page after page, without one tender word, one accent of Divine charity; unmindful of the Apostle who sent back Onesimus to his master, "*not now as a servant, but a most dear brother*," and entreating, "if he hath wronged thee in any thing, put that to my account;" unmindful, too, as Mr. Olmsted happily observes, of the admonition of St. Gregory, that "slaves should be restored to that liberty in which they were born."* But Dr. Meade was content to take a lower model than St. Paul or St. Gregory, and to resemble a jailer rather than an apostle. If his language, as we are informed, be a specimen of the "most careful kind of preaching" to negroes, we may easily understand what notions they form of the religion of the Gospel, as presented to them by Protestant teachers.

But the Episcopalians,—the majority of whose clergy, we are told by one of their own members, "may be seen ministering at the altar of slavery,"†—are not the only monitors of the American negro. Baptists, Methodists, and others, dispute their influence; and if the latter refuse to choose as their solitary text, "Your bodies are not your own," it does not appear that the fruits of their instruction are more advantageous to the welfare of the slave. "It is evident," says Mr. Olmsted, "of the greater part even of those received into the fellowship of the churches, that their idea of religion, and of the standard of morality which they deem consistent with a profession of it, is very degraded;"—another proof of the impotence of Protestantism to deal with those fallen races whom it is the special

* *Our Slave States*, by Frederick Law Olmsted, ch. ii., p. 122.
† Quoted by Helper, *The Impending Crisis of the South*, ch. v., p. 262.

glory of the Church, as we have seen in these pages, to raise to the dignity of men and Christians.

"The testimony of slaveholders," says Miss Martineau, "was most explicit as to no moral improvement having taken place in consequence of the introduction of religion;"* while another eye-witness gives the following description of their public worship: "They leaped aloft, they twisted their bodies round in a sort of corkscrew fashion, and were evidently in a state of convulsion. . . . Whichever way we looked in the church, we saw somebody leaping up and fanning the air; the whole church seemed transformed into a regular Bedlam, and the noise and the tumult was horrible."† One "we saw walking about by himself and breathing hard; he was hoarse, and sighing he exclaimed to himself, 'Oh! I wish I could hollo!'"

Of the use made by negroes of the Bible, which a certain class of missionaries seem to spend their lives in exposing to derision, Mr. Olmsted gives such examples as the following: A baptized negro, addicted to "certain immoral practices," being admonished by a preacher, the following discussion ensued: "Don't de Scriptur say,' rejoined the backslider, 'Dem as bleve and is baptize shall be saved? Want to know dat."

"Yes, but—"

"Dat's all I want to know, Sar; now wat's de use o' talking to me? You aint a going to make me bleve wot de blessed Lord says aint so, not if you trie forever."

The minister attempted to remonstrate, but was finally silenced as follows: "De Scriptur say, if a man bleve and is baptize, he shall—he *shall* be saved. Now, massa minister, I *done* bleve, and I *done* baptize, and I *shall* be saved sure. Dere's no use talking, Sar."

During his researches into the religion of Protestant negroes,—who only faintly resemble the fancy type which Mrs. Beecher Stowe untruthfully drew, in order to promote the selfish designs of a political party,—Mr. Olmsted once asked a black clergyman if he was a preacher. "'Yes, massa,' he replied, 'Kordin to der grace.' He commenced to reply in some scriptural phrase, soberly; but before he could say three words reeled off like a drunken man, entirely overcome with merriment."‡

The white teachers of the same unfortunate race sometimes fall below even this specimen. Thus Mr. Buckingham notices the case of a female slave, solicited to sin by her master's son, to whose earnest entreaty for succor in this emergency "her

* *Society in America*, vol. ii., ch. i., p. 160.

† F. Bremer, *Homes of the New World*, vol. iii., p. 38.

‡ *Our Slave States*, ch. ii., p. 123; ch. vi., p. 377.

religious teacher, the minister of the church she had joined," replied, "that her duty as a slave was clearly passive submission, and that resistance or refusal could not be countenanced by him."*

On the whole, the colored people of Protestant America may be ranged into three classes: the multitude, who have learned nothing, and whom Mr. Howison describes as "a huge mass of mind almost entirely unenlightened;" the few, who, as a capable witness affirms in the *New York Times*, "join the church, perhaps in the great majority of cases, with *no idea* of religion," and only display, as Mr. Olmsted observes, "maniacal excitement," and "a miserable superstition, the more painful that it employs some forms and words ordinarily connected with true Christianity;" and lastly, the free negroes of the North, whose lot is perhaps still more full of ignominy, whose liberty is a mockery and a delusion, and who display so little capacity of social progress that they have actually decreased in numbers, during the decennial period ending in 1860, even in the cities of Boston and New York.

In the island groups of the Atlantic, where perhaps a majority of the negroes have been induced to accept various modifications of Christianity, the same facts recur. It may seem ungracious to find fault with an act upon which England prides herself so much as the emancipation of her West Indian negroes, yet it seems to be her fate, even when she strives to do a good work, to do it in the wrong way. "This English negro emancipation," observes Dr. Waitz, "will remain to all time as one of the most stupendous moral, economical, and political follies which the history of human culture has to point to."† And then he proves, by arguments of which it is impossible to deny the force, the "utter irrationality" of the mode in which this act of sentimental but short-sighted and blundering benevolence was effected. The result of abandoning to the difficult task of self-government, without an hour's previous discipline, a population so absolutely void of foresight or self-control, has been in every way deplorable, and not a few of the negroes, who have quitted the towns for the interior, are said to have already retrograded into utter barbarism. "A race has been freed," said Lord Harris in an official report, "but a society has not been formed; they are only capable of enjoying its vices." In the French colony of La Martinique, where emancipation was proclaimed with equal folly by the Provisional Government of 1848, ruin and chaos have ensued. Mr.

* *America*, vol. i., ch. xix., p. 361.
† Quoted in *The Rambler*, vol. iii., p. 323.

McLeod has recently described the singular condition of the free blacks at Mauritius, and the virtual slavery of the *white* population.* The solitary exception is said to be found in the Danish island of Santa Cruz, where, although the negroes were emancipated, they were wisely left under the action of a special code, which *forces* them to labor, while it permits them to labor for their own advantage.

There is a remarkable concurrence of opinion as to the religious condition of the free blacks, in the islands as well as on the mainland. Dr. Dalton has told us that the Protestant negro considers "good works superfluous," and Mr. Trollope that "he never connects his religion with his life." Like his white co-religionists in other climes, he bursts into violent religious excitement on Sunday, but is apt to relapse into something worse than forgetfulness during the rest of the week. Mr. Coleridge adds the following information.

"The evil which the Methodists have done upon the long run is but scantily counterpoised by a certain sobriety of exterior which they have inflicted on their sect." "The ministers," he adds, always true to this ineradicable instinct, "*sell* to the poor negroes what are called 'tickets of membership,' a sort of certificates of the purchaser's righteousness;" by which ingenious plan one of them confessed that he had amassed, in the course of twelve months, and from a single congregation, six hundred and twenty-four pounds.† Of the Baptists, the most active rivals of the Wesleyans, Lord Metcalfe reported officially, as Sir Benjamin D'Urban reported from South Africa, "Instead of being ministers of peace, they are manifestly fomenters of discord."‡ Of the native preachers, who are often represented in English missionary reports as models of zeal and piety, Mr. Knibb, a Protestant minister, informed the House of Commons that "the majority lead very unholy lives, and allow sins of various kinds in their different churches." It is true that Mr. Wildman gave much the same account, before the same committee, of "the immorality among the ministers of the Established Church."§

It is evident, then, that neither the past history nor the present condition of religion among the classes referred to are pleasant subjects of reflection. Protestantism has failed as completely with the Negro as with the Chinese, the Hindoo, and the Sioux. And with all it seems to have employed the same class of emissaries. A Protestant minister informs us, in

* *Travels in Eastern Africa*, vol. ii., ch. v., pp. 162–5.

† *Six Months in the West Indies*, by Henry Nelson Coleridge, p. 172.

‡ *Papers of Lord Metcalfe*, edited by J. W. Kaye, p. 337.

§ *Parliamentary Reports*, 16 July, 1832; vol. xx., pp. 278, 535.

a recent work, that in the island of St. Thomas, speaking of the middle of the eighteenth century, "concubinage at that period, and afterwards, was not looked upon as a sin, and in no way detracted from the standing and moral estimation even of clergymen." We need not ask him, therefore, what was the character of their congregations. He even names some of the clergy whose irregularities were most notorious, and then adds, apparently as a melancholy illustration of the fact, that whereas "the Roman Catholics, in 1701," were too few to be counted as an element in the population, "the congregation for many years has embraced at least a fourth of the inhabitants of the island, and is therefore very large."*

Perhaps the Anglican operations in the West Indies may be thought to deserve special mention. It is true that the negroes have very little share in the enormous expenditure which distinguishes, here as elsewhere, the barren labors of the parliamentary church. M. Victor Schœlcher notices with astonishment, that the annual cost of the "Establishment in Jamaica is fifty thousand pounds,"† and Mr. Underhill relates that it once reached a still higher sum, and that in a single year "seventy-four thousand pounds was expended on the Church of England."‡ In spite of this vast revenue, and as a proof of the worthlessness of such machinery in promoting religion, we are assured in 1862, that "if the cities of the Dead Sea were *half* as bad as Port Royal in the way of morals, they richly deserved their fate."§

Of Barbadoes, Mr. Coleridge frankly reports, that "the Codrington College is at present all but useless." Though it offers the Principal "one of the most delectable houses in the Antilles," he considers it "quite monstrous that the object of so magnificent a charity, and such large actual funds, should be the support of fourteen or fifteen boys, who might be educated much better elsewhere in the island. . . . . What is done there is not done well, and yet done at an enormous expense." It is just the history of the Protestant colleges at Malacca, Calcutta, Hong-Kong, and elsewhere; they consume, but never produce.

Of Dominica, Mr. Coleridge gives the usual account, in speaking of his co-religionists, and then adds, in spite of violent prejudice, "I am bound to say that a general good report was given of the sobriety and temperate zeal of the Romish priests

* *Historical Account of St. Thomas*, by John P. Knox, Pastor of the Reformed Dutch Church, ch. x., pp. 139, 141 (1852).

† *Colonies Etrangères*, p. 59 (1843).

‡ *The West Indies*, by E. B. Underhill, p. 220.

§ *The Cruise of the St. George*, by N. B. Dennys, R.N., ch. v., p. 76.

in the colony."* Of Bermuda, another English writer records the characteristic fact that when Dr. Field, an Anglican bishop, visited the island to open a new church at Hamilton, and took the opportunity of mildly recommending "Church principles," he had scarcely departed, before the Colonial Assembly voted —for the first time in the history of Bermuda—a respectable stipend to the Presbyterian minister at Hamilton!"† This was their answer to his appeal.

But if the Anglican authorities in these islands can only spend money, without attracting the sympathy either of the colored races or their own nominal disciples, other sects exert a more energetic if not a more beneficial influence. "Completely organized espionage," Mr. Coleridge says, "is a fundamental point in the system of the Methodists; the secrets of every family are at their command; parent and child are watches on each other; sister is set against sister, and brother against brother; each is on his guard against all, and all against each." "The Baptist and Methodist clergy," according to Mr. Olmsted, "spend most of their force in arguing against each other's doctrines," so that the amused negroes acquire "a great taste for theological controversy." The Methodists, however, are generally worsted by the Baptists, because "immersion strikes the fancy of the negroes." Mr. Cartwright, a celebrated American preacher of the Methodist denomination, whose "autobiography" appears to have found a larger number of readers than the Memoirs of Guizot or the History of Macaulay, is particularly severe on the Baptists. They were always opposing him, Mr. Cartwright complains, "and would try to take our converts off into the water; indeed they made so much ado about baptism by immersion, that the uninformed world would suppose that heaven was an island, and that there was no way to get there but by *diving* or *swimming*."‡ But Mr. Cartwright, who has probably had a larger number of hearers than any living man, and has been a celebrity in Boston and Philadelphia as well as in the wilds of Illinois, was a formidable opponent, and rarely mentions a conflict with the Baptists without adding cheerfully, that they were "annihilated," or "finally evaporated and left for parts unknown." His own preaching, on the other hand, was followed by results which, though not witnessed in the apostolic age, are certainly impressive. His hearers, he tells us, and it is perfectly true, sometimes "fell in every direction, right and

* *Six Months*, &c., p. 153.

† *Bermuda*, by a Field Officer, ch. v., p. 93 (1857).

‡ *The Backwoods Preacher; an Autobiography of Peter Cartwright*, ch. xi., p. 71; 31st edition (1858).

left, front and rear. It was supposed that not less than three hundred (after one sermon) fell like dead men in a mighty battle; they were strewed all over the camp-ground."* "The power of God," he says on one occasion, "fell upon the people gloriously. I kept my eye on William P——, and suddenly he fell at full length, and roared like a bull in a net, and cried aloud for mercy. . . . Just about daybreak, Monday morning, William P—— raised the shout of victory, after struggling hard all night."† William P—— had "got religion."

It is fair to hear the Baptists in their turn. In 1862 the Baptist Missionary Society sent Mr. Underhill to visit their congregations in the West Indies. Two main facts may be gathered from his story,—the one, that the Negro Baptists were originally attracted to that sect by the unpopularity of its preachers both with the government and the planters; the other, that as soon as the first excitement of emancipation had subsided, their brief religious fanaticism gave place to indifference and immorality. "Three years after emancipation, in 1841," says Mr. Underhill, speaking of Trinidad, "the condition of the island was most deplorable;" while twenty years later he found that they "stood aloof from the missionary," in consequence of "the introduction of fanatical excesses among them." Mr. Dennys relates in the same year, speaking of Jamaica, that it is impossible to "conceive the horrible state of society to which the so-called revivals gave rise, or the awfully blasphemous language made use of by their promoters."

From Mr. Underhill we learn that, in a multitude of places they oscillate between this loathsome fanaticism, generated by a form of religion which can only appeal to the feelings without illuminating the soul, and its natural sequel, apathy and vice. At Old Harbor Bay, the Baptist agent "lamented the decay of piety among the people; said that they were not so attentive to religious duties as in years past, and that many of the young people were very careless and irregular in attendance at public worship. The Wesleyan congregation also has much declined."

At another place, the "Deacon" "lamented the degeneracy of the people, and their inattention to religion. 'They have got no heart in it,' he said."

At Clarksonville, "backsliders do not return to the Church in such numbers as is to be desired."

At Bethany, "the Church is weak . . . there are few candidates for fellowship."

In another town, "they complained of a general want of

* Ch. viii., p. 46.
† Ch. xii., p. 77.

life in religion; there did not appear any real love for public worship."

In another, "There has been a very large diminution in the number of members since 1845."

Finally, of the native preachers, who are a great majority in the Baptist community, Mr. Underhill gives this candid account. "Instances were related to me where such had been the vanity, the ridiculous assumptions, the extravagance, and the instability of the native ministers, that confidence in their usefulness, and in their fitness for an employment so grave and responsible, was utterly destroyed." Yet they do not cease to employ them.

On the whole, it does not appear that Mr. Cartwright had much reason to envy the success of the Baptists, nor even their theory that "heaven was an island" only to be reached by swimming. One triumph, however, they seem to have enjoyed, which it is due to Mr. Underhill to notice. That gentleman assures his society, as a counterpoise to much gloomy information, that the best results may be anticipated from the extensive circulation of the "*Gospel Trumpet*," a periodical, "portions of which are read at each meeting" in the West Indies, though it is probably less widely known in colder climes.*

The Methodists in the West Indies have invented, perhaps to counterbalance the superior attractions of the Baptists, an entirely new sect, under a certain Mr. Penwick; of which M. Schœlcher lightly observes, "If God grants life to this sect, which has already *fourteen* chapels, before half a century England will have its Penwickians, as it has already its Wesleyans." He notices also that the Baptists, whom he calls "the radicals of Christianity," "attack without mercy the Established Church, which revenges itself by discrediting them without pity." And thus the Negro learns Christianity.

But there is a happier class of negroes, who have Catholic masters, who have received the faith in its fulness, and whose condition has been thus described even by those Protestant witnesses whom alone we have determined to hear in this controversy. "The Roman Catholic Church," says Professor Merivale, in spite of vehement prejudice, "has always proved a protector and a friend to these unfortunates."† In Spanish South America, says Sir Woodbine Parish, "slavery was always more a name than a reality. The negroes were treated with even more consideration than the hired servants of the country. The laws protected them from ill usage, and religious feeling,

* *The West Indies*, by Edward Bean Underhill, pp. 58, 229, 250, 303, 309 346, 430 (1862).

† *Lectures on Colonization*, lect. ii., p. 49.

in a state of society over which the priests had paramount influence, operated still more in their favor."* And the same contrast is noticed, even by American writers, in every other region. In Brazil, where nearly half of the slave population have already acquired freedom, Dr. Kidder, an American preacher, who vainly recommended to them his own religious ideas, confesses, in 1857, that "some of the most intelligent and best educated men I met in Brazil *were of African descent;*" and that "*fuit* will be written against slavery in this empire before another century rolls round." He even adds, "Some of the closest students are Mulattoes."† Mr. Gardner, an English Protestant, declares that "the condition of the domestic slave in Brazil is perhaps even better than that of others; . . . . on estates where there has been no medical attendant, I have often found the lady of the proprietor attending to the sick in the hospital herself."‡ Their masters, says Mr. Walpole, "with an eye to the everlasting welfare of their slaves, always have them baptized on their arrival in the Brazils."§

"If what we see here," says Mr. Mansfield, "is any thing like a fair specimen of slavery, my opinion is that the cry against slavery, as raised in England, *is a vile sham, and lip worship;*" while he observes of the negroes themselves, "I only wish such cheerful faces were to be seen among our English poor."‖ "Any comparison," adds Mr. Anthony Trollope, referring to another part of the same continent, "between the material comfort of a Kentucky slave and an English ditcher and delver would be preposterous."¶

At Bogota, we learn from Captain Cochrane, "the emancipation of slaves has been very great, and but few remain; the course of time will see them all set at liberty."** In Central America, the negroes are all free, slavery having been declared "illegal." In Peru, negroes imported as slaves at once acquire their freedom, without injury to themselves in a society which is profoundly Catholic.

"Avoiding on the one hand the precipitate measure of the English reform ministry, and on the other the ribald effrontery

* *Buenos Ayres,* part ii., ch. ix., p. 115.

† *Brazil and the Brazilians,* ch. viii., p. 133. "As a proof that the Brazilians have thoroughly abandoned the traffic in human flesh, it may be stated, that a slaver taken in January, 1856, into Bahia, and condemned, had touched at five places along the coast previous to her detection, but had not succeeded in selling a single slave." Lempriere, *Mexico in* 1861, ch. i., p. 15.

‡ *Travels in the Interior of Brazil,* ch. i., p. 19.

§ *Four Years in the Pacific,* vol. i., ch. ii., p. 47.

‖ *Paraguay, Brazil,* &c., by C. B. Mansfield, Esq., M.A., ch. ii., p. 29.

¶ *North America,* vol. ii., ch. iv., p. 117.

** *Residence in Colombia,* vol. ii., p. 38.

of the slave statesmen of North America," says Mr. Markham, "the Peruvians have steered a middle course between the extremes," and while the slave population is "becoming gradually accustomed to liberty," they are treated with such charity and consideration that "it is anticipated that few on receiving their liberty will leave their masters, to whom they are endeared by their almost paternal kindness and the recollections of their earliest childhood."*

In Chili, they "are treated with a degree of tenderness and humanity," says Mr. Hill, an ardent Protestant, "that greatly alleviates their servitude. A law has been passed declaring that no slave can henceforth be born in Chili, so that slavery may be regarded as virtually abolished in this fine country."† In the province of La Plata, some of the Mulattoes have already become "professors and teachers of the liberal arts,"—a wonderful example of the civilizing influence of the Catholic religion. In Venezuela, slavery was abolished in 1854. "The Mexicans," observes Mr. Featherstonhaugh, for in every *Catholic* province the facts are uniform, "stand at a proud moral distance from the Americans in regard to slavery, which is abolished in their Republic."‡ Even in Cuba—where the culpable effeminacy of a wealthy and luxurious class diminished in some degree, in former years, the beneficial operation of the excellent code which regulates slavery—Mr. Olmsted notices that "every slave has the liberty of emancipating himself, by paying a price which does not depend upon the selfish exactions of masters. . . . The consequence is, that emancipations are constantly going on, and the free people of color *are becoming enlightened, cultivated, and wealthy;*" while "in no part of the United States do they occupy the high social position which they enjoy in Cuba."§ "There are circumstances of great superiority," observes another American writer, with equal candor, "in the condition of the Cuban over that of the American slave."‖

"Here," says Miss Bremer, in illustration of the same contrast, "the judges are commanded to watch over the rights of the slave. Here a mother may purchase the freedom of her child, before its birth, for fifteen dollars; and after its birth, for double that sum, *she may emancipate her child.*" "These laws of emancipation have caused the negro population of Cuba to amount to nearly five hundred thousand souls, about one-half of the whole population of the island, and near one-third free negroes.

* *Cuzco and Lima*, ch. ii., p. 28.
† Quoted in *The Rambler*, vol. iii., p. 330.
‡ *Excursions Through the Slave States*, vol. ii., ch. xxxiv., p. 188.
§ *Our Slave States*, ch. vi., p. 445.
‖ *Gan-Eden, or Pictures of Cuba*, ch. xiii., p. 189 (1854).

And the free negro of Cuba is the happiest of all created beings."* We know what the free negro is in the Protestant States of America—an object of contempt even to the slave.

Long ago Burke remarked, "As to the negroes (in the French colonies), they are not left, as they are with us, wholly, body and soul, to the discretion of the planter. Their masters are *obliged* to have them instructed in the principles of religion."† At Ceuta, says Mr. Urquhart, "the Spaniards allow them progressively to repurchase their liberty, and when they have done so, admit them to perfect equality of consideration with the white men."‡ Lastly, Mr. Sullivan dares to indicate distinctly the pregnant contrast which Mr. Olmsted and others only venture to insinuate. In Catholic Cuba, he says, "the slaves are allowed to be instructed in their Bible, and are not kicked out of the cathedrals and churches, like so many dogs, as they are in America;"§ he means in the cities where Protestantism reigns, for in New Orleans, Mr. Olmsted relates, apparently with admiration, that in the Catholic cathedral the negro and white man knelt side by side, a spectacle which the writer of these pages has often witnessed in the Catholic churches of New York.

Such, in its outlines, is the contrast between the lot of the negro under Catholic and Protestant masters respectively. A blessing and a curse represent, in this as in every other field, the relative action of the Church and the Sects. In Protestant America, we know what has been the history of the African; in every Catholic State, even on the same continent, he has found either prompt and complete liberty, or a constant and rapid approximation towards it, not by a violent and irrational emancipation following hard upon a debasing servitude, but by gradual culture and wise discipline; and even while still a bondsman, "religious feeling," as Sir Woodbine Parish observes, secures for him such tender care and wakeful solicitude as is rarely conceded in England or America to free laborers. But if we have now sufficient evidence with respect to the fortunes of this section of American society, we have still to show, in conclusion, what Protestantism has done for the original tenants of the land, after slaughtering the pastors who were gathering them by thousands into the fold of Christ, and what has been its final influence upon races whom the missionaries of the Cross would have everywhere converted into a generous, a civilized, and a believing people.

* *Homes of the New World,* letter xxxiii., p. 111; letter xxxvii., p. 244.
† *European Settlements in America,* vol. ii., ch. vi., p. 47.
‡ *The Pillars of Hercules,* ch. vi., p. 104.
§ *Rambles in N. and S. America,* ch. iii., p. 60.

AMERICAN INDIANS.

"The Europeans," says M. de Tocqueville, and Humboldt has used almost the same words, "after having banished the Indian tribes to remote deserts, have condemned them to a wandering and vagabond life full of inexpressible miseries. European tyranny has rendered them more disorderly *and less civilized* than they were before." We have seen that in *South* America, hundreds of thousands of savages were raised to such a degree of virtue, civilization, and prosperity, that "they enjoyed, for many generations," even by the confession of a Southey, "a greater exemption from physical and moral evil than any other inhabitants of the globe." "The moral and physical condition of *this* people," continues M. de Tocqueville, "*has not ceased to degenerate in equal measure*, and their barbarism has increased in proportion to their sufferings." And then, contrasting their woful decay with the unparalleled material progress of their Protestant lords, he adds this cry of righteous indignation: "Never has there been witnessed in any nation either so prodigious a development or so rapid a destruction!"*

The story of that destruction is soon told. The Atlantic States had already been emptied of their inhabitants by the English; but many a tribe still remained, though in diminished numbers, by the banks of the Ohio and the Mississippi, as well as in the wide regions which lie between the confluence of the latter river with the Missouri and the far distant provinces of Oregon and California. In these remote tribes was vested the possession of lands of vast extent and incalculable value. As the flood of emigration rolled onwards, and, bursting one barrier after another, sought an issue in the wide plains of the West, the Indian found himself once more in the presence of men stronger and fiercer than himself, and able to wrest from him the lands which he was unable to guard.

We have learned from American authorities how his race has been exterminated,—men, women, and helpless babes,—that Anglo-Saxon lords might the sooner divide his inheritance; and Mr. Julius Froebel assures us, in 1859, that they have found still more expeditious modes of removing tribes who could have taught them a lesson in humanity, if they had been willing to profit by it. "It is a fact," he says, "that the whites have attempted to poison *whole tribes* of Indians, and I have myself often heard the question discussed how this could be effected

* *De la Démocratie*, &c., tome iii., ch. v., p. 109.

in the best manner. A story of the designed introduction of the small-pox amongst a remote Indian tribe is current in the west, and I have heard it related with every particular."*

If the Indians, provoked by such atrocities, have begun to retaliate, this can hardly excite surprise. In 1862, Commander Mayne relates, that "scarcely a paper reaches Victoria from Oregon or Washington States that does not contain an account of some brutal murder of whites by the Indians, or some retaliatory deed of blood by the troops of the United States. So confirmed, indeed, has this enmity become, that what is little short of *a policy of extermination* is being pursued towards the aborigines."†

It was not, however, always by open violence, but more often by the fiction of a simulated purchase, that the Indian was deprived of his hunting-grounds, and driven to wander again towards the setting sun. In vain he sometimes affected to adopt the nominal religion of his encroaching guests, in the hope of snatching from their sympathy the respite which their avarice denied. "I was struck with amazement," said Dr. Wolff, fifteen years ago, "to find in the United States of North America, that many of the Indians, especially among the Cherokees, adopted outwardly the Protestant religion, in order, as they hoped, to prevent Congress from sending them further into the interior."‡ Feeble device! which did not postpone even for an hour their inevitable doom. There was no Vicar of Christ here, as of old in Mexico and Brazil, to launch the sentence of excommunication against all who should wrong the Indian, nor would such a sentence have had any terrors for those who were now gathering round him. There was no Las Casas to defend, no Vieyra to instruct, no Baraza to die for him. The sons of St. Francis and St. Ignatius were far away, and the Indian was left to struggle alone. And so, in his own touching words, "the tree which was continually transplanted quickly perished." "The Americans acquired," says M. de Tocqueville, "almost for nothing—*à vil prix*—whole provinces which the richest sovereigns of Europe are too poor to purchase." Mr. Everett reminded Congress on the 19th of May, 1830, that they had already seized, by pretended treaty with the Indians, two hundred and thirty millions of acres,—an amount increased, when Mr. Schoolcraft compiled his statistical tables, to more than four hundred millions. The Osages alone gave up twenty-nine million acres for an annuity of a thousand dollars—which

* *Seven Years in Central America*, ch. v., p. 272.
† *Four Years in British Columbia*, ch. xiii., p. 356.
‡ *Narrative of a Mission to Bokhara*, vol. i., ch. ii., p. 54.

would hardly pay for the strong drinks by which the treaty was consecrated.* Many cases were still more flagrant in their mockery of justice. During the whole period of the Anglo-Saxon rule the same policy was pursued, and for nearly two hundred years men bearing the name of Christians have scandalized the pagan tribes of America by their unscrupulous fraud. "Your people," said the orators of the Six Nations to Sir William Johnson, in 1755, "when they buy a small piece of land from us, by stealing they make it large;" and Sir William confessed that it was true. The Delawares, he told the English authorities, "would never leave off killing the English;" for "they were determined to drive all Englishmen off their lands which the English had cheated them out of."†

The Americans have imitated the English, and defraud the Indian, now at their mercy, without even the affectation of justice. The second article of the "Treaty with the Winnibagoes," in 1846, imposes upon them the resignation "of all lands, wherever situated, now or heretofore occupied by said Indians," and assigns, "as their home," a tract west of the Mississippi, "*provided* such land can be obtained on just and reasonable terms."‡ *Twelve* treaties, we learn, "have been made by the United States with the Muskogee nation (Creeks), and each of them has been a treaty of cession;" while the *remnant* of their lands was "in each case solemnly guaranteed to them by the United States." At length, they were slain to the last man, not by hunters or pioneers, whose lawlessness might have found an apologist, but by an organized military force, under the command of General Jackson, afterwards President of the United States!§

The Cherokees also, though their territory had been guaranteed to them "forever" by a formal act of the United States government, were ordered, in spite of their comparative progress in civilization, to be sent to a district west of the Arkansas, which Major Long had reported to be "uninhabitable," being "nearly all a boundless prairie, and destitute of running water during a part of every year."‖

The treatment of the Senecas was of the same kind. They had already been banished from the homes of their fathers, but still possessed more than one hundred thousand acres of "reserved" land, secured to them by solemn treaties. In the

* De Tocqueville, tome iii., ch. v., p. 123.

† *Doc. Hist. N. York*, vol. ii., pp. 750–52.

‡ *The Statutes at Large and Treaties of the U. S. of America*, 1846–7; ed. Minot.

§ Featherstonhaugh, vol. ii., ch. 41.

‖ *Rights of the Indians*, a Memorial to Congress, p. 9 (Boston, 1830).

lapse of time this land had increased in value, and the "Land Company," an association of speculators, resolved to rob them of it. "The United States Commissioner," we are told, "entered into the scheme." Ashamed to appear openly as a party to a nefarious fraud, this officer hid himself in a tavern at Buffalo, and directed his operations from that place of concealment. The design was to bribe, cajole, or compel the Senecas to resign their inheritance. "Runners were hired to scour the forests, and bring in every chief who could be prevailed upon, by fair means or foul, to sign the assent. Spirituous liquor was employed to intoxicate them, false representations to deceive them, threats to intimidate them, and vain hopes to allure them." But after every effort, only thirty-one out of eighty-one chiefs could be induced to sign, and finally they were forced to remove, as American witnesses complain, "by deception and fraud perhaps without parallel in the dark history of oppression and wrong to which the aborigines of our country have been subjected."*

And even these facts do not complete the contrast which marks the history of Catholic and Protestant colonization on this continent; for in the rare cases in which a tribe is permitted for a season to occupy some remote tract, insufficient for their wants unless they till the soil, and which their rulers are not yet prepared to utilize, the niggard concession, as even American writers complain, is only made a pretext for new frauds. "The governmental philanthropy," says Mr. Olmsted in 1857, "*is in practice only a job*, in which, as usual, the least possible is done, and the utmost possible is paid."† The annuity system, which the most eminent authority calls "that delusive means of Indian subsistence," is in practice only profitable to the agents employed under it, while "few of the annuitants reach their home with a dime. Most of them have expended all, and lost their time in addition."‡

A few, indeed, such as the Kikapoos, live as yet on the reserved lands of the "Indian territory," but, as an English traveller informs us, they "are greatly demoralized," precisely because they are "in the vicinity of civilization!" The men are addicted to intoxication, and the women to unchastity; "both sexes and all ages are inveterate beggars, whose principal industry is horse-stealing."§

The Americans, then, by their own confession, have only

* *The Case of the Seneca Indians*, p. 7 (Philadelphia, 1840). Cf. *Plea for the Indians*, addressed to Congress, by the Citizens of Hartford, Connecticut, p. 8.

† *Texas*, p. 298.

‡ Schoolcraft, *Notes on the Iroquois*, ch. i., pp. 12–13.

§ Burton, ch. i., p. 25.

pursued in their dealings with the Indians the cruel policy bequeathed to them by the English. Refusing to adopt from them other precedents, they have imitated them too well in this. And the inevitable result has been to add a deeper intensity to the scorn and disgust which the savage, not without cause, had already conceived for a religion which he was told was Christianity, and for the agents who were presented to him as its teachers. Such a religion, and such teachers, seemed to him so little Divine, that he scarcely deemed them human. "By Christians," observes Mr. Möllhausen, "they have been cheated and betrayed—driven from the grounds of their fathers, and cut down like wild beasts—and for this reason they have repelled missionaries with displeasure and contempt." They saw in such missionaries only traders and speculators, whose largest conception of purity, justice, and self-denial only consisted in constantly violating the two first in their own practice, and never recommending the last save to their victims. In 1821, the Indians had seen a band of so-called missionaries appropriate "a tract of land, consisting of about fifteen thousand acres, from the Osage Indians."* Ten years later, when a tribe in Indiana spontaneously offered land to the governor of the State for the maintenance of *Catholic* missionaries, their petition was answered by an embassy of Protestant ministers, attracted by the prospect of gain, and who contrived to filch from them by fraud one thousand eight hundred and twenty acres.† "Genuine religion has suffered much," says Professor R. Bishop, the historian of *The Sects in Kentucky*, from "the money-making and speculating spirit" of these singular "missionaries."‡

There is something terrible in the disdain which, in our own as in other times, the Indian manifests towards the emissaries of Protestantism. "They treat me," Mr. Kirkland has candidly told us, "with no more respect than they would show to a dog." Many years after, in 1821, a famous chief thus expressed to the Governor of New York his opinion of the same class: "I have observed that whenever they came among the Indians, they

* *Fathers of the London Missionary Society*, vol. ii., app., p. 604.

† *Annales*, tome vi., p. 158.

‡ Quoted by Spalding, ch. vi., p. 88. Considering the character which a multitude of witnesses give of the American clergy, it is not surprising that the so-called missionaries of the same nation should be what an English writer calls "*itinerant livelihood seekers*." Mr. Tilley mentions that he heard one of them lecture at St. Francisco. "His lecture commenced, *secundem artem*, by well abusing the Romanists. He then proceeded to a relation of his own 'call.' He had been a common sailor and a vagabond, but had become a Protestant missionary. His logic was sublime. 'I waited,' said he, 'till I received promises of support to the amount of one thousand dollars a year, and then I started off.'" *Japan, the Amoor*, &c., ch. x., p. 185.

always excited enmities and quarrels amongst them, . . . and that the Indians *were sure to dwindle and decrease* in proportion to the number of preachers that came among them." And then he noticed a recent case: "We have been threatened by Mr. Hyde, that unless we listen to his preaching and become Christians we shall be turned off our lands. We wish to know from the governor if this is to be so; and if he has no right to say so, we think *he* ought to be turned off our lands, and not allowed to plague us any more. We shall never be at peace while he is among us."* Mr. Hyde was removed.

Ten years later, the celebrated *Black Hawk* accepted a treaty with the United States at Prairie du Chien, and in the presence of the American officials the noble savage spoke as follows of the colleagues of Mr. Hyde: "The white men are bad schoolmasters. They smile in the face of the poor Indians, to cheat them, to deceive them, and ruin their wives. They poisoned us by their touch. We were not safe. We were becoming like them, hypocrites and liars, adulterers, lazy drones, all talkers, and no workers."† Is it wonderful if the chiefs sometimes said, in words which have already been quoted, "Our young men do not listen to *them* any better than to ourselves; we wish for Catholic priests?"

Almost at the same moment the chief of the Kansas went to St. Louis to obtain a missionary. A Protestant minister offered to return with him to his tribe. "The chief, eyeing him, said with a smile, 'This is not what I ask; this man apparently has a wife and children, like myself and other men of my tribe. I do not wish him. Whenever I come to St. Louis I go to the great house (church) of the French. There I see Blackrobes who have no wives or children. These are the men I ask.' "‡ A few hours later, Father Lutz was descending the Mississippi with the Kansas chief. "Brother," said the most famous of all the Seneca chiefs, at a great meeting held at Buffalo by the request of the missionaries, "you say you have not come to get our land or our money, but to enlighten our minds. I will now tell you that I have been at your meetings, and saw you collecting money from the meeting. I cannot tell what this money was intended for, but suppose it was for your minister; and if we should conform to your way of thinking, perhaps you may want some from us."§

"My friends," replied an Ojibbeway chief not long ago to the invitation of some English ministers, "we believe that

* Drake, book v., ch. vi., p. 103.
† Id., ch. x., p. 161.
‡ Shea, *Catholic Missions*, &c., ch. xxv., p. 457.
§ Id., ch. vi. p. 103. Cf. *Events in Indian History*, ch. vi., p. 246 (1842).

the white people have two tongues." And then he gave the following reason for thinking so: "A black coat came amongst us in the town where I live, and told us the same words as you have spoken this morning. He said that the religion of the white men was the only good religion; and some began to believe him, and after a while a great many believed him, and then he wanted us to help him to build a house, and we did so. We lifted very hard at the logs, and when it was done many sent their children to him to learn to read, and some girls got so as to read the good Book, and their fathers were very proud of it; and at last one of these girls had a baby, and not long after another had a baby, and then the black coat ran away, and we have never seen him since. My friends, we do not think this right. I believe there is another black coat now in the same house. Some of the Indians send their boys there to learn to read, but they dare not let their girls go. My friends, this is all I have to say."*

The estimate which the Indians have formed, after an unvarying experience of two centuries, of the habits and character of the Protestant emissaries, has naturally created in them, as in the pagans of every other land, the invincible repugnance which their sullen attitude attests, and has aggravated tenfold their passionate aversion to Christianity. If preachers of another order, men of austere virtue, admirable patience, and unwearied charity, could only win them to the Cross at the price of prodigious labors and sufferings, and often at the cost of life itself, we may easily comprehend the failure of another class, who only excite, as we have seen, their contempt and abhorrence. "The American Indian," says a late report of one of the most opulent missionary associations of the western continent, "are, for the most part, yet unblessed with the knowledge of Jesus Christ!"† What more effective proof can we desire of the monstrous contrast which we have traced in these volumes, and of which the history of missions in North and South America supplies the last, and perhaps the most impressive example?

There might still be hope of the effectual conversion of the few remaining tribes, though the task becomes more difficult every year, if Catholic missionaries were the sole representatives of Christianity. It is by the presence of the agents of Protestantism, and not by the indifference or obduracy of the Indian, that their labor is now frustrated. When Father Laverlochère

* Catlin, vol. i., p. 165; 2d edition.

† Western Foreign Missionary Society; see *Foreign Missionary Chronicle*, p. 51 (Pittsburgh).

visited the Sioux at Fort Albany, in 1849, amongst whom a Protestant missionary had dwelt for many years, and urged them to embrace the Faith, this was their reply: "The prayer-man who has been with us is only a rogue and a pretender. *You, too, may be the same.*" And they refused to listen to him.* Such is the fatal result of the presence of Protestant missionaries. They make the conversion of the heathen *impossible.*†

Yet it is in this point alone that the American government, rarely unjust to Catholics, uses all its influence on the side of evil. When the Ottawas applied, in 1829, for Catholic missionaries, their petition was answered, as usual, by a prompt dispatch of Protestant ministers. It is true that the Indians drove them away, with this emphatic admonition: "Keep your errors for yourselves; our nation does not want missionaries with wives and children, but the *Blackrobes*, like those who visited our grandfathers."‡ And three years later, Father Rézé could say, writing from New York, "It is truly admirable to see these good Ottawas all converted in the space of three years, and become excellent Christians."§ We have seen that Mrs. Jameson confirms this account of the Ottawas, from her own observation, in 1852. But the executive authorities,—and this is perhaps the heaviest reproach which they have incurred,—though all these facts are known to them, and have been confessed without reserve, still neglect too often the prayer of the Indian, even while admitting that it is just. They know that Catholic missionaries alone can win him to Christianity, and they continue to send him men who bind his neck with chains while they talk of liberty, who create a desert and call it civilization. The Winnebagoes were not only refused the services of Father Petiot, but forced to pay for a Protestant missionary whom they despised; and this although Mr. McGregor, the agent, reported in 1844, that "it was questionable policy to force them to receive instruction from a class to whom they objected."‖ When the chief of the Kansas nation wrote to General Clark for a *Blackrobe*, the agent, though a Protestant, reported officially in forwarding the application, that "only Catholic priests can succeed in these missions." When

* *Annals*, xii., 163 (English edition).

† It is worthy of observation that the Sioux nation, originally capable of a high degree of civilization, are described by a well-known writer in 1853, as "degraded *by their intercourse with the whites*," and that in 1862 they showed their appreciation of the latter, by massacring five hundred of them at once in the State of Minnesota. *Homes of the New World*, by Frederika Bremer, vol. ii., p. 291, letter xxvii.

‡ *Annales*, tome iv., p. 475.

§ Tome vi., p. 180.

‖ Shea, ch. xxi., p. 400.

Monseigneur Dubourg, the venerated Bishop of New Orleans, visited the President and his ministers at Washington, "it was readily admitted that Catholic priests were fitter for the work than Protestant ministers;" and the Minister for War, frankly confirming the admission, said to the bishop, "Above all, try to procure Jesuits."*

It is confessed, then, by all that is noble and high-minded in the United States,—though the confession comes many years too late,—that while the influence of Protestantism has only tended, during two hundred years, to propagate corruption, disorder, and death among the native tribes, the Catholic missionary, alone and unaided, as destitute of all material resources as his Indian disciple, but filled with the power of the Holy Ghost, has never failed to win him, by the force of his own example, and the Divine gifts of which he is the steward and minister, to peace, contentment, industry, and virtue. What Protestantism has done for the Red Man is written in history. Even its professional advocates confess the truth which they dare not deny. "Alas!" exclaimed one of them fifty years ago, "what has not our nation to answer for at the bar of retributive justice!"

Nearly half a century later, the same confession was once more repeated, in presence of the American Senate, with especial reference to the Florida war, and its disastrous results. "The origin of this war is the same with all our Indian wars. It lies deep, beyond the power of eradication, in the mighty wrongs we have heaped upon the miserable nations of these lands. Three hundred years have rolled into the bosom of eternity since the white man put his foot on these shores, and every day and hour, and every moment, has been marked with some act of cruelty and oppression. . . . . I consider the fate of the Indian as inevitably fixed. He must perish. The decree of extermination has long since gone forth, and the execution of it is in rapid progress. Avarice, Sir, has counted their acres and their power; force and avarice march on together to their destruction."†

Finally, in the year 1861, one of the most conspicuous religious teachers of Protestant America thus estimates, once more, in the presence of his congregation, the unrepented guilt of which the final reckoning is still to come. "Our nation has more sins than one. Its criminal treatment of the Indians is a fit subject for shame. *Every crime in the calendar has been*

* Henrion, tome ii., 2de partie, p. 664.

† *Speech of the Hon. Mr. Hopkinson,* quoted by Macdonald, *British Columbia, &c.,* ch. v., p. 133.

committed against them: slow persecution; the breaking of every treaty made with them when found convenient; and the robbery of their lands."* He only omits the worse crime of all—the cruelty which deprived them of the very teachers who had proved a thousand times, that they, and they alone, could have done for them exactly what their fellow-apostles had done for their more favored brethren in the South.

Such is the contrast, immense and irreparable, which may be resumed in these two admitted results—that while in the *South*, nearly sixteen hundred thousand Indian Catholics are found at this day, though robbed for sixty years of their pastors, still inflexible in the faith, and proof against the assaults of heresy and unbelief, besides whole nations in Central America, Mexico, and California; in the vast territories of the *North*, from Oregon to Florida, and from Boston to Santa Fé, barely three hundred thousand Indians, remnant of a thousand tribes, now survive, of whom nearly all who are not Catholics are pagans. In 1851, the total number of Indians in the territory of the United States was three hundred and eighty-eight thousand two hundred and twenty-nine.† In 1858, they had dwindled to three hundred and fourteen thousand six hundred and twenty-two, being a diminution of nearly *seventy-four thousand* in seven years! while, "in Mexico and South America," as one of the latest writers on the Western Continent observes, "*they still thrive, or increase*, and amalgamate and intermarry with the European races."‡ Such, once more, is that prodigious contrast between the work of the Church and the work of the Sects which we have now traced in every region of the earth, and which, while it has everywhere revealed to us the incurable impotence of human Sects, has displayed in their incomparable beauty those apostolic triumphs of the Christian Church, "to which," by the confession of a hostile witness, "nothing similar has occurred in the whole course of history."§

CONCLUSION.

And now we may conclude this long but imperfect history, of which all the phases were sufficiently known to an English

* Rev. Henry Ward Beecher, quoted in *New York Evening Express*, January 5, 1861.

† Schoolcraft, *Historical and Statistical Information*, &c., part i.

‡ *Life and Liberty in America*, by Charles Mackay, LL.D., ch. xii., pp. 145, 123.

§ Professor Merivale, *Colonization*, &c., lect. x., p. 286.

writer, familiar with men and their works in the United States, to elicit the most remarkable confession ever wrung from a Protestant conscience, and to constrain the unbought avowal, "*The Catholic Faith is the Shield of America.*"* It was, not possible that enlightened men, capable of distinguishing between good and evil, should fail to mark the contrast between the Catholic and Protestant teachers in America. Hence the declaration of Mr. Washington Irving, too strong and free to be caught in the meshes of sectarian bigotry, that the former labored "with a power that no other Christians have exhibited." Hence the homage of Dr. Channing to the Catholic Church, when he said, without deriving instruction from his own words, "Her missionaries who have carried Christianity to the ends of the earth; her Sisters of Charity who have carried relief and solace to the most hopeless want and pain; do not these teach us, that in the Romish Church the Spirit of God has found a home?"† Hence also the sympathy of the just and upright Washington, when he exclaimed, in his "Address to the Catholics of the United States," "May the members of your Society in America, animated alone by the pure spirit of Christianity, enjoy every temporal and spiritual felicity!"‡ Hence too those later confessions of American Protestants, disdaining the peevish malice of their English co-religionists, and frankly expressing the honest admiration which they cherished, not only for the martyred apostles who have long since finished their career, but even for some of their latest successors. "In seeing such men as Cheverus and Matignon," said a Boston writer, when his city hardly knew the Catholic religion but by their labors, "who can doubt that it is possible for human nature to approach and to imitate the God-Man?"§ "Who can forget," says Professor Walters in our own day, with equally generous enthusiasm, "Father Farmer, still venerated by all who knew him;" or "John Carroll, the first Roman Catholic Bishop of Baltimore, the model of prelates, Christians, and scholars," who was sent by Congress to Canada, in 1776, as joint commissioner with Franklin;‖ or "Bishop England, beloved and honored by men of every religious denomination, and even now lamented in the South as one of her best and noblest sons?" Such are the testimonies of men convinced, by actual

* *Englishwoman in America*, ch. iii., p. 95.

† *Works of W. E. Channing*, p. 275; People's edition (1843).

‡ Quoted by Rupp, p. 165.

§ *Boston Monthly Magazine*, June, 1825; quoted in *Vie du Cardinal de Cheverus*, liv. ii., p. 52.

‖ Franklin's *Works*, vol. viii., p. 178; ed. Sparks.

observation, of the truth of that judgment proclaimed by a Protestant writer, in words of almost astonishing candor, "The priesthood of the Catholic Church bear the griefs and carry the sorrows of their infirm and ignorant neighbors, and assuredly come nearer, in their walk through life, to the Saviour's model, than any clergy of any religion whatever;"* an opinion avowed with equal energy by one who had also dwelt in America, and who was constrained by experience to exclaim, "Catholicism seems to me at this time to go beyond Protestantism in the living imitation of Christ in good works."†

It is not in vain, then, that men of God, filled with their Master's presence, and living only for His glory, have evangelized America. The harvest of which they planted the seed has been blighted as far as the natives are concerned, and has still to be reaped and garnered by the race which has cast them out; but already men predict its golden fulness. "If religion, with its immortal hopes," says one of the leading organs of Protestantism in New York, "is to be preserved in the world, and cold infidelity is not to overrun all Europe and America, *there is nothing left but a return to the Catholic Church.*"‡

It is after a journey which has led us through many climes, and carried us into the presence of many nations, that we arrive at length at the close of our long travel. But if we have left far behind, and well-nigh forgotten, such men as Nobrega and Azevedo, Ortega and Baraza, Betanzos and Las Casas, the Blessed Peter Claver and St. Francis Solano,—the evangelists of Brazil and Peru, of Paraguay and Mexico,—it may be permitted to turn once more a parting glance of love and reverence towards the heroes and apostles whom other men and other scenes have almost pushed from our memory. What words can express, what judgment measure, the immense and indelible contrast between the religious history of Brazil and New England, of Paraguay and Virginia, of Peru and Canada? Who but God shall judge between the two classes of men who lived to glorify Him in the one, to dishonor Him in the other? What less unerring and deep-searching eye can penetrate, in all their details, the secret motives, unpublished thoughts, and unrevealed desires, which *we* can only judge in part by their exterior signs? Who shall estimate, on the one hand, the martyr's love, the apostle's toil, the disciple's faith, victorious in suffering and triumphant in death; or take note,

* *Englishwoman in America*, ch. ii., p. 78.
† Bremer, *Homes of the New World*, vol. ii., p. 344.
‡ *New York Herald*, quoted in *Morning Star*, August 23, 1859.

on the other, without partiality or excess, of the cowardice which trembled even in its safe retreats, the luxury which cried piteously for more delicate fare, the avarice which cheated the pagan of his lands, and the cruelty which robbed him of his life? Who shall recompense the labor which won a thousand tribes to the Cross, and converted the waste places of the earth into a smiling garden; or chastise the sloth, the meanness, and the treachery which could turn a paradise into a desert, uproot the fair plants which gentler hands had reared, and make the conversion of the heathen impossible even while pretending to secure it? Lastly, who but God who gave it shall assay the almost omnipotent charity which could knit together ten thousand savages in mutual love, and in the bonds of that indissoluble unity which two centuries of trial could not rend; who but He, the supremely Just, shall compare with His own gifts to His apostles, the vanity, fickleness, and caprice of another order of men, who were so little able to devise a definite and uniform doctrine, that they could only invent new forms of error in which there was nothing permanent but the pride which conceived and the malice which begot them, and which moved even the derision of the mocking savage, and forced from him at last the bitter taunt, "If I should have a mind to turn Christian, I could not tell what religion to be of!"

Such is the contrast which we have attempted to trace, in every state and province of this vast continent, and which may again be summed up in this pregnant conclusion—that in America, the Church has created a hundred Christian nations, while the Sects have not only failed to build up one, but have destroyed even those which the missionaries of the Cross had begun to form, and have made a waste and a desert where *they* would have planted a paradise.

In reviewing such a history, which has conducted us by a gradual progress from the glories of Brazil and Colombia, of Peru and Paraguay, to the shameful annals of Virginia and Maryland, of New England and California,—from the fruitful toils of the apostles of Jesus to the sordid and sterile schemes of human sects,—we have exhausted, within the compass of a single continent, every proof which history can furnish of the momentous truth which it has been our purpose to illustrate in these volumes. The story of American missions, even if it borrowed no light from the exactly parallel records of every other land, would constitute a revelation of the Divine mind as clear and distinct as that which was delivered amid the thunders of Mount Sinai, or announced in softer accents from the summit of Mount Thabor. It tells us, as plainly as if the voice were that of Moses or Elias, of St. Luke or St. John, that in our own age, as in every other, the God of Christians works by the Church and not by the Sects; and it does this with such an overwhelming array of evidence, that while the barbarians of a hundred tribes have attained to eternal life by joyfully confessing it, men whose prejudices are deeper and more incurable than theirs have at least been so far impressed by it as to declare, but only with barren and unavailing regret,—"It must be allowed to reflect honor on the Roman Catholic Church, and to cast a deep shade on the history of Protestantism."*

* Prichard, *ubi supra.*

CHAPTER X.

SUMMARY.

WHEN our Lord would instruct His children how to distinguish, in every age, between true and false apostles, He gave them this precept—*By their fruits ye shall know them.* It is by this test that we have estimated the work of Catholic and Protestant missionaries in all parts of the world, and it is time to review the conclusions to which it has brought us. This shall be our present attempt.

Two classes of men have appeared before us in the history which we have now completed. Both claimed to be ambassadors from God to the lands of the heathen. Brothers in outward form, and kinsmen in the order of nature, in all else they have differed so widely, that we might almost deem them beings of a separate race. Every thing in them exists only in contrast,—faith and works, motive and action, life and death. The one, models of sanctity, of prudence, and heroism, have run through all lands like tongues of fire, kindling every dry branch, bidding the sleeper awake, subduing the fierce and bowing down the strong; the others, often profoundly immoral, and in their highest mood only patterns of domestic propriety, have moved even the pagan to doubt whether they professed any religion whatever. Yet both were children of a common parent, subject to the same infirmities, and filled, at the outset of their career, with the same natural gifts. In spite of this common nature and origin, the one became apostles and martyrs, the others only tourists and merchants.

Whence this prodigious contrast between men otherwise equally endowed? What is that mysterious gift which has been imparted to the one, and refused to the others? What but the call and election of Him whom both profess to serve, but who has said to the first, "*Go, teach all nations;*" while He has declared of the last, "*I did not send them, yet they ran: I have* *not spoken to them, yet they prophesied.*"* Herein lies the interpretation of the mystery. Let us consider, then, what is the vocation to the apostolate, and what are its fruits.

There was one of old, in the very beginning of Christianity, whose claim to the title of Apostle no man has ever doubted. In the broad light of day, in the midst of his companions, the hand of God fell upon him. From that hour, blind and stunned, but soon to be filled with a heavenly light, the persecutor began to be an apostle. And what were the marks of his vocation? He, who best knew, has told us. Though "the least of the apostles" in the order of election, he could offer, when provoked to compare himself with others, these proofs of his calling. "Are they ministers of Christ? I am more. In many more labors, *in prisons more frequently, in stripes above measure, in deaths often.* Of the Jews five times I received forty stripes save one. Thrice was I beaten with rods, once I was stoned; . . . ." and then this man—already eight times scourged to blood; perpetually imprisoned; expelled by force from Antioch; cruelly assaulted at Iconium; let down in a basket by night from the walls of Damascus, because the Jews "watched the gates that they might kill him;" mangled with stones at Lystra, and dragged out of the city by a furious rabble, "thinking him to be dead;" brutally flogged at Philippi, where a jailer washed his bleeding back; hardly escaping with life from Thessalonica; almost torn to pieces in Jerusalem; bound again with fetters in Cæsarea; always in perils, in vigils, and labors; "in hunger and thirst, in fastings often, in cold and nakedness;" and at last, after long years of suffering, to be cut asunder by a pagan sword—could venture to say, "Let no man trouble me: I bear in my body *the marks of the Lord Jesus.*"

Such, in the judgment of St. Paul, are the signs of an apostle. To labor, to suffer, to die; to "fill up those things that are wanting of the sufferings of Christ;" yet in suffering to rejoice, and in dying to overcome; these are the fruits of his vocation. And for this reason it is that the history of the evangelization of the heathen in every land, and in every age, is simply a martyrology. The path of the true apostle, like that of his Master, is a path of blood. Everywhere you may track his steps by that sign. At Jerusalem as at Rome, at Smyrna as at Antioch, at Lyons as at Corinth, by the rivers of Germany as in the plains of Poland, in the forests of Hindostan as in the cities of China, by the mountains of Brazil and Peru as by the frozen lakes of Canada—everywhere there is blood. Xavier and de Britto, Sanz and Dufresse, Ortega and Baraza, Brebeuf and Lallemand,

* Jeremias xxiii. 21.

and a thousand more, what are they but heirs of St. Paul, displaying the same vocation, accepting the same torments, and able to affirm with him, "Are they ministers of Christ? I am more."

And it is by virtue of this vocation alone that they, and such as they, "wrought justice," and "conquered kingdoms." Yet who can tell us all which that vocation includes? Evidently, if we would attempt to describe, or even to comprehend, a state and calling so far above our own,—to know what it is to be summoned by God to the sublime dignity of the apostolate,—we must interrogate that illustrious company upon whom the lot has fallen. From *them* we learn how the apostle of Jesus Christ has received, often from his earliest youth, sometimes even in childhood, a vocation to the immediate service of the King of kings. And this first call, they tell us, is only the beginning of that supernatural career to which the chosen one is now destined. The gift of God is not barren, but a very fountain of power and life. With the vocation, therefore, He confers, in due season, all which it implies and presupposes; death to self and the world, boundless charity, and invincible fortitude. Then follow, in their harmonious order, the spirit of wisdom, of counsel, and of strength; until at length the elect messenger, docile to every inspiration of grace, and armed with the whole panoply of apostolic gifts, begins his appointed work. From that hour he no longer knows, except in God, father, or mother, or kinsfolk; for he can say with St. Paul, "Henceforth we know no man according to the flesh,"—and with the first apostle of China, "We have God for our Father, all mankind for brothers, and the world for a home." Charged to offer henceforth a sacrifice of expiation, suffering is not the object of his dread, but of his ardent desire; and death, no matter in what form, so it be that of martyrdom, is now the prize which he covets, the destined crown of all his toil. "I have specially solicited this grace," says one of whom we have read in these pages, "every time I elevated the Precious Blood in the holy sacrifice of the Mass." To "die daily" is henceforth the very condition of his life, and this he consents to do, by virtue of that mighty interior grace, without which the existence of the Catholic missionarywould be simply impossible to human nature.

Such is the vocation to the apostolate, the highest to which mortal man can aspire, and compared with which regal or imperial state is paltry and obscure. To God alone it belongs to choose those who shall be admitted to this superhuman life, because He alone can give the wisdom and strength which make such a life possible to a fallen race. "Woe to the priest," says one who evangelized India, "who comes to this land without being called of God. He would be the most unfortunate of men, and would provoke his own downfall and that of many others."* But if he be called indeed, then the apostle may set forth on his journey, for the hand of God is upon him, and he must go whithersoever it shall lead him. Whether his path be over the burning sands of India, or along the ice-bound shores of northern climes, or in the far-off islands of the great sea, his mission is sure. He may succeed, or he may seem to fail; but if he triumph, the glory belongs to his Master; if he fall, as sooner or later he will do, his fall shall win an eternal crown for himself. Such is the vocation, such the destiny, of the apostle of Christ.

And now if we inquire, on the other hand, by whom the false apostles are commissioned, and under what auspices they set out, a monstrous contrast is revealed. If we would interrogate these men, or watch them at their work, we must quit the paradise of holy thoughts and pure desires, and descend to the dismal regions of vanity, covetousness, and caprice. Speak not to *them* of that dread apostolic vocation which to their apprehension is only a fiction, and which Protestant missionaries are so far from asserting, that they would be the first to disclaim it, some with fear, others with passionate contempt. "The very notion of a *call* to the ministry," their advocates now admit, "*seems to have died out* in English society."† "Our clergy," says another, "as a sacred order or class, *have ceased to exist*."‡ Ask them not, therefore, who called, or who sent them? If they bear in their body "the marks of the Lord Jesus?" If they have "made themselves eunuchs for the kingdom of heaven's sake?" With fluent jest, or angry taunt, they will mock you; perhaps even defame the gifts and graces which such as they neither possess nor understand. In accepting the wages of some "missionary society" they have only chosen a craft or calling, like any other; they have secured a livelihood, and usually a more luxurious one than they could have obtained at home. It is their own employers who declare it. Many of them, we have been told by Berkeley, "quit their country on no other motive." "It is only a certain kind of business with most of them," says a living writer who had watched their proceedings in many lands, "a calling by which, as in commerce and trade, to make a living."§ Accordingly, before they set out, bound and fettered in every limb with worldly ties, they have

* *Annales*, iv., p. 155.
† *Saturday Review*, January 21, 1860.
‡ Laing, *Notes of a Traveller*, ch. xxi., p. 433.
§ Gerstaecker, vol. ii., ch. vii., p. 234.

carefully arranged, with minutest detail, the salary which they are to receive, and the mode of payment; perhaps even, like the Anglican clergy in India, the exact allowance upon which they are to retire—for they have learned from the "Bishop of Calcutta" that "asceticism is no part of the Gospel system." Plague and pestilence are excluded by the terms of their contract; and if. in spite of every precaution, the unwelcome visitor appears, they flee before it. The sickness of a wife or a child terminates their mission at once. They are only men, fathers of a family, or solicitous to become so, and do not profess to be apostles. To be pensioners of God,—to hunger and thirst,—to be scourged or imprisoned,—this is an enthusiasm which only excites their disdain. To be "in fastings often," to "endure hardness," to have "no fixed abode," not even "where to lay the head,"—this is an "asceticism" which they condemn, a "fanaticism" which they despise, though it be the asceticism of St. Paul, the fanaticism of the Son of God. It would evidently be irrational to talk of a "*vocation*" here. God does not take counsel in heaven about the going forth of such men as these. They have, like the birds of the air and the beasts of the field, the protection of His ordinary providence; more they do not desire or expect.

This, then, is the first point of contrast which the facts reviewed in these pages have disclosed to us between Catholic and Protestant missionaries to the heathen. The one have a vocation from God, the others have not. And both the tenor of their life and the fruits of their labor reveal the influence of this original disparity. They are Protestant witnesses who have told us, in every land, what is the character of either; how the servants of the Church show the marks of *vocation*, how the agents of the Sects display the absence of it. They are Protestants who have unconsciously described to us the phases of that conflict, in which, though all human means were on one side and none on the other, the issue was always the same; and in which we seem to witness in our own day, but on a larger scale and with more impressive results, the application of that terrible test which Elias dared to propose, long ages ago, to the servants of Baal, when he said, "Call ye on the names of your gods, and I will call on the name of my Lord: and *the God that shall answer by fire*, let him be God."* Once more we have heard the false prophets calling, "from morn even till noon," for the fire from heaven which will not descend at their cry. Once more we have listened to the prayer of the true apostle, sure of his own vocation, and venturing to

* 3 Kings xviii. 24.

deluge the sacrifice, the altar, and the trench round about it, with floods of water; but at whose word "the fire of the Lord fell, and consumed the holocaust, and the wood, and the stones, and the dust, and licked up the water that was in the trench." They are enemies, more implacable than the ministers of Baal, who have unwittingly recounted for us this memorable scene, not, as of old, in the solitudes of Mount Carmel, but in every continent of the earth, and every island of the sea. Let us review again, for the last time, a few of the testimonies which we have heard, and visit once more, but only for a moment, the lands which we have already traversed.

GENERAL CONTRAST.

I. During half a century, Protestant writers, filled with the same involuntary admiration which the pagans had often manifested with greater energy, have not ceased to celebrate the courage, devotion, and charity of the Catholic missionaries in China. From Ricci to the latest martyr who gained his crown only yesterday, they have recognized, without understanding, the same tokens of a supernatural calling. Even Morrison was constantly comparing them with himself, though apparently without deriving instruction from the contrast. "He is willing to sacrifice himself—he offers himself up to God," is his account of one whom he could agree to admire, at a safe distance. "They will be equalled by few, and rarely exceeded by any," is the joint confession of Mr. Milne and Mr. Medhurst, "for they spared not their lives unto the death, but overcame by the blood of the Lamb." "That they were holy and devoted men," says Mr. Malcolm, in spite of rooted antipathies, "is proved by their pure lives and serene martyrdom." "They appeared to me," observes Mr. Power, "to surpass any men I ever met with, they were so forgetful of self, so full of pity and compassion for others." "Their self-denying hard labor is truly wonderful," says Mr. D'Ewes. "It is a pity that all missionaries are not equally self-sacrificing," adds Mr. Scarth. "We cannot refuse them our respect," says Colonel Mountain. "To such men," observes Captain Blakiston, "is due praise which I am unworthy to proclaim." "*They* regard neither difficulties nor discouragements," writes Mr. Sirr, who vainly sought the same qualities in their luxurious rivals. "I cannot refrain," exclaims Mr. Robertson, "from admiring the heroism, the devotedness, and the superiority of the Catholic missionaries." And the pagans repeat, but with deeper emphasis and more exact discrimination, the reluctant eulogies of Protestants, humbly begging forgiveness of the apostles whom they torment, or asking a blessing from those whom they murder.

On the other hand, the same impartial witnesses, who had seen them at their work, speak only with sorrow or disgust of the Protestant missionaries in China, in spite of active sympathy with their religious opinions. Morrison, they tell us, "never ventured out of his house," preached only "with the doors securely locked," gave books with such precautions that "it could not be traced to him," and only ventured on operations which were "not of a dazzling or heroic order." Milne "found preaching the Gospel difficult in China," and ran away. Gutzlaff made his fortune, and then "ceased to call himself a missionary." Medhurst could only repeat, "Why are we not successful in conversions?" Tomlin abandoned the work to "the Pope, Mahomed, and Brahma." Smith was content to revile the men whom he dared not imitate, to fling Bibles on "dry banks," and to provoke the scornful rebukes of his own flock. The rest "listened to far-off tidings of what was happening in the interior," or "drank wine and played at cards on Sunday," or "refused to visit the sick in the hospitals," or accepted "a skulking and precarious sojourn in obscurity and disguise." Such is the *Protestant* account of them. "They surround themselves with comforts," says Mr. Power, "squabble for the best houses, higgle for wares, and provoke contempt by a lazy life." "We are grieved to the heart's core," writes Mr. Sirr, "to see too many of the Protestant missionaries occupy their time in secular pursuits, trading and trafficking." "They are mere stipendiary agents of a company," says one Protestant writer. "They will not encounter risks or hazard dangers like the Catholics," reports a second. "They adopt a low tone of morality and bring humiliation on their order," writes a third. "They have no more devotion than a boot-jack," says a fourth. And the pagan Chinese, quite as discerning as these English and American Protestants, and much more exacting in their estimate of religious teachers, speak of them in their houses, and greet them in the streets, with the title of "*Lie-preaching devils.*"

The contrast exhibited in these testimonies need not surprise us. How should even Protestants consent to employ milder terms in describing the two classes, of whom the one consists of such men as Ricci and Schaal, Verbiest and Parennin, de Rhodes and de Fontaney, Borie and Imbert, Jaccard and Gagelin, de Maistre and Chapdelaine, Marette and Perboyre, Sanz and Dufresse, Melchior and Diaz, and hundreds like them; and the other of such as Morrison and Gutzlaff, Tomlin and Kidd, Gillespie and Williams, Edkins and Smith?

The converts, as we have seen,—of whom a million belong to the Church, and "five," by a sanguine estimate, to the Sects,—display the same difference of character as their teachers. What the *Catholic* Chinese were, from the sixteenth to the nineteenth century, we know; what they have been since 1805, hostile witnesses have told us. In spite of torments never exceeded in duration and intensity, more than seven hundred thousand have been added to the Church since Timkowski visited Pekin, and found that "many thousand persons had embraced Christianity, even among the members of the imperial family;" and that the President of the Criminal Tribunal in that city was obliged to relax his severity, because "nearly all his relations and servants were Christians." And so exactly have these Chinese neophytes, in every province of the empire, resembled the primitive disciples by the ardor of their faith, the lustre of their piety, and their constancy in torture and death, that even the mandarins, yielding to involuntary enthusiasm, have been forced to confess from their judgment-seats, in presence of so much virtue and heroism, "Truly this Christian religion is a good religion!" while the incessant conversion of their heathen neighbors, in all parts of the empire, has been due, not only to the apostolic zeal of the missionaries, but perhaps still more to the fascination of the unwonted heroism displayed by their own countrymen, and of the sanctity which revealed even to their gross perceptions the mystery of Divine grace, of which they were in turn to become examples.

The rare Protestant converts, on the other hand, the scum of a Chinese seaport, dishonest pensioners of an immoral bounty, objects of suspicion to those whose wages they consented to receive, and of ridicule to those whose religion they affected to adopt; who at one time "run off with the communion plate," at another with "cases of type," or whatsoever else they can lay their hands upon; have been everywhere of such a class, that, in the words of a candid witness, "anxiety to obtain them has been converted into anxiety about those who were obtained." And even the "teachers" and "catechists" employed by English or American missionaries, brutalized by opium, and quite as willing, as Dr. Berncastle observes, to teach Buddhism as Anglicanism or Methodism for the same wages, only accept Protestant baptism as a condition of their employment, and appreciate it so warmly, that, as we have been told, their whole care thenceforth is to prevent others from sharing the baptism with them, lest they should share their wages also.

II. The contrast revealed to us in the Trans-Gangetic provinces is not less complete in those which lie to the west of the Himalays. To compare St. Francis Xavier with Dr. Thomas

Middleton,—de' Nobili with "the rich and fashionable" Kiernander,—the martyr de Britto, who won tens of thousands to Christ, with Schwartz, whose salaried converts "were proverbial for their profligacy,"—Laynez, majestic as the patriarchs of old, with the love-sick and tearful Martyn,—Borghese, who smiled at torture, with the ex-minstrel Buchanan,—Martin, "the martyr of charity," with the vain and flippant Rhenius,—Bouchet, whom men compared to St. Gregory Thaumaturgus, with the refined but semi-pagan Heber,—Belmonte, the martyr, and Bouttari, the "penitent without spot," and Carvalho, beaten to death, and Beschi, at whose feet the wisest Hindoo was content to sit as a scholar; and hundreds more, who lived like St. Paul or St. John the Baptist, with Corrie, or Wilson, or Cotton, respectable fathers of families, who consider that "asceticism is no part of the Gospel system," and live in harmony with their creed—this would be both irksome and unprofitable. By the first the Gospel was preached in India with such irresistible power, in spite of the absence of all human aids, that but for the events in Europe which tore away the apostles from their unfinished work, even Protestants have frankly confessed, "the whole land would probably have been converted." As late as the middle of the eighteenth century, they were still laboring with such astonishing success, still fascinated the Hindoo with such persuasive holiness, that "no missionary converted less than a thousand pagans annually," while some gained almost as many every month. And if the work of these sublime preachers of the Cross, which survived the combined neglect and oppression of sixty years, has been suspended or only imperfectly resumed, it is not that the race of heroes and martyrs is extinct, but because the Hindoo has learned, from the example of his English teachers, to regard Christianity with such ever-deepening contempt and abhorrence, that, as he has often declared, he "would rather go down into hell" than accept such a religion or consort with its professors. When the English are driven out of India, an event which we may anticipate from the justice of God, the apostles of the Church will contend a second time, on more equal terms, with the evil spirits who rule her. Then the Hindoo will have before him once more only teachers whose lives illustrate their doctrines, and manifest, even to his dull gaze, the presence of God; then he will have seen the last, both of the so-called missionaries whose luxury shocks and whose contradictions revolt him, and of their wretched disciples, atheists and outcasts, who only "become worse and worse," as one witness has told us, whom the Anglo-Indians themselves refuse to admit into their houses, "whose lax morality," as

English writers have honestly proclaimed, "shocks the feelings of even their *heathen* countrymen," and whom the missionaries are often obliged to dismiss, "lest they should ruin all their pagan workmen."

III. The Island of Ceylon fills but a small place on the earth's surface, yet if we seek a demonstration that God works by the Church, and not by the Sects, we may find it here. There is no need to compare again the two classes of missionaries, but who can be insensible to the contrast in their disciples? How uniformly they display their respective characteristics! What history is more noble, more suggestive of Divine gifts and influences, than that of the Catholic Cingalese, as narrated by Protestant writers? "Neither corruption nor coercions," says Sir Emerson Tennent,—and we know how freely both were used,—"could induce them to abjure their faith." For three hundred years these feeble Asiatics, by nature effeminate and pusillanimous, have endured every imaginable trial; first the fierce opposition of their pagan countrymen, which they soon wore out by joyful martyrdom; then the merciless cruelty, or more demoralizing bribery, of the Dutch; and finally, during the present century, the patient artifices of the English and Americans, lavishing gold on every side, setting traps for them at one time in the shape of a school, at another of a hospital, and always beginning again to-day, with fresh resources, the project which they tried in vain yesterday. Yet the Cingalese, even peasants and fishermen, only smile at the policy which costs so much and effects so little. Filled, like their fathers, with that supernatural faith which outlives all assaults, they compel their most cruel adversaries to confess their inflexible stability, religious zeal, and unbroken unity, while even their pagan neighbors openly compare their loving obedience, generosity, and devotion, with the dissensions, incredulity, and indifference of their English rulers.

And what has Protestantism effected, with its gold and its tracts, its government patronage and missionary pensions, among the natives of Ceylon? It has gathered, as its own advocates tell us, at enormous cost, and after the incessant efforts of half a century, a handful of degraded followers, whose allegiance is never secure for twenty-four hours, who worship devils in secret, hurry from the Protestant temple to *purify* themselves in their own, and when sickness or sorrow comes upon them, abandon in all haste the impotent religion which they had affected to adopt, but which has made no impression on their heart, has left their conscience untouched, their intellect uninformed, and their will unsubdued.

IV. In the Antipodes, England and Protestantism found three

nations expecting their rule: two they have already destroyed, and the third is making haste to disappear. Nothing, we learn from official authority in 1860, can now save "a population which has once reached such a state of decrepitude." And their moral corresponds with their physical condition. "Uncleanliness," says one of their Protestant teachers, "outwardly and inwardly, in body and mind, in all their thoughts, words, and actions," is as rottenness in the bones of this doomed people. "Their *spiritual* declension," also, says another missionary, in 1862, "*is general;*" so that, in the words of Archdeacon Brown, "the wheels of our missionary chariot drag heavily." After the efforts of fifty years, and an expenditure which baffles computation, this is their condition, by the confession of the missionaries themselves, who confess in their latest reports not only "the nominal Christianity" of those who still profess it, but the still graver fact of "the *return* of many individuals to the native customs," and their refusal to hold any further intercourse with the missionaries; while the *religion* of their ill-fated disciples, though educated by them from infancy, is frankly described by still more competent witnesses as "*a mere name*," or, at best, "a rude mixture of paganism and the Cross." When sick or afflicted, "they appeal," says Dr. Thomson, like the Protestant Cingalese, "to their old gods for health;" while in the hour of prosperity, they still secretly honor them with prudent foresight, "lest they should punish them with sickness!" Yet New Zealand, to which Protestantism has proved so deadly a malediction, enjoys the presence of five Anglican bishops, besides a multitude of preachers of various sects; whose combined labors have been so utterly barren of all but woe to this once noble and vigorous race, that a Protestant writer could unwittingly publish in 1859 this bitter satire: "The work of Christianity in New Zealand is only begun!" It will be finished, we may anticipate, when the last New Zealander has sunk into the grave which is already yawning for him.

Such, by Protestant testimony, has been the conclusion of all missionary labors in these islands, as far as the natives are concerned; while the British colonists themselves, we are told by those who know them best, "have no religious character," except what Mr. Cholmondeley considers peculiar to his Anglican co-religionists, and which he briefly describes as "the pretence and hypocrisy of the whole thing." These offshoots of the English Establishment are destined, he fears, to become "either Roman Catholics, or atheists and materialists;" while other writers deplore that they are so incurably apathetic or perfidiously insubordinate, that not only "no interest was taken by the public" in any of the projects by which Dr. Selwyn vainly essayed to stimulate their languid zeal, but the iteration of fervent appeals to their "Church principles" only led to their ostentatiously sharing their funds with "the ministers of different religious bodies." Such is the appropriate conclusion of a history which began, as Dr. Lang has informed us, by adultery, drunkenness, and fraud in the "heads of the mission;" and which has exhibited to us Protestant missionaries, during thirty successive years, stumbling over one another in their hot haste to amass gold, and to rob the unsuspecting native both of his land and its produce; while it displayed the same class to the astonished New Zealander as chiefly occupied "in neutralizing each other's labors," or, in the words of Dr. Selwyn, "in inflicting upon them the curses of disunion," and introducing "a counterpart of our own divided and contentious church." Is it wonderful that the sagacious Maori, more impressed by these phenomena—the only results of Protestantism which are absolutely uniform—than Dr. Selwyn, perhaps because less familiar with them, should decide at last, that "Heathenism with love is better than Christianity without it?"

What Bishop Pompallier and his colleagues would have done for these noble savages, now corrupted almost beyond cure, we may easily infer from the triumphs of missionaries of the same order, in many a land, among aboriginal tribes immeasurably more ferocious and degraded. The Omagua was more brutal, the Guarani more bloodthirsty, the Huron less intelligent, than the savage of New Zealand; yet these and a hundred other tribes accepted Christianity and civilization when offered to them by Monroy or Cavallero, by Rasles or Mesnard, and with such fruit, that in vast communities of men so lately sunk in barbarism "not a single mortal sin was committed in twelve months," and that at the present hour their piety and docility are still scoffingly attested by Protestant travellers. But the Catholic missionary in these less favored islands, encountered by weapons more fatal than the knife or the axe, has struggled with only partial success against the more terrible martyrdom of universal corruption which he came too late to heal, of sordid avarice which even his example failed to admonish, and of the incessant religious dissensions which had already reared the pinnacles of the City of Confusion, before he had time to lay the foundations of the City of God.

V. There is no need to trace again the contrast noticed by De la Gravière and Laplace between the natives of the Philippines and of Tahiti, of Wallis and Rarotonga, of Futuna and Hawaii,—between Christians exulting in the faith, and willing to die in its defence, and savages, robbed even of their natural virtues, abhorring the human religion which they were paid to profess, and flinging it away with disgust when the power to control them was lost. Why should we compare again such men as Medina and Sanvitores, Chevron and Bataillon, Chanel and Epaille, Grange and Bachelot, *all martyrs* in fact or desire; with such as Cheever and Bingham, Henry and Williams, Lawry and Bicknell,—traders and adventurers, with hardly an exception, hateful to the barbarians whom they oppressed, as well as to the English and American merchants, who found in them their keenest rivals? What is there in common between missionaries who are described by the *same* Protestant witnesses, on the one hand, as "men of learning and agreeable manners," "exemplary in all their actions," who "astonished the natives by their enthusiasm in the cause of Christ," and won such universal sympathy, that, as Dr. Rae has candidly told us, "I never encountered any one who did not speak in terms of respect of the Catholic priesthood;" and, on the other, according to Sir Edward Belcher and Mr. Forbes, Sir George Simpson and Mr. Melville, Dr. Ruschenberger and Mr. Wheeler, Dr. Meyen and Captain Erskine, and twenty more, as "tyrannical fanatics," or "madly intolerant," or defiled by "monetary dirtinesses," or blind with "greedy cupidity," or fornicators like Lewis and his companions, or apostates like Veeson and Broomhall, or, at best, as intent only upon "enjoying their rich farms,"—so that, as Dr. Rae testifies, "either a sneer, a sarcasm, or a reproach" was always connected with their names in every Protestant society, while their Catholic rivals were held in such esteem, that, as Mr. Walpole unwillingly confessed, "between the men themselves no comparison could be dared?"

What marvel if the difference in the final results obtained by Catholic and Protestant missions respectively in the islands of the Pacific, and recorded by Protestant witnesses, correspond exactly with that which the same writers detected with sorrow in those by whom they were conducted? During a quarter of a century the Society Islands were held in lease by an army of Protestant missionaries. Every temporal advantage, including an enormous annual revenue, amounting as early as 1832 to one hundred thousand pounds, was on their side, and there were none to contest their influence or dispute their sway. And what were the fruits of their long reign? It is their own associates and advocates who have assured us that, while they grew rich themselves at the expense of their disciples, whose most fertile lands they appropriated, and whose humble commerce they wrested from them,—"all being engaged in trade," as their friend Captain Waldegrave discovered, some having seized "the monopoly of cattle," others dealing "in cocoa-nut oil and arrowroot," others, like Williams, "speculating largely in tobacco," and struggling, as even the London Missionary Society complained, "in invidious and degrading competition with their own people,"—the only legacies which they bequeathed at their departure to this once happy and contented population were, as Mr. Bennett relates in 1840, "riot and debauchery that would have disgraced the most profligate purlieus of London;" "nothing," as Mr. Walpole reports in 1849, "but many of the vices of civilization, and most of the follies of the savage;" "little," as Mr. D'Ewes adds in 1855, "except in name and outward observances, of the real spirit of Christianity." At length they were ejected, amid the acclamations of the "haggard and diseased" remnant of the population, among whom, in the words of Mr. Pridham, they had only "added by their own presence a new plague to the evils they had come to cure;" and whereas, as Mr. Wilkes and Mr. Melville noticed, they had "kept their own children aloof" from all intercourse with the natives, because of the universal immorality of which the worst examples had been given by Protestant "missionaries," such as Lewis, Veeson, and Broomhall, so prompt was the regenerating influence of Catholic France, that, in 1861, Mr. Tilley found amongst the once degraded women of Tahiti refined and educated mothers, "admirable specimens of the commingled European and Tahitian blood," while Mr. Therry ascertained in 1863, that "this important island is now," in spite of all which had been done to pollute and destroy it, "a civilized and prosperous community!"

The Sandwich Islands, again, to take but one other example, have been for nearly half a century the spoil and prey of missionaries of the same class. In vain during thirty years they strove to hide both their own proceedings and the real condition of their disciples, by describing, in official reports addressed to the English and American societies, "the extensive prevalence of piety among them," and "the signal triumphs of Divine grace." At length the veil was torn away, and the heartless fiction exposed. Mr. Olmsted, Mr. Hines, and Mr. Dana revealed, one after the other, "the astonishing depopulation without a parallel in the history of nations." Others recorded with surprise the luxurious lives and unblushing greed of the missionaries, "seeking wealth diligently," in the words of Mr. Manley Hopkins, in spite of their ample salaries, "and investing it in very remunerative securities;" a proverb, as Mr. Walpole discovered, for "undenied monetary dirtiness;" abandoning mission work, as Dr. Seemann remarked, to seize upon official positions, and "reducing the natives to penury," as

Dr. Meyen observed, "by their detestable frauds." And though it is just to admit that such men would be cast out as a reproach and a scandal by conscientious Protestants, it must be remembered that they were the confidential agents, during a long series of years, of missionary societies composed of leading clergymen and influential laymen, who willingly augmented their revenues by propagating the shameless "reports" of these very men, and even when compelled to denounce, from motives of worldly prudence, their greedy speculations, still continued to employ them, and pointed to their fictitious successes with a dishonesty at least equal to theirs, in justification of their annual appeal for fresh contributions to their own exhausted treasury.

Yet their employers were not ignorant, as we have seen, of the narratives, which had been multiplying during many years, of a crowd of impartial Protestant travellers, ardently sympathizing with the missionaries whose career they described. As early as 1831, Captain Beechey had observed "what little effect the exertions of the missionaries had produced." In 1832, as we learn from the British Consul-general, though the official reports spoke only of "the triumphs of Divine grace," "moral anarchy prevailed throughout the group; schools were deserted, the teachers themselves falling away; buildings for worship were burned; the dark habits of heathenism sprang up again." A little later Captain Sherard Osborn heard so-called Protestant natives "singing the sixty-fourth Psalm to soothe the heathen goddess who presides over their volcano." In 1840, Commodore Read reported that the nominal Christians were "still licentious, and quite ignorant of the term virtue." In 1843, Sir Edward Belcher recorded his own observation, that "the greatest excesses are committed *within the missionary circle*, which includes the king and chiefs." In 1850, Dr. Seemann confirmed his report. In 1851, the Rev. Mr. Hines ascertained the hopeless degradation of the whole people, "from the hut of the menial to the royal palace," and quoted the *private* confessions of missionaries, that "*none* gave evidence of being Christian." Lastly, in 1862, Mr. Manley Hopkins declared with sorrow that the long reign of Protestantism had only produced "*a nation of hypocrites*;" Mr. Wyllie added that it was "impossible to preserve" a people so universally demoralized; the *Polynesian* and other authorities publicly declared that the most assiduous frequenter of the Protestant church on Sunday would sell his wife or daughter on Monday; and Dr. Rae asserted in the government journal, without challenge or reply, that the missionaries were everywhere objects of disgust or derision.

On the other hand, the missionaries themselves confessed that their disciples were deserting them by thousands to become Catholics; Mr. Walpole and Sir George Simpson expressed their reluctant admiration of the latter, ventured to avow that they were "strongly prepossessed in their favor," and related, with natural surprise, that *they* resisted "even to death" every attempt to force them to apostasy; while Mr. Dana, commissioned by the Protestant societies to visit and report upon all the facts, gave such an account of the success of the Catholic missionaries, of their overflowing churches, and the universal esteem which they had acquired among all ranks of Protestants, that his employers, less candid and truthful than their agent, suppressed, as Mr. Hopkins has told us, all these passages of his unwelcome report as "unsatisfactory to the supporters of the mission!"

VI. What, again, is the history of African missions but a contrast from the first page to the last? Who is so blind as not to behold God on one side, with all His gifts; and on the other, only man, naked and feeble, busy in a work which always fails, and sowing the seeds of a harvest which he never reaps? See in North Africa the sons of St. Francis and St. Dominic, gladly dying by hundreds, that so, by this sacrifice of propitiation, the wrath of God may one day be appeased, a Christian nation rule from the sea to the foot of the Atlas, and light dawn again over the land where once St. Augustine preached. In the East, see the same apostolic workmen braving all dangers and enduring all afflictions,—in Egypt and in Nubia, in the mountains of Abyssinia and by the shores of the White Nile,—passing through Gondar and Sennar, Enarea and Kaffa, and daring to penetrate even to Darfour and the distant Soudan,—patient in all temptations, returning to-day to the spot from which they were driven yesterday, doing battle with Pagan, Moslem, or Monophysite, and deeming the toils of a life too richly recompensed if they can gather together a few hundreds here, a few thousands there, first-fruits of a richer harvest, and presage of greater victories to come. And in this warfare of heroes, too often "victims," as an English writer has told us, "to the excessive austerity of their lives," but "leaving a memory venerated even by the pagans," let us note once more what men can become whom God has raised to the dignity of apostles, and "whose funeral chant is sung," as Mr. Hamilton relates, by the Negro and the Nubian, kindled to love and admiration by virtues which they justly deemed more than human, and by sacrifices which are precious enough to win a blessing even for the race of Cham. Who among modern missionaries comes nearer to the old heroic type than Jacobis, anointed on the rock of Dhalac by a prelate a fugitive like himself, yet winning homage from German *savans* and English tourists as well as from the kings of Tigrè and Shoa, and enthroned at last in Gondar as high-priest of God, and delegate of the Vicar of Christ; or Massaia, for fifteen years a wanderer between the Arabian Gulf and the mountains of Ethiopia, insensible to pain and want, "sorrowful yet always rejoicing, needy yet enriching many, having nothing yet possessing all things," and willing to live thus to the end, that so, in his own words, he may "plant the Cross and kindle the evangelical fire" in that rude Gallas nation, whose fierce tribes have already yielded to the service of God five priests, and twice as many aspirants to the ecclesiastical state.

Compare this history, which begins with St. Francis of Assisi, and ends with Massaia and Jacobis, with those records of weakness and shame, of strife and impurity, which make up the tale of Protestant missions in Africa, as related by Protestant historians. It is from *them* that we have learned, for we have used no other testimony, what their co-religionists are, and what they have done, in Africa. In Morocco you will hear, not of martyrs or confessors, but of the solitary Protestant minister, who scattered Bibles which were thrown into the fire, and then ran away amid the hisses of the people; in Algeria, of Mr. Ewald, whose operations were of the same nature, and led to the same result; in Tunis, of the Scotch mission, "since abandoned," and of certain pretended converts whom the British Consul briefly described as "those wretches." In Egypt you will find the English engaged in their usual work, and avenging their own religious misadventures by intriguing to prevent the reconciliation of the Coptic nation with the Catholic Church, content to mar in all lands what they imitate in none; or educating a few Egyptians and Arabs at Cairo, who, as Dr. Durbin has told us, "resume," when they quit the school,—like the Protestant students in China, India, Ceylon, and everywhere else,—the habits and principles which their unfruitful education was designed to correct. In Abyssinia you will meet Dr. Gobat and Dr. Krapf, both now reposing amid other scenes, of whom the first failed to attract the sympathy of the Abyssinians, who refused to believe that he was not a "Mussulman," and the last has left nothing more notable on record than the prodigious statement, which would have surprised the disciples of St. Paul, that "an unmarried missionary cannot eventually prosper;" while each gained a solitary convert, of whom one "turned Muhammedan at Cairo," and the other was "the unrenewed and unregenerate Wolda Gabriel." In the West, where the sons of St. Ignatius, before they were banished, won whole nations, who still strive, after the lapse of three-quarters of a century, to repeat their half-forgotten lessons, —Mr. Murray tells us of "the flagrant misconduct" of the first Protestant emissaries, and of Mr Horneman who developed into "a highly respectable marabout, or mussulman saint;" and Mr. Moister celebrates the Anglican chaplain who never made a convert in fifty years, and, unmindful of Oxford theology, worshipped the *fetish* on his death-bed; and Mr. Walker commemorates the Anglican "communicants," who "obstinately adhered to their superstitious usages;" and Mr. Cruickshank the "converts," who "exhibited a uniformity of weakness truly humiliating and deplorable;" and Mr. Duncan the "scholars," whose knowledge only made them "more perfect in villany;" and Captain Hewett the "missionary protégés," brought up under their own eye, but "invariably found to be lying, cunning, and utterly worthless." Lastly, Dr. Armstrong and Mr. Calderwood lament that "the Caffres have refused the Gospel," with the exception of a very small number of nominal disciples, who, as a multitude of eye-witnesses declare, "are the worst behaved of the whole tribe;" while the Protestant Hottentots, in whom Mr. Moffat detected "the unction of the Spirit," are described by the same authorities as "notoriously the most idle and worthless of their nation;" and even their teachers are said to be so incurably addicted to agricultural and trading pursuits, in preference to missionary toils, that Mr. Merriman reproachfully observes, "I meet with examples of this wherever I go." They are Protestants, once more, from whom we learn these facts, and without whose testimony it would have been impossible to prove them.

VII. In the Levant, where "British protection is fully enjoyed," we have seen the usual enormous and perfectly useless expenditure, by agents whose "utter unprofitableness," as Admiral Slade relates, "cannot be sufficiently pointed out." We have witnessed the customary distribution of thousands of books, during more than a quarter of a century, which nobody read, and which it was discovered too late, when half a million volumes had been printed, that nobody was allowed to read. We have seen American missionaries courting their Athenian hosts with flattering speech, till the latter cast them out as "heresiarchs from the caverns of hell," and then repaying the unexpected affront by reviling the contemptuous Greeks as "worse than Romanists." We have visited the Malta College, with its ardent professors and ingenious lodgers, speculating with unfailing success upon the well-known qualities of their English benefactors, and always repeating with quiet assurance the artifices which experience had taught them would never be practised in vain. We have seen too its choicest guests,—

Achilli, who fascinated the too credulous Anglican with dexterous hints "that he would join himself to our church," but who chose at last, when English benevolence decayed, the church of Mr. Swedenborg; and Naudi, instructing an imaginary congregation of ideal converts, and repaying the bounty of the Church Missionary Society with "annual reports," till Dr. Wolff discovered, many years too late, that Levantine Protestantism was a pleasant fable, and Naudi a prosperous cheat.

In Turkey, we have found the missionaries from beyond the Atlantic attracted in crowds by "the comforts and pleasant things about this life in the East," and celebrating the "moral sublimity" of missionary nuptials; but not even attempting, as Mr. Walpole remarks, "any conversion except of the Christians." We have been introduced also to their "converts," a few score of shrewd Armenians, "infidels and radicals," as one of their own preachers has assured us, "who deserve no sympathy from the Christian public," but who never ask it in vain from men who are too much in want of disciples not to judge their frailties with indulgence, even when they are so notorious that, in the candid words of Dr. Joseph Wolff, "the *worst* people among the Eastern natives are those who have been converted to Protestantism." In Syria, as Dr. Durbin deplores, "they have come into collision with each other," disputing before the Turk and the Greek about "the validity of their respective ministries." In Jerusalem, where they inhabit palaces with "marble floors," and bid against one another for Hebrew catechumens, who have learned to consider Christian baptism "the only good business they have," they run away, as Dr. Robinson notices, at the first rumor of pestilence, and leave the missionaries of the Cross to die amidst the sick whom *they* have abandoned. Lastly, in Armenia, where Mr. Perkins and his opulent colleagues disposed of about twice the revenue which the great Republic allots to its President, and rode forth on "horses of every breed" of which a monarch might have envied the possession, though half the hierarchy of Armenia accepted their pensions, "their expensive establishments," as their friend Dr. Wagner detected, "have made no converts." Such, as their own witnesses relate, is the history of Protestant missions in the Levant, Syria, and Armenia,—of what even their warmest advocates call in derision "their useless missions in the East."

On the other hand, we have seen missionaries of a different class, more solicitous to abide in poverty than their rivals to secure luxury and ease, toiling during three centuries in the same lands,—dying in the galleys of Constantinople, or in the plague-stricken cities of Syria,—spreading far and wide the blessings of education, from the shores of the Bosphorus to the mouth of the Euphrates, and from the coasts of Palestine to the borders of the Caspian Sea,—attracting scholars "from Beyrout and Damascus, from Persia and Egypt, and even from Nubia and Abyssinia,"—"saving millions of souls," as a generous English writer has told us, and "spreading a sea of benefits, silently and unostentatiously," wherever Mussulmans rule and Christians suffer; till at length they have won to the faith, and are daily winning out of every eastern nation, that multitude of disciples whose "liberality and intelligence," "decided superiority," and "elevation in the scale of civilization," even the most hostile witnesses reluctantly attribute to their reconciliation with the Catholic Church. Already, as we have seen, "nearly all Syria," the whole of Chaldea, and the greater part of Armenia, have accepted their message, or announced their willingness to do so; while every oriental tribe, easily discriminating between the lowly ambassadors of the Church and the worldly and contentious prophets of the Sects, draws nearer to them year by year; and even the Turk, moved by the exceeding charity of those ministering angels who labor with them, and rebuking by a purer instinct the insatiable malice which can revile even such as these, asks in astonishment, "whether they came down thus from heaven?"

VIII. Lastly, in America,—but why should we resume a history so lately reviewed, in which there is *all* on one side, and *nothing* on the other? Why should we compare again the Divine ministry which has added millions of Indians to the fold of Christ, with the unblest efforts of men who have outraged many, but converted none; have depopulated regions wider than the empires of the old world; and have left at last, as a record and monument of their work, only a miserable remnant alive, till they have time to destroy *them* also, throughout the whole vast continent where the Anglo-Saxon reigns?

THE CITY OF GOD AND THE CITY OF CONFUSION.

It has been our attempt in these volumes, neglecting the familiar controversies of other days, to display the Church and the Sects *in action*, in every land where there were gentiles to be converted; nor can that be deemed a partial or inadequate test of both which has had three centuries for its period, and the world for its sphere. The general results of its application are now sufficiently manifest, but there are still certain points of detail which claim a moment's attention, even in this rapid summary.

That the agents of the Sects, having neither the gifts nor the calling of apostles, should have failed to convert the heathen, will surprise none who believe that such a work can be accomplished only by the co-operation of God. But the results of their intrusion into the apostolic office have not been simply negative. This would be an imperfect estimate of their failure. It is to their presence in every pagan land that their own disciples attribute, in moments of candor, what even they call the *growing hatred* of the pagan world towards Christianity and its professors. Protestantism, we have said, is the last scourge of Heathenism; and this is true in many ways, but especially in this,—that it has everywhere set up, not only a spurious type of Christian life, indolent, effeminate, and luxurious, which even the barbarian has ridiculed as scarcely less earthly than his own; but a miserable caricature of the Christian Church, in which he has detected only weakness and confusion, ceaseless strife and unappeasable disorder. Everywhere, therefore, he has confounded in a common disdain the few whose natural gifts might have merited his respect, with the crowd of adventurers who accompanied them. Martyn and Schwartz, like Tomlin and Gutzlaff, were equally in his eyes the salaried agents of some impure sect; Heber and Selwyn, no less than Morrison or Edkins, only amused him by the incoherence of their doctrine and the inconsistency of their practice, or revolted him by the effeminacy of their domestic life. They were too like himself to suggest the belief that they had a mission from heaven, and too eagerly solicitous about common joys to encourage the idea that they had divorced themselves from earth. He perceived also that even these few, in spite of their higher qualities, came to him, like all the rest, with a "Protest" written on their foreheads against the only Church which he could have venerated; and when he saw these men, the chiefs of their sect, tearing the Seamless Robe into a thousand fragments, and running to him with the pieces in their hands to show him what they had done,—can we marvel if he turned his back upon them, or answered with scorn, like the Jews of old, *Quid ad nos? What is that to us?* or if, as we have been told, the subtle Hindoo, keenly appreciating the mingled folly and violence of their anti-Catholic harangues, satirically asks, "Why should we become Christians, when *you* tell us that three-fourths of the Christian world have adopted a creed no way superior to our own?" Let us see, then, once more, how the heathen have judged the Sects, and the incessant mutual conflicts which even they can trace to their true source, and in what language they have expressed their judgment.

I. It was an observation of Leibnitz, that "the want of union among Protestants" would always suffice to ruin any work which they might undertake. If he had lived to mark their attempts to convert the heathen, he would have seen his prediction fulfilled. "The existence of *profound divisions among ourselves*," Lord Elgin observed during his residence in China, "is one of the first truths which we Christians reveal to the heathen." "There is no greater barrier," says an intelligent British official in that country, "to the spread of the Gospel than the division and splitting which have taken place among the various orders of Christians themselves." "The great and fatal error," adds a third witness, "is the *rivalry of religious sects*, and the attempt to gain followers at the expense of each other's tenets." We have seen that Mr. Medhurst could only explain his own failure and that of his colleagues by the "sad disunion" which prevailed among them. The Chinese, who contemplates this singular spectacle with a sentiment of compassion for the "outer barbarian" who cannot even agree about his religion, judiciously remarks, as Mr. Colledge relates, "that Europe and America," which have already sent him more than twenty different sects, "*must have as many Christs as China has gods.*" Yet the *Catholic* Chinese, united in every province of the empire in the same unvarying faith, have displayed during three centuries such inflexible unity, and such ardent charity, that while the pagans themselves, as Commander Brine relates, have learned to contrast their "great unanimity" with the "variety of sentiment" which excites their contempt for Protestantism, one of the most cruel of their emperors declared in a public proclamation, "All who become Christians, whether rich or poor, directly they embrace this religion have such an affection for one another, that they seem to be of one bone and one flesh." Never, since the primitive ages, was that word of our Lord more impressively fulfilled, "By this shall all men *know* that you are My disciples, if you have love one for another."

II. "The discordant tenets of the missionaries" in India was deplored long ago by Dr. Middleton with unavailing regret; and in our own day, Mr. Russell still notes "the astonishment of the Asiatics" at the implacable divisions of the various sects, "all claiming to be of one religion." "Their observation uniformly is," says Mr. Le Bas, "that they should think much better of Christianity, if there were not quite so many different kinds of it." It is a well-known jest among the Brahmins, who have contemplated the various English, German, and American religions in the cities of Bengal and Madras, and have watched with amusement their fretful jealousies and eager rivalry, that "their professors would do far better to agree among themselves what Christianity *is*, before they pretend to teach it to others;" while men of lower caste find in the same portent only a motive for deriding the Gospel, and "many of the Hindus," we are told, "knowing the differences amongst Christians, ask, '*To which Sect would you have me adhere?*'"*

III. In Ceylon, we have learned from Sir Emerson Tennent, "the choice of sects leads to utter bewilderment." "The native," says another, "is *perfectly aghast* at the variety of choice." Can we blame him if he concludes that Christianity is a mere imposture, unworthy of his serious attention; until he comes in contact with that ancient form of it which, like God, "is the same yesterday, to-day, and forever," and which has already captivated the allegiance of so many of his countrymen? "The Protestant Church," says an Anglo-Cingalese writer, who had heard the pagan comments upon "her multitudinous sects and schisms," "has no chance in competition with the Roman Catholic;" but he does not appear to have asked himself, like the more discerning pagan, why the one is a very symbol of confusion and disorder, while the other remains eternally unchanged?

IV. The bitter fruits of Protestantism in New Zealand have been described to us by Dr. Selwyn. "The spirit of controversy," he says, "is everywhere found to prevail, in many cases to the entire exclusion of all simplicity of faith." We have seen what was his own mode of dealing with the evil. "The spirit of Christianity," observes the Rev. Elijah Hoole, "is lost in the form, and the very form itself has become the subject of incessant and angry dispute." "We have the awful sight," adds the Rev. Mr. Turton, "of father and son, mother and daughter, hating each other with a mortal hatred." Such is, in all the earth, the deadly influence of Protestantism, the observation of which forced one New Zealand chief to say, in reply to the overtures of a missionary, "When you have agreed amongst yourselves which is the right road, I may perhaps be induced to take it;" and suggested to another, whose experience of Protestant Christianity had only occasioned a speedy relapse into heathenism, the ingenious taunt, "One beehive is good, but many are troublesome."

V. In the islands of the Pacific, where, as Mr. Walpole observes, "every variety of Dissenters exists among the teachers," who, as Dr. Ruschenberger adds, "deal damnation in a peculiar slang to all whose opinions differ from their own," the poor savage makes the usual reflections, "as one sect succeeds another;" but as he is perfectly indifferent to all of them, and

* *Ancient and Modern India*, p. 520.

only estimates them according to their relative wealth, the varieties of their chameleon creed add nothing whatever to the contempt which he feels for the worldliness, cupidity, and injustice which is common to them all.

VI. In Africa, which abounds, as Dr. Armstrong and his companions lamented, in "church troubles," where "the competition between the Church and the rival sects of Dissenters," as Captain Hewett observes, "*must* militate against the success of missionaries," and where Mr. Merriman deplores the constant ineffectiveness of English operations, "in consequence of their religious divisions," Dr. Livingstone has told us, that "the mission stations are mere *pauper establishments*," unlike "the self-supporting primitive monasteries, pioneers of civilization and agriculture, from which we even now reap benefits;" and that one result of "such a variety of Christian sects," each maintaining a pauper establishment for the disciples whom they would never attract without it, is this—"that converts of one denomination are eagerly adopted by another," to the great detriment, as he intimates, of their spiritual progress. The Presbyterian Hottentot, whatever his frailties, knows that the rival Wesleyan "Establishment" is always open to him; the disorderly Baptist is sure of a hearty welcome among the Anglicans; the refractory Anglican is embraced with joy by the American Congregationalists; the United Brethren dispute the honor of entertaining him with the Rhenish Missionary Society; and the Hottentot himself, solicitous only about his next meal, rejoices in the multiplicity of institutions where a new profession of faith will at least allay the pangs of hunger, perhaps even secure the luxury of a change of diet. Yet he uses these advantages without an emotion of gratitude, and "the moment the food and lodging are discontinued, he does not scruple," says Mr. Andersson, "to treat his benefactor with ingratitude, and to load him with abuse." So that even the savage of South Africa, gross and irrational as he is, takes exactly the same view of his relation to the various Protestant sects as the more subtle Chinese or Hindoo; while his rival hosts, unable to heal what even they call their "accursed divisions," make ineffectual attempts to hide them, like the Anglican archdeacon who humbly suggested a *joint service* to the Wesleyan preacher, lest the barbarians should detect the discord which he devised this characteristic mode of concealing.

VII. In Syria, as Dr. Durbin has informed us, the Protestant missionaries, doomed to eternal warfare, "have come into collision with each other in the midst of these ancient churches,"—for it is the will of the imperious master whom they unwittingly serve, that they should display his banner in all lands. In Turkey, as Dr. Southgate angrily records, they are only busy in promoting "horrid schism," though he has no rebukes for the schism which he vainly struggled to establish himself, till his expensive failure led to his recall. In Armenia, as Mr. Badger relates, the Americans proposed to veil the unwelcome fact "that there are *rival* Protestant sects and interests," by warning the Anglicans off the field—a suggestion which was perfectly unnecessary, as they never thought of entering it, but which Mr. Badger warmly resented, and which he considered "as presumptuous as it is ludicrous."

VIII. Lastly, America exhibits, on a still larger scale, and with the same fatal results which we have witnessed in every other land, the phenomena which mark the presence of Protestantism, and which make Christianity a laughing-stock among all the races of the earth; so that one Indian sachem observed, "If there is but *one* religion, why do white men differ so much about it?"—and another exclaimed, with a feeling of superiority which he did not attempt to conceal, "If I should have a mind to turn Christian, I could not tell what religion to be of." A third displayed a still keener irony, when he retorted upon a Protestant missionary the lesson which he had taught him too well, and positively declined to become a Protestant, on the Protestant ground, that "Every man should paddle his canoe his own way." Finally, a fourth, the chief of the Cree nation, after noticing the varieties of doctrine proposed to his tribe, lately assured Mr. Kane, that "as he did not know which was right, he thought they ought to call a council amongst themselves, and that then he would go with them all; but that *until they agreed*, he would wait."* Yet we have seen *Catholic* Indians, of many nations and climes, steadfastly adhering, generation after generation, under all difficulties and temptations, to one unvarying doctrine, and rejecting with vehement repugnance all the bribes and seductions of error; we have found Catholic Cherokees converting the Pagan Flatheads without the assistance of a missionary, and Christian Huron captives performing the same office for their Mohawk masters; nay more, we have seen the Indian warrior, in the fierce excitement of battle, embrace as a brother the fallen foe who had just aimed at his own life, because the sign of the cross had revealed to him that his enemy was a Catholic like himself.

Yet Protestant controversialists assure us, that this marvellous unity—which links in one brotherhood the savages of a hundred tribes, which suffering cannot rend nor corruption dissolve, and which *looks* so like the mysterious unity of the

* *Wanderings*, &c., by Paul Kane, ch. xxiii., p. 393.

disciples of St. John and St. Paul—is only a trick of priestcraft, the result of some subtle organization, some deep device of human policy! If it were so, we might be permitted to ask, why *they*, who boast of reason as if it were a gift peculiar to themselves, have never been able to imitate it?—why a purely human art, as they deem it, should baffle their most skilful analysis?—why the Church can so easily unite all hearts, whether of bond or free, savage or civilized, in China and Peru, as easily as in France or Ireland, in one immense harmony of faith, love, and adoration; while the Sects, a portent to themselves and a jest among the heathen, cannot so much as persuade the members of the same household to be "of one mind?"

It is true that Protestants have anticipated this inquiry, which does not occasion them a moment's embarrassment. Unity, they reply, is a chimera, and truth itself mutable and progressive. "Emulations, quarrels, dissensions, and sects," which St. Paul classed as "works of the flesh," *they* commend as both good and expedient—though they admit that they somewhat impede the diffusion of the Gospel among the heathen. "The diversity of our sects," says M. Coquerel, a conspicuous French minister, "is our most honorable distinction."* "Far from blushing," exclaims another, "at these variations of creed, Protestants expect to derive glory from them."† The Germans, we are told, "boast of it as their very highest privilege, and the very essence of a Protestant Church, that its opinions should constantly change."‡ "The Protestant Church," says M. de Sismondi, "admits that she herself may be mistaken; she claims only that liberty of thought which the Catholic Church renounces."§ "Scotland and England," observes a British Protestant, deeply impressed with the advantages of disunion, "without their seceders and dissenters, would have been countries in which the human mind slumbered."‖ Lastly, the Swiss, speaking by the mouth of their supreme ecclesiastical organ, frankly proclaim, that "the right of examination is the only element of fixedness which belongs to the Protestant religion."¶ Is it possible to admit more candidly that Protestantism is the negation of the

* *L'Ami de la Religion*, tome xxii., p. 208.

† *Mélanges de la Religion*, tome i., p. 84.

‡ See *The State of Protestantism in Germany*, by Rev. H. J. Rose.

§ *Progress of Religious Opinion during the Nineteenth Century*, p. 79; English edition.

‖ Laing, *Residence in Norway*, ch. xi., p. 447.

¶ *Défense de la Vénérable Compagnie des Pasteurs de Genève, à l'occasion d'un écrit intitulé* "Véritable Histoire des Momiers."

work of Christ, and that the pagan world has reason to ask its representatives, "whether they profess any religion whatever?"

RESULTS OF CATHOLIC AND PROTESTANT EDUCATION.

There is nothing to which the Sects have professed to attribute so much value, among all the means by which they seek to extend their influence, as the diffusion of knowledge. One might suppose, in listening to their orators, that the history of those long ages during which the Church alone cultivated human science, and was the sole sanctuary both of learning and holiness, found no place in their ungrateful memory. Yet even enemies have confessed, that "law, learning, education, science, *all* that we term civilization in the present social condition of the European people, spring from the supremacy of the Roman Pontiffs and the Catholic priesthood over the kings and nobles of the middle ages."* Guizot, Haxthausen, and other writers of their class, men of vigorous intellect and inexorable candor, have declared, that, but for the humanizing influence of the Church, mind must have been everywhere beaten down by brute force, and have freely confessed, that when we thank God for all the treasures of knowledge and art which we now possess, we should thank Him also for the wakeful and generous providence of the Church to which we owe them. It is true that the Protestant revivers of pagan literature in the sixteenth century affected, for the first time in the history of the world, to regard Catholics as obscurantists, though the revival was chiefly due to the ceaseless activity of the latter, and the classical court of Leo X. welcomed with almost as much enthusiasm the discovery of a new manuscript as that of Pius IX. does the triumph of a new martyr. Yet even the most eminent of their own teachers have avouched, that, in spite of their eager self-laudation, the Church beat them out of the field with their own weapons; and that not only, in the words of Ranke, "Rome *continued* to be a metropolis of civilization, *unrivalled* in minute and various erudition," but that the Jesuit schools throughout Europe, as Bacon easily discovered, were so immeasurably superior to those of their complacent rivals, that "it was found that their scholars learned more in one year than those of other masters in two, and even Protestants *recalled* their children from distant gymnasia, and committed them to their care."†

* Laing, *Observations on Europe*, ch. xv., p. 394.
† Ranke, book v., vol. i., p. 379; book viii., vol. ii., p. 208.

But it is not only in the higher spheres of intellectual culture that men who received their noblest inspirations from that illuminating faith which, while marking the limits, has indefinitely extended the domain of reason, have served as models to the ungrateful rivals who affected, often with powers ludicrously disproportioned to their claims, a universal supremacy. Even in lower fields of mental toil, the vain clamor of her boastful accusers has been perpetually rebuked by the calm but sleepless energy of the Church, as their costly but sterile efforts have been surpassed by her silent and peaceful triumphs. "In Catholic *Germany*," says a well-known Presbyterian writer, "in *France*, in *Italy*, and even in *Spain*, the education of the common people is *at least* as generally diffused, and as faithfully promoted by the clerical body, as in Scotland. . . . Education is in reality not only not repressed, but is encouraged, by the Popish Church, and is a mighty instrument in its hands, and ably used." At this hour, he adds, "Rome has above a hundred schools *more* than Berlin, for a population little more than *half* of that of Berlin;" and "if it is asked what is taught to the people of Rome by all these schools—precisely what is taught at Berlin!"*

And the same thing is equally true of every other Catholic land. "Neither in England, nor even in Prussia," says an English traveller in *Austria*, "is education more universally and strictly attended to among the poor;"† while Mr. Kohl observes, that not only are there schools in every village, but that even on the remote Transylvanian frontier "the school-buildings are not only good, but excellent," and the instruction also.‡ So little reason or modesty is there in the insular conceit of Englishmen, who themselves entered later into the field of public education than any other people of Europe, and who have been obliged to confess, in 1862, after immense expenditure, directed by unquestionable administrative skill, that their own tardily devised national system, though it deals only with a fraction of the primary schools, and these the most efficient of their class, has issued in such lamentable failure, that a "new Code" is imperatively needed to secure an improved teaching of the barest elements of human knowledge!

"It is now half a century," says a competent witness, "since education became one of the great objects of social and political enterprise in this country. What is the result? . . . . . Our agricultural population . . . are still generally so ignorant, that

* *Notes of a Traveller*, ch. vi., p. 167; ch. xxi., pp. 439–41.
† *Vienna and the Austrians*, by F. Trollope, vol. ii., letter lvii., pp. 267, 339
‡ *Austria*, by J. G. Kohl, p. 300 (1843).

no reasonable being, for pity's sake, would ask them a question of history or geography out of their own village, or more than fifty years back. They are still a prey to the first fanatic or impostor that chooses to work upon them. . . . This is the case of our now *educated* peasantry. When we turn to the artisan the case is certainly worse."* Yet the very men who make these confessions not only discourse with an air of complacent superiority on the civilization of Protestant Britain, but affect to disparage the peasantry of France or Austria, of Spain or Canada, ten times better instructed even in the arts of common life, and illuminated moreover by that Divine faith of which the English peasant is as void as the herd of which he seems to form a part, or the plough which is scarcely more inanimate than himself.†

Such facts, which we cannot pursue further in this place, would acquire tenfold gravity, if we were to investigate them in relation to the moral results of education, as dispensed by the Church and the Sects respectively, whatever field we might select for the comparison. Prussia and Holland, with their systems of compulsory education, and, still more, Sweden and Denmark, have reached, as we shall learn presently, the lowest moral condition to which nominally Christian nations can sink; while in America, where universal education is said to have created among Protestants a generation of "cold, calculating scoundrels," we have been told that "the only really *useful* and *corrective* education is that of the Catholic schools and colleges."‡ It is, however, with the education of the *heathen* that we have been concerned in these volumes, and which appears, by the confession of adversaries, to have accomplished such results as the following.

I. In China, where Mr. Oliphant, Mr. D'Ewes, Mr. Minturn, and other Protestant travellers, could not but admire "the able and distinguished masters" who taught, not only the highest Chinese classics, but European languages, and the arts of music, painting, and sculpture, with a success which was "*truly won-*

* *The Times*, October 15, 1862.

† Some Englishmen were present a few years ago, at the International Cattle Show in Paris. They saw the herdsman or the drover of France, Belgium, Austria, or Spain, advance with easy self-possession and manly grace, to receive his prize, and they marked in his face what *they* knew not to be the light of the life-giving Sacraments, by which, in the language of St. Peter, he had become a "partaker of the Divine nature."

They saw also the English peasant present himself, with downcast eyes and shambling gait, less comely than his own animals, and brutalized by the influence of a purely human religion; and as the sorry troop advanced, in dismal contrast to their Catholic competitors, they heard the whisper which passed from mouth to mouth, on all the benches where the spectators sat, and it said, "*Comme c'est brute le peuple Anglais.*"

‡ See page 331.

derful;" where even women, like the French Sisters of Charity, had no need of native aid; and where the compositions of native pupils, "who evidently regarded their spiritual masters with feelings of affection and gratitude," won the applause of the pagan professors in the Imperial Academy of Pekin: the educational efforts of two hundred Protestant missionaries, almost all of whom were obliged, from lack of knowledge, to teach only by the aid of salaried Chinese, whose success they could not appreciate, and whose defects they could not correct, are thus estimated by the same friendly witnesses. "The children are taught only the most rudimentary works in their own classics. Their education seems likely, therefore, to be of little service to them, either amongst their own countrymen or foreigners." They only learn English, says Dr. Ball, the solitary accomplishment which their masters can dispense, "to turn it afterwards to their own advantage for trading purposes." "In too many instances," adds the candid Mr. Oliphant, "the knowledge they have acquired only serves to increase their evil influence." The sole effect of their "English education," says another, is "*to qualify them for hypocrites or sharpers.*" Finally, the fruits of Protestant education in China, upon a large scale, and in their latest development,—the ultimate results of half a century of "bible-teaching, essentially Protestant in its principles and tendency,"—have been the mental cultivation and Christian virtues of the Tae-ping rebels!

II. In India, the effects of Protestant education, conducted by a thousand agents, during successive generations, and at prodigious cost, have been simply appalling. The scholars, we are told by one English authority, "reject heathenism without embracing Christianity, and become conceited infidels, worse to deal with than pagans." They may have "a thorough knowledge of Holy Scripture," and "explain in the clearest manner the cardinal point of justification;" they may even rebuke "Popish idolatry" by a suitable array of texts; but in spite of these accomplishments, derived from missionary preceptors, "they have no more faith in Jesus Christ," we are told, "than in their own religion. They believe the Jesus of the English, and the Krishna of the Hindus, to be alike impostors." Lastly,—for it would be idle to recapitulate testimonies which we have found to be absolutely uniform,—"the *educated* native is either a hypocrite or a latitudinarian, with the heart of an atheist under the robe of an idolater. The greater body are but too surely tending to a state morally *lower* than that from which education rescued them."*

* A still later testimony is given, in March, 1863, by the Calcutta correspond-

III. In Ceylon, we have been told by Sir Emerson Tennent, "the moral results of education have been limited and unsatisfactory." The Americans alone are said to have had more than one hundred thousand pupils in their schools; and though they, like the other sects, have had supreme control over this vast mass of scholars from infancy to manhood, they cannot touch their hearts! "The schools have done little good," says Dr. Brown; "even the children educated in them, when they grew up, frequented the idol temples, and scarcely a youth was to be seen at chapel, unless he was still a scholar." We have been informed on the other hand, by Protestant witnesses, how uniformly the *Catholic* pupils illustrate their belief by their practice, and that "neither corruption nor coercion could induce them to abjure their religion."

IV. In Australia, we have heard of natives who had been "*educated* at the mission," not only living naked in the woods, but "murdering their children in after years." In New Zealand, where multitudes have been the apt and intelligent pupils of Protestant missionaries, an official report affirms, in 1859, that simultaneously with "a remarkable activity of mind directed to the development of political ideas," their education has only made them worse, morally, socially, and physically, than they were fifty years ago; while it has rather stimulated than repressed the universal impurity and corruption which they now display, "in body and mind, in all their thoughts, words, and actions."

V. In the islands of the Pacific,—where Catholic missionaries have educated even the barbarous tribes of the Philippines with such success, that a Protestant traveller notices with admiration "that there are very few Indians who are unable to read,"—the emissaries of another faith print, in a single group, and in every successive year, more than twenty thousand volumes; yet we know, by their own confession, what their scholars have become, "from the hut of the menial to the royal palace;" and a native authority assures us that, in spite, or as he seems to think because, of this educational process, "every thing that concerns the native race is both physically and morally *retrograde*."

VI. In Africa, we have seen the Protestant scholars at Cairo resuming their original habits as soon as their education was finished; in the West, it only "enables them to become more

ent of the *Times*, in describing the ceremony of conferring academical degrees upon the native graduates in the Calcutta University. "The youths so educated," he says, "become Deists.... This Deistical state is marked by no little immorality; English vices are fashionable as well as English literature. Their fathers bewail the errors of the rising generation."—*The Times*, April 27, 1863.

perfect in villany," while, as Mr. Cruickshank laments, "the *best educated* men, who some years ago were distinguished for zeal for Christianity, are now living without its pale," and "the missionary protégés," as Captain Hewett records, are so "invariably found to be lying, cunning, and utterly worthless, that no dwellers in the colonies wish to employ as servant a native educated in the missionary schools," and the Governor of Sierra Leone reported officially, that "the children turned out of missionary schools are vagabonds." In the South—but we have heard enough of the Protestant Hottentot, who, as an English writer has told us, "can sing all day long about 'the sufferings of the Lamb,' but knows no more about the Lamb, or His sufferings, than one of the lower animals;" so utterly unprofitable is the instruction of missionaries who can only succeed, as a crowd of impartial witnesses attest, after the labors of three-quarters of a century, in making their disciples "*the most idle and worthless of their nation.*"

VII. In Greece, Protestant education appears to have collapsed as soon as the schoolmasters began to be missionaries. In Syria, as Dr. Valentine Mott reports, "even the Armenians, though professing Christianity, joined with the deluded Turks in suppressing Protestant schools;" but he does not seem to have understood that it was their profession of Christianity which inspired the act, and that even Armenians might reasonably combine to reject what Dr. Wolff calls "the vague and uncertain creed" proposed for their acceptance, and doubt the value of instruction of which the recipients, as the same witness has told us, become "the worst people among the Eastern natives." In Armenia, in spite of the attractive bribes distributed by missionaries of the school of Mr. Justin Perkins, not only was every effort to protestantize the natives perfectly fruitless, but they admit, by the mouth of their friend Dr. Wagner, that if they ceased to pay the scholars their weekly tribute, "the schools would become directly empty."

VIII. Lastly, a great English authority has recorded the same uniform result of Protestant education in the case of the American Indians, who, when their pupilage was over, "returned to their naked brethren the most profligate and the most idle members of the Indian community." It was the observation of these invariable facts which provoked a famous Seneca chief to remind certain missionaries, who urged him to adopt their religious opinions, that "such of the Senecas as they nominally converted from heathenism to Christianity only disgraced themselves by attempts to cover the profligacy of the one with the hypocrisy of the other;"* and of which the

* *Indian Biography,* by B. B. Thatcher, Esq., vol. ii., ch. xvi., p. 290.

universality was candidly admitted by the Rev. Dr. Wheelock, even with respect to his own Indian pupils, who so far surpassed all others that they "had made considerable progress in Latin and Greek." "Some who on account of their parts and learning," says this missionary, "bid the fairest for usefulness, are sunk down into as low, brutish, and savage a manner of living as they were in before."* Yet "several of them," as Dr. Dwight confesses, "were placed in colleges, and received *the usual degrees.* Almost all of them, however, renounced ultimately the advantages which they had acquired, *and returned to the grossness of savage life.*"† Two Dutch ministers also relate, for all the sects record the same unwelcome facts, that after carefully educating an Indian, so that, besides other accomplishments, "he could read and write good Dutch," and manifested his piety by "answering publicly in the church," they "presented him with a Bible, in order to work through him some good among the Indians; but it all resulted in nothing. He has taken to drinking of brandy; he pawned the Bible, and became a real beast, who is doing more harm than good among the Indians."‡

There is a strange uniformity in these disastrous results of Protestant teaching, attested by Protestant writers, upon all classes of scholars, and in every region of the world, which might almost provoke mirth, if such an emotion were possible in the presence of evils so enormous. When we consider that millions of money are being expended by the various Sects, with ostentatious disdain of the Church, and expressly to impede her work in the world; and that after all their clamorous boasts and anticipations of triumph, after all their complacent eulogies of their own skill and enlightenment, they have succeeded at last in educating a few Chinese, whose knowledge "only increases their evil influence;" or Hindoos, only to render them "conceited infidels, worse than pagans;" or Cingalese, that when they quit school, they may with greater zest "frequent their idol temples;" or Maoris, that they may become utterly defiled, "in mind and body, in all their thoughts, words, and actions;" or Hawaiians, that they may "plunge voluntarily into every species of wickedness and excess;" or Africans, that they may "become more perfect in villany," and unfit to be employed even as domestics; or Americans, that they may surpass in vileness "the most profligate and the most idle" of their uneducated brethren; we should be more blind and

* *Documentary History of New York,* vol. iv., p. 506.

† *Travels in New England,* by Timothy Dwight, LL.D., letter ix., vol. ii., p. 99.

‡ Ibid., vol. iii., p. 108.

undiscerning than even these unfortunate pupils if we failed to derive instruction from such facts. That Protestant missionaries have neither vocation nor mission, though it may explain many points of the contrast which we have been tracing, hardly accounts for such phenomena as these. A certain number of them are at least very superior, both in morals and intellectual power, to their scholars. Some of them are even sincere and zealous men, honestly purposing to improve those whom they instruct. Yet every humane effort is baffled, every benevolent aim intercepted; and they educate whole generations, with every appliance which experience can suggest or wealth accumulate, but always with these results! They can only turn pagans into atheists, and honest men into rogues, and it is from themselves that we receive the confession. Whence this frightful uniformity of disaster? If they are without apostolic gifts, and do not even claim them, yet by purely natural means alone they might have been expected to accomplish something better than this! Whence then, let us ask once more, this immense and universal blight, which pursues them everywhere like the cloud of darkness which hung over the Egyptians, and withers every flower and plant which their hands have touched? Is it not that in denying them all *supernatural* gifts, God has resolved to suspend and neutralize even those *natural* powers which, as they confess with dismay, they everywhere employ only to inflict upon the heathen world a deeper curse, a more irreparable woe?

The special advantage of the investigation which we have pursued in these pages, and which, as we have said, it would have been impossible, for want of materials, to conduct with success at an earlier date, consists in this,—that it has led us out of the region of speculative controversy into that of historical facts. We have not debated claims or doctrines which a text may prove or disprove, but we have contemplated the Church and the Sects *in action*. This is the test, complete and decisive, which was indicated by our Lord Himself, and we have seen what it has revealed. Everywhere He has manifested, by manifold and persuasive tokens, His unceasing presence with the Church; everywhere He has refused so much as to recognize the barren ministry of the Sects. In presence of such facts, uniform in their character and universal in their range, we may not unreasonably ask our Protestant adversaries, whether they expect us any longer to treat seriously pretensions which history has disposed of, and which God has judged before our eyes? Even they can hardly feel surprise if henceforth we decline an unprofitable and monotonous discussion which has lost all meaning, because a Divine sentence has closed it forever;

even they can no longer complain, if when they affect to teach us, we are now content to smile; when they provoke, to keep silence; when they revile, to pardon; when they blaspheme, to pray for them.

CELIBACY AND MARRIAGE.

It would be tedious to notice, one by one, all the points of contrast between Catholic and Protestant missionaries, and having sufficiently illustrated throughout these volumes those of greatest moment, it may seem superfluous to speak of some which have less gravity. Yet there are still two which claim a few words.

When St. Paul, the great exemplar of Christian missionaries, exhorted all men to whom effectual grace was given to abstain from marriage, because it was fitting, since the Creator assumed the nature of His creature, to aspire to a more angelic life than was possible under the earlier dispensation, the Church, though proclaiming it one of the Sacraments of the New Law, naturally proposed the higher state of celibacy to all who should aspire to the dignity of the Christian priesthood. If Protestants were content to plead that this is no Divine command, but only an ecclesiastical precept, we might regret their inability to comply with it, but could not justly reproach them with preferring the lower calling which they instinctively appropriate as most suitable to themselves. That Almighty God should always refuse them the special grace which he always grants to His own ministers, would still be a significant fact; but a married clergy, though utterly unable to do the work of God in the world, would only be a humiliating spectacle, not a denial of any revealed truth. But if the "counsel" of St. Paul concerning "virgins" refers to all who would "attend upon the Lord without impediment," and in a special manner to ministers of religion; much more to those who, like himself, are set apart for the perilous toils of the apostolate, and charged to display before the eyes of the heathen the loftiest type of Christian perfection. The disciples of St. Paul knew nothing of Protestant missions, nor of the principles upon which they are conducted, nor of that "strange compound of piety and irreligion" which, as one of their own agents has said, they everywhere present to the pagan world. They knew, however, that even soldiers were not accustomed to take their wives and children into the battle-field; and the proposal to send apostles to the heathen attended by such companions would have seemed to *them* an unseemly jest on a grave subject.

It would not perhaps be impossible to fill a considerable volume with impressive examples, recorded by Protestant writers, of the inconveniences which even they have detected in the employment of married missionaries. The enormous and perfectly useless *cost* which such a system involves will occur to every one, but this is not the chief objection to it. The married missionary, as St. Paul intimates, is simply incapable, even with the best intentions, of performing duties which always demand the sacrifice of ease and comfort, and often of life itself. "He is divided," as the apostle says, and is too "solicitous for the things of the world," to have much leisure for other thoughts, or to preach Christian virtue and heroism, upon which his own life affords such an ambiguous commentary, without the risk of exciting laughter even in a pagan auditory. Indeed, he is very apt to give up preaching altogether for less toilsome recreations. Even Dr. Krapf, of whom we heard in Abyssinia, tells us, that "the wish to settle down as comfortably as possible, and to marry, entangles a missionary in many external engagements which may lead him away from his Master and his duty;" and then he enumerates not only "house-building," but other "irrelevant and subordinate matters." Dr. Morrison found it necessary to recommend "a committee (in England) to attend to the petty wants of young missionaries." Dr. Colenso, speaking from experience, deplores the fact that "wives often ruin a mission by their tempers and animosities." Sometimes they produce the same effect without displaying such moral infirmities. "For nearly three months," says an amiable missionary, "I was confined almost exclusively to the sick-chamber of Mrs. S.,"—a duty which he did well to perform, but which can hardly be said to have promoted his efficiency as a preacher of religion; indeed, he adds that he abandoned the work, because, for the lady's sake, "medical advisers interdicted any future exposure to the privations of a missionary life."* We need not multiply such examples; they occur at almost every page of Protestant missionary annals.

Yet the disciples of the so-called Reformation, though they admit and deplore such results, have adopted other maxims than those of St. Paul, and not satisfied with choosing the least excellent calling, always proceed to defame that which they have not grace to adopt. Celibacy, mortification, and confession are repugnant to mere human nature, and therefore the most convenient process is to condemn them at once. The Bible,

* *Journal of a Residence in the Sandwich Islands*, by Rev. C. S. Stewart, p. 394, 2d edition. *Visit to the South Seas in the U. S. Ship Vincennes*, by the same author; introd.

which Protestantism has skilfully converted into a huge code of self-indulgence, will easily furnish a pretext. Like the pagans of old, who deified their own vices, and consecrated their favorite crimes by dedicating each to a particular demon, Protestants first reject some evangelical truth, and then worship the opposite error in its place. If they cast away the healing Sacrament of Penance, one of the most precious fruits of the ineffable tenderness of Jesus, they do so in a lofty spirit of morality, for "the practice of confession is immoral and degrading." If they shrink from mortification, and even their missionaries occupy sumptuous dwellings, battle for augmented salary, and fare delicately every day, it is only by way of manly and intelligent protest, for, as their bishops considerately remind them, "asceticism is no part of the Gospel system." If they refuse all filial love and honor to the most Blessed Mother of God, they are not content without adding,—if we may without defilement repeat words actually employed by a well-known Anglican dignitary,—that "She," who once "*covered with kisses the lips which shall pronounce the doom of all men*," "is expecting her judgment like any other woman!" If they take away the Daily Sacrifice, and, surpassing all human ingratitude, scoff even at that Sacramental Presence which constitutes the most amazing excess of Divine love, and converts this dreary world into a true paradise, they presently cry out with the Church of England, that the Adorable Mystery "is a blasphemous fable." They do not do things by halves. *Abyssus abyssum invocat*—"*one deep calls to another*,"—and they are bent on sounding them all. If St. Paul says, without limitation or reserve, "It is good for a man not to touch a woman;"* *they* answer with one voice, "It is evil!" Nay more, fulfilling the sacred proverb, and resolved to justify the mode of life which they choose for their portion, they assert, with a perversity which even the savage rebukes, that a married is a *more* acceptable servant of God than an unmarried minister. Who can estimate, they say, the advantage of teaching the heathen the sober joys of domestic life?—even at the risk of teaching them at the same time, as Ricci observes, that "conjugal fidelity" is the summit of Christian perfection. "The wives of missionaries," one Protestant clergyman has assured us, "exalt the dignity of the pastoral character!" "An unmarried missionary," says another, as if he thought Christianity began with such men as Cranmer and Beza, "*cannot* eventually prosper." And though all Protestant missionaries are not so enamored of human infirmity, and would not so openly deify it, yet almost all have shown,

* 1 Cor. vii. 1. Cf. Apoc. xiv. 4.

by actions more impressive than words, how extravagant they deem the injunction of St. Paul, how fastidious his example.*

It is true, as we have seen, that they sometimes bear witness against themselves. All the non-Catholic communities which have lost the grace of celibacy, and especially the Greek and Russian, still render homage to it after their manner. The latter, despairing of the continence of her ministers, yet abhorring the incongruity of priestly nuptials, compels all her secular clergy to marry *before* they enter the ecclesiastical state. "Is not this," asks Mr. Ivan Golovine, himself a Russian priest, "an explicit recognition of celibacy as the more perfect calling?"† Is it not also, we may ask in our turn, an equally explicit confession of inability to attain it? The Russian Church has no missionary organization, or she would have learned, by actual experience, that even the instincts of the pagan world reject with scorn a married priesthood. "Directly the savage hears," says an apostolic missionary in America, "that a teacher of religion has a wife, he regards him as on a level with himself." When a Protestant missionary told a Chinese shopkeeper, in answer to an inquiry, that he was "a priest,"—"a priest," said the Chinaman, "and yet married!"‡ Even the heathen witnesses against the uxorious effeminacy of the Sects, and has a deeper sympathy with the ethics of St. Paul than the most refined and educated Anglican, who *now* confesses that the grace of celibacy, without which missionary success is a pure chimera, is so wholly beyond his reach, that the very pretence of it ought to be discouraged. "The mere declaration" of an Anglican minister, says a conspicuous organ of the Establishment, "that he intends to lead a celibate life is worth nothing."§ Yet one of the ablest advocates of Protestantism in its most intellectual form, has lately announced, not as a religious truth, but as a postulate of common sense, that "one of the very first requisites for the ministry is a capacity for celibacy."‖ How, then, shall we be indifferent to the fact, that our Blessed Lord, who expressly declared this to be a *special* gift, which "all men take not, *but they to whom it is given*,"¶ has always conferred this necessary grace upon the Catholic missionary, and always refused it to the Protestant?

* "Sed quid mirum, si tam perversè ratiocinentur hæretici, quos impuritas excœcavit. Adeo verum est hæreticum vix fuisse qui non fuerit impudicus." Bernardinus a Piconio, in 1 Cor vii.

† *Mémoires d'un Prêtre Russe*, ch. x., p. 167.

‡ Tradescant Lay, *The Chinese as they are*, ch. ix., p. 100.

§ *Christian Remembrancer*, vol. xxxvii., p. 241.

‖ *Saturday Review*, January 21, 1860.

¶ S. Matt. xix. 11.

or how shall we doubt, with the history of Christianity before us, that where His gifts are always found, there He is Himself?*

CONTRAST IN SOCIAL RESULTS.

If it were still possible to doubt, in presence of the facts which have now been reviewed, whether God works by the Church or the Sects, there is yet a final consideration which will perhaps be accepted as conclusive. When we have stated it, we shall have completed our task.

In the first ages of Christianity, while that battle was raging which deluged Western Asia and the Southern provinces of Europe with blood, the victims were always and everywhere of one class. Not a pagan fell during three centuries by the hand of a Christian. The new Faith produced martyrs, but not a single assassin. And even when its preachers were able to remind Consuls and Senates that their disciples had become a mighty multitude, and a Roman army saw with astonishment in its ranks a Legion composed of Christians, not a hand was lifted in anger against the persecutor, even in self-defence. Such is the history of the first three centuries. Everywhere blood was shed, but it was the blood of apostles and martyrs.

In later ages, when the Church and the world were no longer two distinct camps, except in the sight of the Angels, and the corruptions of the last had overflowed, like a sea of mire, and left their stain even on the steps of the temple, the preachers and confessors were still the same, but the heathen saw them accompanied by men, also calling themselves Christians, who brought reproach on the name of Christ. "Take away your Spanish soldiers," said Las Casas, " or we will not go among this people, for we should fail to persuade them." In spite of this new difficulty, the heathen world was converted; and if blood was shed, it was still, as of old, the blood of preachers and confessors. Everywhere, as we have seen, the native races grew and multiplied, as they continue to do at this hour, under the shadow of the Cross. It was not spiritual blessings only which the messengers of the Church bore to them, but temporal also; and as the soul of the savage was renewed by grace, so the very

* "It is a vulgar prejudice," observes a Presbyterian traveller, " to suppose that the Catholic clergy of the present times are not as pure and chaste in their lives as the unmarried of the female sex among ourselves. Instances may occur of a different character, but quite as rarely as among an equal number of our unmarried females in Britain of the higher educated classes." Laing, *Notes of a Traveller*, ch. xxi., p. 432.

land in which he dwelt seemed to blush at its former barrenness, and "the wilderness blossomed as the rose."

They are enemies who have attested these facts. There were even cases, when the apostolic laborers had been removed by violence, in which, as they relate, "Nature herself resumed her original aspect." The very earth seems to have mourned their absence, and once more hid her face from the sun under a robe of briers and thorns. In every pagan land, we have been assured by Protestants, the presence of the Catholic missionary has been fruitful only in benefits to its native tribes. Everywhere they increase under their Christian pastors, in numbers, in intelligence, and in prosperity. Everywhere also they mingle harmoniously with their Catholic rulers, and are amalgamated with them, not only by the bonds of a common faith, but even by the ties of marriage, and by community of social habits and interests.

On the other hand, the same witnesses avouch, that there is not so much as a solitary example of a Protestant conquest, leading to the introduction of Protestant ministers, which has not been *fatal* to the aboriginal tenants of the land. If there be an exception, let it be named. In China and India they could not indeed wholly destroy the natives, because they were themselves only a handful in the midst of millions; but even here they have succeeded in inspiring them with that mingled aversion and contempt to which the lapse of every successive year only adds new intensity. The Chinese, shocked, like their European co-religionists, by their worldliness and cupidity, and by the too evident contrast between their profession of ardent piety and the actual tenor of their daily life, still calls them, after an acquaintance of fifty years, "Lie-preaching devils." Nor has this unfavorable estimate of the teachers been modified by his observation of their disciples. He has seen that in the cases in which they have acquired a temporary influence over a few individuals, it has only tended to lower their moral character, and "to qualify them," as even Protestant witnesses complain, "for hypocrites or for sharpers;" while their most conspicuous followers, brought up under their own eye and in their own dwellings, and long employed by them as paid catechists or assistant missionaries, have recruited the ranks of the Tae-pings, and have attained an infamous notoriety even in that worse than pagan rabble of incendiaries and assassins. Such have been the social results of Protestantism in China.

How widely different the influence of Catholic teachers upon the same people has been, we learn, not only from the testimony of their own actions and of the virtues which have so often attracted the admiration of their pagan countrymen, but also from the generous admissions of intelligent English travellers, such as Dr. Barton and Captain Blakiston, Mr. Oliphant and Mr. D'Ewes, and many others. From them we learn the impressive fact that, as Mr. Oliphant observes, "habits foreign to the Chinese domestic character" have been formed among them; that woman has gained the dignity with which the progress of Christianity always invests her; and that all the other social phenomena which accompany a healthy civilization are now witnessed in many a Chinese household. What the Catholic religion is destined to accomplish ultimately in this land, from which the latest accounts report fresh and almost unprecedented conversions wherever order prevails, we may judge from the peaceful triumphs which it has already secured in so many provinces of the empire. Meanwhile, it is needless to insist further upon this feature of a contrast which, if all other evidence were wanting, would be sufficiently proved by the emphatic verdict of the pagans themselves.

Every land, as we have seen, furnishes the same examples, of which a brief recapitulation may not be deemed superfluous.

In India, where the missionaries themselves complain that many of their disciples "are more depraved even than the heathen around them," and that "instruction appears to have rendered them 'twice dead;'" while Rammohun Roy declares that "they are not only idle, debauched reprobates, but gross railers against the truths of Christianity;" where they are obliged to "suspend" such establishments as the Santipore Training Institution because of peculation and immorality, and maintain other colleges only to create atheists, devoid even of natural religion, the final results of English rule have been thus appreciated by various witnesses. "Were we to be driven out of India," said Edmund Burke long ago, "nothing would remain to tell that it had been possessed by any thing better than the ourang-outang or the tiger." "Few vestiges would remain," an ardent Protestant adds once more in 1860, "as evidence of its *ever* having been under Christian rule." The natives, Mr. Gibson has told us, "are uninfluenced to the slightest extent by European dominion and enlightenment." "We have lowered," says another, "instead of raising the standard of morality." "Far from having effected any serious change in the manners or customs of the East Indians," observes Mr. Warburton, "we have rather assimilated ours to theirs. Were the English rule over India suddenly cast off, in a single generation, the tradition of our Eastern Empire would appear a splendid but baseless dream."*

* *The Conquest of Canada*, by T. Warburton, introd., p. 17

In Ceylon, as Dr. Scherzer remarks, English industry and enterprise have been profitable to the colonists themselves, but "productive of small results as a civilizing element." In Australia, while the aborigines "have persistently withstood," as Dr. Jobson observes, "all attempts to civilize them," and are almost extinct within the bounds of the original colony, a committee of the Colonial Council, in recommending "the abolition of the Protectorate," as a proved failure, urgently advise the adoption of instant measures "to promote the interests of religion and education among the *white* population," lest they should retrograde into barbarism, since they already "live and die," as Mr. Henderson has told us, "without education or any degree of religious instruction." In the new English colony of Victoria, nine-tenths of the whole native population perished, as Mr. Westgarth relates, in twenty years. In Van Diemen's Land, a nation went down into the grave within the same period, literally hunted to death, as Mr. Lloyd has told us, by British soldiers and settlers. The later accounts from New Zealand speak of the decay even of the "nominal Christianity" which had hitherto prevailed, and of "the *return* of many individuals to the native customs," after an uninterrupted intercourse of fifty years with Anglican missionaries, superintended by five bishops and a crowd of archdeacons; and an official document discloses the customary fact, that even "their *social condition* is inferior to what it was five years ago," notwithstanding the benefits of English rule, "their houses worse, their cultivation more neglected," and that nothing can now save what Mr. Cholmondeley calls the "mean, squalid, and sickly" remnant of "a population which has once reached such a state of decrepitude," in spite, as Dr. Dieffenbach notices, of their "disposition for assuming a high degree of civilization."

In every island of the Pacific which has found Protestant masters, the same ruin and demoralization have overwhelmed the natives. The depopulation in the various groups of Eastern and Western Oceanica is declared by Protestant writers to be "as ominous as it is unaccountable." In the Society Islands, two-thirds of the whole population disappeared in thirty years, while their English teachers were busy in depriving them of their lands and their commerce, "to possess themselves of it." In the Sandwich Islands, the natives perish so rapidly that, as Mr. Hines observes, "Anglo-Saxons will convert them into another West Indies," or, as Mr. Olmsted adds, "the total extinction of the nation is *inevitable*." Everywhere, the aboriginal races, once models, as Lisiansky and Von Langsdorff noticed, of athletic beauty, melt away by thousands, as if smitten by some destroying angel, before the face of "missionaries," who, as their own friends bitterly complain, can only teach them new vices, and when they have plundered them of all they possess, inform them in their sermons, that "offended Heaven is about to cut them utterly off from the land." A few years hence, as all the Protestant witnesses agree in predicting, the natives of every island under English or American rule, having passed through all the successive grades of degradation and ruin, will be extinct. Protestantism will have created a desert.

On the other hand, wherever Catholic influence has prevailed, material has advanced *pari passu* with spiritual progress. In the Philippines, as Mr. Crawford, Sir Henry Ellis, and others have told us, "an immense improvement *in their social condition*" has attended the conversion of millions of barbarians to the Christian faith. "Joyous and free to this hour," as Admiral Jurien de la Gravière observes, "under the yoke of the law which they confess," they are still living monuments of the civilizing power of true religion; while another French writer, contrasting the effects of Catholic and Protestant missions, refers to this impressive example: "The natives of the Philippines, converted to Catholicism, furnish devoted soldiers to Spain; the natives of India, still Pagan or Mussulman, revolt in the name of their religion, and declare a war of extermination against England."*

In the Gambier Archipelago and the Marquesas, also converted by Catholic missionaries, "the control they have acquired," an English Protestant has told us, "must be seen to be believed." In the Lobos Islands, Mr. Bennett, who has recorded the prodigious immorality and sordid avarice of the same class in the Protestant groups, found the Catholic natives "contented and happy, courteous and hospitable, notable and modest." In Wallis, Futuna, and New Caledonia, where a few years ago their barbarism was a proverb, the heathen, after slaying their first apostles, have accepted both Christianity and civilization, and are steadily increasing, not only in religious fervor, but in material prosperity. In the Sandwich Islands, a multitude of Protestant witnesses have proclaimed the same invariable contrast. Lastly, in Tahiti, known, during the reign of the Protestant missionaries, by the shameful designation of "the brothel of the Pacific," Catholic influence has in a few years been so fruitful in healing power, that while many of its women, as one English writer has told us, have become "admirable specimens" of their sex, the island itself, in the

* *La Cochin Chine et le Tonquin*, par Eugène Veuillot, preface, p. 14, (1859).

words of another, "is now a civilized and prosperous community."

Of Western Africa, we receive, in 1862, from Captain Napier Hewett, a report founded on careful observation, of which the following may be taken as the summary. "Have missionary labors produced any beneficial effect in the colonies themselves? *They have not?*" "Most of the so-called converts have relapsed into barbarism." "Though the country exhibits a teeming fertility, unsurpassed by any thing on earth, the greater part lies an uncultivated waste; the lands once tilled are abandoned, and the houses, *except those inhabited by the missionaries*, desolate and decaying. It seems as though, like some of the West India islands, *a blight had fallen on the place.*"

In South Africa,—where another pagan race has enjoyed for nearly a century the advantages of English rule, while witnesses of every rank and class declare that the natives have only become more and more depraved, that the worst cases of all are found in those who have been in closest contact with the missionaries themselves, and that, in the words of Dr. Livingstone, "the mission stations are mere pauper establishments,"—the Rev. W. Ellis was brought, no doubt unwillingly, to this conclusion: "Without a change, they *must* either become mere hewers of wood and drawers of water to others, or, as a race, *gradually melt away.*"

In Syria and Armenia, where the sole influence of Protestantism, as we have learned from so many witnesses, has been to create a few worthless and immoral pensioners, full of trickery and fraud, "infidels and radicals," as Dr. Southgate admits, "the worst natives of the East," as Dr. Wolff deplores, Mr. Curzon and Captain Wilbraham, Dr. Durbin and Dr. Robinson, Dr. Wolff and Admiral Slade, and even such vehement Protestant writers as Messrs. Smith and Dwight among American, and Mr. Badger among English travellers, confess the "decided superiority" of all, from whatever sect, who have been reconciled to the Church, that "it is not to be denied that their intercourse with the Roman Catholic Church tends to elevate them in the scale of civilization," and that while "the native Christians of the Turkish empire in general, where Roman Catholic missionaries have not penetrated, are ignorant, rude, and uncouth, like buffaloes, Roman Catholic missionaries *have carried everywhere the light of civilization.*"

Finally, in America, the same contrast assumes dimensions which have arrested the attention even of the tourist and the idler. Even they have noted with amazement that, under Catholic rulers, not a tribe has perished; under Protestant, not a tribe has survived; that in the Catholic provinces men of pure Indian blood, whose fathers were converted two centuries ago, rival those of European descent, as Mr. Markham notices, in mental cultivation, and sometimes, as in Peru and Central America, rule armies and govern States; that wherever the Catholic religion prevails, the natives, as Dr. Mackay and others observe, "*still thrive or increase;*" while in the territory of the United States, as Mr. Schoolcraft shows, they have diminished by seventy-four thousand in seven years, and are doomed, as all the authorities agree, to final extinction; that whereas the Indian, under Protestant patronage, has become everywhere a beggar and a sot, even the occupants of the "reserved lands," who have some tincture of civilization, being described by Mr. Burton and others as drunken, squalid, and unchaste; and the residents in the "missions," in the words of Mrs. Jameson, as "objects of compassion," and in those of Mr. Kingston and Mr. Kane as "a very inferior race," and "wallowing in beastly drunkenness;" "the work effected by the Catholic missionaries," as Governor Stephens reports to the President of the United States, "*is really prodigious.*" Hindered rather than assisted by the civil authorities, and destitute of temporal resources, the latter have employed the higher gifts which they are able to dispense with results which this official might well call prodigious; and the fiercest tribes of the West, subdued by their persuasive charity, are thus described by the same competent and impartial witness: The *Flatheads*, he says, once brutal and sanguinary, "are the best Indians in the territory, honest, brave, and docile, and strongly attached to their religious convictions;" the *Cœurs d'Alène*, polygamists and steeped in barbarism, have not only learned to cultivate the soil and live on its produce, but "their morals have become pure and their conduct edifying;" while the *Potawottomies*, destined under other masters to speedy destruction, have been so effectually converted and civilized, that, according to the same authority, "*they are hardly Indians now.*" It would be barely credible, if we did not learn it from the same official report, that all these tribes, aided only by their spiritual teachers, build churches in these far distant solitudes, "of which all the ornaments are so well executed, that one is tempted to suppose they must have been imported."

Lastly, on the opposite frontier of the same continent, nearly three thousand miles from the western regions just referred to, while all the witnesses agree in describing the nominally Protestant Indians as the most abject of their race, and predict their inevitable annihilation, Miss Martineau tells us of Indian villages "full of orderly and industrious inhabitants;" and

Mr. Buckingham that the missionaries are at this day even "more than usually successful;" and Mr. Kane praises "the agricultural skill and industry" of their disciples; and Mr. Kingston unwillingly reports that "they are said to be a very obedient, industrious, and intelligent set, and superior to the Protestants;" and Miss Murray regrets that "Roman Catholicism is best adapted for civilizing the Indians;" and Mrs. Jameson honestly declares, after minute examination, "One thing is most visible, certain, and undeniable, that the Roman Catholic converts are in intelligence and general civilization superior to all the others."

Even in Central America, and among tribes once so ferocious and degraded as the Caribs, Mr. Stephens has told us, not only of their piety, and of their reverence both for the offices and the ministers of religion, but that "we were exceedingly struck with the great progress made in civilization by these descendants of cannibals, the fiercest of all the Indian tribes."*

Thus, in every region of the earth, by the testimony of hostile or prejudiced witnesses, the same mysterious contrast is revealed. The Church, they confess, has brought to all lands unity, progress, and peace; the Sects, the same annalists avouch, have sown only discord, corruption, and death. Which, shall we deem, has been the work of God?

THE CHURCH AND THE SECTS.

Such, in its general outlines, is the contrast between the work of the Church and the work of the Sects, between the fruitful ministry of apostles, lifted by omnipotent love above human infirmity, and the sterile craft of "mere stipendiaries," who have failed, by the testimony of their co-religionists, in every object which they undertook, except the promotion of their own temporal fortunes. But if these latest adversaries, like the

* It is usual, among Protestants, to point to the history of Spanish colonization as an exception; "yet to Spain," as an ardent Protestant observes, "the credit is due, in spite of numerous shortcomings, and notwithstanding the oppression of her subordinates, of having endeavored to establish *the wisest, the most humane, and the only successful system* of treating natives of an inferior race. . . The Indians," in her colonies, "have continued to form the laboring class; amalgamation has taken place, to a very large extent, with Europeans, and the native race has thus been preserved from extinction. In the English colonies, on the other hand, owing to the influx of settlers of the laboring class,"—he omits all the more important and influential points of contrast,—"the aborigines have either been exterminated, or, through a system of isolation, are rapidly and inevitably advancing on the melancholy road to *final annihilation.*" *Travels in Peru and India,* by Clements R. Markham, F.S.A., F.R.G.S., ch. viii., p. 132 (1862).

Arian and Nestorian missionaries of earlier times, have vainly disputed with the Church her office as Teacher of the Nations, and have not even snatched the transient successes which *they* contrived to obtain, there has been another conflict, waged not in pagan but in Christian lands, which seemed once to promise a different issue, and of which we must attempt, in conclusion, to trace the beginning and the end.

More than two centuries before the missionary schemes of Protestant communities, of which we have now investigated the results, and which owed their tardy origin to the rivalry of conflicting sects rather than to religious zeal, had made their first appeal to Protestant sympathy, a more momentous struggle, which had the whole of Europe for its field, and sucked into its vortex one after the other all the civilized nations of the earth, threatened to subvert the whole existing order of things, to annihilate at one blow all the religious institutions of the past, and even to reconstitute the foundations of civil society. Certain names have been always associated with this famous struggle, as if it had been due solely to the influence and energy of those who bore them. But this is probably an error. The age in which Luther and his companions appeared was already ripe for the movement which their followers regarded as a triumph, and the rest of the world as a catastrophe. The relaxation of discipline and the decay of virtue, which at that time found a home chiefly in the cloister, beyond which, as St. Bernard had said, with a lawful exaggeration, it could hardly be found; the intrusion of worldly and even licentious men, generally of high birth, into the offices of the Church, which they coveted only for the wealth and power of which they were the too copious sources; the neglect of preaching and catechetical instruction, and all that long catalogue of abuses against which theologians had written and saints had supplicated during two centuries, and which the Council of Trent was to reform with such masterful severity, that hardly the faintest vestige of them has been apparent from that date; these, and not the talent of a few individuals, were the true causes of that deplorable revolution which without them would have had neither meaning nor possibility of success.

It was from this vantage ground that Protestantism commenced its warfare against the Catholic Church. For a moment it appeared about to triumph, but in the very hour in which victory seemed most assured, and Europe resounded with the acclamations of a hundred exulting sects, the world was to witness the apparition of that awful Power which alone survives all human vicissitudes, and whose seeming inaction is as the brief slumber of Jesus in the vessel of Peter, from which

He is sure to awake, at the prayer of the Church, to the confusion of His enemies and hers. Once more, in the hour of her greatest need, she was to gain one of those victories which are never so near at hand as when, to human eyes, she seems about to perish. The new religion, like Arianism and Islamism, had already overrun Christendom, but only to give place to the Church against whose life it conspired, and to show that, strong in her union with God, she could both vanquish heresy in its strongholds, and kindle the light of faith simultaneously in new worlds, in China and India, in Canada, Brazil, and Paraguay. Let us contemplate for a moment this latest victory of the Church, of which even the facts recorded in these volumes leave more than half untold.

In *Germany*, as early as 1558, "only *a tenth part* of the inhabitants," as Ranke observes, "had remained faithful to the old religion." Twenty years later, "Protestantism was the dominant creed of *all* the *Austrian* provinces, whether of the German, Slavonic, or Hungarian tongues." Before the end of the century, "nearly the whole nobility of Austria, and even of Styria, had embraced the reformed faith."*

In *France*, so general was the movement, that "for some time *the whole people* seemed to lean towards the Protestant confession." As late as the year 1600, "there were seven hundred and sixty parish churches belonging to the Protestants of France, all in good order; four thousand of the nobility belonged to that confession."

Poland and Saxony, Belgium and Holland, Sweden and Denmark, England and Scotland, were swallowed up in the same vortex, and of all the nationalities of Europe, only Spain, Italy, and Ireland remained wholly faithful, in this universal apostasy, to the Catholic Church.

The victory seemed complete and final; yet men had hardly begun to count its gains before it was converted into hopeless and irretrievable defeat. In Germany, as early as 1622, "Catholicism poured in a mighty torrent," says a well-known Protestant writer, "from the south to the north, and the work of conversion advanced *with resistless force*."† First Austria cast out the unclean spirit which had entered into her. One after another all the provinces of that great empire returned to the faith. In 1620, "all Bohemia," as the Protestant Krasinski notices, "was, with the exception of some nobles and monks, Protestant; in 1637," only seventeen years later, "it was entirely Roman Catholic!"‡ So utterly was heresy

* Ranke, i., 364, 412; Kohl, p. 413.
† Ranke, ii., 77.
‡ *Panslavism and Germanism*, by Count Valerian Krasinski, ch. ii., p. 160.

vanquished, and so effectual was the reconversion of all the Austrian races, after the momentary frenzy of delusion had passed away, that in our own day, even in Bohemia and Moravia, once entirely Protestant, the new religion claims in the latter only six, and in the former only two and a quarter per cent. of the whole population !*

In Hungary, which had become the spoil of the destroyer, the apostles of the Society of Jesus, filled with the might of God, scourged the evil spirits from the land, and preached with such irresistible unction and power the ancient faith, that, after the lapse of two centuries, a German Lutheran thus describes the relative power of the two confessions: "There is a great difference," says Mr. Kohl, "between the Catholic and Reformed clergy in Hungary; the former are *incomparably* more learned and more imbued with the Western European civilization than the latter." "The great convents and abbeys in Austria," he adds, content to adopt a human explanation of the contrast, "have been at all times the nurses and cherishers of science and art. . . Each boasts its celebrated names, either of those who have long departed from this world, and live only in the affection and respect of posterity, or of those still living and actively engaged in the service of their order." Then ridiculing "the notions which Protestants entertain" of these sanctuaries of labor, science, and virtue, he gives this characteristic proof of the universality of their influence. "I asked," he says, while travelling in Hungary, "whether Catholics were not sometimes converted to the reformed faith. '*No, never*,' was the answer; but the contrary sometimes happens. A reformed nobleman, when he is on his death-bed, will sometimes send of a sudden for a Catholic priest, but it never occurs to a Catholic that a Protestant minister can be of any service to him."†

In Poland, where the reformed doctrine developed almost at its birth into Socinianism, and a once faithful nation seemed forever lost to God, the exorcism was equally swift and potent. So completely has heresy died out, in spite of its early triumphs, that while an English writer observes that "the great body of the Polish nation consists of *Catholics*," he adds, that even "of the remainder the majority consists of *Jews*."‡ Count Krasinski, though a Protestant, confesses that this reconversion of a whole nation was effected by the same apostolic ministry which triumphed in so many other lands, and that owing to

* Kohl, p. 70.
† Kohl's *Austria*, pp. 98, 375.
‡ *An Inquiry*, &c., by Herbert Marsh, D.D., p. 67.

the influence of the Jesuits, whom the Spirit of God inspired to reconquer kingdoms and to add to the Church more souls than she had lost, "domestic life in Poland," as soon as heresy was cast out, "was graced by truly patriarchal virtues."*

Everywhere the snare was broken in which the enemy had captured the nations, and millions of souls awoke, at the voice of this new company of apostles, from the trance which had surprised for a moment the conscience of mankind. From one end of Europe to the other, rose up, in every city and village, preachers who emulated the austerity of St. John the Baptist, and the fiery zeal of St. Paul. In obedience to their word, Saxony, Bavaria, and half Prussia returned to the Church. Belgium, which had been half Protestant, "was transformed," as Ranke observes, "into one of the most Catholic countries of the world." Even Holland, which had been so completely subjugated by the enemy that her recovery might well be deemed hopeless, was destined, by a miracle of Divine grace, to welcome once more her sacred hierarchy; and after losing, by a religious revolution, Flanders and Brabant, and every thing south of the Scheldt and the Rhine, has seen fully one-half of the shorn remnant of her population embrace in their turn the Catholic faith.

In France, in the course of a few years, says Ranke, "the number of Protestants decreased *seventy per cent.;*" and only twenty years after the new religion had devastated the land with civil war, and sent forth its armed hosts under the command of kings and princes, men were already predicting, what has long since been accomplished, "the inevitable and final downfall of Protestantism in France."

In every land, except Sweden and England,—where the civil authority prohibited the freedom of conscience which Protestantism was supposed to guarantee, and where the rack or the gibbet supplanted reason, and for a time extinguished faith,—the same swift decay commenced which from that hour no effort has been able to arrest, and of which Macaulay wrote the pregnant summary when he said: "Fifty years after the Lutheran separation, Catholicism could scarcely maintain itself on the shores of the Mediterranean; a hundred years after the separation, *Protestantism could scarcely maintain itself on the shores of the Baltic.*"†

Such was the latest of that long series of victories, renewed in every successive age, of which the all-sufficient explanation is found in the magnificent promises of the Eternal Word:

* *The Religious History of the Slavonic Nations*, ch. ix., p. 197.
† *Essay on Ranke's History of the Popes.*

"*Every tongue that resisteth thee in judgment thou shalt condemn.*" "*Behold, I am with you all days, even to the consummation of the world.*" And even this, as we have seen, was only the half of her triumph. It was not enough that she should recover millions from the apostate races over whom the enemy had begun to reign, and restore repentant nations to the family of God. A more perfect satisfaction was due both to Him and to her; and therefore she received power, while baffling the most formidable conspiracy which had ever assailed her life, to add at the same moment to her communion, by an effort not too great for this mighty Mother, such a multitude of new believers in the East and West, of every people and tongue, as to fulfil once more in the face of the world that double prophecy, "*The nation and kingdom that will not serve thee shall perish*," and "*the strength of the gentiles shall come to thee.*" This was the last and greatest of her triumphs. Ten thousand apostles rose up to do her bidding in the Old World, and twice ten thousand to carry her message to the New. In the very hour of her sorest need, while her Lord seemed to sleep in the vessel round which the storm was raging, a double victory over her enemies was preparing for her, a double confusion for them; for while they could neither recruit a solitary disciple in the other hemisphere, nor maintain their brief conquests in this, she did both at once; and as Moses with one hand gave the Covenant to his people, and lifting up the other "*put Amalec to flight*," so she presented at one moment to a thousand pagan tribes the Gospel of Christ, and the next drove back from the Mediterranean to the Baltic the swarming legions who were arrayed against her. Once more the word came to her, "The Lord will fight for you, and you shall hold your peace," and in patience and confidence she awaited the issue.

THE END OF THE CONFLICT.

It is not at the close of a work already extended to extravagant dimensions that we can attempt to review all the phases of that new combat to which the Church was now challenged, nor to trace the gradual decay and present condition of the Sects which from that hour conspired against her. Yet without a few words on both points this summary would be incomplete. Founded on the common basis of hostility to the Catholic Church, and breathing out destruction against her, the Sects had already lost all cohesion before they had been ten years in the world, and were busy even at that date in those implacable mutual conflicts by which God devoted them to destruction, and which at a later period they were to renew, to the dishonor of Christianity, before the face of the heathen. A brief array of testimonies will suffice to convince us how exactly their later fortunes have accorded with this beginning, and that the domestic history of Protestantism, always "divided against itself," is at least as significant a revelation of its inability to maintain religious life in its own disciples, as its failure among the heathen is of its incapacity to communicate it to others. Three centuries have passed away since they commenced their career, and not one promise which the Sects made to a foolish generation has been kept, even in part. They boasted that they would restore Christian doctrine to its primitive purity, and have only destroyed the faith of whole nations, reducing their masses to a condition almost below that of the heathen, while they have everywhere revived blasphemies against the Blessed Trinity and the Incarnation which had been well-nigh unknown for a thousand years. "The ancient controversies on the Trinity," as Mr. Hallam observes, "had long subsided, ... and Erasmus, when accused of Arianism, might reply with apparent truth, *that no heresy was more extinct.*"* With the new religion it revived, under various names and disguises, in every land, was diffused like a deadly plague wherever the Reformation found disciples; and now at the end of three centuries, the Church is found to be defending in all Protestant lands, against the contemptuous mockery of the Sects, those very truths of revelation of which their founders claimed, with eager imprecation and clamorous taunt, to be the exclusive advocates! They have failed to teach the Gospel to the heathen, but they have failed not less signally to preserve it from the outrages of their own friends. This is their twofold shame. "Men are doubting," said Melancthon, with real or affected horror, "about the most fundamental truths!"† Even in that early day he foresaw what the end would be. It has come at last.

GERMANY.

In Germany,—where the Reformation found its earliest advocates, and where it has been so fruitful of enmity and division, that "there are now about *thirty-eight* Protestant churches, each of which is independent of every other,"—so

* *Introduction to the Literature of Europe*, vol. i., ch. v., p. 507.

† Quoted by Starck, *Theodul's Gastmahl*, p. 246; ed. Kentzinger. "Vides quo tendat petulantia multorum." *Homæ Matthiæ Epist.*, p. 252.

notorious is the decay of all positive religion, and so universal the extinction of Christian faith and piety, that while one German writer declares of its empty and prayerless temples, "one could not bring a heathen inside of them without blushing for shame," another has lately announced, in the face of his co-religionists, and in allusion to phenomena with which they are familiar, "it must be plainly seen that the days in which we live *are ripe for the great apostasy*."*

In 1825, a German theologian, "in recounting the professors who could any how be considered orthodox, that is, those who *in any way* contended for the doctrines of the Gospel, or its very truth, counted, in all Protestant Germany, *seventeen*."† What further proof do we need that Protestantism has been in Germany the destroyer of Christianity?

And what, meanwhile, have been in the same land the fortunes of that Church which Protestantism undertook to reform or supplant, and whose downfall it predicted three centuries ago as just at hand? Teaching at this hour the same doctrines which she taught before the Sects came into being, and which she will still be teaching when they have vanished from the world, she has not only reconverted a majority of the German race, including even in Prussia one-half of the entire population, and recovered the filial homage of such men as Stolberg and Schlegel, and others hardly less illustrious; but has heard at last the sorrowful confession of her adversaries that she alone can now illumine the darkness which hangs like a pall around them, or save them from the deluge of unbelief which, as Messner observes in 1861, "is filtering through and wasting away those protecting dykes, the Family, the State, and the Church."‡

From every quarter the same cry of alarm is heard, and the partisans of a religion once so arrogant and menacing no longer blush to declare, while they contemplate the ruins around them, that the Church alone can now save society from dissolution and chaos. "Two of the most determined political opponents of Catholic interests," we learn from Dr. Döllinger, "both zealous friends and supporters of the Evangelical," or official Church of Prussia, are the well-known President of the Council Von Gerlach, and the Privy Councillor Eilers. "We daily see," says the former, whose whole public life has been an attack upon the authority of the Vicar of Christ, "how small, in comparison with the power of the Catholic Church, is the

* Quoted by Döllinger, *The Church and the Churches*, pp. 275, 308, 330.
† *A Letter to the Archbishop of Canterbury*, by Dr. Pusey, p. 123.
‡ Döllinger, p. 204.

influence which the Evangelical has upon the enlightenment and sanctification of the mass of the population, and upon the majority of its own members." "I have made it my study," adds the latter, who has founded three journals to perpetuate the opposition to the Catholic Church, "to ascertain the connection that exists between what is the Christian life of the Catholic population, and its institutions and practices; and, *with an unwilling heart*, I am compelled to admit that in general a far more Christ-like life is led by those who belong to the Catholic than to the Evangelical Church."*

Whoever desires to obtain an exact conception of the actual condition of Protestant Germany, which appears even to such men as Rudelbach significant of the coming Antichrist, will find in the latest work of Dr. Döllinger at once the most minute and the most authentic narrative which has ever been published. The facts recorded in that remarkable work are entirely derived, and to this they owe their special value, from the spontaneous testimony of a multitude of writers whose names are eminent in the ranks of those who still affect to deem the Reformation a benefit to mankind. It is impossible to repeat them here. Yet there is one, curiously illustrating the real nature of Protestantism, which must be briefly noticed.

Of all the promises which the leaders of the Reformation gave to their followers in every land, the most attractive perhaps was that which offered them liberty of thought and opinion, and complete emancipation from ecclesiastical control. Protestants will tell us how they have kept this promise. "The whole of the northern people of Protestant countries," says Lord Molesworth, "*have lost their liberties* ever since they changed their religion for a better." "Sweden, Denmark, Prussia, and all the Protestant States of Germany," adds a well-known Presbyterian writer, "are at this day, in all that regards freedom in social action, *freedom of mind and opinion*, more enslaved than they were in the middle of the middle ages."† Such is the destiny of those who sell their birthright to the teachers described by St. Peter, "who bring in sects of perdition, *promising them liberty*."

From the hour in which Protestantism acquired supremacy in any land, there has been more audacious tyranny, more arrogant and oppressive "priestcraft," in the most odious sense of the word, than was ever possible in the Catholic Church, or ever tolerated in any human society, pagan or Christian. In

* Döllinger, p. 334.

† Laing, *Observations on Sweden*, ch. i., p. 11. *Observations on Europe*, ch. xv., p. 394.

the State Churches of Germany, where Protestantism began its career, the civil power, to which it transferred the religious supremacy once exercised by the Vicar of Christ, has never thought it necessary to flatter its subjects with even the semblance of ecclesiastical liberty. "The Protestant princes," as Moehler observes, "thought they were bound to decide for their subjects all religious controversies, and to make their own individual opinions the property of all." When Frederic III., Count Palatine of the Rhine, abandoned the Lutheran for the Calvinistic doctrines, in 1562, he compelled his people to do the same. Eight years later, his son Louis banished all the Calvinist preachers and reinstated the Lutherans. Six years after, Frederic IV. restored the Calvinists, and dealt with their rivals just as his ancestors did with the partisans of Geneva. The people of the Palatinate were not even consulted, and would probably have been surprised if they had been.

It was stated at the Westphalian Peace Congress, that the city of Oppenheim, pawned to the Palatinate, has been forced to change its religion ten times since the Reformation. In Anhalt and in Hesse Cassel, the preachers were silenced, deposed, or restored at the pure caprice of the Landgrave. In Prussia, and at the present hour, the same almost ludicrous commentary on the so-called Reformation is still displayed. The Prussians, says Mr. Laing, "are morally slaves, of enslaved minds." In 1834, a Prussian monarch, without even the affectation of consulting the nation, peremptorily suppressed, by a stroke of the pen, both the Lutheran and Calvinistic Churches, in order to substitute a new one of his own invention. When the people of Silesia hesitated to obey the royal edict, or to "fall down and worship the golden image which the king had set up," with the usual accompaniment of "harp, and sackbut, and all kinds of music," they were promptly instructed in the nature of the "liberty" which the Reformation had acquired for them. "Coercion, imprisonment, *military force*, and quartering of troops on the recusant peasants, were resorted to, in order to *force* the ministers and people to receive this new service." The process was characteristic, and "to resist this monstrous tyranny and persecution," adds the Protestant observer, "there was no Rome, no Vatican, no Pope or head of the Church to appeal to. How different, in the same country, at the same period, was the exertion of the autocratic power of the same Prussian monarch over his Roman Catholic subjects! *They* had protection at Rome, and consequently in the whole Catholic world, against such arbitrary violence. He could not even appoint to any clerical office independently of Rome, although he could, and actually did, imprison and dismiss

Protestant clergymen, for refusing to adopt a new Church Service, which, as head of the Church and State, he composed and promulgated by royal edict!"

Is it possible to confess more frankly, that true religious liberty has no existence out of the Catholic Church, and that the Vicar of Christ, after defending the weak against the strong for nearly two thousand years, is still the solitary bulwark against spiritual oppression? "Catholicism is, in fact," adds this Presbyterian witness, "the *only* barrier at present in Prussia against a general and debasing despotism of the State over mind and action,"*—an admission that Protestants still derive a partial protection from the very authority which they once attempted to destroy, while it illustrates the remark of M. Guizot, that "people who aspire to liberty run the risk of deceiving themselves as to the nature of tyranny," and justifies the reproach of Father Faber, that "men would rather be enslaved by the State than owe their emancipation to the Church."

SWITZERLAND.

In Switzerland, the second conquest of the Reformation, the Gospel was finally ejected more than a century ago, and the Holy Name delivered by apostate preachers to the derision of the people. "O Bossuet," said the infidel D'Alembert, exulting in the impieties which had made Geneva the Sodom of Christendom, "where art thou? Eighty years have passed away since you predicted that the principles of the Protestants would conduct them to Socinianism: what gratitude do you not owe to an author who has attested before all Europe the truth of your prophecy!"†

The Redeemer of the world is now declared by the University of Geneva to be "a mere man," and the students for the ministry, the future teachers of a Protestant people, are told by their masters and professors, "Make any thing you like of Jesus Christ, so that you do not make him God."‡ So universal is the apostasy, that the "Berne Synod" could lately report, "Of every ten householders there is scarcely to be found one who now believes in God and Christ, or makes any use of the Scrip-

* Laing, *Notes of a Traveller*, ch. vi., pp. 171, 212.

† *Ouvres de D'Alembert*, tome v., p. 272.

‡ *Sketch of the Religious Discussions which have lately taken place at Geneva*, pp. 4–5. Cf. *Considerations sur la Diviniét de Jésus Christ*, par H. L. Empaytaz.

tures." "There no longer exists in the Protestant Rome," said de Lamennais, "I do not say any Christian faith, but any faith whatever."* "The earthly source, the pattern, the Rome of our Presbyterian doctrine and practice," adds Mr. Laing, "has fallen lower from her own doctrine and practice than ever Rome fell. Rome has still superstition; Geneva has not even that semblance of religion."†

But perhaps the Swiss Protestants, though they have abandoned the Gospel, still retain the "*liberty*" for which their fathers deserted the Catholic Church? Thirty years ago, a few ministers in the Canton de Vaud, who labored under this delusion, ventured to criticise the statement of the "Venerable Company of Pastors," that, "to reject the doctrine of the Trinity is necessary on our principles." They were committed to prison.‡

Perhaps the clergy retain the power and influence which they once possessed, and which they exercised with a fierce and insolent intolerance never matched except in Scotland and in the Puritan hierarchy of New England? So complete is the degradation of this once rampant class, that it was lately discussed in the public journals, "Whether it was proper that clergymen's daughters should be publicly advertised for as housemaids."§

Perhaps, at least, they have the consolation of knowing that they have effectually rooted out the ancient faith, and that their victory over the Catholic Church is complete and undisputed? In 1860, the Protestant population of Switzerland only exceeded the Catholic by one-fifth! In the city of Geneva, the metropolis of Calvinism, where once a Catholic was hunted as a wild beast, and St. Francis de Sales was an object of fear and aversion, while there are forty-two thousand two hundred and sixty-six infidels or Arians, there are forty-two thousand three hundred and fifty-five zealous Catholics.‖ In the ten years from 1850 to 1860 nearly thirteen thousand were added to their number in this one city, in which they at length form a majority of the population. On the other hand, a Protestant minister, who still professes to believe the Gospel while he rails at the Church, the solitary advocate of that doctrine which Servetus was burned for denying, counts about one hundred and fifty followers!

* *Histoire des Momiers*, p. 391.

† *Notes of a Traveller*, ch. xiii., p. 325.

‡ *Défense de la Vénérable Compagnie des Pasteurs*, &c. Cf. *Feuille d'Avis de Genève*, Octobre 7, 1818; *Mélanges de Religion*, tome ix., p. 342; *Genève Religieuse*, par M. A. Bost, p. 12; *Ouvres de M. de Lamennais*, tome viii., p. 392; Halda e's *Letter to M. J. J. Chenevière.*

§ Döllinger, p. 219.

‖ Id., p. 214.

FRANCE.

In France, we have been already told that "hardly twenty *pasteurs* confess the doctrines of the Trinity and the Atonement;" and even the few who think themselves entitled to defend the Christian religion do so in language so full of arrogance and malice, that their writings are, if possible, more odious than those of its professed adversaries. "Christianity," says an English Protestant traveller, "must appear to the great majority of French Protestants to have in it nothing positive or defined at all. . . . On entering a French temple, one experiences the same sensation as on entering a Jewish synagogue. Its services appear like a wretched effort, not to serve, but to keep up the memory of an abolished religion."*

HOLLAND.

"Religion in Holland," says Huber, "has never, since the Reformation, continued the same for thirty years together."† As early as 1655, an English traveller reported that "the sect of Socinianism bears great sway, and is assented to by most there."‡ "At present," says a Dutch writer in 1856, "every one teaches and preaches what he likes."§ Of its fifteen hundred ministers, fourteen hundred are said to deny the Incarnation.

"The Dutch Reformed Church," says Niebuhr, and we have had in these volumes sufficient evidence of the truth of his statement, "has always, wherever it was free, become coarsely tyrannical, and has never, either for the spirit it manifested, or the good dispositions of its teachers, deserved any great esteem."‖ Yet this coarse tyranny, which is the characteristic of "reformed" communities, has not prevented half of its population from becoming Catholic, nor preserved among the remaining moiety even the barest elements of Christianity.

* *Blackwood's Magazine*, April, 1836, p. 470.

† *Bibliothèque Universelle*, tome xxiv., p. 181.

‡ Thurloe's *State Papers*, vol. i., p. 508; vol. iii., p. 50. Cf. Winwood's *Memorials*, vol. iii., p. 340; Gerard Brandt, *History of the Reformation in the Low Countries*, vol. iv.; Grotius, *Ordin. Hollandiæ et Westfrisiæ Pietas*, p. 123; *Encyclopédie Méthodique*, Art. *Sociniens;* Vedelius, *De Arcanis Arminianisme*, lib. i.; Pluquet, *Dictionnaire*, tome I., p. 78; Bossuet, *Histoire des Variations*, &c., tome iv., p. 510.

§ Döllinger, p. 201.

‖ Quoted by Döllinger, p. 100.

"There has been," says Dr. Candlish, a well-known Presbyterian preacher, "a grievous declension and departure from her first faith in the Dutch Church."* "The death-waters of unbelief," adds Messner in 1861, "of Rationalism, Pantheism, and Materialism are in Holland, as in Germany," sweeping all before them; while Groen freely confesses that "the Dutch Church is a chaos, and should not any longer be called a Church."†

ENGLAND.

It is not within the compass of a few pages that we can appreciate the phenomena which betray the real influence of the Reformation in England. One of her own clergy, the Rev. Dr. Pusey, described her population, a few years ago, as "a numerous nation of heathens." A little later, an official census, which revealed the fact that five millions "profess no religion whatever," confirmed his account, and added, that in spite of a religious Establishment which has at least one representative in every village in the land,—in Leeds and Liverpool *forty*, in Manchester *fifty-one*, in Birmingham *fifty-four*, in Lambeth *sixty-one*, and in Sheffield *sixty-two* per cent. of the inhabitants neither have nor profess to have any religion whatever; so that, speaking generally, "heathenism is fast prevailing over Christianity," or, as the Bishop of Exeter expressed it in one of his Charges, "a fierce hatred against the Christian faith rages in many parts of England."

It is in England, again, that the masses have sunk into such a condition of purely animal existence, that the official descriptions, including those of the Assistant Commissioners employed during the late Education Inquiry, are almost incredible. "In this great Christian nation," we are told, "vice exists to an extent *utterly unknown in pagan countries*."‡ And the proofs of this statement are found, not only in the rural and mining districts, but, as an eminent advocate of the Establishment admits, "in the fairest portions of this magnificent city." "A frightful amount of infidelity," says the Rector of one of the most important London parishes, in which Exeter Hall is a conspicuous monument, "infidelity in all its shapes, extending not only to the denying of the Christian revelation, but even to *the grossest and darkest heathenism*," prevails among the lower,

* *The Scottish Christian Herald*, vol. iii., pp. 199, 504; 2d Series.

† Döllinger, p. 204.

‡ *The Times*, April 11, 1862.

"and actually extends among the better classes."* "We could name entire quarters," observes a great authority, and this "within easy walk of Charing Cross," "in which it seems to be a custom that men and women should live in promiscuous concubinage—where the very shopkeepers make a profession of atheism, and encourage their poor customers to do the same." In more obscure districts, he adds, "there are whole streets, nay miles and miles, where the people live literally without God in the world."†

In 1856, a learned English traveller described in these words the impression which he had formed of the comparative civilization of the mass of the British population and "of the black African, or the red American Indian." "I was compelled to come to the conclusion, after fairly investigating the question, that the physical, moral, intellectual, and educational state of the lower orders in England *was the lowest on the scale I had ever witnessed* ..... quite on a par with that of the savage, and sometimes even below it."‡ "Bad," says an Anglican clergyman, who had also gathered knowledge from foreign travel, "as the moral effects of the Jewish and Mohammedan religions are, it must strike every traveller that the people are under the influence of religion, such as it is, more than they seem to be in the great towns of England."§

And what, meanwhile, is the condition of that so-called National Church, which, after a reign of three centuries, has brought to this pass a land once known as "the Isle of Saints?" "Half the inhabitants of this island," we are told, "are Dissenters, and of the rest the greater part take the Establishment simply as it comes, with very mixed feelings, and certainly not loving it as the thing of their choice."‖ After fighting during so long a period for supremacy, and refusing to all others, while she had the power, the smallest liberty of conscience, the so-called Church of England has accepted, says an official organ, "a servitude which the lowest sect of Jumpers would not subject itself to,"¶ and the only religious freedom, as Döllinger observes, which has survived so many conflicts, is "the liberty of *not* belonging to the State Church!"

In the Sects which have separated from its communion, though their members are in bondage to their own conceits or enslaved by human traditions, they persuade themselves that

* *Quarterly Review,* April, 1861, pp. 432–63.
† Ibid.
‡ *The United States,* &c., by John Shaw, M.D., F.G.S., F.L.S., ch. x., p. 244.
§ *The Canary Isles,* &c., by the Rev. Thomas Debary, M.A., ch. xxi., p. 255.
‖ *The Times,* February 28, 1862.
¶ *The Globe,* quoted by Döllinger, p. 156.

they still retain their freedom, because they can exchange one crude opinion for another, whenever they have a mind to do so; but the Church which they have quitted has lost even the right to determine its own confession of faith, and is content to solicit from a lay tribunal the solution of the gravest questions which can agitate the conscience of mankind. The Russian Church has a "Synod," of which it cannot even appoint the secretary and subordinate officials, "who are all nominated and displaced by the Czar," while its president, a Lutheran and a cavalry officer, "presents to benefices, decides upon the degradation of a clergyman, or submits to the Emperor subjects for canonization!"* The Church of England, whose bishops are selected by the Minister of the day, has also a "Convocation," of which the members hardly dare open their mouths, lest they should betray to the world that no two of them are of the same mind, and which assembles only when a lay voice permits it to meet, and retires with equal docility when it bids it depart. Unable to decide even the most fundamental points of faith, its members who are curious to know what is its doctrine of Baptism or of the Inspiration of Scripture, or of the Eucharistic Sacrifice, must now address their inquiries to a learned gentleman, who decides on Monday whether an Anglican minister is a heretic, and on Tuesday whether a patent has been infringed or a charter-party violated. So completely has the Established Church lost the character of a *teacher*, that, as an organ of the government contemptuously observes, "the thousands of its declared adherents laugh aloud whenever its ministers overstep their humble sphere as officers of a national institution."† The clergy of the Establishment know their position, and accept it.

It is true that the official Church, unlike that of Holland or Prussia, has nominally maintained its original formularies; but this is only because they are a burden to nobody, and because experience has shown that even its clergy are at liberty to interpret their vague and contradictory phrases almost at pleasure, while among its lay members every one is free to commend or revile, to accept or suppress them, according to his private humor. "There is scarcely a form of religious imposture," says one of the chief authorities recognized by Englishmen, "and perhaps no set of religious or irreligious opinions, that does not number among its adherents some priest or deacon of the English Church."‡ Differing in this respect from every

* *The Russo-Turkish Campaigns*, by Colonel Chesney, D.C.L., F.R.S., ch. x., p. 313.

† *The Globe*, ubi supra.

‡ *The Times*, April 9, 1862.

other religious community which has hitherto appeared in the world, the outward profession of membership with *this* Church implies absolutely *nothing* as to the belief of those who make it. The titles of "Wesleyan," or "Unitarian," or "Baptist," indicate at least something of the religious opinions of those who bear them; not so that of a member of the Establishment, who may hold the same opinions as either of the classes named, or their contraries, or any conceivable modification of them, without injury to his profession as an Anglican. There is probably less difference of sentiment between any two members of any religious community in the world than is every day announced, not only between the laity, but between the clergy and the bishops of the Anglican body. The Church of England—which neither teaches nor rebukes, neither approves nor condemns, neither canonizes nor excommunicates, and is represented at the same moment, and with equal confidence, by Gorham and Philpots, by Hampden and Keble, by Jowett and Wilberforce, by Whately and Denison, that is, by men whose respective creeds are the formal negation of one another,—confessedly numbers within her undefined pale partisans of *every* religious tenet, theory, or opinion, however opposite and contradictory, which Protestantism has at any time or by any agency introduced into the world. The history of Christianity records no parallel case. "The religion of the Church of England," said Lord Macaulay, "is, in fact, a bundle of religious systems without number; . . . . *a hundred Sects battling within one Church*."*

It is to be observed, moreover, that however significant may be the lessons which we derive from the past history and present condition of a Church which, in spite of its pretensions to be "National," is probably, if tried by any rational test of Church membership, one of the smallest Sects in the kingdom, a new and more formidable era than any which it has hitherto traversed is now about to begin. Neither the past nor the present of this Church are cheerful subjects of contemplation, but the future is more gloomy still. Scientific discoveries, which constitute a real intellectual difficulty for all, and perhaps a fatal one for those who have only private and traditional interpretations of Scripture to fall back upon, are claiming to correct and readjust the popular belief in the Mosaic record. To such an enemy, a religion founded solely on the capricious and fallible interpretation of the Bible, and already losing its hold on the minds of its professors, can offer but a feeble resistance. The Catholic alone, to whom the infallibility of the Church is as certain as

* *Essay on Church and State.*

the attributes of God, has independent proofs of the truth of Christianity, which, though moral rather than scientific, no assault can destroy nor even impair; and moreover, he can always propose to the unbeliever far greater difficulties than any which science can urge against himself. To say nothing of the long history of the Church, with all its magnificent disclosures of the sleepless tenderness and irresistible power of God, the life of a single saint, or even of a consistently good Catholic steadfastly growing in grace by the use of the Sacraments, and perhaps still more of a penitent recalled by the creative voice of the Church from the grave of sin, is to the Christian an immeasurably more convincing evidence of the truth of his religion than any researches in geology or palæontology can be of its falsehood. Except for their probable effect upon others and their deep scientific interest, such researches would be to a Catholic simply indifferent. The very Scriptures whose authority they menace, and which a majority of the Protestant world have already begun to treat with contempt, have sufficiently prepared him for a controversy which they clearly predict, and which seems to have been fitly reserved for an epoch like this, and for "the infidelity of an age so largely engaged as the present in physical pursuits."* Here is their warning against the snare in which it is too probable that many of this generation will be caught.

"Seek not the things that are too high for thee, and search not into things above thy ability; but the things that God hath commanded thee, think on them always, and in many of His works be not curious."

"For it is not necessary to see with thine eyes those things that are hid."

"In unnecessary matters be not over curious, and in many of His works thou shalt not be inquisitive."

"For many things are shown to thee above the understanding of men."

"And the suspicion of them hath deceived many, and hath detained their minds in vanity."†

Such a warning, coupled with the illumination of Divine faith, and the teaching of a Church which can neither deceive nor be deceived, suffices to the Catholic. Difficulties may remain, of which the solution must be deferred for a time, but they will be harmless to him who can say, "I know whom I have believed." With the Protestant,—whose faith is a jumble of unstable opinions, and whose Church can only deal with two

* Hugh Miller, *Footprints of the Creator*, p. 18.
† Ecclesiasticus iii.

contradictory doctrines by deciding, as in the case of Baptism, that both are equally true,—the case is far otherwise. Already some of the ablest partisans of theories fatal to the popular religion are found among those who hold high office in the Established Church. Their number is increasing, and the poor, to whom that Church has been so cruel a stepmother, are said to be catching the infection. Even in circles where their principles are still faintly condemned, their influence becomes more and more visible. One result of it, as we learn from the public press, is the growing disinclination among Protestant gentlemen to become ministers of the Established Church. "The dearth of clergymen," we are told, "is loudly proclaimed from the Episcopal Bench, and wherever clergymen assemble, as a grave and growing evil. The speculative questions that have been stirred within the last twenty years have directly tended to bring about a result which every churchman must deplore. It is not only that the faith of many has been shaken, but that a still larger number shrink from the responsibility of teaching dogmatically *that which others doubt*."* If Rudelbach could say of Protestant Germany, "the day is ripe for the great apostasy," others may soon be saying of Protestant England, "the day has come." The Church can still save her, but her people must choose, and choose quickly. While they hesitate, eternity lies in wait for them.

One class indeed remains, already endowed with many virtues, and capable of aspiring to the highest, whose attitude suggests hope in the midst of the general discouragement. Unconscious that God has devised for His creatures any better thing than the human religion which they profess, they have only to entertain more worthy thoughts of His majesty and of their own destiny, to discover that they have judged too meanly of both. The Church is not the lamentable caricature with which alone they are familiar. There is a paradise even in this world for the children of God, of which they may easily find the entrance. Their danger lies in continuing to accept a counterfeit after having begun to suspect, even for a moment, its true character. That momentary doubt may suffice to condemn them. They need also to be reminded that the good which they discern in non-Catholic communities, and which their ignorance of higher good leads them to exaggerate, is nothing but the fruit of Catholic traditions not yet extinguished, and of those fragments of Catholic truth which have not wholly disappeared in Protestant lands. In every sect, however

* *The Times*, April 7, 1863.

deeply tainted with error, the real source of such religious life as its members display is found, not in their human traditions, but in the power of some Catholic doctrine which heresy has obscured or distorted, but has not entirely defaced. If they "wrest the Scriptures to their own destruction," they still owe to the Church both the Scriptures themselves, and the pious thought that, to the pure in heart, a special and almost sacramental blessedness attends the study of them. If they affect, in rare cases, to imitate Catholic rites, and even the Sacraments of Penance and the Altar are represented in their external forms by men whose act would be a sacrilege if it were not a delusion, this playing with shadows, though it too often leads the principal actors to spiritual blindness and death, engenders in others an insatiable longing for realities, of which the final grace of conversion is not unfrequently the blessed sequel. So true it is that all the evil which exists in heretical communities is due to their own errors, while the good which struggles with it is the alien's portion of those lavish benedictions which the Church scatters with Divine prodigality over the whole earth. She is a savor of life even to those who know her not. In that last hour of His agony, says one who was privileged to know some of its bitter details, when the lot of every creature whom He was yet to call into being was present to His omniscient gaze, "Jesus beheld them all: He wept over those whom He saw wandering with closed eyes outside the garden of the Church, *and only living on the perfumes which were diffused beyond it*."*

SWEDEN, NORWAY, AND DENMARK.

In Sweden, whose religious history so closely resembles that of England, we discover once more all the characteristic phenomena of "reformed" communities, ecclesiastical serfdom, extinction of faith, and prodigious immorality. The State Church has no existence apart from the sovereign. The "House of Clergy," which is supposed by a legislative fiction to regulate its affairs, has as much independence and vitality as the Russian Synod or the Anglican Convocation. "The king," a Protestant writer observes, "has the power of absolute veto on all bills which affect the change or the forming of ecclesi-

* *La Douloureuse Passion de N. S. Jésus Christ*, d'après les Méditations d'Anne Catherine Emmerich, p. 71, 3me edition.

astical laws." "The first conception of religious freedom," he adds, "has scarcely entered the Swedish mind."*

Of the decay of all positive doctrine, which has given way to blank indifferentism, Liebetrut says, "The Swedish Church is a Church desolate! dead! lying under the anathema of God. The Church's unity is the unity and peace of the graveyard."† "It lies in the nature of things," Dr. Döllinger remarks, "that a State Church," which is a revival of the pagan notion of *National* in opposition to *Christian* unity, "can no longer in its isolation inspire piety, or evoke veneration." "I found," says Mr. Loring Brace in 1857, in illustration of this fact, "the same feeling, which seems almost universal through the middle and upper classes, of *utter distrust and dissatisfaction* towards their religious teachers." "The Swedish Church," Mr. Bayard Taylor repeats in 1858, "is slowly ossifying from sheer inertia."‡

The only signs of life are found among a section of the peasants, over whom, as Mr. Brace observes, "the formalism of the Church has lost its hold," and who, in spite of severe penalties, are beginning to substitute *Läsarne*, a kind of Methodism, for the State religion. This new "reformation," he says, "has already produced sad results physically," including hysteria, and raging madness.

Lastly, as to the moral state of this Protestant land, in which the profession of the faith of its first apostles is still punished by confiscation and exile, we have the following accounts by Protestant writers: "In no Christian community," says Mr. Laing, "has religion less influence on the state of public morals." As you stand in the streets of Stockholm, this witness adds, you may make this unusual reflection: "One out of every *three* persons passing me is, on an average, the offspring of illicit intercourse; and one out of every *forty-nine* has been convicted within these twelve months of some criminal offence."§

An American traveller reported in 1857, that so common are the retributive forms of disease which accompany crime, that "it was rare to see a tall, strong, well-made man unflecked with sickness, and without some kind of deformity." In England the Assistant Commissioners under the Education Inquiry reported that, in certain counties, "adultery is made

* *Home Life in Norway and Sweden*, by Charles Loring Brace, ch. xxiii., p. 184; ch. xxxix., p. 311 (1857).

† Ap. Döllinger, p. 259.

‡ *Northern Travel; Sweden, Lapland, and Norway*, by Bayard Taylor, ch. xxviii., p. 285.

§ *Tour in Sweden*, ch. iv., pp. 115, 125.

a mere matter of jest, and incest also is frightfully common;" in Sweden, where Mr. Brace noticed the universality of the same facts, he adds, yet they all take what they call "the Sacrament," "*as a sort of business*," at the periods prescribed by law. "The number of broken-down young men, and blear-eyed hoary sinners," says another Protestant observer, "is astonishing. I have never been in any place where licentiousness is so open and avowed, and yet where the slang of a sham morality was so prevalent."* Even Miss Fredericka Bremer, herself a Swedish Protestant, relates, in confirmation of these dismal facts, that while in America she "heard it lamented that Scandinavian immigrants not unfrequently come hither with the belief that the State Church and religion are one and the same thing, and when they have left behind them the former, they will have nothing to do with the latter. Long compulsion of mind," in a country which boasts of Protestant freedom, "has destroyed to that degree their powers of mind, and they come to the west very frequently in the first instance as rejecters of all Church communion, *and every higher law*."†

On the whole, we can hardly be surprised if Protestant writers, familiar with this exclusively Protestant land, sum up in such words as the following their impressions of its actual condition: "The Reformation," says Mr. Laing, "as far as regards the moral condition of the Swedish people, has done harm rather than good." "The Reformation," Mr. Taylor observes, "needs to be reformed again." "This century," Mr. Brace declares, "will see the disruption and convulsion of the Swedish State Church."

It might seem impossible to draw a darker picture of a "reformed" community; yet Mr. Inglis, another Protestant traveller, advances the remarkable proposition that, vile as is the condition of Sweden, "the standard of morals is considerably higher than in Norway!" In the latter country, he adds from personal observation, "general indifference is manifested for religion."‡

Finally, Denmark is no exception to the other lands in which the Reformation has preserved its fatal dominion. Barthold confesses, in energetic language, "*the dog-like servitude*" of the Danish peasantry which followed immediately upon its intro-

* Bayard Taylor, ubi supra.

† *Homes of the New World*, vol. ii., letter xxiv., p. 219. Cf. *Chronique Religieuse*, tome ii., p. 495; *Memorial Catholique*, tome vi., p. 130, *De l'État Religieux de la Suède*.

‡ *Norway, Sweden, and Denmark*, by H. D. Inglis, part ii., ch. i., p. 142, 4th edition.

duction;* and an English traveller adds, "to this day it is often amusing, or rather deplorable, to witness the overbearing behavior of some wealthy noblemen towards the poor fellow who officiates in the church, and the latter's obsequiousness."† "Bishop" Pontoppidan declared, in one of his pastorals, that, by the eighteenth century, there reigned in the land "an almost heathen blindness." "Towards the close of the last century," says Mr. Hamilton in 1852, "the progress of stupor was complete, and vital Christianity seemed to have departed from the land." "According to Danish accounts," observes Dr. Döllinger, "the great majority of the clergy have fallen as completely into the infidel new theological views as their Lutheran brethren, the clergy of Germany;" while the Schleswig preacher, Petersen, reports that "among the Danish clergy religious and moral conduct is the exception, not the rule."‡

Attempts have been lately made to restore this dead body to life, chiefly hy Grundtvig, a man of zeal and talent, but unfortunately on principles which must inevitably be fatal to his project. The only appreciable result of his labors, Mr. Hamilton confesses, is this, that "the whole intellectual world is split up into opposing sections," and that "they hate one another heartily."§

Such have been, in every country of Europe, by Protestant testimony, the results of the so-called Reformation. Everywhere it has generated, by the confession of its own advocates, sterile fanaticism in the few, hopeless unbelief in the many; and while the Church was able in the same hour to convert whole nations of barbarians to God, and to recover Christian kingdoms from the bondage of heresy, the Sects have not only failed to propagate Christianity in a single heathen land, but have everywhere taught the pagan world to hate and despise the religion of Jesus, while they have been powerless to maintain, even among their own disciples, its most fundamental truths.

* Ap. Döllinger, p. 84.

† *Sixteen Months in the Danish Isles*, by Andrew Hamilton, vol. i., ch. xxiii., p. 390.

‡ Döllinger, pp. 253–5.

§ The case of the United States has been omitted, having been sufficiently considered in a previous chapter. "The state of Christianity in America," as Dr. Döllinger has lately observed, "is an awful and serious warning, and will in future become still more so." In that country every blasphemous and heretical opinion has found a home, but the mass of the people may, perhaps, be most truly described as having no religious opinions whatever. "The doctrines of *materialism*," says one who knows them well, "are perhaps more widely embraced at this day than almost any other religious error." *The Religion of Geology*, by Edward Hitchcock, D.D., LL.D., President of Amherst College, pref., p. 11

Such, once more, has been the double infamy of the Protestant Sects.*

THE REFORMATION HYPOTHESIS.

Yet the religion which has proved so fatal at home, so impotent abroad, is still declared by its professors to be something higher and holier than primitive Christianity. It is nothing less, they everywhere proclaim, than a *second revelation*, designed to correct the failure of the first; a *reformation* of that marred and tainted Gospel which, according to the Lutheran or Anglican hypothesis, its unsuccessful Author vainly strove to preserve from corruption and decay; a *new Ark* for perishing souls, constructed to replace one which foundered long ages ago; a *more perfect redemption*, to remedy that which Jesus wrought and Peter announced, but which, according to the Anglican Reformers, had miserably lost, "*by the space of nine hundred years and odd*," its power and efficacy.

It was to remedy the failure of this earlier religion, which nevertheless was still professed by all the civilized nations of the earth, and to gather the remaining gentiles into the fold of Christ, that the Lutheran and Anglican communities were called into being. The Author of Christianity, according to the Reformation hypothesis, had proved either unable or unwilling to fulfil His promises to the Christian Church. The last and most cherished work of His redeeming love, for which His prophets had anticipated so magnificent a destiny, was abandoned as soon as formed. The Church was suffered to lapse, almost at the moment of her creation, into shameful apostasy. The gates of hell prevailed against her. Her pretended Supreme Pontiff was only a self-elected impostor. Her bishops and priests, without exception, had meanly conspired to sell their birthright to a mitred usurper, whom the weakest of them could have defied with impunity, since he appealed only to the ordinance of God, and the conscience of Christian men. Her doctrines, as the new Anglican Church loudly de-

* Every student of ecclesiastical history knows that the history of the Protestant communities, of which we have noticed only the final chapter, exactly corresponds with that of earlier sects, which invariably lapsed, one after another, into the same shameful disorder and impiety. When the great Sir Thomas More replied to one of those frantic libels of Luther which Mr. Hallam described as "bellowing in bad Latin," he reminded the apostate monk, that "not only there never was an enemy to the Christian faith who did not at the same time declare war against the Holy See, but also that there never has been one who professed himself an enemy of that See, without shortly after declaring himself signally a capital foe and traitor of Christ and our religion." Quoted by Allies, *St. Peter, His Name and Office*, ch. ix., p. 263.

clared, were "blasphemous fables," and her worship had degenerated into "damnable idolatry." "The theology of the Reformers," as Döllinger observes, "established the idea that God had withdrawn Himself from the Church after the death of the apostles; that He had resigned His place to Satan, and so established a diabolical millennium." When the reign of Satan came to an end, Luther, Zwingle, and Cranmer appeared, to inaugurate a new Dispensation.

Such is the theory which the Protestant Churches rightly maintain, because it is the only one which can explain or justify the rebellion of the sixteenth century. Yet if it be true, we shall be compelled to admit, in presence of the facts reviewed in these pages, that the God of Moses and St. Paul has utterly failed, in a *second* attempt as feeble and fruitless as the first, to found a stable religion, or to build up a permanent Church, by whose ministry the Incarnation should be glorified in Christian lands, and the pagan world brought to a knowledge of its Creator. For they are Protestant witnesses who have convinced us, by testimony which is equally copious and decisive to whatever region of the earth it applies, that while the Incarnation has been exposed to impious derision in the majority of Protestant communities, and barely saved from oblivion in the rest, the efforts of the same communities to propagate their opinions in heathen lands have had no other result than to make Christianity the scorn of the gentile world, and to inspire the "growing hatred" of all pagan races towards both the doctrine and its professors, whose incessant divisions provoke them to contemptuous mirth, and whose effeminate lives tempt them to inquire, "whether they believe their own Scriptures?"

The second revelation, then, has proved as unsuccessfnl as the first. And this is not all. In spite of the new Dispensation of the sixteenth century, its supposed Author still permits the Old and "corrupt" Faith, which, according to the hypothesis, it was His purpose to reform, to gain victories, both in the old and new world, which all His efforts cannot secure for the New! Not only is the Catholic Church defending at this hour the Scriptures, the Incarnation, and the whole blessed Gospel, against the ribald assaults of the "reformed" communities, but her missions to the heathen, as her worst enemies confess, are still, both in their agents and their results, absolutely identical with those which subdued the Roman empire to the law of Christ, and carried the Cross in triumph from Jerusalem to Rome and Constantinople, and from the shores of the Euphrates and the Nile to the forests of Scandinavia and the isles of Britain. Nay more, the work which she has accomplished during the last three centuries, beginning from the very date of the so-called Reformation, actually surpasses all which she had done in earlier ages, even in those which witnessed her first combats with the powers of evil. It would seem that, quickly abandoning the new religion, just as He is represented to have formerly abandoned the old, and repenting of the project of a tardy Reformation, the Almighty began from this hour to lavish in more abundance than ever upon the ministers of the Ancient Church the apostolic gifts which He peremptorily refused to their rivals; resolved to make the first types in every land of the supernatural life, and the last everywhere monuments of incorrigible humanism; and while in the one He ceased not to fulfil the word of His prophet, "They shall know their seed among the gentiles, and their offspring in the midst of peoples," He left the other so entirely void of all but purely natural gifts, that they became a jest even to the Chinese and the Kaffir. The "diabolical millennium," as the Anglican Church teaches her members to regard the reign of the Vicar of Christ, gave place to a still more lamentable era; and the Most High, if the Protestant theory be true, having made a Church which brought only evil into the world, first retired in disgust from His own work for a thousand years, and then attempted an abortive Reformation which only served to discredit Christianity in all pagan lands, and to introduce far more grievous calamities, wherever it prevailed, than those which it was designed to remedy.

Such, once more, is the hypothesis on which the Lutheran and Anglican communities are formed. If, therefore, that hypothesis be true, and it was really the Divine purpose, on a certain day and hour of the sixteenth century, to supersede the Church by the Sects, and henceforth to save Christians and to ransom heathens by the agency of the latter, we are brought to this inevitable conclusion,—that there is nothing more infirm and impotent, nothing more inconstant and vacillating, than the imaginary Potentate from whom Protestants profess to derive their religion, but whom they represent as always stumbling from one failure to another; who is perpetually planning some good thing for the sons of men, and as often abandoning the project in despair; who can create but cannot sustain, can resolve but never accomplish; who projected, as they teach, for the salvation of believers, a Church which should last through all time, whose unfading triumphs were announced by a long line of Hebrew prophets, and whose laws were framed by a glorious company of apostles, but whose virgin lustre, in spite of prophets and apostles, was marred by a hideous leprosy, and whose bridal hour was expiated by ten centuries of such unutterable shame, that the Bridegroom turned away his eyes, that he might not even look upon the ruin which he could neither avert nor repair. Protestantism, which takes all this for granted, and finds in it the sole explanation of its own being, can only be admitted to be true on the supposition that there is no God.

It might seem impossible that any one acquainted with the actual state of Protestant Europe, and the history of Protestant Sects, or familiar in any degree with the work of the Catholic Church during the last three centuries, should still believe the so-called Reformation to be the product of omnipotent wisdom and love. It would indeed be absolutely impossible, if we did not know that neither the most attractive natural virtues, nor the rarest mental gifts, suffice to preserve men from almost incredible errors,—that Aristotle believed in the eternity of matter, and Pericles offered sacrifice to Minerva, and Cicero wrote a treatise on "The nature of the gods." But whatever may have been the religious chimeras of past ages, there is not a pagan absurdity ridiculed in the *Stromata* of St. Clement,—neither the copious banquets of Olympus, nor the infirmities of Jupiter, nor the turpitudes of Venus Genetrix,—which reveals more of the abysses of human credulity, or the possible depths of human delusion, than the modern fable of the Reformation.

If, on the other hand, we believe with St. Francis and St. Bernard, with Bossuet and Fenelon, with Peter Claver and Las Casas, with De Brebeuf and Lallemand, with the doctors and evangelists, the saints and martyrs, of every age and every land, that it is by the Church and not by the Sects that the God of Christians seeks His own glory and man's salvation; if we confess that He who is Truth cannot lie, nor the Immutable break His promise; then we shall judge more worthily of the majesty of the Creator, and the dignity of the creature. We shall perceive, on this supposition, that every contradiction disappears, and every difficulty is removed; that God has accomplished every purpose, and fulfilled every promise; that the so-called Reformation, which has annihilated the Gospel in so many Christian and stopped its progress in so many pagan lands, was only a fresh conspiracy of the powers of evil which God has baffled and confounded, and that His love still broods over the Bride of whom He once said, and has now again proved, "No weapon that is formed against thee shall prosper, and every tongue that resisteth thee in judgment thou shalt condemn."

CONCLUSION.

Three classes of men, we may perhaps anticipate, will pronounce judgment upon the facts which we have reviewed in these pages, and upon the argument which we have founded upon them. The first,—of whom a well-known Anglican clergyman has observed, "their existence depends on the success of the system" by which they profit so largely,—making, as St. Paul says, "a gain of godliness," and finding in heathen lands the livelihood which they could not obtain in their own; incapable of accepting the lesson which the barbarians of Asia and America, less blinded by prejudice and self-love, have derived from facts of which even barbarians could appreciate the gravity; vexed and irritated, but not instructed, by the shameful contrast which their co-religionists have reluctantly revealed; will only espouse more passionately the earthly cause with which their interests are associated, and nourish a deeper malice towards the apostles whom God has filled with His Spirit, but whose virtues they hate and whose triumphs they envy, without so much as the wish to emulate the one, or the hope of rivalling the other. To such men it will be simply intolerable that their carnal ministry should be "reputed for nothing," and their lucrative craft "in danger to be set at naught;" nor may we reasonably expect from *them* any other argument than that of the silversmiths of Ephesus, "Sirs, you know that our gain is by this trade."*

A second class, more impartial because less interested, but profoundly indifferent to the supernatural character of actions which confound their reason while they leave their conscience untouched, will smile with lenient contempt at the tale of Protestant missions, confess with a kind of peevish applause the sublimity of the Catholic, and then, "caring for none of those things," will presently forget both the one and the other.

But there is a third which, it is permitted to hope, will discern at length, by the light of history, the truth which they have often suspected, but have hitherto been reluctant to confess. Halting between two opinions, and neither frankly Protestant nor effectually Catholic; urged by a secret instinct

* Acts xix. 25. A clerical officer of the Church Missionary Society, and a suitable champion of the class referred to, has justified this anticipation by a work which prudently ignores the whole history of Christian missions, while it has scandalized even his co-religionists by an appreciation of the life and character of St. Francis Xavier which a moderately virtuous pagan would fear to write, and blush to avow.

to cast in their lot with the Church, yet constrained by lingering prejudice, or the tyranny of habit, or the fascination of domestic ties, or haply by less venial motives, to waste their gifts in the service of a Sect; *they* may comprehend at last on which side is God, and hasten to seek in the Church Him who has announced, by acts which even savages have understood, that they shall not find Him elsewhere. Hitherto they have been blind to the truth, because they have closed their eyes, or because they have misused graces which were designed, not to adorn a Sect, but to lead them out of it. "Comparing themselves with themselves," and carefully adjusting their vision to the narrow field of their own interests and occupations, they have refused to turn one glance towards that mournful desert which hems them in on every side, and which represents, more truly than their own imperceptible spheres of action, the real work of their Sect, and the final issue of its unblest career, against which their own is often an insincere, and always an unavailing protest. Busy with some local scheme, large enough for their narrow sympathies, but which the next hour may subvert and destroy; insensible to signs which God submits to their investigation, and attentive only to those which come not from Him, but are full of deceit and illusion; waiting always for more light, and losing, while they wait, the light which they already possessed; slow to reason when the Church invites them to ponder her message, but swift to dispute when she adjures them not to despise it; borrowing her doctrines to "adapt" them to their private conceits, but always converting them into heresies before they make them their own; boasting of "Orders" which even Indo-Syrians disdain to recognize, and which, if they were as genuine as they are spurious, would only put them on a level with Arians and Monophysites, who possessed them to their greater condemnation; playing at consecrations which consecrate nothing, and rehearsing absolutions which absolve nobody; claiming to hold truths which their Sect abhors, but only to use them *against* the Authority which delivered them to the world, and often more self-willed in maintaining than their co-religionists in rejecting them; never so incurably Protestant, in all their thoughts, words, and actions, as when most they affect to be Catholic; fretfully subject to "bishops" whose heresies they profess to deplore, but always make their own by submission, and meanly loyal to rulers who endure only because they cannot eject them, but whose forbearance they purchase by hiding the truth, and whose judgments they avert by betraying it; differing from other Protestants chiefly in this, that while the rest follow false teachers supposing them to be true, *they* willingly communicate with the same teachers proclaiming them to be false; content to whisper a hollow protest against their companions who deny the most fundamental truths, but not to cry anathema for the love of God upon the Sect which refuses to defend them;* burdening their souls with the guilt of others as well as their own, with the heresies which they privately disclaim as well as those which they publicly avow, and accountable before God for every impiety which is uttered around them, and most of all for the impiety which they ostensibly condemn, but which they do more to confirm by their voluntary acts than to discourage by their unmeaning words; such men, unless their day of grace be already closed forever, may perhaps learn at length from the history which we have reviewed the lesson which their own failures and calamities, the phenomena of their age and country, and even the admonitions of conscience, have hitherto taught them in vain.†

It is not indeed a new truth which the events of the last three centuries, and the intimate union of God with the Church and her ministry have taught the world, though perpetually confirmed by a new series of facts. A thousand years ago, our fathers were already proclaiming it with admiration, for *they* detected on little evidence what has been announced to ourselves by greater. The first victories of the Church had hardly been gained, and paganism was still a mighty power in the world, when St. Augustine was telling the faithful in Africa that Christians of his age had this advantage over the disciples of St. Peter and St. Paul, that whereas the latter could only look *forward* to the promised glories of the Bride of Christ, the former could already look *back* to their partial fulfilment. Fifteen centuries have passed away since then, and each has only accumulated fresh evidence of the same truth. For what additional testimony are men waiting? What fresh proof do they require of her indefectibility? What new snare can they devise for the Church which she has not already broken? What

* When the highest tribunal recognized by the Anglican Church decided that the doctrine of baptism was, within the limits of her communion, "an open question," a solemn protest, which bore the names of Mr. Keble, Dr. Pusey, and other leaders of the same school, announced the conviction of the subscribers that, unless the impious decision was annulled, the Church of England would forfeit all claim to be considered, in any sense whatever, a part of the Church of God. Of those who signed that protest, one-half have become Catholics, one is dead, and the rest are still ministers of the Established Church!

† How should they not be taught in vain, to whom the Tempter has artfully suggested, that it is their *duty* to abstain from all inquiry? "There is an essential irreverence, similar to that false devotion which the prophet rebuked in Achaz, when he refused to ask a sign of God, though God through His prophet bade him do so; the irreverence of *not investigating the signs which God gives us for the purpose of being investigated*, as if we knew better than He, and were more delicate and circumspect in our operations." *Bethlehem*, ch. vi., p. 324.

new adversary can they bring from the ends of the earth whom she has not already overcome? Perpetually assaulted, she has outlived every enemy, and though they have predicted, one after another, her approaching end, she has chanted her *de profundis* over them all. "When we reflect," said the great English essayist, suggesting truths which bore no fruit in his own soul, "on the tremendous assaults which she has survived, we find it difficult to conceive in what way she is to perish." What indeed is the history of the world, for well-nigh two thousand years, but the history of her combats and triumphs? Arian and Nestorian, Vandal and Donatist, Hun and Goth, Greek and Moslem, vainly leagued together against her. Every assault which could menace, at one time her faith, at another her existence, has only served to show, again and again, that "whosoever shall fall upon this stone shall be broken." Vainly the enemy arrayed against her the hosts of northern barbarians, merciless and sanguinary as beasts of prey, trusting to overwhelm by brute force what all the subtle heresies of Greece, Egypt, or Syria had failed to undermine; they came only to lay their spoils at her feet, and finished by adoring the Cross which they had been sent to destroy! Vainly the armies of the false prophet blotted out the corrupt churches of the East, made Greece their prey, and set up a throne in Byzantium, the metropolis of the oriental schism, for these were the bounds beyond which they might not pass. From that hour the Moslem, checked in mid career by the invincible legions whom the Vicar of Christ had sent forth against him, understood that faith was more than a match for fanaticism, that Catholic unity was a more impenetrable barrier than human or satanical confederacy, and that it was time to sue for peace with a Power which neither might nor artifice could hope to subdue, and with a Church whose supreme Pontiff could predict in the same breath, and with equal confidence, the triumph of Rome and the captivity of Constantinople. In vain, lastly, did the enemy, baffled in so many encounters, head the most formidable revolt against which she has ever contended; for in that sixteenth century, in which the gates of hell were thrown wide open, and a legion of unclean spirits received permission to make war upon her, in the very hour in which their loud cry of triumph was heard in half the kingdoms of Europe, a new army of apostles came out of the sanctuary, clothed in the armor of God, and charged by Him to reconquer at the same moment the apostate races of the North, and to gather in the East and West, out of all nations and people, that vast company of new believers to whom He resolved to transfer the inheritance which Swedes and Saxons, drunk with the enchanter's cup, were now casting away.

Such was the latest victory of the Church, of which we have attempted to trace the details in these pages. Three centuries have elapsed since the conflict began, and while the Sects have putrified, filling the air with the odor of death, *she* has remained unmoved upon her eternal foundations; teaching everywhere the same unalterable faith; "spreading everywhere," as one of her enemies has told us, "the light of civilization;" "diffusing," as another has confessed, "a sea of benefits," and "saving millions of souls," by a ministry so full of truth and power, that even the most degraded races of the human family,—the Annamite, the Huron, and the Guarani,—have confessed that God was with her, and have found in her communion a light to their feet, "the promise of the world that now is, and of that which is to come."

What further evidence do we seek? What sign can we ask or conceive of the presence and the power of God which is not found in the long history of the Catholic Church? There are, as St. Leo said in his generation, mysterious workings of Providence of which man cannot penetrate the secret plan; and there are more intelligible operations, clear as the lightning which shines out of heaven, which even a child can mark and interpret. Such have been the works of God by the Church. "Non intelligimus judicantem," said the same Saint, "*sed vidimus operantem.*" This is the truth which it has been our purpose to illustrate in these pages. *Vidimus operantem!* We have *seen* Him, who knows how to dispense His own gifts, pouring out in all lands the most precious graces on one class, and constantly refusing them to every other. We have *seen* Him, when the enemy seemed about to triumph, summoning His apostles by thousands, to declare in all the world the very message against which the apostate had closed his ears. We have *seen* Him, so openly has He wrought this work, send forth a new Paul or Barnabas, filled with their spirit, and preaching their doctrine to every province of the earth, from the populous homes of the East to the scattered tents of the savage in the distant West. And everywhere He has made the disciples worthy of such teachers. We have *seen* the weak become valiant and the timid strong, so that they could smile at torture and rejoice in death, because His grace was in their hearts, kindling both the apostle's courage and the martyr's hope. We have *seen* in the cities of China and India, in the islands of the Southern Ocean, and by the banks of the Plata and the Uruguay, of the Mohawk, the Huron, and the Genesee, the same mysterious sacrifices by which nations live and kingdoms are won to Christ, and which once crimsoned at the same hour the waters of the Rhone and the Tiber, of the Abana and the Orontes, and were offered for the same end in the streets of Lyons, Rome, and Jerusalem, and in the capitals of Lydia, Pontus, and Syria.

Lastly, we have seen all these marvels, which are "the work of the right hand of the Most High," renewed in our own day, by our own brothers and kinsmen, still filled with the Holy Ghost as their fathers were, still accepting the same almost incredible sacrifices, and accomplishing the same Divine victories. And while the emissaries of the sects,—salaried apostles of a mutilated Gospel, from which they have excluded all which might disturb their repose or restrain their earthly appetites; to whom even Divine bounty refuses all but purely natural gifts, and deprives even these of their efficacy,—are everywhere making Christianity a proverb, its cruel dissensions a by-word, and its ministers a jest among the heathen; the Church is still sending forth, as she did in the beginning, apostles upon whom God is never weary of lavishing a father's gifts, and of whom He still lovingly proclaims, "*They* shall know their seed among the gentiles, and their offspring in the midst of peoples: All that shall see *them* shall know them, that these are the seed which the Lord hath blessed."

Vidimus operantem! What our fathers saw we have seen, but with clearer evidence, and in a more dazzling light. The counsels of God are hidden, but his works are plain, and wrought for our instruction. They teach what they have ever taught. It is still in the Church that He lives and acts. We have *seen* that it is there He dwells. She is still the sole sanctuary which He illumines with His presence. She is still "the Bride adorned for the Bridegroom," "the City which the glory of God hath enlightened."* Search not for Him elsewhere, for He has shown in a hundred lands, by signs which even pagans have understood, how vain the search would prove. As well might the followers of Moses have returned to seek light in Egypt, over which Divine wrath had spread a supernatural darkness; as wisely might the companions of Josuè have sought teachers among the Amorites, already devoted to destruction, as Christians forsake the Church to find God in the midst of perishing Sects,—Lutheran, Anglican, or Calvinist,—which He abandoned from the first moment of their existence to mutual hate and shameful disorder, and which have at length reached that final stage of corruption from which even Protestants recoil with dismay, while they cry out, with a sorrow which comes too late, "The days in which we live are ripe for the great apostasy!"

On the eve of that conflict of which so many voices herald

* *Apoc.* xxi. 2, 23.

the approach, and in which, though we may be sure only for a moment, Science is to be arrayed against Revelation; at a moment of which the gravity is apparent, even to men not easily interested in questions of the soul, and which seems to presage a still more rapid decomposition of the Protestant Sects than that of which we have already traced the progress; it is more than ever evident that only one refuge remains for the human communities which have lost all power of resistance from within, and which appear, even to their own members, to be swaying to and fro in the first throes of approaching dissolution. They must choose between the Church and chaos, for they may soon have no other choice. Happy they who have already chosen, and chosen aright. The winds may blow and the floods rage, but *their* house will stand, for it is built upon a rock. As to the rest, who have never known the Church, and seem to ask, before the final catastrophe is upon them, for fresh proofs that she is indeed the true Spouse, the appointed ark of refuge, the "garden inclosed" which is watered by the river of life,—to them she addresses once more, it may be for the last time, her gentle expostulation. Calm and unmoved, sure of God and of herself, she will still save them, if they will consent to be saved. She bids them ponder her history and their own. She rehearses again for their admonition all which she has done among men since the hour when the Son of God committed them to her charge, and chiefly what He has done in and by her during the last three centuries, all the nations she has begotten to Him, all the apostles she has nurtured, all the martyrs she has blessed. She reminds them of their own history during the same period, full only of malediction both to themselves and to the heathen who have caught the infection from them; and then, comparing with it that healing ministry of power and love upon which God has set visibly the seal of His acceptance, using it in all lands for the salvation of His creatures and the manifestation of His own glory, she leaves judgment to Him, and only borrows words which He has put into her mouth, to say to those who still affect to doubt,—"If you believe not my words, *believe the works that I do.*"

THE END.

INDEX OF CONTENTS.

A.

Anglicanism, Hindoo estimate of; I. 317, 18.
Anglican Establishment in India; I. 327.
" Missionaries in America; II. 356, 361, 365.
Asceticism, "part of the ignominy of the Cross;" I. 315.
Aleppo, Catholic Missions in; II. 35–37.
Achilli, Dr., his esteem for the Church of England; II. 4.
Armenia, Catholic Missions in; II. 84, 99, 105.
" Protestant " II. 110–119.
Armenians, Catholic, their superiority; II. 107.
Algeria, conduct of French soldiers in; I. 553.
" " " Government in; I. 554, 5.
Arabs, predict the downfall of Islamism; I. 558.
" their submission to France; I. 560.
Arab Christians; II. 44, 96.
Algeria and India compared; I. 560.
Abyssinia, early Missions in; I. 573.
" present state of; II 582.
" failure of Protestant Missions in; I. 589.
Africa, Eastern, Protestant Missions in; I. 585–591.
Africa, Western, Protestant Missions in; I. 591–3.
" " Catholic " I. 603–10.
Africa, Southern, Sects in " I. 617.
" " Results of Protestant Missions in; I. 641.
African Protestant Converts, specimens of; I. 562, 85, 86, 95, 99, 601, 14, 15, 20–39.
Africaner, character of; I. 623.
Armstrong, Dr., his experience in Africa; I. 617, 637.
Atheism of pagans, a result of Protestant Education; I. 348–55.
Australia, no Protestant converts in; I. 414–16.
" Anglican Clergy in; I. 410.
" Catholic Missions in; I. 420–22.
Australian Natives, their belief in immortality; I. 411.
Aborigines, their extermination in Protestant colonies; I. 416, 17, 495, 510, 514; II. 124, 5, 8, 314, 440–6.
Acquisitiveness of Protestant Missionaries; I. 163, 181, 312, 13, 425, 495, 513, 516, 524, 633; II. 350, 351, 369, 391.
Anchieta, his labors in Brazil; II. 137–140.
Azevedo, and the sixty-eight Martyrs; II. 147.
Amoy, Protestant Missions in; I. 168.
Anouilh, Bishop, on the Chinese conversions in 1862; I. 139.
American Protestants, their general candor; II. 221.
" " " " its explanation; II. 222.
Anglican Reformers, impieties of; II. 207, 8.

Alvarado; II. 232.
Arctic regions, early Missions in; II. 331.
American Indians, their actual condition; II. 387–91.
" " their prosperity in the Catholic provinces; II. 396.
" " their contempt for Protestant Missionaries; II. 391–4.
America, contrast between Catholic and Protestant Missions in; II. 398–400.
Anderson, Rev. J. S. M., on Anglo-American Missions; II. 353–6.
Athens, American Missions at; II. 11–14.

B.

Bibles, how used by the heathen in China; I. 20.
" " " " India; I. 26.
" " " " Africa; I. 35.
" effects of their dispersion in European lands; I. 40–2.
" best versions Catholic reprints; I. 53.
Bossuet, his opinion of the Society of Jesus; I. 94.
Beuth, Martyr; I. 83.
Berneux, Bishop and Confessor; I. 117.
Burke, Edmund, on English in India; I. 208.
" " state of Greek Church; II. 8.
Bonnard, Martyr; I. 133.
Bowring, Sir John, on Catholic Missionaries; I. 161, 480, 482.
Bettelheim, Dr., his operations in Loo-Choo; I. 176, 7.
Bang-kok, Catholic and Protestant Missions at; I. 161.
Bagdad, Catholic success in; II. 104.
Brazil, Catholic Missions in; II. 131–141.
" Anglican " II. 163.
" Huguenot " II. 162.
Brazilians, their estimate of Protestant Missionaries; II. 164.
Baraza, Cyprian, Martyr; II. 203.
Brooke, Sir James, on Anglican Missions in India; I. 345.
Benyowski, Count, on Dutch Missions; I. 361.
Baptism, sacrilegiously administered; I. 369, 375, 379, 380; II. 49.
Broughton, Dr., his despair of converting the Australians; I. 411.
" Protestant estimate of him; I. 412.
Bathurst, anecdote of Missionaries at; I. 615.
Belcher, Sir Edward, his opinion of Protestant Missionaries; I. 519.
Borneo, Missions in; I. 544.
Blakesley, Rev. Mr., on French Mission in Algeria; I. 555.
Bonar, Rev. Dr., his remarkable fanaticism; I. 564–6.
Beke, Dr., his candor; I. 574, 8.
Boré, Eugène, on state of Greeks; II. 9.
Beyrout, Missions in; II. 35.
Badger, Rev. G. P., his admiration of Nestorians; II. 111, 112.
Broomhall, Rev. J., his conduct in Tahiti; I. 485.
Bread-fruit, Protestant use of; I. 491.
Bennett, Mr., his account of Tahiti; I. 501.
" " the Sandwich Islands; I. 518.
Bingham, Mr., his conduct in the Sandwich Islands; I. 512, 531.
Britto, Venerable John de, Martyr; I. 231.
Borghese, Xavier, Confessor; I. 239.
Beschi, Hindoo admiration of; I. 240.
Buchanan, Dr. Claudius, his career; I. 293–6.
Buchanan, Dr. Francis, on Indian Catholics; I. 255.
Burmah, Missions in; I. 297.
Baptist Missions in India; I. 319.
Baptist Converts, specimens of; I. 321–3, 388.
Bombay, failure of Anglican Missions in; I. 336.

Baltic Provinces, influence of Russo-Greek Church in; II. 74.
Beechey, Captain, on Protestant Missions in Tahiti; I. 494.
Borie, Bishop and Martyr; I. 124.
Betanzos, Domingo de; II. 239.
British Columbia, Missions in; 276–281.
Brebeuf, Jean de, his martyrdom; II. 295.
Bressany, Confessor; II. 296.
Bellamont, Lord, his treatment of Catholic Missionaries; II. 299.
Bancroft, Mr., on character of Catholic Missions in America; II. 300.
Buckingham, Mr., on contrast between Catholic and Protestant Missionaries in Canada; II. 315.
Brainerd, his character; II. 369, 70.
Barbadoes, Anglican College in; II. 380.
Bermuda Colonial Assembly, its view of "Church principles;" II. 381.
Beecher, Rev. Henry Ward, on treatment of American Indians; II. 395, 6.
Baltimore, Lord; II. 360.

C.

Colleges, Missionary, Protestant; their cost and failure; I. 154, 155, 178, 179, 199, 309, 331; II. 380.
Church Missionary Society, its wealth, I. 4; its defence of the luxury of its agents, I. 374; its untruthfulness, I. 471.
Chinese Women, their constancy; I. 128, 136, 137.
" Religious; I. 138.
" Pagans, arguments of; I. 128.
Chapdelaine, Martyr; I. 135.
Chinese Treaty of 1860, effects of; I. 139.
Caste; I. 219, 229.
Conversion of the Gentiles, a mark of the true Church; I. 57.
China, early preaching of the Faith in; I. 61. Stability of Missions in; I. 65.
Canghi, his relations with the Catholic Missionaries; I. 72.
Chinese, heathen, their testimony to the truth; I. 32, 97.
Chinese Christians, constancy of; I. 84, 87.
" their innocence; I. 89.
" Christian exiles; I. 89, 103, 160, 162.
" Martyrs, letters of; I. 109, 122, 123.
Corea, Missions in; I. 113.
Cornay, Martyr; I. 121.
Cuénot, Bishop and Confessor; I. 125.
Chanel, Abbé, his martyrdom; I. 531.
Copts, their degradation; I. 563.
Cairo, failure of Protestant Missions in; I. 567, 568.
" Specimen of Protestant converts; I. 569.
Congo, Missions in; I. 605.
Colenso, Dr.; I. 634, 5.
Calderwood, Rev. H., the Kaffirs; I. 640.
Ceylon, Martyrs in; I. 358.
" Anglican Missions in; I. 380, 381, 3, 386.
Cingalese Converts, devil-worshippers; I. 377, 8, 9.
" Catholics, their zeal and fervor; I. 392.
Ceremonial, not an instrument in converting the heathen; I. 398.
" Catholic use of; I. 402, 3.
Carnarvon, Lord, his defence of the Druses; II. 98.
Chaldea, wholly Catholic; I. 104.
Cayenne, Jesuits in; II. 168.
Claver, Blessed Peter; II. 169–172.
Chili, Religion in; II. 186–7.
Chiquitos, the; II. 201, 2.

Cavallero, Lucas, Martyr; II. 202.
Crawfurd, Mr., account of the Philippines; I. 479.
Campbell, Dr., on Polynesian Missions; I. 484.
Cruickshank, Brodie, on West African Missions; I. 600.
Close, Dr., on English rule in India; I. 261–3.
Cotton, Dr., his Gospel; I. 314.
Carey, Dr., his translations of the Bible; I. 320.
Campbell, Mr., on Protestant Missions in India; I. 331.
Converts, Protestant; conversion makes them "twice dead;" I. 331.
Clarkson, Rev. W., failure of Anglo-Indian Missions; I. 333.
Calcutta, Anglicanism in; I. 317, 18.
Carne, Dr., Syrian Protestants; II. 5, 99.
Constantinople, Patriarchate of, actual condition; II. 9.
Cachod, R. P., "Father of the Slaves;" II. 21.
Castlereagh, Lord, on Jerusalem Mission; II. 46.
Caucasus, Russian influence in; II. 82, 83.
Crimea, Religion in; II. 85.
Christian Remembrancer, its admission of Anglican failures; I. 7, 339, 346.
" " its opinion of Anglican celibacy; II. 438.
China, Nestorian Missions in; I. 61.
Cartwright, the Backwoods preacher; II. 381.
Cuba, Negroes in; II. 385.
Cheverus, Cardinal, American esteem for; II. 309, 397.
Chateaubriand, his journey with a Catholic Missionary; II. 308.
Canadians, French, their character; II. 324.
Cortez, his character; II. 231, 2.
Cancér, Luis, Martyr; II. 226.
Crowe, Rev. F., his misadventures in Central America; II. 227.
California, Missions in; II. 250.
" " destruction of, by the Americans; II. 253, 259.
" " results of their secularization; II. 254–258.
" character of Indians; II. 261.
" Protestant Missions in; II. 261.
Canada, Catholic Missions in; II. 283.
" Disunion of Protestants in; II. 319, 20.
" Social state of; II. 326.

D.

Daniel, Antoine, his martyrdom in Canada; II. 294.
Dwight, Dr. Timothy, on Protestant Indians; II. 311, 12.
Durham, Earl of, on Canadian clergy; II. 320.
Duff, Missionary voyage of; I. 484.
Divorce, among Greeks and Anglicans; II. 9, 15.
De Hell, Hommaire, on Russian clergy; II. 69, 85.
Diaz, Bishop and Martyr; I. 136.
Dominicans, their controversy with the Jesuits; I. 141.
Dominicans, their missions in Mexico; II. 238.
Du Chaillu, on West African Missions; I. 612.
Desveaux, General, his way of converting the Arabs; I. 554.
Dupuch, Bishop, his work in Algeria; I. 555.
D'Abbadie, on the Abyssinians; I. 575.
Druses, their opinion of Protestantism; II. 97.
" English sympathy with the; II. 97, 8.
Donoso Cortes, on the Miracles of the Church; II. 146.
Dutch, character of their missionaries; I. 360.
" cruelties of " II. 149, 150, 151.
" their proceedings in Japan; I. 362.
" " in Ceylon; I. 360–69.

Dutch, their proceedings in South America; II. 149–51
D'Orbigny, on the Catholic Indians in South America; II. 129, 219.
Dieffenbach, Dr., on New Zealand Missions; I. 431.
Damascus, Catholic Missions in; II. 38.
Denmark, state of religion in; II. 467.
Dana, Mr., on the success of Catholic Missions in the Sandwich Islands; I. 524.

E.

Elias, his challenge to the priests of Baal; II. 405.
Eliot, Rev. John, his preaching in America; II. 368, 9.
England, effects of the Reformation in; II. 459–65.
Edkins, Rev. Joseph, his observations in China; I. 193.
Ellis, Sir Henry, his account of the Philippines; I. 481.
Ellis, Rev. William, his proceedings in Tahiti; I. 491.
" " his real history in Madagascar; I. 543.
English, conduct of, in India; I. 269, 275.
" " in Australia; I. 418, 19.
" " in America; II. 302, 305, 358, 365, 372.
Education of the heathen, by Catholics; I. 178, 9, 180, 420, 22, 533, 72; II. 28, 39, 93, 94, 210, 427–431.
" " by Protestants; I. 178, 180, 348, 355, 385, 413, 414, 418, 568, 599, 600; II. 427–435.
Education, character of, in Catholic lands; II. 428.
" results of, in England; II. 428.
Earl, Mr. Windsor, his account of Protestant Missions; I. 155.
Ewald, Rev. Mr., his misadventures; I. 561.
Egypt, Missions in; I. 563.
" Martyrs in; I. 569.

F.

"Feelings," religious; I. 598–II. 54.
Fisk, Rev. Pliny, his history in Palestine; II. 29.
Frankl, Dr., character of Hebrew Protestants; II. 49.
Farley, Mr., his account of Syria; II. 59.
Finland, religion in; II. 75.
Fox, Mr., his account of New Zealand; I. 445.
Feejee Islands; I. 508, 541.
Fontanier, Pondicherry Mission; I. 257.
" Pulo Pinang " I. 162.
Fénélon, on the Society of Jesus; I. 94.
Féron, Abbé, his account of Corea; I. 116.
Forbes, Alexander, on Californian Missions; II. 251.
Fenwick, Bishop of Boston; anecdote of an Indian Catholic; II. 307.
French, love of American Indians towards the; II. 284, 304, 341.
Florida, Missions in; II. 358.
Frye, Rev. Mr., specimen of an Anglo-American Missionary; II. 364.
Francis, Conyers, English opinion of Protestant Indians; II. 369.
France, Protestantism in; II. 458.
" " influence of, in Society Islands; I. 510.
" " " in Sandwich Islands; I. 531.
Futuna, Conversion of; I. 531.
Falkland Islands; I. 542.
Fasting, Heathen comments on Protestant neglect of; I. 590.
Franciscan Missions in the Holy Land; I. 553.

G.

Gambier Islands; I. 537.
Guiseppe, R. P., his work in Algeria; I. 559.
Guizot, on the Society of Jesus; I. 94.
" on the Christianity of the sixth century; I. 565.
Gallas, Missions among the; I. 582.
Gobat, Dr., in Abyssinia; I. 584, 5.
" in Jerusalem; II. 46.
Gagelin, Venerable François, his martyrdom; I. 106.
Gutzlaff, Dr., his history in China; I. 159–163.
Grant, Archdeacon, on Luthero-Anglican Missionaries; I. 277.
Guyana, Missions in; II. 164.
Guaranis, Conversion of; II. 197.
Gonsalvez, Martyr; II. 198.
Golownin, on Dutch Missions; I. 360.
Gerstaecker, " " I. 361.
Gibraltar, Anglicanism in; II. 2.
Greeks, their religious condition; II. 6–9.
" their feelings towards Protestantism; II. 12–15.
Greek Monks, their character; II. 44, 86.
Greek Easter, imposture of the "holy fire;" II. 59, 60.
Georgia, Russian influence in; II. 82.
" Catholic Missions in; II. 119.
Galton, Mr. Francis, quoted; I. 632.
Garnier, Martyr; II. 296.
Greenland, results of Protestant Missions in; II. 337–9.
Germany, present state of religion in; II. 452–4.
Gravière, Admiral Jurien de la, on contrast between Catholic and Protestant Missions; I. 525.

H.

Holy City, conduct of Protestants in; II. 54–58.
Heber, Reginald, his life in India; I. 310–316.
Hobson, Dr., his invention of a Sacrament; I. 492.
Hill, Dr., his proceedings in British Columbia; II. 280.
Heki, specimen of a New Zealand "convert;" I. 444.
Harvard, Rev. W., his account of Cingalese Protestants; I. 377.
" " his account of Cingalese Catholics; I. 391.
Heathens, their estimate of Protestants; I. 167, 258, 269, 270, 272, 274, 275, 353, 393, 402, 453; II. 348, 391.
Humboldt, moral degradation of American Indians; II. 128.
Holland, Lord, quoted; II. 217.
Hindoos, piety of; I. 221.
Horneman, Fredrick, his "great courage;" I. 593.
Havard, Bishop and Martyr; I. 124.
Hopkins, Manley, on religion in the Sandwich Islands; I. 516, 522.
Hines, Rev. Gustavus, on Anglican Missionaries in China; I. 190.
" " " on religion in Hawaii; I. 521, 2.
Hewett, Captain Napier, West African Missions; I. 613.
Haxthausen, success of Catholic Missions in China; I. 90.
Henarez, Bishop and Martyr; I. 124.
Hurons, character of the; II. 310.
Holland, state of religion in; II. 488.
Hall, Judge, on contrast between Catholic and Protestant Missionaries; II. 301.
Hawkins, Rev. Ernest, on Anglo-American Missions; I. 351–4.

Howison, on the true causes of the enmity of Red Indians towards the English; II. 365.
Heaven, Protestant view of; I. 404.

I. & J.

Ignorance, effects of, in Missionaries; I. 197, 328, 329; II. 17.
Irving, Washington, his eulogy of Catholic Missionaries; II. 291.
Iroquois, ruined by the English; II. 301, 2.
Indians, American, their reverence for Catholic Missionaries; II. 304.
Iceland, Missions in; II. 335.
India, character of Protestant converts in; I. 343, 4.
Indo-Syrians, their rejection of Anglicanism; I. 295.
Indian Catholic Mission, present state of; I. 247–258.
Islamism, its victory over the Greek schismatics; II. 25.
Johnson, Rev. Mr., his autobiography; I. 597.
Judd, Rev. Dr., anecdote of; I. 521.
Jacobis, Bishop, his toils in Abyssinia; I. 577–80.
Jaccard, Martyr; I. 108.
Japan, Missions in; I. 241, 2.
Judson, Dr., his life and character; I. 296–303.
Jowett, Rev. Mr., his intercourse with the Greeks; II. 15.
Jerusalem, Luthero-Anglican Missions in; II. 43–53.
Jones, Peter, Protestant Indian Missionary; II. 312.
Jameson, Mrs., on contrast between Catholic and Protestant Indians; II. 314.
Jogues, Martyr; II. 293, 4.
Jesuits, effects of their suppression; I. 244, 5, 481; II. 157, 166, 167, 212, 219.

K.

Klaproth, on worldliness of Moravian Missionaries; II. 77.
" on Russian intolerance; II. 84.
King, Dr., his adventures at Athens; II. 12.
Kiernander, the "fashionable missionary;" I. 278.
Kaye, J. W., his intemperance; I. 227, 8.
Khoan, Father Paul, his discourse and martyrdom; I. 129.
Kien Long, persecution by; I. 177.
King, Father Thomas, Martyr; I. 113.
Krapf, Dr., his proceedings in Abyssinia; I. 585–8.
Kicherer, Rev. Mr., his ingenuity; I. 621.
Kohl, Mr., on Catholic Missions in Canada; II. 316–19.
Kirkby, Rev. W., on Anglican Missions in British America; II. 334, 5.
Kurds, their opinion of Protestants; I. 585.
Kirkland, Rev. Mr., his account of his own failure; II. 370.

L.

Laing, Major Gordon, his experience of Protestant Missionaries; I. 594.
Livingstone, Dr., his testimony to Catholic Missionaries; I. 603–6.
" " his account of Protestant " I. 638–40.
" " his own failure and recall; I. 639.
Lichtenstein, on African Missions; I. 620.
Le Comte; I. 92.
"Lie-preaching Devils," Chinese name for Protestant Missionaries; I. 167.
Lahore, Missions in; I. 231.
Lombard, R. P., his labors in Guyana; II. 166.
Lang, Dr. J. D., on Protestant Missions; I. 418, 423.

Lawry, Rev. Walter, his commercial activity; I. 429, 30.
Ladrone Islands, conversion of; I. 478.
Lewis, Rev. Mr., his way of converting heathens; I. 485.
Las Casas; II. 225.
Laplace, Captain, his liberation of the Hawaiian Catholics; I. 530.
Laynez, Francis, Bishop and Confessor; I. 237.
Luthero-Anglican Missionaries; I. 276, 7; II. 34, 5.
" " " Dr. Wolff's opinion of; I. 278.
" " " American comments on; II. 15.
Ludlow, English irreligion in India; I. 209.
Liberty, destroyed by the Reformation; II. 454–6.
Lemprière, Dr., his views of Christianity; II. 242, 244.
Lallemand, Gabriel, his martyrdom; II. 295.
Luxury of Protestant Missionaries; I. 181, 182, 190, 313, 314, 373, 374; II. 116.
" " " remarks on, by the Church Missionary Society; I. 374.

M.

Malta, Protestant College of; II. 3–5.
Montesquieu, condition of the Greeks a Divine judgment; II. 7.
Margoliouth, Rev. Moses, on frailty of Hebrew Protestants; II. 47.
Mount Sinai, Greek Monks at; II. 86.
Mackintosh, Sir James, on Jesuit Missions; II. 129.
" " his opinion of Henry Martyn; I. 289.
Martyn, Henry, his life and character; I. 286–92.
Middleton, Dr., his career in India; I. 303.
Marshman, Dr., state of his Mission; I. 321.
Madras, Anglican Mission in; I. 335.
Mass, the only true worship; I. 401.
Menzel, on the character of Protestantism; I. 401.
Man, the only object in Protestant worship; I. 404.
Melbourne, state of; I. 419.
Marsden, Rev. J., his proceedings in New Zealand; I. 424.
Maronites, their character; II. 87–95.
Miller, Hugh, miracles "not impossibilities;" II. 146.
Modern missionaries in South America; II. 189–192.
Monroy, Gaspard de, his heroism; II. 196.
Moxos, their conversion; II. 204.
Medical Missionaries, their failure; I. 196.
Minh, Father Philip, his martyrdom; I. 135.
Mongolia, Christians in; I. 137.
Melchior, Bishop and Martyr; I. 138.
Morrison, Dr., his life in China; I. 153–6.
Malcolm, Rev. Howard, his confessions; I. 154, 5, 9.
Missions, unexampled stability of; I. 95.
" fruitless without martyrs; I. 9.
" useless without vocation; II. 401, 2.
Marsh, Dr., his testimony against the Bible Society; I. 51.
Marette, Martyr; I. 103. 123, 125.
Miracles; I. 105, 140, 233; II. 133, 143, 146.
Minh-Menh, his cruelty; I. 110.
Marchant, Abbé, his martyrdom; I. 111.
Meyen, Dr., on Protestant Missionaries; I. 516.
Mofras, Duflot de, on Sandwich Islands Missions; I. 519.
Mangareva, conversion of; I. 537.
Marquesas; I. 542.
Madagascar; I. 543
Morocco; I. 550.

Mussulman sympathy with Protestants; I. 562.
Massaia, Bishop; I. 579–581.
Moffat, Rev. Robert; I. 619, 625, 629.
Moravians, traders and mechanics; I. 621.
" their conduct in Abyssinia; I. 588.
" their cupidity; II. 77, 8.
Moodie, Mr., his account of South Africa; I. 625–627.
Merriman, Archdeacon, on Anglican Missions in South Africa · I. 622.
MacMicking, Mr., account of the Philippines; I. 481.
Melville, Herman, Polynesian Missions; I. 503, 513.
Maistre, Abbé de, his labors in Corea; I. 113.
Manitouline Islands, Mission in; II. 311.
Martineau, Miss, on Missions in Canada; II. 315.
Mather, Cotton; II. 343, 346, 8, 9.
Mather, Increase; II. 347.
Maryland, infamy of Anglican Clergy in; II. 361.
" present state of Catholics in; II. 362.
Meade, Dr., his way of evangelizing Negroes; II. 375, 6.
Marriage, inconsistent with missionary labors; I. 455; II. 436.
Mexico, conversion of; II. 229–243.

N.

Nukahiva, failure of Protestant Mission at; I. 630.
Navigator Islands, Catholic Mission at; I. 542.
Napier, Colonel, his opinion of Protestant Missionaries; I. 630.
Neale, Mr., his account of Bang-kok; I. 161.
Narses, Armenian Patriarch, his confessions; II. 101, 107.
Nestorian heresy, Anglican sympathy with; I. 295; II. 111, 112.
Nobrega, his Mission in Brazil; II. 131.
Negroes, capable of conversion; II. 171.
" comparison of their state in Catholic and Protestant lands; II. 373–386.
Néel, Martyr; I. 140.
Norbert; I. 226, 7.
New Zealand, first Missions in; I. 423.
" actual state of; I. 470, 71.
" degradation of natives; I. 438, 448.
Nobinkissen, Hindoo testimony to Catholic Missions; I. 258.
Neilgherries, Mission in the; I. 324.
Naudi, Dr., his services to the Church Missionary Society; II. 4.
Nazareth, Catholic Arabs; I. 44.
Nobili, Robert de; I. 218.
Nacchi, R. P., his ministry in Aleppo; II. 22, 3.
North American natives, their friendly reception of the first Missionaries; II. 284, 5, 340.
" " their cruel treatment by the English; II. 285–8.
" " their appreciation of Catholics and Protestants; II. 273, 7, 287, 8, 370.
Newfoundland, decay of Anglicanism in; II. 333.
" present Anglican Missions in; II. 333.
Narragansetts, destruction of, by the English; II. 358.
Norway, state of religion in; II. 467.

O.

Orleans, Archbishop of, his life in Texas; II. 248.
Ortega, his labors in South America; II. 195.

Oregon, failure of Protestant Missions in; II. 263–7.
" success of Catholic " II. 267–276.
Oriental Church, its actual state; II. 64, 5.
Ostiaks, how converted; II. 79.
Ossets, " II. 82.
Oceanica, final result of Protestant Missions in; I. 546.
Ouvea, complete conversion of; I. 536.
Osborn, Captain Sherard, on Sandwich Islands Protestants; I. 515.

P.

Parennin, R. P., his labors in China; I. 76.
Perboyre, Martyr; I. 126.
Pompallier, Bishop; I. 466.
Polynesian ethnology; I. 475.
Philippine Islands, Martyrs in; I. 477.
" " present state of; I. 479.
Perrin, on the Society of Jesus; I. 236.
Possevin, on the Indian Mission; I. 243.
Perrone, on result of Missions; I. 326.
Porte, the, its relations with Protestants; II. 19.
Parsons, Rev. Levi; II. 30.
Palmerston, Lord, his pontifical decree; II. 48.
Panslavist movement, motive of; II. 65.
Paraguay, Missions in; II. 193–220.
Pridham, Mr., on Cingalese Missions; I. 359.
Pilgrim Fathers, their character; II. 342.
" " results of their influence; II. 349.
Prussia, religious bondage in; II. 455.
Pizarro; II. 233.
Peter of Ghent, his work in Mexico; II. 239.
Picquet, Abbé, his character and labors; II. 297, 307, 8.
Prince Edward's Island, Anglicanism in; II. 366.
Portugal, her former missionary zeal; I. 217.
" her present degradation; I. 604; II. 328.
Protestantism, fatal to the conversion of the heathen; I. 449, 611; II. 394, 421.
Philip, Dr.; I. 622, 4.
Polygamy, Protestant defence of; I. 634.
Paris, Rev. Mr., specimen of his preaching; I. 518.
Polynesian Religious; I. 537, 8.
Parkyns, Mansfield, on Abyssinian Missions; I. 588.
Porter, Rev. D. L., how he resented his failure; II. 90–96.
Perkins, Rev. Justin, his palace and stables; II. 113–119.
Persia, Missions in; II. 119–122.
Parish, Sir Woodbine, his testimony to the Jesuits; II. 148, 214.
Pombal; II. 158, 9.
Peru, Missions in; II. 172–5.
Patagonia, Jesuit martyrs in; II. 201.
Puritans, American, their cupidity; II. 350.
Protestant disunion, Pagan comments on; I. 195, 307, 308, 394, 395, 396, 444, 453, 633; II. 348, 425.
Poverty of Catholic Missionaries; I. 399.

Q.

Queen of Hawaii, her view of Christianity; I. 515.
Quake, story of; I. 592.

Quakers, never molested by the Indians; II. 341.
" failure of their efforts in America; II. 370.

R.

Retord, Bishop; I. 131..
Ranke, on Indian Missions; I. 229, 30, 42.
" on American " II. 142.
Robinson, Dr., on Jerusalem Missions; II. 51.
Russian Missions; II. 74–87.
" " Dissenters in; II. 61, 62, 81.
" Church, state of; II. 68–71; teaches Ultramontane doctrine; II. 72.
Russell, Dr., on English support of idolatry; I. 267.
Rhenius, his services to the Anglican Church; I. 280.
Rammohun Roy, on Protestant converts; 322, 342.
Rauperaha, his conversion; I. 445.
Religious dissensions in New Zealand; I. 450.
Richler, Henry, his work in South America; I. 55.
Race, Missionaries of every; II. 201.
Robertson, on the Jesuits; II. 215.
Ricci, his labors in China; I. 63–66.
Rhodes, Alex. de, his ministry; I. 85.
Ruschenberger, Dr., on Polynesian Missions; I. 517.
Rae, Dr., comparison of Catholic and Protestant Missionaries; I. 524.
Ravignan, de, R. P., his petition to preach to the Arabs; II. 555.
Reade, Sir Thomas, on Algerian converts; I. 562.
Rebmann, Rev. Mr., his "Ebenezer;" I. 586.
Reformation, early triumphs of; II. 448.
" their rapid decay; II. 448, 451.
" final results of; II. 451–69.
Reformation hypothesis; II. 469–72.
Rocky Mountains, Catholic Missions in; II. 268–276.
Rasles, Sabastian, his martyrdom by the English; II. 305–6.
Rupert's House, Anglican Mission in; II. 335.

S.

Switzerland, state of religion in; II. 456, 7.
Sweden, state of religion in; II. 465–7.
Stephens, J. L., Central America; II. 228.
Stephens, Governor, his report on Catholic Missions in the Far West; II. 275.
Scotland, moral state of; II. 329.
" decay of religion in; II. 330.
Seminoles, Protestant influence upon; II. 359.
Sierra Leone, failure of Protestant Missions; I. 615.
Simpson, Sir George, character of Protestant Missionaries; I. 514.
Seeman, Dr., on Sandwich Islands Missions; I. 520.
Samoan Group; I. 539, 540.
Snow, Captain Parker, on Falkland Island Mission; I. 542.
St. John, Spenser, account of Borneo; I. 544, 5.
Staoueli, monastery; I. 557.
Sicard, Claude; I. 570.
Samuel, Rev. J., his fictions; I. 44.
Schaal, Adam, his labors in China; I. 68.
Sanz, Bishop and Martyr; I. 81.
Staunton, Sir George, on Catholic Missions in China; I.
Shoolcraft, Mr., his opinion of Catholic Missionaries; II. 122.

Santa Cruz, Raymond de, Martyr; II. 154.
Southey, Mr., his intemperance; II. 156, 208.
Smith, Dr., on Peruvian Missions; II. 173.
Solano, St. Francis; II. 174.
Scarlett, Hon. Campbell, his rest disturbed; II. 179.
Smith, Dr., his travels in China; I. 167.
" Protestant estimate of him; I. 176.
Siam, Missions in; I. 159.
Singapore, Missions in; I. 162.
Scripture, study of, among Hindoos; I. 351.
Selkirk, Rev. James, on Missions in Ceylon; I. 378, 9.
Sterility of Missions due to conflicts of sects; I. 307.
Speculations of Anglican Missionaries; I. 429.
Shortland, Rev. Mr., his account of New Zealand; I. 444.
Selwyn, Dr., his life in New Zealand; I. 453–462.
Society Islands, Missions in; I. 483.
Sandwich Islands, cost of Missions in; I. 511.
" " final state of; I. 521, 227, 29.
" Islanders, Catholic virtues of; I. 528
" " persecutions of; I. 529, 30
Schwartz, his life in India; I. 282.
" failure in Ceylon; I. 369.
Sabat, his conversion and apostasy; I. 291.
Serampore College, state of; I. 323.
Santipore Training College, its failure; I. 331
Serampore Missions, failure of; I. 323, 334.
Sects in China; I. 194.
" India; I. 307.
" Ceylon; I. 395.
" Antipodes; I. 420, 450.
Satan, power of, in heathen lands; I. 224.
Schouvaloff, Catholic devotion and Greek levity; II. 3.
Slade, Sir A., his account of Protestant Missionaries in the Levant; II. 17.
Southgate, Dr., his failures in Turkey; II. 18.
Sisters of Charity in Turkey; II. 26.
" " in Beyrout; II. 27.
" " in Smyrna; II. 34.
Smyrna, Protestant Missions in; II. 29, 32, 34.
" Catholic " II. 33, 34.
Sidon, Missions in; II. 35.
"Simplicity" of Protestant worship; II. 38.
Society for the conversion of the Jews, its history; II. 49, 50.
Samoyeds, nominal Christians; II. 79.
Siberia, Catholic priests in; II. 80.
Schoeffer, Martyr; I. 133.
Scherzer, Dr., resources of Catholic and Protestant Missions; I. 532.
Stowe, Mrs. Beecher, her political romance; II. 377.
Seward, Mr., his view of Negroes and Indians; II. 373.
St. Paul, on the signs of an apostle; II. 402.
Social results of Missions; II. 439–446.

T.

Tocqueville, de, fate of American Indians; II. 341, 387.
Texas, Missions in; II. 244–250.
" conduct of Americans in; II. 245.
Talbot, Rev. Mr., his account of Catholic Missions in America; II. 299.
Turks distinguish between Catholics and Greeks; II. 8.
Turkey in Europe, Protestant Missions in; II. 15 20.

Turkey, Americans in ; II. 16. Catholics ; II. 20, 29.
Taylor, Bayard, character of Latin Monks ; II. 47.
Taeping rebels, their religion derived from Protestant Missionaries ; I. 99–205.
Thomas, St., the Apostle of India ; I. 210.
Torrette, Martyr ; I. 126.
Thibet, Christians in ; I. 137.
Tanjore, Protestant Missions in ; I. 337.
Tinnevelly, " " I. 337, 8.
Tupper, Rev. W. G., on Ceylon Missions ; I. 381.
Tennent, Sir Emerson, Ceylon Missions ; I. 382, 396.
Taylor, Rev. Richard, his fortunes in New Zealand ; I. 427.
Tomlin, Rev. T., his account of his own labors ; I. 163.
Trollope, Anthony, on the Negroes ; II. 165.
Tong-King, Missions in ; I. 85.
Timskowski, constancy of Chinese ; I. 98.
Turner, Rev. George, history of Samoan Group ; I. 539.
Tunis, Missions in ; I. 561, 62.
Tristram, Rev. Mr., on Algerian Protestants ; I. 562.
Tzatzoe, his comedy at Exeter Hall ; I. 622.
Thompson, Mr., his revelations ; I. 625.
Tinh, Father Paul, Martyr ; I. 136.
Tahiti, original state of ; I. 487. Catholic Missions in ; 506. Final state of ; 569, 10.
Therry, Mr., account of Tahiti in 1863 ; I. 510.
Tabert, Bishop, his labors and writings ; I. 103.
Thomas, St., Protestant clergy in ; II. 380.
Temple, Rev. Daniel, his likeness to Abraham ; II. 31.
Thomson, Rev. Dr., on motives of Hebrew converts ; II. 53.

U. & V.

Unity of Catholics, Heathen comments upon ; I. 97, 195, 394.
" " Protestant " " II. 425, 6.
Unitarianism in the United States ; II. 349.
United States, state of religion in ; II. 339.
Underhill, Rev. Mr., on Baptist Missions in the West Indies · II. 382, 3.
Virginia, history of Anglicanism in ; II. 363.
" cradle of American Revolution ; II. 368.
Voltaire, on Paraguay Mission ; II. 193.
Vieyra, Antony, his apostolate in Brazil ; II. 151, 3, 6.
Victoria, fate of natives in ; I. 417.
Vaz, Joseph, his labors in Ceylon ; I. 359.
Valentia, Lord, on Indian Missions ; I. 283.
Veeson, Rev. Mr., his crimes ; I. 486.
Von Kotzebue ; I. 488, 493.
Verbiest, F., his labors in China ; I. 70.
Vera Paz, origin of the name ; II. 225.
Virtues of Catholics confessed by the heathen ; I. 98, 101, 125, 6, 7 132, 3, 189.
Vocation, its effects ; II. 403.
" not recognized by Protestants ; II. 404, 5.

W.

Wolff, Dr. Joseph, his fictions ; I. 45, 6.
Wilks, Mark, his view of apostles ; I. 526.
White Nile, Mission on the ; I. 571.
Wilson, Rev. Leighton, on West African Missions ; I. 611.

Worship, real; I. 401.
Williams, Archdeacon, his history in New Zealand; I. 426, 7, 433.
Wilson, Dr. Daniel, his experience in India; I. 316.
Wilkes, Commodore, account of Protestant Missions; I. 441, 2, 488, 502.
Waldegrave, Lord, " " " I. 489, 493.
Williams, Rev. John, his real history in Polynesia; I. 496–500.
Wheeler, Mr., Polynesian Missions; I. 501, 513.
Walpole, Hon. F.; I. 503, 520.
Wallis Island, Missions in; I. 507, 535, 6.
Williams, Rev. George, his opinion of Protestant Missionaries in Syria; II. 42, 52.
West Indies, Anglican Church in; II. 380.
Washington, his address to American Catholics; II. 397.
Wilberforce, Dr. Samuel, on American Puritans; II. 345.
" " on Anglicanism in Virginia; II. 363.
" " on the value of endowments; II. 363.

Y.

Yong-Tching, persecution by; I. 73.
Yate, Rev. Mr., on New Zealand Missions; I. 428.
" " specimen of his converts; I. 439.
Young, Cuthbert, Protestantism in Turkey; II. 19.
Young, Rev. Mr., Australian Missions; I. 412.

INDEX OF AUTHORITIES.

A.

Annales de la Propagation de la Foi.
Annuaire Historique Universel.
Asseman; Dissert. de Syris Nestorianis.
Allatius, Leo; De Eccles. Occident. et Orient. Perpet. Conseensu.
Ami de la Religion.
Augustini Opera.
Asiatic Journal.
Asiatic Researches.
Argensola, B. L. de; Discovery and Conquest of the Molucca and Philippine Islands.
Anderson, C.; Annals of the English Bible.
Angas, George French; Savage Life in Australia.
Atkinson, T. W.; Oriental and Western Siberia.
Ainsworth, H.; Travels in Asia Minor.
Adalbert, Prince of Prussia; Travels in Brazil, &c.
Acts of the Government of the Cape of Good Hope.
Alexander, Sir James; Voyage among the Colonies of Western Africa.
Andersson, Charles John; Lake Ngami, &c.
" " The Okavango River.
Arundell, Rev. J.; Discoveries in Asia Minor.
Aspinall, Clara; Three Years in Melbourne.
Auber, Rev. Peter; China.
Abeel, Rev. David; Journal of a Residence in China.
Addison, Lieut.-Colonel; Traits of Anglo-Indian Life.
A Glance at the East; by a retired Bengal Civilian.
Arnold, Edward; The Marquis of Dalhousie's Administration of British India.
A Voyage to the Island of Ceylon in 1747.
Anderson, Rev. Philip; The English in Western India.
Anadol; by the Author of "Frontier Lands."
Achilli, and the Malta Protestant College.
Adam, Rev. John; Memoir of.
Allies, T. W.; St. Peter, His Name and Office.
Astley; Voyages and Travels.
Anderson, Rev. J. S. M.; History of the Colonial Church.

B.

Brasseur de Bourbourg; Histoire du Canada et de ses Missions.
Bressany, R. P.; Missions dans la Nouvelle France.
Bertolacci, A.; View of Ceylon.
Björnstjerna, Count; The Theogony of the Hindoos.
Blumhardt; Christian Missions.
" Histoire Générale de l'Etablissement du Christianisme.

Bernouilli; Description de l'Inde.
Bost, M. A.; Genève Religieuse.
Bertrand, R. P.; Histoire de la Mission du Maduré.
Baudicour, Louis de; La Colonisation de l'Algérie.
Baude, Baron; L'Algérie.
Beke, C. J., Ph. D.; Mémoire Justificatif en réhabilitation des Pères Paëz et Jérome Lobo.
" " " Statement of Facts relative to the British Mission to Shoa.
" " " Christianity among the Gallas.
Biographie Universelle.
Boué, A.; La Turquie d'Europe.
Bourassé, l'Abbé; La Terre Sainte.
Bonald, M. de; Législation Primitive.
Boré, Eugène; Correspondance et Mémoires d'un Voyageur en Orient.
" " Arménie.
Brosset, M.; Histoire de la Georgie.
Brossard, Alfred de; Les Républiques de la Plata.
Bohusz, Mgr. de, Archevèque de Mohilew; Recherches Historiques sur l'Origine des Sarmates, des Esclavons, et des Slaves.
" " " " Histoire du Royaume de la Chersonèse Taurique.
Bodenstedt, Friedrich; Life in the Caucasus and the East.
Bossuet; Œuvres.
Bridgman; Chinese Chrestomathy.
Benyowski, Comte; Travels.
Bancroft, George; History of the United States.
Beecham, John; Ashantee and the Gold Coast.
Burchell, William J.; Travels in the Interior of Southern Africa.
Bannister, S.; Memoir respecting the Colonization of Natal.
Backhouse, James: Visit to the Mauritius and South Africa.
Bunbury, Charles J. F.; Journal of a Residence at the Cape of Good Hope.
Baldwin, W. C.; African Hunting from Natal to the Zambesi.
Browne, J. Ross; Yusef.
Badger, Rev. G. P.; The Nestorians and their Rituals.
Bremer, Fredericka; Travels in the Holy Land.
" " Homes of the New World.
Borror, Dawson; Journey from Naples to Jerusalem.
Barrow, Sir George; Ceylon, Past and Present.
Brace, Charles Loring; Home Life in Norway and Sweden.
Brown, Rev. William; History of the Propagation of Christianity among the Heathen.
Bowring, Sir John; The Kingdom and People of Siam.
" " A Visit to the Philippine Islands.
Bradshaw, W. S.; Voyages to India, China, &c.
Bidwill, John Carne; Rambles in New Zealand.
Brodie, Walter; Remarks on the Past and Present State of New Zealand.
Bright, John; A History of New Zealand.
Bligh; Voyage to the South Sea.
Byron, Lord; Voyage of H.M.S. Blonde to the Sandwich Islands.
Bennett, F. Debell; Narrative of a Whaling Voyage.
Belcher, Sir Edward; Narrative of a Voyage round the World.
Barth, Dr.; Travels in Africa.
Blofeld, J. H.; Algeria, Past and Present.
Blakesley, Rev. J. W.; Four Months in Algeria.
Broughton, Mrs.; Six Years' Residence in Algiers.
Bonar, Rev. H., D.D.; The Desert of Sinai.
Burton, James; First Footsteps in East Africa.
Bruce; Travels, &c.
Blackiston, Captain Thomas W.; Five Months on the Zang-Tsze.

Bingham, Commander Eliot; Narrative of the Expedition to China.
Barrow; Travels in China.
Bernard; Services of the Nemesis.
Berncastle, Dr.; A Voyage to China.
Burke, Edmund; Works.
Bartoli and Maffei; Life of St. Francis Xavier.
Binning, Robert B. M.; Two Years' Travel in Persia, &c.
Buchanan, Dr. Claudius; Christian Researches in Asia.
" " The Star in the East.
Brine, Commander Lindesay; The Taeping Rebellion in China.
Ball, B. L., M.D.; Rambles in Eastern Asia.
Bartlett, John Russell; Personal Narrative of Explorations in Texas, &c.
Boston Pilot.
Bradford, William J. A.; Notes on the North West.
Barker, Charles Fiott; Memoir on Syria.
Buckingham, J. S.; America.
" " Canada.
Babbage; Ninth Bridgewater Treatise.
Brown, William; New Zealand and its Aborigines.
Braim, T. H.; History of New South Wales.
Brief View of the operations of the B. and F. Bible Society, 1862.
Baird, Rev. Robert; Religion in the United States of America.
Burton, Lieutenant; Sindh.
Bennett, J. W.; Ceylon and its Capabilities.
Beechey, Captain; Voyage to the Pacific.
Buchanan, Dr. Francis; Journey through Mysore, &c.
Barrett, Joseph; The Duty of Britons to promote Christianity in India.
Bell, Captain Evans; The English in India.
Bellew, H. W.; Journal of a Mission to Afghanistan.
Bevan, Major; Thirty Years in India.
Bateman, Rev. Josiah; Life of Daniel Wilson.
Briggs, Lieut.-General; India and Europe compared.
Bowen, John; Missionary Incitement and Hindoo Demoralization.
Baker, Lieutenant; Rifle in Ceylon.
" " Eight Years' Wanderings in Ceylon.
Burton, Judge; State of Religion in N. S. Wales.
Bennett, George; Wanderings in N. S. Wales.
Byrne, J.; Twelve Years' Wanderings, &c.
British Colonization of New Zealand.
Barca, Madame Calderon de la; Life in Mexico.
Boudinot, Elias, LL.D.; A Star in the West.
Beecham, John; Colonization.
Berkeley, Hon. Grantley F.; The English Sportsman in the Western Prairies.
Bouchette, Colonel; British Dominions in North America.
Bradford, Wm. J. A.; Notes on the North West.
Baltimore Metropolitan Catholic Almanac.
Burke, E.; An Account of the European Settlements in America.
Burton, Richard F.; The City of the Saints.
Berkeley; A Proposal for the better supplying of Churches in our Foreign Plantations, Works, 1784.
Bermuda; By a Field Officer.
Brandt, Gerard; History of the Reformation in the Low Countries.

C.

Compans, H. Terneaux; Voyages, &c., pour servir à l'Histoire de la Découverte de l'Amérique.
Chronique Religieuse.
Charlevoix; Histoire du Paraguay.

Charlevoix, Histoire du Japon.
" Histoire de la Nouvelle France.
Chabrol, M. de; Essai sur les Mœurs, &c., ap. Pancoucke.
Cortes, Donoso; Œuvres.
Casalis, E.; Les Bassoutos.
Compendio della, Vita del B. Pietro Claver.
Chateaubriand; Génie du Christianisme.
Cordara; Historia Societatis Jesu.
Cochin, Augustin; L'Abolition de l'Esclavage.
Carette, M. E.; Algérie.
Callander; Terra Australis Cognita.
Calvin; Comment. in Nov. Test.
Custine, Marquis de; La Russie en 1839.
Cruickshank, Brodie; Eighteen Years on the Gold Coast.
Colenso, J. W., D.D.; Ten Weeks in Natal.
Calderwood, Rev. H.; Caffres and Caffre Missions.
Clark, J. A., D.D.; Glimpses of the Old World.
Coleridge, S. T.; Literary Remains.
Crowe, Rev. F.; The Gospel in Central America.
Cochrane, Captain Charles Stuart; Journal of a Residence in Colombia.
Colton, Rev. Walter; Incidents of a Cruise to California.
Chinese Repository.
Christmas, Rev. H.; The Hand of God in India.
Campbell, Colonel; Excursions in Ceylon.
Cordiner, Rev. James; A Description of Ceylon.
Caldecott, R. M.; Life of Baber, Emperor of Hindostan.
Close, Dr.; An Indian Retrospect.
Cameron, Charles Hay; The Duties of Great Britain to India.
Clarkson, Rev. William; India and the Gospel.
Cormack, Rev. John; Abolition of Female Infanticide in Guzerat.
Charlesworth, Miss; Africa's Mountain Valley.
Carter, Rev. T. T.; Memoir of Bishop Armstrong.
Cole, Alfred W.; The Cape and the Kafirs.
Chase, John C.; The Cape of Good Hope.
Carne, John; Letters from the East.
Cox, Samuel; Wanderings in Europe and the Orient.
Curzon, Hon. F.; Monasteries of the Levant.
" " Armenia and Erzeroum.
Castlereagh, Viscount; A Journey to Damascus, &c.
Clark, E. D., LL.D.; Travels in Various Countries.
Cheever, George B., D.D.; The Pilgrim Fathers.
Curtis, G. W.; The Wanderer in Syria.
Chesney, Colonel; The Russo-Turkish Campaigns.
Cameron, Lieut.-Colonel Poulett; Personal Adventures in Georgia, Circassia, and Russia.
Chamerovzow, Louis; The New Zealand Question.
Church in the Colonies.
Cruise, Captain; Journal.
Cholmondeley, Thomas; Ultima Thule.
Campbell, Rev. John, D.D.; Maritime Discovery and Christian Missions.
Coulter, John, M.D.; Adventures on the Western Coast of South America.
" " Adventures in the Pacific.
Cheever, Rev. Henry T.; The Island World of the Pacific.
Caswall Rev. H.; The Western World Revisited.
Churton, Rev. H. B. W.; The Land of the Morning.
Crawford, M. S.; Through Algeria.
Churchill, Colonel; Mount Lebanon.
Chasseaud, George Washington; The Druses of the Lebanon.
Carnarvon, Earl of; Recollections of the Druses.
Colton C. · Thoughts on the Religious State of America.

Calcott, Lady; Journal of a Voyage to Brazil.
Courtot; Life of St. Francis Solano.
Cleveland, Richard J.; A Narrative of Voyages.
Campbell, George; India as it may be.
Crawfurd; Embassy to Siam and Cochin China.
China and the Missions at Amoy.
Colonial Church Chronicle.
Colledge; Suggestions with regard to employing Medical Practitioners as Missionaries in China.
Cobbold, Rev. R. H.; Pietuves of the Chinese.
Cunynhame, Colonel Arthur; Recollections of Service in India.
Calcutta Review.
Callery and Yvan; History of the Insurrection in China.
Churchill; Collection of Voyages.
Christian Remembrancer.
Cuningham, Rev. J. W.; Christianity in India.
Chinese and General Missionary Gleaner.
Cape and Natal News.
Causes of the Indian Revolt; by a Hindu of Bengal.
China, Last year in; by a Field Officer.
Chandless, William; A Visit to Salt Lake.
Church, the, in Canada.
Cockburn, Henry; Memorials of his Time.
Coxe, Rev. A. C.; Statements and Documents concerning the Board of Managers of the American Bible Society.
Chalmers; History of the Revolt of the American Colonies.
Church Advocate.
Colton; Church and State in America.
Castell, William; A Petition exhibited to the High Court of Parliament, 1641.
Colton, Mrs. Ann; An Account of our late Troubles in Virginia, 1676.
Coleridge, Henry Nelson; Six Months in the West Indies.
Cartwright, Peter; The Backwoods Preacher.
Catlin; American Indians.
Channing, W. E.; Works.

D.

D'Orbigny, Alcide; Voyage dans l'Amérique Méridionale.
Duflot de Mofras; Exploration du Territoire de l'Orégon.
Didier, Charles; Cinq Cents Lieues sur le Nil.
David, Jules; Syrie Moderne.
D'Hericourt, Rochet; Second Voyage dans le Pays des Adels et le Royaume de Shoa.
D'Istria, Comtesse Doria; Les Femmes en Orient.
Daumas, General E.; Les Mœurs du Désert, &c.
De Maistre; Lettre à une Dame Russe sur le Schisme et sur l'Unité Catholique.
Déluzy, Léon; La Russie, son Peuple et son Armée.
Desvergers, A. N.; Abyssinie.
D'Orleans, R. P.; Vie du Père Ricci.
Du Halde; Description de l'Empire de la Chine.
Domenech, l'Abbé Emanuel; Journal d'un Missionaire au Texas et au Mexique.
De Guignes; Voyages à Pékin, Manille, &c.
Défense de la Vénérable Compagnie des Pasteurs de Genève.
Divers Voyages de la Chine.
D'Herbelot; Bibliothèque Orientale.
D'Alembert; Œuvres.
Davis, Sir John; Sketches of China.
" " China since the Peace.

Duyckink; Cyclopædia of American Literature.
Davidson, F.; Trade and Travel in the Far East.
Downing, H.; The Fan Qui in China.
Dallas, Rev. Alexander; The Missionary Crisis.
Dublin Review.
De Bults, Lieut.; Rambles in Ceylon.
Dorr, Benjamin, D.D.; Notes of Travel in the East.
Dwight, Rev. H. G. O.; Christianity in Turkey.
" " " Christianity Revived in the East.
Drew, G. S.; Scripture Lands in Connection with their History.
Dalgairns, Rev. F.; The Holy Communion.
Duncan, W.; Travels in Western Africa.
Drayson, Captain Alfred; Sporting Scenes among the Kaffirs of South Africa.
Du Chaillu, Paul B.; Equatorial Africa.
Durbin, Rev. J. P., D.D.; Observations in the East.
Drake, Samuel G.; History of the Indians of North America.
Döllinger, Dr.; The Church and the Churches.
Dibble, Rev. Sheldon; History of the Sandwich Islands.
Dieffenbach, Dr. Ernest; Travels in New Zealand.
Dillon, Captain P.; Narrative of the Discovery of the Fate of La Pérouse.
D'Ewes, J.; China, Australia, and the Pacific Islands.
Dana; Two Years before the Mast.
Debary, Rev. Thomas; The Canary Isles, &c.
Davies, Rev. E. W. L.; Algiers in 1857.
Davis, N.; Ruined Cities within Numidian and Carthaginian Territories.
Demidoff, Anatole de; Travels in S. Russia.
Denton, Rev. W.; Servia and the Servians.
Documentary History of New York.
Dalton, Henry G.; History of British Guiana.
Damer, Mrs. Dawson; Tour in Greece.
Dobrizhoffer; Account of the Abipones.
Dalcho, Frederick, M.D.; An Historical Account of the Protestant Episcopal Church in South Carolina.
Dwight, Rev. Timothy, D.D.; Travels in New England.
Durham, Earl of; Report and Despatches.
Dennys, N. B.; The Cruise of the St. George.

E.

Evagrius; Hist. Ecclesiast.
Epistolæ Indicæ.
Encyclopédie Méthodique.
Epistolæ Præpos. General. ad Patres et Fratres Soc. Jesu.
Empaytaz, H. L.; Considérations sur la Divinité de Jesus Christ.
Emmerich, Anne Catherine; La Douloureuse Passion de N. S. Jesus Christ.
Ewbank, Thomas; Life in Brazil.
Elwes, Robert; Tour Round the World.
Ewald, Rev. F. C.; Journal of Missionary labors.
Earle, Augustus; Nine Months' Residence in New Zealand.
Excursion in New Zealand.
Ellis, H. T.; Hong-Kong to Manilla.
Ellis, Rev. William; Polynesian Researches.
" " Three Visits to Madagascar.
" " Brief Notice of China and Siam.
Ellis, Sir Henry; Journal of an Embassy to China.
Erskine, J. Elphinstone; The Islands of the Western Pacific.
East, J. D.; Western Africa.
Essay on the Religious Prejudices of India.
Eclectic Review.

Edinburgh Review.
Edinburgh Christian Instructor.
Earl, George Windsor; The Eastern Seas.
Elwood, Mrs. Colonel; Narrative of a Journey to India.
Edkins, Rev. Joseph; The Religious Condition of the Chinese.
Evangelical Christendom.
Elphinstone, Hon. Mountstewart; History of India.
Edwards, Frank S; A Campaign in New Mexico.
Englishwoman, The, in America.
Events in Indian History.

F.

Frank, Dr. Louis; Déscription de la Régence de Tunis.
Fontanier, V.; Voyage dans l'Archipel Indien.
" Narrative of a Mission to India.
Fénélon; Œuvres.
Fardoonjee Nowrosjee; The Civil Administration of the Bombay Presidency
Froebel, Julius; Seven Years' Travel in Central America.
Fowler, George; Three Years in Persia.
Ferrier, General; Caravan Journeys in Persia, &c.
Fletcher, Rev. J. C., and Kidder, Rev. D. P.; Brazil and the Brazilians.
Fox, W.; The Six Colonies of New Zealand.
Farley, J.; Two Years in Syria.
Frankl, Dr.; The Jews in the East.
Frontier Lands of the Christian and the Turk.
Foote, Commander; Africa and the American Flag.
Forbes, Commander; Dahomey and the Dahomans.
Forbes, James; Oriental Memoirs.
Forbes, Colonel; Recent Disturbances in Ceylon.
Forbes, Major; Eleven Years in Ceylon.
Forbes, Lieutenant; Five Years in China.
Forbes, Alexander; California.
Forbes, J.; Unrefuted Charges, &c.
Faber, F. W., D.D.; The Creator and the Creature.
" " The Blessed Sacrament.
" " Bethlehem.
Freeman, Rev. J. J.; Tour in South Africa.
Fisk, Rev. George; A Pastor's Memorial.
Flanagan, Roderick; History of New South Wales.
Fitton, Edward Brown; New Zealand.
Fletcher, Rev. Joseph; A Voice from New Zealand.
Fitzroy, Robert; Remarks on New Zealand.
Fuller, Francis; Five Years' Residence in New Zealand.
Fanning, R.; Voyages round the World.
Fremantle, Rev. W.; The Eastern Churches.
Fast Day Sermons.
Fuller, Andrew; Apology for the Christian Missions in India.
Foreign Missionary Chronicle.
Fraser, James B.; Travels in the Persian Provinces.
Fifteen Years in India, by an Officer, &c.
Fleuriau; Life of B. Peter Claver.
Finlayson; Mission to Siam.
Fonblanque, Edward Harrington, de; Niphon and Pe-che-li.
Frontier Lands of the Christian and the Turk.
Fishbourne, Captain; Impressions of China.
Fearon, Henry Bradshaw; Sketches of America.
Francis, Conyers; Life of Rev. John Eliot.
Featherstonhaugh; Excursions through the Slave States.

Franklin; Works, ed. Sparks.
Feuille d'Avis de Genève.

G.

Gironière, P. de la; Vingt années aux Philippines.
Golovine, Ivan; Mémoires d'un Prêtre Russe.
Gerebtzoff, Nicolas de; Histoire de la Civilisation en Russie.
Guizot; Histoire de la Civilisation en Europe.
" " " en France.
Gennadius; Adversus Græcos.
Galitzin, le Prince Augustin; Un Missionaire Russe.
Grotius; Ordin. Hollandiæ et Westfrisæ Pietas.
Godard, Léon; Le Maroc.
Giesler; Ecclesiast. Hist.
Grosier; Voyage en Chine.
Golownin, Captain; Recollections of Japan.
Gardner; Travels in the Interior of Brazil.
Gardiner, Captain Allen; A Voice from South America.
" " " A Visit to the Indians of Chili.
Gilliam, Albert M.; Travels in Mexico.
Grant, Asahel, M.D.; The Nestorians.
Grey, Sir George; Overland Expedition from Auckland to Taranaki.
" " Journals of Two Expeditions in Australia.
Gobat, Samuel, D.D.; Journal of a Three Years' Residence in Abyssinia.
Graham; Letters on India.
Gouger, Henry; Two Years' Imprisonment in Burmah.
Garston, Edgar; Greece Revisited.
Gibson, William; Recollections of other Lands.
Godlonton, R.; Narrative of the Kaffir War.
Galton, Francis; Tropical South Africa.
Grant, Rev. Anthony, D.C.L.; Bampton Lectures for 1843.
Gibbon; Decline and Fall.
Gibson, Walter; Glance at the East Indian Archipelago.
Gillespie, Rev. William; The Land of Sinim.
Geddes, Rev. Michael; History of the Church of Malabar.
Gerstaecker, F.; Voyage round the World.
Gutzlaff, Rev. Charles; China Opened.
" " History of China.
" " Journal of Three Voyages along the Coast of China.
Gookin; Historical Collections.
Godley; Letters from America.
Gillies; Historical Collections.
Gan-Eden, or Pictures of Cuba.

H.

Hoefer, F.; Afrique Australe.
Hammer, J. Von; Histoire de l'Empire Ottoman.
Hell, Xavier Hommaire de; Les Steppes de la Mer Caspienne.
Hoornbeek, De Conversione Indorum et Gentilium.
Haafner, M. J.; Voyages dans la Péninsule Occidentale de l'Inde.
Hogendorp, Comte de; Coup d'œil sur Java.
Huc; L'Empire Chinois.
" Le Christianisme en Chine.
Humboldt; Asie Centrale.
Henrion; Histoire Générale des Missions Catholiques.
Haxthausen; Etudes sur la Russie.

Haxthausen ; Transcaucasia.
Histoire Apologétique de la Conduite des Jesuites de la Chine.
Histoire des Momiers.
Hausmann ; Voyage en Chine
Histoire de ce qui s'est passé au Royaume d'Ethiopie.
Hong-Kong Daily Press.
Hamberg, Rev. Thomas ; The Chinese Rebel Chief, Hung-Siu-Tsuen.
Hough, Rev. James ; History of Christianity in India.
History of the Tartar Conquerors of China.
Hamilton, Rev. James ; China and the Chinese Mission.
Holmes ; American Annals.
Hodgson, Pemberton ; Residence in Japan.
Hines, Rev. Gustavus ; Life on the Plains of the Pacific.
Henderson, John ; Excursions in New South Wales.
Heaphy, Charles ; Narrative of a Residence in various parts of New Zealand.
Hursthouse, Charles ; New Zealand, the Britain of the South.
Hodder, E. ; Memories of New Zealand Life.
Hodgkinson, S. ; A Description of the Province of Canterbury
History of the Mutiny of the Bounty.
Hopkins, Manley ; ; Hawaii, an Historical Account of the Sandwich Islands.
Hamilton, James ; Sinai, the Hedjaz, and Soudan.
Henderson, E. ; History of Brazil.
Holland, Lord ; Foreign Reminiscences.
Helps, A. ; Mexico.
Hopkins, David ; The Dangers of British India.
Hoffmeister, Dr. ; Travels in Ceylon and Continental India.
Hudson, Major ; Memoir of.
Hartwig, Dr. G. ; The Tropical World.
Hendon, Lieut. ; Valley of the Amazon.
Hooker, Sir William ; Himalayan Journals.
Hood, John ; Australia and the East.
Hervey, Captain Albert ; Ten Years in India.
Head, Rev. Erskine ; The Right of a Clergyman to Oppose the Errors of his own Church.
Heber, Reginald ; Indian Journal.
Hamilton. J. ; Letters of a Hindoo Rajah.
Hawes, J., D.D. ; Travels in the East.
Hahn-Hahn, Countess ; Letters, &c.
Harris, Major Cornwallis ; The Highlands of Æthiopia.
Hewett, Captain J. F. Napier ; European Settlements on the West Coast of Africa
Holden, Rev. W. C. ; History of the Colony of Natal.
Hawker, Rev. Robert, D.D ;. Works.
Haolé, A. ; Sandwich Island Notes.
Hoole, Rev. Elijah ; Year Book of Missions.
Howitt, W. ; Colonization and Christianity.
Hislop, Sir Thomas ; Summary of the Mahratta Campaign.
Hill, S. S. ; Travels in the Sandwich and Society Islands.
Hawks, Francis L., D.D. ; American Expedition under Commodore Perry.
Harvard, Rev. William ; Narrative of the Mission to Ceylon.
Henderson, E. ; Biblical Researches in Russia.
" The Turkish New Testament Incapable of Defence.
Hawkins, Alfred ; Picture of Quebec, with Historical Recollections.
Hawkins, Rev. Ernest ; Missions of the Church of England in the North American Colonies.
Howison, Robert R. ; History of Virginia.
Halkett, John ; Notes on North American Indians.
Hildreth, Richard ; The History of the United States of America.
Head, Sir Francis ; Narrative, &c.
Hutchison Papers ; New York.

Héron, H. de Courcy, de Laroche; The Catholic Church in the United States, ed. Shea.
Heckewelder; Narrative, &c.
Helper; The Impending Crisis of the South.
Hallam, Henry; Introduction to the Literature of Europe.
Haldane; Letter to S. J. Chenevière.
Hamilton, Andrew; Sixteen Months in the Danish Isles.
Hitchcock, Edward, D.D.; The Religion of Geology.

I. & J.

Jancigny; Ceylon.
Journal d'un Voyage au Levant.
Journal d'un Voyage en Orient.
Joly, Crétineau; Histoire de la Compagnie de Jesus.
Jacquenet, Abbé; Vie de M. l'Abbé Gagelin.
Jouvency; Hist. Soc. Jesu.
Journal Asiatique.
Jobson, Rev. F., D.D.; Australia, with Notes by the Way.
Johnson, George W.; The Stranger in India.
John, C. S.; On Indian Civilization.
Jones, Rev. George; Excursion to Cairo.
Journal of the Royal Geographical Society.
Journal of the Asiatic Society of Bengal.
Journal of the American Oriental Society.
Jocelyn, Lord; Six Months in China.
Jones, Rev. H. Berkeley; Adventures in Australia.
Jarues, James J.; History of the Sandwich Islands.
Jacobs, Thomas Jefferson; Incidents and Adventures in the Pacific Ocean.
Johnston, Charles; Travels in Southern Abyssinia.
Journal of a Deputation to the East.
Jowett, Rev. W.; Christian Researches in the Mediterranean.
Indian Mutiny, Thoughts and Facts.
Isaacs, Nathaniel; Travels in Eastern Africa.
Irving, Washington; Knickerbocker.
Irving, B. A.; The Theory and Practice of Caste.
Indian Religions, The; by an Indian Missionary.
Inquiry into the Causes of the Alienation of the Delaware and Shawanese Indians from the British Interest.
Jameson, Mrs.; Sketches in Canada.
Indians of North America; by the Religious Tract Society.
Indians, Plea for the; by the Citizens of Hartford, Connecticut.
Inglis, H. D.; Norway, Sweden, and Denmark.

K.

Kéroulée, Georges de; Un Voyage à Pékin.
Klaproth, Jules; Voyage au Mont Caucase et en Georgie.
Krasinski, Count Valerian; Montenegro and the Slavonians of Turkey.
" " " Panslavism and Germanism,
" " " The Religious History of the Slavonic Nations
Kohl, J. G.; Russia.
" " Austria.
" " Wanderings round Lake Superior.
Krapf, Rev. Lewis; Travels in Eastern Africa.
King, Rev. S. W.; The Italian Valleys of the Pennine Alps.
Kennedy, Captain J. Clark; Algeria and Tunis.
Kotzebue; New Voyage round the World.

Krusenstern; Voyage round the World.
Kesson, J.; The Cross and the Dragon.
Kidd, Samuel; Critical Notices of Dr. Morrison's Literary Labors.
Kaye, J. W.; Christianity in India.
" " Life of Sir John Malcolm.
" " History of the Administration of the East India Company.
" " Papers of Lord Metcalfe.
Kipp, Rev. W. Ingraham; The Early Jesuit Missions in North America.
Knighton, William; Tropical Sketches.
" " Forest Life in Ceylon.
Knox, Captain; Captivity in Ceylon.
Kolff, D. H.; Voyages of the Dourga.
Kerr, Rev. Dr.; Report on the State of the Christians of Cochin and Travancore.
Kelly, Walter Keating; Syria and the Holy Land.
Kinglake; Eothen.
Kendall, George Wilkins; Narrative of the Texan Santa Fé Expedition.
Kane, Paul; Wanderings of an Artist among the Indians of North America.
Kingston, W. H. G.; Western Wanderings.
Knox, Rev. John P.; Historical Account of St. Thomas.

L.

Lettres Edifiantes et Curieuses.
Labat, R. P.; Nouvelle Relation de l'Afrique Occidentale.
Lamennias; Œuvres.
Leonardus Echiensis; De Captivitate Constantinopolis.
La Russie, Est-elle schismatique?
L'Univers Pittoresque.
Lange, Laurent; Journal du Voyage à la Chine.
Laurent, Achille; Relation Historique des Affaires de Syrie.
Laplace; Campagne de Circumnavigation de la Frégate l'Artémise.
La Croze; Histoire du Christianisme des Indes.
Levaillant; Voyage dans l'Intérieur de l'Afrique.
Livingstone, Dr.; Missionary Travels in Southern Africa.
Lay, G. Tradescant; The Chinese as they are.
Lang, John; Wanderings in India.
Le Bas, Rev. C. Webb; Life of Bishop Middleton.
Letters from Wanganui.
Lancelott, F.; Australia as it is.
Lang, John Dunmore, D.D.; New Zealand in 1839.
" " History of New South Wales.
Lawry, Rev. W.; Friendly and Feejee Islands.
Latham, Dr.; The Ethnology of the British Colonies.
" Ethnology of India.
" The Nationalities of Europe.
" The Natural History of the Varieties of Man.
Lee, Dr.; History of the Church of Abyssinia.
Le Comte; The Present State of China.
Life of St. Dominic.
Lockhart, William; The Medical Missionary in China.
Lyell, Sir Charles; The Antiquity of Man.
Ludlow, John Malcolm; British India.
" " Policy of the Crown towards India.
Laing, S.; Notes of a Traveller.
" Residence in Norway.
" Observations on Europe.
" Observations on Sweden.
Layard; Nineveh and its remains.

Life of Anchieta.
Lockman; Travels of the Jesuits.
Latrobe, Rev. J. C.; Letters on the Nicobar Islands.
Life in Bombay.
Lewin, Malcolm; The Way to lose India.
Lloyd, George Thomas; Thirty-three years in Tasmania and Victoria.
Laurie, W. F. B.; Orissa.
Laing, Major Alexander Gordon; Travels in Western Africa.
Leyden, Dr. J.; Discoveries and Travels in Africa.
Lichtenstein; Travels in Southern Africa.
Life of Africaner.
Locke, Captain Granville; The Campaign in China.
Lempriere, Charles, D.C.L.; Mexico in 1861 and 1862.
Lee, Rev. D., and Frost, Rev. J. H.; Ten Years in Oregon.
Lennard, Barrett, Captain C. E.; Travels in British Columbia.

M.

Montezou, F. de; Mission de Cayenne et de la Guyane Française.
Mohl; Rapports faits à la Société Asiatique.
Mission de la Cochin-Chine et du Tonquin.
Moges, Marquis de; Souvenirs d'une Ambassade en Chine et au Japon.
Mémorial Catholique.
Muratori; Relat. delle Missioni.
Maimbourg; Histoire du Schisme des Grecs.
Montesquieu; Grandeur et Décadence des Romains.
Missions du Levant.
Mélanges de la Religion.
Michaud et Poujoulat; Correspondance d'Orient.
Melancthon; Epistolæ.
Munk, S.; Palestine.
Marcel, J. J.; Histoire de l'Egypte.
Mislin, Mgr.; Les Lieux Saints.
Mosblech; Notice sur la Langue de l'Océanie Orientale.
Merolla; Voyage to Congo.
Menzel; German Literature.
Mendoza; Historie of the Kindome of China.
Minturn, Robert B.; From New York to Delhi.
Moseley, William; Memoir on Sending the Scriptures to China.
Madras Catholic Directory.
McGhee, Rev. R. J. L.; How we got to Pekin.
Mountain, Colonel Armine; Memoirs of.
Missionary Records of the Religious Tract Society.
Merriman, Archdeacon; Journals of.
Malan, Rev. S. C.; Who is God in China.
Macfarlane, Charles; The Chinese Revolution.
Macfarlane, Rev. James, D.D.; Indian Missions of the Church of Scotland.
Macfarlane, Charles; History of British India.
Morrison, Dr.; The Fathers of the London Missionary Society.
Markham, Clements; Travels in Peru and India.
" " Expeditions into the Valley of the Amazon.
" " Cuzco and Lima.
Mullens, Rev. Joseph; Missions in S. India.
Missionary Herald.
Morell, J. Reynell; Algeria.
Margoliouth, Rev. Moses; A Pilgrimage to the Land of my Fathers.
Murray, Hugh; Discoveries in Africa.
" " Historical Account of Discoveries in Asia.
" " Descriptive Account of China.

Morrell, Abby Jane; Narrative of a Voyage.
Melville, Herman; The Marquesas Islands.
" " Omoo.
Mac Micking, Robert; Recollections of Manilla and the Philippines.
Missionary Voyage to the South Sea.
Missionary Transactions of the London Missionary Society.
Merivale, Professor Herman; Lectures on Colonization, &c.
Monk, Charles James; The Golden Horn, &c.
Marsh, Herbert, D.D.; An Inquiry relative to the B. & F. Bible Society.
" " History of the Translations of the Scriptures.
Marshman, J., D.D; Chinese Grammar.
Milner, Rev. Thomas; The Crimea, its Ancient and Modern History.
Martin, Montgomery; British India.
" " China, Political, Commercial, and Social.
Malcolm, Rev. Howard; Travels in S. Eastern Asia.
Moehler; Symbolism.
Medhurst, Rev. W. H.; China, its State and Prospects.
Morrison, Dr.; Memoir of, by his Wife.
Mackintosh, Sir James; Works.
Milne, Rev. W. C.; Life in China.
Meadows, Taylor; The Chinese and their Rebellion.
" " Desultory Notes on the Government and People of China.
Monthly Review.
Montauban, Mrs. Eliot; A Year and a Day in the East.
Mackenzie, Mrs. Colin; Six Years in India.
Möllhausen, B.; Journey from the Mississippi to the Coasts of the Pacific.
Macdonald, Colonel; The Civilization and Instruction of the Natives of India.
Mills, Arthur, M.P.; India in 1858.
Mansfield, C. B.; Paraguay, Brazil, &c.
Mollien, G.; Travels in the Republic of Colombia.
Mayhew, Henry; London Labor and the London Poor.
Mayer, Brantz; Mexico, Aztecs, Spanish and Republican.
Monro, Rev. Vere; Travels in Syria.
Maury, S. M.; Statesmen of America.
Miers, John; Travels in Chili.
Macaulay, Lord; Essays.
Marco Polo; Travels.
Maximilian, Prince of Wied-Neuwied; Travels in Brazil.
Miller, Hugh; Footprints of the Creator.
" " The Testimony of the Rocks.
" " Rambles of a Geologist.
Moister, Rev. William; Memorials of Missionary Labor in W. Africa.
Moodie, Lieut. J. D. W.; Ten Years in South Africa.
Moffat, Rev. Robert; Missionary Labors in Southern Africa.
Mason, John; Three Years in Turkey.
Mott, Valentine, M.D.; Travels in Europe and the East.
Morris, E. Joy; Tour through Turkey, Greece, &c.
Millard, D.; Journal of Travels in Egypt.
Monteith, General; Kars and Erzeroum.
Martineau, Harriet; Suggestions towards the future Government of India.
" " Society in America.
Marjoribanks, Alexander; Travels in N. S. Wales.
Mundy, Colonel; Australasian Colonies.
Mead, Henry; The Sepoy Revolt.
Marshall, Henry; Ceylon.
Mackenzie, Kennett; Burmah and the Burmese.
McKillop, Lieut. H. F.; Reminiscences of Twelve Months' Services in New Zealand.
Minge, Abbé; Dictionnaire des Apologistes Involontaires.
" " Dictionnaire des Conversions.

Macartney, Lord; Embassy to China.
Morelle, Captain; A Narrative of Four Voyages.
Mayne, Commander, R. C.; Four Years in British Columbia and Vancouver Island.
Macdonald, Duncan, G. F.; British Columbia and Vancouver's Island.
Massachusetts Historical Collections.
Morse, Rev. Jedidiah, D.D.; A Report to the Secretary of War of the United States on Indian Affairs.
Murray, Hon. Charles A.; Travels in North America.
Murray, Hon. Amelia; Letters from the United States, Cuba, and Canada.
Memoirs of a Church of England Missionary in the North American Colonies.
Mitchell, D. W.; Ten Years in the United States.
McLeod, W.; Travels in Eastern Africa.
Mackay, Charles, LL.D.; Life and Liberty in America.

N.

Nettement, Alfred; Histoire de la Conquête d'Alger.
Nouveaux Mémoires du Levant.
Nouveaux Mémoires de la Moscovie.
Nouvelles Lettres Edifiantes.
Norbert; Mémoires Historiques sur les Missions des Malabares.
Notice sur le Chili; par un Voyageur Français.
Newbold, T. J.; British Settlements in the Straits of Malacca.
Neale, J.; Residence in Siam.
North American Review.
Naval and Military Gazette.
Narayan Sheshadri; A Sermon by.
Norton, Bruce; Topics for Indian Statesmen.
Narrative of a Yacht Voyage in the Mediterranean.
Neale, E.; Syria, Palestine, &c.
Napier, Lieut.-colonel E. Elers; Excursions in Southern Africa.
Napier, Colonel; Reminiscences of Syria, &c.
Neander; History of the Christian Religion and Church.
New Glories of the Catholic Church.
Nicholas, J. L.; New Zealand.
New York Herald.
New York World.
New York Evening Express.
New York Churchman.
Nicolay, Rev. C. J; The Oregon Territory.
New England's Plantations; by a Reverend Divine now there resident, 1630.
Nicolini, G. B.; History of the Jesuits.

O.

Orateurs Sacrés.
Orlich, Leopold von; Travel in India.
Olmsted, Francis; Incidents of a Whaling Voyage.
Olmsted, F. Law; Our Slave States.
" " Journey through Texas.
Olin, Stephen, LL.D.; Works.
Oakeley, Canon; Life of Sir Charles Oakeley.
Osborn, Rev. Henry; The Pilgrim in the Holy Land.
Oliphant, Laurence; Lord Elgin's Mission.
" " The Russian Shores of the Black Sea.
Oliphant, Sir Oscar; China, a Popular History.
Osborne, Captain Sherard; The Past and Future of British Relations in China.

Overland Bombay Times.
Owen, Robert Dale; Footfalls on the Boundary of another World.
Observations on India; by a Resident there many Years.
Owen, Rev. J.; History of the British and Foreign Bible Society.
Osborn, Rev. E., D.D.; History of the Objibway Indians.
Onderdonck, Dr.; Sermon preached at the Consecration of Christchurch, New York.

P.

Perrone; Prælect. Theolog.
Proyart; Histoire de Loango, Kakongo, &c.
Panthéon Littéraire.
Pouqueville; Grèce.
Pluquet; Dictionnaire.
Persécutions et Souffrances de l'Eglise Catholique en Russie.
Pauthier; La Chine.
Penhoën, Baron Barchou de; L'Inde sous la Domination Anglaise.
Prat, R. P.; Histoire du Bienheureux Jean de Britto.
Perrin; Voyage dans l'Indostan.
Poujoulat, Baptistin; La Vérité sur la Syrie.
Poitou, Eugène; Un Hiver en Egypte.
Ponlevoy, R. P; Vie du R. P. Xavier de Ravignan.
Pelissier, E.; La Colonisation Militaire en Algérie.
Parkyns, Mansfield; Life in Abyssinia.
Putnam, G.; American Facts.
Percival, Rev. Peter; The Land of the Veda.
Periodical Accounts of the Serampore Mission.
Parliamentary Papers.
Patagonian Missionary Society.
Porter, Captain David; Cruise to the Pacific Ocean in the U. S. frigate Essex.
Pulszky, Francis; The Tricolor in the Atlas.
Patterson, J. Laird; Journal of a Tour in Egypt, &c.
Petherick, John; Egypt, the Soudan, &c.
Paul, R. B.; Australia, Tasmania, and New Zealand.
Puseley, D.; Australia and Tasmania.
Polack, J. S.; Manners and Customs of the New Zealanders.
Power, W. Tyrone; Sketches in New Zealand.
Prichard; Natural History of Man.
Purchas; Pilgrims.
Palmer, Aaron H.; Letter to the Hon. C. J. Ingersoll.
Prout, Ebenezer; Life of Rev. John Williams.
Philalethes; History of Ceylon.
Pearson; Memoirs of Swartz.
" Memoirs of Buchanan.
Peggs, John; Pilgrim Tax in India.
Pinkerton; Collection of Voyages.
Pfeiffer, Ida; Voyage round the World.
" Last Travels of.
Pridham, Charles; Ceylon and its Dependencies.
Percival, Captain; Account of the Island of Ceylon.
Pringle, R.; Narrative of a Residence in S. Africa.
Philip, Rev. John, D.D.; Researches in S. Africa.
Prime, Samuel Irenæus; Travels in Europe and the East.
Perkins, Rev. Justin; Residence in Persia among the Nestorian Christians.
Pietrowski, Rufin; Story of a Siberian Exile.
Porter, Rev. J. L.; Five Years in Damascus.
Pierson, Rev. H. W.; Biographical Sketches of Distinguished American Missionaries.

Power, T.; Residence in China.
Points about China and the Chinese.
People of China, The; by the Religious Tract Society.
Parish, Sir Woodbine; Buenos Ayres, &c.
Parker Society; Works of the English Reformers.
Progress and present Position of Russia in the East.
Paton, G.; Modern Syrians.
Parrot, Dr.; Journey to Ararat.
Porter, Sir Robert; Travels in Georgia.
Parlby, Major-general; The Establishment of the Anglican Church in India.
Palmer, William; Dissertations on the Orthodox Church.
Proceedings of the South India Missionary Conference.
Parton, J.; The Life and Times of Aaron Burr.
Pusey, Rev. E. B., D.D.; A Letter to the Archbishop of Canterbury.

Q.

Quick; History of the Reformed Churches in France.
Quarterly Review.

R.

Relations des Jesuites dans la Nouvelle France.
Richarderie; Bibliothèque Universelle des Voyages.
Revue Orientale et Algérienne.
Revue des Deux Mondes.
Rienzi, G. L. Domeny de; Océanie.
Ruchat; Histoire de la Réformation de la Suisse.
Rorhbacher; Histoire de l'Eglise Catholique.
Rozet, P.; Alger.
Reynolds; Voyage of the Potomac.
Refutation of the Charges brought by the Roman Catholics against the American Missions at the Sandwich Isles.
Richardson, James; Narrative of a Mission to Central Africa.
" " Travels in the Great Desert of Sahara.
Russell, Rt. Rev. M.; Nubia and Abyssinia.
" " Polynesia and New Zealand.
" " Palestine, or the Holy Land.
Rights of the Indians; A Memorial to Congress.
Russell, Joshua; Missionary Tour in Ceylon and India.
Rovings in the Pacific; by a Merchant long resident at Tahiti.
Rough, David; Narrative of a Journey through part of the North of New Zealand.
Rochfort, John; Adventures in New Zealand.
Reed, Andrew, D.D.; Visit to the American Churches.
Robinson, Dr.; Biblical Researches in Palestine.
Rochau, A. L. von; Wanderings through the Cities of Italy.
Rose, Rev. H. J.; The State of Protestantism in Germany.
Revelations of Russia.
Ranke, Leopold von; History of Servia.
" " History of the Popes.
Recollections of Russia; by a German Nobleman.
Robinson, Rev. Edward; Romanism in Ceylon.
Russell, W. H.; Diary in India.
Raikes, Charles; Notes on the N. W. Provinces of India.
Ross, Charles; The Cornwallis Correspondence.
Rammohun Roy; Defence of the Precepts of Jesus.
" " Letter to Rev. H. Wade.

Risk, Allah Effendi; The Thistle and the Cedar of Lebanon.
Rupp, J. D.; History of the Religious Denominations of the United States.
Robertson; Works.
Ripa; Residence at the Court of Pekin.
Rickards; India.
Roberts; Hindostan.
Ruschenberger, W. S., M.D.; Voyage round the World.
Ravenstein; The Russians on the Amur.
Reports of the (United States) American Board for Foreign Missions.
" " Malta Protestant College.
" " Debates of the House of Commons on the State of New Zealand.
" " Directors of the New Zealand Company.
" " Church Missionary Society.
" " Baptist Missionary Society.
" " London Missionary Society.
" " Wesleyan Methodist Missionary Society.
" " Foreign Aid Society.
" " Society for the Propagation of the Gospel.
" " Society for Missions to Africa and the East.
" " British and Foreign Bible Society.
" " Executive Committee of the American Unitarian Association.
Ritchie, Leigtch; The British World in the East.
Rhodes, Alexandre de; Voyages et Missions de.
Rose, Cowper; Four Years in Southern Africa.
Rattray, Alexander, M.D.; Vancouver Island and British Columbia.
Remarks on the Moral and Religious Character of the United States.

S.

Schnitzler, J. H.; La Russie, la Pologne, et la Finlande.
" " Histoire Intime de la Russie.
St. Sauveur, J. Grasset de; Encyclopédie de Voyages.
Salvado, Mgr. Rudesindo; Mémoires Historiques sur l'Australie.
Schœlcher, Victor; Colonies Etrangères.
Schouvaloff, R. P.; Ma Conversion et ma Vocation.
Starck; Theodul's Gastmahl.
Saint Cyr, Louis; La Mission de Maduré.
Sainte-Foi, Charles; Vie du R. P. Ricci.
Salverte, Georges de; La Syrie avant 1860.
Smet, R. P. de; Cinquante Nouvelles Lettres.
Szyrma, Colonel Lach; Revelations of Siberia.
Schedel, Dr. H. E.; The Emancipation of Faith.
Schlegel, F. von; Philosophy of History.
Scherzer, Dr. Carl; Voyage of the Novara.
Saulcy, F. de; Narrative of a Journey round the Dead Sea.
Stanley, Rev. Arthur Penrhyn, D.D; Sinai and Palestine.
Southgate, Rev. Horatio; Narrative of a Tour in Turkey and Persia.
Southgate, Mr., and the Missionaries at Constantinople.
Swinhoe, Robert; Narrative of the N. China Campaign of 1860.
Speir; Life in Ancient India.
Sleeman, Lieut.-colonel; Rambles and Recollections of an Indian Official.
Sleeman, Sir William; Journey through the Kingdom of Oude.
Sargent, Rev. H.; Memoir of Rev. H. Martyn.
Staunton, Sir George; Laws of China.
Smith, Rev. George; Visit to the Consular Cities of China.
Sirr, Henry Charles; China and the Chinese.
Shuck, Henrietta; Scenes in China.
Scarth; Twelve Years in China.
Shiel, Lady; Life and Manners in Persia.

Tiffany, Osmund; The Canton Chinese.
Townshend, J.; Rocky Mountains.
Traits of American Indian Life.
Thacher, James, M.D.; History of the Town of Plymouth, U. S.
Talvi; History of America.
Thatcher, B. B.; Indian Biography.
Trollope, F.; Vienna and the Austrians.
Thurloe; State Papers.

U. & V.

Vie du Cardinal de Cheverus.
Valbezen, E. de; Les Anglais et l'Inde.
Vedelius; De Arcanis Arminianismi.
Voyage de la Favorite.
Ventura, R. P.; La Bellezza della Fede.
Veuillot, Louis; Les Français en Algérie.
Veuillot, Eugène; La Cochin Chine et le Tonquin.
Urquhart, David; The Pillars of Hercules.
Underhill, Rev. Edward Bean; The West Indies.
Ullathorne, W., D.D.; A Reply to Judge Burton.
" " The Catholic Mission in Australia.
Valentia, Lord; Travels.
Van Lennep, Mrs.; Memoir of.
Venn, Rev. H.; The Missionary Life and Labors of Francis Xavier.
Valdez, Francisco Travassos; Six Years in Western Africa.
Universal History.
Ubicini; Letters on Turkey.
Vaux, W. S.; Nineveh and Persepolis.

W.

Wittman; Storia Universale delle Cattoliche Missioni.
Wadstrom, C. B.; Précis sur Sierra Leona.
Warren, Comte Edouard de; L'Inde Anglaise.
Werne, F.; Expedition to discover the Sources of the White Nile.
Warburton; The Crescent and the Cross.
Wilson, Rev. J. Leighton; Western Africa.
Ward, Mrs.; Five Years in Kaffir Land.
Westgarth; Victoria and the Australian Gold Mines
Wilson, Daniel, D.D.; Prehistoric Man.
Wheeler, Daniel; Memoirs.
Wilks, Mark; Tahiti, &c.
Walmsley, Colonel; Sketches of Algeria.
Wilkinson, Sir Gardner; Modern Egypt.
Wilson, John, D.D.; Lands of the Bible.
West, Rev. D.; Life and Journals of.
Walker, Rev. S.; The Church of England Missions in Sierra Leone.
Wilson, Dr. Rae; Travels in the Holy Land.
Wortabet, G.; Syria and the Syrians.
Waring, Major Scott; Observations on the Present State of the East India Company.
" " Letter to the Rev. John Owen.
Wilkinson, Rev. M.; Sketches of Christianity in India.
Wayland, Francis; Memoir of the Rev. Adoniram Judson.
Wilson, John, D.D.; The Darkness and the Dawn in India.
Williams, Rev. John; Narrative of Missionary Enterprises in the South Sea Islands.

Williams, Dr. Wells; The Middle Kingdom.
Wakefield, E. Jerningham; Adventures in New Zealand.
Widdrington, Captain; Spain and the Spaniards in 1843.
Walsh, Rev. R., LL.D.; Constantinople, &c.
Wilbraham, Captain Richard; Travels in the Trans-Caucasian Provinces of Russia.
Walpole, Hon. F.; Four Years in the Pacific.
" " The Ansayrii, &c.
Walsh, Rev. R., LL.D.; Notices of Brazil.
Williams, Rev. George; The Holy City.
Whitehead, Rev. Edward; Sketch of the Established Church in India.
Wilks, Colonel Mark; Historical Sketches of the South of India.
Wilkes, Commodore; U. S. Exploring Expedition.
Wellsted, J. R.; Travels, &c.
Wolff, Dr. Joseph; Travels and Adventures of.
" " Journal.
" " Mission to Bokhara.
Wagner, Dr. Moritz; Travels in Persia, &c.
Wingfield, W. F.; A Tour in Dalmatia.
Wallace, Alfred R.; Travels on the Amazon and Rio Negro.
Ward, Rev. F. de W.; India and the Hindoos.
Wilson, Robert; Mexico and its Religions.
Wylie, M.; Bengal as a Field of Missions.
Weitbrecht, J. T.; Missions in Bengal.
Winthrop, Theodore; Adventures among the North-Western Rivers and Forests.
Wyse, Francis; America, its Realities and Resources.
Wilberforce, Samuel, D.D.; A History of the Protestant Episcopal Church in America.
Warburton, T.; The Conquest of Canada.
Winwood; Memorials.

Y

Yanoski, Jean; L'Afrique Chrétienne.
" " Histoire de la Domination des Vandales en Afrique.
Yates, W. Holt, M.D.; Modern History of Egypt.
Yate, Rev. William; An Account of New Zealand.
Young, Rev. R.; The Southern World.
Young, Cuthbert; The Levant and the Nile.

N. B. Of eleven hundred works cited in these volumes, *nine hundred and forty-seven* are by non-Catholic writers.

www.ingramcontent.com/pod-product-compliance
Lightning Source LLC
LaVergne TN
LVHW021314110826
845150LV00003B/567

9781425558000